New Views on Pornography

New Views on Pornography
Sexuality, Politics, and the Law

Lynn Comella and Shira Tarrant, Editors

 PRAEGER

AN IMPRINT OF ABC-CLIO, LLC
Santa Barbara, California • Denver, Colorado • Oxford, England

Library of Congress Cataloging-in-Publication Data

New views on pornography : sexuality, politics, and the law / Lynn Comella and Shira Tarrant, editors.
     pages cm
   Includes bibliographical references and index.
   ISBN 978-1-4408-2805-8 (print : alk. paper) — ISBN 978-1-4408-2806-5
(e-book)   1. Pornography—United States.   2. Sex—United States.   I. Comella, Lynn.
II. Tarrant, Shira, 1963–
   HQ472.U6N485 2015
   363.4'70973—dc23   2014028964

ISBN: 978-1-4408-2805-8
EISBN: 978-1-4408-2806-5

19 18 17 16 15   1 2 3 4 5

This book is also available on the World Wide Web as an eBook.
Visit www.abc-clio.com for details.

Praeger
An Imprint of ABC-CLIO, LLC

ABC-CLIO, LLC
130 Cremona Drive, P.O. Box 1911
Santa Barbara, California 93116-1911

This book is printed on acid-free paper ∞

Manufactured in the United States of America

Contents

SECTION I: FOUNDATIONS AND CONTROVERSIES

SECTION II: CULTURAL ISSUES AND EFFECTS

Section I

Foundations and Controversies

Introduction

This collection takes a fresh look at a provocative topic. *New Views on Pornography* brings together current scholarship that covers a range of issues regarding pornography's relationship to cultural, political, and legal debates. This comprehensive and interdisciplinary collection is a timely resource for students, researchers, and journalists who write about pornography and sexuality. We hope this collection also appeals to the general reader who is interested in learning more about a topic that is both compelling and controversial.

Recent years have seen an uptick in media attention, online articles, academic research, popular books, and everyday conversations about pornography. The chapters in this collection challenge many arguments and longstanding beliefs about pornography by addressing questions such as who uses pornography, why they use pornography, in what kinds of contexts, and with what kinds of social and psychological effects. Academic departments across the United States and internationally are increasingly incorporating a focus on pornography as part of broader projects in gender and sexuality studies, as well as film, media, and legal studies. With easy access to online pornography, discussions about perceived harms and benefits are rapidly growing. These conversations, however, often are based on conjecture, moral outrage, and bias rather than well-researched facts and data. The topic of pornography—as contentious and intriguing as it is—warrants sophisticated methods and frameworks for addressing dilemmas regarding ethics of production, sexism, racism, compulsive use, consent, and the law. *New Views on Pornography* explores the robust relationship between sexuality, politics, and the law, demonstrating just how intertwined these domains actually are.

These chapters are deeply interdisciplinary. They utilize a variety of methodological approaches, both qualitative and quantitative, including ethnography, interviews, survey measurements, archival research, and other methods. This is a collection that asks new questions about an industry that has been around for a long time. The authors engage with pornography from a variety of vantage points: gender studies, history, sociology, media studies, philosophy, politics, psychology, and criminology. In addition, chapters also include first-person perspectives from industry performers and directors. Complex sets of sociopolitical questions, such as those invoked by pornography, require that "different research traditions talk to each other and begin to learn from each other, not so that we all speak the same language or that we all agree, but so that our analysis grows."[1] As editors we see this tenet as central to cultivating new views on pornography.

Section I, Foundations and Controversies, begins with three chapters that present important legal, historical, and political overviews of pornography. In Chapter 1, First Amendment attorney Kimberly Harchuck summarizes key legal issues that surround sexually explicit content, including obscenity, child pornography, and online piracy. She discusses a series of significant legal decisions that interpret the First Amendment, before turning her attention to current issues in obscenity and government censorship. In Chapter 2, film historian Kevin Heffernan explores the shifting conditions of production and distribution that occurred as pornography increasingly moved into the public sphere. He focuses on the period beginning with stag films in the early 20th century and ending with the ascendance of home video in the 1980s. Heffernan argues that examining pornography as a business, including changes in porn distribution, provides important clues about the history of the industry, including the emergence of new forms of infrastructure, institutions, and censorship battles. In Chapter 3, Carolyn Bronstein examines the history of feminist confrontations over pornography. Why did pornography emerge as such a central concern for feminist activists and scholars in the 1970s? What were the competing claims advanced by feminists fighting to eradicate pornography versus those opposing censorship?

The next three chapters build upon these foundations, and grapple with issues of antiporn scholarship and activism. In Chapter 4, Christopher Boulton examines the antiporn agendas and strategies put forth by feminist activists and scholars, government measures surrounding Internet filtering initiatives, and tactics used by Christian-based ministries, which offer porn-using heterosexual men an alternative route to redemption and salvation. In "Strange Bedfellows: Black Feminism and Antipornography Feminism," Jennifer Nash traces antipornography's and black feminism's respective engagements with racialized pornography. She offers an alternative strategy for understanding how black women's bodies are portrayed in pornography, and carves out space for black spectators to view themselves—and each other—as sexual subjects. In Chapter 6, Jessica Johnson discusses the production, consumption, and online circulation of sexualized doctrine and public confessions by the pastors and congregants of Mars Hill Church. She analyzes the highly gendered logic of the church's brand of "biblical porn"—an antipornography discourse through which sexual sins and fantasies are collectively generated for online dissemination. Johnson argues that Mars Hill, and its charismatic yet controversial former leader, pastor Mark Driscoll, is shaping and transforming evangelical congregations on regional, national, and global scales.

The next set of essays surveys the history of "queer smut," lesbian pornography, and alternative porn production, including bisexual pornography. Historian Whitney Strub investigates the political contribution of "queer smut" to the queer civil rights movement. He argues that queer erotic expressions, from lesbian pulp fiction to beefcake magazines and beyond, were personally empowering, community building, and, for some, life-saving expressions of same-sex desires. In "Steamy, Hot, and Political: Creating Radical Dyke Porn," lesbian porn producers Shar Rednour and Jackie Strano offer a first-person account of creating DIY lesbian porn in San Francisco during the late 1990s and early 2000s. They describe this venture as both a labor of love and a political statement. In Chapter 9, author and cultural sexologist Carol Queen discusses the role that San Francisco-based sex toy retailer Good Vibrations played, from the mid-1980s onward, in creating both a cultural space and distribution network for alternative porn. Queen describes Good Vibrations' forays into porn production and its efforts to create greater diversity in pornography.

In Chapter 10, Georgina Voss takes us behind the scenes to explore stakeholder responsibility in the pornography industry. Voss considers the practices of three of the industry's most historically influential trade organizations. She argues that the notion of responsibility is shaped by multiple, intersecting, and sometimes contradictory considerations to protect against harm and legitimize a stigmatized industry. In Chapter 11, feminist philosopher Margret Grebowicz confronts issues of sexual agency, consent, and responsibility in a posthumanist environment by analyzing the topic of "zoo porn." And finally, authors Michael Salter and Thomas Crofts tackle the topic of revenge porn, and discuss the law's responsibility to protect those harmed by nonconsensual online behavior. Their analysis treats revenge porn as a highly gendered form of coercion, stalking, interpersonal harm, and violence. As digital and online technology is integrated into social and sexual life this behavior warrants effective solutions.

Section II includes eleven chapters focusing on cultural issues and effects. The section begins with Ronald Weitzer's chapter, "Interpreting the Data: Assessing Competing Claims in Pornography Research." Weitzer highlights issues of empirical data, explaining the methodological shortcomings of research limited by ideological frameworks that presuppose pornography's harmful effects on individuals and society. In questioning methodologically embedded bias, Weitzer calls for objective approaches to research on pornography.

In the second chapter, Clarissa Smith, Martin Barker, and Feona Attwood ask the key question posed by the title: "Why Do People Watch Porn?" Using survey data collected under the auspices of PornResearch.org, the authors analyze how individuals describe their motivations and reasons for watching pornography. These findings challenge prior assumptions and stereotypes about who watches porn and why. In Chapter 15, media scholar

Andy Ruddock investigates the academic research on pornography's effects. He outlines what cultivation theory can contribute to our understanding of pornography's significance. In "Pornography and Effects Studies: What Does the Research Actually Say?" Ruddock compares different research paradigms, highlighting what they share and how they differ in order to discern the most productive approaches for assessing the social impact of pornography.

In "'She's Totally Faking It!' The Politics of Female Pleasure in Pornography," Emily Crutcher draws from focus-group responses. Crutcher showed participants both mainstream gonzo and feminist pornography to analyze how viewers interpret the authenticity of female pleasure. Crutcher suggests that, in certain social contexts, feminist pornography succeeds in depicting genuine female pleasure, and may have a positive impact on female sexuality. In "Lust, Love, and Life" (Chapter 17), Lotta Löfgren-Mårtenson and Sven-Axel Månsson report on qualitative findings about Swedish adolescents' perceptions of pornography. Noting the widespread concern in Western society about easy access to porn, the authors conclude that teens experience both normalizing effects and ambivalence about pornography. Their research also finds that adolescents have the necessary skills to handle exposure to pornography in a sensible manner.

The following two chapters highlight first-person perspectives from performers and directors working in the industry. Mireille Miller-Young's interview with Betty Blac addresses the politics of race, size, and agency in porn and cam work. In Chapter 19, Lynn Comella explores the politically transgressive potential of queer pornography in her interview with performer and director Courtney Trouble. Trouble discusses how fat-positive, transracial, and transgender pornography challenges normative cultural assumptions.

In Chapter 20, Gregory Storms compares condomless gay male porn from the pre-HIV/AIDS era with contemporary bareback porn. The former films were made before condoms became mandatory in mainstream gay pornography following the rise of HIV/AIDS. Storm's enthnographic research grapples with nostalgia, censorship, and history. "Bare-ing Witness: Bareback Porn and the Ethics of Watching" advocates for new modes of spectatorship that place precondom pornography in historical context and do not erase the reality of potential HIV/AIDS in the gay community.

In "Ambient XXX: Pornography in Public Spaces," Ryan Bowles Eagle draws upon interviews and fieldwork to explore the dynamics of pornography as a public phenomenon. Given the availability of pornography on digital devices, in public libraries, and in the context of a gay leather-fetish bar, Bowles Eagle considers how the ambient porn screen in public spaces becomes a site of struggle between the possibilities and limits for public sexualities.

In Chapter 22, "Pornography and Pedagogy: Teaching Media Literacy" political scientist Shira Tarrant positions pornography as an important media genre for both questioning normative expectations and exploring forms of resistance to intersectional subjugations. Tarrant suggests that media literacy provides tools for critically analyzing the gender and sexual politics that infuse our culture. In the closing chapter to the volume, "The Science and Politics of Sex Addiction Research," Nicole Prause and Timothy Fong discuss their neuroscience findings on visual sexual stimuli. In rejecting arguments that favor the porn addiction model, the authors discuss the backlash to their findings and expose the politics of sex-addiction research.

NOTE

1. Feona Attwood and Clarissa Smith, "Porn Studies: An Introduction," *Porn Studies* 1, no. 1–2 (2014): 3.

I

Pornography and the First Amendment Right to Free Speech

Kimberly A. Harchuck

> I disapprove of what you say, but I will defend till the death your right to say it.[1]

The First Amendment, like any other constitutional provision, especially that which is located in the Bill of Rights, represents an overarching statement of the people's will. Among the most important aspirations of the First Amendment is the desire to give citizens a voice, as well as a means of accessing information vital to maintaining a truly democratic government. The Freedom of Speech guarantee contained within the First Amendment allows the citizenry to remain as informed as possible by creating a truly open marketplace of ideas and a priceless ability to discover the truth. By allowing for and protecting a wide range of speech, the First Amendment promotes tolerance, advances personal knowledge, and facilitates self-development.

This chapter examines the most important judicial decisions interpreting the First Amendment, including the methodology by which courts analyze First Amendment issues. We will study the impact of some of these decisions on sexually oriented speech and consider the concept of obscenity, eventually turning to the legislative decisions made in an effort to curb child pornography and online piracy. This will lead into a discussion of current issues in governmental censorship, including contemporary obscenity case law and technological attempts at blocking Internet content. Finally, this chapter concludes with the future outlook of the relationship between pornography and the First Amendment.

FIRST AMENDMENT METHODOLOGY

> Congress shall make no law respecting an establishment of religion, or prohibiting the free exercise thereof; or abridging the freedom of speech, or of the press; or the right of the people peaceably

to assemble, and to petition the Government for a redress of grievances.[2]

The plain language of the United States Constitution's First Amendment documents a seemingly simple ideology that many of us unconsciously classify as a divine right: the pledge by our government guaranteeing the preservation of expressive[3] and religious freedoms. However, the scope of such guarantees is determined by an array of delicate balancing tests implemented by the judiciary. Practically speaking, the judicial branch of our government is tasked with deciding whether such notions of self-governance assured to the Republic in the Bill of Rights must be qualified in the name of the greater good. At its core, free speech doctrine is merely an ever-evolving portfolio of case law defining the contours of one of the most sacred and essential liberties of U.S. citizens.

In analyzing freedom of speech protections guaranteed by the First Amendment, there are three primary considerations:

1. Is the action in question one taken by the government (state or federal), or by someone acting on behalf of the government?[4]
2. Is the speech at issue entitled to protection under the First Amendment?[5]
3. Is the government's action content-based or content-neutral?

The second and third prongs are often the heart of most First Amendment assessments, as the answers to those inquiries determine the standard of review employed by the judiciary in evaluating the law in question. The three standards of review are rational basis, intermediate scrutiny, and strict scrutiny.[6] The standards of judicial review utilize varying degrees of a balancing test between the constitutional right and regulatory concern at hand. In other words, every First Amendment issue calls on the courts to determine if the government's regulatory interest should outweigh the public's right to freedom of expression in that particular instance.

In order to examine what is protected, we must first determine the speech that is considered to fall beyond deserving constitutional protection. Unprotected speech is that which contains "no essential part of any exposition of ideas."[7] The well-settled basic categories of unprotected speech include obscenity, defamation,[8] and fighting words. Given the low-value label of these speech categories, they are subject to rational basis judicial review. Under rational basis review, the court is to uphold the regulation if it is rationally related to a "legitimate government interest."[9] This evidentiary threshold is often met with ease, thus, the law in question is presumptively constitutional unless it is shown that the causal link between the government's action and goal is essentially arbitrary. As a result, speech that is categorically excluded from constitutional protection may be regulated by the government, so long as the regulation in question does not discriminate based on the viewpoint of such speech.[10] This means that even if the speech falls within an unprotected category, the government must still regulate it in a content-neutral manner.

This leads directly into the third prong of the analysis: asking if the action is content-based or content-neutral. All expression not falling within one of the designated unprotected categories qualifies as protected speech. A content-based regulation is one that aims specifically at impairing the communicative impact of the speech or expression, while a content-neutral restriction does not. If a law regulates protected speech with the basis for the infringement being the content of such speech, the law is presumed to be unconstitutional and thus, examined under the strict scrutiny standard of review. To survive strict scrutiny, the government action must satisfy two extremely difficult requirements, resulting in such action rarely being upheld. The regulation at issue must:

1. Serve a compelling government interest; and
2. Be narrowly tailored to achieve that particular government interest.[11]

Practically speaking, the second element mandating that the law be narrowly tailored means that the action is the least restrictive manner in achieving the government's objective. In other words, there may not be a less restrictive method in which the government can effectively achieve its desired goal. Furthering its title as the most stringent standard of judicial review, strict scrutiny also places on the government the burden of proving the constitutionality of the act in question.

Conversely, content-neutral policies are aimed at something other than the communicative impact of speech and, therefore, subject to a much less rigorous test in determining constitutionality. The core of an analysis of a content-neutral regulation evaluates the nature and scope of the speech, because the regulation restricts only the manner in which the speech is communicated, not the speech itself. Governmental entities often restrict speech without directly targeting it by regulating conduct that combines speech and non-speech (often referred to as "expression"),[12] the secondary effects, or the time, place, and manner of speech occurring in a public forum. Such regulations are examined under a standard that falls between strict scrutiny and rational basis, often referred to as *intermediate scrutiny*. Intermediate scrutiny requires that the regulation serve an important government interest by means that are substantially related to that interest. An example of such a content-neutral regulation would be a city's complete ban on leaflets, due to its ultimate goal of preventing littering. The city's restriction is not based on any one person or group's communicative speech. Although the regulation may ultimately burden freedom of expression, the purpose of it is other than to do so.

Notably, there are types of speech that are less protected, but still within the purview of the First Amendment. Arguably, the most controversial of such less-protected free speech is indecent sexual speech, commonly referred to as sexually oriented speech. Because sexually oriented speech does not rise to the level of obscenity, it technically is lawfully protected speech, but because of its perceived low value, the government is granted more latitude in regulating it.[13] Thus, the First Amendment protection and associated regulation of pornography was, is, and will continue to be a constant legal debate inherent in the existence of pornography itself.

SEXUALLY ORIENTED SPEECH

> [A]bove all else, the First Amendment means that government
> has no power to restrict expression because of its message, its ideas,
> its subject matter, or its content.[14]

Offensive or indecent speech, although just that, is fundamentally protected by the First Amendment. The importance of such protection is rooted in the very nature of the alleged offensiveness. Unpopular and controversial speech often is considered the most offensive, and yet the most crucial for public dissemination.

In the 1971 case of *Cohen v. California*, the Supreme Court held that the plaintiff, Paul Cohen, could not be convicted for wearing a jacket stating "Fuck the Draft" in a courthouse corridor.[15] The Court's majority opinion noted that "one man's vulgarity is another man's lyric," and set the tone for First Amendment protection of what was eventually dubbed "emotive" speech.[16] Justice Harlan went on to state that California could regulate the time, place, or manner of Cohen's speech, but only if such regulation was content-neutral, as any further restriction would be an imposition on Cohen's First Amendment rights.

The vital protection of offensive speech encompasses language or images that are considered sexually oriented and even sexually explicit. Whether it is by use of zoning ordinances, licensing mandates, or invasive antiprivacy policies, the government has found many ways to circumvent free speech principles and regulate sexually oriented speech. Despite the fact that all such regulation arguably is done for the greater good, the Supreme Court has yet to categorically define lawful sexually oriented speech.[17] Without a concrete definition, many constitutional scholars question the Court's rationalization in justifying regulation of such speech, thus, ultimately questioning why sexually oriented speech, if not obscene, is subject to this "low value" label.

Black's Law Dictionary defines pornography as "material (such as writings, photographs, or movies) depicting sexual activity or erotic behavior in a way that is designed to arouse sexual excitement."[18] As referenced above, pornography is protected by the First Amendment, unless the material falls within a categorical exclusion of one's right to free speech. There are two types of pornography that are not constitutionally protected: obscenity and child pornography. Determining what material actually crosses the line into unprotected speech is a task that has plagued the legal system for decades, thus constantly positioning pornography at the forefront of First Amendment law.

UNPROTECTED SPEECH

> Constitutionally protected expression . . . is often separated from obscenity only by a dim and uncertain line.[19]

Obscenity

It has been expressly acknowledged that sex and obscenity are not tantamount to each other. Therefore, although all obscene material is sexually explicit, not all forms of sexually explicit speech are necessarily obscene. The justification for distinguishing between the once seemingly identical terms is that obscene material constitutes "no essential part of any exposition of ideas" and contains "such slight social value as a step to the truth."[20] Although the Court has created this expansive classification that is undeserving of constitutional protection, given the innately subjective nature of individual perception, it has struggled for decades to actually define the term.[21]

The 1957 Supreme Court case Roth v. United States decided for the first time with certainty that obscenity, as evaluated by the test announced in that case, was not a protected form of speech under the First Amendment.[22] The facts of the case involved Samuel Roth, a vendor in New York City. Roth was convicted under the federal obscenity statute, which made it illegal to send "obscene, lewd, lascivious or filthy" materials through the mail.[23] Together with Roth's case, the Court also examined that of David Alberts, a man who ran a mail-order business out of Los Angeles, and was convicted under the California Penal Code for "lewdly keeping for sale obscene and indecent books, and with writing, composing and publishing an obscene advertisement of them."[24] The Supreme Court in *Roth* ultimately affirmed both convictions and defined obscenity as material that is "utterly without redeeming social importance."[25] The test that was announced for determining what could be considered obscenity was material whose "dominant theme taken as a whole appeals to the prurient interest" when judged by "the average person, applying contemporary community standards." This test was meant to be applied on a case-by-case basis, rather than as an objective definition. Justice Brennan, writing for the Court, held that obscenity was not "within the area of constitutionally protected speech or press."

It wasn't until 1973 that the Court abandoned its efforts to find a strict, bright line definition of obscenity, and constructed a multi-tiered formula to be used as criteria in identifying obscene material. This test was the result of the seminal obscenity case of *Miller v. California.*[26] In *Miller*, the owner/operator of a mail-order pornographic film and book store sent a brochure advertisement in the mail depicting acts of graphic sexual activity. Miller was arrested and eventually convicted of violating a California statute that criminalized the sending of "any obscene matter."[27] Recognizing the need to clarify the legal meaning of obscenity, the Supreme Court granted review of the controversial case. The *Miller* court ultimately decided that the distribution and sale of obscene material was not protected as free speech under the First Amendment. Acknowledging, however, that regulating any form of expression could be problematic, the Court set forth the three basic guidelines that would ultimately become known as the Miller Test. The three-part test delineates when speech qualifies as obscene, thus removing it from the purview of the First Amendment and subjecting it to potential regulation. The Miller Test is as follows:

1. Whether the average person, applying contemporary community standards, would find that the work, taken as a whole, appeals to the prurient interest;
2. Whether the work depicts or describes, in a patently offensive way, sexual conduct specifically defined by applicable state law; and
3. Whether the work, taken as a whole, lacks serious literary, artistic, political or scientific value.[28]

Although it clearly built upon previous case law, the Court made several notable changes in obscenity jurisprudence when creating the Miller Test. For example, until *Miller*, it was unclear as to whether the "community standards" utilized in measuring "appeal to the prurient interest" were national or local community standards. The *Miller* Court roundly rejected the notion that such a standard could be at a national level and still be "constitutionally sound."[29] Accordingly, *Miller*'s "contemporary community standards" are exactly those—*community* standards of what constitutes material appealing to one's prurient interest in sex. Further, the *Miller* Court noted the foundational First Amendment principle of value-based protection in abandoning the previous classification of material "utterly without" social value to that which lacked "serious" social importance.[30] This seemingly minor shift in language created a much lower threshold for unprotected speech, thus resulting in an expanded scope of obscenity and, ultimately, subjecting much more expression to government regulation.

The Supreme Court further examined the issue of obscenity in *Stanley v. Georgia*, this time introducing the right to privacy as a catalyst.[31] Unlike *Roth* and *Miller*, which dealt with the issue of public distribution and advertising of obscene material, *Stanley* exclusively examined the issue of private possession. During the execution of an unrelated search warrant at his private residence, Georgia police discovered pornographic material belonging to Robert Stanley. Stanley was charged with violating a state law for possession of obscene materials. Upon reaching the Supreme Court, Stanley's conviction was overturned in a unanimous decision by the justices, thus invalidating all state laws that criminalized the possession of obscene materials.[32] According to the opinion, criminalizing the private possession of obscene material in one's residence violates the homeowner's right to privacy. Although acknowledging the state's continued "broad power" to do so, the Court decided that preserving one's privacy rights outweighs the state's interest in regulating obscenity.[33]

Child Pornography

Another category of pornography that falls outside the purview of First Amendment protection is child pornography. The constitutionality of laws prohibiting this controversial type of material was addressed by the Supreme Court in the landmark case of *New York v. Ferber*.[34] Specifically, *Ferber* analyzed a New York state criminal statute that prohibited knowingly promoting material depicting a sexual performance by a child.[35] While it acknowledged the potential for overbroad laws to suppress valid expression, the Court ultimately upheld the New York statute.[36] It found that the State has a "particular and more compelling interest in prosecuting those who promote the sexual exploitation of children."[37] The Supreme Court deemed the state's duty in "safeguarding the physical and psychological well-being of a minor" as tantamount to all other interests, and specifically rejected the need to apply the Miller Test to such material.[38] As a result of *Ferber*, child pornography is removed from First Amendment protection and therefore categorically outlawed despite the fact that it may not necessarily qualify as legally obscene.[39]

Osborne v. Ohio, like the Stanley case, examined the issue of private possession, but in Osborne the possessed material at issue was child pornography.[40] Following its own logic from Ferber, the Supreme Court found that the "interests underlying child pornography prohibitions" far exceed the state's interest exhibited in Stanley.[41] Confirming previous opinions regarding child pornography, the Court described its social value as "exceedingly modest, if not de minimis."[42] The state's interest was to eliminate the "market for the exploitative use of children."[43] The Court stated that it could not fault the state for "attempting to stamp out this vice at all levels in the distribution chain," and therefore outlawing even mere possession of child pornography was reasonable in this regard.[44] By upholding the Ohio law as constitutional, this ruling expanded the Ferber decision by criminalizing even the mere possession of child pornography.

INTERNET CENSORSHIP

> The First Amendment exists to protect offensive, disgusting and even vile speech. . . . A free society does not guarantee safety. It guarantees liberty, which includes inherent risks.[45]

Traditionally, the Supreme Court has maintained the premise that the medium of communication used to convey speech inevitably customizes such speech and therefore triggers different levels of First Amendment scrutiny.[46] Needless to say, the technological boom of the last thirty years has thrown this ideology into a bit of a tailspin. The marketplace has demonstrated a limitless ability to create novel methods of communicating, thus tasking legislative authorities to redefine and re-evaluate established legal analyses. The Internet, unquestionably, is at the top of the list of catalysts. It practically goes without saying that the Internet, by mere existence, presents significant and increasing challenges to well-settled First Amendment jurisprudence on a daily basis.

The Internet has been called "the most participatory form of mass speech yet developed."[47] Less than two decades ago, the Supreme Court itself acknowledged the groundbreaking avenue of speech as the first of its kind and deemed the Internet a "unique and wholly new medium of worldwide human communication."[48] The Internet, if not by choice then most certainly by default, has become the preferred venue for dissemination of speech. Megaphones and telephones have given way to keyboards and forum boards—the Internet has forever revolutionized the flavor of public discourse.

First Amendment legal doctrine, for the most part, has always maintained a consistent state of progression. The Internet has only furthered this constant evolution. Since its inception, lawmakers have attempted to keep pace with the technological advancements cultivated in cyberspace. With such efforts bordering on legislative hysteria, or simply missing the mark completely, the United States' regulation of the Internet has been an exercise in trial and error. Contemporary attempts to discern the fundamental purpose and intended scope of free speech rights only generate more legal uncertainty when incorporating the online world. It is safe to say that the drafters of the Bill of Rights could not have conceptualized the expansive nature of expressive freedom provided by the digital age. Despite the lack of a germane connection with the nation's founding fathers, the Internet is and will continue to be the preferred venue of modern free speech; our laws should reflect as much. Logic tells us that there undoubtedly exists a compromise between permissive online anarchy and the stifling of speech and innovation. When it comes to adult-themed content, Congress has struggled to find that middle ground and, in some ways, still continues to do so.

SOCIAL HARMS: PROTECTING MINORS FROM THE INTERNET

Communications Decency Act of 1996

In 1996, Congress passed the Communications Decency Act (CDA).[49] Certain portions of the CDA's Section 223 were Congress's first attempt at regulating the Internet, by requiring that minors essentially be blocked from all adult Web sites. The provisions made it a federal crime to transmit or allow transmission of any "indecent" material on any public computer network.[50] More specifically, the Act prohibited anyone from knowingly using "an interactive computer service to send to a specific person or persons under 18 years of age"[51] or "using any interactive computer service to display in a manner available to a person under 18 years of age, any comment, request, suggestion, proposal, image or other communication that, in context, depicts or describes, in terms patently offensive as measured by contemporary community standards, sexual or excretory activities or organs."[52]

The CDA's questionable language was examined and ultimately held unconstitutional by the Supreme Court in *Reno v. American Civil Liberties Union*.[53] In its first case applying free speech principles to the Internet, the Court invalidated the problematic provisions of the CDA in a 7–2 decision. The language was deemed unconstitutional on the grounds that it created criminal penalties for transmission of obscene or indecent communications, but was not narrowly tailored to serve a compelling government interest.[54]

Therefore, less restrictive alternatives were available to accomplish the same goal of protecting minors.[55] Justice Stevens, writing for the Court, found that in attempting to "deny minors access to potentially harmful speech," the CDA effectively suppressed "a large amount of speech that adults have a constitutional right to receive and to address to one another."[56] Acknowledging the distinction in media, Stevens nonetheless analogized sex on the Internet with sex on prerecorded phone messages, a form of speech that was deemed constitutionally protected in *Sable Communications of California v. FCC*.[57] Following the reasoning in *Sable*, the Court recognized that the indecent nature of many forms of sexual expression does not automatically elevate the material to the level of obscenity or child pornography. Essentially, this means that the government may not use the protection of minors as rationale for suppressing the lawful—albeit indecent—speech of adults.

Child Pornography Prevention Act of 1996

Another important piece of legislation is the Child Pornography Prevention Act (CPPA), which expanded the definition of child pornography to include new forms of media (i.e., virtual pornography).[58] This Act was a notable step for Congress, as it claimed to further the government's underlying interest in protecting children, the same rationale used in the *Ferber* and *Osborne* decisions. Specifically, the CPPA extended the scope of child pornography prohibitions to encompass "any visual depiction" that is, "appears to be," or "conveys the impression" of a "minor engaging in sexually explicit conduct."[59] Given the breadth of the language, the CPPA classified certain material as child pornography even though no actual minors were involved in its creation.

In 2002, the Supreme Court struck down provisions of the CPPA in *Ashcroft v. Free Speech Coalition*, calling the Act overbroad and stating that it criminalized "the freedom to engage in a substantial amount of lawful speech."[60] Despite the government's claims that the CPPA was necessary for the law to keep pace with technological advancements[61] and combat the growing problem of virtual child pornography, the Court opined that the law prohibited speech that "records no crime and creates no victims."[62] The Court addressed the points made in *Ferber*, but ultimately refused to extend the same analysis here. The *Ferber* decision was rooted in concern for the victims of child pornography, and gave no indication that similar government action would be permitted absent such victims.[63] Meaning, if the material at issue did not portray actual children, the government's interest in protecting children could not be used as rationale for regulating such material. Additionally, the Court found that the suppressed speech could possibly have redeeming value, as the law could easily be applied to certain Hollywood movies that use youthful adult actors in sexual scenes or even to Renaissance paintings.[64] The Court noted that the CPPA "proscribes a significant universe of speech that is neither obscene under Miller nor child pornography under Ferber."[65] The provisions were therefore struck down, with *Ashcroft* being one of the first cases before the Supreme Court to evidence that not all child pornography statutes are immune from a successful First Amendment challenge.

Child Online Protection Act of 1998

After the Supreme Court struck down key "anti-indecency" provisions of the CDA in *Reno*, Congress responded by passing the Child Online Protection Act (COPA).[66] Intended to protect minors from exposure to sexually explicit material on the Internet, the Act required commercial Web site operators to restrict minors from accessing online content that would qualify as "harmful to minors."[67] The online material was harmful to minors if the average person "applying contemporary community standards" would view the material as knowingly appealing to the "prurient interest" of a minor.[68] After successfully surviving the legislative branch, COPA struggled its way through almost ten years of judicial challenges in the *Ashcroft v. American Civil Liberties Union* line of cases.[69]

The ACLU sought to prevent enforcement of COPA via a court ordered preliminary injunction, arguing that the Act was unconstitutional under the First Amendment because of its restrictions on lawfully protected Internet speech. After a District Court judgment for the ACLU, the case made its way to the United States Court of Appeals for the Third Circuit. The court of appeals affirmed the ruling, reasoning that the application of "contemporary community standards" to a Web site on the Internet would allow the "most puritan of local communities" to shield "vast amounts of material."[70] The Supreme Court reversed the Third Circuit's ruling, finding that the "contemporary community standards" portion of the Act was not unconstitutionally vague.[71] On remand, the Third Circuit reaffirmed the lower court's ruling by upholding the pending preliminary injunction, thereby continuing to prevent enforcement of the Act.[72]

By the time COPA made its second appearance in front of the Supreme Court, the Act had been pending for over five years. In a narrow 5–4 decision, the Court affirmed the grant of injunctive relief, finding that there was a substantial likelihood that COPA would be declared unconstitutional if enacted into law.[73] Given COPA's limited application to sexually explicit material distributed via the Internet, the Court found COPA to be a content-based restriction, thus triggering the strict scrutiny standard of review.[74] Although acknowledging the government's compelling interest in preventing minors from accessing harmful material on the Internet, the Court rejected the claim that COPA was the least restrictive means of serving that interest.[75] In affirming the judgment of the Court of Appeals, Justice Kennedy remanded *Ashcroft* back to the lower courts, where it spent the next five years navigating the judicial system once again, only to be stricken from the United States Code, having never taken effect.[76]

ECONOMIC HARMS: PROTECTING BUSINESS FROM INTERNET PIRACY

Legislative Censorship

In recent years, under the guise of such noble causes as consumer protection, battling piracy, reducing unemployment, and even combating terrorism, the U.S. government has permitted legislative censorship to take center stage on Capitol Hill. With the majority of the bills labeled as antipiracy laws, SOPA, PIPA,[77] CISPA,[78] and OPEN[79] afforded the federal government with broad regulatory powers over online content. Given the scope of such power, it didn't take long for the public to recognize the high potential for abuse enabled by the bills. Fortunately, this widespread public backlash resulted in the bills being abandoned or tabled indefinitely.[80]

The main bill that had the most momentum among the bunch and made it the furthest through the legislative process was SOPA, the Stop Online Piracy Act. SOPA would have given the U.S. government almost total control in blocking access to Web sites that exhibit potentially infringing activity.[81] Under SOPA, copyright holders of allegedly pirated material were permitted to get such material removed from a Web site, along with getting the entire Web site taken down, all without even notifying the site owner.[82] Further, in such circumstances the Department of Justice was given the authority to block the domain housing the alleged infringing material, effectively removing an entire Web site from the Internet without affording any due process rights to the Web site's owner.

For all practical purposes, these bills died in committee, but that status is only applicable for these versions of the bills. Meaning, with just a few minor amendments, SOPA-like regulations may be reintroduced at any time during a federal legislative session. In fact, this form of bait-and-switch policymaking is employed all too often with controversial bills like SOPA. So often we hear the war-cry of grass roots movements, reminding us that all citizens have a voice. The unfortunate reality is that although it's true that activism starts at home, so does sanctimonious complacency. In today's overstimulated Information Age, the inadvertent label of "old news" would be the proverbial golden ticket for suspect proposals like SOPA. Legislative Internet censorship is a very real concept—one that, if dismissed by citizens, will undoubtedly find itself buried within the folds of yet another massive bill in the name of the greater good. As technology continues to flourish on a daily basis, it's all but certain that the law will continue its struggle to keep pace with innovation. However, the answer to the global piracy epidemic is not systematically eradicating an entire venue of speech and justifying it as a means to the end of online piracy.

Abuse of Current Regulations

There is no denying the detrimental impact that piracy is having on the adult industry. Copyright infringement should be punished like any other crime. But the punishment, like that for any other crime, must be consistent with due process principles. Allowing the government to shut down Web sites by seizing domain names based on allegations of piracy and preliminary investigations sets a dangerous constitutional precedent, as it runs directly counter to all free speech principles. Unfortunately, domain name seizures (among other excessive sanctions) are becoming a disturbing trend in the online war against infringement.[83]

With a large portion of the Internet still a proverbial Wild West, legally speaking, it's easy to disregard constitutional rights for the sake of creating order. However, simply taking the activity beyond the brick-and-mortar world to the Internet does not negate the requirement that government action must abide by rights afforded to citizens by the Constitution. For example, there is case law telling us that the government may not shut down an entire bookstore retail location merely because there was a sale of an allegedly illegal book. This specifically prohibited government act parallels domain seizures. These domains are platforms displaying constitutionally protected speech; therefore, their seizure by the government before any defenses are heard could easily be deemed an illegal prior restraint on free speech.[84] An unconstitutional prior restraint is essentially a government action that prevents certain lawful communication from entering the marketplace of ideas. In the example above, law enforcement is not permitted to shut down the bookstore, as it denies access to potentially legitimate and legal books while it is determined whether the one sold is legal. Even if the government eventually reinstates a Web site, once the domain is seized, the damage is already done. This process makes domain name seizures resulting from piracy allegations the furthest thing from a simple administrative procedure, as is often portrayed. Seizure of a domain name prior to adjudication of guilt is one of the most egregious attacks on the First Amendment today.

The government is paying close attention to the expanding role that the Internet plays in business, political, and human affairs. The natural temptation is to assert more control and seek to protect assets and the bottom line. That said, the global inability to effectively address the current piracy situation likely will result in more attempts at passing draconian laws like the ones referenced above, or continued abuse of current regulations in the name of preventing piracy. The unfortunate reality is that these overbroad regulatory attempts are just the beginning of what promises to be a long legislative battle. The future of free speech on the Internet will turn largely on the ability to balance the rights of content producers with the rights of publishers or service providers. Without this balance, the result is practically guaranteed to be significantly restricted free speech rights.

CONTEMPORARY CENSORSHIP

> We only have as much freedom as we demand in this country. Government, by its very nature, will always seek to stifle individual freedoms . . . It is essential that citizens of this great country stand up, speak up, and be heard. We have the right not to remain silent in America.[85]

Recent Obscenity Prosecutions

Modern-day obscenity law was largely formed via case law of the 1960s and 1970s. The federal court system eagerly applied the modernized theories with a series of federal prosecutions through the 1980s. Much to the satisfaction of the adult entertainment industry, it appeared that obscenity prosecutions had reached a plateau, particularly at the federal level. Enter the Internet. Surprisingly or not, the adult entertainment industry has frequently been found at the forefront of developing technology and affording it to the masses; the mainstream globalization of the Internet was no different. With the unwitting assistance of their Web sites as sales hubs, adult content producers now were reaching previously untapped markets and making every jurisdiction in the country a potential distribution point. As the first term of the George W. Bush Administration was coming to a close, it was clear that obscenity prosecutions were back on the agenda.

In 2003, after a raid by federal agents, husband and wife business partners, Rob Zicari and Janet Romano, the owners of Hollywood-based Extreme

Associates, Inc., were indicted in Pittsburgh, Pennsylvania, on ten counts of obscenity charges. *U.S. v. Extreme Associates* was the federal government's first major obscenity prosecution in over a decade.[86] The couple faced an astounding maximum sentence of fifty years in prison, a fine of $2,500,000, or both. Extreme Associates, Inc. faced a maximum total sentence of a term of probation of fifty years and a fine of $5,000,000.[87] The case remains, arguably, one of the most significant legal attacks against the adult entertainment industry, as it was essentially a test case to determine the acceptable limits of contemporary pornography due to the hardcore nature of the material in question.

The defense, citing the Supreme Court rulings in *Lawrence v. Texas* and *Stanley v. Georgia*, argued the existence of a fundamental right to sexual privacy,[88] which includes the right to privately possess and view sexually explicit material.[89] *Extreme Associates* claimed that this right existed, regardless of whether the material lacked literary or artistic merit, thus calling into question the well-settled tenets of the Miller Test.[90] The trial court agreed, and the case was dismissed in January 2005, with a finding that the federal obscenity statutes were unconstitutional, as they violated an individual's right to privacy. On appeal, the Third Circuit found that the federal obscenity laws remained wholly constitutional, and thus overturned the lower court's ruling. With the U.S. Supreme Court declining to hear the case, the reinstated obscenity charges were sent back to the District Court. After a six-year battle in the court system, the couple and the corporate entity pleaded guilty to the charges, which led to their imprisonment shortly thereafter.

Similarly, in 2005, Paul Little (stage name: Max Hardcore) and his California-based company, Max World Entertainment, were charged in Tampa, Florida, for violating federal obscenity laws.[91] The indictment consisted of five counts of transporting obscene matter by use of an interactive computer service and five counts of mailing obscene matter. Little was subsequently found guilty on all charges and sentenced to forty-six months in prison.[92]

Although there have been no federal obscenity prosecutions initiated during either of the Obama terms, the administration continued with all the obscenity cases brought by its predecessor. Since 2009, the Obama Administration's prosecutors have tried only two adult obscenity cases, in contrast to the volumes of obscenity prosecutions that took place under President George W. Bush.[93]

In 2008, adult entertainment producer John Stagliano was indicted on seven counts of violating federal obscenity laws.[94] The charges stemmed from the sale and distribution of adult films by his company Evil Angel. Two years later, a federal district court judge dismissed the case. In his ruling, U.S. District Judge Richard Leon chastised the government, calling the prosecution's evidence "woefully insufficient" to link Stagliano (and two corporate defendants) to the production and distribution of two videos alleged to be obscene. Touted as an extremely embarrassing loss for the federal government, the *Stagliano* case was perceived to be the culmination of Bush-era obscenity oppression. This notion was furthered shortly thereafter when Attorney General Eric Holder disbanded the Obscenity Prosecution Task Force of the Department of Justice.[95] In April 2011, amidst allegations of being "soft on porn," the attorney general issued a public letter of reply, stating that the Department of Justice had made the realistic decision to focus its "limited investigative and prosecutorial resources on the most egregious cases, particularly those that facilitate child exploitation."[96] Given the Department of Justice's very high-profile loss in the *Stagliano* trial, the attorney general's decision to concentrate attention on prosecuting media involving children, as opposed to consenting adults, was completely logical. Whether such actions were the politically motivated byproduct of a presidential administration on the cusp of campaigning for a second term, or the result of a shift in public perception of erotic material, the adult industry was hopeful that obscenity prosecutions finally were a thing of the past.

With the Obama Administration kept busy with a second-term presidential election, an unemployment crisis, and healthcare reform, the adult entertainment industry was enjoying the relative silence from the Department of Justice on obscenity issues. Scholars and industry participants were wondering if the Internet Age had finally accomplished the impossible and altered the sex taboo once and for all, at least legally. Then, in early 2014, the adult industry was reminded once again that evolution in technology does not necessarily equate to parallel cultural progress.

After seven years navigating the federal court system, fetish film producer Ira Isaacs's battle against censorship finally came to an end. On March 25, 2014, the Ninth U.S. Circuit Court of Appeals affirmed Isaacs's 2012 obscenity conviction, sending the industry veteran to prison for up to four years.[97] Isaacs was originally charged with violating federal obscenity statutes in 2007, after the distribution of several of his fetish films via U.S. mail. Isaacs's 2008 trial was placed on hold and eventually resulted in a mistrial, amid judicial controversy. Judge Alex Kozinski, who was presiding over the obscenity prosecution, recused himself within days of commencing the trial after it was discovered that the judge had been maintaining a personal Web site exhibiting sexually explicit images.[98] The 2012 guilty conviction was Isaacs's third trial over the obscenity charges, and the basis for his appeal to the Ninth Circuit. The unsuccessful appeal relied more on procedural due process arguments, as opposed to disputing his guilt of violating obscenity laws. Notably, however, the numerous due process claims were rooted in allegations of uncertainty directly related to the Miller Test—specifically, the concept of "prurient interest," as set out in the first prong of the Test.[99]

Historically, *Miller* has not worked in the industry's favor on numerous levels, and as exhibited in the Isaacs case, it has failed to do so again. Because the Miller Test was, arguably, inherently flawed from inception, many in the adult industry believe that the Internet has blatantly exposed such flaws and left it practically obsolete. Specifically, the intrinsic vagueness that plagues almost every facet of the multitiered formula makes it difficult to reconcile with practical application and almost impossible when such application involves technology that evolves on a daily basis.[100]

Porn Bans and Filtering

Although always a concern, especially for the adult entertainment industry, speculation of significant antiporn censorship policies by European governments started coming to light at the beginning of 2013. In March of the same year, the EU Parliament voted on a proposal that would have set out the path for laws "banning pornography in all media" across the European Union, including the Internet.[101] Fortunately, the controversial "porn ban" section of the proposal was struck down "amidst censorship concerns."[102] In the wake of the EU controversy, the United Kingdom's Prime Minister, David Cameron, proceeded to implement his own censorship policies, a "voluntary" Internet filtering plan.[103]

In just a few short months, over 90 percent of UK-based Internet service providers had already implemented the default blocking of a wide variety of controversial content, including pornography. Many of the UK's anticensorship groups were alarmed by the lack of resistance from larger service providers, which would have forced the program to weather the formal parliamentary legislation route, as opposed to integration as mere policy. Notably, the preselected filtering system restricts several other categories of allegedly problematic material such as that related to alcohol, drugs, tobacco, political extremism, violence, gaming, and social networking.[104] Only by contacting one's Internet service provider and choosing to opt out of the default filter system will Internet users in the UK get full access to the Web.[105] These filters are being presented to Britain as the saving grace of the Internet, despite the paradoxical reality that network-level algorithmic blocking will almost certainly not catch everything it's supposed to, while inevitably blocking material it shouldn't.

Not long ago, Australia also implemented a countrywide filtering system.[106] Within months, legitimate sex education sites, gay and lesbian support sites, and even medical forums discussing sexual issues slowly started disappearing.

Fortunately, Australia has since tempered its filters, but not after causing a serious erosion of digital freedom. Aside from the immense privacy and liberty issues, there promises to be inevitable collateral damage resulting from the imperfect logistics of the system. For example, it is not clear whether the Internet service providers—or any entity, for that matter—are responsible (financially and otherwise) for overzealous blocking and timely correction of filter errors. The repercussions are by no means restricted to the United Kingdom, and its efforts have already spawned new calls for service provider-level porn filtering in Iceland and several other "progressive" countries.[107] Ultimately, the United Kingdom is highly unlikely to become a porn-free zone irrespective of the new filtering policies.[108] If history has taught us anything, it's that if there's a will, there's a way.

CONCLUSION

The price of freedom is eternal vigilance.[109]

Constitutional law, generally, is one of the most complex areas of legal doctrine today; its subset of First Amendment jurisprudence clearly is no different. Given the breadth of free speech principles, this chapter was restricted to providing an overview of the legal issues surrounding sexually oriented material only. Just as with any other scholarly discipline spanning centuries, understanding the origins and evolution of constitutionally protected speech is central to the study and, even more so, the practice of First Amendment law. Although the timeline of case law evidenced a remarkable progression in free speech tenets throughout the years, the Supreme Court has noticeably chosen to rest on the laurels of relatively dated litigation. Such obsolescence unquestionably occurred at the hands of the Internet. This allegation is painfully apparent when witnessing contemporary examples of the judiciary acting as morality police, or exploring the struggle of lawmakers in applying antiquated legal regulations to the actions of a technology-driven society—just two examples of the continued censorship problem of the 21st century.

The First Amendment is rooted in the notions of personal autonomy and the unencumbered marketplace of ideas. Lively and honest public discourse has been recognized as something of vital importance throughout history. It is the obligation of the government not to burden such discourse through legal regulation, and it is the responsibility of the American public to question such suppression, should it exist. The liberty of free speech charges citizens with the task of holding the government accountable for its actions. Expressing thought and conveying speech is a fundamental right granted to the people regardless of whether such speech is offensive, controversial, or sexual in nature.

Pornography is the physical manifestation of one of the most—if not the single most—controversial categories of free speech. The mere existence of the content itself is meant to push the envelope and test the boundaries of convention. Despite the respective opinions that members of the public may have of the various types and genres of pornography, the material, no matter how offensive, nonetheless is completely legal with extremely limited exceptions. Antipornography sentiment is not novel by any means; the United States has long participated in frantic hyperbole demanding the collapse of the adult entertainment industry as a means of finally ending the alleged social and moral corruption cultivated by sexually oriented materials. Such outrage and disgust, bolstered by forewarning of corrupted children and the moral decay of society, is the perfect example illustrating why expansive free speech principles are a societal necessity. Pornography often embodies some of the most offensive and disturbing existing speech. These characteristics make defending it that much more crucial in the battle against censorship. Protecting the most egregious and distasteful speech ensures that all other speech unquestionably remains within the purview of the First Amendment.

Although we have shown some advancement in the court of public opinion, the discussion and depiction of sexual activity still remains a social and cultural taboo in the United States on many levels. At the risk of sounding colloquial, the Internet was a game changer—socially, economically, culturally, and legally. With technological innovation propelling the path of society like never before, it stands to reason that the fabric and mores of a culture would evolve as well. The online world transformed inconceivable concepts of technological and global convenience to standard operational orthodoxy in just a matter of years. The Internet brought luxuries like constant and limitless accessibility, instant gratification, and nonexistent geographic boundaries to the masses—all with just the click of a button. Sexually oriented material is no longer confined to the walls of bedrooms or sordid establishments on the outskirts of towns; pornography is at the public's disposal anytime, anywhere, and on the palm of the hand.

Traditional views and methods of regulating pornography are no longer applicable. In fact, many legal scholars argue that maintaining this sheltered mentality in the age of the Internet potentially rises to the level of ethically questionable hypocrisy. Regulation of online speech inevitably mandates a delicate balance between privacy, security, and freedom. Sacrificing privacy and freedom, regardless of the reason for doing so, undoubtedly leads to censorship on some level. Although such actions may seem insignificant in isolation, when one looks at the overall impact on the marketplace of ideas, there is an unmistakable chilling effect as each action erodes many core First Amendment principles. While the Constitution proffers an inalienable protection of lawful sexually oriented speech, the United States continues to preserve a strong puritanical vein running through its culture. As a result, it seems that no matter how progressive technology has encouraged U.S. society to be, there will still be a constant battle to maintain constitutional protection over pornography.

Although pornography has become considerably more accepted in mainstream society as a result of widespread exposure via the Internet, sluggish social tolerance does not necessarily equate to judicial or legislative acceptance. The Internet has provided the public with an unprecedented venue for the dissemination of speech. Regrettably, as with most novel platforms of speech, some parties desire to misuse such venues for illicit purposes. The government—and, at times, the public as well—forgets that lawful pornography is not analogous to criminalized unprotected sexual speech like obscenity and child pornography. Therefore, suppression of pornography via government action amounts to nothing but an unconstitutional infringement of free speech rights. The adult entertainment industry retains its familiar position on the front lines of the battle against censorship. Almost at ease operating with a target on its back, the industry seemingly thrives on being forced to operate on the periphery of convention. Pornography, holding firm as one of adult entertainment's primary commodities, is no different. With the law consistently struggling to catch up to technology and the existence of an entire industry willing to test those shortcomings time and again, the battle against censorship wages on and the only thing to expect is the unexpected.

NOTES

The author would like to thank the following individuals: Lawrence G. Walters, Esq., for providing me with the opportunity to be part of the small, esteemed group of attorneys whose client is the United States Constitution and the privilege of practicing every day knowing that I'm fighting the good fight; Lisa Brown, whose watchful eye kept my billables on track throughout this drafting process; Anjali Sareen, Esq., whose detail-oriented MENSA training was invaluable in editing this chapter; and my parents, Bob and Lee Ann Harchuck, for teaching me the value and pride of a blue-collar work ethic and always knowing the perfect timing for a Give 'Em Steel! pep talk.

1. Evelyn Beatrice Hall (pseudonym Stephen G. Tallentyre), *The Friends of Voltaire* (London: Smith Elder & Co., 1906).

2. The First Amendment of the United States Constitution.

3. The fundamental rights that comprise the legal concept of "freedom of expression" are freedom of speech, press, assembly (and association), and petition.

4. The constitutional guarantee of free speech does not apply to infringement of speech by private parties or entities, unless such parties or entities are acting in conjunction with the state or federal government. The action taken by the government

or government actor can be, for example, a law, regulation, bill, legislative act, or some form of regulatory restriction.

5. Categorizing speech as protected or unprotected is rooted in determining the value such speech brings to society.

6. "There may be a narrower scope for operation of the presumption of constitutionality when legislation appears on its face to be within a specific prohibition of the Constitution, such as those of the first ten amendments, which are deemed equally specific when held to be embraced within the Fourteenth [...] It is unnecessary to consider now whether legislation which restricts these political processes such as voting, expression, and political association which can ordinarily be expected to bring about repeal of undesirable legislation, is to be subjected to more exacting judicial scrutiny under the prohibitions of the Fourteenth Amendment than are most other types of legislation [...] Nor need we inquire whether similar considerations enter into the review of statutes directed at particular religious [...] or national [...] or racial minorities [...]: whether prejudice against discrete and insular minorities may be a special condition, which tends seriously to curtail the operation of those political processes ordinarily to be relied upon to protect minorities, and which may call for a correspondingly more searching judicial inquiry." *U.S. v. Carolene Products Co.*, 304 U.S. 144, 152 (1938). Footnote Four of the Carolene Products case, written by Justice Harlan Stone, was the Supreme Court's first suggestion that several levels of judicial scrutiny should be utilized when determining the constitutionality of a governmental action.

7. "There are certain well-defined and narrowly limited classes of speech, the prevention and punishment of which have never been thought to raise any Constitutional problem. These include the lewd and obscene, the profane, the libelous, and the insulting or fighting words—those which by their very utterance inflict injury or tend to incite an immediate breach of the peace. Such utterances are no essential part of any exposition of ideas, and are of such slight social value as a step to truth that any benefit that may be derived from them is clearly outweighed by the social interest in order and morality. Resort to epithets or personal abuse is not in any proper sense communication of information or opinion safeguarded by the Constitution, and its punishment as a criminal act would raise no question under that instrument." *Chaplinksy v. New Hampshire*, 350 U.S 568, 572 (1942).

8. Constitutionally unprotected defamatory expression excludes libel or slander of public figures or officials.

9. A "legitimate government interest" is an extremely broad constitutional concept, and fully intended as so. Arguably, almost any government objective associated with health, safety, or the general welfare of the public can qualify as legitimate for the purposes of rational basis review.

10. *R.A.V. v. City of St Paul*, 505 U.S. 377, 383 (1992). In instances where the government discriminates based on viewpoint, despite the fact that the speech at issue may be unprotected, the courts often will employ strict scrutiny review.

11. The strict scrutiny standard of judicial review is applied most often in the context of government restriction on a fundamental constitutional right; thus, it is consistently applied to First Amendment jurisprudence.

12. See *U.S. v. O'Brien*, 391 U.S. 367, 377 (1968). In *O'Brien*, the Supreme Court compiled a test to be used in analyzing regulations that indirectly burden speech via intended regulation of conduct. To surpass the O'Brien test, the law at issue must fulfill the following requirements: (1) Be within the constitutional power of the government to enact; (2) Advance an important or substantial government interest; (3) Such interest must be unrelated to the suppression of free expression; and (4) Any incidental burden on speech is no more than is necessary to further that interest.

13. "Moreover, even though we recognize that the First Amendment will not tolerate the total suppression of erotic materials that have some arguably artistic value, it is manifest that society's interest in protecting this type of expression is of a wholly different, and lesser, magnitude than the interest in untrammeled political debate that inspired Voltaire's immortal comment. Whether political oratory or philosophical discussion moves us to applaud or to despise what is said, every schoolchild can understand why our duty to defend the right to speak remains the same. But few of us would march our sons and daughters off to war to preserve the citizen's right to see 'Specified Sexual Activities' exhibited in the theaters of our choice. Even though the First Amendment protects communication in this area from total suppression, we hold that the State may legitimately use the content of these materials as the basis for placing them in a different classification from other motion pictures." *Young v. American Mini-Theaters, Inc.*, 427 U.S. 50, 70–71 (1976).

14. *Police Dept. of Chicago v. Mosley*, 408 U.S. 92, 95 (1972).

15. 403 U.S. 15 (1971).

16. *Id.* at 25–26.

17. *Erznoznik v. City of Jacksonville*, 422 U.S. 205, 207 (1975). Although the Supreme Court has yet to define the informal category of "low level value sexually oriented speech," it has been clear that nudity, alone, does not warrant such a label.

18. *Black's Law Dictionary*, 9th ed. (St. Paul: West Publishing, 2009).

19. *Bantam Books, Inc. v. Sullivan*, 372 U.S. 58 at 66 (1963).

20. *Chaplinksy v. New Hampshire*, 350 U.S 568, 572 (1942).

21. *Jacobellis v. Ohio*, 378 U.S. 184 (1964). When the Supreme Court was "faced with the task of trying to define what may be indefinable," Justice Potter Stewart ambiguously defined obscenity with the infamous "I know it when I see it" quote.

22. 354 U.S. 476 (1957).

23. "This Court, as early as 1896, said of the federal obscenity statute: 'Every one who uses the mails of the United States for carrying papers or publications must take notice of what, in this enlightened age, is meant by decency, purity, and chastity in social life, and what must be deemed obscene, lewd, and lascivious.'" Ibid., 491. See also footnote 28 citing *Rosen v. United States*, 161 U.S. 29, 42, 16 S.Ct. 434, 438, 480, 40 L.Ed. 606.

24. *Id.* at 481.

25. *Id.* at 484.

26. 413 U.S. 15 (1973).

27. Cal. Pen. Code § 311.2

28. *Miller* at 24.

29. "To require a State to structure obscenity proceedings around evidence of a national community standard would be an exercise in futility." See also, *Id.* at 33. "Nothing in the First Amendment requires that a jury must consider hypothetical and unascertainable 'national standards' when attempting to determine whether certain materials are obscene as a matter of fact. It is neither realistic nor constitutionally sound to read the First Amendment as requiring that the people of Maine or Mississippi accept public depiction of conduct found tolerable in Las Vegas or New York City." Ibid., 31.

30. *Id.* at 21, citing *Memoirs v. Massachusetts*, 383 U.S. 413 (1996).

31. 394 U.S. 557 (1969).

32. *Id.*

33. *Id.* at 568.

34. 458 U.S. 747 (1982).

35. "At issue in this case is 263.15, defining a class D felony: 'A person is guilty of promoting a sexual performance by a child when, knowing the character and content thereof, he produces, directs or promotes any performance which includes sexual conduct by a child less than sixteen years of age.'"

36. *Ferber* at 756.

37. *Id.* at 761.

38. *Id.* at 756–757, citing *Globe Newspaper Co. v. Superior Court*, 457 U.S. 596 (1982).

39. When *Ferber* reached SCOTUS, forty-seven states and the federal government had already passed laws prohibiting child pornography (thirty-five of those states also addressed distribution of such material), with most of the laws requiring little or no consideration as to whether or not the material at issue was legally obscene.

40. 495 U.S. 103 (1990), citing Ohio Rev. Code. Ann. § 2907.323(A)(3). The Ohio Supreme Court, before the issue went to the U.S. Supreme Court, read the statute as applying specifically and exclusively to lewd exhibitions of a minor's genitals, or a depiction with a graphic focus on a minor's genitals. Therefore, the Supreme Court found that the statute could not be considered overbroad, due to the Ohio court's narrow interpretation.

41. *Id.* at 108.

42. *Id.*

43. *Id.* at 109.

44. *Id.* at 110.

45. Lawrence G. Walters, "Walters: Florida CP Bill Goes Too Far," *XBIZ* 2014, http://www.xbiz.com/news/177314%20.

46. *Red Lion Broadcasting Co. v. Federal Communications Commission*, 395 U.S. 367, 386 (1969).

47. *Reno v. ACLU*, 521 U.S. 844, 863 (1997) (quoting *ACLU v. Reno*, 929 F.Supp. 824, 883 (E.D. Pa. 1996)).

48. *Id.* at 850.

49. Communications Decency Act of 1996; Title 47 U.S.C. § 223.

50. Specifically, §§223(a) and 223(d); the so-called "anti-indecency provisions."

51. 47 U.S.C. § 223(a)(1)(B)(ii).

52. 47 U.S.C. § 223(d).

53 521 U.S. 844 (1997).

54. *Id.* at 846.

55. *Id.* at 874–879.

56. *Id.* at 846; 874.

57. *Id.* at 868–870, citing *Sable Communications of California v. FCC*, 492 U.S. 115 (1989). Sable Communications, a company in California, had operated a "dial-a-porn" business for profit since 1983. In 1988, Congress amended the Communications Act of 1934 to ban obscene and indecent interstate commercial phone messages, thereby making Sable's business illegal. Ultimately, the Supreme Court determined that it is constitutional to ban obscene telephone communications, but not indecent ones. The Court there drew a distinction between these two types of speech, ultimately explaining indecent speech as that which may not rise to the level of obscenity but was still sexually charged.

58. Child Pornography Prevention Act of 1996; 18 U.S.C. § 2251; 18 U.S.C. § 2256(8)(C).

59. *Id.* Section 2256 of the CPPA prohibited a specific manner of creating virtual pornography, commonly referred to as "morphing" (altering images of minors in such a manner that the images appear to be engaging in various forms of sexually explicit activity).

60 535 U.S. 234; 256 (2002).

61. *Id.* at 264. The government asserted that the particular provisions in question were necessary, as it was becoming harder to distinguish whether or not digital images depicted actual children.

62. *Id.* at 250.

63. *Id.*

64. *Id.* at 241.

65. *Id.* at 240.

66. Child Online Protection Act of 1998, 47 U.S.C. § 231.

67. *Id.* The penalties for violating the Act were up to $50,000 in fines and/or six months imprisonment.

68 47 U.S.C. §609.

69. 542 U.S. 656 (2004).

70. *Ashcroft v. ACLU*, 535 U.S. 564 (2002).

71. *Id.*

72. *Ashcroft* (2004).

73. *Id.* at 666. In deciding whether to grant preliminary injunction, district court must consider whether plaintiffs have demonstrated that they are likely to prevail on the merits.

74. *Id.* at 670.

75. *Id.* at 667; 670. The Supreme Court believed that autonomous alternatives like parental supervision and filtering software would yield more successful results than such an expansive Act by Congress.

76. *Id.* at 673. The Supreme Court sent the *Ashcroft* case back to the District Court for a full trial regarding certain factual disputes (e.g., the effectiveness of filtering software). This time, the trial court granted not only a preliminary injunction, but a permanent injunction, meaning the enforcement of the Act would be permanently blocked. In 2007, the ruling was again upheld by the Third Circuit and the government appealed to the Supreme Court for review once again. In 2009, the Supreme Court officially refused to hear the case, thereby effectively blocking the enforcement of COPA and, by extension, its lawful enactment.

77. Preventing Real Online Threats to Economic Creativity & Theft of Intellectual Property Act. While PIPA was labeled as the Senate version of SOPA and almost identical in language, it contained two significant differences from the House bill: (1) PIPA did not prohibit third-party Internet service providers from doing business with banned Web sites; and (2) PIPA required greater court intervention (e.g., formal court orders) when pursuing copyright infringement allegation under the Act.

78. Cyber Intelligence Sharing & Protection Act.

79. Online Protection and Enforcement of Digital Trade Act. The OPEN Act was introduced to the U.S. House of Representatives on January 18, 2012, the same day that several major Web sites went dark in protest of SOPA and PIPA. The bill was intended to deliver stronger intellectual property rights for American artists and innovators while protecting the openness of the Internet, and would give enforcement powers to the International Trade Commission instead of the Department of Justice.

80. The public fought back with a world-wide Internet blackout campaign, wherein hundreds of service providers (ranging from Google to Wikipedia) went offline or posted "CENSORED" messages on their sites. After January's historic public outcry, SOPA and PIPA were removed from their respective legislative committee schedules.

81. It also gave copyright owners the power to lodge complaints that Web sites infringed on their copyright and seek compensation from any company that did business with the Web site.

82. If a court grants an injunction against a site, associated Internet providers and intermediaries have five days to take specific actions against "foreign infringing sites" or risk being sued themselves: (1) Internet service providers must take measures designed to "prevent access" to the site (including blocking the domain name completely); (2) search engines must take measures designed to prevent the site from "being served as links in search results"; (3) payment processors must take measures designed to "prevent, prohibit, or suspend transactions" between the site and U.S. customers; and (4) advertising networks must take measures designed to stop serving ads on the site, or third-party ads on the site (including sponsored links), and cease all compensation to or from the site.

83. *U.S. v. Megaupload Ltd.*, E.D. Va., No. 1:12CR3 (Jan. 5, 2012). Although not specifically limited to adult material, the Megaupload case was one of the most notable seizures of recent times. Megaupload is a digital locker that allows users to store files that can then be streamed or downloaded by others. The Web site allowed

users to download some content for free, but made money by advertising and charging subscriptions to people who wanted access to faster download speeds or extra content. Although located overseas and, arguably, compliant with the relevant laws of its host nation, the U.S. government indicted the company (along with certain owners/board members) on charges of racketeering and conspiracy to commit copyright infringement, and subsequently seized eighteen top-level domain names belonging to the company.

84. *Near v. Minnesota*, 283 U.S. 697 (1931). In *Near*, the U.S. Supreme Court recognized the freedom of the press by roundly rejecting prior restraints on publication, a principle that was applied to free speech generally in subsequent jurisprudence. See also *Neb. Press Ass'n v. Stuart*, 427 U.S. 539, 559 (1976) ("[p]rior restraints on speech and publication are the most serious and the least tolerable infringement on First Amendment rights."); *Alexander v. United States*, 509 U.S. 544 (1993) (describing temporary and permanent injunctions that forbid speech activities as "classic examples of prior restraints").

85. Lawrence G. Walters, "10 Questions with a First Amendment Lawyer," *The Magical Buffet* 2008, http://themagicalbuffet.com/blog1/2008/11/26/10-questions-with-a-first-amendment-lawyer.

86. *U.S. v. Extreme Associates*, 431 F.3d 150 (3d Cir. 2005). Despite the fact that Extreme Associates, Inc. was located in California, the indictment and trial took place in the Western District of Pennsylvania; the location where undercover agents had ordered the offending materials, and video clips had been downloaded.

87. The prosecution also sought forfeiture of the films charged in the indictment, all gross profits from the distribution of the films, and all property used to facilitate the alleged crimes, including the domain name extremeassociates.com.

88. *Lawrence v. Texas*, 539 U.S. 538 (2003). The Supreme Court invalidated all state sodomy laws as an unconstitutional infringement on individual privacy rights pursuant to the principles set forth in the First and Fourteenth Amendments.

89. The defense claimed that the fundamental right to privacy gave individuals the constitutional right to view offending materials in private, a right that cannot be meaningfully exercised without a corresponding right of companies to distribute such materials. The Department of Justice rebutted, claiming that an individual's right to privacy is unrelated to a company's right to commercial distribution.

90. The defense argued that this right was not affected by the fact that the material does not have any literary or artistic merit, and that because the federal obscenity laws imposed a complete ban on materials that people have the right to possess, they were unconstitutional.

91. *United States v. Little*, 365 F. App'x 159 (11th Cir. 2010).

92. The 11th Circuit Court of Appeals upheld Little's obscenity conviction, and the producer began serving his sentence on January 29, 2009.

93. "U.S. Department of Justice statistics show prosecutors charged 361 defendants with obscenity violations during President George W. Bush's years in office, nearly twice as many as under President Bill Clinton. In 2009, 20 defendants were charged, compared with 54 the previous year." Spenser S. Hsu, "U.S. District

Judge Drops Porn Charges Against Video Producer John A. Stagliano," *Washington Post,* 2010, http://www.washingtonpost.com/wp-dyn/content/article/2010/07/16/AR2010071605750.html.

94. *United States v. Stagliano,* 729 F.Supp.2d 215 (D.D.C. 2010).

95. The Obscenity Prosecution Task Force of the U.S. Department of Justice was a special interest unit of the DOJ, formed under the first George W. Bush Administration. The Task Force was said to be created to combat the overabundance of allegedly obscene material available on the Internet. Upon its dissolution in April of 2011, the Task Force was absorbed into the Child Exploitation and Obscenity Section (CEOS) of the U.S. Department of Justice.

96. Josh Gerstein, "Eric Holder Accused of Neglecting Porn Fight," *Politico* 2011, http://www.politico.com/news/stories/0411/53314.html.

97. *United States v. Isaacs,* No. 13-50036, 2014 WL 1201134 (9th Cir. March 25, 2014). Isaacs was convicted of two counts of mailing obscene matter (18 U.S.C. § 1461); one count of engaging in the business of producing and selling obscene matter (18 U.S.C. § 1466(a)); one count of transportation of obscene matter for sale or distribution (18 U.S.C. § 1465); and one count of transportation of obscene matter (18 U.S.C. § 1462(a)).

98. Judge Kozinski, a well-known conservative, later shifted partial responsibility for the images to his adult son.

99. The defense claimed that the lower court erred in altering jury instructions over the concept of "prurient interest" as used in the Miller Test for obscenity.

100. For instance, the prong relating to "contemporary community standards" arguably is nonexistent in the Internet information age of the 21st century. Given the right to possess even obscene materials in the privacy of one's home and the developing right to sexual autonomy, distribution of sexually explicit material via the Internet completely alters the perception of presence within a geographic community. Taking into account the boundlessness of the Internet, there is no doubt that certain adult-oriented materials transmitted via the Internet should not implicate the same concerns that were addressed in *Miller* and its progeny (relating to each community's right to regulate the type of erotic material whose presence is tolerated within the confines of the local community).

101. "Report on Eliminating Gender Stereotypes in the European Union (2012 /2116(INI))," *European Parliament* 2012, http://www.europarl.europa.eu/sides/getDoc.do?pubRef=-//EP//TEXT+REPORT+A7-2012-0401+0+DOC+XML+V0//EN.

102. *Id.*

103. Jim Killock, "Sleepwalking Into Censorship," *Open Rights Group* 2013, https://www.openrightsgroup.org/blog/2013/sleepwalking-into-censorship. Some Internet service providers have gone to the extent of blocking so-called esoteric material by default. Because no definition of that term is provided in Prime Minister Cameron's filtering policy, this grants the service providers broad discretion in determining which sites to block.

104. "Blocking Categories on Parental Controls," *BT Group* 2013, http://bt.custhelp.com/app/answers/detail/a_id/46809/kw/parental%20controls/c/346,6679,6680/

related/1. The referenced Internet filtering system is the policy enforced at the time of publication.

105. Oliver Duggan, "'Active Choice+' vs 'Default On': How Cameron's Crackdown on Internet Pornography Became a Rebranding Exercise," *The Independent* 2013, http://www.independent.co.uk/news/uk/politics/active-choice-vs-default-on-how-camerons-crackdown-on-internet-pornography-became-a-rebranding-exercise-8710076.html.

106. Jerry Barnett, "Opinion: Claire Perry's 'Porn Filter' Is Internet Censorship v1.0," *Pirate Party* 2013, http://www.pirateparty.org.uk/blog/editor/opinion-claire-perry%E2%80%99s-%E2%80%9Cporn-filter%E2%80%9D-internet-censorship-v10.

107. Iran, China, and North Korea have limited citizens' access to online content (including pornography) as well, but such restrictions have been in effect in those particular countries essentially since the Internet's inception.

108. The ability to control infiltration of the banned content leads directly to the next hurdle—the black market. In the Internet age, every technological restriction is met with a response circumventing that restriction. Whether it's a scrubbing tool used to mask IP address identification or software that scrambles collected geo-location location, there are countless techniques enabling the average Internet user to evade government-imposed limitations.

109. Lawrence G. Walters, "Anatomy of an Obscenity Prosecution: The Tammy Robinson Case Study," *Adult Industry Update*, 1999, http://www.adultindustryupdate.com/archives/Anatomy%20of%20an%20Obscenity%20Prosecution.pdf.

2

Seen as a Business: Adult Film's Historical Framework and Foundations

Kevin Heffernan

> I write about porn as an industry because I want people to under-
> stand that it needs to be seen as a business whose product evolves
> with a specifically capitalist logic.
>
> —Gail Dines[1]

INTRODUCTION

Ever since theatrical distribution of hardcore pornography raised the profile of sexual media in the early 1970s, most research on the subject has treated it as a set of social problems to be solved by the broad, overlapping domains of ethics, free expression, censorship, human rights, psychology, and the law.[2] In response to this trend, since around the mid-1990s, there has emerged an increasing number of fine-grained analyses of erotic art and media from a more focused perspective that fold both the study of pornography and porn itself into questions posed by art history, anthropology, literary criticism, moving-image studies, and, most recently, computer science.[3] As film scholar Peter Alilunas notes,[4] much of this scholarship falls somewhere on a continuum between Walter Kendrick who, in *The Secret Museum*, defines the object of study by its hidden, surreptitious, or regulated nature,[5] and Linda Williams who, in *Hard Core*, outlines the textual features that constitute hardcore narrative cinema and provides a model of how these elements change over time.[6] Both Kendrick and Williams, and the scholars who have drawn upon their distinctive models, incorporate a sophisticated and nuanced discussion of the role that larger commercial media and their successive technological forms play in both the individual moments of erotic media and the often nonlinear way media texts and their circulation and reception change over time. But all in their own way treat economic change as an epiphenomenon of the engines that drive the pornographic process: Kendrick's master narrative is one of social control drawn along lines of class, and *Hard Core* treats moving-image pornography as a deeply ambivalent heir to conflicting early-20th-century discourses about technology, gender, and the visible body. Shifting contexts of production, distribution, and exhibition provide successive iterations of these dominant themes, although Williams's later book, *Screening Sex*, analyzed key shifts in the media industries in much greater detail.[7]

But what happens if we place economics at center stage in the historical narrative?[8] First, from the *Regents v. Exelsior* decision of 1955 to the Communications Decency Act of 1996, it becomes clear that most of the signature censorship struggles faced by the adult film industry appear after major changes in modes of distribution. Second, each shift in porn distribution produces a new set of infrastructure and related institutions as producers, distributors, exhibitors, retailers, and Webmasters attempt to standardize trade practices after distribution moves into a new phase. These institutions include the trade press, lobbying groups, and publicity and promotion consisting of industry awards and appearances of industry figures in the mainstream media. Finally, changes in distribution have major effects on the aesthetic conventions of adult films, including generic norms, film style, and the star system. This chapter highlights the period of hardcore cinema's distribution from stag films that appeared in the early 20th century to their later incarnation as loops distributed to peep-show booths in the 1960s, the porno-chic era in the 1970s, and the decline of adult film's theatrical distribution at the dawn of the home video era in the 1980s.

STAGS, BEAVERS, LOOPS, AND BOOTHS: HARDCORE CINEMA MOVES INTO THE PUBLIC SPHERE

According to contemporary accounts, which tend to be spotty at best, the earliest short commercial films showing unsimulated sexual intercourse appeared during the nickelodeon era of 1905 to 1915.[9] Because of these films' clandestine and illegal status as commercial entertainment, the personnel, business practices, and audiences of this era of moving-image pornography have been notoriously difficult for historians to reconstruct. Indeed, many 35 mm nitrate prints of the films have congealed or combusted. That said, much bold and innovative scholarship is being conducted on this period in adult film history. According to author Dave Thompson, European exhibition of many of these early films took place in an underground network of secret cinemas that rarely "operated from the same premises more than once. Like modern raves, their locations were fiercely guarded secrets until as close to screening time as possible."[10] Their contemporary nonerotic nickelodeon counterparts also exhibited above ground; early sex films were usually sold rather than leased to the venue that exhibited them. From the beginning, these screenings were associated with the presence of female sex workers, either through screenings conducted in proximity to brothels or through sex workers hired as subcontractors by the impresario presenting the films. In Germany, the United States, and France, stag films were screened inside brothels, sometimes showcasing onscreen talent and specialized services provided by the establishment. Thus, in many secret cinemas as well as "houses of ill fame," the films served as loss leaders designed to market the services of sex workers and the establishments that employed them. This framing context of the films' exhibition and economic function helps to explain two of the most remarkable features of stags from this era—their often high production values, and the performers' unusually wide sexual repertoire.

The immense social changes in the United States after World War I drastically altered the commercial landscape in which stag films were distributed and exhibited. When American women won the right to vote in 1920, many activists began to apply political pressure to Congress, state legislatures, and municipal governments in an effort to ameliorate a crowded urban environment associated with sexual exploitation of the poor and alcohol-fueled violence against women. Passage of the Eighteenth Amendment in 1920, which outlawed the production and sale of alcohol, gave federal, state, and local authorities sweeping new powers to control, search, sanction, and close a huge range of urban leisure establishments, in effect shuttering many of the venues that had been crucial to the exhibition of stag films.

The other major social change in this period, which forever altered the landscape of erotic entertainment, was the rise of the automobile. As male-centered entertainment establishments left the increasingly scrutinized urban leisure core and became more dispersed, the automobile enabled members of fraternal orders, police and firefighting units, college social clubs, and World War I veterans groups to replicate the shifting locales of the prewar secret cinemas in a members-only homosocial environment, with each member providing his own transportation to the temporary exhibition venue. The automobile was also indispensable to the new means of distributing the stags: The model of established venues buying prints of sex films outright was replaced by the model of the itinerant showman, who drove across states and regions with a car trunk full of 16 mm film prints, a projector, and a screen, which he deployed for one evening at a set fee. An evening's program could be quite eclectic, featuring both stag films and more conventional fare, all of which was tailored to the needs and desires of those who hired his services. Although these traveling programmers were mostly publicized by word of mouth, repeat business seems to have been crucial to their success. There is evidence that some of these itinerant showmen had a well-cultivated circuit of clubs and lodges to whom they offered their services on an annual or semi-annual basis during their long drives across the region.[11]

The 8 mm film gauge provided hardcore cinema an entrée into the booming 1960s public retail environment in the form of the arcade viewing booth. Although introduced in 1932, the 8 mm film camera and projector did not become a fixture in middle-class American homes until the post–World War II period.[12] Regular 8 mm film consisted of a 16 mm reversal film strip run twice through the camera, processed, split down the middle, and spliced together for projection. Short hardcore films on 8 mm appeared above ground in the 1960s after legalization of pornography in several European countries made sexually explicit magazines available for import, to be sold in specialized adults-only retail outlets established in American urban areas. After a rapid period of consolidation and expansion in the adult bookstore market in the late 1960s, several firms, including a subsidiary of Reuben Sturman's Cleveland-based *Sovereign News*, began to lease 8 mm viewing booths to adult bookstores for patrons' private enjoyment of short hardcore films.[13] Initially, the booths were constructed out of the old post–World War II "soundie" video jukeboxes modified to accommodate 8 mm film[14] after the soundies were crushed by French competitor Scopitone in the 1960s.[15] The exploding popularity of the arcade booths created an insatiable demand for the short loops (so called because they were spliced head to tail and could be run through the projector repeatedly without a reel change). In a typical arrangement, the arcade owner would contract with Sturman's Sovereign Agency, the Gambino crime syndicate's Star Distributing, or another firm to install the booths, and the proceeds would be split 50/50 with the supplier. The supplier would furnish some of the films, but the huge turnover in product made it virtually certain that retailers would acquire product from other sources.

The involvement of organized crime in this aspect of adult cinema provides an example of the Mob's ability to establish a significant presence in the adult industry but its inability to dominate or monopolize all aspects of production or distribution. Because it was still illegal in the late 1960s to manufacture hardcore pornography, the Mafia controlled many of the New York labs that processed the raw 16 mm footage shot by the loop makers. In exchange for safe return of their footage, which a non-Mafia connected lab likely would have seized and turned over to the police, filmmakers paid drastically inflated rates for film processing. Further down the pipeline, Sturman, Robert DiBernardo, and their associates in the Gambino and Colombo families directly controlled the installation and fee collecting of the machines in several regions of the country. They also controlled Wholesale Books, one of the larger companies supplying 8 mm films to the marketplace.[16] Organized crime flourished in the porn business when it could control a carefully selected choke point in the production or distribution pipeline and exact tribute for allowing unprocessed film, boxed and labeled 8 mm product, and the viewing machines to reach their final destination—the adult bookstore where customers waited with pockets full of quarters. Even the well-financed and connected Mob interests were unable to feed the insatiable maw of the loop machines, however. A number of competitors emerged in machine installation, and adult bookstores bought their arcade movies not just from major suppliers such as Wholesale Books and others but also from independent "rack jobbers," itinerant sales associates who traveled the country by region selling film out of the trunks of their cars.[17] Adult filmmaker Cass Paley, who shot and sold loops in this period, recalls that some 2,000 named firms provided product to the market.[18] Similarly, some filmmakers avoided the inflated fees of the connected labs by paying conventional lab technicians under the table to run their reversal reels through the bleaching, processing, and fixing baths after hours. This often resulted in distorted color values and washed out images because the film was processed using lab chemicals at the very end of their daily replacement cycle.[19]

During this period, bookstores bought rather than leased the arcade films, which were sold by the foot,[20] and chain stores could buy films in volume and switch them out between stores to meet the consumer demand for new product. Then, the 1965 introduction of Super 8 mm—a single strip of film with smaller sprocket holes preloaded into a camera-ready cartridge that provided a larger, brighter image—led to an explosion of interest in home movie making and viewing. Just as the introduction of the arcade machines had created a film product shortage for the adult bookstores, so the introduction of Super 8 created a shortage of movies for home viewing as consumers using the new gauge sought to augment their home movies with cartoons, condensed feature films, sports highlights, and pornography. Although sex shops had been selling 8 mm loops to customers for some time, hardcore loops in the new Super 8 format became a major source of profit for the bookstores as demand skyrocketed. This expanded means of distribution, caused by product shortage, had two predictable consequences: First, some firms attempted product differentiation through the development of a star system. The Sweetheart line featured newcomer John Holmes, who performed with female costar Linda McDowell in a very popular series, which began in the late 1960s.[21] In 1973, Sturman and partner Al Bloom started the long-running Swedish Erotica series, which was located not in Scandinavia but in the San Francisco Bay area. Sturman and Bloom cultivated a stable of performers who split their time between performing in the company's loops and starring in theatrically exhibited features. Several major stars of the seventies such as Seka and Juliet Anderson (aka "Aunt Peg") first achieved popularity in Swedish Erotica loops, and megastar Annette Haven eventually served as production manager on many of the company's more ambitious shoots in the late 1970s.[22] Second, this change in distribution and the attendant wider circulation of 8 mm hardcore led to a key censorship case. In 1969, after a Georgia man was arrested when police found hardcore 8 mm reels in his home office while executing a search warrant for bookmaking records, the U.S. Supreme Court ruled in *Stanley v. Georgia* that possession of hardcore pornography in the home was protected under the First and Fourteenth Amendments.[23]

Film historian Eric Schaefer has shown that the initial public exhibition of hardcore pornography emerged from a space in between 8 mm loops and 35 mm theatrical exhibition, namely the screening of color 16 mm "beaver films" in storefront theaters in San Francisco around 1967. These short, initially silent films featured full frontal nudity, much writhing and grinding, and direct looks into the camera as the female talent disrobed and eventually spread her legs for the camera.[24] Both the beaver film as a genre and the exhibition context of small storefront theaters or "mini-cinemas" spread from the Bay Area to other cities, and more films were needed to fill the growing demand. Some exhibitors, such as Lowell Pickett and Arlene Elster's Sutter Cinema, Alex DeRenzy's Screening Room, and the Mitchell Brothers' O'Farrell Theater, began producing their own beaver shorts, which were sold to other exhibitors after the conclusion of their run.[25] Competition between filmmakers, who sold their films outright to the theaters, as well as competition between theaters, led to rapid innovation and a ratcheting up of explicitness. The films became longer, and women appeared first onscreen with other women, then with men, and finally in groups. By 1969–1970, some companies, such as the exhibitor-financed Cosmos Films, began producing feature-length narrative films in 16 mm, which featured the full nudity of beaver films along with a story line and scenes of simulated sex.[26] The "distribution" of these prints consisted of shipping a carton of 16 mm film in mailing containers often disguised as other kinds of freight.[27]

Manufacturers soon realized that some geographic locations were more apt to prosecute storefronts than others, so they began to send different versions of some of their titles to different customers.[28] Over the next year, some storefronts began showing films with edited inserts of visible penetration and fellatio, while more demure versions showing whole-body simulation were shipped to other locations. By 1971, some theaters that had been showing 35 mm sexploitation films (discussed in the following section) installed 16 mm projection equipment and began screening an increasingly available array of hardcore features, including *Mona* (1970), *School Girl* (1971), and *The*

Coming Thing (1972), which were leased like theatrical features rather than sold outright as the beaver films had been.

Many of the early mini-cinema situations later became famous as specialist or low-end 16 mm houses after the rise of the hardcore feature. These exhibition sites included the couples-friendly Sutter Cinema, the wilder O'Farrell cinema in San Francisco,[29] and New York City's Avon, Cameo, and Tivoli theaters, the last of which became a legendary cruising spot for men after changing its name to the Adonis and adopting a policy of screening gay hardcore. As Schaefer notes, the simulation features such as The Line Is Busy (1969) and Model Hunters (1970) provided a range of stylistic and narrative elements that hardcore features would eventually inherit, most notably the intercut close-ups of penetration, which had their origin in the multiple versions of prints shipped out to storefronts but that continue as a stylistic device in hardcore movies to this day.

THE POSTWAR AMERICAN FILM INDUSTRY, THE ART THEATER, AND THE SEXPLOITATION FILM

Another important set of historical changes that eventually led to hardcore adult cinema's appearance above ground in traditional American movie houses occurred after World War II. The vertically integrated Hollywood studio system, which had been the subject of lawsuits by independent exhibitors for over a decade, was ruled illegal restraint of trade by the Supreme Court in the 1948 decision U.S. v. Paramount Pictures et al. The major studios were ordered to sign consent decrees stating that they would sell their theater chains and desist from booking films in large blocks to exhibitors. In addition, the spun-off exhibitor companies were forced to divest themselves of theaters whose location and market position gave them a de facto local monopoly in the profitable first-run engagement of major studio releases. At the same time, a massively subsidized shift of the population from urban areas to newly constructed suburbs relocated much of the movie audience away from both first- and second-run movie theaters in the city, and new theater construction in suburban areas lagged far behind this shift. Disposable income was now used to purchase consumer durable goods, including television sets, which further removed movie-going from its long-accustomed central role in American culture and the entertainment business. Although film financing and production processes changed,[30] Hollywood still dominated the most profitable sectors of the film industry because of its powerful system of national distribution. Both studios and independent producers began producing fewer films, with higher budgets, and often showcased new technologies of presentation such as color, widescreen, stereo sound, and 3-D.

The years between the introduction of CinemaScope in 1953 and the appearance of theatrically exhibited hardcore cinema in 1970 constituted the most sustained and precipitous decline in movie attendance in American film history.[31] The major distributors ruthlessly increased rental terms for their big hits and booked them for extended first runs at confiscatory terms, and many of the most popular films entered subsequent-run engagements completely played out. Former sub-run theaters also had fewer releases from which to choose, resulting in a severe product shortage that plagued even large circuits well into the 1970s. Some new players such as American International Pictures (AIP) were able to exploit this situation by making films for the youth market touted with sensational, carnival-like publicity. AIP successfully booked its films into many hungry neighborhood theaters and drive-ins and had achieved mini-major status by the 1960s, complete with a national distribution network of regional film exchanges. Some exhibitors began to book an increasing number of films from abroad and touted their difference from Hollywood products by emphasizing the foreign films' franker treatment of sexual and violent themes. Many of the smaller distributors of these movies lacked the national distribution infrastructure of even an AIP and had to rely on regional subdistributors to book their films into local circuits and independent exhibitors. Some theater chains specializing in broadly defined foreign films, such as Midwesterner Louis Sher's Art Theater Guild, entered distribution to secure films for their own and other theaters. It is this last, "foreign art film" model—hand-to-mouth exhibitors renting movies from regional subdistributors without an orderly system of runs and clearances through national film exchanges—that would characterize hardcore cinema well into the 1970s. In fact, some of the same key figures from the art cinema market reappear in the porno chic era and beyond.

The world of art-film distributors and struggling exhibitors forms the background for the three signature movie censorship cases of the postwar period. The 1952 U.S. Supreme Court ruling in *Joseph Burstyn, Inc. v. Wilson* (known as the *Miracle* decision) extended First Amendment protection to motion pictures. The Court ruled unconstitutional the use of a New York education law to bar art film importer Joseph Burstyn from screening Roberto Rossellini's short film *Il Miracolo*, originally part of the omnibus feature *L'Amore*, on the grounds that it was "sacrilegious."[32] Then, in 1955, Excelsior Pictures, a small distributor of imports and low-budget films, produced and released *Garden of Eden*, a family drama largely set in a nudist colony. New York tried to ban the film, but the New York State Supreme Court ruled the following year in *Excelsior v. Regents* that in motion pictures, "nudity per se is not obscene." The film played the circuit of former subsequent-run theaters, which had come to specialize in imports and exploitation films.

In 1957, the U.S. Supreme Court's decision in *Roth v. United States* made the "dominant theme of a work, taken as a whole" the subject under discussion in obscenity cases—in this case, the entirety of a book in a case involving the printed word. Five years later, the Court overturned a decision by the Supreme Court of Ohio convicting Cleveland exhibitor Nico Jacobellis of obscenity for showing the French import *The Lovers* (1958) at his Heights Art Theater, an outpost of Louis Sher's Art Theater Guild chain. *Jacobellis v. Ohio* failed to reach a consensus among the nine justices regarding what specifically constituted obscenity in movies, but its precedent raised the bar for local prosecution of movies with nudity and sexual themes.

By the early 1960s, moviegoers and distributors could recognize an entire circuit of what was known as "art theaters"—a term often uttered with a smirk or a roll of the eyes. Many of these subsisted on an eclectic program of imports and exploitation films, and some of them came to specialize in adults-only films such as the nudist camp films that followed in the wake of *Garden of Eden*, the "nudie cuties" that followed the success of Russ Meyer's *The Immoral Mr. Teas* in 1959, and the later "roughies" or sexploitation films. Sexploitation films attempted to unite the partial, nonfrontal nudity of its predecessors with downbeat, violent themes derived from the thriller, the film noir, the melodrama, and the urban crime drama in films such as *Lorna* and *Sin in the Suburbs* (both 1964), *Aroused* (1966), *The Agony of Love* (1967), and others. By 1967, almost every city had a theater specializing in such films, and distributors such as Entertainment Ventures, Inc. (EVI), Cambist Films, Distribpix, and Box Office International distributed their product through these theaters either through regional subdistributors or by leasing the national film exchanges of AIP and other companies. To keep production budgets low in what became a high-output business with frequently changed double features, there was little promotion of stars in the period of softcore sexploitation. Some performers, however, such as Marsha Jordan of *The Wild Females* (1968), *Lady Godiva Rides* (1969), and other films, developed a sizeable fan base and made promotional appearances at engagements of their films.

Although explicitness, including full frontal nudity, gradually increased, most changes in the form resulted from slightly higher budgets following the shift to color around 1968 and the gradual consolidation of production into a smaller group of larger firms. In 1969, many larger distributors and theater chains specializing in softcore adult films created the Adult Film Association of America, a trade organization designed to pool resources in the fight against censorship, lobby elected officials on behalf of the industry, gingerly begin advocacy of adult movies to the general public, and ensure more orderly distribution and accounting of ticket sales in a Wild West–like business environment. As Eric Schaefer has shown, the largest and most influential AFAA members initially resisted the intrusion of hardcore cinema into the existing system of distribution and industry legal defense and advocacy.[33] EVI head and future AFAA president David F. Friedman, in an adage taken from his mentor in the exploitation business, summarized the role of hype and tease in a sexploitation industry that refused to reveal the primal act on the screen: "Sell the sizzle, not the steak."

THEATRICALLY EXHIBITED HARDCORE IN THE 1970s AND 1980s

Only after the financial and legal success of Sturman's private viewing booths, the business model of producer/exhibitors such as the Mitchells and DeRenzy, and the proven viability of 16 mm distribution and exhibition, did hardcore filmmakers begin to more widely distribute 35 mm release prints to conventional movie theaters. DeRenzy himself made *Sexual Freedom in Denmark* (1970), a documentary film about Sex 69, Copenhagen's international convention of the sex industry. Using the *Roth* and *Memoirs* obscenity standards to situate the explosive explicit imagery in his film within a context of documentary exploration, DeRenzy enjoyed not only spectacular success in his own Screening Room but also many lucrative independent and circuit bookings with a 35 mm blowup of the movie. For the next year, many films that couched their hardcore footage in the documentary format, usually deploying tropes of sociological inquiry or sex education, secured successful bookings in a range of theaters during the depths of the 1968 to 1971 film industry recession.

The big breakout of hardcore cinema in 1971 and 1972 relied heavily on the culture, infrastructure, and major players of the art cinema movement of the previous twenty years. First, the *succès de scandale* of Grove Press's 1969 release of the Swedish import *I Am Curious (Yellow)* cemented the decades-long association of the art theater with explicit imagery and sexual themes.[34] In fact, the Motion Picture Association of America (MPAA)'s 1968 replacement of the Production Code Administration with the age-based rating system of the Code and Ratings Administration (CARA)—still in use today—was Hollywood's attempt to establish a competitive beachhead against independent films and imports, which had differentiated their product through sexual frankness. While the Grove Press import was wending its way through the courts, Midwestern exhibitor Louis Sher, whose distribution arm Sherpix had supplied both his own Art Theater Guild circuit and other theaters since 1965, announced an expansion of his company with films designed for much wider release. These included the 3-D feature *The Stewardesses* (1969) and the explicit hardcore feature *Mona, the Virgin Nymph* (1970). A year later, *Mona* went into much wider release on a double bill with the cofeature *School Girl* (1971). Sherpix and several other defendants were indicted by a federal grand jury in Memphis in *U.S. v. Jerome Sandy et al.* for distributing the allegedly obscene film *School Girl* in interstate commerce. Among the codefendants were AIP's Washington, D.C., film exchange and other subdistributors of the film.[35] For years, Sherpix, along with other distributors of imports and exploitation films, had relied on AIP's film exchanges to secure bookings for their films, which followed the broad outlines of an orderly national release—often with spectacular success in films such as *The Stewardesses*. After the debacle of the *Sandy* case, AIP's distribution arm quietly withdrew from allowing hardcore films to pass through its film exchanges, and for the remainder of the decade explicit films relied on a patchwork of regional subdistributors to book them into the growing but loosely affiliated circuits of porno houses.

The American art cinema exhibition context of the 1950s and 1960s also gave hardcore cinema its highest profile and most important exhibition venue—the 300-seat World Theater on New York City's West 44th Street. This had been the house where many of the signature art films of the era, including those of Ingmar Bergman and the French New Wave, had made their American debuts.[36] In 1965, the theater was bought by a partnership headed by Distribpix chief Arthur Morowitz and shifted its program to releases from Distribpix and other sexploitation companies. The famous year-long run of *Deep Throat* at the World in 1972–1973 shows how even organized crime interests, often mischaracterized as the most powerful players pulling the strings in the adult film industry, had to accommodate the pattern of distribution and exhibition established over the previous twenty years. When the Peraino brothers, producers of the film and members of the Colombo crime syndicate, sought theatrical exhibition for the film, they turned to East Coast subdistributor Terry Levene, whose Aquarius Pictures secured bookings for *Deep Throat* in an ad hoc circuit of theaters in the New York and New Jersey area, including the World.[37]

The reliance of filmmakers on subdistributors, many of whom also owned regional chains of adult theaters, plagued the orderly distribution and accounting of receipts throughout the porno chic era of the early 1970s. The Mitchell Brothers took out full-page ads in *Variety* to warn exhibitors not to book *Behind the Green Door* and *Resurrection of Eve* (1973) from named bootleggers often tied to states-rights distributors. The Perainos subcontracted nationwide for a team of "checkers" and "sweepers" to count theater attendees and later collect the 50 percent of receipts due to the company (terms extraordinarily generous to theater owners, who would have paid up to 90 percent to the major studios for a box-office hit of *Deep Throat*'s magnitude). Even the threat of Mob muscle was not enough to prevent millions of dollars of runoff.

After the Perainos entered mainstream distribution with Bryanston Pictures, they enjoyed major hits in 1974 with *The Texas Chainsaw Massacre*, *Andy Warhol's Frankenstein*, and Bruce Lee's *Return of the Dragon*. The company's most ambitious (and ultimately fatal) endeavor was the expensive introduction of a computerized box office accounting system that Bryanston hoped would become the industry standard[38] and stave off the millions in losses the company had sustained through subdistributor and exhibitor hijinks.

Many hardcore exhibitors continued showing their films in 16 mm. While larger distributors such as Sherpix and Cambist blew up 16 mm negatives to 35 mm for distribution, an increasing number of production companies made reduction prints from 35 mm to 16 mm to secure bookings in the smaller houses that proliferated in the first half of the decade. In some of these smaller situations, other theaters in their city or region had already sewn up the current high-profile releases likely to sustain weeks-long bookings, so they adopted a strategy of programming a new double feature every week, booking almost everything they could get their hands on, sometimes buying 16 mm prints outright from other theaters. This sellers' market supported many low-budget "one-day wonders" shot and released in 16 mm. Adult filmmaker Carter Stevens recalls that many directors and cinematographers worked on both 16 mm features and loops well into the 1970s. "The loops were our bread and butter," he remembers, "but features were like a steak dinner."[39] By the middle of the decade, there was a sufficient backlog of older "A" releases in reduction prints, which could be slotted into double bills with newer films. The one-day wonders began to disappear, and Carter and his colleagues increasingly worked in the theatrical gauge of 35 mm.

Ancillary institutions such as trade groups and the star system changed rapidly in this period. The Adult Filmmakers Association of America (AFAA) was crucial to imposing some measure of order to the commercial breakout of hardcore cinema. Many of the major players in AFAA were some of the larger regional circuit owners and subdistributors, including Sam Lake's Maturpix on the East Coast (later absorbed into Distribpix), the California-based Essex Films, and Sherpix in the Midwest. These firms established something like a trustworthy relationship with many of the production companies over a three- or four-year period of "trust but verify" in which rental figures from individual houses and regional circuits could be compared over time and something like an orderly accounting of receipts was established. Also, the star system arose in this period of adult film's efforts to secure the distribution necessary to create and sustain box office hits. Performers such as Linda Lovelace of *Deep Throat*, Georgina Spelvin of *The Devil in Miss Jones* (1973), and Marilyn Chambers of *Behind the Green Door* (1972) achieved national name and face recognition (and more in men's magazines). These high-visibility performers were crucial in the industry's efforts to maintain at least a national profile, if not a traditional national distribution, for its releases.

Two events in the middle of the decade had incalculable effects on the distribution of hardcore adult cinema. In 1973, the Supreme Court's *Miller* decision ruled that "contemporary community standards" in the legal definition of obscenity were local rather than national. As with the *Regents* and *Jacobellis* decisions of the previous decades, *Miller* occurred after the distribution context of hardcore films had changed from the itinerant and jobber mode of stags and loops to high-profile distribution and booking into theater circuits. Now, filmmakers could not be certain that films made in New York or San Francisco would not be ruled obscene in Minneapolis or Memphis after prints had played for only a week's engagement. This in effect strengthened the hand of subdistributors, who often were either exhibitors themselves or in close contact with them and thus were the best judges of what kinds of films were likely to "bring on the heat." After *Miller*, the star system began to wane as name performers retired, tried to cross over into mainstream films, or became integrated into the small stock company of performers appearing in dozens of features. Then, in 1976, Congress repealed the tax shelter laws allowing investors to write off multiples of their share in feature films if the movies proved unprofitable.[40] This was a hidden—but deliberate and devastating—blow to hardcore film financing, because filmmakers in New York and California had relied on production financing from silent partners in real estate, investment banking, advertising, and retail who had sought to wipe out declared income from their more lucrative business dealings.[41] The repeal of the tax shelter affected not only pornographers but also filmmakers in other modes and genres on the low end of the production budget spectrum. George Romero, John Waters, Wes Craven, and Tobe Hooper either fell silent for a time after 1977 or allied themselves with financing from Hollywood and Europe once the tax shelters that had helped finance films such as *Night of the Living Dead* (1968), *Pink Flamingos, Last House on the Left* (both 1972), and *The Texas Chainsaw Massacre* were no longer available to investors.

Silent partners seeking tax shelters had been crucial for smaller 16 mm producers in overcoming barriers to entering the business of feature film production. With this mode of film financing no longer available, the number of low-end, one-day wonders produced and exhibited in 16 mm continued to diminish. Simultaneously, mainstream cinema's recovery from the pre-1972 recession on the backs of blockbusters such as *Jaws* (1975) and *Star Wars* (1977) was not extending to many subsequent-run theaters in city neighborhood and suburban shopping complexes. Between 1975 and 1979, an increasing number of subrun theaters screening films in 35 mm converted to adult houses, relying on the smaller but consistent porn audience's willingness to pay ticket prices still about twice as high as those for conventional Hollywood fare. By 1977, the adult film industry was characterized by fewer annual releases, most of which were shot on 35 mm with larger budgets. In terms of distribution, there were smaller print runs and a much more orderly system of circulation of prints in which successive runs of a film proceeded in concentric circles outward from heavily populated urban areas, to the suburbs, and finally to rural theaters,[42] including drive-ins, which frequently (but not always) screened alternative "cooler" versions of the films with hardcore inserts removed.[43] Many of these coordinated regional releases constituted a de facto national release, often timed to coincide with nude photo spreads of a film's female lead in men's magazines such as *Penthouse*, *Gallery*, and *Hustler*. This proved to be an important and profitable synergy.[44]

This shift in distribution resulted in a number of efforts by adult filmmakers and their trade groups and ancillary institutions to present their releases as part of the wider American landscape of popular film. First, the star system returned to hardcore cinema. Annette Haven had made her debut in a lead role in 1975 with *China Girl*. By 1977, her films, such as *Desires Within Young Girls* (an uncredited, high-budget hardcore reworking of the 1953 Fox hit *How to Marry a Millionaire* with Haven in the Betty Grable role), were on *Variety*'s top rental charts, and she was touring to support the releases of her films. Samantha Fox and Seka first appeared onscreen in 1977. Veronica Hart and Kelly Nichols made their hardcore bows in 1979, and theatrical porn's last megastar, the notoriously underage Traci Lords, appeared on the scene four years later. Second, the AFAA began hosting its annual Erotic Film Awards ceremony based on the Oscars in 1977. The awards were used by the industry to draw the public's attention to the acting and filmmaking skills visible in adult cinema in its continuing efforts to cross over to a larger and more diverse audience.

As with every change in distribution, the move toward high-profile releases and wide promotion brought with it increasing calls for censorship, this time from Women Against Pornography and other feminist groups. Although opposed from the beginning by women's groups such as Feminists for Free Expression and the Feminist Anti-Censorship Task Force, antipornography feminism generated many important book-length political and philosophical critiques of pornography including Susan Griffin's *Pornography and Silence* and Andrea Dworkin's *Pornography: Men Possessing Women*.[45] Women Against Pornography's most high-profile event was a March 1979 demonstration in New York's Times Square, which drew over 5,000 participants. The feminist sex wars were at least partially an outgrowth of the changes in adult film distribution, which brought the industry's products and public figures into public view, and into the cultural and cinematic mainstream to an unprecedented degree.[46]

Initially, home video—introduced in 1976 with the Sony Betamax—coexisted with the successful theatrical exhibition of hardcore cinema. Companies such as Quality X and VCX issued a back catalog of older films on home video at prices of $70 to $100 apiece. By the early 1980s, video was beginning to replace 8 mm and 16 mm in viewing booths and arcades, but big-budget films with major stars were still hugely popular at the box office.[47] By 1983, the home video market had transformed from a high-end, consumer sale model to a rental model,[48] and video stores that carried both adult product and mainstream releases became the major customers for adult video companies. In 1983, several employees of Movies Unlimited—a large Philadelphia video distributor, which supplied films of every description to video rental shops—began to publish the newsletter Adult Video News (AVN) to help mom-and-pop video stores buy and market adult films on home videotape to their rental customers. Meanwhile, companies such as Swedish Erotica—who bought out a catalog of several companies for home video release and changed its name to Caballero Control Corporation—and VCA Labs, a tape duplicating service that began to distribute acquired titles to retailers, entered feature film financing. Caballero produced early-1980s films including the box-office hit Sorority Sweethearts (1983), and VCA both financed Chuck Vincent's award-winning In Love (1983) and produced the films of the Dark Brothers, most notably the hugely influential New Wave Hookers (1985), the last major box-office hit of the theatrical era. By 1986, productions shot on videotape for the rental market had begun their ascendancy, and the industry moved into a high output mode of production. As adult video became more popular, the exhibition circuits began a steady decline into oblivion. A glossy, monthly AVN had become the ancillary trade institution most important to the adult film industry; the Reagan-era Meese Commission began its investigation, with venue-shopping prosecutions and a public relations campaign against the industry; and the cycle described throughout this chapter repeated itself yet again.

CONCLUSION

Changes in distribution often prompt institutions as varied as advocacy groups, the legal system, and the production and exhibition branches of the film industry to adjust and reorient. For example, if we situate the history of film censorship in the context of distribution, we see that censorship battles function as both effects and causes of many important changes in the distribution branch of the adult movie business: The wider availability of moving-image erotic media in the late 1960s and early 1970s led to increased calls for its suppression. Conflicting court rulings—even on the same movie or printed text—led to the *Miller* decision that "community standards" were local. This, in turn, made expensive infrastructural changes necessary for the industry to move from a diffuse model of distribution to a more centralized national one, which was less attractive to many of the industry's larger players: If a national circuit of dedicated film exchanges tied to a centralized distributor could be raided by local prosecutors and the films seized as evidence, there was no incentive to change the existing model of shipping prints as individual items of freight or even hand-delivering them to theaters. Venue-shopping obscenity prosecutors continued to exploit the fragmented national market for adult film—from the Memphis *Deep Throat* case, to the Department of Justice's RICO-inspired prosecutions during the Meese Commission era, all the way to the failed Communications Decency Act of 1996.

A second pattern that emerges is the product shortage, which almost always follows in the wake of major shifts in distribution. The distribution of commercial moving image media, including Hollywood films, through television ultimately resulted in former subrun theaters scrambling for product and eventually embracing art cinema and its next-generation heir, softcore and hardcore adult films; the shift to 16 mm distribution of more explicit films created a huge demand of product to fill the play dates of storefront theaters and enabled small-scale producers of one-day wonders to enter production; and the *Miller* decision and the consolidation of production after the tax-shelter changes ultimately created a sellers' market for more ambitious 35 mm movies after many failing subrun theaters converted to porn in the mid-1970s. This trend continued as porn moved into the home: The explosion in VCR sales was seized upon by adult film companies, first under the high-end sales model established by VCX and Quality X in the early 1980s[49] and later under the high-output production model brought on by consumer rental-driven patterns of distribution later in the decade. Like the model of historically situating censorship battles described above, this approach to cyclical product shortages provides one possible account of historical change in moving-image erotic media up to the contemporary period.

Although many of adult film's most vituperative critics describe the genre as a locus classicus of capitalist predation and alienation, few have explored the economic history of the industry in any great detail.[50] Sociologist Gail Dines has conducted primary research into the porn industry by interviewing producers and filmmakers (as well as fans), but she has never seriously heeded her own call for an analysis of the "capitalist logic" behind adult cinema, nor has she written about adult film "as a business" in terms that provide a nuanced model of historical change. The narrative in Dines's book *Pornland* is one of an alarming proliferation of destructive images and access thereto exponentially expanding to younger eyes.[51] According to her model of history, changes in communication technology have made this static, one-dimensional, Velveeta-like cultural toxin virtually ubiquitous. The only historical change visible under this model is the escalating barbarism in the images and sounds themselves and their increasingly immoderate and impulsive "use" (as in, "I used an Agnès Varda movie late last night before bed."). This sort of outrage itself is one of the highly predictable epiphenomena of changes in the distribution of erotic media—one that was seen previously in the shuttering of brothels and secret cinemas after World War I, the campaign by Morality in Media to eradicate adult theaters in the 1970s, and the alliance of the Meese Commission and antiporn feminism during the home video era. Historians have traced this cycle back at least as far as the establishment of the New York Society for the Suppression of Vice after post-Civil War changes in printing and transportation made penny dreadfuls and other salacious printed matter available to young men in urban environments.[52] But still, it is wise to heed Dines's call, because historical research, especially that of the economics of erotic media, helps us avoid oversimplification in our engagement with texts and the range of likely social meanings in their circulation. The rich and varied body of adult film scholarship that will exist one day will include fine-grained historical studies of economic changes within the industry and trace these changes and their symbiotic relationship with aesthetic conventions, cultural background sets, and changing technologies of production, distribution, and consumption.

NOTES

I am grateful to many people who helped me in researching this essay. Adult film preservationist Joe Rubin of Vinegar Syndrome, adult film historian Casey Scott, and retired adult filmmaker Carter Stevens provided a wealth of information on the theatrical distribution of hardcore cinema in interviews conducted in March 2014. Retired adult filmmaker Cass Paley shared his extensive knowledge of the production, distribution, and sale of 8 mm loops and home movies in the 1960s and 1970s. Finally, my lifelong friend Barry Solan employed me for several years at our beloved State Theater in Newark, Delaware, and at Video Américain in Baltimore, Maryland, giving me a front-row seat to several of the changes I describe in the movie and home video business.

1. Gail Dines, "Stop Porn Culture Conference, Wheelock College, June 2010," June 22, 2010. http://gaildines.com/2010/06/stop-porn-culture-conference-wheelock-college-june-2010.

2. See Michael J. Goldstein and Harold Sandford Kant, with John J. Hartman, *Pornography and Sexual Deviance; A Report of the Legal and Behavioral Institute, Beverly Hills, California* (Berkeley: University of California Press, 1973); Ray C. Rist, ed., *The Pornography Controversy: Changing Moral Standards in American Life* (New Brunswick, NJ: Transaction Books, 1974); David Copp and Susan Wendell, eds., *Pornography and Censorship* (Buffalo, NY: Prometheus Books, 1983); Neil M. Malamuth and Edward Donnerstein, eds., *Pornography and Sexual Aggression* (Orlando, FL: Academic Press, 1984).

3. Many of these approaches can be found in Linda Williams, ed., *Porn Studies* (Durham, NC: Duke University Press, 2004). The massive Internet data aggregation made possible by contemporary computer science is used as raw material for an anthropological investigation of porn search habits in Ogi Ogas and Sai Gaddam, *A Billion Wicked Thoughts: What the Internet Tells Us About Sexual Relationships* (New York: Plume, 2011).

4. Peter Alilunas, "Conspiracy or Regulation: Floyd Bloss and the Complexities of Adult Film Historiography," Society for Cinema and Media Studies Conference, Seattle, Washington, March 20, 2014.

5. Walter Kendrick and Steve Renick, *The Secret Museum: Pornography in Modern Culture* (Berkeley: University of California Press, 1997).

6. Linda Williams, *Hard Core: Power, Pleasure, and the "Frenzy of the Visible,"* expanded edition (Berkeley: University of California Press, 1999).

7. This is one of the approaches Williams herself implores adult film studies to use in a recent survey of the field. Linda Williams, *Screening Sex* (Durham, NC: Duke University Press, 2008).

8. Linda Williams, "Pornography, Porno, Porn: Thoughts on a Weedy Field" *Porn Studies* 1, no. 1–2 (2014): 26. Online at http://dx.doi.org/10.1080/23268743.2013.863662.

9. Dave Thompson, *Black and White and Blue: Adult Cinema from the Victorian Age to the VCR* (Georgetown, Ontario: Jaguar Book Group, 2007), 16.

10. Ibid., 33.

11. Russell Schaeffer, "Smut, Novelty, Indecency: Reworking a History of Early Twentieth-Century 'Stag' Film," Society for Cinema and Media Studies Conference, Seattle, Washington, March 20, 2014.

12. For a history of 8 mm and Super 8 mm home movies as a technological and cultural form, see Patricia R. Zimmerman, *Reel Families: A Social History of Amateur Film* (Bloomington: Indiana University Press, 1995) and Karen L. Ishizuka and Patricia R. Zimmerman, eds., *Mining the Home Movie: Excavations in Histories and Memories* (Berkeley: University of California Press, 2007).

13. The early career of so-called King of Pornography Reuben Sturman and his role in the adult retail, sex toy, and loop machine business is synopsized in John Heidenry, *What Wild Ecstasy: The Rise and Fall of the Sexual Revolution* (New York: Simon and Schuster, 1997), 47–50, 73.

14. For a history of the soundies up to their eventual relegation to the porn industry, see Scott MacGillivray and Ted Okuda, *The Soundies Book: A Revised and Expanded Guide* (New York: iUniverse, Inc., 2007).

15. Cass Paley interview, March 2014.

16. Cinematographer and director Larry Revene recounts the process of loop manufacture and sale in a 2013 interview with adult film historian Ashley West on The Rialto Report podcast, available online at http://www.therialtoreport.com/2013/05/12/podcast-010-larry-revene-loops-and-organized-crime-2. For a much more detailed account, see Larry Revene, *Wham Bam $$ Ba Da Boom: Mob Wars, Porn Battles, and a View From the Trenches* (New York: CreateSpace Independent Publishing Platform, 2013).

17. Carter Stevens interview, March 2014.

18. Cass Paley interview, March 2014.

19. Carter Stevens interview, March 2014.

20. Cass Paley interview, March 2014.

21. Holmes's career in loops for *Sweetheart, Swedish Erotica,* and other lines is recounted in Jennifer Sugar and Jill C. Nelson, *John Holmes: A Life Measured in Inches* (Albany, GA: Bear Manor Media, 2007), 35–52, 438–443, 551–581.

22. Annette Haven interview, April 2014.

23. See *Stanley v. Georgia* - 394 U.S. 557 (1969), http://supreme.justia.com/cases/federal/us/394/557/case.html.

24. Eric Schaefer, "Gauging a Revolution: 16mm Film and the Rise of the Pornographic Feature" *Cinema Journal* 41, no. 3 (Spring, 2002): 9–10.

25. Ibid., 10.

26. Ibid., 12–13.

27. Cass Paley interview, March 2014.

28. Schaefer, op. cit., 18.

29. For a comparison of the self-consciously crass O'Farrell Theater and the self-consciously classy Sutter Cinema, see Joseph Lam Duong, "San Francisco and the Politics of Hardcore" in Eric Schaefer, ed., *Sex Scene: Media and the Sexual Revolution* (Durham, NC: Duke University Press, 2014).

30. For a detailed account of the changes to film financing and the rise of independent production in postwar Hollywood see Tino Balio, *United Artists, Vol 2, 1951–1978: The Company That Changed the Film Industry*, with an expanded introductory section (Madison, WI: University of Wisconsin Press, 2009). The effects these changes had on low-budget genre cinema is in Kevin Heffernan, *Ghouls, Gimmicks, and Gold: Horror Films and the American Movie Business, 1952–1968* (Durham, NC: Duke University Press, 2004), 90–98.

31. Ibid., 7.

32. See *Joseph Burstyn, Inc. v. Wilson* - 343 U.S. 495 (1952), http://supreme.justia.com/cases/federal/us/343/495/case.html.

33. Eric Schaefer, op. cit., 18–19.

34. Kevin Heffernan, "Prurient (Dis) Interest: The American Release and Reception of I Am Curious (Yellow)" in Eric Schaefer, ed., *Sex Scene: Media and the Sexual Revolution* (Durham, NC: Duke University Press, 2014).

35. See *United States v. Jerome Sandy, American International Pictures Exchange of Washington, D.C. et al.*, http://www.plainsite.org/dockets/index.html?id=886564.

36. Tino Balio, *The Foreign Film Renaissance on American Screens, 1946-1973* (Madison, WI: University of Wisconsin Press, 2010).

37. Casey Scott interview, March 2014.

38. See "Year-Old Bryanston: $20-Mil Rentals," *Variety*, October 20, 1974, 3, 32; and Harlan Jacobson, "Bryanston in Computer Turnstile 'Detecting'," *Variety*, April 7, 1975, 3.

39. Carter Stevens interview, March 2014.

40. See "Business: Cinematic Shelter," *Time*, January 19, 1976.

41. Addison Verrill, "Review: *Wet Rainbow*," *Variety*, October 30, 1974.

42. Joe Rubin interview, March 2011.

43. Adult film actress Sharon Mitchell discusses shooting both softcore and hardcore versions of films in her 2014 interview with Mike White and Robert St. Mary on The Projection Booth podcast, available for download at http://www.projection-booth.com/audio/Ep158-Smoker.mp3.

44. Joe Rubin interview, March 2014.

45. Susan Griffin, *Pornography and Silence: Culture's Revenge on Nature* (New York: Harper Collins, 1982) and Andrea Dworkin, *Pornography: Men Possessing Women* (New York: Plume, 1991).

46. Many key documents from both sides of the feminist debate on sexuality and pornography have been collected in Lisa Duggan and Nan Hunter, eds., *Sex Wars: Sexual Dissent and Political Culture* (New York: Routledge, 1996).

47. Joe Rubin interview, March 2011.

48. A detailed contemporary account of the shift to a rental market for home video is James Lardner, *Fast Forward: Hollywood, the Japanese, and the Onslaught of the VCR* (New York: W. W. Norton and Co., 1987).

49. An account of the changes home video brought to the world of adult film distribution is David Jennings, *Skinflicks: The Inside Story of the X-Rated Video Industry* (AuthorHouse, 2010), 71–90.

50. A fascinating early instance of this style of critique is Todd Gitlin, "The Left and Porno" in Michael Kimmel, ed., *Men Confront Pornography* (New York: Plume 1991), 102–108.

51. Gail Dines, *Pornland: How Porn Has Hijacked Our Sexuality* (Boston, MA: Beacon Press, 2010), 68–92.

52. For an account of 19th-century sex panics about the penny dreadfuls, see Nicola Kay Beisel, *Imperiled Innocents: Anthony Comstock and Family Reproduction in Victorian America* (Princeton, NJ: Princeton University Press, 1998).

3

Clashing at Barnard's Gates: Understanding the Origins of the Pornography Problem in the Modern American Women's Movement

Carolyn Bronstein

On April 24, 1982, rival groups of feminists clashed outside the gates of New York City's Barnard College as the annual Scholar and the Feminist conference was about to begin. For almost a decade, this important conference had brought together activists and academics to explore the relationship between feminist scholarship and practice. This year, the conference theme was an explosive one: sexuality. The planning committee had designed a meeting that would focus on sexual pleasure, exploring questions of women's sexual desire, fantasies, and transgressive sexual practices, such as using pornography and practicing lesbian sadomasochism. The conference would address the question of how to expand women's access to pleasure in a patriarchal environment, not an easy feat at a time when antisexual, conservative political forces were gaining ground under the Reagan Administration.[1] This "prosex" or "sex-positive" orientation was not simply a benign approach to inquiring about lesser-known areas of female sexuality, but was also recognized within the women's movement as an explicit political challenge to a different, influential type of thought: antipornography feminism.

The conference planners sought to emphasize sexual pleasure that year as a direct move to counter a conservative feminist discourse around sex that framed pornography as a dangerous political and cultural agent of female subordination and oppression. They were alarmed that the expansive feminist agenda around sexuality and sexual rights seemed to be collapsing in favor of a repressive and moralistic focus on controlling pornography and protecting women from sex and its alleged harms. This seemed especially unwise given the rising power of the religious right by the early 1980s and the Republican "family values" platform, which was widely recognized as a backlash campaign against women's rights and important feminist gains, such as the legalization of abortion, the creation of battered women's programs, and the establishment of no-fault divorce, which enabled women in many states to end abusive marriages without proof of harm.[2] By the end of the 1970s, however, such gains were in peril. In 1980, the Supreme Court handed down a decision in *Harris v. McRae* that affirmed the constitutionality of the 1976 Hyde Amendment banning the use of federal funds (Medicaid) to pay for abortions, leaving 44 million poor women without essential reproductive options. In 1981, the Reagan Administration shuttered the federal Office of Domestic Violence, which had been created two years earlier under President Carter, a move that was interpreted as openly hostile to feminist achievements in documenting and fighting male violence in the family context.[3]

Given this alarming political environment, the conference planners worried that the most visible arm of the women's movement at this volatile moment was the antipornography campaign, whose members did not publicly advocate for women's rights to enjoy sexual pleasure and desire free of shame and legal persecution. Instead, the antipornography movement emphasized a vision of sex as a danger to women, and pornography as a driver of uncontrollable male lust that stimulated aggression and encouraged men to control women through sexual violence. This view of unrestrained sexuality and pornography as corrupting social forces dovetailed with right-wing attacks on homosexuals and gay rights, and efforts to preserve and protect the heterosexual nuclear family. By the time of the Barnard Conference, leading voices within the antipornography movement were arguing that government censorship was a potential fix, a solution that would bring pornography—never easily defined or delimited—under the control of a conservative, patriarchal state. The sex-positive feminist agenda of the Barnard Conference was a defiant response—an attempt to recuperate the positive aspects of sexuality for women and challenge the mounting calls for government protection.[4]

As hundreds of Barnard conference attendees arrived at the gates, they were met by protesters holding picket signs, many of whom were affiliated with the powerful New York-based group, Women Against Pornography (WAP). WAP had emerged in 1979 as the most influential organized feminist group promoting antipornography ideas and activism, as its name clearly proclaimed, and it counted important feminist authors and movement intellectuals like Susan Brownmiller, Andrea Dworkin, and Robin Morgan among its founders and supporters. The protesters wore T-shirts emblazoned "For a Feminist Sexuality" on the front and "Against S/M" on the back. They handed out a leaflet that denied the possibility of woman-positive pornography and attacked the feminist credentials of particular conference session speakers on the basis of their chosen sexual practices (e.g., some were lesbian sadomasochists, some participated in gendered butch/femme eroticism, and others were vocal about using and enjoying various forms of pornography).[5] The ugly confrontation outside the gates that day forever changed American feminism, bringing out into the open a deep schism over questions of sexuality, and initiating a period of personal and ideological conflict called the Sex Wars that was discernible through the 1990s, and still reverberates today.

How did this schism develop over time in the women's movement? What social, cultural, political, and legal developments in American life fostered the creation of two very different, yet identifiably feminist, positions on the question of pornography? This chapter looks backward in time from the starting point of the historic confrontation outside the Barnard gates to offer a context for answering that question and for understanding how and why pornography made its way to the forefront of American feminism by the early 1980s. It presents the issues that both camps saw at stake for the future of women, and explains why pornography was dangerous and unsalvageable in the eyes of one group, yet worthy of consideration to the other. The account begins with development of antipathy to pornography within the radical feminist wing of the women's liberation movement, based on changes in radical feminist theory that gave new insight into the institution of heterosexuality and the role of sexual violence in maintaining the patriarchal order. Next, it considers the growth and greater visibility of the pornography industry in mainstream American society through the 1970s, a shift that opened many women's eyes to the sexist and violent character of mass-market porn. Once feminist antipornography activity began to take on urgency and frequency in the women's movement through the establishment of activist groups, the counter-movement began rolling in defense of erotic rights. The chapter ends with a look at the years immediately following the Barnard Conference, when the antipornography movement faced the problem of advances in technology that made pornography more accessible to Americans. Leading antipornography feminists sought to bring pornography under state control via a civil rights ordinance developed by the legal scholar Catharine MacKinnon and the author and radical feminist activist Andrea Dworkin.

ON THE ROAD TO ANTIPORNOGRAPHY: RADICAL WOMEN, SEXUALITY, AND SEXUAL VIOLENCE

The road to antipornography theory and activism was a long one, and it began in earnest more than fifteen years prior to the Barnard Conference. From the late 1960s onward, American men and women experienced a freer sexual culture in the United States as the sexual revolution took hold and uprooted long-standing norms, such as the proscription against premarital sex. These changes had a liberating potential and were welcomed by young people who sought to distance themselves from their parents' rigid sexual codes and to embrace their bodies as a source of wellness, good feeling, and personal fulfillment. Fueled by the cultural radicalism of the Civil Rights movement, student protest against the Vietnam War, and feminism, the sexual revolution was touted as an immediate way to create social change. Free love challenged a patriarchal order that used monogamy and marriage to force men into the role of head-of-household and breadwinner (which supported capitalism, another social ill), and women into the domestic sphere as wives and mothers, often with unhappy results.

Yet, for all its promise, the sexual revolution delivered mixed results. Instead of creating sexual and social equality, many women found that the sexual revolution was primarily benefitting men, putting women at even greater disadvantage. Among teenage girls and college women, whose rates of premarital sex doubled between 1960 and 1970, rates of venereal disease and unplanned pregnancy soared. Women complained that the new no-strings-attached ethos and the political climate against sexual repression gave them fewer grounds on which to say "no" and put them at physical risk. Many felt used in an environment where expecting a relationship in return for sex was ridiculed as uptight and old-fashioned. Historian Jane Gerhard analyzed the pressures that young women encountered and concluded that many recognized a bad bargain: "Opportunities for more sex with more partners did not necessarily translate into sexual liberation for women. Many women rejected accounts of their 'liberation' that viewed them as *Playboy* bunnies."[6] Married women also were affected by the changing times; some resented the new sexual norms and greater expectations to be free-wheeling in the bedroom, engaging in behaviors like oral sex and even swinging, which entailed sleeping with someone other than one's spouse.[7] By the mid-1970s, the sexual revolution was a source of disillusionment for many women who perceived expanded sexual rights for men, but not for themselves.

The radical feminist women's liberation movement spread across the nation after 1970, and its signature method of consciousness-raising became a popular way for women to share personal experiences, especially those around sex. Consciousness-raising involved small-group, face-to-face discussions in which women shared everyday and intimate experiences, ranging from growing up under the thumbs of controlling fathers, dealing with husbands who would not share the housework or child care, facing barriers to advancement at work, acquiescing to unwanted sexual encounters, and undergoing illegal abortions. The behavioral scientists Morton A. Lieberman and Gary R. Bond described consciousness-raising in 1976 as women discussing their "problems in living," but a more accurate description would have indicated that they were discussing their problems in living *as women*.[8] In these safe, small-group spaces, a generation of women discovered feminism and saw for the first time that their "personal" problems were widely shared and were actually political in nature, stemming from the systemic subordination of women in a patriarchal society. The feelings of disappointment and anger that many experienced around heightened male sexual expectations and the negative consequences for women emerged in these consciousness-raising groups, and stimulated theory development. Women could see clearly that sexuality was a powerful locus of male control and they began to connect sexuality to the widespread condition of female oppression.

Through the process of consciousness-raising, feminists also exposed an epidemic of male sexual violence. Black feminists had long called attention to the use of rape as a form of terror during slavery, but the full extent of the political uses of rape had not been thoroughly articulated.[9] Categories of rape, such as marital rape and date rape, had yet to be named and perceived legally and socially as "true" rapes and crimes. Within the small groups, women also shared experiences of other types of sexual violence, including battering, incest, child sexual abuse, and sexual harassment, and realized how their lives and freedoms had been circumscribed by these experiences and their efforts to avoid further exploitation. Male sexual violence began to emerge as a web of related, strategic acts that kept girls and women under male control.

Beginning in the early 1970s, radical feminist authors like Susan Griffin, Robin Morgan, and Susan Brownmiller translated the discoveries about male sexual violence into theory. They introduced a new perspective on female vulnerability to sexual coercion as a "male protection racket" as Griffin described it, which ensured female subordination.[10] The threat of sexual violence—what might befall a woman who ventured out on the street at night without a male escort—was the root oppression and it kept women in a constant state of fear. The concept of rape benefitted all men, even those who did not rape or commit other acts of sexual violence, by forcing women to seek relationships with men for security; a woman alone was an easy and obvious target for attack. Susan Brownmiller forcefully articulated this viewpoint in her landmark 1975 book *Against Our Will*, which reached a national audience. Describing the power that the threat of violence held over women, she wrote: "It is nothing more or less than a conscious process of intimidation by which *all men* keep *all women* in a state of fear" (emphasis in original).[11] Brownmiller also argued that pornography and prostitution exacerbated the rape problem by objectifying women and teaching young men that sexual access to women's bodies was always available, and was a male right.

Discovering the extent of the male violence problem was empowering for some women in the sense that they invented feminist institutions like battered women's shelters and rape crisis centers to provide support. But at the same time, it was terrifying for many to face unpleasant realities about the scope of male sexual violence. The new radical feminist theories implicated all men and claimed that every man had a stake in the perpetuation of violence in support of patriarchy. Early radical feminists had rejected blanket antimale ideas and saw the differences between women and men as socially constructed (artificial gender roles), not as due to biology. But, as radical feminism moved into its later stage in the mid-1970s, often called cultural feminism, men were vilified as aggressive, rapacious, brutish, genitally focused, and driven to sexual violence and war by testosterone-fueled urges. Women, on the other hand, were depicted as very different sorts of creatures: nurturing, passive, benevolent, and more interested in emotional connection than physical gratification.[12] These stereotypes about male and female nature would help support opposition to pornography as the decade progressed, with the women featured in pornography perceived as helpless victims of uncontrollable male lust, and the men who used these materials as predators, seething with violent intent.

Armed with new insight into the ways that men controlled women, radical feminists turned a critical eye to media depictions to try to understand how boys learned to be violent and girls learned to be victims. This was an obvious next step—trying to identify the popular culture "curriculum" that taught contempt for women and encouraged sexual violence, and it was an important step that solidified antipathy to pornography. Feminists began by connecting mass media representations of gender to rape. Andra Medea and Kathleen Thompson wrote in 1974: "As long as we accept the stereotypes that are presented to us in everything from pulp detective stories to Oscar-winning films—that women are naturally passive, childlike, and vulnerable, and that men are naturally aggressive, brutal, and uncontrollable—the rape situation will not change."[13] They regarded media images as a textbook for patriarchy, and focused new attention on the role of media in perpetuating patterns of violence against women.

New questions emerged. Was pornography a *cause* of male sexual violence, such as rape? Was *pornography itself a form of male sexual violence*—done first to the woman forced to film the sexual acts, and then to all women forced to watch it, and/or to live in the sexist, violent culture that pornography created? These were remarkable new ways of thinking that reflected the feminist critique of heterosexuality and new understandings of the transhistorical function of violence in maintaining and reproducing patriarchy.

THE GROWTH OF THE COMMERCIAL SEX INDUSTRY

At the same time that feminists were concentrating new energies on theorizing media and media effects, the American media landscape was undergoing dramatic change. Encouraged by a national decline in prosecution of obscenity cases, the pornography industry entered a period of unprecedented expansion in the mid-1970s. This was due to a series of modifications in the 1960s to the test for obscenity first established by the Supreme Court in *Roth v. U.S.* (1957), which gradually enlarged the range of sexually explicit materials that were guaranteed First Amendment protection. These modifications introduced the concept of social worth as applied to pornography, meaning that the presence of any redeeming social value in a creative work taken as a whole meant that it could not be classified as obscenity. The producers and sellers of sexually explicit materials enjoyed a greatly reduced threat of prosecution, and favorable grounds for legal defense. As the political scientist Donald A. Downs has explained, "the presence of virtually any idea 'or any other form of social importance' would salvage constitutional protection for a sexual work," taking it out of the reach of the courts.[14]

The effects of the new legal climate were visible through the mainstream national attention paid to the 1972 blockbuster X-rated film *Deep Throat*. This film, which played in regular movie theaters as well as adult theaters, spent 96 weeks on *Variety*'s list of the 50 top-grossing films and was reputed to have earned more than $100 million worldwide.[15] *Deep Throat* starred Linda "Lovelace" Marchiano and Harry Reems in the story of a woman who sought sexual ecstasy with a multitude of lovers, but somehow never achieved orgasm. Marchiano sought medical advice from Reems, who made a startling anatomical discovery: Her clitoris was located in the base of her throat rather than at the top of her labia, meaning that orgasm required stimulation by deep fellatio. Marchiano had been taught (she later claimed force and abuse) by her then-husband and manager to do the "sword-swallowing" act featured in the film, taking the entire length of an erect penis into her mouth and throat. She became a celebrity on the basis of *Deep Throat*, and appeared on the covers of *Esquire*, *Time*, and *Newsweek* magazines, and as a guest on *The Tonight Show* with Johnny Carson, where she was praised for her sexual prowess. The public hailing of this new "liberated" oral-sex goddess was a wake-up call for feminists. Around the nation, women denounced the film's convenient plot for glorifying an act typically associated with male sexual pleasure as something that a woman would be endlessly delighted to perform.[16]

Deep Throat introduced a national American audience to pornography, and in so doing revealed mass market pornography as sexist and male-oriented. When the social value of *Deep Throat* was called into question, women saw many male lawyers, journalists, intellectuals, artists, and former allies from the Left rise up to defend their rights to enjoy this type of content, while remaining silent on women's demands to be depicted responsibly, with bodily integrity. Linda "Lovelace" Marchiano, they were told, was a liberated woman who exploited men as sex objects for her pleasure just as men used women.[17] On college campuses, female student groups protested screenings of *Deep Throat* on the grounds that the film objectified and dehumanized women, only to be ridiculed by male classmates as enemies of sexual freedom.[18] This was, for many women, the beginning of a realization that men were their allies in the quest for political and social equality only to the extent that such demands did not interfere with unfettered male sexual rights.

As the decade wore on, and consumers expressed a taste for increasingly graphic content, pornographers churned out sexualized images of women unapologetically, looking for new ways to attract their male customer base. Women watched with horror, anger, and shame as their naked and abused bodies were packaged like consumer goods and sold for profit in the name of "sexual freedom" and "free speech." The radical feminist antipornography activist Sheila Jeffreys has observed that the ubiquity of pornography in the 1970s drove women to take it seriously as a political issue and a concrete threat to women's health, safety, and rights as citizens. "The sheer visibility of the porn industry had a consequence which the pornbrokers may not have intended," she wrote. "Women were able to look at pornography and for the first time had at their disposal a panoramic view of what constituted male sexuality."[19] Radical feminists connected pornography with the theoretic critique of male violence and began to regard it with hatred and fear as a potent teaching tool of patriarchy, and a set of texts that oppressed women and denied their basic humanity.

THE FEMINIST ANTIPORNOGRAPHY MOVEMENT MOBILIZES

Although *Deep Throat* inspired new feminist thinking, the film did not generate lasting action against pornography. Several years later, feminists on the West Coast were the first to mobilize a sustained campaign against sexually violent media images, planting the seeds of what would become by 1980 a full-fledged feminist antipornography campaign.[20]

The first major group, Women Against Violence Against Women (WAVAW), organized in Los Angeles in 1976. Their initial effort focused on preventing Southern California screenings of a brutal X-rated film titled *Snuff*. The producer of this low-budget B feature claimed that the film depicted the actual murder of a young woman during sexual intercourse. Publicity materials for *Snuff* boasted that it had been filmed in South America "where life is cheap." The new organization coordinated demonstrations outside movie theaters showing the film, protesting that it glorified and trivialized sexual violence against a woman. WAVAW called for a boycott of Mann Theatres, a Southern California chain that refused to stop showing *Snuff*. On March 18, 1976, female protesters associated with WAVAW hurled bricks through the lobby and box office windows of three Mann establishments. WAVAW members also persuaded an Orange County municipal judge to find *Snuff* in violation of state obscenity statutes and the public nuisance provision of the California penal code. Using a mix of tactics, primarily based around consumer education and boycott, WAVAW was able to rid Southern California of *Snuff* in just over one week and provided a model for other feminist groups fighting the film in cities around the nation.

WAVAW achieved national prominence several months later, when its members protested Atlantic Records' advertising campaign for the Rolling Stones album, *Black and Blue*. The campaign featured print ads, radio spots, in-store displays, and most famously, a giant billboard above the Sunset Strip in Los Angeles that showed a woman in a ripped white bodice, breasts exposed, and body covered with bruises. Her legs were spread apart and her wrists were tied with ropes, arms immobilized overhead. The woman, a future *Playboy* model whom Mick Jagger himself had reportedly trussed up on set, was shown with her eyes closed and mouth hanging open in an expression of unadulterated sexual desire.[21] Next to her picture, the billboard text read: "I'm Black and Blue from the Rolling Stones and I Love It!" Members of WAVAW saw a celebration of sexual violence and a message that made light of battering, encouraging men to beat women to make their natural, animal sexual appetites emerge.

The organization took immediate action, urging Atlantic Records to cancel the campaign and explaining that it sent a message that it was socially acceptable, even glamorous given the Rolling Stones connection, to regard violence against women as sexy. Neither Atlantic Records nor the members of the Rolling Stones were responsive to WAVAW's concerns. Jagger told *Rolling Stone* magazine that a lot of women enjoyed that kind of treatment: "Well, there are a lot of girls into that, they dig it, they want to be chained up."[22] Keith Richards ridiculed the WAVAW activists as annoying "marchers with bees in their bonnets."[23] WAVAW launched a successful national three-year boycott of Atlantic Records' parent company, Warner Communications, to force the company to adopt a policy barring the use of sexually violent images in its marketing and advertising materials, including album covers.

Although WAVAW did not identify itself as against pornography per se, this was nonetheless a decisive moment for the burgeoning antipornography movement. Women around the nation interpreted this advertising campaign through the lens of feminist theory about sexually violent media images and the role of heterosexuality in the oppression of women. WAVAW saw this campaign as a perfect example of a mass media message that glorified sexual violence, objectified women's bodies, taught women to think of themselves as powerless victims, and encouraged men to rape.

Feminist attention to pornography increased in 1977, as a second feminist organization formed to fight abusive media images. Women Against Violence in Pornography and Media (WAVPM) was a Bay Area group and sister organization to WAVAW, but as the group's name proclaimed, its members were explicitly concerned about pornography. WAVPM initiated a number of media actions against advertising that trivialized violence against women, such as a Max Factor moisturizer campaign for a product called "Self-Defense," which seemed to mock women's efforts to learn karate and judo to keep themselves safe from male attackers on the street and at home.[24] But the organization also focused its energies on pornography, leading protest marches through San Francisco's North Beach and Tenderloin adult districts and picketing the Ultra Room, a live sex act club where women engaged in sadomasochistic sex play, using paddles, whips, and leather swings. Viewing this kind of activity, WAVPM members insisted, taught men that women found pain and torture erotic, and contributed to a social environment that condoned sexual violence against women. In opposing S/M, WAVPM honored its mission to eradicate portrayals of women being bound, raped, tortured, or killed for sexual stimulation or pleasure. The organization also pressured the *San Francisco Chronicle* and the *San Francisco Examiner* newspapers to limit the size and format of ads for adult films and theaters, following the adoption of a similar policy at the *New York Times* in 1977. This campaign was unsuccessful, largely due to the revenue loss that the Bay Area papers would have sustained without adult-themed ads, and the need to serve the city's significant gay community, but it nonetheless cemented the idea that many feminists opposed pornography.

The shift to antipornography organizing began in earnest in 1978. First, *Hustler* magazine—one of the raunchiest and most popular adult titles—published a cover illustration showing a naked woman being fed head first into a meat grinder. Her legs were sticking out of the top of the grinder, but her head and torso had already been churned into bloody hamburger meat. WAVPM coordinated pickets of Bay Area stores selling *Hustler*, and the organization earned national attention for its leadership around protest efforts. Arguments about the woman-hate and violence present in pornography gained traction as a result of the *Hustler* cover image.

Next, WAVPM organized the first national feminist conference on pornography, held in San Francisco in November 1978. The conference brought together such leading feminist thinkers as poets Audre Lorde, Adrienne Rich, and Susan Griffin; authors Susan Brownmiller and Andrea Dworkin; and sociologist Diana Russell, each of whom articulated feminist opposition to pornography. It was here that feminists began for the first time to discuss openly the possibility of seeking state action against pornography, seeking to rescind its First Amendment protection as a form of speech and to reclassify it as a form of gender discrimination. This was a cultural moment when feminist lawyers were bringing about dramatic changes in rape trial proceedings, establishing sexual harassment as a crime, and redefining domestic violence. Using the law to restrict the production and distribution of sexually violent pornography seemed to many activists like an empowering course of action. The WAVPM conference ended with the first national *Take Back the Night* march, which expressed women's desire to be free from sexual violence and the threat of assault. Andrea Dworkin emphasized the dangers of pornography to the 3,000 women who assembled to march. "The most terrible thing about pornography is that it tells male truth," she said. "[P]ornography functions to perpetuate male supremacy and crimes of violence against women because it conditions, trains, educates, and inspires men to despise women, to use women, to hurt women."[25]

LAUNCHING WOMEN AGAINST PORNOGRAPHY

The national WAVPM conference was an electrifying event for attendees, who witnessed major directional changes toward a movement focus on pornography and legal strategies to control it. But the event was not covered by the national news and received limited local coverage. Susan Brownmiller declared in her memoir, *In Our Time*, that Bay Area newspapers "had blanked out the nation's first feminist antipornography conference and march."[26] She was convinced that the movement, then headquartered on the West Coast, needed to create a presence in New York City to get national attention. New York was home to the best-known adult entertainment district—Times Square—as well to as the national media and many of the country's best-known feminists, such as Gloria Steinem, Bella Abzug, Andrea Dworkin, Letty Cottin Pogrebin, and Brownmiller herself. In March 1979, Brownmiller invited WAVPM's two chief organizers, Laura Lederer and Lynn Campbell, to come to New York City to lead this effort. Campbell, a dynamic young woman who organized California agricultural workers in the grape boycotts prior to joining the women's movement, accepted and moved to New York City in the spring of 1979. Although she had technically been recruited to establish an East Coast chapter of WAVPM, by that summer it was clear that the New Yorkers were creating an independent organization solely focused on pornography: Women Against Pornography (WAP). They intended to make pornography the number-one women's rights issue in the nation.

Over the course of the next few years, WAP began to present the anti-pornography analysis as the authoritative feminist position. This raised concerns as WAP leaders sought support from government officials and encouraged discussion of legal controls. Members of WAP appeared on the national *Phil Donahue* talk show where Brownmiller insisted that pornography did not deserve First Amendment protection and ought to be legally defined as obscene and banned from public display. In 1979, WAP opened an office on the edge of Times Square and allied itself with the mayor's office, which supported sweep arrests of prostitutes and gentrification plans to turn Times Square into a tourist mecca, both of which were policies at odds with feminist politics. The organization began leading guided education tours of the adult establishments in Times Square that emphasized how the pornography industry exploited and victimized women—actions which heightened tensions with unrepentant sex workers and feminists concerned about the tours' antisexual tone.[27] The focus on Times Square culminated with a major march and a national conference in autumn of 1979 that established WAP as the new leader of the feminist antipornography movement. Over the course of the next few years, WAP and its goals often were portrayed—incorrectly—as in line with those of right-wing moralist groups who condemned pornography for leading men and women into sinful sexual encounters, a category that lumped together all gay and lesbian activity, youth sexuality, and sex outside of marriage. WAP came under fire for sexual conservatism, gender essentialism, racism, and classism, and found its relationship with sectors of the women's movement strained by the early 1980s.

THE CLASH AT BARNARD'S GATES: CHALLENGING THE ANTIPORNOGRAPHY DISCOURSE

As WAP grew in national influence and visibility, and took on new targets such as *Playboy* magazine, pornography became the most central and contentious subject facing the women's movement in the 1980s. Many issues were at stake in the battles over sexuality that comprised the sex wars, including erotic rights, sadomasochism, butch/femme sexuality, and the possibility of feminist agency in sex work and heterosexual encounters, but no issue was more explosive at that historical moment than pornography.

By the time of the Barnard Conference, the idea that violent male sexuality and its cultural propaganda—pornography—were powerful agents of female oppression was a subject of conversation and debate everywhere that white, middle class feminists gathered. Many poor women and women of color across all socioeconomic classes, however, were less interested in the pornography question and antipornography organizing. This was due to competing, and arguably more urgent, issues of poverty and racism affecting their communities, as well as the reality that a number of poor, young women, frequently women of color, had to cycle in and out of sex work to earn money. The antipornography movement regarded sex workers only as victims rather than women making rational economic decisions given limited choices, and this mantle of "victimhood" did not sit well with all. Antipornography was also antimale in its formulation, and feminists of color balked at declaring men of color as oppressors rather than oppressed. These realities made pornography a complicated issue for feminists of color, and not one that held wide appeal.

Among sex-positive feminists, there was increasing interest in exploring erotic diversity for women rather than focusing exclusively on questions of violence and danger in the sexual exchange. Paula Webster, a contributor to a 1981 issue of *Heresies* magazine that focused on female sexual desire and pleasure, argued that antipornography feminism was a movement bent on controlling male vice, leaving no space for women to enjoy sex. Voicing burgeoning concerns, she argued that feminists ought to regard pornography with a greater degree of openness, recognizing its potential to thrill and excite, to diversify women's erotic lives, and to encourage sexual experimentation. Webster refuted the antipornography movement's claim to know the difference between woman-hating "pornography" and woman-positive "erotica," pointing out that "[t]here are no universal, unchanging criteria for drawing the line between acceptable and unacceptable sexual images."[28] Women deserved the opportunity to explore their sexuality without fear of running afoul of the women's movement.

The sex-positive feminists were not by definition enthusiastic about mass-market pornography. Many perceived this material to be heterosexist and far less concerned with women's sexual desire and pleasure than with male ejaculation. Ellen Willis, a leading radical feminist activist who became a major voice of sex-positive feminism and an opponent of antipornography efforts, found most mass-market pornography intolerable. Writing in 1979 for the New York alternative weekly, the *Village Voice*, she noted that sadistic and dehumanizing pornographic images had become such a ubiquitous feature of popular culture that they qualified as a form of "psychological harassment" of women.[29]

But, at the same time, the sexual revolution had empowered women to throw off the shackles of heterosexual, marital, procreative sex, and sex-positive feminists recognized a precious opportunity. The Barnard Conference planners maintained that women had been denied exposure to sexual diversity and sexual variety for too long, and closing off any avenue that might stimulate exploration would be detrimental to their emerging sexual freedom. Pornography was hateful in many respects, but it was a set of erotic texts that could help women be sexual, and that alone was sufficient reason to protect it from state censorship, a favored tactic of antipornography leaders throughout the mid-1980s.[30] Sex-positive feminists argued that women could use male-oriented pornography in a resistant way, subverting dominant constructions of female and male sexuality. This was the perspective that informed the planning of the Barnard Conference, and this set of ideas helped to provoke the bitter clash outside Barnard's gates that April morning.

Traitors to the Movement

For the WAP members and other antipornography activists who turned out to protest the Conference, emphasizing sexual pleasure and the potential benefits of pornography seemed dangerous and irresponsible, even sickening. Some were especially incensed that sex-positive feminists defended women's rights to participate in sadomasochism (including S/M-themed pornography) and to insist that role-playing rituals and voluntary exchanges of power could be carried out in feminist ways.[31] This ignored the realities of life under patriarchy, where power was never held by women, where gender roles were fixed, not mutable, and where a flood of pornography encouraged (and possibly caused) the epidemic of male sexual violence. Following the influential theories of Andrea Dworkin and Catharine MacKinnon, they argued that pornography harmed women as a class, robbing them of speech and their rights to meaningful citizenship in a democracy. Pornography turned all women into subjugated objects under male control.[32] How could women who called themselves feminist ignore the role of pornography in silencing and intimidating women?

This perspective was well supported by radical feminist theory that portrayed male sexuality as the root source of women's oppression. Men made pornography with political intent—they created the dominant sexual images of women as panting, empty vessels, as slavish whores whose sole purpose was to satisfy male sexual desires. Men were the primary consumers of pornography. Men's sexual needs and fantasies came first in pornography—witness *Deep Throat*'s plot—just as their needs came first in all other sectors of American life—marriage, the family, the workplace, education, and government. Pornography taught men from an early age that it was their right to be catered to by women, in the bedroom and in every other arena of social life. When they looked at pornography and saw "men as inexhaustibly desiring, tumescent and irresistible; women insatiably available," antipornography feminists saw a pattern of sexist discrimination that taught men to view women with contempt, as objects fit only for sexual use.[33] These were core antipornography ideas circulating among WAP members and other protesters as they approached the Barnard gates that April morning. They were incensed that the conference organizers had turned their backs on pornography's harms, choosing instead to focus on pleasure, a luxury that women could ill afford in the midst of a war for survival.

POST-BARNARD: CHANGES IN TECHNOLOGY AND TACTICS

The events at Barnard did not mark the end of the conflict between anti-pornography and prosex feminists. Instead, the post-Barnard years were the most divisive of the sex wars. Antipornography feminists lobbied for new laws to protect women from pornography, successfully introducing model civil rights ordinances in several cities around the nation. Meanwhile, changes in technology affected both how pornography was delivered and the quantity of production, allowing greater reach.

Video Technology and Cable Television

In the period following the Barnard Conference, the antipornography forces encountered an even more challenging obstacle than a feminist coun-ter-movement opposed to their politics. Efforts to stem the flow of pornog-raphy were greatly hampered by advances in technology that made sexually explicit material more accessible to Americans. Newly developed videocas-sette recorder (VCR) technology and premium cable television subscription services like HBO and Cinemax began bringing pornography directly into American homes, defeating one of the last barriers to enjoyment: the fear of getting caught.[34] The shift to private viewing increased the demand for adult content exponentially because it eliminated the serious risk attached to seeking out pornography in a public theater. In 1991, the career of actor Paul "Pee-Wee Herman" Reubens was irrevocably damaged when undercover detectives engaged in a sting operation at a Sarasota, Florida, adult theater and arrested him for indecent exposure (public masturbation). CBS stopped airing reruns of Reubens's television show, *Pee-Wee's Playhouse*, Disney-MGM Studios removed a video featuring Reubens from its studio tour, and the store chain Toys-R-Us pulled all Pee-Wee Herman toys and dolls from its shelves permanently.[35] The risks of viewing pornography in public were considerable, and this reality had previously helped to constrain the industry.

Once adult material was available discreetly and privately for home use, the battle to control pornography became much harder to fight. The price of VCRs began dropping steadily in 1977 because of competition between Betamax and VHS video technology, and within a decade close to 90 percent of American homes featured at least one VCR. XXX videos could be ordered through the mail wrapped in plain brown paper packaging at a cost of about

$70 per title in the mid-1980s; adult titles accounted for about 75 percent of all prerecorded tapes sold.[36] Cinema historian Peter Alilunas has documented the economic vitality of independent video stores featuring significant "back rooms" filled with adult titles, which managed to outlast corporate chains like Blockbuster and Hollywood Video that featured only "family friendly" rentals. By 1987, American customers were renting more than 100 million adult videos per year.[37] Pay cable services like the *Playboy* Channel—which debuted the same year as the Barnard Conference—or Cinemax's *Max After Dark*, which was first offered in 1984 and was credited with the network's strong early growth—brought pornography into people's homes at unprecedented rates.[38]

New forms of pornography also abounded in the 1980s. Feminist pornographer Candida Royalle founded Femme Productions in 1984, producing adult videos targeted to women that were based on sex-positive ideas about female desire. Her films were free of the conventions of traditional pornography such as the obligatory "money shot" where male ejaculation is visible on screen. Her first film, *Femme*, contained six short vignettes that emphasized foreplay, fantasy, and erotic daydreams.[39] The publisher of *High Society* adult magazine invented a new genre of pornography in 1983; she turned a 900-number pay telephone service that people typically called to hear the time or the weather into an erotic resource. Callers could dial up 24 hours a day, 7 days a week to hear recordings of women describing sexually graphic scenarios and moaning to climax.[40] Pornography was morphing in format and increasing in accessibility. From the WAP perspective, we could compare the situation to bailing water out of a sinking ship with a single bucket—there was no way to keep up with the flood.

The MacKinnon and Dworkin Civil Rights Ordinance

In more than a symbolic way, the confrontation at Barnard between sex-positive and antipornography feminists received a definitive public hearing in 1986. That year, the Supreme Court affirmed a lower court decision in *American Booksellers v. Hudnut* that the Antipornography Civil Rights Ordinance, enacted in Indianapolis in 1984, was unconstitutional. Crafted by the feminist legal scholar Catharine MacKinnon and radical feminist author and activist Andrea Dworkin, the ordinance made individual instances of pornography actionable as violations of women's civil rights.

Building on earlier radical feminist theory, MacKinnon and Dworkin argued that pornography should not be treated as a form of speech deserving First Amendment protection, but as a form of sex discrimination— "the graphic sexually explicit subordination of women through pictures or words."[41] Pornography actively taught men that women were inferior and harmed all women by creating gender inequality; the pervasiveness of pornography's message made it impossible for women to claim equality with men. Pornography also linked male sexual arousal to degrading and violent images of women, especially images that showed women tied down, whipped or chained, and forcefully restrained by others. The ordinance empowered injured individuals—potentially all women, everywhere—to seek damages through the courts from producers, sellers, and distributors of pornography.[42]

This move to bring sexual expression under the control of the state and effectively curtail sexual freedom motivated sex-positive feminists to organize the Feminist Anti-Censorship Taskforce. They rejected the description of women as powerless against pornography's harms, and insisted that women could exert agency, even in the face of sexism. They argued that sexually explicit speech and images were not in and of themselves harmful to women, and that the ordinance would allow for overly broad state suppression of sexual material, including gay, lesbian, and feminist expression. Conservative courts would be empowered to interpret ambiguous terms such as "degradation" against marginalized groups, which included anyone outside what feminist theorist Gayle Rubin has described as the "charmed circle" of marital, heterosexual, procreative sex.[43] Indeed, this has come to pass in Canada, where portions of the MacKinnon-Dworkin ordinance were adopted into law in 1992; mainstream heterosexual pornography is flourishing there whereas gay and lesbian and other minority sexual expression faces censorship.[44]

CONCLUSION

The Barnard Conference provides a useful point of entry for understanding the origins of the sex wars in the modern American women's movement. Tensions between antipornography and sex-positive feminists over the issue of pornography, its role in stimulating male violence and creating conditions of female subordination, and the advisability of seeking state protective action reached a boiling point in the weeks leading up to the conference. Sex-positive feminists used the conference as a means of opening up a dialogue about the possibility of sexual pleasure and desire under patriarchy, an approach that infuriated feminists on the front lines of antipornography organizing.

In the post-Barnard years, these two camps would battle over the MacKinnon-Dworkin civil rights ordinance, with both camps claiming periodic victories. Antipornography forces seemed to have the upper hand when the ultra-conservative Attorney General's Commission on Pornography

(Meese Commission) released its report in 1986 advocating stricter enforce-ment of existing obscenity laws and expanding definitions of obscenity to make additional forms of pornography illegal.[45] Yet sex-positive feminists triumphed when the Supreme Court agreed that the MacKinnon-Dworkin ordinance was unconstitutional. The sex wars continued throughout the 1990s and beyond, with the central battle over pornography playing a major role in promoting new academic fields of inquiry, such as queer theory, and new forms of activ-ism, such as third wave feminism, whose activists embrace sexual diversity in direct response to the sex wars and the contentious issue of pornography. [46]

NOTES

1. Carole S. Vance, "Pleasure and Danger: Towards a Politics of Sexuality," in *Pleasure and Danger: Exploring Female Sexuality*, ed. Carole S. Vance (Boston: Rout-ledge and Kegan Paul, 1984).

2. On the rise of the right, see Whitney Strub, *Perversion for Profit: The Politics of Pornography and the Rise of the New Right* (New York: Columbia University Press, 2010). On no-fault divorce, see Stephanie Coontz, *Marriage, a History: How Love Conquered Marriage* (New York: Penguin, 2006).

3. Nancy Whittier, *Feminist Generations: The Persistence of the Radical Women's Movement* (Philadelphia: Temple University Press, 1995), 85–91.

4. An influential argument about the counter-productive effects of state protec-tion on women's sexual freedom came from historians Ellen DuBois and Linda Gor-don in an essay prepared for presentation at the Barnard Conference. See "Seeking Ecstasy on the Battlefield: Danger and Pleasure in Nineteenth-Century Feminist Sexual Thought," in *Pleasure and Danger: Exploring Female Sexuality*, ed. Carole S. Vance (Boston: Routledge and Kegan Paul, 1984), 31–49.

5. The academic journal *Feminist Studies* reprinted the leaflet in its entirety fol-lowing the conference. See The Coalition for a Feminist Sexuality and Against Sado-masochism Leaflet, *Feminist Studies* 9, no. 1 (Spring 1983): 180–82.

6. Jane Gerhard, *Desiring Revolution: Second-Wave Feminism and the Rewriting of American Sexual Thought, 1920 to 1982* (New York: Columbia University Press, 1982), 87. On the relationship between *Playboy* and the women's liberation move-ment, see Elizabeth Fraterrigo, *Playboy and the Making of the Good Life in Modern America* (New York: Oxford University Press, 2009), 167–204.

7. See Lillian B. Rubin, *Worlds of Pain: Life in the Working-Class Family* (New York: Basic Books, 1976), 137–44.

8. Morton A. Lieberman and Gary R. Bond, "The Problem of Being a Woman: A Survey of 1,700 Women in Consciousness-Raising Groups," *The Journal of Applied Behavioral Science* 12 (1976): 372.

9. The rape of female slaves was a dehumanizing and stigmatizing tactic that often broke up families and destroyed communities. Rape was also a charge leveled against

black male slaves by white women and white men as a means of social control, and was punishable by lynching. See Jacqueline D. Hall, "The Mind that Burns in Each Body: Women, Rape, and Racial Violence" in *Powers of Desire: The Politics of Sexuality*, ed. Ann Snitow, Christine Stansell, and Sharon Thompson (New York: Monthly Review Press, 1983), 328–49.

10. Susan Griffin, "Rape: The All-American Crime," *Ramparts* 10 (1971): 30.

11. Susan Brownmiller, *Against Our Will: Men, Women and Rape* (New York: Simon & Schuster, 1975), 15.

12. Historian Alice Echols has documented the shift from radical feminism to cultural feminism and their respective views of biological versus socially constructed views of male and female nature. See Alice Echols, *Daring to Be Bad: Radical Feminism in America, 1967–1975* (Minneapolis: University of Minnesota Press, 1989).

13. Andra Medea and Kathleen Thompson, *Against Rape* (New York: Farrar, Straus, and Giroux, 1974), 7.

14. Donald A. Downs, *The New Politics of Pornography* (Chicago: University of Chicago Press, 1989), 15. This book is an excellent source for understanding the legal changes that affected pornography from the 1950s through the 1980s.

15. Frederick S. Lane III, *Obscene Profits: The Entrepreneurs of Pornography in the Cyber Age* (New York: Routledge, 2000), 29–30.

16. For a more complete account of the effect of *Deep Throat* on feminist attitudes toward mass-market pornography, see Carolyn Bronstein, *Battling Pornography: The American Feminist Anti-Pornography Movement, 1976–1986* (Cambridge UK: Cambridge University Press, 2011), 78–81.

17. For this perspective, see Vincent Canby, "What Are We to Think of Deep Throat?" *New York Times*, January 21, 1973, section 2:1.

18. For an example of such a protest at Michigan State University, see Marianne Rzepka, "'Throat' Not Sexist?" *Her-Self: Women's Community Journal* 3, no. 2 (1974): 6.

19. Sheila Jeffreys, *Anticlimax: A Feminist Perspective on the Sexual Revolution* (New York: New York University Press, 1990), 250.

20. I detail the evolution of this antipornography campaign from its roots in feminist media antiviolence organizing in *Battling Pornography*, chapters 4–9.

21. For a more detailed account, see Bronstein, *Battling Pornography*, 93–98.

22. Quoted in Ricardo A. Forrest, "Women in Rock: Artsy Image or Insult?" *Neworld: The Multi-Cultural Magazine of the Arts* 4, no. 5 (1978): 43.

23. "Hot Stuff," *Rolling Stone*, July 29, 1976, 25.

24. See Bronstein, *Battling Pornography*, 127–39.

25. Andrea Dworkin, "Pornography and Grief," in *Take Back the Night: Women on Pornography*, ed. Laura Lederer (New York: William Morrow, 1980), 289.

26. Susan Brownmiller, *In Our Time: Memoir of a Revolution* (New York: Dial Press, 1999), 302.

27. Claire Bond Potter, "Taking Back Times Square: Feminist Repertoires and the Transformation of Urban Space in Late Second Wave Feminism," *Radical History Review* 113 (Spring 2012): 67–80.

28. Paula Webster, "Pornography and Pleasure," *Heresies 12: The Sex Issue* (1981): 50.

29. Ellen Willis, "Feminism, Moralism and Pornography," *The Village Voice*, October 15, 1979, 8.

30. On this perspective, see the essays in *Pleasure and Danger: Exploring Female Sexuality*, ed. Carole S. Vance (Boston: Routledge and Kegan Paul, 1984).

31. Many prosex feminists defended lesbian sadomasochism as a way of allowing women to play with power in a safe space, an option never granted in patriarchal society, and provided an opportunity to be boldly sexual, leaving aside the passive behaviors typically expected from women in sexual encounters. On the critique of S/M, see Robin Linden, Darlene R. Pagano, Diana E. H. Russell, and Susan Leigh Star, eds. *Against Sadomasochism: A Radical Feminist Analysis* (East Palo Alto, CA: Frog in the Well, 1982).

32. For a comprehensive account of this position, see Andrea Dworkin and Catharine A. MacKinnon, *Pornography and Civil Rights: A New Day for Women's Equality* (Minneapolis: Organizing Against Pornography, 1988).

33. Lynne Segal, "Only the Literal: The Contradictions of Anti-Pornography Feminism," *Sexualities* 1, no. 1 (1998): 46.

34. Peter K. Alilunas, "Smutty Little Movies: The Creation and Regulation of Adult Video, 1976–1986" (PhD dissertation, Northwestern University, 2013), 3.

35. Ty Burr and Mark Harris, "Pee-Wee and Sympathy," *Entertainment Weekly*, August 16, 1991, http://www.ew.com/ew/article/0,,315140,00.html.

36. Bruce C. Klopfenstein, "The Diffusion of the VCR in the United States," in *The VCR Age: Home Video and Mass Communication*, ed. Mark R. Levy (Newbury Park, CA: Sage, 1989), 30.

37. Alilunas, "The Death and Life of the Back Room," 3. See also Joshua M. Greenberg, *From Betamax to Blockbuster: Video Stores and the Invention of Movies on Video* (Cambridge: The MIT Press, 2010).

38. James Cook, "The X-Rated Economy," *Forbes*, September 18, 1978, 85.

39. Alilunas, "Smutty Little Movies," 284.

40. Bronstein, 309–10.

41. Downs, 44.

42. Downs, 95–143.

43. Gayle Rubin, "Thinking Sex: Notes for a Radical Theory of the Politics of Sexuality," in *Pleasure and Danger: Exploring Female Sexuality*, ed. Carole S. Vance (Boston: Routledge and Kegan Paul, 1985), 281.

44. A definitive account of the Canadian situation is Brenda Cossman, Shannon Bell, Lise Gotell, and Becki Ross, eds. *Bad Attitude/s on Trial: Pornography, Feminism, and the Butler Decision* (Toronto: University of Toronto Press, 1997).

45. Strub, 198–206.

46. On the differences between second and third wave feminism and third wavers' views on sexuality and pornography, see Astrid Henry, *Not My Mother's Sister: Generational Conflict and Third-Wave Feminism* (Bloomington: Indiana University Press, 2004).

4

Antiporn Agendas: Feminism, Internet Filtering, and Religious Strategies

Christopher Boulton

As an object of analysis for cultural studies, Internet pornography is uniquely positioned as both an enormously popular media genre and a deeply despised idea. It is a contested textual space, opposed from various angles by grassroots activists, opportunistic politicians, and religious conservatives; each group evokes, and sometimes even displays, pornographic images in order to spark the shock and disgust of a supposedly respectable public and then rearticulates this affective response with its own larger programs of social reform. This chapter looks specifically at how the evolving agenda of the feminist antiporn organization Stop Porn Culture (SPC) has helped enable government-mandated Internet filtering along with other attempts to quarantine adult content online. It also considers how some conservative churches have, in addition to filtering, turned toward sex-positive language as a religious strategy for opposing pornography. Moreover, in light of this recent confluence of events, it now seems an opportune time to revisit and update "Porn and Me(n),"[1] my analysis of the 2007 national antipornography conference held at Wheelock College—an event that drew in both feminists and religious conservatives alike and served as the launch pad for SPC and its emerging legislative agenda.

I initially attended the 2007 Wheelock conference with an antiporn agenda of my own. Up to that point, my personal experience with Internet pornography had long been a deeply irrational and contradictory one—a repeated cycle of ecstasy and despair. First would come the titillation of search and discovery for a suitably arousing image to accompany masturbation. The Web offered an infinite and ever-expanding virtual universe of willing bodies at-the-ready; but then, once the selection was made and orgasm achieved, would always come the inevitable crash—the switch from an all-consuming passion for a pornographic image to utter disgust for the same could be brutal and abrupt. The process often was impulsive, rushed, and frantic. In the end, I would find myself alone, depressed, and full of regret, sometimes resolving never to do it again, until I did. I wanted to stop, but I couldn't. Although I came from a religious background, I did not experience shame or guilt so much as pain and longing. The women in these pictures and videos were not, after all, available to me in the flesh and never would be. The fantasy that they were—while exciting for a moment—would, over time, cultivate dissatisfaction with my potential and actual sexual partners by offering explicit visions of ones that would never be.[2] I should note here that Internet pornography is a broad and blunt term, comprising a wide range of queer, alternative, and otherwise subaltern practices that offer unique opportunities for sexual identification and instruction, both to and from sexual minorities. Indeed, I often defend the Internet pornography industry on these grounds alone—that it has opened up a space capable of accommodating such a wide range of sexual tastes, desires, and practices that otherwise would go unrepresented and remain hard to find. In short, there are surely a variety of porn viewing practices that fall well outside the realm of my own experience. And yet, when I read debates between so-called antiporn and prosex feminists, I often got the sense that neither side had an appreciation for men—like me—who use Internet porn, but, for a variety of reasons, wish that they didn't. Neither side had very much to say about changing porn's effect on *my* life. John Stoltenberg[3] and Robert Jensen[4] offered empathy, but, in terms of solutions, both seemed to believe that merely knowing the antiporn analysis and subscribing to the correct politics would, alone, be sufficient for the enlightened feminist male to reconcile the contradictions of his desires and live a porn-free life of sexual integrity. I went to Wheelock College in 2007 looking for a third way.

After the conference, I conducted several rounds of interviews with four other male attendees, whose political and spiritual commitments ranged from conservative Christian to progressive secular humanist, asking them about their own consumption of porn as well as their experience of Wheelock. I wrote up my findings in an article entitled "Porn and Me(n)." In it, I argued that the radical feminist analysis of pornography not only failed to account for the pleasures of objectification, but also created a hostile environment by provoking—then quickly shaming—heterosexual male desire while refusing to stipulate the bounds of an acceptable alternative. I then compared the relatively diminished and marginal position of the Wheelock approach with the wildly popular and mainstream success of the Christian antipornography movement across a range of media-friendly initiatives. I concluded that the religious formula of confession and redemption offered a more effective rhetorical and practical appeal that bound men together through a process of communal catharsis, spiritual exorcism, and a collective return to the dignity and respectability so clearly delineated by what Gayle Rubin has called the "charmed circle" of monogamous, heterosexual coitus freely exchanged within the privacy of the home and the sanctity of marriage.[5] In contrast, Wheelock not only sacrificed intellectual rigor by pandering to a populist stance of disgust toward male sexual deviance, but, more crucially, failed to offer those men—even the most well-meaning and feminist identified of the men actually in attendance—a clear pathway toward sexual self-actualization. In sum, I argued that this theoretical retrenchment has allowed conservative Christians to successfully take one of feminism's most popular issues from its larger political program and rearticulate it as a religious one.[6]

When I initially presented this work at an academic conference in 2008, Robert Jensen, one of the founders of SPC, spoke up during the Q&A to address my argument that the Christian antiporn agenda was more flexible, welcoming, and popular than the current feminist approach. Jensen explained as follows:

The Wheelock conference—for all of its ideological uniformity—also had conflicting strains in it. Some were rooted more in an older antago-nism. There were people who didn't even think I should be on the stage speaking [because I'm a man] . . . but in defense of the movement, because the feminist antipornography movement is part of a broader left feminist movement and the goal isn't just to critique pornography, it's to undermine patriarchy, white supremacy, and corporate capitalism in the imperial culture—slightly more ambitious goals than just get-ting people to stop using porn. So, not surprisingly, if you're rooted in that kind of political analysis, the mainstream culture ain't much inter-ested in talking to you! . . . . But I think your point is well taken about how you formulate a rhetoric to men that is—at least—not alienating. Whether it's easy to create this sort of 'here's a land of milk and honey' or 'walk over here and it's a land of endless orgasms' is another question [audience laughs].[7]

Jensen's clever comment offers three important insights that preview the main sections of this chapter. First, antiporn feminism often conjures the kind of identity politics that makes it difficult for men to speak out openly and honestly about their often contradictory experiences with pornography. Second, in trying to keep other axes of oppression on the agenda along with collectivist society-level reforms, the feminist antiporn movement may have a structural disadvantage compared with government and religious antiporn Internet filtering efforts that locate choice at the level of what Margaret Thatcher called "individuals and their families."[8] Finally, antiporn feminists need to develop a way to offer porn-using men a value-added proposition for changing their behavior; even religious reformers realize that shame is not enough. In what follows I begin with a recent trajectory of how the antiporn feminist movement, as led by Gail Dines and SPC, has generally failed to open up more space for men or offer them a less alienating framework. What the movement has achieved is an influential position in the public debate over regulating pornography, aided by religious and political organizations that do not share what Jensen described as their "slightly more ambitious goals" of undermining "patriarchy, white supremacy and corporate capitalism in the imperial culture."[9]

ANTIPORN FEMINISM: A RESURGENCE

Much has changed for SPC since 2007. For one thing, their critique has gone mainstream. As Clarissa Smith and Feona Attwood noted in 2013, "the last five years have seen a flood of news reports, observations, policy documents, and calls for increased legislation against the 'pernicious tide' of sexually explicit representations in music, film and new communication technologies."[10] In 2010, Beacon Press published Gail Dines's *Pornland*,[11] which summarizes the radical feminist account of how pornography has evolved from skin magazines into a vast and diversified commercial space expanding into ever more niche and brutal porn subgenres that degrade and debase women. Arguing that this "industrialization of sex" provides inexhaustible supply chains for Web site proprietors while, at the same time, profiting the bankers, hotels, and home cable operators that fund and distribute adult media content, Dines then turns from porn's political economy to the effects of its content, asserting—largely on the basis of anecdotal evidence—that sexualized violence or "torture porn" can turn boys into aggressive and selfish brutes, both in and out of bed. Notably, Dines neglects to define exactly what she thinks proper sexual decorum and decency might look like, but laments that porn—once shamed to the periphery and difficult to access—is now so widely available and accepted that explicit sex, kink, fetish, and other alleged perversions of what sex ought to be have now achieved a degree of legitimacy in popular culture. Moreover, Dines's call for collective action in response to porn as a public health problem indulges in the public's common sense around the vulnerability of others—especially children.

Later in 2010, Routledge published Karen Boyle's edited volume *Everyday Pornography*.[12] And while the contributions address a variety of topics and critical perspectives ranging from methods for analyzing content and interpreting meanings to porn's impacts on men, women, and youth, the first chapter, entitled "Arresting Images: Anti-pornography Slideshows, Activism and the Academy," pays particular attention to the revival of antipornography feminism and features a roundtable interview with Gail Dines and Rebecca Whisnant, two of the principal organizers of the Wheelock Conference. In addition to rehearsing their now-familiar critique of pornography as a sexist industrial product that exploits and objectifies female bodies, Dines and Whisnant argue that academics need to get beyond textual analysis and start interrogating pornography as a particular kind of industrial practice. Textual analysis is not enough, they argue; scholars must also work to translate their work beyond the academy in order to promote activist attempts to regulate or outlaw the porn industry. When Boyle poses a question about how this translation has led to a conservative co-optation of feminist antiporn discourse, Dines offers this response:

> We've had very little contact with the Christian right. They stay away from us . . . what they have done, though, is adopt some of our language, and that's not a terrible thing, because we got them thinking about harm to women . . . The main [religious] focus at the moment seems to be pornographic addiction, and one of the reasons is that there are so many religious men who are addicted. I was speaking to someone whose husband runs an addiction group for Mormons—for addictions to any substance or behavior—and yet the room is full of men wanting to talk about their addictions to pornography.[13]

If the Christian right, does, in fact, "stay away" from Dines, she doesn't stay away from them. Just a few months before the publication of *Everyday Pornography*, Dines accepted an invitation to appear at a briefing alongside conservative political action committees, interfaith coalitions, and faith-based charities at the U.S. Capitol sponsored by *PornHarms.com*.[14] PornHarms is an initiative of Morality in the Media, a group launched in 1962 by a group of clergy who worked with both the Nixon and Reagan administrations "to curb traffic in obscenity and uphold standards of decency in the media [using] common sense, anecdotal evidence and social science research."[15] The founder and president of PornHarms, former Department of Justice official Patrick Trueman, personally lobbied Republican Presidential Nominee Mitt Romney[16] and has declared that "all the efforts of Morality in Media, and groups, churches and individuals will come to naught unless our Lord is directing them [toward] a great awakening to the harms, spiritual and physical, of pornography."[17] Trueman opened the briefing by insisting that hardcore pornography was obscene and therefore should be prosecuted as illegal under existing law, whether distributed through the Internet, television, hotels, or retail stores.[18] In her presentation, Dines followed suit, listing a series of hardcore pornography Web site titles as self-evident proof of sexual assault and thereby translating the feminist analysis of pornography into a format designed to shock and mobilize an audience of conservative—and largely Christian—legislative activists.[19]

More books by antipornography scholar-activists were to follow. In 2012, Zed Books published Julia Long's account of the history and newfound energy of public protest against pornography based largely on Long's participatory observation within the UK antiporn feminist groups OBJECT and Anti-Porn London.[20] Long chronicles radical feminist responses to pornography—from the genesis of the women's liberation movement in the 1970s through a new generation objecting to lad magazines on sale in Tesco supermarkets. For Long, pornography is not just a highly lucrative and prolific industry; it has led to the normalization of erotic venues (strip clubs and *Playboy* brand stores), risqué media (music videos that objectify women and Page 3 topless photos in British tabloids), and even sexual self-improvement (labiaplasties, breast enlargements, and pole-dancing exercise classes). Long contends that these trends have sparked a resurgence of the antiporn agenda and the infectious *jouissance* of feminist activists participating in a range of antiporn tactical repertoires.

In that spirit, Long calls for increased international networking among groups such as Norway's Otter, Australia's Collective Shout, and SPC in the United States.[21] In addition to rave reviews from Dines and Whisnant championing her book as a rejoinder to the academy's general acceptance of pornography and a welcome revisionist history of the antiporn movement, Long boasts a strong endorsement by Clare Short, a former member of the British Parliament,[22] which is important because it foreshadows SPC's legislative agenda—one that, as we shall see, would soon bear fruit.

In the summer of 2012, SPC hosted Long, among others, during a four-day event at the University of San Diego.[23] The first half, described as "Anti-Porn Activist Training," included an antiporn slide show presentation along with practice Q&A sessions to help participants "speak publicly against pornography in your community." As others have argued, this slide-show-as-consciousness-raising strategy addresses audiences as good and upstanding citizens naïve to what's "out there" and therefore in need of exposure to a "thrilling" truth that will radicalize and rally them to rise up and oppose porn in all its forms.[24] The second half, "Contemporary Radical Feminism in the Age of Porn," featured scholars from the United States, Australia, Norway, and the UK presenting scholarship and discussing past successes and future tactics for legal recourse and public policy gains.[25] For instance, after presenting an update on SPC, Dines proposed taking legal action against the industry—not the enforcement of obscenity laws, as proposed by Patrick Trueman at the U.S. Capitol briefing back in 2010, but rather class action lawsuits seeking compensation for bodily damage to porn workers. She also emphasized the importance of global alliances, noting that the "Who wants to be a porn star?" slide show and accompanying script first introduced at Wheelock in 2007 remains "the absolute central piece of our activism and education." This slide show is now used and adapted by colleges, social service agencies, and churches throughout the UK, Canada, Scotland, Ireland, Australia, and other countries.[26]

The following year would bring more international alliances for SPC, along with a shift in focus from lawsuits to legislation. In March 2013, Dines posted a petition on the organization's Web site in support of Iceland's efforts to enact legislative limits on violent Internet pornography.[27] Several months later, in June, MP Claire Perry invited Dines to present to members of the British House of Commons as part of a forum titled Generation XXX: *Sunday Times* Symposium on How to Save Our Children From the Dangers of Online Porn.[28] Just days after her presentation, Dines would be quoted in the *Guardian* regarding another petition,[29] this one calling on Routledge press to diversify what the petition's organizers called a "uniformly pro-porn" editorial board of its recently announced *Porn Studies* academic journal. The petition recalls similar tactics used by Women Against Pornography to try to prevent the convening of the 1982 Barnard Conference on Sexuality through phone calls, letter writing, and eventually picketing the venue.[30] And while SPC's petition against *Porn Studies* did not get much traction at the publishing house,[31] the group's efforts to build international alliances in the UK were about to gain a powerful ally at 10 Downing Street.

INTERNET FILTERING: GOVERNMENT RESPONDS

On July 22, 2013, British Prime Minister David Cameron called a press conference: "I'm not making this speech because I want to moralise or scaremonger, but because I feel profoundly as a politician, and as a father, that the time for action has come."[32] Concerned with how online pornography was "corroding childhood," he had worked out a deal with Internet service providers (ISPs) to place automatic, family-friendly, network-level filters on domestic Internet connections by default, thus affecting all devices in the home and meaning that customers would have to actively opt-out of the protection in order to access legal porn and other adult material online.[33] Cameron's announcement made waves overseas. A few months later, in November 2013, Canadian MP Joy Smith invited Dines (and Julia Beazley of the Evangelical Fellowship of Canada) to Ottawa to present to parliamentarians on the necessity of the government's building a "pornwall" to protect children.[34] Later that month, *PornHarms.org*, which had sponsored the Capitol Hill briefing where Dines appeared back in 2010, launched a petition to bring Britain's opt-out model to the United States.[35] In March 2014, SPC launched the group's first European chapter (Stop Porn International UK) at an antipornography conference bringing together feminists from five nations (including Norway, Iceland, Sweden, and Austria) in London, just a five-minute drive from Mr. Cameron's residence.[36]

This confluence of proposed legislation and activist activity placed Britain at the forefront of government responses to Internet pornography; however, many doubts remain as to how such an opt-out filtering program would actually work. For instance, what, exactly, would be blocked? The BBC reported that the very same family filters already in place on public Wi-Fi spots in the UK stopped users from accessing news articles about Cameron's plan—presumably due to the articles' inclusion of the term "pornography."[37] Furthermore, studies of filters currently in use by some UK ISPs found that well-known porn sites came through just fine while educational sites about reproduction or sexual health sites are rendered invisible.[38] And while boasting that he had closed a loophole to make it "a criminal offense to possess Internet pornography that depicts rape," Cameron did not explain the criteria for what constitutes "rape porn."[39] When pressed, he admitted that there could be "problems down the line," adding that he didn't believe that the *The Sun's* Page 3 topless pictures or written erotica would be blocked, but this would ultimately depend on decisions made by third-party vendors:

> The companies themselves are going to design what is automatically blocked, but the assumption is they will start with blocking pornographic sites and also perhaps self-harming sites . . . It will depend on how the companies choose how to do it. It doesn't mean, for instance, it will block access to a newspaper like *The Sun*, it wouldn't block that— but it would block pornography.[40]

Britain's largest Internet provider, BT, complied with Cameron's request by offering their 6.8 million broadband customers a filter designed to control all Internet-enabled devices using the same home network. The filter comes with three predefined settings (strict, moderate, and light) covering seventeen categories. And while all three of these settings restrict pornography, they can also exclude sites promoting drugs, alcohol, tobacco, hate, and self-harm. For instance, the moderate setting excludes "sites featuring nudity, weapons and violence, gambling and social networking" and the strict setting even blocks "fashion and beauty sites, file-sharing, games and media streaming."[41] As the *Guardian* observed, other potential blocks range from "anorexia and eating disorder websites" to "suicide related websites" and even include such vague categories as "extremist related content," "web forums," and so-called "esoteric material."[42] Adding to the confusion, the lowest setting of BT's opt-in filtering system blocks "obscene content," which, oddly enough, also covers file-sharing sites commonly used for downloading music and software.[43] And while BT retracted a controversial category that initially blocked sites featuring a "gay and lesbian lifestyle,"[44] the filtering is run by a private third-party supplier and so its criteria, as well as coding, key terms, and other algorithmic formulas, are not necessarily subject to either government or public oversight.[45]

In addition to vague filtering categories and criteria, there are also troubling privacy issues. For starters, the UK model requires that each family subscribing to an ISP home network connection would have to make one decision about whether they want access to "obscene material." This decision would then affect everyone trying to access the Internet through this home network. When asked whether this decision could force some awkward conversations among spouses, such as a husband having to "fess up" to his wife if he wanted to opt-out of the filters to look at porn, Cameron responded flatly, "Yes, it does."[46] It is also unclear just how much of British citizens' surfing, or even that singular act of opting-out, would be reported to the government or perhaps stored and thus made vulnerable to future surveillance. Recent events should give us all good reason for caution in this regard. NSA documents leaked by Edward Snowden in late 2013 describe how the agency tracked online porn viewing as a way to discredit six suspected Muslim "radicals" by exposing their hypocrisy and thereby undermining their influence through social media.[47] This tactic recalls the Hoover-era FBI surveillance of Martin Luther King's alleged affairs and the subsequent attempt to use this information to blackmail him.[48] In sum, governments cataloging so-called obscene content and potentially tracking private Internet use could lead to all sorts of mischief.

And yet, despite the haunting specter of government abuse, Cameron's attempt to regulate Internet pornography reveals less about state power than it does about the state's ever-increasing dependence on the private sector to help mediate—and indeed arbitrate—the public's access to online information, whether pornographic or otherwise. For instance, within the Tumblr Web site, bloggers can use tags to identify adult content and readers can set a "safe mode" search to limit their own access to that content; but the Tumblr mobile app automatically blocks porn-related search terms[49] for fear of violating the antiporn marketplace parameters imposed by the oligopoly of the Apple App Store and Google Play. As the two major players in smartphone operating systems, Apple and Google police both the content and capability of their applications—prohibiting the apps in their stores from either containing or even searching for pornographic content. This is another, if perhaps unintended, effect of the push for Internet filtering as a means to protect and preserve "family friendly" spaces. It incentivizes social media platforms such as Tumblr to ban a wide variety of search terms—again determined by an unaccountable third party—and render their mobile apps porn-free.[50]

Internet filtering can be justified either by governments as a necessary measure to protect the innocence of children or by corporations as a technique for preventing unwanted exposure to what they categorize as offensive content. The prevailing assumption throughout is one of victimization through accidental incursion and ignores the intentional Web searches of healthy, curious children. The logic underpinning many Internet filtering initiatives is thus less about protection and more about control: Childhood interest in sex is deemed dangerous for fear that unfettered access to Internet pornography will allow kids to seek out images and ideas that may intrigue at first but may, over time, also damage them. The assumption here is that children have no impulse control. But what if the presumably more responsible and rational adult behaves in the same way?

RELIGIOUS STRATEGIES: ACCOUNTABILITY, CONFESSION, AND ADVICE

As I mentioned in the introduction, the feminist antiporn agenda at the Wheelock Conference condemned my desire for pornography and expected me to control my impulses through sheer force of will, but the conservative Christians in the audience had a different strategy. While at Wheelock, I met members of XXXChurch, an upstart Christian antipornography organization that, in addition to holding "Porn and Pancakes" events at churches and distributing "Jesus Loves Porn Stars" bibles at sex-industry conventions, also developed X3Watch, a free accountability software program to help people practice a porn-free life. The program—which launches at start-up and appears ever-so-discreetly in your computer's system preferences as a groovy purple "W" logo—tracks users' Web activity and notifies your self-appointed "accountability champions" of any visits to "inappropriate sites" by e-mailing users a bimonthly report. If any porn sites pop up on the report, the understanding is that the champions will confront you. In addition—and this is key—the program is based on the assumption that you are an addict; your resolve will weaken and, if given the chance, you will succumb to temptation.

To prevent a "relapse," X3Watch alerts all champions when you make any modifications such as deleting a champion or uninstalling the software; there is no privacy, and that is precisely the point.[51] Even if you activate Safari's private browsing or Chrome "incognito" in order to turn off your browsing history and thus visit pornographic sites off the record, X3Watch keeps running in the background and records every page. As XXXChurch founder Craig Gross explained in 2013, the software now has over a million users and "the mere knowledge that someone else will be seeing where you go online—will be virtually looking over your shoulder as you browse the Internet—is a huge deterrent to leaping down the rabbit hole of porn. It just works."[52]

Well, not exactly. Because Apple does not permit third-party applications to run in the background on iOS devices, XXXChurch had to create a new version of X3Watch for iPhones that, after disabling Safari, functions as an alternative, and vastly inferior, browser (e.g., slow performance, frequent crashes, no tabs, no bookmarks, and URLs from other applications must be copied and pasted). So, while the software is free, users pay a hefty price in terms of inconvenience. That being said, it was good enough for me.

Covenant Eyes is a similar accountability service named after the biblical verse, "I made a covenant with my eyes not to look lustfully at a young woman."[53] In 2013, the company grew by 18 percent to over 125,000 paid subscribers, with expectations that it will grow by another 30 percent in 2014.[54] The service uses an algorithm that sends spiders across the Web to analyze text, links, domain names, search terms, and even YouTube video titles in order to rate every page in real time according to categories drawn from video games and TV shows (E for everyone, T for Teen, M for Mature, etc.).[55] An in-house team can then further refine these ratings with user feedback about the algorithm's accuracy. Like X3Watch, Covenant Eyes can filter content and/or send out synopsis reports of browser histories categorized by rating to accountability partners who often are parents or spouses.[56] According to Sam Black, an Internet Safety Consultant and a manager at Covenant Eyes, some technical loopholes remain: Social media sites' log-ins can block tracking, and mobile apps with built-in browsers can allow users to work around both the filtering and accountability functions. Despite these limits to the software's capability, Black insists that the principle of accountability is always more effective than filtering because it incorporates the Christian strategies of confession and rebuke: Subscribers must first admit their sins in order to secure an accountability partner and then be prepared for a rebuke if they sin again. But Christian software solutions are only one of the more recent religious antiporn strategies. For many Christian speakers, authors, and pastors, pornography is not just a problem, it's a hook.

At the time of the Wheelock Conference in 2007, Michael Leahy, a born-again Christian and self-proclaimed "fully recovered pornography addict," was wrapping up Porn Nation, an evangelical college tour of more than eighty campuses that, along the way, had collected porn-use surveys from over 24,000 college students and been featured on ABC's *20/20* and *The View*.[57] Since then, other Christian leaders have followed Leahy's lead, pulling porn out of the shadows and up into the pulpit. In 2007, Craig Groeschel, senior pastor at Life Church, one of the largest churches in America with a weekly attendance of 52,000 across 18 different campuses,[58] preached a sermon series entitled "My Secret," which invited people to get their pornography addictions out in the open by making an anonymous confession. It was a successful formula for Groeschel, inspiring him to preach other series, such as Satan's Sex Ed, and to host XXXChurch events like The Porn Event and National Porn Sunday.[59] Others, like Fred Stoeker, have co-written Christian antiporn self-help books such as *Every Man's Battle: Winning the War on Sexual Temptation One Victory at a Time*,[60] a title that has been translated into six languages and has sold nearly 900,000 copies worldwide.[61] Still others have tried to start a movement. In 2010, Jay Dennis, a megachurch pastor in Florida, asked a stadium-style church auditorium of Christian men to bow their heads, close their eyes, and stand if they were struggling with porn. After a brief pause, all you could hear was the sounds of seats flipping up as the men stood "and it was almost like the chains were falling off and there was a sense of revival."[62] Three years later, Dennis took on what he called "the new Bubonic Plague" by writing *Our Hardcore Battle Plan: Joining in the War Against Pornography*.[63] Later that summer he launched Join One Million Men,[64] a national campaign urging men to make "a porn free commitment" by posting their names to an online Internet "wall."[65] The Southern Baptist Convention,[66] an annual gathering that represents "forty-five thousand churches and church-type missions with nearly sixteen million members,"[67] endorsed and promoted Join One Million Men, calling it "a Godsend" because "the devil has figured out that the greatest weapon in his arsenal to destroy families and to destroy lives in 21st-century America is hardcore Internet pornography."[68]

So what does all this saber rattling mean? In 2007, XXXChurch and Porn Nation were controversial in evangelical circles. Today, men talking about porn in public is a mainstream religious strategy for attracting younger members. Indeed, by 2012, the sheer volume of conservative Christian antiporn accountability software hacks, college tours, sermons, books, and online confessionals prompted the *Daily Beast* to observe that "straight talk about sex" could now be considered a new "feature of evangelical cool."[69]

And there's been yet another important shift in religious antiporn strategies. In "Porn and Me(n)," I critiqued XXXChurch and Porn Nation's taboo testimonials and titillating confessions as a kind of double bait-and-switch that, not unlike SPC's slide show, would lure prurient curiosities with the promise of "thrilling" discourses and imagery safely ensconced within the socially acceptable confines of critique, only to then shame any resulting arousal and, finally, offer conversion (whether political or spiritual) as the only way out.[70] But, just as with antiporn feminism, much has changed since 2007 and many conservative Christians now are pivoting from prohibition to instruction.

For instance, Groeschel preached "God Love Sex," a six-part sermon series that drew on both his own, personal experiences and one of the most poetic books of the Bible, the Song of Solomon.[71] Taunting prudes with a warning that some had deemed the biblical passages as "not suitable for reading in church," Groeschel just smiled and gave the following advice: (1) because the bible uses the metaphor of "fawns" for breasts, men should sneak up on them "gently" like a hunter would approach a deer; (2) if parents want thirty minutes of privacy for sex during the day, they should plop their kids in front of an episode of *Barney*; (3) if "ladies" want to initiate sex, they should drop their clothes when their husbands walk in the door and "watch him just worship right there!"[72] Mark Driscoll, the head pastor at Mars Hill Church,[73] wrote a blog with his wife entitled "Christian Sex: Frank Answers to Honest Questions" and rated MH-17 (Under 17 Requires Adult Permission),[74] with some of the entries referring readers to Covenant Spice (a Christian sex toy shop)[75] and Christian Nymphos (a blog with categories ranging from "position of the week" to "creative sexual techniques").[76] Driscoll then wrote *Porn Again Christian*,[77] a book that, while condemning masturbating to pornography, strongly endorses adventurous, albeit marital, sexual exploration.[78] In January of 2012, Driscoll and his wife published *Real Marriage: The Truth About Sex, Friendship, and Life Together*, a book that endorses role-playing, cybersex, and wives anally penetrating their husbands—all to keep marital sex vital and help couples avoid "The Porn Path."[79] That same month, Ed Young, another megachurch pastor who has preached against porn,[80] with a congregation spread over ten campuses in three states plus a satellite in London, also published a book with his wife called *Sexperiment: 7 Days to Lasting Intimacy with Your Spouse*.[81] Ahead of the book's release, Young and his wife staged a twenty-four-hour "bed-in," inspired by John Lennon and Yoko Ono,[82] on the roof of their Fellowship Church flagship building.[83] Propped up on pillows, tucked under the covers, and surrounded by lights, cameras, and crew, the couple entertained Skype calls from sympathetic church leaders and fielded questions from local and international media about how having sex for seven days in a row renews and restores Christian marriages because "God is pro-sex."[84]

Whether it's Groeschel's "God Love Sex," Driscoll's "Frank Answers," or Young's "Sexperiment," these three famous pastors of very large conservative congregations don't stop at accountability or confession when it comes to sexual sin; they go on to offer concrete advice to help the men in their flock redirect their desires away from pornography and back towards their wives. Sex, they promise, when confined within a Christian marriage, can be kinky and abundant. Whether this actually works or not is an open question, but this shift in religious strategy matters because it fills an important gap left by the radical feminist analysis of pornography—namely, sex education. While SPC has gained ground with powerful political allies in furthering their supply-side regulatory reform agenda against "bad sex," their silence on both defining "good sex" and teaching the public how to get it has allowed conservative Christians to claim it as their own. And despite SPC's tendency to describe porn use as an addiction, the organization does not include any accountability software (such as 3XWatch or Covenant Eyes) on its resource page nor has it publicly asked browsers to grant users the ability to maintain browsing history as an accountability device—indeed, given Apple and Google's prudish attitude towards apps in their own stores, it is surprising that, as of this writing, it is impossible to turn off the "incognito" or "private browsing" option on either Chrome or Safari.[85] The radical feminist analysis of pornography, in choosing a collective top-down strategy, has failed to provide either a concrete, appealing, and sex-positive vision of the porn-free life or any accountability tools for helping all those irresponsible and irrational individuals with no impulse control, such as myself, hoping to get to the promised land.

CONCLUSION

The antiporn agendas examined in this chapter are never just about sex. Some feminists, governments, and Christians use Internet pornography as a means to a much larger end, whether it be challenging the existing social order, consolidating political power, or spreading the gospel of Jesus Christ. In this way, porn remains a powerful, and contested, signifier—loved by its fans, feared by its enemies. Thus, the current state of affairs is an ironic one. On one hand, sectors of the megachurch evangelical right are embracing a more sex-positive discourse as both a media-friendly tactic for selling books and a practical—and very popular—instruction manual for their congregations to find sexual agency within the structure of heterosexual marriage.[86] On the other hand, politicians in both the UK and Canada have repurposed one very limited aspect of feminism in order to pander to their constituents' panic around Internet pornography and children. Due to the technological challenges in mapping and categorizing the Internet, the state's efforts to regulate adult content may ultimately fail, but Cameron's move has placed antiporn feminism at the center of the public policy sphere. Personally, I am sympathetic. As an X3Watch user, and someone who does not *want* to want to see porn, I welcome any ironclad mechanism whereby, in a moment of moral fortitude, I could scrub my Internet experiences clean and, despite myself, never go back. For me, porn is much more than simply a text;[87] it is an embodied practice that associates familiar scripts with physical pleasures again and again. It is precisely the reliability of porn's unique value proposition (e.g., instant access to images of women ready to do whatever it takes to help you attain orgasm) that makes it so attractive to men and so repulsive for those wary of how men might apply it to their personal and professional lives.

At the end of "Porn and Me(n)," I concluded that there is a problem among those feminists publicly condemning the representation of certain sexual practices as misogynist while refusing to offer constructive alternatives. In naming the bad, but refusing to define the good, it is no wonder that the radical feminist analysis of pornography at the Wheelock Conference had all the guilt and none of the pleasure. Such an approach suggests that the only kind of healthy sexual activity is exclusive, scarce, noncommercial, and invisible. It is an agenda that dovetails with that of moral conservatives. In response, I asked SPC to consider a critical men's porn conference that would focus more on explicit sex education—a safe place for men to share good techniques, consider the benefits of forgoing masturbation, and generally inspire each other to move from spectatorship towards embodiment.[88] SPC has gained influence in legislative circles, yet it has neglected to help men imagine a viable alternative, ceding even more valuable ground to conservative Christians like Groeschel, Driscoll, and Young who have been much quicker to adapt to the needs of ambivalent audiences. Indeed, while media fans and antifans may be familiar to cultural studies scholars who are interested in learning more about them, we are less familiar with reluctant fans who, like me, regret the ritual consumption of particular media genres and wish to interrupt the cycle. In short, porn can be a source of both momentary pleasure and enduring pain. Pastors get this, but many feminist antiporn academics don't.

NOTES

1. Chris Boulton, "Porn and Me(n): Sexual Morality, Objectification, and Religion at the Wheelock Anti-Pornography Conference," *The Communication Review* 11, no. 3 (2008): 247–73.

2. The men I spoke to at Wheelock told similar stories. Boulton, "Porn and Me(n)," 2008.

3. John Stoltenberg, *Refusing to be a Man: Essays on Sex and Justice* (New York: Penguin, 1990).

4. Robert Jensen, *Getting Off: Pornography and the End of Masculinity* (Cambridge, MA: South End Press, 2007).

5. Gayle Rubin, "Thinking Sex: Notes for a Radical Theory of the Politics of Sexuality," in *The Lesbian and Gay Studies Reader*, ed. Henry Abelove et al. (New York: Routledge, 1993), 666.

6. I sent copies of my "Porn and Me(n)" article to both Gail Dines and Rebecca Whisnant, two of the principal organizers of the Wheelock Conference, hoping that my analysis would be welcomed as constructive criticism; I never heard back. The article did, however, generate great interest during my time on the academic job market. While I initially worried that such a taboo subject could jeopardize my career prospects, I encountered many search committees eager to bring a critical engagement with pornography to their campuses. Boulton, "Porn and Me(n)," 2008.

7. Robert Jensen, face-to-face communication, June 13, 2008.

8. Margaret Thatcher quoted in Stuart Hall, "And Not a Shot Fired," *Marxism Today*, December 10, 1991. http://www.amielandmelburn.org.uk/collections/mt/pdf/91_12_10.pdf.

9. Jensen, June 13, 2008.

10. Feona Attwood and Clarissa Smith, "Emotional Truths and Thrilling Slideshows: The Resurgence of Anti-Porn Feminism," in *The Feminist Porn Book: The Politics of Producing Pleasure*," ed. Tristan Taormino, et al. (New York: The Feminist Press, 2013), 43.

11. Gail Dines, *Pornland: How Porn Has Hijacked Our Sexuality* (Boston: Beacon Press, 2010).

12. Karen Boyle, *Everyday Pornography* (New York: Routledge, 2010).

13. Gail Dines quoted in Boyle, *Everyday Pornography*, 28.

14. Concerned Women for America Legislative Action Committee Staff, "Congress Told of Pornography's Harms," http://www.cwfa.org/congress-told-of-pornographys-harms.

15. "About Morality in Media," http://pornharms.com/history.

16. Steven Nelson, "Romney Campaign Quietly Promised 'Vigorous' Porn Crackdown, Reagan Prosecutor Says," http://dailycaller.com/2012/07/18/romney-campaign-quietly-promised-vigorous-porn-crackdown-reagan-prosecutor-says/#ixzz2rbgisJzJ.

17. "National Day of Prayer," http://pornharms.com/prayer.

18. PornHarms, "Pt 1 PornHarms.com founder Patrick Trueman, Attorney at Law, at Briefing on Capitol Hill," https://www.youtube.com/watch?v=1irif6u4wmg.

19. According to at least one observer, Dines's tactic worked: "Several members of the audience were noticeably affected by the repulsive, violent, degrading acts [Dines] described to demonstrate that today's pornography is not traditional *Playboy*-style images." PornHarms, "Pornography Debases Men, Women & Culture. Dr. Gail Dines at PornHarms.com Briefing GailDines.com," https://www.youtube.com/watch?v=aaA1Y-aypD0&feature.

20. Julia Long, *Anti-Porn: The Resurgence of Anti-Pornography Feminism* (New York: Zed Books, 2012).

21. Ibid., 207.

22. Clare Short, quoted in Long, *Anti-Porn*, back cover.

23. A very similar event, entitled "Challenging Porn Culture," took place in London the previous December. Feminist Brighton, "Report from the Challenging Porn Culture Conference 3rd December," http://feministbrighton.wordpress.com/2011/12/07/report-from-the-challenging-porn-culture-conference-3rd-december.

24. Given the popularity of the genre, it is certainly possible that such "exposure" could backfire by arousing audience members—a finding I came across at Wheelock. Moreover, while the presenters did display sensitivity towards sexual assault victims, warning them that some of the slide show imagery could "trigger" past trauma, there seemed to be little thought of how images, so popular with men, might affect male audience members.

25. Feminist Philosophers, "Stop Porn Culture: Conference and Training," http://feministphilosophers.wordpress.com/2012/03/16/stop-porn-culture-conference-and-training.

26. stoppornculture, "6/19/12 Part 3," http://www.livestream.com/stoppornculture/video?clipId=pla_0831f323-8a0e-45d0-9d27-3b4f9b3ac385&utm_source=lslibrary&utm_medium=ui-thumb.

27. Gail Dines, "Letter of Support for Iceland's Anti-Pornography Initiative," http://gaildines.com/2013/03/letter-iceland.

28. Safer Media for a Safer Society, "Safermedia News - 20 May 2013," http://www.safermedia.org.uk/news15june2013ar.htm.

29. Stop Porn Culture and concerned academics, "Routledge Pro Porn Studies Bias," http://www.ipetitions.com/petition/porn_studies_bias.

30. See *The Communication Review*, "Special Issue: Commemorating the Barnard Conference" 11, no. 3 (2008); and Carole Vance, ed., *Pleasure and Danger: Exploring Female Sexuality* (Boston: Routledge & Kegan Paul, 1984).

31. The careful reader will notice, however, that Routledge did publish *Everyday Pornography*, which features an interview with Dines and other antiporn feminists in the first chapter.

32. Ross Hawkins, "Online Pornography to Be Blocked by Default, PM Announces," http://www.bbc.co.uk/news/uk-23401076.

33. Ibid.

34. Link Byfield, "A raft of good Internet intentions is coming to the U.K.—and Canada?" http://thechristians.com/?q=node/942.

35. Morality in the Media, "Petition: Make Porn Opt-In Only," http://pornharms.com/petition-make-porn-opt-in-only.

36. Stop Porn Culture, "Events," http://stoppornculture.org/events.

37. BBC News Technology, "Q&A: UK Filters on Legal Pornography," http://www.bbc.co.uk/news/technology-23403068.

38. Ibid.

39. Hawkins, "Online Pornography."

40. Oliver Wright, "Family Filters Won't Block 'Soft' Porn: David Cameron Retreats in War on Internet Porn, Admitting There Will Be 'Problems Down the Line,'" http://www.independent.co.uk/news/uk/politics/family-filters-wont-

block-soft-porn-david-cameron-retreats-in-war-on-internet-porn-admitting-there-will-be-problems-down-the-line-8726991.html.

41. Sophie Curtis, "BT Forces Porn Filter Choice," http://www.telegraph.co.uk/technology/internet-security/10520537/BT-forces-porn-filter-choice.html.

42. Martin Robbins, "Cameron's Internet Filter Goes Far Beyond Porn—and That Was Always the Plan," http://www.newstatesman.com/politics/2013/12/camerons-internet-filter-goes-far-beyond-porn-and-was-always-plan.

43. Laurie Penny, "David Cameron's Internet Porn Filter Is the Start of Censorship Creep," http://www.theguardian.com/commentisfree/2014/jan/03/david-cameron-internet-porn-filter-censorship-creep.

44. Robbins, "Cameron's Internet Filter."

45. Such secrecy has led to fears that filters could have other unintended consequences such as the infringement of unpopular speech. Citing how MP Joy Smith's failed attempt to pass a Clean Internet Act in 2007 did not stop at porn but "would also have banned material deemed to advocate or incite racial hatred or violence against women (neither of them defined)" and how often "Canadian Christians have been hauled before Human Rights Commissions and judges for alleged extremism and hatred against homosexuals, abortion clinics, and Muslims," a contributor to *TheChristians.com* worried that letting government censors determine what constitutes extremist material could eventually lead to filtering prolife and profamily sites on the basis of speech deemed to be too radical. Byfield, "A Raft of Good Internet Intentions."

46. Wright, "Family Filters."

47. Glenn Greenwald, Ryan Gallagher, and Ryan Grim, "Top-Secret Document Reveals NSA Spied on Porn Habits as Part of Plan to Discredit 'Radicalizers,'" http://www.huffingtonpost.com/2013/11/26/nsa-porn-muslims_n_4346128.html.

48. P. J. Vogt, "The NSA Spies on People's Porn Habits," http://www.onthemedia.org/story/nsa-spies-porn.

49. Prohibited search terms are not limited to sexual organs or acts, but also include sexual minorities such as "#gay, #lesbian, and #bisexual." Kit Eaton and Gabe Stein, "Tumblr's Porn Filter Backfires In LGBTQ Community," http://www.fastcolabs.com/3014581/yahoo-owned-tumblrs-clever-new-way-of-porn-filtering.

50. Steve Kovach, "Tumblr Users Are Revolting over Anti-Porn Policies (YHOO)," http://www.sfgate.com/technology/businessinsider/article/Tumblr-Users-Are-Revolting-Over-Anti-Porn-4676581.php.

51. X3Watch Support, "Can X3Watch Premium Easily Be Bypassed or Removed?" http://support.x3watch.com/entries/22603879-Can-X3Watch-Premium-easily-be-bypassed-or-removed.

52. Craig Gross, *Open: What Happens when You Get Real, Get Honest, and Get Accountable* (Nashville, TN: Thomas Nelson, 2013), 6.

53. Job 31:1, NIV.

54. Sam Black, Internet Safety Consultant and a manager at Covenant Eyes, personal phone conversation, February 10, 2014.

55. Covenant Eyes Newsroom, "Parents Need Help Protecting Kids on iPod®, iPhone®, iPad® Devices," http://www.covenanteyes.com/newsroom/parents-need-help-protecting-kids-on-ipod-iphone-ipad-devices.

56. Ibid.

57. Porn Nation Website, "About," http://www.pornnation.org/about.htm.

58. Lifechurch.tv, "Statements of Activities," https://s3.amazonaws.com/ext. lifechurch.tv/pdf/2013_Financial_Statements_unaudited.pdf.

59. "Search Sex," http://open.lifechurch.tv/search?page=1&q=sex&x=0&y=0.

60. Stephen Arterburn, Fred Stoeker, and Mike Yorkey. *Every Man's Battle: Winning the War on Sexual Temptation: One Victory at a Time* (Colorado Springs, CO: WaterBrook Press, 2000).

61. "About Author Fred Stoeker," http://www.fredstoeker.com/about.shtml.

62. For Faith and Family, "Pornography Is Death to Relationships," http://faithandfamily.com/fff/program/pornography-is-death-to-relationships.

63. Jay Dennis, *Our Hardcore Battle Plan: Joining in the War Against Pornography* (Birmingham, AL: New Hope Publishers, 2013).

64. "About Pastor Jay Dennis," http://www.churchatthemall.com/about-us/about-pastor-jay-dennis.

65. "Men's Porn Free Commitment," http://www.join1millionmen.org/get-on-the-wall.

66. David Roach, "Anti-Pornography Initiative Launched at SBC," http://www.sbcannualmeeting.net/sbc13/newsroom/newspage.asp?ID=39.

67. "About Us," http://www.sbc.net/aboutus/default.asp.

68. Roach, "Anti-Pornography Initiative."

69. David Sessions, "Mark Driscoll's Sex Manual 'Real Marriage' Scandalizes Evangelicals," http://www.thedailybeast.com/articles/2012/01/13/mark-driscoll-s-sex-manual-real-marriage-scandalizes-evangelicals.html.

70. Boulton, "Porn and Me(n)," 2008.

71. "God Love Sex," http://open.lifechurch.tv/groups/1237-god-love-sex.

72. Ibid. See also Jessica Johnson's chapter "Porn Again Christian? Mark Driscoll, Mars Hill Church, and a Pornification of the Pulpit" in this volume.

73. "Pastor Profile: Mark Driscoll," http://marshill.com/pastors/mark-driscoll (accessed February 3, 2014).

74. Pastor Mark Driscoll, "Question #28: How Can I Get My Wife to Be More Adventurous?" http://marshill.com/2008/12/04/question-28-how-can-i-get-my-wife-to-be-more-adventurous.

75. "Homepage," http://www.covenantspice.com.

76. "Homepage," http://christiannymphos.org.

77. Pastor Mark Driscoll, "Porn-Again Christian," http://theresurgence.com/books/porn_again_christian.

78. "The Bible is, quite frankly, more liberated on the matter of sex than most Bible teachers. In the Song of Songs alone, we see the condoning of marital kissing (Song 1:2), a sexually aggressive wife (throughout the Song of Songs), a wife who likes to perform oral sex/fellatio (Song 2:3), masturbation performed on one spouse by another (Song 2:6, 5:4–6), massage and petting (Song 4:5), a wife who enjoys her husband performing oral sex/cunnilingus (Song 4:12–5:1), a wife who performs a strip-tease (Song 6:13b–7:9), a husband who enjoys his wife's breasts (Song 7:7–8), erotic conversation (throughout the book), and ongoing variety and creativity that includes

new places and new positions such as lovemaking outdoors during a warm spring day (Song 7:11–13). The bottom line is don't sin, but have fun." Pastor Mark Driscoll, "Chapter 5: Masturbation," http://theresurgence.com/books/porn_again_christian/ch5.

79. Mark Driscoll and Grace Driscoll, *Real Marriage: The Truth about Sex, Friendship & Life Together* (Nashville, TN: Thomas Nelson, 2012).

80. Ed Young Television, "Prime Time Porn: Escaping the grips of pornography" http://edyoung.com/series.php?id=133.

81. Ed Young and Lisa Young, *Sexperiment: 7 Days to Lasting Intimacy with Your Spouse* (New York: FaithWords, 2012).

82. Molly Hennessy-Fiske, "'Sexperiment': Texas Pastor Beds Down With Wife Atop Church," http://latimesblogs.latimes.com/nationnow/2012/01/texas-pastor-sexperiment.html.

83. "The Sexperiment," http://thesexperiment.com.

84. "24 hr Bed-in, with Ed and Lisa Young," http://thesexperiment.com/bedin.

85. Stop Porn Culture, "For Partners/Spouses," http://stoppornculture.org/resources-2/for-partnersspouses.

86. Of course, conservative Christians are "sex-positive" only within limits. The "walled garden" they build around Rubin's "charmed circle," strictly forbidding any premarital and/or queer sexual expression, makes it possible, in turn, for media outlets to pique their audiences' licentiousness by covering pornographic content laundered by the legitimacy of religious restraint. Rubin, "Thinking Sex," 1993.

87. Indeed, as a commercial industry, porn's fantasies may be invented and its pleasures exaggerated, but the abode of porn's production—that is the assembly of its own manufacture—is an embodied activity that tends to be represented through a set of supposedly self-evident physical responses to sexual stimulation by sex workers aimed to facilitate an embodied reception (from arousal through masturbation to orgasm) by its vastly male audience.

88. Boulton, "Porn and Me(n)," 268.

5

Strange Bedfellows: Black Feminism and Antipornography Feminism*

Jennifer C. Nash

Saartjie Baartman, the so-called Hottentot Venus, has emerged as one of the most significant figures in contemporary black feminist thought.[1] The recent explosion of interest in Baartman can be traced, at least in part, to Sander Gilman's seminal article "Black Bodies, White Bodies: Toward an Iconography of Female Sexuality in Late Nineteenth-Century Art, Medicine, and Literature." Gilman documents the 19th-century European fascination with Baartman, a Khoikhoi[2] woman who became an object of caged display at exhibitions in London and Paris. Baartman's body functioned as a "master text,"[3] allowing European audiences to cast their collective gaze on the racially and sexually marked Other in an era where locating the Other's imagined differences justified the project of exporting "civilization."

The "Black Venus narrative," which linked black women's bodies with sexual deviance and moral pathology, provided the European audience an analytic framework for interpreting Baartman's display.[4] Foundational to this narrative was Baartman's imagined "steatopygia"—the term used to describe (and denigrate) her "deviant" buttocks—which was taken as evidence of her aberrant sexuality.[5] The racialized fictions surrounding both Baartman's buttocks and her allegedly abnormal genitalia transformed Baartman from a cultural curiosity into an object for "scientific" exploration.[6] "Scientific" interest in Baartman continued even after her death in 1815, as French scientist Georges Cuvier produced a plaster mold of her body and dissected her genitalia, allowing the European audience to continue their search for "proof" of racial-sexual difference.

Gilman's canonical work offers the important insight that Baartman's body became the quintessential Hottentot body, and the Hottentot body became the quintessential African body, such that "in the course of the 19th century, the female Hottentot comes to represent the black female *in nuce*."[7] In other words, Baartman became a symbol of a symbol, the primary metaphor for imagined racial and sexual difference.

Ironically, Gilman's critique of European uses of Baartman's body as the proto-typical representation of difference has produced a "veritable theoretical indus-try," where feminists use Baartman's story as a metaphor for theorizing black women's perceived otherness.[8] In fact, Baartman's story has become a kind of black feminist "biomythography," a ritualized retelling of a political parable that demonstrates the dangers of the dominant visual field for black female subjects.[9]

Recent scholarship calls attention to Baartman's privileged analytic sta-tus within feminist work, inviting scholars to critically examine the contin-ued deployment of Baartman's story as the primary framework for theorizing black female sexuality. Zine Magubane writes: "The question must be asked why this woman has been made to function in contemporary academic debates as the preeminent example of racial and sexual alterity. This ques-tion becomes even more compelling when we consider that Sarah Baart-man was one of thousands of people exhibited and transformed into medical spectacles during the course of the nineteenth century."[10] Magubane's work foregrounds the politics of *selection*, suggesting the importance of scholarly attention to the rationale underpinning the retelling of Baartman's story and the politicized use(s) that the retelling of Baartman's story serves.

This article takes up Magubane's challenge by examining the rhetorical and political work that the retelling of Baartman's story performs for both anti-pornography and black feminist scholarship.[11] In particular, I argue that the constant invocation of the Hottentot Venus has enabled an antipornography theoretical formation to flourish within the parameters of black feminism. Pulling back the curtain on the intimate relationship between these schol-arly projects spotlights how antipornography feminism's fingerprints smudge the lens through which black feminism examines sexuality, pornography, and pleasure.

This article focuses on two significant theoretical and political conse-quences of the traffic between black and antipornography feminisms. First, in mobilizing the Hottentot Venus to critique dominant representations of black women's bodies, black feminism has permitted a pernicious sexual conservatism, wearing the guise of racial progressivism, to seep into its ana-lytic framework. By sexual conservatism, I refer to black feminism's tendency to foreground examinations of black women's sexual exploitation, oppres-sion, and injury at the expense of analyses attentive to black women's sexual heterogeneity, multiplicity, and diversity.[12] In emphasizing black women's continual sexual degradation, rather than the complex interplay between "pleasure and danger"[13] that constitutes black women's sexual subjectivity, black feminism has become steeped in an "epistemological respectability,"[14] producing an intellectual formation that tends to avoid questions about black women's sexual desires, black queer subjectivities, and the various forms of black women's pleasures.

While my critique of black feminism's sexual conservatism emphasizes the importance of theorizing pleasure, I do not imagine sexual pleasure as a site of liberation wholly outside of domination. In fact, my emphasis on pleasure is informed by antipornography feminism's important insight that pleasure can obscure inequality, eroticize subordination, and entrench hierarchy, functioning as a "velvet glove on the iron fist of domination."[15] While mindful of the ways that dominance can disguise itself as pleasure (and to the ways in which dominance and pleasure are often coconstitutive), I turn my attention to pleasure in the hopes of creating a rupture in the dominant subordination narrative, a gap that can produce space for imagining the critical linkages between black female sexuality and black female subjectivity.

The second effect of the traffic between antipornography and black feminism has been the production of *normative*, rather than iconographic or analytical, engagements with racialized imagery in pornography. To that end, both scholarly traditions pose the perennial question "is pornography racist," and answer that question in the affirmative by drawing connections between Baartman's exhibition and the contemporary display of black women in pornography. However, merely affirming pornography's alleged racism neglects an examination of the ways that pornography mobilizes race in particular social moments, under particular technological conditions, to produce a historically contingent set of racialized meanings *and* profits.

This article begins by tracing antipornography's and black feminism's respective engagement with racialized pornography. It then examines the theoretical traffic between these scholarly conceptions of racialized pornography, revealing the centrality of the Hottentot Venus to both projects' critique of racialized pornography. In particular, I argue that the Hottentot Venus acts as an antipornography and black feminist reading practice, the primary analytic tool used for exposing the racism that continues to haunt the pornographic visual field.

Finally, I suggest an alternative reading practice—racial iconography—to supplant the dominance of the Hottentot Venus reading strategy. As a reading practice, racial iconography grapples with the multitude of meaning-making purposes that black bodies perform in the visual field in a panoply of social, historical, and technological moments, and the complex and multiple interpretative frameworks that spectators deploy to interpret these racialized meanings. In examining pornography's strategic use of black women's bodies in particular historical and technological moments, racial iconography asks new questions about the pleasures racialized pornography can produce for minoritarian viewers, carving out representational space for black spectators to view themselves and each other as sexual subjects.

ANTIPORNOGRAPHY FEMINISM

Antipornography feminists have strategically mobilized claims about race to bolster their arguments about the *gendered* harms of pornography.[16] These scholars imagine racialized pornographic representations as produced through gendered pornographic representations, asserting that "pornography contains a racial hierarchy in which women are rated as prized objects or despised objects according to their color."[17] For antipornography feminists, pornography oppresses all women, yet it subordinates women differently based on "racial hierarchy." Ultimately, this body of scholarship treats race as "an intensifier" that demonstrates the severity of pornography's gender-based inquiry and as an analytic tool that helps antipornography feminists secure their claims to pornography's harms.[18]

Despite its interest in using race to bolster claims about pornography's sexism, antipornography feminism has been inattentive to pornography's mobilization of *particular* racial and ethnic differences. Antipornography feminists conflate the variety of racial and ethnic representations within pornography under a theory that the deployment of any racial or ethnic trope necessarily renders pornography pernicious sexist representation. MacKinnon's description of racialized pornographic tropes is emblematic of this approach: "Asian women are bound so they are not recognizably human, so inert they could be dead. Black women play plantation, struggling against their bonds. Jewish women orgasm in reenactments of Auschwitz."[19] For MacKinnon, there is a basic fungibility to racialized tropes in pornography: All racially or ethnically marked women are exploited "as women" and are the most exploited of *women*.

Despite the interchangeability of racial and ethnic tropes in antipornography theory, black women have held a special rhetorical status for this project. To secure their claims that pornography is a particularly undesirable form of sexist representation, antipornography scholars compare the pornographic treatment of black and white women, advancing the claim that the presence of black bodies in the pornographic visual field makes pornography *more* sexist. Luisah Teish's work epitomizes this trend, arguing that "the pornography industry's exploitation of the Black woman's body is qualitatively different from that of the white woman. While white women are pictured as pillow-soft pussy willows, the stereotype of the Black 'dominatrix' portrays the Black woman as ugly, sadistic, and animalistic, undeserving of human attention."[20]

This interest in the "qualitative differences" in representations of black and white women has two significant implications. First, antipornography scholars argue that black women are represented "worse" than white women. To that end, Alice Walker's notion that "where white women are depicted as human bodies if not beings, black women are depicted as shit" has become the standard antipornography method of investigating the meaning-making work that race performs in pornography.[21] This comparison ultimately yields the insights that pornography is doubly dangerous as it is racist and sexist, and that black women are exploited *worse* than white women in pornography, with little examination of the processes or mechanisms through which black women are represented differently.[22] Second, womanhood functions as a unifying common denominator across racial difference. That is, while black women are treated worse than white women, both black and white women are oppressed *as women*. The difference in their treatment is a difference in degree, not in kind.

When antipornography scholars focus their attention on pornography's "differential" treatment of black women, they draw analytical linkages between contemporary pornography and Baartman's display. In particular, antipornography feminists have anthologized Patricia Hill Collins's essay "Pornography and Black Women's Bodies," an excerpt from *Black Feminist Thought*, in a number of antipornography edited collections, including *Making Violence Sexy* and *Violence against Women: The Bloody Footprints*, rendering Collins's essay the decisive text on pornography and black women.[23]

Collins's essay traces contemporary pornography's roots to 19th-century Europe, precisely the moment when European audiences were fascinated by the ethnopornographic display of Baartman's body. Locating pornography's genesis in Baartman's historical moment suggests that "the treatment of Black women's bodies in nineteenth-century Europe and the United States may be the foundation upon which contemporary pornography as the representation of women's objectification, domination, and control is based. Icons about the sexuality of Black women's bodies emerged in these contexts."[24] Contemporary pornography has cultivated a "full-scale industry" that reenacts Baartman's display, featuring black women in positions that glamorize subordination and reify racial mythologies of black women's hyperlibidinousness. To that end, contemporary pornography continues to shore up conceptions of black women's sexual alterity, and black women's bodies act as the "key pillar on which contemporary pornography itself rests."[25]

While Collins's essay insists on the importance of race to pornography's history, her essay neglects to investigate how viewing technologies and historical moment[26] shape the relationship between the viewer and the viewed, fundamentally altering the psychic labor of interpretation.[27] Considering the *differences* between the live display of Baartman's body in 19th-century Europe and the computer-mediated pornographic displays of black women's bodies in our current moment would allow an analysis of how technology shapes both racial fantasies and spectators' viewing pleasures. Ultimately, if interpretation is a process of "shuffling and collating and transcription of images or words so that they have effectivity within one's own fantasy universe," it becomes critical to engage with how the form of pornographic viewing alters spectators' pleasures and fantasies.[28]

Collins's essay has been strategically taken up by antipornography feminists precisely because it performs antipornography work under the guise of racial progressivism. If pornography has historical roots in Baartman's display, any sexualized representation of the black female body contains that same impulse to locate, display, and verify black women's imagined racial-sexual differences. To that end, eliminating pornography serves an antiracist purpose: it eradicates texts that shore up conceptions of black women's alterity.

BLACK FEMINISM

Black feminism has committed itself to drawing attention to "mainstream" feminism's neglect of questions of racial difference and its exclusion of the experiences of women of color—which are always already multiple and heterogeneous—from the dominant feminist project. With a particular interest in exploding the various incarnations of race-versus-gender logic, black feminism has recently mobilized "intersectionality" to describe the coconstitutive nature of experiences of oppression and identity.[29] That is, identity is understood to comprise the intersections of multiple constructed categories including, but not limited to, race, gender, sexuality, class, and nation.

While black feminism's practical goals—explicating the relationship between race and gender, recovering black women's stories, and challenging both feminism and antiracist projects to meaningfully include black women— have been clear, it has struggled since its inception to define the contours of its theoretical project. This has been a particular challenge because of black feminism's interest in crafting a grounded theory, producing linkages between "the real" and "theory."[30]

This fundamental interest in translation, in rendering black feminism "real" to the imagined black female subject (whether the romanticized black "Folk"[31] or the equally romanticized figure of "Shequanna on 142nd"[32]), has often placed black feminist thought in an oppositional relationship to conventional conceptions of theory. Black feminists have argued that dominant notions of theory privilege institutionalized forms of knowledge, ignoring the panoply of ways in which black women have produced theory. Barbara Christian's work epitomizes this position, asserting that institutionalized forms of knowledge overlook the ways that "people of color have always theorized—but in forms quite different from the Western form of abstract logic. And I am inclined to say that our theorizing (and I intentionally use the verb rather than the noun) is often in narrative forms, in the stories we create, in riddles and proverbs, in the play with language, since dynamic rather than fixed ideas seemed more to our liking."[33] Christian's work persuasively argues that prevailing conceptions of theory deemphasize, if not devalue, the theoretical richness of experience. Yet her formulation of "narrative forms" and "riddles and proverbs" as theory suggests that *every* cultural product black women create is a kind of theory. This incredibly expansive conception of the theoretical tends to overpoliticize black women's cultural production, suggesting that we can distill theoretical meanings out of black women's seemingly quotidian social practice.

Where black feminism has functioned as a kind of "critical social theory"[34] is in its critical engagement with visual culture, with the (re)production of what Patricia Hill Collins terms "controlling images."[35] Collins describes "controlling images" as dominant representations that produce and entrench racial-sexual mythologies. These images depict black women as licentious, animalistic, libidinous Jezebels; as asexual, comical, masculinized Mammies; or as tough, detached, "strongblackwomen."[36] Collins envisions these "controlling images" as serving a social purpose: they provide a justification for the state's continued disciplining of the black female body. That this discipline has most often focused on black women's sexuality, linking black women's reproduction to the moral and fiscal "deterioration of the state," demonstrates the ideological power these images have in securing conceptions of black women's sexual deviance.[37] Ultimately, the regulation of the black female body has rendered it a public site, a space onto which social debates and collective anxieties about morality, religion, policy, and the state are inscribed.

For black feminists, Baartman is the quintessential symbol of both the public nature of black women's bodies and the power that "controlling images" have over the collective imagination in both producing fears of difference and legitimizing racist-difference narratives. Mobilizing Baartman's story as an analytic point of departure has enabled black feminism to offer a "real" theory of the public nature of black women's bodies, a theory rooted in the practice of Baartman's exhibition. This "real" theory emphasizes the ways that black women's bodies have been unshielded by the privilege of privacy afforded to majoritarian subjects, rendering the contemporary black female body exposed and displayed.[38]

THEORETICAL TRAFFIC

While antipornography and black feminisms are often imagined as discrete intellectual projects, there are three significant theoretical strands of continuity between these theoretical regimes. First, both antipornography and black feminist projects imagine black women's bodies as inherently "overexposed."[39]

According to this logic, racialized pornography secures black women's status only as objects to be gazed upon in the ostensibly white spectator's unrelenting search for proof of racialized mythologies. Second, both regimes implicitly pathologize interracial voyeurism, suggesting that the ostensibly white male viewer's gaze at the black female body is motivated by "racial fetishism," and thus constitutes a reductive, objectifying form of looking.[40] Finally, scholars working out of both traditions imagine sexualized representations as the linchpin in the perpetuation of white supremacy and racial inequality. To that end, the theoretical and political work of both projects is to dismantle dominant sexualized representations of black bodies and to encourage black women to launch a "visual defense" rooted in self-representation.[41]

The Logic of "Overexposure"

Both black and antipornography feminism take black women's visual "overexposure" as an analytic point of departure. Rooting "overexposure" in slavery, scholars argue that white slave owners' unmitigated sexual access to black women's bodies rendered exploitation, violation, and literal bodily *exposure* central to black women's experiences of their sexuality.[42]

Both camps extend this "overexposure" framework into our contemporary moment, arguing that black women's bodies continue to function as cultural spectacles that are called upon to provide evidence of black subjects' deviance. For antipornography feminists, black women's inherent "overexposure" renders them the prototypical antipornography subject. It is precisely because black women are already hypervisible that they are an ideal case study for antipornography feminism: if all women are "exposed" and objectified, black women's hyperexposure makes them the ideal metaphorical vehicles for exposing pornography's harms.

For black feminists, terms like the "culture of dissemblance,"[43] the "beached whale" of black female sexuality,[44] and the "politics of silence"[45] have provided frameworks for considering how black women strategically avoid describing their own sexuality as a way of guarding against "overexposure." That is, black women are imagined to have adopted a deliberate "politics of silence" as a way of shielding themselves from further scrutiny and exploitation.

However, the predominance of these terms often obscures the historical specificity with which they were originally used. For example, Darlene Clark Hine's notion of the "culture of dissemblance" seeks to describe the noneconomic rationales for black women's migration in the decades following the Civil War, yet has been expanded to function as a transhistorical description of black women's sexuality. As Michele Mitchell warns, "it remains crucial to consider how analytical frameworks can obscure as well as reveal."[46] Considering the constitutive power of concepts like the "culture of dissemblance" reveals that the strategic "silence" that black women are imagined to have taken on as a result of "overexposure" requires analyses of the mechanisms of "dissemblance" and "silence" and the variety of ways that black women both took on and resisted "silence."

Because both projects are concerned with black women's hypervisibility, their incessant cultural and representational exposure, they suggest that the work of radical political projects is to shield the black female body from the exploitation inherent to dominant representation by encouraging black women to represent themselves, on their own terms.

However, this strategy has two significant shortcomings: first, considering the case of pornography suggests that black women are not always "overexposed" in the visual field. In fact, there are historical moments when black women are wholly absent from the pornographic visual field. Comparing black women's relative absence from pornography's early stag films to black women's presence as pornographic protagonists in Golden Age films—the era spanning the 1970s when pornographers self-consciously challenged the boundary between the pornographic and the mainstream, producing films that resembled conventional Hollywood films—compels us to ask how we might understand the black female body as *both* under- and overexposed. An attention to historical and technological variability would allow black feminists to interpret black women's absences from the pornographic visual field in particular historical moments, and to read those against pornography's strategic (and profitable) mobilizations of black women's bodies in other social, historical, cultural, and technological moments.

Debates about the over- *and* underexposure of the black female body extend far beyond the pornographic visual field.[47] Art historians have a long-standing interest in the *de*sexualization of the black female body in the history of Western art and the invisibility of black women's bodies from visual representation outside of roles as servants, mammies, or handmaids.[48] In particular, the paucity of representations of the black nude has been a source of tremendous interest to art historians, with Judith Wilson noting that "apparently, the black nude only becomes a permissible subject for black artists in the twentieth century."[49] This absence is of particular significance because of the centrality of the nude to the history of Western art and to Western conceptions of beauty, suggesting that black female bodies might be "underexposed" in sites conventionally associated with desirability, femininity, and sexuality. The striking lack of sexual representations of black bodies, and of representations of the "black body beautiful" more generally from visual culture, suggests the need for conceptualizing both visibility and *in*visibility in more historically contingent and specific terms.[50]

Second, both projects' advocacy of a "black liberation discourse on the black body beautiful" ignores the problems inherent to visuality itself, neglecting questions about the violence that representation can inflict, particularly on minoritarian subjects.[51] Because the visual is underpinned by an incessant plea for legibility and intelligibility, it often requires bodies to confess, to provide "proof" of the difference that race, gender, and sexuality produce. This appeal to making bodies' workings visible can compel minoritarian subjects to provide evidence of precisely the "truths" that can inflict injury: race, gender, and sexuality.

Moreover, appeals to self-representation often neglect that *what can be seen* is colored in a visual economy that is structured by race.[52] Judith Butler argues that we inhabit a "racially saturated field of visibility," where race fundamentally alters the conditions under which viewing takes place.[53] Given that visual lenses are so thoroughly smudged by race, even images that black women have produced are subject to (mis)readings informed by the dominant conception of black women's sexual deviance.

Ultimately, feminist appeals to perpetuating "positive images" of the black female body through self-representation assume that the task of black cultural production is to contest racism[54] and ignore the homogenizing effects that "positive images" can have.[55] In encouraging black women to create images of "the black body beautiful" that disrupt racial fictions and mythologies, appeals to "positive" self-representation discount the significance of images of black female heterogeneity and diversity to the "inauguration of a public black female subjectivity."[56]

Racial Fetishism

Both antipornography and black feminist traditions argue that racialized pornography is produced for a white spectator, whose desire to gaze at the black female body's imagined difference is motivated by a reductive "racial fetishism." Looking across the racial border is thought to be undergirded by a pernicious inequality, one where part of the pleasure-in-looking that the white male viewer achieves is the reification of his position of social dominance.

For antipornography feminists, interracial inequality bolsters gendered inequality; the interracial gaze and the male gaze coalesce during consumption of racialized pornography, entrenching white male power. Because pornography is imagined to be produced for a white male viewer, antipornography feminists draw connections between the fact that "we [women] are pussy, beaver, bitch, chick, cunt" and the fact that "pornography is a major medium for the sexualization of racial hatred. Every racial stereotype is used."[57] MacKinnon makes explicit the imagined connections between sexism, racism, and representation:

Perhaps sexuality is a dynamic in racism and ethnic prejudice as well as in gender bias. Upon examination, much racist behavior is sexual. Consider the pure enjoyment of dominance that makes power its own reward, reports of the look of pleasure on the face of racist torturers, accounts of the adrenalin high of hatred and excitement that survivors of lynchings describe having seen, the sexual atrocities always involved. Recall the elaborate use of race, ethnicity, and religion for sexual excitement in pornography and in much racist harassment.[58]

To that end, sexism and racism are theoretically run together, with pornography bolstering both male privilege and white privilege simultaneously.

Scholars working out of the black feminist traditions have imagined the white viewer's visual pleasure as rooted in a pathological "racial fetishism," one that renders particular body parts—the buttocks, in particular—a metonymy for the entirety of the black female body. For these scholars, the black body is an object for white viewing pleasures, enabling white spectators to entertain a kind of "imperialist nostalgia" for a moment like the one when Baartman was displayed, and black female bodies were literally objects to be consumed.[59]

In ignoring both the possibilities of black spectatorship and non-"fetishistic" white spectatorship, the "racial fetishism" logic suggests both that block bodies inhabit the visual field *for* white viewing pleasures, and that interracial viewing is inherently problematic as it is steeped in inequality. This theoretical framework leaves little room for white visual pleasures that are not degrading, objectifying, or fetishizing, foreclosing the possibility of white spectators gazing at, and taking pleasure in, black women's bodies without reducing the black female body to its constitutive parts.

The Danger of Images

Finally, scholars working out of both traditions conceive of sexualized representations as the linchpin in the perpetuation of white supremacy and racial inequality. In advocating the eradication of these images, either through legal abolishment (antipornography feminism) or the creation of counterimages produced by minoritarian subjects (black feminism), these projects envision sexualized representation as integral to structures of domination and hegemonic control.

For antipornography feminists, sexuality is the primary locus of patriarchal power, and pornography functions as the most vivid representation of phallic power. Underpinning this conceptualization of sexuality is a critique of the heterosexual sex act as an enactment of male power and dominance, whereby women are rendered "occupied."[60] For antipornography feminists, heterosexual sex epitomizes and reenacts the social conditions of male dominance because man functions as the active penetrator and woman as the passively penetrated. This rhetorical critique of the heterosexual sex act has been broadened to envision normative heterosexuality, rather than simply heterosexual intercourse, as the locus of patriarchal power. Sexuality is a "dynamic of control" whereby male dominance produces, eroticizes, and maintains gendered inequality and constitutes a political system that entrenches male dominance.[61]

This "dynamic of control" is made particularly visible in pornography where "man fucks woman; subject verb object."[62] Pornography reinforces a "dynamic of control" because it is not simply a cultural product; instead, it is a cultural practice and a patriarchal tool where power and inequality innocently masquerade as sex. Because pornography is a kind of "doing," a visual advocacy of violence, the work of the antipornography project is to eliminate pornographic representations entirely.

While antipornography feminism imagines pornography as the linchpin in female subordination, it gestures to the "erotic" as a benign site where women can cultivate their sexuality subjectivity.[63] For example, MacKinnon's condemnation of pornography is coupled with a celebration of erotica, "sexually explicit materials premised on equality," as erotica is imagined to permit women to explore their sexual subjectivities unencumbered by the violence of phallocentric patriarchy.[64]

Yet, absent from MacKinnon's formulation of the egalitarian possibilities of erotica are an engagement with what equality means in sexual representation, and an analysis of the plethora of pornographic products designed for the pleasurable consumption of women, couples, and sexual minorities. MacKinnon's conception of "equal" sexual representation is too vague to be conceptualized, neglectful of the potential importance of domination and subordination to the cultivation of sexual subjectivity, and inattentive to the sheer variety of pornographic products that "speak sex" to a host of consumers.[65]

Finally, MacKinnon's powerful critique of pornography as an advocacy of "man fucks woman; subject verb object" neglects the material realities and visual diversity of pornography: a representational site that increasingly features images of women pleasuring each other (which often predict a male viewer, but nonetheless center female pleasure) and "speaks sex" in *particular* vernaculars to *particular* imagined communities including, but not limited to, queer communities,[66] women,[67] and couples.[68] Considering pornography as a diverse market, which alters its vocabulary for "speaking sex" to appeal to a variety of consumers, challenges the seemingly universal claims that MacKinnon marshals against pornography.

Similarly, black feminism's emphasis on the perils of representation suggests that "controlling images" are the linchpin of black women's subordination.

Collins argues that an examination of the resilience of "controlling images" is particularly important, as "even when the initial conditions that foster controlling images disappear, such images prove remarkably tenacious because they not only subjugate U.S. Black women but are key in maintaining intersecting oppressions."[69] In legitimizing black women's social marginalization, "controlling images" are integral to the production of a "highly effective system of social control designed to keep African-American women in an assigned, subordinate place."[70]

Both antipornography and black feminism conceptualize representation as a critical site in the reproduction of racist and sexist inequality. In particular, sexualized representations are imagined to function as sites that exclusively entrench dominant regimes, securing white patriarchal power. While the two scholarly traditions conceive of the work that sexualized representation performs in securing the dominant regime's power differently, both ultimately embrace a normative goal of eradicating sexualized representations, at least those that are produced for the voyeuristic consumption of the dominant white male subject.

RACIAL ICONOGRAPHY AS A READING PRACTICE

Locating the racist and/or sexist practices of heteropatriarchal, white-dominated society is a project that has been of tremendous interest to a number of progressive intellectual traditions. While usefully demonstrating the multiplicity of sites in which processes of domination exert their control, this task contributes to "the logic of the trial," to the production of a normatively driven intellectual project that condemns unequal practices in lieu of locating the *mechanisms* through which structures of domination are articulated in varying social moments.[71] In the context of pornography, scholarship inspired by the "logic of the trial" permits asking certain questions ("is pornography racist?") and systematically avoids questions about the social, historical, and technological specificity of pornography's racialized meanings, the possibilities of black pornographic spectatorship, and the pleasures black bodies might take *in* pornographic representations that include them.

In place of the normatively driven Hottentot Venus reading practice, a framework undergirded by the "logic of the trial," I advocate a reading practice of racial iconography. Racial iconography is a critical hermeneutic, attentive to the nonracist meaning-making work that black women's bodies perform in pornography and to the historical contingency of racialized pornographic texts. Ultimately, in posing unasked, indeed unthinkable, questions about the multiplicity of pornography's racialized meanings, racial iconography shifts black feminist thought toward what Rinaldo Walcott calls "the unthought of what might be thinkable."[72]

The remainder of this essay will deploy racial iconography as a reading practice, engaging in close analyses of two Golden Age films. I have specifically chosen to focus on Golden Age pornography as it marked a significant shift in both the quantity and type of pornographic representations of black women's bodies. During the Golden Age, a period spanning the 1970s, moving-image pornography was transformed from an underground genre to a mainstream genre whose feature-length, narrative-driven films like *Deep Throat* (directed by Gerard Damiano, 1972) and *Behind the Green Door* (directed by Artie Mitchell and Jim Mitchell, 1972) resembled Hollywood films.

Significantly, black women were ushered on-screen as pornographic protagonists after their relative absence from the short, anonymously produced stag films that constituted the moving-image pornography market prior to the advent of the Golden Age. In films like *Lialeh* (directed by Barron Bercovichy, 1973) and *Sexworld* (directed by Anthony Spinelli, 1978), the pornographic presence of black female protagonists became significant for the formation of Golden Age narratives.[73]

Using racial iconography as an interpretative device permits asking previously unasked questions about Golden Age films. First, racial iconography examines how Golden Age films coupled pornographic genre conventions with the genre conventions of mainstream cinema to produce visual pleasures for new audiences, including black spectators. An examination of Golden Age's interest in producing pornographic films *for* black spectators challenges the prevailing conception that black bodies inhabit the pornographic visual field for the exclusive pleasure of the white spectator and asks how pornography produced an aesthetic for "speaking sex" to a black audience. Second, racial iconography analyzes Golden Age representations of black protagonists taking visual, aesthetic, and sexual pleasure in blackness, troubling the deeply held notion that race is a site of pleasure for whites and an embodied wound for blacks.

Generic Marriages and the "Discovery" of New Audiences: Reading *Lialeh*

The era that produced hits that traversed the boundary between the mainstream and the pornographic also ushered on-screen the first all-black pornographic film. *Lialeh*, the so-called black *Deep Throat*,[74] merges the genre conventions of the pornographic and the blaxploitation to "speak sex" directly to the black spectator. In so doing, *Lialeh* both recognizes a new market—the black spectator—and codifies a pornographic vernacular for "speaking sex" to that audience.

Lialeh's classic blaxpoitation narrative tells the story of Arlo, who produces a black sexual revue, and his perennial conflict with Roger, the white club owner, who insists on receiving payment before the show can continue. Because the ostensibly black spectator is invited—indeed, encouraged—to imagine Roger as an exploitative, racist white man who profits from extracting money from black subjects, Arlo's proclamation that he plans to take "black tits, cunts, dicks, pricks, and mak[e] them into a big-time money-making show" acts as a racially progressive, emancipatory claim.

Of course, the sexual revue hinges on the presence of women's bodies, and Lialeh, the film's black female protagonist, acts as the conduit for connecting the blaxpoitation project of representing the triumph of black business with the pornographic project of displaying the workings of female bodies. Yet, unlike conventional pornographic films, the display of Lialeh's body is explicitly in the service of a race loyalty narrative, with Lialeh using her sexuality to secure black humanity in the face of white dominance.

For example, in the film's climactic scene, Lialeh concludes her on-stage performance at the revue and then enters the audience to perform a strip-tease. First dancing suggestively in front of a black male audience member who puts money into her G-string, Lialeh then dances for a white man. When the white audience member attempts to slide money into her G-string, she reprimands him, exclaiming, "that's a fiver, not a c-note," and stuffs the money into his open mouth. Lialeh's acceptance of money from a black audience member compared to her reproach of a white audience member gestures to the race loyalty that underpins the blaxploitation: Lialeh is willing to sacrifice financial gain for establishing her allegiance to the imagined black collectivity. In coupling the blaxpoitation and the pornographic, *Lialeh* produces a blax-porn-tation aesthetic designed to celebrate the black phallus, race loyalty, and racial authenticity, and to showcase the black female body as an erotic site for the black spectator.

While racial iconography attends to the viewing pleasures created by generic collusions, it also examines generic collisions and the potential visual pleasures produced by the discontinuities between aesthetic projects. In the case of *Lialeh*, black women's sexual pleasures are clearly articulated in the fissures produced by the marriage of the blaxploitation and the pornographic. In the scene preceding the film's climax, Lialeh talks with her minister about her anxiety regarding her upcoming performance. When the reverend interrupts their conversation to use the bathroom, he returns a few moments later in embarrassed agony, explaining that his penis has become stuck in the zipper of his pants. Though the reverend begs Lialeh not to touch his penis, Lialeh and two of her friends dislodge his jammed penis through fellatio, and then Lialeh mounts him and has sex with him.

In this scene, the blaxploitation and the pornographic humorously collide, troubling the aesthetic and meaning-making projects of both genres
and producing visual space for representing black women's pleasures and
desires. First, while blaxploitation uses the elevation of the black phallus as
a metaphor for black male dominance more generally, this scene foregrounds
black male masculinity's vulnerability. In this scene the black male phallus
is *literally* in trouble, and it is black women who are able to loosen (again,
literally) trouble's grip. Mireille Miller-Young describes this scene as a "subversion of the sexual conservatism within the black Church," yet the scene is
also a "subversion" of the blaxploitation foundational myth of black phallic
power.[75]

Moreover, once Lialeh mounts the minister and begins to have sex with
him, the scene concludes without a resurrection of phallic power, usually indicated by the pornographic money shot, the visual evidence of both phallic
presence and phallic pleasure. As a generic convention, the money shot provides quantifiable and legible proof of male pleasure, lending a visual stamp
of authenticity to the pornographic scene. While aural clues suggest that the
minister enjoys a sexual climax, the scene concludes without visual "proof"
of the primacy of the phallus and with no "evidence" that the troubled black
phallus has been restored to its customary position of authority.

Lialeh exploits the interstices of the coupling of the blaxploitation and the
pornographic to carve out space for the black feminine sexual imagination
and for black women's pleasures. Miller-Young's analysis of *Lialeh* suggests
that the film "moves beyond any film in the black, Hollywood, or pornographic 'exploitation' film traditions in advancing a space for the articulation
of the explicit, hardcore sexuality of black women actors."[76] This analysis
underscores *Lialeh's* production of visual space for the articulation of black
women's desire and pleasure. Yet, racial iconography advances this reading
by suggesting that *Lialeh* produces black pleasures on multiple interpretative
levels. Read as a blax-porn-tation film, *Lialeh* celebrates the black phallus and
black women's racial loyalty to men; yet, read with an attention to aesthetic
"failures," to the difficulty of completely coupling the blaxploitation and the
pornographic, it becomes clear that black women's pleasures flourish in the
in-between spaces, in the gaps between two aesthetic projects.[77]

Reading Race-Pleasure in *Sexworld*

While racial iconography recognizes the pleasures of black spectatorship,
it also examines the possibilities of pornographic representations of black
race-pleasure, contesting the dominant conception that blackness is merely
an embodied wound repeatedly inflicted on black bodies by white hegemony.

Rather than reading the black body's presence in the visual field as evidence of white spectators' desires to screen imagined difference, racial iconography asks how the on-screen black body can represent blackness as a locus of pleasure and sexual arousal *in addition to* a classificatory formation that inscribes itself on the flesh of all subjects, conferring benefits and burdens on whites and blacks respectively.

Racial iconography enables reading the Golden Age film *Sexworld*, described by critic Robert Rimmer as "an excellent montage of interracial sexmaking," as a representation of the black female protagonist's taking sexual, aesthetic, and visual pleasure *in* her own blackness.[78] Rather than depicting blackness as a site for white protagonists' and white spectators' pleasure, blackness becomes a locus of sexual enjoyment for the on-screen black protagonist, a "fact" that becomes essential to her arousal and pleasure.

In *Sexworld*, participants travel to a fantasy-sex resort where they are encouraged to abandon "social taboo" and to surrender their free will to the Sexworld "experts" who ensure the fulfillment of their fantasies and desires. The film's predominant narrative vehicle for communicating Sexworld's status as a site where fantasies are realized is an interracial scene between a white man, Roger, and a black woman, Jill. In Roger's initial session with the Sexworld experts, he shares his disgust at the sight of Jill on the Sexworld bus. The experts interpret this confession as a sign of his repressed desire for black women and arrange a sexual liaison with Jill to help Roger unleash his subconscious longings for black women. When Jill enters Roger's room, he mistakes her for the maid, ordering her to clean his room, and Jill responds that she will "clean your wet cock when *we'se* done, sir." The sexual number is then structured by Jill's persistent articulation of her body's virtues, with an emphasis on those body parts usually designated sites of black women's alterity—her "class ass," her "honey pot"—and Roger's conversion from disgust to uncontrollable excitement.

Dominant readings of this interracial scene suggest that Jill performs the role of hyperlibidinous black woman for the pleasurable consumption of both the white male protagonist and the ostensibly white male spectator. Miller-Young's analysis epitomizes this reading strategy, arguing that Jill's racialized performance "illustrates the white pornographic imagination of black women's sexuality" and represents black female sexuality as "something desired that must also be denied."[79]

Racial iconography permits a reading of *Sexworld* that avoids foregrounding the pornographic "use" of black women's bodies and instead imagines that blackness is represented as a pleasurable site for the black protagonist. This new reading requires analyzing the Roger/Jill scene alongside the film's other interracial scene, which features black actor Johnnie Keyes (star of *Behind the*

Green Door) and another white Sexworld guest, Lisa. The scene begins when Lisa confesses her predilection for interracial pornographic films, particularly *Behind the Green Door*, to the Sexworld experts. When Lisa returns to her suite, the experts send Keyes to visit her. Keyes enters Lisa's room wearing his famous *Behind the Green Door* costume: a skin-tight full-body white leotard. While the leotard acts as a kind of racial condom, cloaking his black body in a tight seal of whiteness, it has a hole cut out for his penis to poke through the costume. This hole provides an important visual contrast: the dark black of his penis is accentuated by the stark whiteness of his leotard, visually emphasizing what Lisa deems desirable: the always-erect black penis.

Keyes's purpose on-screen is clear: he exists for Lisa's pleasure. Generally, pornographic genre conventions privilege both aural "proof" of pleasure (in the form of moans, whimpers, and groans) and visual "proof" of pleasure (in the form of the money shot and close-ups celebrating phallic pleasure). The Lisa/Keyes scene is performed to music, rendering aural proof of pleasure impossible. In lieu of visual "evidence" of phallic pleasure, the scene focuses on Lisa's pleasure, featuring close shots of her face, her mouth open in delight as Keyes performs cunnilingus on her, and her teeth grinding into Keyes's shoulder in pleasure. While Lisa's pleasure is centered in the scene, "evidence" of Keyes's pleasure is wholly absent, save from the convention of the money shot, where his ejaculate streams from her mouth. Even this generic convention, normally read as a sign of phallic triumph, is oriented around Lisa's pleasure as it reenacts the climax of *Behind the Green Door*, where actress Marilyn Chambers famously allowed ejaculate to stream from her mouth.

Reading the Lisa/Keyes scene against the Jill/Roger scene makes clear that Jill's body acts as a site of pleasure for *both* Jill and Roger, with both subjects garnering enjoyment from Jill's racialized performance. As Jill urges Roger to "dip into the valley, dally into the valley for a while," she is attempting to "convert" Roger from racial bigotry to interracial pleasure and revealing the pleasure she takes in her own blackness. When Jill declares "now don't these thighs make your peter rise? . . . And ain't this a class ass?" Jill takes up loci of imagined racial difference, claiming them as sites of pleasure, as she proudly displays the virtues of her body.

Whereas the Lisa/Keyes scene is structured by Keyes's instrumental presence—he inhabits the visual field *for* Lisa's pleasure—the Roger/Jill scene is structured by Jill's insistent presence. Keyes plays the role of a present absence; he provides Lisa with the fulfillment of her fantasy to consume the black male body as Marilyn Chambers does in *Behind the Green Door*. In so doing, Keyes is virtually missing from the scene; the scene is performed to music, so his voice is unheard, and the only insistently present portion of his body is the always-erect black penis that protrudes from his white leotard. In contrast, Jill is emphatically present in the Roger/Jill scene, insisting on the potential pleasures of interracial sex *and* the pleasures she takes in her black body.

In reading *Sexworld*'s two interracial scenes against each other, both the potential for pornographic representations of pleasures *in* blackness and the variety of ways that blackness is strategically mobilized for distinct meaning-making ends becomes clear. Jill's articulation of the aesthetic, sexual, and sensual pleasures she takes in her own black body certainly traffics in racialized stereotypes in its incessant invocation of black women's buttocks, "titties," and "honey pots." In so doing, *Sexworld* demonstrates that "fantasies do not merely unleash domination upon people of color. Fantasies can project desire, open the psyche, and work as technologies of imagination for authors, spectators, and critics of color."[80] Racial iconography suggests that race itself can be a "technology of imagination" and that Golden Age pornography can represent blackness as its own locus of pleasure for both black spectators and black protagonists.

Toward the "Unthought"

Racial iconography provides a productive rupture in the dominant black feminist analytical framework that links the contemporary objectification and degradation of black women in the pornographic visual field to Baartman's exhibition. In place of a normative reading of racialized pornography, racial iconography asks new questions about black spectatorship and black visual pleasures, attending to the historical and technological specificity of both. In so doing, racial iconography allows black feminists to break with a lengthy tradition of sexual conservatism and to instead embark on what Evelynn Hammonds has called a "politics of articulation."[81]

This "politics of articulation" insists on unmasking the silence that has cloaked black female sexuality and the sexual conservatism that has been smuggled into black feminism. In its place, racial iconography encourages black feminism to produce rhetorical, theoretical, and imaginative space for describing the heterogeneous and diverse pleasures that mark black female sexual subjectivity. That these pleasures are mediated by the continued violence of white dominance and heteronormativity is, of course, a central component of a black feminist "politics of articulation." Yet, a "politics of articulation" also recognizes the continued power of black sexual imaginations to envision themselves and each other as sexual subjects, as agents of their own pleasure. A "politics of articulation" requires an interrogation of the metaphors, symbols, and tropes—including Baartman's story—that have come to stand in for meaningful engagement with the messy heterogeneity of black female sexuality. Considering the rhetorical and theoretical work that metaphors perform for black feminist politics reveals that even seemingly progressive stories can become "controlling images," limiting the black feminist imagination. It is only when we loosen the stronghold these "controlling images" have on our ability to envision the black body in ecstasy that we can begin to take seriously both the legacy of violent sexist-racist exploitation of black women's bodies and the possibilities, politics, and pleasures of black female sexual subjectivity.

NOTES

1. For a sampling of scholarly work on Baartman, see Anne Fausto-Sterling, "Gender, Race, and Nation: The Comparative Anatomy of 'Hottentot' Women in Europe, 1815–17," in *Skin Deep, Spirit Strong: The Black Female Body in American Culture*, ed. Kimberly Wallace-Sanders (Ann Arbor: University of Michigan Press, 2002), 19–48; Ann du Cille, *Skin Trade* (Cambridge, MA: Harvard University Press, 1996); Susie Prestney, "Inscribing the Hottentot Venus: Generating Data for Difference," in *At the Edge of International Relations: Postcolonialism, Gender, and Dependency*, ed. Phillip Darby (New York: Pinter, 1997), 86–105; T. Denean Sharpley-Whiting, *Black Venus: Sexualized Savages, Primal Fears, and Primitive Narratives in French* (Durham, NC: Duke University Press, 1999); Z. S. Strother, "Display of the Body Hottentot," in *Africans on Stage: Studies in Ethnological Show Business*, ed. Bernth Lindfors (Bloomington: Indiana University Press, 1999); Zine Magubane, "Which Bodies Matter? Feminism, Poststructuralism, Race, and the Curious Theoretical Odyssey of the 'Hottentot Venus,'" *Gender and Society* 15 (2001): 816–34; Janell Hobson, *Venus in the Dark: Blackness and Beauty in Popular Culture* (New York: Routledge, 2005). Also of note is the emerging work on Baartman as an actual person rather than a symbol or political parable. See Rachel Holmes, *African Queen: The Real Life of the Hottentot Venus* (New York: Random House, 2007).

2. While Dutch colonists called colonial subjects on the Cape of Good Hope "Hottentots," the inhabitants called themselves "Khoikhoi."

3. Sharpley-Whiting, *Black Venus*, 17.

4. Zine Magubane's work advocates scholarly investigations of the differences between British and French interpretations of Baartman's body, noting that Baartman's "relatively weak interpellation into British medical and scientific discourses as compared to French" might act as a point of departure for further research ("Which Bodies," 826).

5. Sander Gilman argues that "female sexuality is linked to the image of the buttocks, and the quintessential buttocks are those of the Hottentot." See Sander Gilman, "Black Bodies, White Bodies: Toward an Iconography of Female Sexuality in Late Nineteenth-Century Art, Medicine, and Literature," *Critical Inquiry* 12 (1985): 210. Anne Fausto-Sterling suggests that the fascination with Baartman's buttocks may have had other explanations. She argues that an emerging cultural anxiety about sodomy might suggest "possible relationships between cultural constructions of the

sodomitical body and those of the steatopygous African woman." Fausto-Sterling, "Gender, Race, and Nation," 79.

6. Janell Hobson, "The 'Batty' Politic: Toward an Aesthetic of the Black Female Body," *Hypatia* 18 (2003): 92.

7. Gilman, "Black Bodies," 206.

8. Magubane, "Which Bodies," 817.

9. "Biomythography" is Audre Lorde's term. See Audre Lorde, *Zami: A New Spelling of My Name* (Watertown, MA: Persephone, 1982).

10. Magubane, "Which Bodies," 830.

11. Though I am using the term *black feminist* throughout this article, I am cognizant of debates within black feminist scholarship and sensitive to black feminist diversity.

12. While this article describes the *dominant* black feminist tradition, there are a number of black feminist texts with an interest in black female sexual heterogeneity. See Evelynn Hammonds, "Black (W)holes and the Geometry of Black Female Sexuality," *differences* 6 (1994): 126–45; Tricia Rose, *Longing To Tell* (New York: Farrar, Straus, and Giroux, 2003); Tricia Rose, "Two Inches or a Yard: Censoring Black Women's Sexual Expression," in *Talking Visions: Multicultural Feminism in a Transnational Age*, ed. Ella Shohat (Cambridge, MA: MIT Press, 1999); Mignon R. Moore, "Lipstick or Timberlands? Meanings of Gender Presentation in Black Lesbian Communities," *Signs* 32 (2006): 113–39; Cathy Cohen, "Punks, Bulldaggers, and Welfare Queens: The Radical Potential of Queer Politics?" in *Black Queer Studies*, ed. E. Patrick Johnson and Mae G. Henderson (Durham, NC: Duke University Press, 2005).

13. "Pleasure and danger" is a reference to Carole Vance's edited volume, *Pleasure and Danger: Exploring Female Sexuality* (Boston: Routledge, 1984). Vance's volume asserts that feminist attention to the dangers that constrain female sexuality has overshadowed engagement with the diversity and heterogeneity of female pleasures that flourish even under conditions of patriarchy and heteronormativity. However, with the exception of Hortense Spillers's contribution to the anthology, the *racialized* particularities of *both* pleasure and danger are not analyzed in detail.

14. William Haver quoted in Rinaldo Walcott, "Outside in Black Studies: Reading from a Queer Place in the Diaspora," in *Black Queer Studies*, ed. E. Patrick Johnson and Mae G. Henderson (Durham, NC: Duke University Press, 2005), 93.

15. Catharine MacKinnon, *Feminism Unmodified* (Cambridge, MA: Harvard University Press, 1987), 8.

16. Angela Harris describes antipornography feminism's use of black women as "black women are white women, only more so." Angela Harris, "Race and Essentialism in Feminist Legal Theory," *Stanford Law Review* 42 (1989): 592.

17. Dorchen Leidholdt, "Where Pornography Meets Fascism," *WIN Magazine* (1981): 20.

18. Harris, "Race and Essentialism," 596.

19. Catharine MacKinnon, *Women's Lives, Men's Laws* (Cambridge, MA: Harvard University Press, 2005), 301–2.

20. Luisah Teish, "A Quiet Subversion," in *Take Back the Night: Women on Pornography*, ed. Laura Lederer (New York: Morrow, 1980), 117.

21. Alice Walker, *You Can't Keep a Good Woman Down* (New York: Harcourt, Brace, Jovanovich, 1981), 52.

22. Harris critiques the practice of offering generalizations about women as a class while offering "qualifying statements, often in footnotes, [which] supplement the general account with the subtle nuances of experience that 'different' women add to the mix," arguing that this "nuance theory" reifies whiteness as a norm from which women of color deviate (Harris, "Race and Essentialism," 595). Equally problematic is that this theoretical configuration ignores the complex simultaneity of privilege and oppression for both white and black subjects, neglecting the complexity of positions of marginality (and privilege).

23. I do not take Collins's work to be representative of all of black feminist thought; instead, I am interested in the ways in which her article has been taken up by antipornography feminists as *the* black feminist position on racialized pornographic imagery.

24. Patricia Hill Collins, "Pornography and Black Women's Bodies," in *Making Violence Sexy*, ed. Diana Russell (New York: Teachers College Press, 1993), 98.

25. Ibid.

26. Kobena Mercer's reading and subsequent rereading of Robert Mapplethorpe's photographs of black male nudes convincingly demonstrates how historical moment alters interpretation. Mercer's first reading of Mapplethorpe's work argues that the photographs are steeped in "racial fetishism," permitting the white spectator to view black men's bodies as "abstract, beautiful 'things.'" Kobena Mercer, *Welcome to the Jungle* (New York: Routledge, 1994), 174. Even worse, Mercer argues, is that Mapplethorpe's work bolsters the "primal fantasy of the big black penis," reifying the racial-sexual mythology of the hyperphallic, hypermasculine, black male subject. Mercer's rereading of Mapplethorpe's work is written in the backdrop of a different social moment. In the wake of Mapplethorpe's death and the extensive political debates over funding for Mapplethorpe's exhibitions, Mercer approaches Mapplethorpe's work from a position of "ambivalence" (Mercer, *Welcome*, 189). Mercer suggests that the always-erect black penis might be a way of calling the viewer out on her knowledge of racial mythologies, poking fun at the racial fictions that continue their hold on the collective sexual imagination. Finally, in recognizing the political stakes of reading Mapplethorpe, Mercer notes, "For my part, I want to emphasize that I have reversed my reading of racial fetishism in Mapplethorpe not for the fun of it, but because I do *not* want a black gay critique to be appropriated to the purposes of the New Right's antidemocratic cultural offensive" (Mercer, *Welcome*, 203). Mercer's self-conscious and reflexive reading and rereading of Mapplethorpe only underscore the ways that historical, social, technological, and *political* context shape and alter viewer's engagements with sexualized representation.

27. Jennifer Wicke describes the labor of interpretation as "the shuffling and collating and transcription of images or words so that they have effectivity within one's own fantasy universe—an act of accommodation, as it were. This will often entail wholesale elimination of elements of the representation, or changing salient features

within it; the representation needs to blur into or become charged with historical and/or private fantasy meanings." Jennifer Wicke, "Through a Glass Darkly: Pornography's Academic Market," in *More Dirty Looks: Gender, Pornography, and Power*, ed. Pamela Church Gibson (London: British Film Institute, 2004), 181.

28. Ibid., 181.

29. Kimberlé Crenshaw coined the term *intersectionality*.

30. I am using *the real* in reference to Rebecca Walker's work. See Rebecca Walker, *To Be Real* (New York: Random House, 1995). See also Astrid Henry, *Not My Mother's Sister: Generational Conflict and Third Wave Feminism* (Bloomington, IN: Indiana University Press, 2004).

31. Alice Walker's definition of "womanism" includes "Loves music. Loves dance. Loves the moon. *Loves* the Spirit. Loves love and food and roundness. Loves struggle. *Loves* the Folk. Loves herself. *Regardless*." Alice Walker, *In Search of Our Mothers' Gardens* (San Diego, CA: Harcourt Brace Jovanovich, 1983), xi–xii (italics included in original).

32. Joan Morgan, "Fly-Girls, Bitches, and Hoes: Notes of a Hip-Hop Feminist," *Social Text*, no. 45 (1995): 155.

33. Barbara Christian, "The Race for Theory," in *Making Faces, Making Soul/ Haciendo Caras: Creative and Critical Perspectives by Women of Color*, ed. Gloria Anzaldúa (San Francisco: Aunt Lute Foundation Books, 1990), 336.

34. Patricia Hill Collins, *Black Feminist Thought*, 2nd ed. (New York: Routledge, 2000), 17.

35. Ibid., 84.

36. Joan Morgan, *When Chickenheads Come Home to Roost* (New York: Simon and Schuster, 1999), 109–11.

37. Collins, *Black Feminist*, 80.

38. For more on black feminists' relationship to privacy, see Jennifer C. Nash, "From Lavender to Purple: Privacy, Black Women, and Feminist Legal Theory," *Cardozo Women's Law Journal* 11 (2005): 303.

39. Hobson, *Venus in the Dark*, 1.

40. *Racial fetishism* is Kobena Mercer's term. See Mercer, *Welcome*, 174.

41. Hobson, *Venus in the Dark*, 141.

42. See Deborah Gray White, *Ar'n't I a Woman? Female Slaves in the Plantation South*, rev. ed. (New York: Norton, 1985).

43. See Darlene Clark Hine, "Rape and the Inner Lives of Black Women in the Middle West: Preliminary Thoughts on the Culture of Dissemblance," *Signs* 14 (1988): 912–90.

44. Hortense Spillers argues that "black women are the beached whales of the sexual universe, unvoiced, misseen, not doing, awaiting *their* verb. Their sexual experiences are depicted, but not often by them, and if and when by the subject herself, often in the guise of vocal music, often in the self-contained accent and sheer romance of the blues." Hortense Spillers, "Interstices: A Small Drama of Words," in Vance, *Pleasure and Danger*, 74.

45. Evelyn Brooks Higginbotham, "African-American Women's History and the Metalanguage of Race," *Signs* 17 (1992): 266.

46. Michele Mitchell, "Silences Broken, Silences Kept: Gender and Sexuality in African-American History," *Gender and History* 11 (1999): 440.

47. An interest in the simultaneity of overexposure and underexposure, or hyper-visibility and invisibility, has been of tremendous interest to a number of black feminist scholars. Patricia J. Williams contrasts the "sense of being invisible" that marked her experience as a black female law school student with the "now-heightened visibility" of her experience as a black female professor. Patricia J. Williams, *The Alchemy of Race and Rights* (Cambridge, MA: Harvard University Press, 1991), 55–56. Williams notes, "I know that my feelings of exaggerated visibility and invisibility are the product of my not being part of the larger cultural picture" (ibid., 56).

48. See Lisa Collins, "Economies of the Flesh: Representing the Black Female Body in Art," in Wallace-Sanders, *Skin Deep, Spirit Strong*, 99–127. Kobena Mercer's reading of Mapplethorpe, mentioned above, also describes the absence of the black nude from Western art. In his rereading of Mapplethorpe, Mercer suggests that the elevation of the black male body to the subject of art might act as an "elementary starting point of an implicit critique of racism and ethnocentrism in Western aesthetics" (Mercer, *Welcome*, 196).

49. Judith Wilson, "Getting Down to Get Over: Romare Bearden's Use of Pornography and the Problem of the Black Female Body in Afro-U.S. Art," in *Black Popular Culture*, ed. Gina Dent (Seattle, WA: Bay Press, 1992), 114.

50. Hobson, *Venus in the Dark*, 13.

51. Ibid., 13.

52. Kalpana Seshadri-Crooks's work also reads race and the visible as inextricably bound up, suggesting that race is both a "regime of looking" and a "practice of visibility." Kalpana Seshadri-Crooks, *Desiring Whiteness: A Lacanian Analysis of Race* (New York: Routledge, 2000), 2.

53. Judith Butler, "Endangered/Endangering: Schematic Racism and White Paranoia," in *Reading Rodney King/Reading Urban Uprising*, ed. Robert Gooding-Williams (New York: Routledge, 1993), 15.

54. Michele Wallace critiques this perspective, writing, "Since 'racism,' or the widespread conviction of that blacks are morally and/or intellectually inferior, defines the 'commonsense' perception of blacks, a positive/negative image cultural formula means that the goal of cultural production becomes simply to reverse these already existing assumptions. Not only does reversal, or the notion that blacks are more likeable, more compassionate, smarter, or even 'superior,' not substantially alter racist preconceptions, it also ties Afro-American cultural production to racist ideology in a way that makes the failure to alter it inevitable." Michele Wallace, *Invisibility Blues: From Pop to Theory* (New York: Verso, 1990), 1.

55. Ann Pellegrini captures the "normalizing" effect of "positive images," arguing, "We can no more predict what actions or identifications 'positive' representations will give rise to than we can be certain to capture the all of us in 'our' would-be positive images. Can any campaign for 'positive' images reckon with the unconscious and its unpredictable of 'the' image? Will 'our' images be any less normalizing than 'theirs'?" Ann Pellegrini, *Performance Anxieties: Staging Psychoanalysis, Staging Race* (New York: Routledge, 1997), 81.

56. Wallace, *Invisibility Blues*, 4.

57. MacKinnon, *Feminism Unmodified*, 199.

58. Catharine MacKinnon, *Only Words* (Cambridge, MA: Harvard University Press, 1993), 63.

59. bell hooks, *Black Looks: Race and Representation* (Boston: South End, 1992), 29.

60. See Andrea Dworkin, *Intercourse* (New York: Free Press, 1987).

61. Catharine MacKinnon, *Toward a Feminist Theory of the State* (Cambridge, MA: Harvard University Press, 1989), 137.

62. Ibid., 124.

63. Audre Lorde's canonical "Uses of the Erotic" essay is also strategically taken up by both black and antipornography feminists as an example of the possibilities for feminine sexual subjectivity untainted by the pornographic. See Audre Lorde, *Sister Outsider* (Trumansburg, NY: Crossing Press, 1984).

64. MacKinnon, *Feminist Theory*, 176. Gloria Steinem makes a similar distinction: "Look at or imagine images of people making love; really making love. Those images may be very diverse, but there is likely to be a mutual pleasure and touch and warmth, an empathy for each other's bodies and nerve endings, a shared sensuality and a spontaneous sense of two people who are there because they *want* to be." Gloria Steinem, *Outrageous Acts and Everyday Rebellions* (New York: Holt, Rinehart, and Winston, 1983), 219.

65. Linda Williams, *Hard Core: Power, Pleasure, and the "Frenzy of the Visible"* (Berkeley, CA: University of California Press, 1989), 2.

66. Pornography's importance to queer male subjects has been theorized by a number of scholars (there is considerably less scholarship on lesbian pornographies and their importance for queer women subjects). Richard Dyer captures pornography's analytic and representational importance, arguing that pornography is "the predominant form of how we [gay men] represent our sexuality to ourselves." Richard Dyer, "Gay Male Porn: Coming to Terms," *Jump Cut: A Review of Contemporary Media* 30 (1985): 27. For more on gay male pornographies, see Tom Waugh, "Men's Pornography, Gay vs. Straight," *Jump Cut* 30 (1985): 30–36; John R. Burger, *One-Handed Histories: The Eroto-Politics of Gay Male Video Pornography* (New York: Harrington Park, 1995); Jeffrey Escoffier, "Gay-for-Pay: Straight Men and the Making of Gay Pornography," *Qualitative Sociology* 26 (2003): 531–55; Richard Fung, "Looking for My Penis: The Eroticized Asian in Gay Video Porn," in *How Do I Look? Queer Film and Video*, ed. Bad Object-Choices (Seattle: Bay Press, 1991), 145–68; Daniel Tsang, "Beyond 'Looking for My Penis': Reflections on Asian Gay Male Video Porn," in *Porn 101: Eroticism, Pornography, and the First Amendment*, ed. James Elias et al. (Amherst, N.Y.: Prometheus, 1999), 473–77.

67. Candida Royalle notes that she started Femme Productions, her adult video company, because "I wanted to show that it was possible to produce explicit porn that had integrity, I wanted to show that porn could be nonsexist, and I wanted to show that porn could be life-enriching." Candida Royalle, "Porn in the USA," *Social Text*, no. 37 (1993): 23. There has been considerable feminist attention to Candida Royalle's films, produced specifically for women and couples, precisely because Royalle critiques the hard-core from within its parameters. See Williams, *Hard Core*; Drucilla Cornell, *The Imaginary Domain* (New York: Routledge, 1995); Jane Juffer,

At Home with Pornography: Women, Sex, and Everyday Life (New York: New York University Press, 1998); James K. Beggan and Scott T. Allison, "Reflexivity in the Pornographic Films of Candida Royalle," *Sexualities* 6 (2003): 301–24; Roberta Sterman Sabbath, "Romancing Visual Women: From Canon to Console" (PhD diss., University of California, Riverside, 1994). Some scholars have been quite critical of feminist interest in works like Candida Royalle's. Constance Penley notes that feminists have tended to focus on pornography that falls outside of the mainstream, including Royalle's couple-centered films. She notes, "within mass-commercial videos, the great majority of the titles are seen to merit little critical, much less feminist, interest." Constance Penley, "Crackers and Whackers: The White Trashing of Porn," in *Porn Studies*, ed. Linda Williams (Durham, NC: Duke University Press, 2004), 312. For a sampling of Royalle's films, see *Femme* (1984); *Urban Heat* (1985); *Christine's Secret* (1986); *Sensual Escape* (1988); *Revelations* (1993); *Stud Hunting* (2002).

68. Linda Williams describes couples' pornography as a "softer, cleaner, nicer version of the stock numbers and narratives of feature-length hard core." Linda Williams, *Hard Core*, 232. Yet the emergence of instructional sex-videos for couples, like *Bend Over Boyfriend* (dir. Shar Rednour, 1998) and *The Ultimate Guide to Anal Sex for Women* (dir. Tristan Taormino, 1999), "demonstrating and demystifying anal sex—a sex act with a stigmatized past and (as evidenced by these films) a changing future"— suggests that the couples market has changed significantly since Williams's initial analysis. See Michelle Carnes, "Bend over Boyfriend: Anal Sex Instructional Videos for Women," in *Pornification*, ed. Susanna Paasonen, Kaarina Nikunen, and Laura Saarenmaa (Oxford: Berg, 2007), 151.

69. Collins, *Black Feminist*, 69.

70. Ibid., 5.

71. Loïc Wacquant, "For an Analytic of Racial Domination," *Political Power and Social Theory* 11 (1997): 222.

72. Walcott, "Outside in Black Studies," 91.

73. Mireille Miller-Young's dissertation, "A Taste for Brown Sugar: The History of Black Women in American Pornography" (PhD diss., New York University, 2004), provides tremendously useful details of *Lialeh*'s and *Sexworld*'s plots and production histories.

74. Light in the Attic Records and Productions, distributor of *Lialeh*'s soundtrack, refers to the film as the "black *Deep Throat*."

75. Miller-Young, "Brown Sugar," 139.

76. Ibid., 142–43.

77. While hardcore pornography's celebration of phallic authority and blaxploitation's celebration of black phallic power seem to bolster each other, *Lialeh* gestures to the tensions between these two seemingly related genres. For example, in an early scene, Arlo arrives at Roger's office to find Roger's (white) secretary eating her lunch, insisting that Roger is unavailable. When Arlo tries to side-step her desk, she performs a martial arts move, and the two engage in highly stylized mock-fighting, which eventually yields to kissing and fondling. When the secretary turns to Arlo and queries, "Wait a minute, you mean you're not going to rape me?" Arlo fondles her, and then penetrates her with the remainder of her lunch, a hot dog. Mistaking the hot dog for

Arlo's penis, she continues to moan with pleasure until Arlo jumps up and says, "so long bitch, enjoy your lunch!" Arlo's strategic withholding of sex, while true to blaxploitation's commitments to race loyalty and contesting white dominance, frustrates the pornographic promise of making bodies and their pleasures visible. Arlo's body remains completely covered during this scene, frustrating the spectator's desire to *see* his "cock"—its hardness, its emphatic visual presence—and black phallic triumph is garnered not through sex, but through the *refusal* of interracial sex.

78. Robert Rimmer, *The X-Rated Videotape Guide 1* (Buffalo, NY: Prometheus, 1993), 135.

79. Miller-Young, "Brown Sugar," 146–47.

80. Celine Parreñas Shimizu, *The Hypersexuality of Race* (Durham, NC: Duke University Press, 2007), 146.

81. Evelynn Hammonds, "Toward a Genealogy of Black Female Sexuality: The Problematic of Silence," in *Feminist Genealogies, Colonial Legacies, Democratic Futures*, ed. M. Jacqui Alexander and Chandra Talpade Mohanty (New York: Routledge, 1997), 180.

6

Porn Again Christian? Mark Driscoll, Mars Hill Church, and the Pornification of the Pulpit

Jessica Johnson

Editors' Note: *On Tuesday, October 14, 2014, Mark Driscoll submitted his resignation as an elder and lead pastor at Mars Hill Church. This chapter reflects conditions in the church at the time this volume went to print.*

At Mars Hill Church of Seattle's Ballard Campus, where the sanctuary still bears the high-beamed traces of the warehouse it used to be, several different screens transmit images, colors, and text at once. As Mars Hill's founder, Preaching Pastor Mark Driscoll, sermonizes center stage, a background scrim of images shifts according to emotional register while a flat screen TV to his right flashes Bible verses, talking points, and congregants' questions in real time. On this night, Driscoll preached on Song of Songs 6:11–7:10, verses he dubbed "the most erotic, exotic, and exciting" of scripture, with a take-away message summed up by the "great truth claim" that "all men are visual."[1] "Our world assaults men with images of beautiful women," he warns his audience. "Male brains house an ever-growing repository of lustful snapshots always on random shuffle . . . the temptation to sin by viewing porn and other visual lures is an everyday war." While lingering over an explicit line-by-line reading of an "ancient strip tease" called "Dance of Manahaim," Pastor Mark encourages wives to be visually generous allies—to fight with and for their husbands by providing an archive of redeemed images. Preempting critics who may have "taken a few women's studies classes in college" and would accuse him of objectifying the female body, Driscoll retorts: "pornography turns women into parts and pieces, not image-bearers of God . . . a husband should be captivated by his wife, that's what I'm talking about. I want the proverbial camera of his heart fixated to his wife so that his snapshots are of her."

Driscoll's sermonizing on the everyday sins of mainstream pornography creates opportunities for the proliferation of Mars Hill's own brand of biblical porn—a term I use to index the cultural production, online circulation, and marketing of sexualized doctrine to promote the church's influence in popular culture. Throughout this controversial sermon series, Driscoll encourages wives to be naked without shame in the marital bedroom while graphically depicting biblically ordained fantasies for public dissemination. Although wives are relegated to domestic roles in Mars Hill's complementarian gender doctrine,[2] women are crucial to the production of biblical porn and play a critical role as producers themselves: Their sexual freedom works on behalf of not only their marriages but also the church. I argue that biblical porn is a genre of social pornography,[3] an antipornography discourse through which sexual fantasies are collectively engendered in overt, if mediated, forms for public consumption. Driscoll wants to distance the sinful temptations of worldly porn from the sexy abandon of its Christian expression; yet, as his sermons are shared, edited, and debated through a variety of media channels, members also submit their sexual shame and desires to scrutiny in support of the church's propagation.[4] Until October 2014, Mars Hill boasted fifteen locations in five U.S. states with approximately 15,000 attendees each week, and was partnering with organizations and church planters in India and Ethiopia to build more congregations affiliated with its ministry Mars Hill Global.[5] Not only do video clips of Driscoll's frequent sermons on sexuality glean hundreds of thousands of hits on the church's Web site, but they also pop up in titillating porn searches on YouTube under such titles as "Biblical Oral Sex."[6] While anonymously texting questions during services, congregants confess to sexual sins and fantasies for online distribution in "greatest hits" collections, signaling Mars Hill's entry into the business of producing its own brand of pornography as popular culture without advertising it as such.

As Mars Hill utilizes interactive media technologies and social networks to inspire audience participation in the production and circulation of biblical porn, practices of confession and surveillance commonly understood as institutional mechanisms of self-empowerment and self-governance are transformed to capitalize on the so-called free and open market of the information superhighway. Mars Hill is an innovative leader among a group of theologically fundamentalist yet technologically savvy churches whose pastors market their brand of evangelicalism through publicity stunts and sermon series that highlight a sex-positive doctrine within the confines of heterosexual Christian marriage.

There is evidence that such cultural and political shifts within U.S. evangelicalism have been institutionally endorsed, presenting opportunities for an increasingly sexualized reading of scripture to be preached and published. Since the 1980s, texts such as *The Gift of Sex* promoted the orgasmic pleasure of "godly sex" while offering sex advice based on the understanding that the Bible was in fact "pro-sex" (within heterosexual Christian marriage).[7] Additionally, according to *Christianity Today*, the National Association of Evangelicals is now promoting a theology of sex to encourage healthy, stable marriages.[8] However, Mars Hill's discursive and digital cultural production of biblical porn does more than promote family values or offer tips on how to have hot Christian sex. While Driscoll offers frank counsel on how to embody sexual freedom within the confines of heterosexual Christian marriage, the political scope and value of biblical porn as a social pornography collectively engendered and virtually mediated extends beyond the discursive policing and disciplinary regulation of normative gender and sexuality.

The empirical evidence I have collected, including teaching material endorsed by the church for public distribution, indicates how the strategic use of interactive digital technology and multimodal media integrates audio, visual, and text to engage several sensory registers simultaneously. This practice is impacting the cultural politics of U.S. evangelical congregations:[9] As Driscoll criticizes an evangelical establishment out of touch with popular culture to its own detriment, Mars Hill's production and circulation of biblical porn concurrently functions as a proselytizing and marketing tool that provokes and manipulates globally directed, affective political value under the auspices of sexual freedom that actually amplify control.

This chapter demonstrates how the popularization of biblical porn signals shifting aims and emergent strategies in the cultural politics of conservative evangelicals. These shifts move beyond mobilizing moral-values voters over single issues, such as the legalization of gay marriage, or upholding so-called traditional family values. By couching the temptation to view porn in terms of everyday warfare, Driscoll creates a sense of urgency while suturing wives' sexual freedom to their husbands' visual nature. These embodiments of visual generosity by women meant for the marital bedroom circulate through virtual networks of technology and imagination within and beyond the church sanctuary, as Driscoll's live and remote audiences contribute to the discursive and digital production of a biblically sanctioned social pornography to bodily affect and political effect.

At once visceral and global in scope, biblical porn conflates freedom and control to intensify and extend the cultural value of the Mars Hill brand beyond Christian markets. Concurrently, this evangelical genre of social pornography refashions the act of confession from an institutionally endorsed mode of individual expression that publicly reveals secret sin for purposes of personal transformation and healing into the voluntary labor of a collective "participatory panopticon" that supports the replication and securitization of the church network.[10]

A PORNIFICATION OF THE PULPIT

Since the 1980s, evangelical Christian leaders have co-opted feminist antipornography rhetoric, suturing supposedly normal male sexuality to the obsessive viewing of porn and lustful aggression. For example, in his contribution to U.S. Attorney General Edwin Meese's Commission on Pornography Report in 1986, Focus on the Family's founder James Dobson reiterated Robin Morgan's quote "Pornography is the theory; rape is the practice" without citation.[11] While Driscoll endeavors to "put the fun back into fundamentalism,"[12] his sermons resonate with texts that explicitly describe the spiritual benefits of sexual pleasure shared within Christian marriage. However, as he paradoxically preaches an antiporn dogma using salaciously sex-focused content for online dissemination, he frames Mars Hill's biblical position as more liberal than most churches—a stance that has led many evangelicals to not only criticize but also to censor him. In 2009, after Driscoll's controversial sermon series on Song of Songs was widely publicized in *New York Times Magazine* and on ABC's *Nightline*, an evangelical radio network interrupted its "Family Life" program and truncated the host's interview with Driscoll once founder Dick Bott learned that he was the guest.[13] In the *Baptist Press*, Bott said that he made the decision because of Driscoll's penchant for using vulgarity: Driscoll "interpreted Song of Songs 2:3 as referring to oral sex and then said, 'Men, I am glad to report to you that oral sex is biblical . . . ladies, your husbands appreciate oral sex. So, serve them, love them well . . . we have a verse—the fruit of her husband is sweet to her taste and she delights to be beneath him.'"[14] Bott was also offended by an anecdote Driscoll told about a wife who said that she had won her unbelieving husband to Christ by performing oral sex on him.[15]

That same year Driscoll was vehemently criticized for sexualizing scripture by Phil Johnson, founder of the Calvinist blog site *Pyromaniacs* and executive director of the long-standing evangelical radio program *Grace to You*.[16] In a talk given at a leadership conference and subsequently uploaded to YouTube entitled "Sound Doctrine; Sound Words," Johnson coined the phrase "pornification of the pulpit," to describe "the tendency of so many pastors lately to employ things like profanity, cruel and obscene words, vile subject matter, carnal topics, graphic sexual imagery, erotic language, filthy jokes."[17] While Johnson's belief in the inerrancy of scripture theologically aligns him with Driscoll on paper, their rift signals a culture war among evangelicals. As Phil Johnson states in his YouTube video, the justification usually given for this pornification of the pulpit

> is that course language and sexual themes are the tools of contextualization—it's a way to make us sound more relevant. Lots of voices in the church are insistent that this is absolutely essential if you want to reach certain segments of our culture . . . *New York Times Magazine* recently did a feature article on Mark Driscoll in which this was a

major theme—"Who Would Jesus Smack Down?" was the title of the article, and here's the lead sentence: 'Mark Driscoll's sermons are mostly too racy to post on an evangelical family friendly website' . . . and so this is a subject that almost everyone, including the *New York Times* is already talking non-stop about, and yet it seems to me that people in the evangelical world are not thinking very biblically about it. What language, and what kind of subject matter are suitable for the public, suitable for the pulpit in a public worship service?[18]

In Driscoll's subsequent response to Johnson, the distinguishing character-istics of their physical rather than theological platforms is striking. In the opening moments of Johnson's talk, the viewer's eye is drawn to an aggres-sive bouquet of white, light pink, and dark red roses thrusting from a coffin-sized podium. The mega-sized proportions and meticulous arrangement of the stage and its props invoke institutional authority. By contrast, Driscoll stands against a slightly sponged off-white background that projects the affect of a rustic blank canvas. He does not stand behind a podium but keeps his notes on the kind of clunky music stand found in a junior high band room. Com-paring their fashion choice is a study in generational juxtaposition: Rather than a goatee, Driscoll sports stubble and a fauxhawk; rather than a dark suit, he wears distressed jeans; instead of a tie, he wears an army-green designer shirt embossed with emblems—a minimalist presentation stripped down to its barest essentials, connoting a casual hipster style. Driscoll's comments to his audience convey a similar approachability:

I'll take a few moments to address a few issues in a letter I received from Phil Johnson . . . Most of the questions I think really come down to a misunderstanding . . . One of those is taken from my first sermon on the Song of Songs . . . In that sermon I talk about the fact that we do love Jesus but that we do not love Jesus as if we were his bride . . . Here's the big idea: The church is 60 percent female, between 11 and 13 million more female than male Christians right now attending church . . . I think one of the reasons, and this has been a big aspect of my teaching for a number of years is this, the bride imagery of the church doesn't work real well for an individual application, especially for a man . . . That is not the kind of relationship that a heterosexual man should have with Jesus.[19]

The doctrine at the heart of this evangelical culture war pertains to sexuality but is not framed by unending debates about whether or not homosexual-ity is a sin. Instead, this disagreement centers upon how a theology of sex is preached for public consumption. Driscoll defines his approach to Song of

Songs as the more attractive alternative to allegorical readings that "queer" Jesus' relationship to male congregants. The setting of his presentation supports this assertion by visually demarking his hermeneutic as more culturally current and appealing to masculine men who prefer the raucous ambience of alt-rock to roses. As their dissention extends into online forums, Driscoll's sexy interpretation of Song of Songs is circulated and awarded a catch phrase, fortifying its consumption beyond the pulpit. In fact, Johnson participates in the very pornification that disgusts him. Christians who publicly admonish Driscoll perpetually offer him venues and occasions to emphasize the importance of an active marital sex life in tandem with a call for cultural reformation among evangelical churches.

VIDEOLOGY

Driscoll's sermonizing style bears the traces of Billy Sunday, an evangelical minister who preached to large crowds during revivals in cities throughout the United States in the late nineteenth to early twentieth centuries. Sunday's jeremiad responded to socioeconomic changes resulting from industrialization that impacted normative gender roles divided according to dichotomous private and public spheres. As an increasing number of middle-class women sought jobs in factories and degrees in higher education, Sunday responded to this social "crisis" by naturalizing motherhood as a blessing of the highest calling while mocking "sissy fellows."[20] Driscoll echoes Billy Sunday when he rails against pastors who portray Jesus as "a Richard Simmons, hippie, queer Christ, [a] neutered and limp-wristed popular Sky Fairy of pop culture that . . . would never talk about sin or send anyone to hell."[21] Sunday's version of a "muscular Christianity" was recast in the 1990s by Promise Keepers, which sought cultural transformation "through prayers, accountability groups, and the reclamation of the American home."[22] While the organization gained media attention and monetary profit through football stadium rallies, safe spaces for sharing emotional intimacies apart from the spectacle were cultivated in private huddles where men cried together.[23]

By contrast, Driscoll derides self-help therapy and Christian institutions that utilize its strategies as a means to personal transformation: "We have a whole culture that promulgates self-love, self-esteem, self-help, and self-actualization."[24] Driscoll teaches that undue focus on self-worth detracts from true salvation, framing his jeremiad in terms of a masculinity crisis that must be overcome in order for Christianity to flourish and Mars Hill to multiply. As contextualized by a global war on terror, Mars Hill's incentive to expand is best described by Driscoll during a sermon preached on "Men and Masculinity": "We hold masculine leadership in the highest esteem because the church is almost completely effeminate in America . . . that is why young men in urban centers are attracted to Islam, they want a masculine religion, a powerful God, something that gives them truth."[25] Driscoll does not blame secular culture war adversaries for the events of 9/11,[26] but figures the war on terror as spiritually and culturally waged inside congregations desperate for entrepreneurial masculine leaders. In turn, Mars Hill capitalizes on the decline of denominational churches in Seattle by buying them at a good price to open another campus, circumventing prohibitive city zoning laws while fostering growth in an untapped neighborhood.

As Mars Hill's congregants and online voyeurs consume biblical porn they also participate as producers who contribute to Driscoll's sermons by volunteering their technological acumen. The Mars Hill experience is not expensive—most church events and digital resources are free.[27] Pastors encourage congregants to offer their talents to the church's various ministries and plug in to its many social networks. Followers can access material on YouTube, Facebook, Twitter, and iTunes, as well as *Mars Hill Global*, where people around the world are encouraged to share stories on how the ministry of Mars Hill is transforming their lives; *The Resurgence*, a blogging site where pastors across the nation dialogue, advertise conferences, and promote their books; and *The City*, Mars Hill's own social networking site launched using software developed by a pastor and former Amazon employee (a program later sold by the church for four million dollars to Zondervan, a Christian publishing company).[28]

While Driscoll preaches that scripture is inerrant and man is totally depraved in keeping with Calvinist orthodoxy, the church capitalizes on Seattle's info-tech labor force in fostering a multisite structure that maps its congregation throughout the city by way of autonomous facilities that pipe in video recorded sermons formerly preached by Driscoll from Mars Hill's administrative center in Bellevue, Washington. This organizational framework also informs Mars Hill's presence online, whereby the Internet is approached as a missionary site not unlike the neighborhood block. Driscoll describes the church's development of a videology in this way: "A church must have timeless truth and timely methods—it must contend for the truth but then it must contextualize it in culture. Churches that only contend are fundamentalistic and mean . . . churches that only contextualize invariably become liberal and lose sight of the truth of scripture."[29]

Driscoll couches the current "information age" in terms of an "experience economy" based on "various distribution channels for the communication and articulation of ideas" that create three stages of consumption: observation (watching a video); participation (responding through prayer, the taking of communion, getting to know other congregants); and immersion (helping to create the experience).[30] In describing the Mars Hill experience, Driscoll depicts its videology as a worship practice and community building process through which congregants become not only consumers but also producers of doctrinal teaching—a labor that, as it is integrated to serve the church, is collectively transformative. While he explains the connections between observation, participation, and immersion, Driscoll distinguishes Mars Hill from traditional megachurches that gather followers together en masse; digital technology plays a critical role in eliciting audience participation within and beyond the church's Seattle facilities. This multisite model of physical and virtual expansion is distinct in the way it utilizes multimodal media, while providing opportunities to participate in Driscoll's teaching via interactive forms of mobile communication. The instrumentalization of these everyday digital practices by the church differently constitute and configure Driscoll's audience in relation to and through the Mars Hill experience, by encouraging them to contribute content during question and answer sessions after sermons for online distribution.

As Mars Hill incorporates congregants' voluntary labor into its videology, the church circulates affect by simulating processes of emotion that "*involve subjects and objects* . . . without residing positively within them."[31] Instead of rechanneling feelings of shame that belong to congregants onto less desirable (gay and lesbian) "others,"[32] Mars Hill capitalizes on digital technology to inspire performative confessions to sexual sin and fantasy by congregants for online distribution as a means of collective transformation. As church members voluntarily participate in the circulation of biblical porn, they embody self-sacrifice on behalf of Mars Hill's multiplication. The church's discursive and digital cultural production of biblical porn simultaneously serves as a proselytizing and marketing tool, as it materializes in the worship practices and community building of its congregation on the ground. While arresting and channeling the attention of members and voyeurs who participate in its industry, biblical porn generates and instrumentalizes the visceral and virtual labor vital to Mars Hill's propagation.

PORN AGAIN CHRISTIAN?

In addition to hosting Christian boot camps that train men how to become masculine leaders on the spiritual battlefield, Mars Hill directly ministers to military personnel by gathering donations to ship resources to (male) soldiers around the world. These materials emphasize the need for men to put down porn and take up arms for the sake of spiritual redemption and domestic security. One elder writes on the Military Mission blog: "As a chaplain and pastor to the military community, by far the worst and most common issue I deal with is pornography . . . one of the first and primary ways we reach into the dark world of porn and military life is through two books we send in our initial 'Troop Pack' to every service-member who requests materials from us: [one of which is] *Porn Again Christian* by Pastor Mark Driscoll."[33]

Porn Again Christian was published as a free e-book that challenges the idea that lusting after a women's unclothed body is necessarily sinful. [34] Driscoll assures his male readers that any position is permissible between a husband and wife, punctuating his point by describing a variety of sex acts in vigorous detail. In a question and answer section entitled "Practical and Theological Reasons to Masturbate," a congregant describes a scenario in which his wife slips nude photos of herself in his briefcase so that while away on a business trip he can call her for phone sex and stare at her image as they mutually masturbate. The husband asks Driscoll whether this kind of erotic image, which helps to reduce temptations while he is on the road, is permissible. Driscoll replies that images of one's wife are "redeemed," and that the man need not worry but instead "thank God for the freedom your wife enjoys with you."[35] This sense of freedom, especially as performed by wives while sexually pleasing their husbands, recurs throughout Driscoll's frank advice and counsel. When asked, "Is it ok for my wife and I to masturbate ourselves if we are together and both turned on by it?" Driscoll responds in the affirmative, adding:

> Some couples have cited a number of reasons why this may be helpful. One husband and his wife do not have intercourse during her menstrual cycle and so she cares for him during that time with masturbation. Upon occasion, though, she cannot bring him to climax and so he will do so while fondling her breasts so that the two of them are still participating. Some people report that their spouse simply has no idea how to stimulate their genitals and so they stimulate their own genitals in front of their spouse to teach them what they enjoy so that their spouse could then satisfy them. Some spouses also report that during heavy petting and/ or deep massage they prefer to stimulate their own genitals while their spouse stimulates other erotic zones and enjoy watching their spouse simultaneously enjoy sexual stimuli from many places on the body.[36]

With regards to having "sex according to the Bible," Driscoll assures his readers that they should not be too anxious because "the Bible is, quite frankly, more liberated on the matter of sex than most Bible teachers."[37] For example, Driscoll claims that in the Song of Songs many acts normally considered taboo by fundamentalists are not only condoned but encouraged, including a sexually aggressive wife, a wife who likes to perform fellatio, mutual masturbation, a wife who enjoys cunnilingus, a wife who performs a strip tease, erotic conversation, and "ongoing variety and creativity that includes new places and new positions such as making love outdoors during a warm spring day."[38]

In these passages, Driscoll encourages wives to openly express their sexual desires for the sake of their lustful husbands; however, men are warned away from such visible expressions of sexual freedom. Although he claims that scripture does not prohibit masturbation, Driscoll devotes a whole chapter to discussing the practical and theological reasons for and against its practice.

> [T]here are some additional practical reasons why [masturbation] may not be wise for God's men to do so. First, masturbation is a form of homosexuality because it is a sexual act that does not involve a woman. If a man were to masturbate while engaged in other forms of sexual intimacy without his wife in the room it is bordering on homosexual activity, particularly if he's watching himself in a mirror and being turned on by his own male body.[39]

In *Porn Again Christian*, the male body is figured both as the autoerotic subject and object of a pornographic gaze seductive enough to momentarily turn a straight guy gay. By this formulation, women's "difference" is crucial for reinforcing the uneven, paradoxical logics of gender equality and sexual freedom that inspire the circulation of biblical porn online. This particular passage of *Porn* was widely discussed in blog posts and online periodicals such as *The Huffington Post* as an "anti-gay stance;"[40] however, far more powerfully it signals how biblical porn provokes and manipulates mutually constitutive logics of shame and desire. Instead of proclaiming that masturbation is biblically forbidden, Driscoll asks men to consider whether they experience shame while engaging in its practice. Ostensibly, he goads male congregants to free themselves from addictive, sexualized forms of self-obsession by converting onanistic urges into various forms of voluntary labor that serve Mars Hill, including security detail during sermons, participating in the church's many worship bands that record and tour, community group leadership, and the development and maintenance of the church's presence on social networking channels, its extensive media library, and myriad affiliated Web sites.

Driscoll's teaching on biblical masculinity is shaped by a cultural milieu preoccupied by a "masculinity crisis" that has spurred industries of self-help books, *Jackass* showmen, and prescription drugs to refute media headlines announcing "the end of men."[41] At the time of Mars Hill's beginnings in the basement of Driscoll's Seattle home, the marketing of Viagra was pivotal in proliferating discourses on penile performance anxiety.[42] As unemployment figures rose due to industrial outsourcing, men were encouraged to take command in the bedroom by assuaging their erections and flexing phallic power. Marketing techniques and medical surveillance exerted biotechnological control over men's bodies, while the prowess of the male sexual subject became a matter of primary national concern.[43] Concurrently, porn viewer-ship grew increasingly gender balanced and the market more varied in its depictions of sexual pleasure as innovations in visual and new media afforded more home entertainment options.[44] The "spending penis" of the "money shot" that according to scholar Linda Williams had embodied "all the prin-ciples of late capitalism's pleasure-oriented consumer society: pleasure figured as an orgasm of spending" gave way to the recognition of sexual differences—a movement "from the economy of the [phallic] one to the many."[45] It is this diversification in terms of pornographic representation, performers, markets, and modalities that Driscoll is combating by pornifying the pulpit. Through his sexualized exegesis, the phallic economy becomes redeemed and rechanneled into evangelical pursuits that inspire the circulation of globally directed, affective political value in support of the Mars Hill's propagation.

THE PEASANT PRINCESS

In September 2008, Driscoll began his controversial sermon series on the Song of Songs (alternatively known as the Song of Solomon) entitled *The Peasant Princess*. Interpretations of this book of the Old Testament are con-tested, with some biblical scholars maintaining that the man and woman who metaphorically describe one another's bodies and sex acts in this erotic love poem are unmarried.[46] In addition, Song of Songs is often read as an allegory representing God's love for His people. However, among a growing number of evangelical pastors, including Driscoll, Song of Songs is increasingly preached as a how-to manual for married Christians seeking to spice up their sex lives. The church's production staff created a video introduction for *The Peasant Princess* series based on Driscoll's hermeneutic. A pastor blogging about the creative team's approach wrote:

> [W]e started with a branding that centered on the concept of 'Free Sex.' We went with this title and began working on visual concepts for about three weeks before we found out the name was changed to 'Free Love' to try and tone down the in-your-face title we previously had. Seventy-two hours later we had a third and final title—*The Peasant Princess*. The idea was Vegas 2050 meets Disney meets Mars Hill.[47]

The film's visuals mimic Disney's doe-eyed animation and bright techno-colors while updating this template so its color scheme reflects the techno-infused electronic keyboards pulsating in the background—a catchy, bubble-gum pop vibe with a pronounced bass beat that encourages head bobbing. Green and yellow birds cavort with a pink fawn bounding across a bright meadow where a chesty, grinning apple tree with well-defined pectoral muscles gyrates to the music. *The Peasant Princess* video invites viewers to participate in its pastoral, family-friendly scene, offering a setting that is playfully coy. Frolicking fawns wink at the audience, signifying biblical sex as pure, lighthearted fun. As a background screen of large tube light bulbs in neon blue, green, orange, and yellow oscillates like a Rorschach Lite-Brite, Driscoll preaches in front of a glowing cross. During this series, his audience discovers that the flirtatious deer in the verse signify breasts ("the petting zoo is now open," Driscoll exclaims in week seven) and that the apple tree is a metaphor for oral sex. While the illustrated characters of this animated short may conjure visions of Disney characters, it is up to Driscoll and his congregants to fuel fantasies of Vegas 2050.

In the first sermon of the series entitled "Let Him Kiss Me," Driscoll provides his audience with statistics compiled by a sociology professor on the sexual experiences of young men and women. A great deal of time is spent by Driscoll relaying statistics regarding pornography. According to his data the porn industry generates $60 billion a year on the global market, $12 billion of which is spent by U.S. citizens. Driscoll continues to present numbers that are intended to provoke outrage and fear over the accessibility of online pornography: over 200 porn films are made in the United States every week; porn sites are 12 percent of all Internet sites; porn is 25 percent of all search engine requests; over 40 percent of Internet users view porn; 20 percent of men admit to accessing porn at work; 13 percent of women admit to accessing porn at work; every second $3,000 is spent on porn in America; 28,000 Internet users are viewing porn every second in America; 372 Internet users every second in America are typing words looking for more porn; 90 percent of children between the ages of 8 and 16 have viewed porn online; the average child sees porn online for the first time at age 11; the number-one consumer of pornography is boys ages 12 to 17; and 10 percent of American adults admit to being addicted to Internet porn.[48] If you thought the use of pornography was rampant, his statistics confirm it.

While Driscoll points out that sinful pornographic viewing is an issue for both men and women, its causes and effects differ according to gender: Men are solely consumers and called "addicts" and "abusers," whereas women are "performers" and "prostitutes" victimized by the industry.[49] Driscoll then segues into the next section of his sermon by stating that roughly one-third of the women at Mars Hill have been sexually abused. While lamenting this statistic, he insists that it is critical for female victims to seek biblical counseling in order to "have a fresh perspective on sex."[50] Driscoll also emphasizes that sex is a godly gift to be enjoyed beyond the strictures of procreation: "If it's in marriage, praise God. Have lots of pleasure. God made our bodies for pleasure."[51]

In his sermons on biblical sexuality, Driscoll echoes feminist antipornography campaigns in which porn writ large is understood as a source of misogyny and inevitably exploitive of women.[52] In polarizing debates structured by an oppression/liberation binary, antiporn feminists argue that women are always victims of pornography, whereas sex-positive feminists offer alternative readings of porn scripts and imagery that index sexual agency.[53] However, Driscoll circumvents such dichotomies by preaching a mutually constitutive antiporn/sex-positive doctrine through which the dominant phallic economy of one becomes redeemed in a diversifying global economy. Once male sexuality is directed into wedded bliss, sexually liberated wives secure Mars Hill's most valued asset: entrepreneurial men who volunteer their technological skills and leadership abilities in support of the church network. At Mars Hill, women who have been sexually abused are taught to seek biblical counseling so as to perform their blessed role as sexually available wives that offer salvation to their husbands by embodying the fantasy that sex within Christian marriage is always free and pleasurable. Driscoll succinctly summarized how crucial this women's work is to the future of Mars Hill and its network in a statement to a room full of men aspiring to found churches affiliated with the global church planting network he founded called Acts29. Those who attended an Acts29 "boot camp" in 2007 were told that the church planter's wife has the "most important job" in a new church—"having sex with the church planter."[54]

BIBLICAL PORN AS CONFESSIONAL DISCOURSE AND SURVEILLANCE TECHNOLOGY

Since the mid-2000s public discourse and interventions pertaining to women's sexuality have proliferated at Mars Hill. In the aftermath of a contentious blog post in which Driscoll blamed pastors' wives for their husbands' infidelities,[55] workshops and counseling on female sexual sin visibly increased at the church. A workshop called *Maturity in Singleness* taught by and for women offered strategies for retaining biblical purity before marriage. During a daylong seminar entitled *Redeeming Female Sexuality* women testified to sexual sins past and present including same-sex attraction, promiscuity, and denial of sex within marriage.[56] A blog (no longer in publication) named *Reforming Femininity* appeared on Mars Hill's Web site as a forum for women to discuss a variety of issues, including sexual abuse and shame. Alongside a pronounced increase in the number of opportunities offered by the church for women to publicly confess to sexual sin, female congregants called upon one another to openly acknowledge various "feminine sins" for the salvation of the church. During a "Women's Training Day" I attended called "Christian Womanhood in a Feminist Culture," among those sins considered "feminine" were "romanticism" (a sexually charged fantasy life driven by the passionate pursuit of one's soul mate inspired by the reading of too many romance novels and viewing of too many Hollywood "chick flicks"), "gluttony," "modesty," and "physical and spiritual adultery." The latter included not only premarital sex but "whoring" in terms of one's time and energy—the exhaustive performance of good deeds in order to prove one is worthy of God's love. Women are called on to habitually and pub-licly confess to sexual shame in the unending process of seeking redemption, challenging the misconception that women are not "equal" to men insofar as their capacity to sexually sin is concerned. In effect, by "freely" offering their sexual transgressions and sexualized bodies as signs and commodities through which to discursively and digitally produce biblical porn, women's voluntary labor contributes to its circulation and capacity to accrue political and cultural value. While same-sex attraction, fornication, and consuming pornography (which includes reading romance novels) are all sexual sins women testify to at Mars Hill, it is the withholding of sex by wives from their husbands that is most often highlighted. In a post entitled "Not Tonight Honey, I Have a Headache," one contributor to *Reforming Femininity* wrote:

> Scripture clearly states that men and women who are married are to have sex, and have it regularly (Gen. 1:28, 1 Cor. 7:5). We are not to deprive one another, and what's more, [men's and women's] bodies belong to our spouses . . . scripture does not command us as wives to desire our husbands sexually at all times. It is *not a sin* for a woman to lack sexual desire for her husband. The point at which it becomes a sin is when a wife is unwilling to give her husband access to her sexually. This can lead to many problems including bitterness, resentment, sexual temptation and frustration and a lack of confidence in the husband . . . Make sex a priority, rearranging whatever is necessary in life until you have given it the proper place; remember, it's a priority in God's eyes and an entire book of the Bible is devoted to it! (Heb. 13:4) Here's the hardest part . . . *do not deny your husband* sexually.[57]

According to the doctrinal understanding articulated above, husbands and wives "equally" possess ownership of their spouses' bodies; but, in terms of access to said bodies, wives are more prone to sexual sin than their husbands. This anonymous *Reforming Femininity* contributor reiterates the biblical imperative preached by Driscoll that Christian wives testify to their sexual freedom in the marital bed. Prioritizing sex is ordained by God in order to secure masculine leadership in the home and congregation.

During *The Peasant Princess* series, Driscoll's wife Grace joined him onstage for the first time during a service to provide feminine counsel on questions directed towards women during the Q&A sessions. According to the church's gender doctrine, women are not permitted to hold pastoral positions or preach from the pulpit. Driscoll justified his wife's participation after sermons during the *Princess* series by reminding viewers that a husband and wife narrate the Song of Songs. After Driscoll finished preaching, anonymous text questions materialized like sound-bite confessions on screens throughout the sanctuary, confronting congregants with evidence of their predisposition to sinful lusting as their collective shame and desire concurrently figured them as enslaved by and witnesses to sin. Some examples include the following:

DOWNTOWN: "What if my spouse cannot compare physically to the visual temptations of the world?"

BALLARD: "What resources are available for men with low sex drive?"

BELLEVUE: "Would it be sinful to videotape my wife and I being intimate?"

BALLARD: "Should spouses confess to each other every time they sin visually or sexually?"[58]

As these queries index, Mars Hill's methodology of circulating biblical porn is aligned with technologies of surveillance that resemble reality television rather than group therapy. While inquiring as to the sinful or biblical ramifications of their sexual desires—or shameful lack thereof—congregants testify to the biblical truth of Driscoll's preaching on masculine visuality, producing their own pornographic imaginaries through his antiporn message. Multiple screening and multimodal media processes work in congruency with emergent digital technologies, simultaneously utilizing systems of visibility and surveillance that are panoptic, whereby the many are watched by the few, and synoptic, whereby the few are watched by the many. Mars Hill incorporates the seductive logics of social networks such as Facebook and cultural trends such as reality television to incite congregants' participation in biblical porn. In turn, the church's marketing and proselytizing practices reinforce a panoptic-synoptic relationship through which "surveillance [becomes] progressively more commonplace, unexceptional, and even desirable."[59] The inauguration of yet another church-affiliated Web site was announced in a post that read: "Pastor Mark.tv is Alive—er, Live!"

Pastor Mark is everywhere these days: Ireland, South Carolina, Haiti, Chicago . . . some of you dutifully track Mars Hill Church, Resurgence, Acts 29 channels and more to listen to his messages and read his essays—but that's gotten trickier recently as his content is published across more and more channels every year. So we gave him his own site: PastorMark.tv. This way, all you have to do is come to this one place to find all those teaching pieces. What's more, you'll also get posts from him where he'll be speaking more personally about what's going on with him and his family.[60]

Pastor Mark.tv purports to offer a single portal to his teaching and an all-access pass to his ministry. As Mars Hill continues to grow, Driscoll increasingly lives in public. Pastor Mark.tv is concurrently "alive" and "live"—a process of screening that simulates his real-time presence. Despite the mega-sized proportions of its population, mobile communication fluency and a multisite structure affords Mars Hill the flexibility to accrue and assert cultural capital through a variety of media channels. Emulating a multinational corporate enterprise, Mars Hill relies less on disciplinary models of governance in favor of processes of screening and simulation that free social control from specific territories or territorial logics. As biblical porn excites and exploits digital practices of confession, it echoes and affirms Driscoll's Calvinist-infused message that his audience is sinfully depraved and in need of frank biblical counsel on matters of sex, while supporting the propagation of the Mars Hill network at once virtually and viscerally, globally and bodily circulating and amplifying affect to political effect.

CONCLUSION: A CALL TO ARMS

Any visitor to the Mars Hill Web site is a few clicks away from "Christian Sex Q&A (Mature Content)."[61] Here, a warning box announces that due to the overwhelming volume and explicit content of questions texted during the *Princess* series, the Driscolls have blogged responses to queries. According to the MH-17 rating, anyone under 17 is required to get adult permission before viewing. Given the church's target audience is young, presumably pornographically challenged men, this play on the NC-17 film rating comes across more like a tantalizing teenage joke rather than a serious attempt to warn readers. However, such humor functions not only as a proselytizing tool but a call to arms, as men are instructed to put down the porn and channel their sinful desires into service for the church. Driscoll and his wife Grace replied to inquiries such as, "Can I perform anal sex on my wife?" with frank advice that encouraged further research online: "Do your homework, be careful if [your wife] is willing. . . anal sex is technically permissible, but for a host of reasons may not be beneficial. We do not endorse everything on this website, but if you want to read some commentary on the issue from Christian married women, you can go to *Christian Nymphos*."[62] Questions such as, "My wife likes to masturbate me upon occasion and wants to know how to get better at it. What should she do?" or, "Is it okay for me and my wife to masturbate ourselves if we are together and both turned on by it?" or, "Is it okay for a spouse to masturbate himself or herself during the act of lovemaking?" are also answered with candid encouragement:

> Yes. The combination [of masturbating during the act of lovemaking] may physically heighten the degree of pleasure. For example, many wives cannot climax from normal intercourse but can climax from stimulation of their clitoris, which is not a point of contact during normal sexual intercourse. This can be pleasurable for both spouses, considering that most men are visual and this could be a display of visual generosity for him.[63]

The Driscolls encourage mutual masturbation as a form of couples therapy that encourages those seeking their advice to reach out and touch themselves through the church network. While flexing its phallic power online, Mars Hill promises marital orgasms as explosive as those procured with Viagra. The church circulates biblical porn as a confessional discourse and surveillance technology that concomitantly titillates and monitors as audiences live and remote voluntarily subject themselves to invisible practices of online scrutiny by turning on and plugging into the Mars Hill experience. A holy combination of sexual tease, biblical counsel, and sex education, biblical porn proliferates as and through channels of popular culture each time "porn" is typed into a search engine. While Mars Hill continues to exploit everyday digital practices to deterritorialize and intensify control, it secures the replication of its network like a virus. Transformations in hermeneutical and confessional practices signal changes in the cultural politics of evangelical churches that pornify the pulpit through not simply sexualized exegesis but technological interfaces that corporatize and amplify their stakes in a global economy increasingly manipulated by the virtual and visceral circulation of affective political value.

NOTES

1. Quotes from *The Peasant Princess* series are transcribed from video recordings organized by their weekly titles available in Mars Hill Church's media library, http://marshill.com/media/the-peasant-princess.

2. According to the complementarian gender doctrine that Mars Hill teaches, men and women are "equal but different"—equal insofar as they are made in God's image but different because their roles are distinct. In this theological worldview, men are biblically ordained providers, protectors, and leaders in the workplace, home, and church while women are their submissive helpers whose most blessed function is motherhood.

At Mars Hill, women are permitted to teach about subjects related to biblical femininity in sex-segregated workshops but are prohibited from positions of eldership.

3. Jennifer Wicke, "Through a Gaze Darkly: Pornography's Academic Market,"
in *More Dirty Looks: Gender, Pornography, and Power*, ed. Pamela Church Gibson
(London: British Film Institute, 2004), 184.

4. Evidence of the varied channels through which one can locate video clips and
commentary that criticizes and supports Driscoll's reading of Song of Songs can be found
online at *Christian Nymphos*: http://christiannymphos.org/2009/03/04/the-peasant-
princess; *Pyromaniacs*: http://teampyro.blogspot.com/2009/03/more-on-pornifica-
tion-of-pulpit.html; *The Wartburg Watch*: http://thewartburgwatch.com/2009/04/22/
brother-mark-%E2%80%98s-traveling-sex-show; and *WenatcheeTheHatchet*: http://
wenatcheethehatchet.blogspot.com/2011/10/new-guest-series-is-up-at-from-bitter.
html.

5. http://marshill.com/global.

6. The Mars Hill Web site no longer provides sermon-specific metrics on the
amount of hits garnered by videos. In fact, *The Peasant Princess* and other series audio
and video downloads formerly available at no cost in the church's media library are no
longer available. There is speculation as to why this erasure occurred, but it is difficult
to say for certain. It does seem safe to presume that recent controversies surrounding
confirmed accusations of plagiarism in Driscoll's book *Real Marriage* (2012), as well as
debates concerning his celebrity, dubious marketing strategies to elevate *Real Marriage*
to "Number One *New York Times* Bestseller" status (a moniker no longer attached to
the book), and sexualized exegesis have led to a decision to alter and lower his public
profile. Driscoll himself made such an admission in an "open apology" that was posted
as a letter to a members-only site and quickly leaked on Reddit as well as evangelical
blogs: http://www.reddit.com/r/religion/comments/20gg40/mark_driscoll_addresses_
mars_hill_church. However, Mars Hill's 2013 Annual Report (available online at
http://marshill.com/annual-report-2013) claims that the church Web site attracted
"7,400,000 visits to our website" and distinguishes this figure from the number of
"people who came to our site," which it documents as 2,700,000. These statistics
demonstrate invisible online monitoring practices that the church wants to publicize
without formally revealing. However, a glossy 2009 *New York Times Magazine* profile
of Driscoll entitled "Who Would Jesus Smack Down?" published soon after the *Princess* series ended documents the church's savvy online distribution and marketing of
its video clips beyond Christian media channels: "Mark Driscoll's sermons are too
racy to post on *GodTube*, the evangelical 'family friendly' video-posting Web site.
With titles like 'Biblical Oral Sex' and 'Pleasuring Your Spouse,' his clips do not stand
a chance against the site's content filters. No matter: YouTube is where Driscoll . . .
would rather be. Unsuspecting sinners who type in popular keywords may suddenly
find themselves face to face with a husky-voiced preacher in a black skateboard-
er's jacket and skull T-shirt" (Whorten 2009, 22). Available online at http://www.
nytimes.com/2009/01/11/magazine/11punk-t.html?pagewanted=all. In addition, in
an article published just before he began preaching the Princesses series in 2008,
Driscoll claimed, "I'm big on Facebook and MySpace, YouTube and iTunes. We'll have

100,000 downloads of the sermon each week just off the Internet." http://churchex-ecutive.com/archives/mark-driscoll-senior-pastor-mars-hill-church-seattle-wa.

7. Dagmar Herzog, *Sex in Crisis: The New Sexual Revolution and the Future of American Politics* (Philadelphia: Basic Books, 2008), 31–32.

8. Adele M. Banks, "Evangelicals Push 'Theology of Sex,' Abortion Reduction," *Christianity Today*, http://blog.christianitytoday.com/ctpolitics/2010/05/evangelicals_pu.html.

9. From 2006 to 2008, I conducted ethnographic fieldwork at Mars Hill's Ballard location, including participant-observation at events open to nonmembers such as sermons, workshops on biblical gender and sexuality, and women's training days. My analysis is informed by experiences recorded in my field notes during these events.

10. Mark Andrejevic, *Reality TV: The Work of Being Watched* (Lanham, MD: Rowman and Littlefield Publishers, 2004).

11. Linda Williams, *Hard Core: Power, Pleasure, and "the Frenzy of the Visible"* (Berkeley, CA: University of California Press, 1989), 78.

12. http://marshill.com/media/the-peasant-princess.

13. Don Hinkle, "Bott Network Blocks Driscoll," *Baptist Press*, http://www.bpnews.net/bpnews.asp?id=30700.

14. Ibid.

15. Ibid.

16. Johnson has since stopped blogging on *Pyromaniacs*.

17. Phil Johnson "Sound Doctrine; Sound Words," http://www.youtube.com/watch?v=8EFXP04ke2o.

18. Ibid.

19. Mark Driscoll, "Driscoll Responds to Phil Johnson," http://www.youtube.com/watch?v=GMoEJvHS5x4.

20. David S. Gutterman, *Prophetic Politics: Christian Social Movements and American Democracy* (Ithaca, NY: Cornell University Press, 2005), 62.

21. Molly Whorten, "Who Would Jesus Smack Down?" *New York Times Magazine*, http://www.nytimes.com/2009/01/11/magazine/11punk-t.html?pagewanted=all.

22. Gutterman, *Prophetic Politics: Christian Social Movements and American Democracy*, 95.

23. Susan Faludi, *Stiffed* (New York: William Morrow and Company, 1999).

24. Mark Driscoll, *Luke's Gospel: Investigating the Man Who Is God*, http://marshill.com/media/luke/sermons.

25. Mark Driscoll, *Proverbs: Men and Masculinity*, http://marshill.com/media/proverbs/men-and-masculinity.

26. On Pat Robertson's *700 Club*, Jerry Falwell, founder of the politically engaged conservative evangelical organization known as the Moral Majority in the 1980s, blamed abortionists, feminist, gays and lesbians, and the ACLU for the World Trade Center attacks on 9/11.

27. As previously noted, the "free" and "open" availability of teaching content online no longer exists. While there are several recent sermon series still available

for viewing and as downloads on the church Web site, a wealth of teaching content contributed by Driscoll and other pastors has been stricken from its media library.

28. http://marshill.com/global; http://theresurgence.com; http://marshill.com/about/the-city.

29. Mark Driscoll, "Videology," http://marshill.com/media/special/videology.

30. Ibid.

31. Ahmed, "Affective Economies," italics by author, 119.

32. Arlene Stein, *Shameless: Sexual Dissidence in American Culture* (New York: New York University Press, 2006), 115.

33. Steven Mulkey, "Mars Hill Military Mission: Victory over Porn Through the Gospel," http://blog.marshill.com.

34. Mark Driscoll, *Porn Again Christian* (Wheaton, IL: Crossway Books, 2009), http://theresurgence.com/books/porn_again_christian, 11.

35. Ibid., 22.

36. Ibid., 23–24.

37. Ibid., 23.

38. Ibid., 23.

39. Ibid., 21. This quote is edited from the original for brevity.

40. "Mark Driscoll, Pastor of Mars Hill Church, Says Masturbation Can be a Form of Homosexuality," http://www.huffingtonpost.com/2011/10/21/mark-driscoll-masturbation_n_1023743.html?view=print&comm_ref=false.

41. Hanna Rosin, "The End of Men," *Atlantic*, July/August 2010 http://www.theatlantic.com/magazine/archive/2010/07/the-end-of-men/308135.

42. Susan Bordo, *The Male Body: A New Look at Men in Public and Private* (New York: Farrar, Strauss, Giroux, 1999).

43. Meika Loe, "The Viagra Blues: Embracing or Resisting the Viagra Body" in *Medicalized Masculinities*, ed. Dana Rosenfeld and Christopher A. Faircloth (Philadelphia: Temple University Press, 2006).

44. Jane Juffer, "There's No Place Like Home: Further Developments on the Domestic Front" in *More Dirty Looks: Gender, Pornography, and Power*, ed. Pamela Church Gibson (London: British Film Institute, 2004), 45–58.

45. Linda Williams, *Hard Core: Power, Pleasure, and "the Frenzy of the Visible"* (Berkeley, CA: University of California Press, 1989), 114.

46. Michael Coogan, *God and Sex: What the Bible Really Says* (New York: Twelve, 2010); Jennifer Wright Knust, *Unprotected Texts: The Bible's Surprising Contradictions about Sex and Desire* (New York: Harper Collins, 2011).

47. A. J. Hamilton, "Making the Peasant Princess: Insights into a Mars Hill Sermon Series Part 1," http://theresurgence.com/2008/11/10/making-the-peasant-princess-insights-into-a-mars-hill-sermon-series-part-1.

48. http://marshill.com/media/the-peasant-princess.

49. Hamilton, "Making the Peasant Princess."

50. Ibid.

51. Ibid.

52. Lisa Duggan, "Censorship in the Name of Feminism (1984)" in *Sex Wars: Sexual Dissent and Political Culture*, ed. Lisa Duggan and Nan Hunter (New York: Routledge, 1995), 40.

53. Jane Juffer, "There's No Place Like Home: Further Developments on the Domestic Front," in *More Dirty Looks: Gender, Pornography, and Power*, ed. Pamela Church Gibson (London: British Film Institute, 2004), 47.

54. Acts29 is a global church planting network founded by Driscoll in 2001 that financially supports and trains men who wish to found congregations in the United States and around the world using Mars Hill's theological orientation and organizational structure as a model. While Driscoll is no longer President of Acts29, he is still a member on its Board of Directors and speaks at "boot camps" for potential planters. This particular quote comes from a "boot camp" hosted in Raleigh, NC, in 2007: http://www.acts29network.org/sermon/the-man.

55. "Most pastors I know do not have satisfying, free, sexual conversations and liberties with their wives. At the risk of being even more widely despised than I currently am, I will lean over the plate and take one for the team on this. It is not uncommon to meet pastors' wives who really let themselves go; they sometimes feel that because their husband is a pastor, he is therefore trapped into fidelity, which gives them cause for laziness. A wife who lets herself go and is not sexually available to her husband in the ways that the Song of Songs is so frank about is not responsible for her husband's sin, but she may not be helping him either," from a blog post by Mark Driscoll, "Evangelical Leader Quits Amid Allegations of Gay Sex and Drug Use," http://theresurgence.com/authors/mark-driscoll.

56. These workshops and seminars took place in November 2006 and July 2007, respectively.

57. "Not Tonight Honey, I Have a Headache," *Reforming Femininity*, http://marshill.com.

58. http://marshill.com/media/the-peasant-princess/dance-of-mahanaim.

59. Richard V. Ericson and Kevin D. Haggerty, eds., *The New Politics of Surveillance and Visibility* (Toronto: University of Toronto Press, 2006), 51.

60. "Pastor Mark.tv is Alive—er, Live!" http://marshill.com/2011/09/13/pastormark-tv-is-alive-er-live.

61. Grace Driscoll and Mark Driscoll, "Christian Sex Q&A (Mature Content)," http://marshill.com/categories/christian-sex-qa-mature-content.

62. Ibid.

63. Ibid.

7

Queer Smut, Queer Rights

Whitney Strub

Queer smut. If the phrase resists respectability, that may be precisely the point. From the start, the LGBT battle for civil rights has of necessity been a struggle also for freedom of expression, as a precursor to self-definition, visibility, and the other privileges that accompany social citizenship. Indeed, the historical difficulties in forming community solidarity from a social position of relative invisibility lay at the heart of the early homophile movement as it developed in the 1950s. Trapped in a hostile society that deployed a barrage of laws intended to subjugate queer identity and mandate heteronormative patterns of behavior, gays and lesbians first needed to locate one another before activism could begin. "Perhaps the most stubborn problem faced by homosexuals over the course of the twentieth century," historian Martin Meeker suggests, "has been one of communication." Often stranded in individual closets for fear of sanctions that ran from physical violence to incarceration or institutionalization, gays, lesbians, and other queers struggled valiantly to establish the public visibility necessary for a civil rights movement.[1]

The circulation of erotic texts played a critical role in establishing and perpetuating these social networks. Often mentioned by scholars but rarely studied systematically, such texts, historically derided as trash, in fact performed what gay scholar Michael Bronski calls an "important political function"; in a society that has historically demanded silence and invisibility from sexually noncompliant persons, such "smut" has affirmed identities, promoted visibility, forged community, and combated imposed normativity. "The power of the erotic," as lesbian author Audre Lorde terms it, has informed and shaped gay and lesbian civil rights movements since their emergence in the 1950s, from lesbian pulp fiction novels of that decade to gay male safe-sex porn films of the 1980s, and beyond.[2] Disreputable texts call into question complacent or assimilationist politics, keeping the social power of normality always evident.

This chapter surveys the political contributions of gay and lesbian erotic texts to the queer civil rights movements.[3] It shows how these wide-ranging texts challenged harmful stereotypes, drew gays and lesbians out of the closet, helped shape approaches to activism, and even contributed to lifesaving educational efforts. Emphasizing these positive benefits of erotic expression in no way means that such endeavors were entirely unproblematic; pornography, like all cultural genres and formats, carries a multiplicity of meanings and significations that never reduce to one simple message. But whatever the shortcomings, erotic material played a crucial and too-often overlooked role in the social, legal, and political empowerment of queer Americans, and it fully deserves a place in the history of these struggles.

LESBIAN PULP FICTION: HIDDEN POCKET(BOOK)S OF RESISTANCE

Before the emergence of a formal lesbian rights movement in the 1950s, various forms of "prepolitical" activity set the stage for its mobilization. Butch lesbians, by adopting so-called masculine appearances, claimed the right to queer public visibility; lesbian bars also laid claim to public space and helped foster the sense of community and solidarity crucial to any civil rights movement.[4] Though problematic in many ways, the erotic lesbian pulp fiction that flourished in the 1950s and early 1960s must also be included in these prepolitical institutions that gave rise to a lesbian consciousness. The "lesbianism" of these books remained tenuous, as the genre was dominated by pseudonymous male authors by a ratio that expert Katherine Forrest estimates at five for every one actual lesbian author.[5] Furthermore, pulp often catered to a male consumer base eager for prurient and "exotic" vicarious thrills, offering fetishized depictions of lesbian sexuality and adopting the prevailing pathological psychiatric model of the times. Nonetheless, in spite of these heavy mediating factors, lesbian pulp found an avid audience among isolated lesbian readers, alerting them to the existence of other lesbians and providing insight, albeit sometimes skewed, into the operations of lesbian subcultures.

As the "paperback revolution" began in the late 1930s, publishers enticed readers with lurid and salacious covers. When they realized in the early 1950s that the commodification of lesbianism sold well, a new genre was born.[6] While most lesbian pulp fiction foregrounds erotic elements, framed as tawdry and deviant for a leering male gaze, within the genre's recesses lay more authentic portrayals of lesbian life. It is in these works, superficially indiscernible from their male-oriented counterparts but substantively remote from such exploitative intent, that the political thrust of lesbian pulp resides.

Marijane Meaker, for instance, who wrote under the pen name Vin Packer, earned a cult following for her 1952 novel *Spring Fire*, which exemplifies the thoughtful strategies lesbian authors used to communicate queer themes despite publishing-industry obstacles. Packer's male editor encouraged her to pursue homosexual themes, but he demanded unhappy endings. This constraint consigned Packer's tale of romance between Midwestern sorority sisters Mitch and Leda to a jarring, doomed ending. Within the story, however, Packer sends clear signals to readers. While providing the requisite amount of erotic content, she subversively undermines heterosexuality, framing it as universally unpleasant. Mitch's straight encounters range from rape to awkward failure, and when Leda describes sex with her boyfriend, "dry bread" is her metaphor of choice. In sharp contrast, the two lovers' intimacies act as moments of soothing refuge from a hostile world; "quiet and warm," with gentle touches and ecstatic responses, lesbian sexuality is without doubt the more attractive orientation in *Spring Fire*.[7]

Such tactics distinguished true lesbian pulp. Della Martin's *Twilight Girl*, published in 1961, reiterates the tropes of *Spring Fire*. While a violent conclusion brings to an abrupt end the burgeoning love affair between suburban teenager Lon and twenty-something bohemian Mavis, again the book's thematic endorsement of lesbianism resists its narrative impositions. One lesbian character describes "straight married people" as "stuck," raising children or "payin' on a house an' a car." Again, heterosexual sex is depicted in unflattering terms, as in a lengthy sexual encounter between lesbian character Sassy and her oafish boyfriend Durham that Sassy experiences as "grotesquely laughable." Repulsed by "this perspiring, ungraceful, undemanding ugly body" on top of her, she inadvertently cries out in disgust; Durham vainly mistakes it for an orgasm. Juxtaposed against this are tender, reciprocal lesbian sex scenes. To Lon, embracing Mavis in bed is "like holding a delicate Christmas angel in your arms."[8]

While the tragic endings were an institutional component of lesbian pulp novels, designed to ward off potential censors and obscenity charges by reinforcing heteronormativity, even this device was sometimes challenged. Ann Bannon, perhaps the most valorized author of the genre, published a series of novels in the late 1950s and early 1960s detailing the adventures and affairs of butch heroine Beebo Brinker and her assorted friends and lovers. Bucking trends, Bannon defiantly concluded her books on positive notes. Bannon's 1960 novel *Journey to a Woman* wastes no time in delivering a scathing portrait of contemporary marriage. "She lay in the dark and cried," the novel begins, describing a closeted woman who "had learned to cry without making a sound" while her husband has sex with her. Yet again, lesbianism receives more glowing descriptions as a "fantastic luxury" containing "a thousand sensual subtleties." Unlike other works in the genre, *Journey* ends with lovers Beebo and Beth walking together, "hand in hand."[9]

The political implications of this literature are manifold. Lesbian pulp challenged the pathological model of lesbianism that dominated psychiatric discourse of the era, which framed lesbians as neurotic, frigid, immature, and even psychotic. While the imposed tragic endings often mitigated this challenge, such works as Bannon's offered more direct refutations. Beyond this, as scholar Suzanna Danuta Walters notes, pulp constituted "a sort of 'how-to' of lesbian lust," helping readers learn queer cultural codes from dress style to language to identifying marks of lesbian bars.[10] As such, it assisted numerous women in the transition from the closet to the lesbian bar. Abundant testimonials to this effect ring across the pages of lesbian history and memoirs, from such notable public figures as Dorothy Allison, Barbara Gittings, Joan Nestle, and Kate Millett. Author Donna Allegra offers the most vivid recollection of pulp's importance. "No matter how embarrassed and ashamed I felt when I went to the cash register to buy these books," she writes, "it was absolutely necessary for me to have them. I needed them the way I needed food and shelter for survival."[11] A crucial prepolitical institution, pulp gave lesbians the tools to begin disassembling the oppressive social strictures that confined—or *attempted* to confine—them to isolated closets.

EROTIC POLITICS: FROM BEEFCAKE TO GAY PORN

While gay male pulp never grew as prominent as lesbian pulp, lacking a comparable straight crossover market, gay male erotica has existed since time immemorial, across every medium. Thomas Waugh has documented, for instance, that explicit photographs, often privately circulated, date back literally to the dawn of photography. In various ways, these materials contributed to the rise of a shared gay consciousness by validating gay sexuality, by providing sexual outlets to isolated men, and by establishing a communications infrastructure.[12] As the homophile movement took shape in the 1950s, though, erotic materials initially seemed to be at odds with the movement's agenda. The Mattachine Society, leading homophile organization of the decade, steadfastly insisted on a public respectability that precluded overt displays of sexuality. Instead, homophile publications of the 1950s offered textual discourses on legal, psychiatric, and political matters. Only in the 1960s would homophile activism converge with erotic celebration to give rise to a gay liberation movement that affirmed sexuality as central to gay identity.

Incremental steps toward this convergence took place on both sides. On the homophile end, *ONE* magazine, founded by Mattachine-affiliated activists in 1953, encountered repeated obstacles at the hands of postal inspectors who found it obscene simply by virtue of its homosexual themes. While *ONE* carefully asserted that "being 'against smut' is entirely praiseworthy," it also noted the prevailing double standard that "what is permissible in hetero-sexual literature is *not* permissible in *ONE's* case."[13] Resisting all the way to the Supreme Court, *ONE* won its lengthy battle with postal censors in 1958; after losing at every prior judicial level, the magazine was finally exonerated.[14]

As homophile groups reached a tangible understanding of the critical importance of free expression, the superficially more frivolous world of gay erotica learned the necessity of political mobilization. While "beefcake" magazines such as Bob Mizer's *Physique Pictorial*, founded in 1951, often seemed content simply to revel in the undraped beauty of scantily clad men, government obscenity charges frequently targeted gay materials. After newspaper columnist Paul Coates attacked *Physique* in 1954, suggesting its readers were "brutal, horrifying sex criminal[s]," Mizer was arrested, tried, and convicted on obscenity charges. When an appeal effort argued that Mizer's beefcake photos were close in nature to the "agonized muscular activity" in Biblical motion pictures like *The Robe* (1953), his conviction was reversed the next year, but the case nonetheless served as a warning to beefcake publishers.[15]

If Mizer's local Los Angeles case went unheralded at the national level, Washington, D.C. publisher Herman Womack escalated the legal battle to the highest court of the land. A former philosophy professor whose beefcake magazines such as *MANual* and *Grecian Guild Pictorial* were deemed obscene by postal inspectors in 1960, Womack was distraught over the unjust double standard that allowed such naked pictures of women as those in *Playboy* to circulate but proscribed equally and less explicit pictures of men. Challenging this discrepancy in court, Womack lost repeatedly before finally appealing to the Supreme Court, which rendered a decision in 1962. While the language used was hardly supportive of gay eroticism, calling Womack's works "dismally unpleasant, uncouth, and tawdry," the Court nonetheless ruled in his favor, exonerating his magazines of obscenity and averring that they "cannot fairly be regarded as more objectionable than many portrayals of the female nude that society tolerates."[16]

Womack's victory constituted a major landmark. Whereas the 1958 *ONE* case had been decided without a written opinion, thus holding limited precedential value, *MANual Enterprises* firmly and unequivocally stated that gay male publications were to be held to the same stringent standards of obscenity as their straight counterparts. Thanks to Womack, no longer could physique magazines be targeted simply for catering to a gay consumer base.

Meanwhile, as the 1960s progressed, the homophile movement grew more aggressively militant but maintained its rigorously asexual public front. Beginning in 1965, public protests brought homophile groups to newfound levels of visibility, but self-regulation within the movement demanded the highest standards of respectability at all times. As late as a 1969 homophile picket in Philadelphia, even meager physical contact was emphatically barred by the organizers, leading to conflict among the ranks when a young gay couple, arguing that "Our message is that homosexual love is good," insisted on holding hands.[17]

It took Philadelphia activist Clark Polak to finally fuse the two distinct threads, acknowledging both that the erotic is inherently political and that queer political activism necessarily includes sexual corollaries. Polak embodied this framework in *Drum*, which he began publishing under the auspices of the homophile Janus Society in 1963. While carrying on the homophile tradition, *Drum* unapologetically incorporated beefcake photos. Polak's editorials condemned the "gestapo-like tactics of US Postal inspectors," and also lamented that "there has been little activity in attempting to establish the legitimacy of interest in photographs of the nude body." Framing such interest as more than mere legal right, but rather a politically meaningful expression of gay identity, *Drum* found an avid readership. By the mid-1960s its subscriptions had eclipsed all other homophile publications combined.[18]

Polak's reconceptualization of prurience as valid and political rather than shameful reached its apex when *Drum* boldly began including full-frontal nude photos for its subscribers at the end of 1965. *Drum*'s contents directly challenged the established homophile principle of respectability, and the challenge was met with disapproval; earlier in 1965, the East Coast Homophile Organizations, a collective umbrella group, voted to expel Polak's Janus Society from its ranks. Not all gay men shared that attitude, as clearly indicated by *Drum*'s wide readership. One supporter, "glad to see an organization put sex back into homosexuality," felt *Drum* advanced gay causes more effectively than homophile groups that obscured "the fact that we homos like to gratify our sexual desires."[19]

Incubating in the pages of *Drum*, then, was a new vision of gay rights. As the homophile model of political rights abstracted from bodily pleasures grew obsolete, in its stead emerged the new paradigm of "gay liberation," ushered in by the spontaneous June 1969 Stonewall rebellion. The riots, initiated to resist an all-too-common New York City police "vice raid" of the queer Stonewall Inn, were seen as a decisive breaking point with respectable homophile tactics. A new radical consciousness infused gay liberation, recognizing that "politics" extended far beyond the traditional realms of civil and legal rights; like the concurrently developing women's liberation movement, gay liberationists saw the personal as political. Sexuality figured prominently in this new analysis, as gay liberationists eagerly endorsed public expressions of desire, lust, and pleasure. Long denied the right to enjoy their sexuality, by measures from sodomy laws to threats of violence, gay liberationists reconfigured sex itself into an act of political resistance.[20] Polak's work in *Drum* did much to facilitate this liberationist synthesis, forging an erotic politics that saw the right to sexual pleasure as inseparable from (and intertwined with) other forms of legal rights.

Los Angeles filmmaker Pat Rocco provides an effective complement to Polak's efforts; while *Drum* pushed the reluctant homophile movement toward an acknowledgment of sexuality, Rocco's films politicized beefcake. Nearly wordless and plotless, Rocco's short films centered on the amorous embraces of naked, attractive young men. Strolling in Griffith Park, swimming in the Pacific Ocean, and even kissing at Disneyland, Rocco's unabashed lovers rejected long institutionalized stances of shame and secrecy. Unlike physique magazines, Rocco made no pretense of disguising his work as depicting "physical culture" or "artistic modeling." When he began exhibiting his shorts in 1968, he labeled it a "homosexual film festival." Without delivering any verbal manifestoes, Rocco forcefully asserted an affirmative vision of gay male sexuality, doing "more to lift the morale and self-image of American homosexuals," New York underground magazine *Screw* declared, "than a thousand Mattachine orators."[21]

If Rocco helped empower gay men on the brink of Stonewall, gay pornographers who followed him embodied the liberationist ethos. Rocco's work featured extensive nudity but downplayed sex acts, privileging soft-hued romanticism over sweaty physicality. His successors took a different approach. Buoyed by 1960s legal advances, the first hardcore films, featuring graphic depictions of unsimulated sex acts, began to appear at the dawn of the 1970s. Early gay hardcore features often evinced drab imagery and negative attitudes, inspiring Broadway choreographer and dancer Wakefield Poole in 1971 to create the iconic work of liberationist gay porn, *Boys in the Sand*.[22]

Featuring the attractive male model Cal Culver and set on longtime New York gay resort locale Fire Island, *Boys* offered an idyllic portrait of gay life, explicit sex included. Poole saw the film as reflective of the gay liberation slogan "Gay Is Beautiful." As the director told an interviewer, "I wanted a film that gay people could look at and say, 'I don't mind being gay—it's beautiful to see those people doing what they're doing!'" Rejecting low-rent Times Square porn venues, Poole premiered *Boys* at a respectable uptown theater in December 1971. The approach proved massively effective, drawing large crowds and even mainstream media coverage; in an oft-quoted review, *Variety* proclaimed, "There are no more closets."[23]

Other gay pornographers also helped smash the closet. Fred Halsted, for instance, demanded that advertisements for his 1972 porn epic *L.A. Plays Itself* carry the word "homosexual" rather than the euphemistic "all male cast" that generally signified queer films. The *New York Times* initially rejected the ad but subsequently relented, marking the first time the term "homosexual" appeared in its film ads. After gay activists were beaten at the New York Hilton Hotel in April 1972, proceeds from *L.A. Plays Itself* screenings were donated to the Gay Activists Alliance Legal Defense to defray litigation costs.[24]

The advent of gay liberation and hardcore pornography seemingly marked a clear break with homophile activities of the past, but continuities bound the two eras together. Perhaps the best illustration of this comes from the career of Hal Call. As president of the Mattachine Society in the 1950s, Call had fervently argued for the maintenance of respectability as the most effective means of advancing gay rights. Switching gears as liberationist groups superseded Mattachine in the late 1960s, Call opened the Adonis Bookstore in San Francisco. The nation's first exclusively gay-themed bookstore, Adonis sold a range of materials both erotic and political. In 1968 Call began hosting a series of graphic sex films, some shot by himself, eventually termed CineMattachine; if the tie to the past was not abundantly clear, well into the 1970s advertising material noted that "Adonis is more than a gay bookstore—it helps support Mattachine Society, Inc., [the] oldest gay-freedom organization in the USA."[25] At a glance, Call's commercial work in pornography would seem to be directly antithetical to his earlier Mattachine stance of respectability. In the context of evolving gay-rights activism, though, it indicates the shift from that of respectability to a liberationist politics of public resistance, a shift informed and assisted by affirmative gay erotic imagery.

"BULLDAGGERS OF THE SEASON": LESBIAN PORN AND SELF-DEFINITION

Committed, like gay men, to radical liberationist ideals, lesbians rarely gave the conceptualization of public sex as an act of political resistance the same position of theoretical centrality. As sexuality became a heated battleground in the late 1970s, though, lesbians began to assert the political value of pornography as a tool of empowerment in the face of encroaching normativity from both a homophobic mainstream society and an overly prescriptive feminist movement.

A concerted feminist effort to reclaim the erotic representation of women transpired in the 1970s. Noting the works of artist Judy Chicago and the films at the First International Festival of Women's Films in 1972, a reporter for the feminist paper *off our backs* argued that "this aggressive presentation of the cunt is a first step at self-definition."[26] Certainly lesbians partook in such efforts; as media historian Rodger Streitmatter observes, mid-1970s lesbian periodicals such as *Sisters, The Lesbian Tide, Tribad,* and *Amazon Quarterly* regularly and casually featured naked and erotic photographs, as well as explicit writing, in an effort at "demystifying lesbian sex." *Lesbian News* even avoided euphemism, advertising a new magazine, *Ecstasy,* as "pornography for women" in 1975.[27]

One inhibiting factor in the development of postpulp, lesbian-defined erotic expression was the emergence in the late 1970s of the feminist antipornography movement. Antiporn feminism considered pornography categorically antiwoman, an oppressive cultural blight that normalized objectification, reducing women to sex objects and fostering attitudes that rape and violence were acceptable. At times the antiporn feminists found receptive lesbian audiences; the litany of pornographic sexual horrors chronicled in such influential books as Andrea Dworkin's *Pornography: Men Possessing Women* (1979) and Susan Griffin's *Pornography and Silence* (1981) offered compelling critiques, and such prominent lesbian activists as Charlotte Bunch showed support, contributing an essay to the widely read 1980 antiporn anthology *Take Back the Night.*[28]

By the late 1970s, though, deep tensions between lesbians and antiporn feminists began to surface. The antiporn definition of "pornography" carried a great deal of semantic fluidity, referring to nonviolent but ostensibly misogynistic porn fare one minute, and nonsexual but violent or degrading imagery the next. Problematic as this was, more troubling to lesbians was the refusal of antiporn feminists to recognize a substantive difference between male-produced, male-oriented porn and that made by and for women. *The Lesbian Tide* ran several articles equating antiporn feminists with the conservative activists of the politically ascendant New Right, noting that both sought to impose restrictive new standards on queer sexual expression.[29] Leading group Women Against Pornography did little to assuage these suspicions when it omitted the word "lesbian" from publicity materials and declined to endorse the National March on Washington for Lesbian and Gay Rights in 1979, offering the unsatisfying explanation that WAP was a single-issue group.[30]

Normative corollaries of the antiporn movement also left many lesbians distressed. Critiques of butch/femme roles and sadomasochism (s/m) in particular generated much antagonism. These critiques came from both within and outside lesbian communities, but they were firmly associated with the antiporn movement. Susan Brownmiller, a WAP leader and bestselling author, caused controversy in 1979 when she mocked a confrontational butch critic at a conference by telling the crowd, "See, she even *dresses* like a man." Such actions did little to endear the antiporn movement to ambivalent lesbians. Antiporn feminists also figured prominently in the 1982 anthology *Against*

Sadomasochism, which described lesbian s/m as "firmly rooted in patriarchal sexual ideology."[31]

Dissent from these positions echoed throughout the lesbian-feminist press, but as the 1980s began, lesbians opposed to the antiporn positions found themselves consistently marginalized. As antiporn leaders like Andrea Dworkin and Catharine MacKinnon attained national public prominence, claiming a monopoly on feminism in their widely read books from major publishers, no nationally recognized forum disseminated opposing perspectives. When lesbian s/m supporter Pat Califia wrote a scathing critique of the antiporn movement in 1980, denouncing its "Victorian imagery" as a reiteration of traditional gender norms of women in need of protection, it ran in the gay male *Advocate*.[32]

In 1984, the year that the "sex wars" hit a fever pitch as Dworkin and MacKinnon helped draft a restrictive antiporn ordinance in Minneapolis, lesbians who defined themselves as "sex positive" finally found an organized avenue for self-expression. *On Our Backs* debuted that year. Frustrated by the antiporn feminists who sought to dictate proper sexual behavior, *On Our Backs* (OOB) declared the "Year of the Lustful Lesbian," opening its first issue by exclaiming, "Yes, finally a sex magazine for lesbians!" Gleefully tawdry, the magazine's very title parodied the long-running feminist paper *off our backs*. Featuring a "Bulldagger of the Season" photo spread, OOB lived up to its lustful aspirations, but sutured into its graphic photographs were sharp sexual politics. Unlike the male-oriented world of the mainstream porn industry, with its oppressively rigid standards of female beauty, OOB models encompassed a diverse range of ages, races, styles, and body types. Lauding 1950s lesbian pulp as its predecessor, the magazine took a measured stance toward pornography, complaining of the prevalence of "boring, dick-centric" smut but nonetheless dredging up moments of genuine eroticism buried within the dreck, all the while offering itself as an alternative.[33]

Premised on the right to sexual self-determination, *On Our Backs* met fierce resistance on both ends of the political spectrum. On the right, social conservatives, using the rhetoric of Christianity to mask an antigay agenda, opposed both lesbianism and pornography as antithetical to "family values." Meanwhile, on the left, feminists denounced the magazine for approaching pornography and s/m irreverently rather than antagonistically. Many bookstores, such as Spinsters, a lesbian-run collective in Lawrence, Kansas, were boycotted by feminists for carrying OOB.[34]

Despite such obstacles, OOB struck a responsive chord in its readers, and its success at amassing subscriptions proved indicative of a wider lesbian resistance to normative impositions. Sex-war factions often aligned across issues not just of smut and bondage, but also transgender and butch/femme identities and practices, which were frequently condemned by self-declared radical feminists. OOB celebrated self-determination on all fronts, embracing sex toys and butch/femme aesthetics even before Elizabeth Kennedy and Madeline Davis's landmark 1993 study of working-class lesbian history reclaimed the crucial "pre-political" role butches played in asserting a public lesbian presence. Meanwhile, in writer and editor Susie Bright, OOB launched one of the most powerful sex-positive lesbian voices; in her numerous columns and books, Bright mercilessly lampooned the "Prime of Miss Kitty MacKinnon."[35]

Bad Attitude, an s/m-themed magazine that also began in 1984, rejected the antiporn analysis, arguing that "good sex" could include "objectification, fantasies, surprise and an exchange of power," illustrating this by featuring graphic photographs of "deviant" sexual behavior ranging from bondage to fisting.[36] That same year, Nan Kinney of OOB launched Fatale Video, a film company dedicated to reclaiming control over erotic lesbian representations from the straight-male oriented mainstream porn industry. Joan Nestle's autobiographical book *A Restricted Country* (1987) defended butch/femme roles as subversive, rather than supportive, of patriarchy, and Pat Califia's fictional *Macho Sluts* (1988) unapologetically indulged in elaborate s/m fantasies. Collectively, these works rejected antiporn dogma while still fulfilling feminist goals of women's autonomy.

While lesbianism had long been a staple of straight male porn, "there are no lesbian sex movies made *by* lesbians," an *On Our Backs* reporter complained in 1985. OOB cofounder Debi Sundahl helped change this in 1990, directing Fatale's *Suburban Dykes* to tremendous acclaim. Film scholar Heather Butler calls the film an "important stepping-stone" in the history of lesbian sexual expression, because it employs butch/femme roles, dirty talk, and other transgressive behavior to repudiate stereotypical notions of an essential female sexuality based on presumably feminine qualities.[37] Once established, lesbian pornography expanded rapidly over the 1990s. As sex-positive feminism supplanted antiporn feminism in the public eye, with woman-friendly sex shops Good Vibrations and Toys in Babeland becoming lucrative entities, lesbian porn catered to an ever-growing market. A "shocking political coup" for lesbian pornographers occurred in 2001, when *Hard Love & How to Fuck in High Heels*, made by "100% dyke produced" San Francisco company SIR, won the best all-girl feature award from *Adult Video News*, a leading publication of the mainstream porn industry.[38] Having seized the means of production, lesbians now exerted some control over their erotic representation. Like Clark Polak before them, dyke-porn auteurs fused a progay feminist agenda to an unapologetic celebration of queer pleasure.

LESSONS AND LEGACIES

Erotic texts, queer and otherwise, are often relegated to the social margins, perceived as wallowing in the gutters of culture and holding much less significance than the "high art" against which they are contrasted. Yet the various forms and genres surveyed in this chapter have bolstered queer civil rights struggles in a multitude of manners. This serves as a reminder that a full portrayal of the ongoing struggle must locate its sources of sustenance and fortitude in both realms deemed socially reputable and those deemed not. A brief concluding examination of two further conflicts—responses to the devastating AIDS crisis and the legal right to freedom of expression for s/m lesbians—shows how pornography has continued to act as a site of queer resistance, and also how precarious gay and lesbian rights remain in contemporary society.

While gay and lesbian activism had made great strides by the mid-1970s, the politicization of evangelical Christians, and particularly their consolidation in the Republican Party in the late 1970s, created a strong obstacle to the advancement of queer rights. Most importantly, the 1980 presidential election replaced the ambivalent but modestly supportive Carter administration with the actively hostile Reagan administration.[39]

When AIDS emerged as a deadly epidemic in the early 1980s, the Reagan administration privileged politics over public health. Seen as primarily a gay men's issue, AIDS was given insufficient attention by the administration; indeed, Surgeon General C. Everett Koop was even ordered not to make speeches on the topic, and his attempts to promote the distribution and use of condoms were fought vigorously by administration staffers.[40] Furthermore, when Reagan finally established federal education policy guidelines in 1987, they were premised on "placing sexuality within the context of marriage," an absurd framework for the at-risk gay men who were entirely excluded from that very institution.[41] While Reagan's AIDS policies thus catered to Christian Right demands that homosexuality not be condoned, they did so at the cost of effectiveness.

In the absence of a useful government response to the growing crisis, gay and lesbian activists established support systems. Medical, educational, media, and political campaigns took shape thanks to tireless activists, and pornography too contributed to the battle against AIDS. An organized effort to eroticize safe sex, promoting "the idea that safe sex is perverse and fun, not boring or limited," was underway by the mid-1980s. In *Play Safely*, a 1986 porn film, characters actually verbalize their anxiety about contracting HIV before engaging in steamy but safe sex; in the popular 1988 film *Top Man*, "condoms are completely normalized," as AIDS scholar (and *Bad Attitude* cofounder) Cindy Patton writes.[42] While the gay porn industry had arguably lost its liberationist impulses as it moved from the fringe into profitable capitalist currents during the 1970s, this attempt to integrate condoms into the gay erotic imagination reflected the ongoing political relevance of porn to gay struggles.

The use of erotic imagery as an educational device extended beyond the porn industry. Gay Men's Health Crisis (GMHC), the most important AIDS activist organization, filed grant proposals with the Centers for Disease Control for its safe sex videos and comics, which used graphic images to convey the message that "there are healthy, satisfying and erotically appealing alternatives" to risky behaviors. Arguing that vague and euphemistic concepts like "bodily fluids" were less useful than discourse framed in direct language with appeal to its target audience, GMHC and other AIDS groups quickly learned what Patton calls "the pornographic vernacular."[43]

Activist campaigns to harness the power of pornography against AIDS found vocal political opponents. North Carolina Republican Senator Jesse Helms proved the most aggressive, introducing a 1987 legislative amendment barring the use of CDC resources for projects that "promote or encourage, directly, homosexual sexual activities." This posed a grave crisis, as public health experts had already well established that the sex-positive messages of GMHC were more effective than moralistic efforts to fight AIDS by simply advocating abstinence. While GMHC challenged the resulting policies in court and won, their videos and pamphlets became rallying points for conservative opponents.[44] California Republican Representative William Dannemeyer, for instance, ignored the lifesaving effects of the materials, reducing them to "pornographic trash published by the homosexual activists with a smirk" in 1991. Despite the GMHC legal victory against the Helms Amendment, AIDS groups in North Carolina, Iowa, and elsewhere reported a "chilling effect," as state and local health commissions continued to reject explicit safe-sex campaigns.[45]

As AIDS activists confronted this antagonism to viable education programs, lesbian porn also encountered the limits of social tolerance for queer sexual expression. Confiscated by Canadian police in Toronto in 1992, *Bad Attitude* was found obscene there early the next year, bringing to the attention of gay and lesbian Americans a systematic targeting of queer erotic materials that had long been underway in Canada. That such efforts were assisted by a 1992 Canadian Supreme Court ruling reading obscenity law in the spirit of American antiporn feminist Catharine MacKinnon only served to reinforce the political urgency of defending freedom of sexual expression. Like the right-wing campaigns against eroticized safer sex educational materials, the Canadian obscenity battles also highlighted the precariousness of gay and lesbian rights, and the susceptibility of queer sexuality to social stigmatization.[46]

This precariousness remained tangible in the new millennium. A 2000 Canadian Supreme Court decision reaffirmed the prevailing obscenity code, despite acknowledging that its criteria of "degrading" and "dehumanizing" had been disproportionately employed against queer materials.[47] Meanwhile, in the United States, the relative open-mindedness of the 1990s Clinton administration gave way to the virulently antigay presidency of George W. Bush. Moralism once again superseded effective public health, as in the case of the San Francisco group Stop AIDS, which underwent multiple investigations after a Bush Health and Human Services inspector found its publications and workshops "too sexy" in 2001; Stop AIDS ultimately lost its CDC grant support in 2004, despite its methodological soundness.[48] As Bush himself propagated antigay messages, proposing a constitutional amendment expressly designed to prevent legal recognition of same-sex marriage, his Justice Department launched a "vigorous crackdown" on adult obscenity in 2004. This represented a distinct shift from Clinton-era policies of focusing obscenity prosecutions on child pornography, and queer media went on heightened alert, recognizing that gay and lesbian erotic expression was often the first target of such crusades.[49]

Under such conditions, queer erotic expression remains an integral component of the ongoing gay and lesbian civil rights movement. Still denied substantive equality, both socially and legally, in the United States, queers must vigilantly safeguard their rights, including free speech. There are dangers in overvalorizing the political significance of pornography; since the 1990s, for instance, the prevalence of barebacking, or unsafe sex, in gay male videos has been "expanding at a rapid pace," counteracting much of the progressive work done by porn of the 1980s.[50] As well, it would be reductionist and misleading to overemphasize the place of the erotic in queer cultural contributions, which have never been predicated exclusively on sex. With those cautions in place, however, the legacy of erotic expression to queer civil rights is extensive, ranging from the personally empowering, to the community-building, to the lifesaving. In the 21st century, the niche-marketing afforded by the Internet has opened cultural space for groups previously marginalized into near-invisibility, with smut often staking out those spaces. Transman Morty Diamond's "gender-fucking porno" *Trannyfags* (2004), for instance, won acclaim for its feminist-informed eroticizing of transgender bodies and desires, while Shine Louise Houston's popular Pink & White Productions emphasizes fluid gender roles and sexual desires. "There is a power in creating images," Houston explained on the company's Web site, finding it "necessary" for "a woman of color and a queer to take that power."[51]

Erotic materials have expanded queer legal rights in hard-won courtroom battles, promoted public visibility, challenged oppressive theories of homosexual pathology, and created a public space for the assertion of marginalized sexual identities and practices. In short, materials ranging from lesbian pulp to safe-sex gay porn have reconfigured prurience from something tawdry, illicit, and shameful to something affirmative, counterhegemonic, and inherently political. By affixing this resistance to a reminder of the pleasures of queerness, these materials ensure motivation for the perpetuation of the long, uphill battle for civil rights and equality.

NOTES

1. Martin Meeker, *Contacts Desired: Gay and Lesbian Communications and Community, 1940s–1970s* (Chicago: University of Chicago Press, 2006), 1. A preliminary bibliography on the travails of mid-century gay and lesbian citizens would include, among many other works, John D'Emilio, *Sexual Politics, Sexual Communities: The Making of a Homosexual Minority in the United States, 1940–1970* (Chicago: University of Chicago Press, 1983); Estelle Freedman, "'Uncontrolled Desires': The Response to the Sexual Psychopath, 1920–1960," *Journal of American History* 74, no. 1 (1987): 83–106; William Eskridge, *Gaylaw: Challenging the Apartheid of the Closet* (Cambridge, MA: Harvard University Press, 1999); David Johnson, *The Lavender Scare: The Cold War Persecution of Gays and Lesbians in the Federal Government* (Chicago: University of Chicago Press, 2004).

2. Michael Bronski, *Culture Clash: The Making of Gay Sensibility* (Boston: South End Press, 1984), 161; Audre Lorde, "Uses of the Erotic: The Erotic as Power," in *Take Back the Night: Women on Pornography*, ed. Laura Lederer (New York: Bantam, 1980), 295–300.

3. It is perhaps worth noting that no single term effectively captures the constantly evolving self-identification of LGBT communities over time. So while my subjects surely would not all employ "queer" to describe themselves, I rely on it as a broad umbrella to signify the continuity of counternormative sexualities over time (as opposed to, for instance, "gay," the anachronistic usage of which C. Todd White critiques in *Pre-Gay L.A.* [Urbana, IL: University of Illinois Press, 2009]). On one social genealogy of "queer," see George Chauncey's brilliant analysis of community formation in *Gay New York: Gender, Urban Culture, and the Makings of the Gay Male World, 1890–1940* (New York: Basic, 1994).

4. Elizabeth Lapovsky Kennedy and Madeline Davis, *Boots of Leather, Slippers of Gold: The History of a Lesbian Community* (New York: Penguin, 1992), 151–190; Nan Alamilla Boyd, *Wide Open Town: A History of Queer San Francisco to 1965* (Berkeley, CA: University of California Press, 2003), 68–101.

5. Katherine Forrest, ed., *Lesbian Pulp Fiction* (San Francisco: Cleis, 2005), xi.

6. Yvonne Keller, "'Was It Right to Love Her Brother's Wife So Passionately?': Lesbian Pulp Novels and U.S. Lesbian Identity, 1950–1965," *American Quarterly* 57, no. 2 (2005): 385–410.

7. Vin Packer, *Spring Fire* (San Francisco: Cleis, 2004 [1952]), vi, 113, 59.

8. Della Martin, *Twilight Girl* (San Francisco: Cleis, 2006 [1961]), 46, 103, 105, 49.

9. Ann Bannon, *Journey to a Woman* (Tallahassee, FL: Naiad, 1986 [1960]), 5, 120, 223.

10. Suzanna Danuta Walters, "As Her Hand Crept Slowly Up Her Thigh: Ann Bannon and the Politics of Pulp," *Social Text* 23 (1989): 90.

11. Donna Allegra, "Between the Sheets: My Sex Life in Literature," *Lesbian Erotics*, Karla Jay, ed. (New York: New York University Press, 1995), 72.

12. Thomas Waugh, *Hard to Imagine: Gay Male Eroticism in Photography and Film from their Beginnings to Stonewall* (New York: Columbia University Press, 1996).

13. William Lambert, "Editorial," *ONE*, April 1958, 4; *ONE's* Legal Counsel, "The Law of Mailable Material," October 1954, 6.

14. *One, Inc. v. Oleson*, 355 U.S. 371 (1958).

15. Paul Coates, "Well, Medium, and Rare," *Los Angeles Mirror*, 4 May 1954; *People v. Mizer* (1954), Case File, Los Angeles County Record Center.

16. *MANual Enterprises v. Day*, 370 U.S. 478 (1962); Rodger Streitmatter and John Watson, "Herman Lynn Womack: Pornographer as First Amendment Pioneer," *Journalism History* 28, no. 2 (2002): 56–65.

17. Marc Stein, *City of Sisterly and Brotherly Loves: Lesbian and Gay Philadelphia, 1945–1972* (Philadelphia: Temple University Press, 2004), 294.

18. "The Visit," *Drum*, October 1965, 5; "Frontal Nudes," *Drum*, July 1965, 2. On Polak and *Drum*, see Stein, *City*, 231–245.

19. Quotes from Stein, 244, 237.

20. Donn Teal, *The Gay Militants* (New York: St. Martin's Press, 1971); Terence Kissack, "Freaking Fag Revolutionaries: New York's Gay Liberation Front," *Radical History Review* 62 (1995): 104–134.

21. "Most Unusual Film Festival" flyer, n.d. (1968); undated *Screw* clipping; Pat Rocco Papers, ONE National Gay and Lesbian Archives, Los Angeles.

22. Wakefield Poole, *Dirty Poole: The Autobiography of a Gay Porn Pioneer* (Los Angeles: Alyson, 2000), 147–48.

23. Donn Teal, "Wakefield Poole Adds New Dimension to Porn," *Advocate*, March 1, 1972, 17.

24. Teal, "Halsted's Porn," *Advocate*, May 10, 1972, 21; Ad for *L.A. Plays Itself*, *New York Times*, April 30, 1972.

25. Adonis leaflet (1975), Hal Call Papers, box 103-197, ONE Archives: Meeker, "Behind the Mask of Respectability," 113–14.

26. Maryse Holder, "Another Cuntree," *off our backs*, September 30, 1972, 15.

27. Rodger Streitmatter, *Unspeakable: The Rise of the Gay and Lesbian Press in America* (Boston: Faber & Faber, 1995), 169–172; "Ecstasy: Pornography for Women?" *Lesbian News*, September 1975, 6.

28. Charlotte Bunch, "Lesbianism and Erotica in Pornographic America," *Take Back the Night*, 80–83.

29. Bloomington Gay Rights Coalition, "Censorship" *Lesbian Tide*, May/June 1978, 10–11; Jeanne Cordova and Kerry Lobel, "Feminists and the Right" ibid., November/December 1979, 17.

30. Lynne Shapiro, "Lesbian-Straight Split," *Lesbian Tide*, November/December 1979, 24. See also Whitney Strub, "Lavender, Menaced: Lesbianism, Obscenity Law, and the Feminist Antipornography Movement," *Journal of Women's History* 22, no. 2 (2010): 83–107.

31. Susan Chute, "Backstage with the Feminist Heroes," *Sinister Wisdom*, Fall 1980, 111; Robin Ruth Linden, "Introduction," *Against Sadomasochism: A Radical Feminist Analysis* (East Palo Alto: Frog in the Well, 1982), 4.

32. Pat Califia, "Among Us, Against Us," *Advocate*, April 17, 1980, 14–18.

33. "Year of the Lustful Lesbian," *On Our Backs*, Summer 1984, 1; Roberta Yusba, "Twilight Tales," ibid., Summer 1985, 30–31, 43; Barbra LaRue, "Video Lesbiana," ibid., Fall 1984, 16.

34. Letter from Spinsters Collective, *On Our Backs*, Winter 1987, 3.

35. Elizabeth Lapovsky Kennedy and Madeline Davis, *Boots of Leather, Slippers of Gold: The History of a Lesbian Community* (New York: Routledge, 1993); Susie Bright, "The Prime of Miss Kitty MacKinnon," *Sexwise* (Pittsburgh: Cleis, 1995).

36. Donna Turley, "Uncivil War," *Bad Attitude*, Fall 1985, 19.

37. Barbara LaRue, "Video Lesbiana," 36; Lisa LaBia, "Fatale Attraction," *On Our Backs*, January/February 1991, 15; Heather Butler, "What Do You Call a Lesbian with Long Fingers? The Development of Lesbian and Dyke Pornography," *Porn Studies*, Linda Williams, ed. (Durham, NC: Duke University Press, 2004), 179.

38. Ragan Rhyne, "Hard-core Shopping: Educating Consumption in SIR Video Production's Lesbian Porn," *Velvet Light Trap* 59 (2007): 42–50.

39. William Turner, "Mirror Images: Lesbian/Gay Civil Rights in the Carter and Reagan Administrations," *Creating Change: Sexuality, Public Policy, and Civil Rights*, John D'Emilio, et al., eds. (New York: St. Martin's Press, 2000), 3–28.

40. William Martin, *With God on Our Side: The Rise of the Religious Right in America* (New York: Broadway, 1996), 241, 249–52; Jennifer Brier, *Infectious Ideas: U.S. Political Responses to the AIDS Crisis* (Chapel Hill, NC: University of North Carolina Press, 2009).

41. Turner, "Mirror Images," 23–24.

42. Cindy Patton, *Fatal Advice: How Safe-Sex Education Went Wrong* (Durham, NC: Duke University Press, 1996), 124, 133–35. Lesbian porn also adopted safer-sex erotics, as in the 1993 Fatale production *Safe is Desire*. On this complicated effort, see Mary Conway, "Spectatorship in Lesbian Porn: The Woman's Woman's Film," *Wide Angle* 19, no. 3 (1997): 91–113.

43. Jack Anderson and Joseph Spear, "Explicit Anti-AIDS Campaign Debated," *Washington Post*, November 21, 1985.

44. Jessica Tourk, "Controlling Expression: The Stagnant Policy of the Centers for Disease Control in the Second Decade of AIDS," *Cardozo Arts & Entertainment Law Journal* 13 (1993): 601.

45. Malcolm Gladwell, "Graphic Safer-Sex Ads for Gay Men Often Judged Offensive," *Washington Post*, March 17, 1991.

46. Brenda Cossman, et al., eds., *Bad Attitude/s on Trial: Pornography, Feminism, and the Butler Decision* (Toronto: University of Toronto Press, 1997).

47. Brenda Cossman, "Disciplining the Unruly: Sexual Outlaws, *Little Sisters*, and the Legacy of *Butler*," *University of British Columbia Law Review* 36 (2003): 77–99.

48. Esther Kaplan, *With God on Their Side: George W. Bush and the Christian Right* (New York: New Press, 2005), 180–82.

49. Mubarak Dahir, "Defending Porn from Bush," *Houston Voice*, April 16, 2004; Mike Hudson and Chad Graham, "Censorship: The Big Chill," *Advocate*, May 11, 2004.

50. Lou Chibarro, Jr., "Bareback Sales Booming," *Washington Blade*, June 2, 2006.

51. http://www.mortydiamond.com/video/trannyfags; Shine Louise Houston statement, http://pinkwhite.biz/PWWP/about.

8

Steamy, Hot, and Political: Creating Radical Dyke Porn

Shar Rednour and Jackie Strano

Shar Rednour and Jackie Strano were at the forefront of lesbian porn production in San Francisco in the late 1990s and early 2000s. They were the architects behind the groundbreaking sex education series Bend Over Boyfriend *and* Bend Over Boyfriend 2: More Rockin', Less Talkin', *and hardcore lesbian features such as* Hard Love & How to Fuck in High Heels *and* Sugar High Glitter City. *Here, Rednour and Strano reflect on the sex-positive queer art and cultural scene in San Francisco in the late 1990s that created the conditions for them to make porn that was both political and deeply personal.*

THE BEGINNING: FATALE MEDIA AND *ON OUR BACKS*

Shar

I arrived in San Francisco before something called "feminist porn" was en vogue, and before the Bay Area was crowned a queer porn Mecca. It was a city that was on the cusp, just waiting for lesbians to make porn. So we did.

In 1990, I moved to San Francisco with a hundred dollars, my typewriter, and a trunk of high heels. I point out the year not only as historical reference but as a matter of social class: I was a poor writer from a blue-collar family in the Midwest. Because of the major earthquake in 1989, I could afford to move to San Francisco the following year. By 1996, the city would have been financially out of reach. This story would not have happened and things would have unfolded differently. Maybe I would have made dyke porn in Chicago or Indianapolis instead. Affordable space is crucial in order to create radical art and imagery.

Along with my day jobs (which just barely covered rent), I needed to jumpstart my writing career. With this in mind I decided to volunteer at the only lesbian sex magazine in existence, *On Our Backs*—a play on the title of the radical feminist news journal called *off our backs*.[1]

At *On Our Backs* (*OOB*) I did everything from answering the phone to taking out the trash. I showed up in femme high heels my first day, which made the staff giggle. They knew they were giving me, like any other volunteer, the messy work, but I didn't care. I sashayed up to the shipping table, grabbed a box cutter and tape gun, and went at it. After that I learned File-Maker, following instructions on dealing with mailing lists. We were a tiny operation, and as the only administrative help I quickly became everyone's girl. I learned how to write press releases from editor Susie Bright; I learned how to talk to potential advertisers from publisher Debi Sundahl; I learned all about desktop publishing and many other aspects of running a small press. These women—my mentors—were lesbian porn pioneers who were redefining lesbian desire on their own terms, creating explicit sexual imagery, and teaching me crucial skills that would come of service when Jackie Strano and I started making porn on our own.

Not long after I started volunteering at *OOB*, Debi offered me a paid position. I worked for a time with Susie, Nan Kinney, and Debi—the original and legendary forces behind *On Our Backs*—along with Lisa Palac, the assistant editor, and Marcy Sheiner, the fiction editor. When radical erotic photographer Honey Lee Cottrell left the magazine, Phyllis Christopher became photo editor and her sleek, specialized style can be credited with creating the 1990s lesbian look that became associated with queer-women's sexual freedom of that era. Looking back, *OOB* was a veritable "Who's Who" of 1990s lesbian pornography.

Phyllis Christopher and I were close in age and went out together all the time. We were in the same dyke scene and shared similar worlds—all of which were about pushing boundaries and creating new sexual and political territory. Our bosses and coworkers at *OOB* were partnered, older than us, and most lived in the suburbs by this time. Phyllis and I used and liked the word "dyke," because it was edgier than "lesbian" and, to our minds, described us better. Although this term was controversial to some older lesbian, gay, bisexual, and transgender (LGBT) people, it didn't concern us. We didn't slow down enough to bother arguing with anyone who was upset that we used words like "dyke" and "fag"; we didn't try to change anyone's opinion; we didn't cater to accusations or, frankly, even care or notice. We were dykes—sexy dykes, bi-dykes, femme dykes, butch dykes, SM dykes—and we were allies and best friends with fags.

I eventually worked my way up to assistant editor, and found that I was a natural at creating a bridge between artistic endeavors and efforts to make the magazine financially viable. I could understand the writers and editorial side of the operation, yet I also understood the needs of the marketing and the ad departments. By the time I was on the scene, Debi and Nan were no longer together as a couple. Nan, still a femme-loving butch, was with a femme woman, while Debi and Susie, who were both bisexual, had partnered with men. Because of the bi-phobic climate within gay culture they both were relatively closeted about this at OOB—at least in print. Moreover, people in the office, as well as our magazine readers and Fatale viewers, debated how, when—or even if—it was okay for men to see Blush Entertainment content (the umbrella name for Fatale Media and On Our Backs magazine). Susie once hinted at her bisexuality in an On Our Backs editorial by revealing that someone had asked her, "Did you inseminate or did you party?" to get pregnant and she replied, "I partied."

DEVELOPING A BUSINESS MODEL AND INCREASING PORN SALES

I loved the video arm of Blush Entertainment. One day I overheard Debi, Susie, and Nan having a heated conversation about money and sales. Soon, the office door swung open and Debi stomped out, coming over to our box of free magazines and catalog mailers from other companies, stuff that often ended up in recycling. She wrestled an armful of the material into a pile that she delivered to my desk with a *thunk*. Debi grabbed a highlighter, flipped pages, and ripped open mailers to show me how to find businesses that might distribute our products. She told me to look past the naked dicks and tits to find out who was an adult store or mail order business. Some ads were less graphic, in which case Debi taught me how to use my creative-writing imagination to read euphemisms to understand they were selling porn or sex toys. We looked for gay stores and women's bookstores that might be willing to sell our products. After that, I was the one circling ads and names, carefully searching listings big and small. I opened up mailers filled with porn images and found an order address or the toll-free 800 numbers. I searched to find names and contacts, and then called 411 to get phone numbers when there wasn't a number in print. Distributors were not going to come to us. If we wanted to make money, we needed to seek them out and pitch our products.

This is how I sold Fatale movies wholesale to businesses. I cold-called every mom-and-pop adult backroom across America. Often, the guys on the other end of the phone laughed at me or at our high prices. One guy said, "Hey, chickie, I already got lezzie stuff. What's so different about yours that makes it so special?" I said, "It's real lesbian sex. We fuck!"

At the time many "lesbian movies" had women doing a few sex acts, but in my opinion, as a lesbian viewer, they didn't fuck. Or, if they did fuck, it didn't look realistic or wasn't a turn-on for me. The ciswomen in these films rarely wore harnesses, and if they did, it was some ugly elastic band thing *and* they wore it wrong.

Among the many successes in marketing and distribution for Fatale Media, there were some failures. Countless times, for example, Nan, Susie, and Debi tried and failed to get *On Our Backs* or Fatale movies onto Olivia Cruises[2]—even as free gifts. They never could go to Michigan Womyn's Music Festival. They were unsuccessful in getting Fatale Videos into the Film Festival circuit. We realized that explicit depictions of lesbian sex made even some lesbians nervous.

One day in early May 1993, I walked through the doors of the Good Vibrations retail store on Valencia Street to get sex toys to use as props for the Fatale movie *Safe Is Desire*, a safer sex movie for lesbians. A very helpful and good-looking clerk waited on me. I never got her name, but she seemed interested both in me and in the film production. I walked out of the store with a bag of goodies as I made promises of onscreen thanks. Weeks later, I found myself face-to-face with that same woman at Club Cream at Eros, the place that was going to be the set for our *Safe Is Desire* shoot the next day. She kissed me and we fucked. We fell in love. The next day I went back in Good Vibrations with lollipops in my hand and a question on my tongue: "What's your name?"

She grabbed me by the back of my head, pulling me half-over the counter for a long wet kiss, right in front of customers and her co-worker. She said, "Jackie, and you are Shar, right?"

Jackie and Shar would always go together after that.

Jackie found herself on the sales floor of Good Vibrations providing the same sex education lesson for certain topics over and over again—like G-spots, pregnancy, and anal sex—especially anal sex for men wanting to be fucked by their female partners.[3] Was there another way that we could get sex information into the hands of the people who needed it the most?

What Jackie and I really wanted to do was make movies. One day Jackie said, "Fuck it. Why are we working all day for other people? Nobody wants to do what we want to do. Let's work for ourselves. We are starting our own business."

HOW WE MADE RADICAL DYKE PORN

Jackie

Shar and I came of age during the Reagan years, and held the hands of comrades who were dying of AIDS. We saw first hand that sex didn't just stigmatize you, it could also kill you. We were under full frontal assault from government organizations and from our own community for being queer and for demanding that our government recognize there was an epidemic that was killing our friends. We faced criticism for publicly insisting that women are sexual beings who should be in charge of their own reproductive rights, that queers deserve to live without fear of death and brutality, and that making porn expressing our actual sexual desire was not violence against women or harmful to others, nor was it aping the patriarchy. From the Meese Commission in the early 1980s to the lesbian sex wars, we had to fight for our right to have an orgasm on our own terms, and not from the vantage point of someone else's mores or laws. We saw making porn as an opportunity to create greater gender equality in the world of erotic imagery.

To make our films, we found real-life couples that were interested in documenting their sexual desires onscreen. We often cast our friends who loved fucking and being part of a political movement. Our crew, too, was made up of our friends whose day jobs involved making documentaries and teaching film and sound at local universities.

We had to rent Avid editing suites, big Betacam cameras, and lots of equipment from Adolph Gasser Photography in San Francisco. We also had to pay for studio time for mixing and postproduction. Easy-access editing software and MacBooks did not yet exist. Ultimately, as we continued, movie-making technology advanced and we used the three-chip camera, Final Cut, and Pro Tools. We were able to edit, render, and create on our own. This meant we no longer had to rent editing studios and we could take that expense line item off of the budget. Changes in technology helped create the conditions where more—and different kinds of—people could now make porn. For us, these technological changes meant that in the span of three years we were able to film, edit, produce, distribute, ship, and market more than seven feature movies.

Shar

With our minds made up to make porn, we made lists of topics that people often asked for help with at Good Vibrations, topics that we found ourselves talking the longest about with customers because they needed the most information. People wanting to know about the G-spot already had Debi Sundahl's *How To Female Ejaculate* movie. Pregnancy would require finding extra-special explicit performers. That left us with the topic of men who wanted to be anally penetrated by their female partners. No educational film existed that tackled this subject. Plus, we really liked the idea of lesbians teaching heterosexual men about receiving penetration. We also knew that if we started with this film, it would sell and we could use the money we made from queering straight sex to fund our dyke porn empire.

This was 1996. Jackie and I looked for investors for eighteen months to make *Bend Over Boyfriend.* We were rejected and laughed at by everyone, with people telling us that no one would want a movie about straight men getting it in the rear. Our plans stalled. The following year, however, Nan Kinney came back to California for a visit. I sat in her tiny black pickup truck and talked her into doing her first project involving men. I told her how much times had changed since she started Fatale in the early 1980s, and if we made this movie, people—well, her lesbian customers, specifically—would not hate her or desert Fatale Media.

Nan signed on the dotted line for a loan from Joani Blank, the founder of Good Vibrations. Joani wouldn't loan money to Jackie and me, because she knew that we couldn't pay her back if our movie did not sell. Nan, on the other hand, was in a position to pay Joani back even if the movie failed financially. This was 1998, and as it turned out, there was no need for anyone to worry. *Bend Over Boyfriend* sold like sweet tea in August. Like hotdogs at the pennant. Like Magic Wands at a Betty Dodson convention. We literally could not keep up stock with our duplicator. To give you an idea of what this meant: Jackie and I were on tour at the time, me with the spoken word troupe Sister Spit, and she with her band, The Hail Marys. One day, we walked into a bar in New Orleans where the friend of a friend had left a message with the bartender saying that Good Vibrations was out of *Bend Over Boyfriend*. The folks at Good Vibrations talked with other businesses and everyone was running out. I called Nan immediately, yelling over the drunk people in the bar and telling her that she needed to get shipments out fast, promising to cover extra UPS fees.

In those days, before the rise of e-commerce, you had to hope that mail-order catalogs would carry your title. This was almost the only way to ensure sales. The steps went something like this:

Get money for production.

Make movie.

Send screeners to buyers for stores and mail order catalogs.

Follow up with calls and beg them to carry your movie if they were not familiar with your work or if you did not have an established reputation.

The title "buyer" often meant the "everythinger" at a small business. Bottom line: One way or another, you needed to get a commitment that your flick would be included in their catalog and carried in their store.

We got on the phone and sold directly to buyers of companies. We relied on their mail order catalogs and retail locations to push our movies to customers. Catalog print runs were scheduled months ahead, so we made sure we knew deadlines of places like Good Vibrations so we could hand them product to be included in that catalog. Artwork and a screener were rushed to editors and reviewers personally so we could count on publicity hitting and preorders to happen, then we had to guarantee the initial run of covers and replicated videos from Los Angeles. From there:

Negotiate wholesale price.

Find out catalog art deadlines and selection deadlines.

Get them everything they need.

Duplicate and ship VHS videos.

Wait for their catalog to be printed and sent out seasonally.

Wait for it . . . wait for it . . .

And, hopefully, get paid within three to six months.

It was a very different business era than what exists today, one where marketing and sales were dependent on the U.S. Postal Service rather than blogs, Facebook, Twitter, and Tumblr. There were no Internet sales or online catalogs. Some stores, including Good Vibrations, had a call center, but that was only one step faster than sending an order envelope and a check through the mail.

But here's the thing: With *Bend Over Boyfriend* Jackie and I owned 25 percent of something for the first time in our lives. I was no longer that working-class girl having nightmares of pushing a timecard at the factory door. I was running a business.

Jackie

After *Bend Over Boyfriend*'s success, we embarked on our mission of making explicit lesbian content, this time with our own brand of hot dyke fucking. With films like *Hard Love & How to Fuck in High Heels* and *Sugar High, Glitter City* we made images that no one had seen before: butch dykes strapping it on and anally penetrating their femme lovers; butches getting fisted by their femmes; we featured drag kings and an Asian Daddy and fierce femme-on-femme fucking. We showed real lovers having real orgasms and talking a dirty blue streak while making no apologies for their sexual desires. Our films were homages and tributes, perverted testaments to butch/femme sex and erotic desire. We considered the porn we were making to be feminist manifestos. And with all of it, we contributed to the growth of independent erotic cinema that was developing in San Francisco, and where there would later be another wave of queer porn fueled by a DIY and feminist porn ethics.

Our company, SIR Video (Sex, Indulgence, and Rock 'n' Roll), helped usher queer porn into the sexual mainstream. Back then the adult industry didn't know what to do with us or how to categorize our films. As a result, our first award nomination for *Bend Over Boyfriend* was placed in the category "Best Specialty Tape." It was still the age of VHS, and "male anal" wasn't an award category. A "how to" movie in which men were anally penetrated by their female partners was, almost by default, just called "specialty." Two years later, in 2001, we continued to blaze trails by being the first independently woman-owned, dyke-owned company to win an AVN Award for "Best All-Girl Feature" for *Hard Love & How to Fuck in High Heels*. Known as the "Oscars of Porn," we were officially recognized by the adult industry for our filmmaking and innovation. The vibe in the room in Las Vegas the night we won was confirmation that something was burgeoning and momentum was growing. Technology would soon allow more artists and performers to make pornography, and sex-positive retailers like Good Vibrations were helping to create new distribution channels. The general public had increasing access to acquiring alternative sexual content. Our movies were not just culturally influential and critically acclaimed, but they also sold well.

This was back when VHS was still king. DVDs emerged around the same time that SIR debuted, which meant that for several years we had two revenue channels for one movie.[4] Even before Video On Demand (VOD), Google, and social media platforms like Facebook and Twitter, our movies got attention. Reviewers wrote about us in industry trade magazines and local weekly newspapers. Shar and I contacted every sex-positive feminist store from coast to coast to find distributors for our films. We hustled and did everything we could to promote our movies through mail order catalogs, zines, film festivals, screenings, and word of mouth among our queer peers.

Shar

It was a crazy, great time. The checks came in and, unlike production among most mainstream porn producers in the San Fernando Valley, Nan agreed that Jackie and I could make *Bend Over Boyfriend 2: More Rockin', Less Talkin'* under our own company name.[5]

In 1999, we made BOB 2, which had a radically different process for casting than the first one. With *Bend Over Boyfriend*, casting (just like funding) took a lot of effort. We looked for real couples to star in BOB; and even if we had the money or wanted to hire professionals from "Porn Valley," the men acting in straight porn movies at the time would not have done anal sex—even with a female partner. This posed some issues for casting talent. First, out of the general population there were only so many women who were curious about fucking their man up the ass. Second, there were even fewer who actually did it. Third, there were even fewer who did it and who happened to know us or know we were casting for a movie about pegging. Casting, therefore, was done largely by word-of-mouth. We didn't have the luxury of the Internet or social media. We also didn't want a bunch of people who wouldn't take the project seriously, so we did not advertise in newspapers. We told our network of sex-savvy associates and friends, which included local prostitutes and dominatrixes, that we were making a movie about pegging. We wanted our performers to be passionate about sex and about promoting queer imagery. It was a job, sure, but not in the typical sense.

Money, it seemed, was always in short supply. In fact, Jackie's band, The Hail Marys, had a song about "doing business on a payphone." While it might have seemed to some like a prison reference, the song was actually about us. We had spent every single dollar we had, and had not paid our phone bill. I stood on a busy street corner at Fell and Gough haggling over prices of the costs of goods on a pay phone, playing it cool when delivery trucks roared by, saying, "Sorry it's so loud—it's boiling hot here in San Francisco—I'm standing by an open window." We did whatever we needed to do to make and sell our films.

We shot *How to Fuck in High Heels* in twelve hours on one day in one studio at 320 Fell Street in an old doughnut factory. Drag queens, hustlers, the latest DJs, cabaret performers, and even politicians sashayed down the haphazard hallways. The studio we shot in had skylights, so chasing the natural lighting was a constant challenge. Our sound person hated us because Jackie kept yelling, "Boom in the shot." We dressed and redressed a simple backdrop and a massage table. We spent all of our money on the crew, on our cast, on lights, and on sound. Our crew consisted of local filmmakers and production people who normally worked on documentaries. We usually had a film student as an assistant. They were very handy to have on set because they got equipment for free from their universities. They would have to lie about that, of course, and act like they were making their own epic film. We never had insurance on set. Jackie and I have never had good credit or credit cards, so it was usually Phyllis Christopher who used her credit card to check out the professional lighting equipment that we rented. We were, to be sure, a real DIY operation. We depended on our own chutzpah, and the good will of others, to bring our dyke visions to life.

LOVE LETTERS TO SAN FRANCISCO

Jackie

We think of our lesbian movies as love letters to San Francisco. When we began our porn adventures, we had a funky old art space on Fell Street. That space is now home to a fancy start-up and a charcuterie that serves San

Francisco's nouveau riche of the tech boom. In those days, though, we lived in a space populated by artists, photographers, and various denizens of the *demi monde*. Raging Stallion Studios hosted its naked porn star photo shoots there. Dan Nicoletta took pictures of Sylvester and Divine there before they passed away, and we shot most of our movies there. We loved, laughed, plotted, and partied in that space. We knew it was a special time of dyke glitterati and butch-femme renaissance. Do-it-yourself artists of every stripe added to San Francisco's rich cultural and creative life.

In 2000, things started to change. Our landlord was in the midst of being committed to a retirement home, and her homophobic nephew was pursuing eviction for us all. Our old landlord was an androgynous bohemian artist who loved that their building was filled with renegades and rule breakers. But our slummy Shangri La came to an end when we got evicted by the descendants and fled our beloved San Francisco with our pit bull in tow. Because we didn't have to pay rent we ended up spending a long delayed honeymoon in Sydney, Australia, after being invited to the Mardi Gras Film Festival. Our movies had toured the queer film festival circuit, which was a first for any porn production company, and we were often invited to appear at the screenings. Our movie, *Hard Love & How to Fuck in High Heels* packed the theater. Women howled and hooted as images of dyke sex and dildos exploded onscreen. We took it as a compliment that theater-goers were canoodling and getting intimate while still in the theater. But not everyone was pleased. Outside in the lobby following the screening I was accosted by a woman who accused me of not being a "real lesbian" since I wore a dildo in the film and, according to her, "acted like a man."

This was before transgender awareness really existed, and dildo use—at least in the eyes of this particularly militant lesbian—was seen as a tool of the patriarchy. There were so many stereotypes about lesbian sex—even among lesbians. We were supposed to engage in slow 69'ing while waterfalls and butterflies swirled in the background. There was not much variation or diversity about what the sex lives of lesbians were supposed to look like. We wanted to change this.

I took a breath and said, "Yes, I have dildos. Many actually." I explained that not only do I do fantasy play, but dildos are an extension of my body; they are my cock. They are also a way that I make my lover come. The sex act is not about my cock, it's about her orgasm, and the cock is a means to her pleasure and orgasm. The woman then asked why I engaged in blow job activities and fucking someone while they were on all fours. I replied that it's hot, it feels good, and that's how we like to have sex. I also told her that my gender identity and hot buttons are not hers—or maybe they are and she hasn't allowed herself to explore it yet. At this point her lover, who had been standing next to her during this exchange, turned purple. The exasperated look on her face let me know that this was not the first time they'd had this conversation.

I share this story because putting our sex lives on screen for all to see meant that sometimes people did not like what they saw—and they were not shy about letting us know. Lesbian porn pioneers Nan Kinney and Honey Lee Cottrell from *On Our Backs* and Fatale Media fame have similar stories about confrontation, negotiation, and making porn during the height of the feminist sex wars. As butch pornographers we shared the need to narrate our love and passion on our own terms.

Shar

Fatale Media was actually the first company to have a lesbian porn film accepted at Frameline Film Festival. It was 1985 and the film was *Private Pleasures and Shadows*. Fatale presumed that because it was a first there were probably some dykes on the curating panel who thought explicit representations of hardcore lesbian sexuality, including SM and butch/femme relationships, should be shown. There were so few films, on any subject, made by lesbians at the time that perhaps that was the reason the review panel gave it the nod. *Private Pleasures and Shadows* screened at the legendary Castro Theater that year.

The screening was sold out, and the films elicited strong responses from those in attendance. People either loved them or hated them. I'd heard Susie and Nan's version of events, but the story is essentially the same: women hissed and threw things at the screen and stalked out to the lobby where Nan was cornered at the merchandise table. Fatale had T-shirts, VHS copies of their films, and posters for sale. Nan was verbally attacked with antiporn vehemence. I remember her laughing when she recalled it decades later, saying, "Hey, I would have understood if they had complained about the production quality!" Nan lived to tell the story, and eventually crawled out from under the merchandise table to enjoy pats on the back from supportive audience members, who were blown away to see lesbian images that they could relate to and that entertained them.

Today, when Jackie and I travel around the country to screen our lesbian clip show *Lesbo Retro: A Dyke Porn Retrospective*, which features footage of lesbian sex made by queer women from the 1960s through the early 2000s, I use this moment as an opportunity to talk about female pleasure. When casting, most feminist pornographers want to know what performers enjoy doing sexually. Finding these things out in advance helps to ensure that we are doing everything we can to capture genuine pleasure on set. For example, we will do everything we can to have the correct size dildos and a Magic

Wand plugged in and at the ready if that's what our performers like. Jackie and I always wrote our shot list keeping the performers' preferences in mind. Why have Betsy Butch do an anal scene when she loves oral sex? And why ask Felicity Feelgood to do a dyke-dick blow job if she loves anal? Our mission was to capture real queers having real queer sex on camera. In order to do that we first needed to know what made our performers tick sexually.

Before casting our performers we did interviews to find out what they loved to do sexually, what they would love to try if they had the chance, and what was absolutely off limits. And finally, we always asked, "What gets you off? What do you love?" For many women having a whole hand in her pussy, usually while she receives stimulation to her clitoris, was the answer. The Fatale movie *Shadows* shows fisting for precisely this reason (even though today many pornographers avoid fisting scenes due to concerns with obscenity prosecution). Fatale wanted to show real lesbians having sex the way they would if the cameras weren't rolling. The reality of lesbian sex—what it actually looked like and the pleasure it could produce—were simply not images that were readily available or accessible in the 1980s and 1990s.

Both Fatale Media and SIR Video wanted to challenge preconceptions about lesbian sex, and we used pornography as a vehicle to do this. For us, our pleasure and our bodies are our politics. That was lesbian porn to us then, and this attention to both politics and pleasure remains the driving force of much feminist and queer porn that is made today.

Jackie

The last film that Shar and I co-produced was *Healing Sex*, of which I am extremely proud. The movie is a mind-body approach to healing from trauma and abuse using somatic practitioner Staci Haines's work in her book by the same name. Haines's work, and our film, strives to help survivors loosen the chains of sexual triggers that inhibit their ability to experience pleasure, find love, or even be mentally stable. We finished this sexually nonexplicit feature right before we started having children and stopped making movies altogether.

Shar and I always knew that before we could entertain people with sexual imagery, we had to educate them. We needed to give viewers permission to experience and receive pleasure. As the late erotic writer Marco Vassi once said, to fuck without reverence is the greatest sin. When I look back at my career as a lesbian pornographer, I am perhaps most proud of giving the people who watched our films permission to be unapologetically sexual in whatever lusty and queer way they wanted. To me, that's revolutionary.

NOTES

1. *Off our backs* remained in print from 1970 to 2008.

2. Olivia Travel was created in 1988 after Olivia Records, which was created in 1973 to circumvent the male stranglehold on music, was no longer financially viable.

3. Now called "pegging," this sex act did not have a name at that time. The name came from a public vote via Dan Savage's "Hey Faggot" newspaper column.

4. VHS and DVD sold simultaneously very well until DVD ultimately won out.

5. Nan acted with honor, breaking the capitalist tradition where the person who pays for it owns all. *Bend Over Boyfriend* was our creative project to nurture and trademark.

9

Good Vibrations, Women, and Porn: A History

Carol Queen

In the summer of 1990, I received a phone call that changed my life. It was from Joani Blank, the founder and owner of Good Vibrations, a women-focused sex shop in San Francisco. Joani, a sex therapist and author, had started Good Vibrations in 1977 to provide women with an alternative to the stereotypical adult stores, places that many women openly admitted they were uncomfortable in and reluctant to patronize. Good Vibrations was different; it was cozy, like a living room scattered with sex toys, and many women (myself included) had made pilgrimages there. From the get-go, Good Vibrations was as much about sex education as it was about getting vibrators into the hands of women. Much to my delight, she was calling to offer me a job.

Good Vibrations was certainly one-of-a-kind, but it wasn't the very first woman-focused sex shop. Fortunately, neither has it been the last.

The first female-centric sex business in the United States was Eve's Garden, founded in 1974 by Dell Williams.[1] Dell was a businesswoman and feminist who'd gone to Macy's in New York City to buy a Hitachi Magic Wand—"the Cadillac of vibrators!"—only to be sexually harassed in the personal care aisle and taunted with "Whaddaya gonna do with *this?*" Dell vowed to create a space where women could access "personal care" items of pretty much any sort without the hassle and shame. A scant few years later, Joani, working with a group of sex educators and therapists led by Lonnie Barbach,[2] head of a groundbreaking program at the University of California, San Francisco medical school to treat preorgasmic women, heard the umpteenth woman say she "could never go into one of *those* places"—referring to an old-school dirty bookstore—to buy a vibrator, and Good Vibrations was born.

Good Vibes' distinctive model was influenced by Joani, her early staff, and also by San Francisco, a singular cultural space for sex-related institutions to flourish. In the late 1970s, when the idea of sex-positive cultures was still in its infancy, Good Vibrations could not have been established anywhere else, really. It joined sister institutions San Francisco Sex Information, the Institute for Advanced Study of Human Sexuality, the Women's Building, the sex-focused counseling Center for Special Problems, and many other recently developed professional or activist organizations that focused on sexuality.

Good Vibrations opened in the Mission District where it joined a neighborhood that already included a woman's bookstore, a women's coffeehouse, a women's bathhouse, and women's bars. Word about this new "friendly, feminist, and fun" sex store spread to various communities that were united by a common sexual interest, like the Bisexual Center, the lesbian BDSM club Samois, clubs for other BDSM players (including the largest, the Society of Janus), Bay Area swingers who met for parties at Barry and Shell's,[3] and many others.

Even though this was a time and place in which the prefix "women's" was often code for "lesbian," one could browse Good Vibrations regardless of one's sexual orientation and interests. The original store was tiny, with relatively few items for sale: several vibrators, a smattering of other toys,[4] sensuality products like massage oils, some books, and erotic literary journals. Men would come to shop occasionally, popping their heads in like Kilroy to ask something along the lines of, "Can I shop here too? You know, I don't like *those* places either."

Eventually Good Vibrations began carrying a few items of special interest to men, though for the longest time they were an afterthought. As much as men might have needed a space like Good Vibrations, women needed it even more. Whether other sex stores were not aesthetically pleasing to women, or led them to feel unsafe from unwanted sexual attention, or because women weren't raised to think they had a right to sexual pleasure, the fact that Good Vibrations was women-owned and women-focused was, at least in the 1970s, nothing short of revolutionary.

NO PORN MOVIES HERE, WE'RE FEMINISTS

When Joani Blank started Good Vibrations, she had no intention of carrying porn. Joani didn't really like porn—and she didn't think other women did, either. Porn was already a fraught issue among feminists when Good Vibrations was founded, and the passing years only made it more so. Early feminist media-focused activism like that of Women Against Violence in Pornography and the Media was an important part of helping women (and everybody else) understand that the media we consume sometimes carries problematic messages. But before long, feminist media activism refocused to specifically work against porn; now the focal organization was called simply Women Against Pornography. Antiporn feminism became practically synonymous in the popular mind and media with feminism itself. The late 1970s kicked off the sex wars, a time when feminists were at each others' throats arguing about not only pornography but other contested sexual practices: BDSM, sex work, butch/femme lesbian identities, even penetrative sex with dildos—all of which were constructed as "anti-feminist." In 1982 the often-bitter disagreements came to a head at the Barnard Conference on Sexuality in New York City, a deeply controversial day of discussions about nonreproductive sexuality that included antiporn activist picketers and the "outing" of individual women's sexual practices. It was no wonder Joani wanted the little utopia of her clean, well-lighted place to be far from those disagreements.

But Good Vibrations was also democratically managed. This meant that Joani's employees had a strong say in the decisions and direction of the business. Staff members could set their own salaries, and Joani didn't just hire clerks; she wanted the women behind the counter to be active participants in the goals and direction of the company. By the time I arrived in 1990, we were a fairly diverse lot: older, younger, gay, straight, and bisexual. One of Joani's staff members, Susie Bright, hired in 1981,[5] was a rising star in the world of women's sexuality. A sex-positive feminist icon, Susie Bright edited *On Our Backs* magazine (subtitled "entertainment for the adventurous lesbian"); she also wrote for *Penthouse Forum*, and had begun to do movie reviews for them.[6] Susie was inspired by one of her girlfriends, the photographer Honey Lee Cottrell, who showed her plot-driven, X-rated movies that were made in the 1970s, before video technology brought sex movies out of the porno theaters and onto the home VCR. Susie liked a lot of what she saw and felt the story of "the Golden Age of Porn"—when filmmakers were sure explicit films were about to become an accepted genre—was very much worth telling.

Susie's role was to convince Joani that not only had visionaries begun to make women-centric porn, but even made-for-men pornography could be seen through a woman's eyes and recontextualized, especially the high-concept films of the Golden Age. Susie soon developed a clip show-with-lecture titled "How to Read a Dirty Movie," which she toured around from city to city. Through this work, Susie became a well-known and highly respected voice of porn analysis, someone whose influence was felt far beyond the lesbian community and borders of San Francisco. On top of that, she worked with Joani to develop *Herotica*, a book of female-written sex stories.

Eventually Joani could see the writing on the wall. Susie was right: There was increasing interest in diverse forms of sexuality and sexual imagery. One paradox of the AIDS years, whose fearsome repercussions engulfed San Francisco, was an increasingly audible discourse about sex and erotic practices. What antiporn feminist Andrea Dworkin thought of as always-harmful material was now listed as a safer-sex alternative in brochures about how to avoid HIV. Additionally, the community of women who identified as "sex-positive" feminists was emerging, many of them women who had been shamed by other feminists for their own sexual identities or interests, and many others women who themselves were porn performers, or sex workers of other stripes. This was the backstory of the Good Vibrations I joined in 1990.

When I arrived in July of that year, Susie had been gone for just a few months, leaving as the fruit of her efforts the inclusion of movies in Good Vibrations' book catalog, The Sexuality Library. I was newly interested in porn myself, thanks to my studies at the Institute for Advanced Study of Human Sexuality and its notorious pedagogical tool, the Fuckarama.[7] I observed that Joani was still no fan of porn—and she never would be. But plenty of our customers had become avid explorers of sexy movies. Susie had left us a curated collection of pornography videos, and she continued to add notable titles even after she was no longer on staff. The collection was eclectic and included almost all the women-made movies that existed, including rare titles like the Austin, Texas-made dyke porno *Waking Up*, which featured (among more explicit scenes) butches and femmes doing a line dance. There were the sexy art films of Annie Sprinkle, Susie's favorite Golden Age dramas, like *The Opening of Misty Beethoven* and all the other Henry Paris/ Radley Metzger flicks in the great XXX director's filmography. Notable newer movies included favorites *Cafe Flesh* and *Smoker*; a couple of gay male movies, including the classic *El Paso Wrecking Company*; transsexual feature *Sulka's Wedding*; and even a few R or NC-17-rated sexy classics that put everything else into context. As the 1990s went on, Susie added plot-based films, like the acclaimed *Masseuse*; explicit educational fare by a number of filmmakers, including porn performer educators Nina Harley and Ona Zee; and female favorites like the films of Andrew Blake, which were so visually beautiful that many women drooled over them the way they might catalogs of beautiful home furnishings or sexy shoes. And, of course, the collection included anything new produced by X-rated feminist foremothers like Candida Royalle's Femme Productions and Fatale Media.

Candida Royalle, a performer and Golden Age porn starlet, had created Femme in 1984 to develop erotic movies specifically intended for women's enjoyment. She drew on her own porn experience but also recruited the brightest of a newly vocal group of feminist porn performers, like Annie Sprinkle, Gloria Leonard, and Nina Hartley. Her films were aesthetically beautiful and sought to depict sex in the context of women's whole lives. Fatale Media, founded in 1984, was closely linked to *On Our Backs* magazine and drew upon the feisty, sex-positive lesbian community in San Francisco. It was particularly important to Good Vibrations that we had women-made porn to offer. But equally notable was the fact that Good Vibrations served as a significant distributor for these movies. Very few porn stores were even willing to carry such films, as women were not yet seen as especially relevant customers for pornography.

Susie—as well as Good Vibrations' customers—had many favorite stars. The notion that porn performers were dragooned into doing humiliating and damaging acts was a staple of mainstream feminism, egged on by the beliefs of antiporn radicals who couldn't conceive of a woman having sex on camera simply because she wanted to. By this time—the early 1990s—Susie, and some of the rest of us, had met many of our porn-performer favorites, like Nina Hartley, Gloria Leonard, Annie Sprinkle, Veronica Hart, Vanessa del Rio, Jeanna Fine, Richard Pacheco, and John Leslie, among many others. Most of these performers turned out to be thoughtful and well-spoken people who had made a home in porn either by accident or by design. They had come to enjoy the creativity, the exhibitionism, the sex, and the First Amendment activism that performing involved. Customers, and Good Vibrations staff alike, sought performances that looked genuine, like real expressions of pleasure. We appreciated actors who could deliver their lines—not to mention scriptwriters who wrote good lines for them to deliver. We liked seeing solid characters for the naked thespians to bring to life. One thing many of the women who rented movies at Good Vibrations sought was diversity. They wanted films that depicted a range of body types. Then, as now, slender, big-breasted women were well-represented in porn, but not all of our customers were entirely happy about that. Women also told us they wanted to see more attractive men in the movies—there was too little diversity there, too.

All this information was shared with Good Vibrations staff as part of our regularly occurring Continuing Education sessions. Here Susie (and later her successor Roma Estevez) would show video clips and talk about salient elements of each newly added video. The goal was to give sales staff the information they needed to talk to customers about the porn collection with ease and confidence. Information was also shared between staff and customers through a special video notebook, which sat in the store near the video shelves. Anyone, including customers, could peruse the notebook, or add their own reviews.

Today, anyone wishing to give feedback on a particular video, or on porn in general, can find a place to do it online. But before the rise of the Internet, the opportunity to make your preferences known in any sort of public forum—especially for women—was rare. I loved flipping through the notebook during slow store hours, seeing my favorite films through other people's eyes. Controversial elements—like the abduction scene in *Behind the Green Door*—were hotly debated on its pages. People often told us who their favorite performers were, and why (e.g., good acting, sexy, believable).

Acting, sexual performance, and the ability to depict genuine sexual pleasure and passion were among the criteria for the curated Good Vibrations film collection. We also looked for smart, interesting, or especially sexy scripts. Diversity, both in terms of performers and of the sexual practices they depicted, also was important. When Susie chose something controversial, which was occasionally the case, she came to the store and told staff why she had picked it. She did not want to coddle her viewers, and often selected dramatic, challenging films because these were among the best ones in the genre.

Susie stopped curating the video collection just about the same time that Joani took her experiment in democratic management to the most extreme, and, some may argue, logical, conclusion. In 1992, she sold the company to her staff, and Good Vibrations became a worker-owned cooperative. It made sense that we would have an in-house representative to sift through new films and, in concert with a team of reviewers, choose additions to the video library. That person was Roma. A movie fan and a great communicator, she was able to glean information constantly about what her fellow worker/owners and our customers wanted to see. One of the questions she had to contend with was, "What do women want?"

While all sorts of people rented and purchased porn at Good Vibrations, the video collection was always curated with women in mind. We were interested in knowing what they rented for solo viewing, to watch with friends, to share with partners. In general, women wanted to see movies in which the sexual pleasure of women performers was given its due. We quickly discovered, however, that a lot of women—of all sexual orientations—really liked gay male porn, which featured beautiful men and generally no women characters at all. We sought out more of these films to add to the collection. Other customers favored the bisexual movies—more pretty men, but with female characters included too. But bi movies were a subset of gay male porn. (Because these movies included men having sex with men as well as women, gay pornographers almost exclusively made them.) Plus, the women performers in them sometimes felt less like focal points and more like additions to the gayboy main event.[8] Candida Royalle's movies were justly popular. Women also responded strongly to movies with plot lines, as though it was preferable to watch a story in which one knew the roles and relationships of the people who were having sex onscreen. It is possible that women (then if not now) were especially willing to watch erotic movies—including very diverse kinds of content—if only they had an idea about *why* these people were fucking in the first place.

We valued the feedback we got from customers and, whenever possible, tried to accommodate their requests for certain types of films, featuring certain kinds of people and certain types of sexual acts. It remained the case, however, that we were limited in terms of what we could offer based on what was being made by most porn production companies. For women as porn consumers, as Gertrude Stein might have said, there was no—or at least hardly any—*there* there.

SEIZING THE MEANS OF PRODUCTION

In 1998 two of my Good Vibrations colleagues, Shar Rednour and Jackie Strano, and I took the role of customer feedback to a new level. It was part of our job at Good Vibrations to help customers purchase all kinds of sex gear, including dildos and harnesses. We began to notice that there was one kind of customer we saw surprisingly frequently: men and women who wanted to buy a strap-on so that she could anally penetrate him. (Well, who knew so many straight and bisexual people did that?) And although it didn't even have a name back then—it's now known as pegging—*Bend Over Boyfriend*, the movie we made with my partner (and anal expert) Robert Morgan Lawrence, helped launch this practice into the public eye and gave people helpful information that was focused on both safety and pleasure.

Bend Over Boyfriend, while not made by Good Vibrations, was inspired by the kinds of interactions that our sales staff regularly had with customers. It was the first and only nonlesbian movie that Fatale Media produced, and it literally would not have been made if Shar, Jackie, and I were not Good Vibrations staffers. We were aware that there was no comparable resource available for people wanting to learn about this nontraditional form of sexual intercourse and anal play. Of course it would have been possible to write a "how to" guidebook; but an explicit movie allowed for all the explanations a book might include, plus visuals. We knew how popular the sex education videos were with customers who wanted to try new erotic practices, and Shar and Jackie were sure that this was a topic that had an audience.

Bend Over Boyfriend was not my first explicit role. My very first time in front of a camera happened back when I was a student at the Institute for Advanced Study of Human Sexuality; I joined a group of women to make a women's safer-sex movie called *Latex and Lace*. I appeared in other explicit movies as well. They were mostly either "ex-ed" movies[9] or alt-porn. *Carol Queen's Great Vibrations*, produced by Good Vibrations founder Joani Blank and inspired by Good Vibrations customer discussions, was a show-and-tell about using vibrators.[10]

I thought of my role in these movies as bringing my sexological training to the screen. I tried to show authentic sexual responses, and to model for viewers how they could communicate about sex. I also liked the camera—I didn't write a book called *Exhibitionism for the Shy*[11] for no reason! I valued the opportunity to blend accurate information and authentic sexual representation with my enjoyment of performing. As I would soon learn, however, not everyone felt comfortable in front of a camera, a point I return to below.

At the request of Good Vibrations, I also began to create clip shows for special events like National Masturbation Month.[12] Watching porn in public is rarely done any more, and it was always interesting to gather people together at San Francisco–area theaters like the Castro, Parkway, or Roxie to watch such a show. For most of these events I worked with then Good Vibrations staff member Sarah Kennedy, who has a background in filmmaking. My favorite show was a big Castro Theatre extravaganza celebrating the Silver Anniversary of the Golden Age of porn. For this, I collected favorite scenes from Golden Age movies and invited a panel of notable stars such as Chris Cassidy, Richard Pacheco, Jamie Gillis, and others.

I worked even more extensively with Sarah and other Good Vibrations staff members when we decided to develop our own movie company, Sexpositive Productions, which made its first film in 2001. Sexpositive Productions was a way for us, as a company, to address the fact that we saw far too few good porn movies featuring bisexual characters and plots, big women performers, diversity, and various kinds of "ex-ed"—all things that customers constantly asked us for. Too often, diversity in mainstream porn took the form of fetish videos. If fat women or older women, for example, were going to be depicted sexually, there would often be disrespectful plot lines, titles, or cover art referencing their performances and bodies. We wanted to address these absences and insults and find new—better, more respectful, and more realistic—ways to represent otherwise underrepresented groups of people. We knew how hurtful or alienating it could be when people who were not accustomed to seeing themselves and their own sexuality depicted on screen watched porn, only to then feel further invisibility.

Diverse and respectful representation was an intentional part of Sexpositive Productions' agenda. It was also necessary, given our company's mission, to work with amateur performers who were not professionals in the industry, and who hailed from various sexuality communities. Sometimes these performers were sex workers or burlesque performers who had some pre-existing level of comfort creating and projecting an erotic persona. Other times, they were sexual enthusiasts who wanted to help us create new and different kinds of porn.

Our first Sexpositive Productions movie was *Slide Bi Me*, a bisexual picnic romp created by a then staffer who went on to have an academic career. The film was nominated for an award—Best Bi Feature—at the Gay AVN Awards show in 2002. Bay Area bisexuals came out in droves to be cast; but finding amateurs who were comfortable performing in front of the camera was not easy. Not just anyone makes porn—no matter how inspired the idea may seem in theory—partly because not just everyone feels comfortable being naked and having sex in front of a camera. And you really *can't* control human sexual response entirely. For example, our movie about the G-spot and female ejaculation, *G Marks the Spot*, starred a number of women who were squirters—but just not on camera. We discovered that for some, the intensity (and perhaps pressure) of appearing in front of the camera sometimes resulted in performance anxiety even when a person was a happy sexual explorer and excited to be there.

Sexpositive Productions cast community members in its movies. We looked for sexually adventurous people who were eager to help promote a sexual style they felt strongly about and identified with. Most of the time, these people were not porn professionals. Some had made one or two other explicit films; many never made another porn movie after their Sexpositive Productions role. To cast them, we had to try to determine whether they really would be comfortable in a sex movie—not just in front of the cameras while we were shooting but over time, including after the film was released. We interviewed potential cast members to try to determine this kind of comfort level. We were also looking for diversity. One of our biggest complaints about mainstream porn was that it included less racial diversity than we wanted to see. We were also invested in showing diversity of body type, too. We wanted to represent a wider range of humanity than we often saw in porn and to do it with respect.

As time went on, many more individuals and small porn companies emerged to make the erotic material that was meaningful to them and to their communities. Shar Rednour and Jackie Strano created their own company, SIR Video, and continued making films. Christopher Lee created *Alley of the Tranny Boys* and other movies starring transmen. Joseph Kramer began making ex-ed for gay men with his Erospirit line. In the era just before it became possible to utilize the Internet to bypass the need for a store, catalog, or distributor, Good Vibrations became a de facto collector and unofficial distributor of indie porn—and we carried as much as we could. But the economics of selling porn, with a high retail mark-up and enough return for the filmmaker, proved to be challenging. "Alt porn," like the kind Sexpositive Productions was making, was almost always more expensive to produce than mainstream studio porn made by companies with the capacity to press exponentially more copies of a movie and sell it everywhere porn was sold. It became clear that we needed a true distributor of alt material to make it more likely that we'd have the diverse porn we wanted to see. But the economics of this were never right; no one entrepreneur or company could make enough money distributing such a small number of these movies to make a viable business of it.

Since that time—from the late 1990s into the beginning of the new century—the economics of all porn production and distribution have changed dramatically. Anyone can put a webcam in their bedroom and produce sexually explicit content. On the consumer side, many people download porn for free, which exacerbates the financial problems of even the largest companies. Large or small, a company spends a lot of money producing content and risks losing much of its economic value to piracy. Today, it is harder for any company producing or distributing content to make the economics of porn work for them. Alternative kinds of porn—such as queer porn and feminist porn—are often made as activist projects, because people do not see themselves represented onscreen and therefore feel a need to create more diverse and varied representations.

Good Vibrations ceased being a cooperative in 2007, and the new management has devoted more economic and staff resources to making the kind of porn that Good Vibrations' customers continue to request. We created Good Releasing in 2009 with three component brands—Pleasure-Ed (offering "a wide range of informational and instructional content to inspire and enhance your sex life"), Reel Queer ("documenting authentic, edgy, queer sex and culture with relevant, intelligent films inclusive of the many sexualities that identify as queer"), and HeartCore ("offering artistic alternatives to formulaic features with films by independent artists with fresh, diverse content"). These films add diverse new offerings to the still fairly small number of alternative porn films that exist. In an effort to cater to customers who want educational movies, queer porn, and more-or-less-heterosexual alt porn, we've made even more movies that explore various facets of sexuality, working with porn professionals as well as with amateurs. Our educational titles include *Going Down*, *Heads Up*, and *Gush* (about cunnilingus, fellatio, and the G-spot and ejaculation, respectively); Reel Queer films include the *Roulette* series, *Speakeasy*, *Bordello*, and *Nostalgia*; and HeartCore titles include *Dangerous Curves*, *Mandy Candy*, and *Behind the Red Door*. Porn auteurs Madison Young and Courtney Trouble have made a new generation of porn far more inclusive of the identity spectrum, which is now represented by the term "queer"; I scripted and host the Pleasure-Ed movies; and porn industry alt-luminaries like April Flores and her late husband Carlos Batts made the movies *they* wanted to see: artistic beauty and hot sex in a racially and body-diverse context. Working with a critical mass of feminist porn creators, sex workers, sex community people, and porn stars, we've collaborated on a new generation of explicit material that Good Vibrations' staff and customers sought to see way back when Susie Bright was still choosing films. We also continue to seek out and carry extraordinary porn made by others, like the movies of Shine Louise Houston's Pink & White Productions and Jennifer Lyon Bell's Blue Artichoke Films.

For queer, feminist, and alt porn, increasingly, there is a *there* there—a critical mass of interest, audience, performers, and material facilitated by the growth in sexual identity communities, the rise of other women's and queer sex toy stores, the Feminist Porn Awards, the Internet, and the ever-growing profile of porn performers and directors who tweet news about their lives, work, and projects. In many ways, it's a great time to be interested in porn. Still, the challenge of selling it and making the economics pencil out persists. What's more, antiporn perceptions and activism still surround the business, in and out of Good Vibrations.

For us to have great porn, the kind of sexual entertainment that turns us on and reflects our interests, our bodies, our politics, and our lives, this critical mass of interest and availability is crucial. When we regard porn as an entertainment medium and expect the best of it, some of that porn gets better and better. That's what I've learned in over twenty years at Good Vibrations of watching, selling, and helping to make pornography. Open discussions about and even critical interest in erotic media will result in more content that is of interest to women, men, and everybody else.

NOTES

1. Lynn Vanucci, *Revolution in the Garden* (Santa Rosa, CA: Silverback Books, 2005).

2. Barbach is a sex therapist and author whose bestselling books include *For Yourself: The Fulfillment of Female Sexuality* (originally published in 1976).

3. Barry and Shell's was the San Francisco Bay Area's preeminent swinger's club, a venue that held couples-based sex parties on weekend nights.

4. In Good Vibrations' early days the dildos that were for sale weren't displayed on the sales floor, but had to be requested.

5. Karen Calabria, "Good Vibrations—The Life and Times of Sexpert and Feminist Susie Bright," *Kirkus Reviews* 2011, https://www.kirkusreviews.com/features/good-vibrations-life-and-times-sexpert-and-feminis.

6. Susie Bright, "The Birth of the Blue Movie Critic," in *The Feminist Porn Book*, ed. Tristan Taormino, Celine Parreñas Shimuzu, Constance Penley, and Mireille Miller-Young (New York: The Feminist Press, 2013), 32–40.

7. I wrote about my reactions to the Fuckarama, which involved a great many porn movies watched simultaneously, in my essay "The Four-Foot Phallus," collected with my other personal essays in *Real Live Nude Girl: Chronicles of Sex-Positive Culture* (San Francisco/Pittsburgh: Cleis Press, 1997, 2002).

8. While women almost always had sex with women in most mainstream porn films, no one really characterized these films as "bisexual," and the plot generally did not emphasize these relationships. Bisexuals wanted films that reflected their interests, identity, and personal connections—not just hot same-sex action.

9. I call these films "ex-ed"—explicit educational—to differentiate them from the genre of sex education movies with a white-coated doctor holding a pointer and explaining the reproductive system.

10. I also shot two movies with Libido Video, one a dramatized erotic story from an issue of *Libido* magazine, the other a couple's enhancement video; and, alone or with my partner Robert, I also signed on for a few videos produced by mail order sex giant Adam & Eve, whose Sinclair Institute how-to movies covered various sexual practices.

11. Carol Queen, *Exhibitionism for the Shy* (San Francisco: Down There Press, 1995, 2009).

12. In 1995 Good Vibrations declared May to be National Masturbation Month to honor former United States Surgeon General Dr. Joycelyn Elders, whose statement regarding masturbation got her fired. Each May, Good Vibrations develops programming and events intended to raise the profile of solo sex.

10

Trade Associations, Industry Legitimacy, and Corporate Responsibility in Pornography

Georgina Voss

> We're a sex positive company that tries to portray porn in a good light. Our company is about goodness and I'm very, very proud of that.
>
> – Dan O'Connell, owner of Girlfriend Films.[1]

If legitimacy is the yardstick for corporate social responsibility,[2] what does responsibility look like in an industry that many consider to be socially deviant? Pornography, together with tobacco, arms, and alcohol producers, is part of a select group of controversial industries whose products and services elicit reactions of "distaste, disgust, offence or outrage."[3] Its benefits—sexual pleasure, consumer satisfaction, employment—are rarely openly discussed; instead, pornography is more often spoken of in terms of harm: harms to those who consume it, harms to those who appear in it, harms to wider society.[4] The ways in which the adult industry elicits moral outrage have been extensively debated. At the most extreme ends, pornography is pushed into the outer limits[5] to become associated in the public eye with an array of illegal and deviant activities including child exploitation, human trafficking, and drug addiction. Despite—or perhaps because of—the fact that the industry appears to be mainstreaming[6] it remains contentious, the center of moral panics around the pornification of society and the sexualization of young people,[7] and untouchable by many mainstream institutions.[8] To achieve legitimacy, the porn industry would need to create the social perception that they are "desirable and proper within some socially constructed system of norms, values, beliefs and definitions."[9] But is this an unlikely goal when its most extreme critics describe the industry as "what the end of the world looks like"?[10]

Controversial industries disrupt many conceptions about what responsible business behavior looks like. While the literature on corporate responsibility clearly delineates the "bad" corporate citizens who are routinely excluded from lists of companies with the best Corporate Social Responsibility (CSR) reputations,[11] many of these so-called bad guys also produce corporate citizenship reports, which muddies the waters.[12] Socially responsible behavior allows companies to legitimize their activities while demonstrating to shareholders that they are "doing the right thing."[13] But evaluating what is "right" rapidly becomes troubled. To their critics, these sectors can never be truly socially responsible because the very nature of their existence is to create offerings that are harmful to humans, society and the environment;[14] to their supporters, these same businesses create jobs, bring in tax revenues, and create products that their consumers enjoy. The nature of ethical violation of social norms also varies by industry.[15] For example, the weapons industry's deadly output has historically been legitimated both through government agencies and appeals to patriotism.[16]

All industries have a variety of stakeholders, including customers, employees, shareholders, and pressure groups, whose perceptions of harm vary across different stakeholders[17] and may only be visible with hindsight,[18] yet whose different concerns and pressure shape how managers conceptualize corporate responsibility.[19] The social construction of the cultural norms that shape notions of "distaste, disgust, offence and outrage"[20] are fluid and context-dependent, allowing controversial industries to wander between legitimate and illegitimate identities. In this complicated space, ethical practices become compressed, challenging, and contradictory. Controversial industries are forced to conceptualize corporate responsibility in a much narrower manner by only responding to a small group of stakeholders and understanding that they are unlikely to achieve the corporate legitimacy that they strive for.[21]

In this chapter I move behind the scenes to explore notions of stakeholder responsibility in the pornography industry by examining the practices of three of the sector's most historically influential trade organizations: the now-defunct Adult Industry Medical Healthcare Foundation (AIM); the Free Speech Coalition (FSC); and the Association of Sites Advocating Child Protection (ASACP).[22] My specific interest is to ascertain how the organizations' concepts of responsibility both align with and detach from harms identified by its critics. These concerns range from the transmission of sexually transmitted infections (STIs), to the exploitation of performers, to the production of child pornography. To do this I first review the specific accusations of harm leveled at the mainstream pornography industry by various critics, including antipornography feminists and AIDS healthcare advocates. I then identify the stakeholders to which industry members hold themselves socially responsible. Finally, I assess how rhetoric and practices of responsibility and legitimacy play out in this industry through the work of these trade bodies, each of which focuses on issues specific to the adult sector: health of performers in a space where condom use is minimal (AIM); legal protection in producing and distributing sexually explicit material as framed by the First Amendment (FSC); and clarification of the difference between legal pornography and illegal child abuse images (ASACP). By exploring how each organization addresses these different issues, I demonstrate that "responsibility" is not a homogenous concept in this stigmatized sector but is instead driven by multiple, intersecting, and sometimes contradictory considerations of protection and legitimacy.

Trade organizations are useful ways of conceptualizing the scope and framing of responsible business practices and priorities within a sector. Their emergence marks the structuration of a field as members become aware of the need to determine a common enterprise.[23] By embedding these processes in formal structures, trade associations can facilitate and reinforce normative institutionalization processes.[24] These bodies can also enable collective action, which is more effective than acting alone.[25] This is an important factor for controversial industries, as questions of legitimacy and threats of state intervention apply across the entire sector, not just to individual firms.[26] In addition, AIM, FSC, and ASACP also have predominantly represented the mainstream pornography industry, at which most of the criticisms are targeted. By exploring their actions within the context of the wider industry, I ask the following: To whom does the contemporary pornography industry hold itself socially responsible, and how do these responsibilities manifest?

PROBLEMATIZING "HARM" AND "RESPONSIBILITY" IN PORNOGRAPHY

Pornography and harm are both fundamentally fluid concepts,[27] yet controversial industries have pariah status imposed on them by the harms their actions allegedly create (or are perceived to create). Entangled in the broader rhetoric of moral panic and culturally specific contexts of "the language of condemnation,"[28] the harms attributed to porn are often socially constructed and principled in tone, and fall broadly into two camps.

Firstly, the production of pornographic content is accused of causing harm to those who appear in it. This line of argument draws on broader debates about consent, exploitation, and physical and emotional health and rarely draws on the lived experience of performers themselves.[29] Female performers in particular are painted as pitiable and abused, coerced into the industry to perform "degrading" acts not representative of "normal" sex.[30] These women are presumed to have been abused as children, engaging in drug use, and mired in a host of psychological problems when compared to women outside the adult industry.[31] Journalism professor Robert Jensen has drawn on conversations with performer and director John Stagliano to argue that the increasingly hardcore tropes of pornography are directly responsible for increased health risks, with performers financially pressured into doing "weirder and weirder stuff"[32] if they want to continue working in the industry.[33]

The second group of harm addresses a much wider range of stakeholders including consumers and civil society. These harms are allegedly caused by exposure to pornographic material. This line of debate is embedded in moral panics that are based on perspectives concerning the intersections of communication technologies and sex, in which porn—like video games, television, and music[34]—can deterministically create wide-sweeping and damaging changes in behavior and social attitudes. Stephen Maddison describes how arguments for greater control of online porn position it as a "corrupting flood," which have the "quality of a biblical plague—abundant, malevolent, mysterious."[35] Much of the blame is laid on the allegedly corrupting depictions in pornography, which its critics argue are produced for the heterosexual male gaze and depict women in ways that are at best passive and at worst dehumanized. Mainstream porn has indeed historically been targeted at straight male consumers, displaying female performers at the center of sexual activity. Noting that the top-selling adult films in the United States depict aggressive acts inducing a response that is either neutral or pleasurable (as defined by the researchers[36]), porn's critics also argue that these representations are transforming into more hardcore gonzo tropes. The term "gonzo" was originally used by the industry to mean an unscripted style of production but has been reappropriated by antiporn scholars to denote material as distinguished by low production values, minimal storylines and "raw and disturbing" depictions of sex.[37] While gonzo—under this reframed meaning—has only been developed by a small number of contemporary producers, notably Max Hardcore and Extreme Associates, antipornography scholars argue that its very existence is the result of the market need to create novel forms of content to satisfy consumers tired of existing offerings.[38]

Establishing causal links between porn consumption and changes in attitudes and behavior, particularly propensities to sexual violence, has been problematic and inconclusive.[39] Instead, a discourse about pornification has emerged, encompassing claims about the ways that Western mainstream culture references pornography through its languages, codes and cultures, and the subsequent ways in which people—particularly young women—are turned into sexual objects potentially without their consent.[40] Yet the rhetoric in these debates demonstrates the challenges in trying to assign a locus of responsibility for the asserted harms of pornographic content. As Clarissa Smith states:

> When pornographication links together Bratz dolls, pornstar T-shirts, Playboy key rings, pole dancing, lads mags, push-up bras for teenagers, breast enlargement, breast reduction, vaginaplasty, Viagra, the sexual self-representations of sexblogs, sexting, Beautiful Agony and Suicide Girls, anime and hentai, burlesque, *Cosmopolitan* magazine, a photograph of Miley Cyrus in *Vanity Fair* and the photographs from Abu Ghraib, Max Hardcore's prolific output, TV programmes like *Girls Gone Wild*, *Sex and the City* and *Porn: A Family Business*, we should be ringing alarm bells at the conflation and supposed obviousness of the connections, not wringing our hands and looking to government for solutions.[41]

Defining the boundaries of any industry—and thus the subjects of its responsibilities—is an imprecise art. Much of the online porn that critics classify as corrupting is uploaded by amateurs and content thieves whose actions have demonstrably reduced rather than boosted the pornography industry's revenues; but in doing so they have also made pornographic material available to a far wider audience than a core group of paying customers. The pornification debates also extend the blame for promoting the tropes of pornography in mainstream creative industries—film, advertising, music—while continuing to blame the porn industry for creating those tropes in the first place. While a heterogeneous mix of content producers are responsible for the porn industry's core product, their practices are embedded in complex global supply chains that encompass a variety of auxiliary services. These include legal support, hosting providers, and mainstream media conglomerates. Examining the tactics of the pornography trade associations, themselves markers of the structuration and maturity of the industry, provides a way of identifying which of the sector's stakeholders its members recognize and address their responsibilities towards.

PRODUCTION PRACTICES IN CONTEMPORARY PORNOGRAPHY

The contemporary pornography industry lies at the center of debates about harms to performers and harms to society, with rhetorics of harm around porn often drawing on fears of a "massive profit-making industry of pictures and words acting as pimp"[42] with enormous turnover and reach. The reality is

more mundane. The core of the North American industry originally developed around Los Angeles in the 1960s and continues to center there. It col-
locates with the mainstream Hollywood movie industry, although porn has,
over the past two decades, shifted further north into the cheaper region of the
San Fernando Valley. Although there is an overlap in the activities and workers in both sectors around aspects of film production, porn continues to be the
more marginal and socially illegitimate of the two and has been dubbed "The
Other Hollywood" by members of both industries to reflect this difference.[43]
The industry profited enormously in the early days of the Internet where the
low barriers to entry and an eager consumer market for online porn made it
possible for industry newcomers to make enormous sums of money with little
effort (or knowledge of either the industry or wider business practices); but
those same factors came back to bite the adult industry in later years as their
customer base and profit margins were savaged by waves of free online content and tube sites.[44]

The current porn industry cluster in Los Angeles comprises several major
content production studios, other media organizations and service providers, and the trade associations themselves. Their activities include creating
content, hosting and distributing it via online or offline means (e.g., DVD,
video), developing online payment, hosting and traffic monitoring tools,
marketing and cross-promotion (predominantly via the affiliate program
scheme), and providing auxiliary legal and financial services.[45] The industry's stakeholders include performers; owners of the various types of companies in the sector, and their employees; customers; the local community
in Los Angeles; and members of the wider general public. The stakeholders that are notably missing are public shareholders, as, unlike companies
in other industrial sectors, very few porn companies have been publically
traded.

Most of the accusations of harm are targeted at the content producers,
encompassing both labor conditions for performers in which they are treated
with a lack of empathy and respect, and exposed to harms to their physical
and mental health; and representations in the content itself that reflect these
working conditions.[46] Addressing falling revenues might seem to be a higher
priority for company owners than addressing these criticisms, yet the two are
often intertwined. A cluster of independent porn producers have emerged
creating alternative, queer-, and female-positive material, which, like gonzo
content, arguably meets consumer needs. Antiporn critics claim that alt- and
feminist porn is still networked into systems of capitalist and cultural production, responding to and shaped by the discourses of the mainstream pornography industry even when positioned as an alternate to it.[47] These critics
further claim that independent porn remains economically and culturally

marginal.[48] In response, porn director Tristan Taormino argues that, in the U.S. sector, there is no clear discreet division between alt-porn and the mainstream, but instead there is a great deal of overlap between production styles, performers, and producers.[49]

Some of the larger mainstream production studios have developed strategies that, intentionally or not, address some of these criticisms around their responsibilities to performers. For example, Vivid Entertainment Group, founded in 1984, is reputed to have worked deliberately to overcome critiques about harms to both viewers and their female performers. Vivid Girls are reputed to be the "best paid and most powerful performers in the industry."[50] The content turned out by the studio also embodies an upscale aesthetic that, David Slayden argues, helps establish the company's products as "safe and mainstream."[51] Many other production companies have begun to introduce behind-the-scenes material, including blooper reels that allow the audience to look behind the camera to see the mundane aspects of pornographic content production. This also creates opportunities for actors to express how they are indeed aware of the limits of the roles and fantasies that they are expected to fulfill, and their own reactions: humor, disgust, enthusiasm, frustration, and sometimes just the sheer boredom of the work itself.[52]

The actions described above are, however, atomized into different production houses. More wide-scale, coordinated efforts to regulate content production have been transitory. Alec Helmy, founder of the adult-focused media organization XBIZ and other affiliate sites, set up the Best Practices in Adult Video (BPAV) initiative in May 2006.[53] When launching BPAV, Helmy invoked the need for industry self-regulation as a means of both improving employment practices and creating legitimacy:

> Considering the amount of scrutiny the adult industry receives from the government and the media, it behooves video producers and content providers to run their businesses ethically. At AVN, we always felt that protecting the working conditions of the performers was of paramount importance, but difficult to monitor . . . the industry needs to set an example and send the message that working in the adult business can be a positive experience.[54]

BPAV advocated several practices targeted at improving the relationship between performers and producers including a Disclosure of Acts stipulation, whereby producers would inform performers of the types of acts they would be asked to do on set.[55] However, despite gaining initial encouragement from content producers and the Free Speech Coalition (FSC), the initiative quietly ended several months later.

There has been no unionization of workers, performers or otherwise, in the industry's history. A number of sex-work advocacy groups exist, including the Desiree Alliance and the Sex Workers Outreach Project-USA, but these predominantly support the rights of escorts and prostitutes—those who have consensual sex with clients for money rather than adult film performers.[56] In addition to avoiding self-imposed controls, the industry has also continuously shied away from top-down government initiatives that would regulate its activities. As *Hustler* editor Ira Levine stated, "This industry . . . has some rather unusual characteristics, one of which is strong resistance to outside intervention."[57] Trade organizations have emerged to take on the collective issues faced by adult film companies. In doing so they occupy a challenging position: representing the interests of a group who want their needs met, but are deeply suspicious.

ADULT INDUSTRY MEDICAL HEALTHCARE FOUNDATION

The Adult Industry Medical Healthcare Foundation (AIM) was founded by Sharon Mitchell and Steve York in 1998 and, until its closure in 2011, provided healthcare services to performers in the adult industry. These services included STI testing, gynecology services, general health check-ups, and educational material. The organization's primary focus was the health and well-being of performers—individuals who were at a much higher risk of contracting STIs due to their number of sexual partners, and the amount and type of sexual acts they performed. In doing so AIM also responded to the needs of studios by enabling content production to continue without widespread transmission of STIs.

AIM's approach to healthcare provision was underpinned by the core supposition that the majority of pornography studios would not use condoms in production[58] because it was both impractical for the types of frequent, intense, and sometimes unusual sexual acts that performers engaged in, and also would allegedly lead to revenue losses. Any healthcare strategy that was targeted at the industry would therefore have to work around this fact. Mitchell had spent over two decades working as a pornography actress before retraining as an HIV and chemical dependency counselor following a near-fatal accident in 1996. AIM was established shortly thereafter during one of the periodic outbreaks of HIV across the industry. At that time, in the late 1990s, there was no centralized or industry-enforced system of STI testing. The Free Speech Coalition contacted Mitchell requesting that she investigate the outbreak because she was one of the few people connected to the adult industry who had the "special combination of clinical awareness and sensitivity to the population"[59] necessary to take on the investigation. Mitchell set up a small clinical office in the Sherman Oaks suburb of Los Angeles in a room donated by a modeling agency that had prior experience engaging with sex workers. After determining the "Patient Zero" of the outbreak,[60] Mitchell transformed the clinic's temporary activities into a permanent fixture by founding AIM. Due to Mitchell's experience and standing in the industry—a community which, despite claims of its size, is small and tight-knit—AIM rapidly became the primary testing facility for industry performers, testing up to 2,000 people per month.[61] While much of the healthcare system in the United States is privatized, few production companies provide performers with healthcare insurance plans, so the costs of testing at AIM were split between the patient and the film studio. The organization developed the AIMCheck database that stored testing results and made them available to both performers and producers.[62]

The mental health of performers was also addressed by AIM. Through her prior work in the industry, Mitchell was skilled in recognizing emotional stresses that performers experienced. As the organization expanded, it provided additional services including drug and alcohol counseling, psychiatric assessments, counseling referrals, and group workshops about "Life After Porn."[63] The latter program included "porn scholarships" for performers who wanted to transition out of porn and into mainstream work.[64] Newcomers to the industry were also given a "Porn 101" DVD that provided them with information about what this line of work would involve. Mitchell made use of the centrality of AIM within the adult industry—and the trust that it had earned with performers—to challenge the "Damaged Goods Hypothesis," systematically testing it against the self-report of actresses who used AIM's services.[65]

Mitchell had always been pragmatic, even critical, when speaking publically about the industry's lack of condom use. As a medical professional, Mitchell understood that mandatory condom use was the most effective form of STI prevention; she also acknowledged, based on her inside knowledge of the industry, that such state-sanctioned measures were likely to force production either out of state or further underground.[66] In the context of the adult industry, AIM argued that they were providing the most effective healthcare they possibly could, and that as a result of their work, the rate of STIs among adult performers was actually lower than the wider average of sexually active young people.[67]

AIM's eventual downfall and closure in 2011 was brought on by a clash with the AIDS Healthcare Foundation (AHF), ostensibly over the differing perceptions of their harm reduction ethos and methods, and those of wider campaigning groups. Prior to this conflict, California's Occupational Safety and Health Administration (Cal/OSHA) had occasionally targeted production studios for health violations,[68] but AIM had managed to go about its business relatively under-the-radar.

In 2009, this changed when the Los Angeles arm of the AHF, led by Michael Weinstein, began to target the local pornography industry, demanding that they use condoms as part of Cal/OSHA regulations on occupational safety and health standards. AHF employees and supporters picketed the AIM offices, made formal complaints about AIM's procedures to several federal and state government agencies, and provided the financial and legal resources for two former adult performers who sued AIM for alleged violations of privacy law.[69] AIM and other industry members maintained their position that enforcing condom use would not protect the health of performers, and argued that AHF's true intention was not to protect adult actors but instead to drive the porn industry out of state, thereby earning fame and plaudits from antiporn activists. In February 2011, AIM attempted to stave off L.A. County regulation of nonprofit clinics by shifting from nonprofit status to a private healthcare provider, AIM Medical Associates PC. But its problems were not over; three months later AIMCheck was hacked and, in what became known as Porn Wikileaks, many confidential medical and personal records were leaked.

Exhausted from the firefighting around Porn Wikileaks and financially compromised by the legal costs from subpoenas, AIM was weakened; and in May 2011, the organization closed and filed for bankruptcy. Following its demise, porn industry blogger Gram Ponante declared, "No successor that can guarantee the performer privacy, medical competence, and medical and legal savvy required of such a lightning rod has asserted itself."[70] As Ponante suggests, AIM had occupied a unique place in the industry, born of a crisis specific to the sector and run by an insider who was able to garner sufficient trust to address the industry's issues while being openly critical of them.

AIM's activities partially aligned with the industry's critics in that it recognized that there were physical health risks associated with the labor of a performer; it also identified the stigma surrounding the industry itself and associated difficulties in finding work outside the industry. However, AIM didn't prevent the types of specific sexual activities themselves from happening (although Mitchell herself identified the changing modes of performance) and, critically, chose to posit its services around the lack of condom use in the industry rather than campaign for their use.

"THE INHERENT RIGHT OF ADULTS TO BE ADULTS"[71]

The Free Speech Coalition (FSC) is the pornography industry's main trade body, and much of its work has been targeted at ensuring that the production, distribution, and sale of pornographic materials (including content and sex toys) can continue lawfully and profitably. As such, the organization poten-tially holds responsibilities to all of the companies in the sector who create and sell sexually explicit materials—including production studios, retailers, and other distributors—and the performers themselves.

The FSC was founded in 1991, following a merger of the Adult Video Association and the Free Speech Legal Defense Fund.[72] The organization is funded through a combination of the membership fees of its estimated 750 members, sponsorship, and donations.[73] In a sector with rapidly chang-ing business models and technologies, the FSC is considered one of the old guard by dint of its longevity. Although relatively small, it is respected and influential.

As its name and history suggests, the FSC's main ethos and strategies have been to fight for the freedoms guaranteed in the U.S. Constitution under the First and Fourth Amendments. The organization aligns its identity with organizations that represent the rights of free speech and civil liberties.[74] The group's early activities included lobbying over the Federal Labeling Law in 1994, and constitutionally challenging the amendment of the federal Child Pornography laws in 1997. The battles continued into the next decade with the 2002 U.S. Supreme Court virtual child porn case, *Ashcroft v. Free Speech Coalition*. This case was taken up after Congress had expanded the definition of "child pornography" in the Child Pornography Prevention Act of 1996 to include computer-generated images and those which appeared to give the impression of minors engaging in sexual activity. After arguing that these definitions were too broad and could potentially have a chilling effect on legitimate work, the FSC won the case, resulting in a decision that struck down the two provisions because they abridged the freedom to engage in a substantial amount of lawful speech. In addition, the FSC filed ongoing complaints against the Department of Justice about the 18 U.S.C. § 2257 regulations,[75] arguing that they endangered the performers' safety and privacy by allowing private information to be accessed through the record-keeping process, and that the regulations were overly complicated such that pornog-raphy producers would be unable to fully comply with the record-keeping system. The FSC also contains a legislative affairs department that lobbies on behalf of the industry at local and national levels, and informs its members of potentially threatening legislative trends. The lines of argument in these legal challenges and lobbying activities have focused on principles around the erotic freedoms of consenting adults in content production and the need to protect the privacy and safety of performers. The organization brands itself by emphasizing patriotism and free speech, using playful stars-and-stripes imagery and anticensorship rhetoric. The FSC firmly opposes government interference, declaring "the inalienable right to liberty includes the right to

explore consensual forms of sexual variety and information free of government interference."[76]

Against a constantly shifting landscape of technological change, the FSC
expanded its remit around supporting the "growth and well-being of the adult
entertainment community" into digital spaces. Following the financially dis-
ruptive effects of tube sites, which were featuring pirated content, the FSC
developed the Anti-Piracy Action Plan (APAP) in 2011. APAP acts as a
mega-affiliate scheme that enables tube sites to generate revenue through
sales, which are then split among the sites, the content providers, Vobile, and
the FSC itself. The plan also includes a litigation component enforceable via
video and screenshot evidence, and distribution of Digital Millennium Copyright Act (DCMA) take-down notices[77] through DCMA's evidence packets.

The second arm of support from FSC emerged following disruption within
the industry itself. After the demise of AIM, FSC worked with the FBI to
analyze AIMCheck for signs of breaches before setting up the Adult Protection Health and Safety Services (APHSS) in May 2011.[78] When Los Angeles
introduced Measure B onto the voter's ballot that would make condom use
mandatory in the industry, the FSC coordinated the "No on Government
Waste—No on Measure B" campaign to take on the initiative proposed by
the AHF.[79] The FSC campaign framed the issue as a waste of government
resources and damaging to the local economy. The FSC noted that the porn
sector contributes an estimated $1 billion and 10,000 jobs to the local econ-
omy, the loss of which could not be afforded by a county where unemployment rates were 12 percent and 4 percent higher than the national average.[80]
"We can't afford the condom police" ran the campaign's tagline at the FSC
stall at the 2013 AVN Expo, illustrated by a man in full bright yellow protective biohazard clothes and brandishing a camera.

As is the role of trade organizations, the FSC reflects the opinions of its
members, ascertained through its Board of Directors who represent all facets
of the industry including performers, directors, CEOs of production studios,
Internet service providers, and representatives from the toys and novelties
sector. At her interview for the Executive Directorship, Diane Duke was
informed by the panel that it was unlikely that any one person or organization would be able to organize the industry in a top-down manner; instead
the industry members would define the issues perceived to be important and
the FSC would then follow that lead.[81] The organization makes statements
about the issues, with which its members broadly agree, such as opposition to
18 U.S.C. § 2257 regulations. However, it has remained neutral on issues that
are more divisive within the industry, such as the content of adult films and
whether content production companies should provide group health insurance. The FSC developed a Code of Ethics for its members in 2009 that

covers aspects of respecting self-determination, protecting minors, safeguarding privacy, implementing professional business practices, promoting social responsibility, and enhancing the industry and its profession. Adhering to these strictures currently remains voluntary.

Some of FSC's activities appear to align with the harms identified by the industry's critics, albeit indirectly. The crackdown on content piracy could be viewed as a way of limiting the amount of content online (although still encouraging high sales volumes), and the organization has also taken on further responsibilities towards the health of performers since the demise of AIM. However, much of FSC's work is diametrically opposed to the opinions of antiporn activists in that the organization actively and visibly campaigns for the very right of the industry to exist and create sexually explicit material containing self-policed representations—as is their constitutional right under the First Amendment.

ASSOCIATION OF SITES ADVOCATING CHILD PROTECTION: PROTECTING CHILDREN ONLINE

The Association of Sites Advocating Child Protection (ASACP)[82] occupies a curious place in the pornography industry. By working with a network of prominent mainstream partners it has achieved levels of recognition and legitimacy that are unusual for a body so closely entwined with pornography; yet this same engagement with the mainstream has not always endeared the organization to actors within the adult sector. Unusually, the organization stakeholders are located both inside and outside the pornography industry and include children who are sexual abuse victims; customers—and would-be customers; and companies that profit from the online sale of pornographic material.

ASACP was founded in 1996 by Alec Helmy. Initially set up as a voluntary organization, its focus shifted with the appointment of its first executive director, Joan Irvine, in 2002. Like FSC, ASACP is also funded through the fees of its members in the adult industry, sponsorship, and donations. It remains a small-staffed enterprise, which was co-housed within the XBIZ offices for several years. Its scope is international, however: In addition to the U.S. advisory board, ASACP also has a European advisory board whose members span content production, billing solutions, and affiliate programs.

The primary aim of ASACP is to eradicate child pornography (CP) from the Internet. In doing so the organization intends to educate the wider public about the efforts of the online adult industry to tackle child sexual abuse,[83] and thus legitimize the industry by working with government bodies to track and report illegal child abuse material, and providing a stamp of approval on approved "clean" adult sites. This two-fold approach underscores the reasons why the organization was founded: Populist assumptions imply an inherent link between the (legal) pornography industry and the (illegal) production of child abuse materials. The need for separation is reflected in the name: originally titled *Adult Sites Against Child Pornography*, the organization later renamed itself (while maintaining the acronym) to remove any possible association with CP. Tackling this assumed association required the industry not only to differentiate and distance itself from criminal activity, but also to openly demonstrate a commitment to stopping it altogether.

Following her appointment Irvine led the development of a multifaceted strategy for the organization, designed to demonstrate that porn could be proactive in addressing issues related to CP rather than simply react to incoming legislation. An Approved Members program was set up to provide reassurance to customers and support for adult Web sites. Once a Web site was approved as "clean" (i.e., contained no CP-related images or text) and the owner paid their membership fees, they were permitted to host an ASACP badge on their sites. ASACP also developed a Code of Ethics, which, unlike the FSC's codes, is mandatory for its members. Much of the code, unsurprisingly, focused on the age—both real and perceived—of performers, as well as viewers of the site.[84] ASACP's code also, however, asks that its members enforce ethical behavior beyond the boundaries of their own firm by "reviewing sites which direct traffic to your site and parse those which feature Unacceptable Terms" (including the terms "Lolita" and "sex with minors") and "Do business with companies that comply with the ASACP Code of Ethics."[85]

In addition to self-regulation, ASACP also encouraged wider reporting of CP by setting up an online hotline, linked to all member sites. Suspect material is then passed on to government agencies, including the FBI and National Center for Missing and Exploited Children. ISPs and payment processors are also informed when their services are used to host this suspect material. Finally, the organization founded the Restricted to Adults (RTA) Label, which allows Webmasters, for a fee, to label their sites as containing "age inappropriate content." The RTA Verified system is portrayed as a way of circumventing heavy-handed and hostile government legislation. As the site states, "No one wants a complicated and mandatory government website label created by the people who want to put you out of business."[86] In contrast with this portrayal of invasive compulsory regulation, the RTA Label is described as "voluntary, easy to use, and it won't interfere with existing tags or traffic—it will just help keep kids off your site!"[87]

ASACP's position in the adult space is unusual and sometimes uneasy. The organization is strongly networked into the mainstream through its work with Internet service providers, charities, and government agencies, more so than the other trade organizations or indeed many of its members. It has also been lauded by the same entities for achieving what are—for a body so publicly associated with pornography—quite extraordinary levels of praise and recognition, garnering several awards including the Associations Advance America 2005 Honor Roll and the California State Assembly Certificate of Recognition. In 2008, Irvine herself was awarded the Certificate of Congressional Commendation by the U.S. House of Representatives. Yet, while these accolades may go some way toward legitimizing ASACP in the mainstream, they do not necessarily have the same effects on the way that the organization is viewed by the industry itself. ASACP provokes a range of responses. At its best it is viewed as doing good work, both in terms of CP reporting and improving the reputation of the adult industry. But, at worst, the organization is viewed as only being out for itself, caring more for accolades than for the industry itself. An element of these responses is born from the difficult space from which ASACP operates: Unlike the tangible activities of FSC and AIM, which directly contribute to the well-being of the industry—both firms and performers—ASACP's work is intended to indirectly support the sector through increased social legitimacy and customer trust. It can be difficult to see the direct impact of this work on the bottom line of revenue streams.

The departure of Irvine from the organization in 2011 exacerbated some of the criticisms around ASACP's perceived loyalties. Irvine left to take up an executive position with the International Foundation for Online Responsibility (IFFOR), the not-for-profit group responsible for monitoring the controversial .xxx domains,[88] which, during her tenure at ASACP, she had vocally opposed.[89] The move raised questions about which stakeholders in the industry Irvine—and by extension ASACP—held responsibilities toward given how harmful the .xxx domains were perceived to be, and how they were being implemented without engagement with the adult industry.[90]

Of all of the trade organizations, ASACP has targeted the broadest range of stakeholders external to the industry and received the largest amount of external validation. It has also directly engaged with the argument that conflates illegal child abuse with legal pornographic content; and, through its membership program, has also gone some way toward regulating the terms used to market pornography. Like the other trade organizations, however, ASACP does not target the nature of the content produced by the pornography industry, nor the conditions by which it is produced.

BUSINESS AS USUAL?

The pornography industry continues to be an extremely controversial sector. As a result, the trade organizations within it are located on a "different legitimacy battlefield"[91] where their actions are balanced and divided between ensuring the continued existence and financial well-being of companies in the sector; caring for the physical and mental well-being of performers; and creating legitimacy for the industry as a whole.

As the representatives of a controversial industry, AIM, FSC, and ASACP have indeed been forced to conceptualize their responsibilities in a narrow manner, responding to a small group of stakeholders. FSC and ASACP are both membership organizations and have, accordingly, targeted their primary responsibilities to the adult companies who make up their member base; and both have also been clear that they only speak for these members and not the wider industry.[92] AIM and FSC's care for performers can also be seen as an extension of the responsibilities toward production companies by protecting the health of the men and women in front of the cameras and sharing this information with their employers. However, looking after the well-being of performers also carries value in its own right as was particularly apparent in AIM's programs around mental health provision and support for future career development.

Stigmatised organizations can find it difficult to openly work with mainstream bodies, and the porn trade associations themselves are subject to "stigma-by-association" effects from the industry that they serve and represent.[93] These issues extend to the manner in which the organizations have less engagement with stakeholders external to the industry. AIM provided sexual healthcare services for members of the local public, although this was an extension of their existing work rather than part of their core purpose and was framed as a general form of healthcare provision rather than anything specifically related to or supporting pornography. ASACP is unusual in having undertaken responsibilities to several external stakeholders. Their work comprises a complex set of interdependent activities in which "doing good" for one group—abuse victims—also directly and indirectly benefits others; customers are alleged to be more confident in viewing porn online, and porn companies themselves have their legitimacy boosted.

Legitimization strategies are therefore a critical aspect of the work of the porn industry's trade organizations. Many other controversial industries such as alcohol, tobacco, arms, or mining comprise large and powerful multinational organizations with large financial prowess and extensive political lobbying embedded into many government systems, which provide them with the political firepower to fight for legitimacy and prosper in the interim. By contrast the porn industry contains fewer large companies, none of which have dedicated corporate social responsibility departments, and whose history of political lobbying in the United States mostly comprises the work done by the FSC and its antecedents. This lack of resources, combined with the widespread social disapproval surrounding the sector, makes it more vulnerable to local and national political targeting when compared to its larger controversial peer industries.

As ASACP's work shows, some legitimation activities can intersect with strategies to protect the interests of stakeholders within the industry. By actively searching for and reporting CP material, ASACP aims to demonstrate that its members strive to be socially legitimate, thus marking its members' sites as clean and even working with the state and federal authorities who might otherwise target them. The strategy depends on the perception that legal pornography is socially acceptable while child pornography is not; and is arguably successful because "protecting the children" is a more appealing prospect than "protecting the pornographer" (and with good reason). FSC has taken a different legitimization approach, which focuses less on the moral qualities of porn and pornographers and more on the legal right of the sector to exist and the financial benefits that a large and successful industry brings to the local region, as demonstrated in the "No to Measure B" campaign. AIM also broadened its appeal beyond the industry's self-concern by extending its sexual health services to the general public. Like AIM's extension of sexual health services, legitimation here comes from providing localized material benefits—both fiscally and physically—as proof that the porn industry "does good" to its local communities, both directly and indirectly.[94]

Despite these activities, pornography's identity as a controversial sector means that full social legitimacy is unlikely to ever be realized.[95] For trade organizations, protecting the well-being of their members can clash heavily with legitimation, and this is particularly true around the industry's core product, porn itself. The production and representations in content draws the greatest fire from critics both in terms of what it depicts and how it is created, yet is an area that remains relatively untargeted by the trade organizations. BPAV failed in its attempts to shift producer behaviors, and FSC's code of ethics is voluntary. ASACP's regulation of content production is allied to its anti-CP cause, which does directly answer the criticisms that women in porn are depicted as underage and that pornography should only be able to be accessed by adults, but doesn't focus on other aspects of production (e.g., types of sexual activities performed). Counter to their critics, AIM and FSC have also continually argued against the use of condoms in content production and associated systems of STI testing. FSC invokes the (erotic) freedoms ensconced in First Amendment rights and the power of the free markets to argue that firms should be free to respond to what the customer wants (or what producers think that customers want) within the hard regulatory limits of obscenity law. Strategies to self-regulate content production are also based around inside knowledge of how the industry works.[96] Sharon Mitchell stated in 2007, "I am a clinician who serves a world that I know very, very well because I come from it."[97] As the individuals who hold most power in dictating what type of content is created and how, managers and directors of production companies often drive these conversations. Chauntelle Tibbals has noted how the voices of performers are marginalized in debates around condom use[98]; and APHSS does not offer the range of mental and social support for performers that AIM did. Performers have also contributed to these debates, achieving a wide level of reach through social media platforms.

The multiplicity of activities that these trade organizations undertake and the variability with which they are received by the wider adult industry demonstrates that, for pornography, "legitimacy" itself is highly fluid and uneven. AIM, FSC, and ASACP have had to manage reputational effects in two directions, demonstrating to their members that they are doing the right thing by them but also demonstrating to the wider public that their members deserve to exist and are "doing good." Walking this line is difficult, particularly given porn's mistrust of the mainstream to see through the stigma and evaluate the industry on its own terms. While Mitchell, Helmy, and Irvine have been openly critical of some of the practices of the pornography industry, all have consistently fought for self-regulation on the grounds that they know better than anyone how change in that space should best be managed. Ultimately, they argue it should not be left to outsiders who would come to the industry with views colored by the industry's deviant reputation.

NOTES

1. Quoted at the State of the Industry panel, *AVN Expo* trade show, Hard Rock Hotel, Las Vegas, January 17, 2013.

2. S. Prakash Sethi, "Dimensions of Corporate Social Performance: An Analytical Framework," *California Management Review* 17, no. 3 (March 1975): 58–64.

3. Aubrey Wilson and Christopher West, "The Marketing of 'Unmentionables,'" *Harvard Business Review* 59, no. 1 (January/February 1981): 92.

4. Gail Dines, Linda Thompson, and Rebecca Whisnant with Karen Boyle, "Arresting Images: Anti-Pornography Slideshows, Activism and the Academy," in *Everyday Pornography*, ed. Karen Boyle (London: Routledge, 2010), 23.

5. Gayle Rubin, "Thinking Sex: Notes for a Radical Theory on the Politics of Sexuality," in *Pleasure and Danger: Exploring Female Sexuality*, ed. Carol Vance (Rivers Oram Press/Pandora List, 1984), 153.

6. Karen Boyle, "Introduction: Everyday Pornography," in *Everyday Pornography*, ed. Karen Boyle (London: Routledge, 2010), 2.

7. Clarissa Smith and Feona Attwood, "Lamenting Sexualization: Research, Rhetoric and the Story of Young People's Sexualization in the UK Home Office Review," *Sex Education* 11, no. 3 (2011): 327–37.

8. Georgina Voss, "'Treating It as a Normal Business': Researching the Pornography Industry," *Sexualities* 15, no. 3–4 (2012): 391–410.

9. Mark Suchman, "Managing Legitimacy: Strategic and Institutional Approaches," *Academy of Management Review* 20, no. 3 (July 1995): 573.

10. Robert Jensen, "Pornography Is What the End of the World Looks Like," in *Everyday Pornography*, ed. Karen Boyle (London: Routledge, 2010), 105–13.

11. Examples of these lists include Reputation Institute's CSR RepTrak. Companies that have regularly been included on this list include Microsoft, Google, Apple, and the Walt Disney Corporation.

12. Subharata Banerjee, "Corporate Social Responsibility: The Good, the Bad and the Ugly," *Critical Sociology* 34, no. 1 (2008): 51–79. For example, British American Tobacco has a CSR committee that produces annual sustainability reports. British American Tobacco, "British American Tobacco: Corporate Social Responsibility," BAT 2011, http://www.bat.com/ar/2011/corporate-governance/corporate-social-responsibility/index.html.

13. Brenda Joyner and Dinah Payne, "Evolution and Implementation: A Study of Values, Business Ethics and Corporate Social Responsibility," *Journal of Business Ethics* 41, no. 4 (2002): 299.

14. Ye Cai, Hoje Jo, and Carrie Pan, "Doing Well While Doing Bad? CSR in Controversial Industry Sectors," *Journal of Business Ethics* 108, no. 4 (July 2012): 467–80.

15. Edmund Byrne, "The U.S. Military-Industrial Complex Is Circumstantially Unethical," *Journal of Business Ethics* 95, no. 2 (August 2010): 153–65.

16. Michael Bellesiles, "The Origins of Gun Culture in the United States, 1760–1865," *The Journal of American History* 83, no. 2 (September 1996): 425–55.

17. For example, communities with strong economic dependency on the mining industry are aware of both the risks of mining, but also the benefits that they reap from it. Barbara Miller and James Sinclair, "Risk Perceptions in a Resource Community and Communication Implications: Emotion, Stigma and Identity," *Risk Analysis* 32, no. 3 (2012): 483–95.

18. This has been exemplified by the embarrassment of the business and management scholars who heaped praise onto Enron prior to its collapse. Banerjee, "Corporate Social Responsibility: The Good, the Bad and the Ugly," 63–64.

19. Archie Carroll, "The Pyramid of Corporate Social Responsibility: Toward the Moral Management of Organizational Stakeholders," *Business Horizons* 34, no. 4 (1991): 39–48.

20. Wilson and West, "The Marketing of 'Unmentionables,'" 92.

21. Guido Palazzo and Ulf Richter, "CSR Business as Usual? The Case of the Tobacco Industry," *Journal of Business Ethics* 61, no. 4 (November 2005): 387–401; Cai, et al., "Doing Well While Doing Bad? CSR in Controversial Industry Sectors," 234–59.

22. This analysis is constructed by drawing on empirical material gathered through ethnographic approaches including interviews with industry members, participant observation at trade events, and document analysis.

23. Paul DiMaggio and Walter Powell, "'The Iron Cage Revisited': Institutional Isomorphism and Collective Rationality in Organizational Fields," *American Sociological Review* 48, no. 2 (April 1983): 147–60.

24. Andrew Tucker, "Trade Associations as Industry Reputation Agents: A Model of Reputational Trust," *Business and Politics* 10, no. 1 (May 2008): 1–26.

25. Shiv Gupta and David Brubaker, "The Concept of Corporate Social Responsibility Applied to Trade Associations," *Socio-Economic Planning Sciences* 24, no. 4 (1990): 261–71; Phillipe Schmitter and Wolfgang Streeck, *The Organization of Business Interests: Studying the Associative Action of Business in Advanced Industrial Societies* (Cologne, Germany: Max Planck Institute for the Study of Societies, 1999).

26. John Campbell, "States, Politics and Globalization: Why Institutions Still Matter," in *The Nation-State in Question*, ed. T. V. Paul, G. John Ikenberry, and John Hall (Princeton: Princeton University Press, 2003), 234–59; Julia Clarke and Monica Gibson-Sweet, "The Use of Corporate Social Disclosures in the Management of Reputation and Legitimacy: A Cross-Sectoral Analysis of UK Top 100 Companies," *Business Ethics: A European Review* 8, no. 1 (1999): 5–13. This is driven in part by pragmatism. In examining the corporate social responsibility strategies of controversial industries, Cai and colleagues (2012) were unable to gather material about pornography companies from the KLD database, as very few are publically traded, and there is also little extant material about the industry and its working practices, due in part to the challenges of gathering such data (Voss 2012).

27. Jeffrey Weeks, *Sexuality and Its Discontents: Meaning, Myths, and Modern Sexualities* (London: Routledge, 1985), 232.

28. Weeks, *Sexuality and Its Discontents*, 44.

29. Jennee Evans-DeCicco and Gloria Cowan, "Attitudes Towards Pornography and the Characteristics Attributed to Pornography Actors," *Sex Roles* 44, no. 5–6 (March 2001): 351–61. One of the few pieces of work that explored the labor of female performers is Sharon Abbott's research on pornography actresses; however, this work examines motivations for entering the industry rather than issues around health and safety. Sharon A. Abbott, "Motivations for Pursuing an Acting Career in Pornography," in *Sex for Sale: Prostitution, Pornography, and the Sex Industry*, ed. Ronald Weitzer (New York: Routledge, 2010), 47–66.

30. Dines et al., "Arresting Images: Anti-pornography Slideshows, Activism and the Academy," 27.

31. Catharine MacKinnon, *Only Words* (Cambridge, MA: Harvard University Press, 1996).

32. "Interview: John Stagliano," *Rogreviews.com*, April 2002, http://www.rogreviews.com/16805/interview-john-stagliano-02.

33. Robert Jensen, *Getting Off: Pornography and the End of Masculinity* (Cambridge, MA: South End Press, 2007), 91.

34. Jodi O'Brien and Eve Shapiro, "'Do It On the Web': Emerging Discourses on Internet Sexuality," in *Web Studies: Rewiring Media Studies for the Digital Age*, ed. David Gauntlett and Ross Horsley (London: Arnold Press, 2004), 118; Michael Newman, "New Media, Young Audiences, and Discourses of Attention: From Sesame Street to 'Snack Culture,'" *Media, Culture and Society* 32, no. 4 (July 2010): 581–96; Feona Attwood, "'Younger, Paler, Decidedly Less Straight': The New Porn Professionals," in *Porn.com: Making Sense of Online Pornography*, ed. Feona Attwood (New York: Peter Lang, 2010), 88–106.

35. Stephen Maddison, "Online Obscenity and Myths of Freedom: Dangerous Images, Child Porn and Neoliberalism," in *Porn.com: Making Sense of Online Pornography*, ed. Feona Attwood (New York: Peter Lang, 2010), 18.

36. A subsector of the mainstream porn industry also produces gay content (i.e., exclusively male actors) for a gay male audience, but there is no equivalent in the mainstream pornography for lesbian material (i.e., depictions of lesbian acts are produced for an expected male viewer). Jennifer Moorman. "Gay for Pay, Gay For(e)play: The Politics of Taxonomy and Authenticity in LGBTQ Porn," in *Porn.com: Making Sense of Online Pornography*, ed. Feona Attwood (New York: Peter Lang), 155–70.

37. Robert Jensen, *Getting Off: Pornography and the End of Masculinity* (Cambridge, MA: South End Press, 2007), 17.

38. Jensen, "Pornography Is What the End of the World Looks Like," 105–13; Ana Bridges, "Methodological Connections in Mapping Pornography Content," in *Everyday Pornography*, ed. Karen Boyle (London: Routledge 2010), 34–49.

39. Berl Kutchinsky, "Pornography and Rape: Theory and Practice?" *International Journal of Law and Psychiatry* 14, no. 1–2 (1991): 47–64; David Jaffee and Murray Strauss, "Sexual Climate and Reported Rape: A State-Level Analysis," *Archives of Sexual Behavior* 16, no. 2 (April 1987): 107–23. Large-scale studies exploring this linkage give mixed results: much of this work is lab-based and doesn't evaluate the highly heterogeneous context of personal use or effects over an extended time period; has a confused correlation between cause and effect; and subjects are often white middle-class male undergraduates. While extensive consumption may have effects on people with a predisposition to sexual violence, high pornography use in itself is not necessarily indicative of high risk for sexual aggression for the wider heterosexual male population. Michael Seto, Alexandra Maric, and Howard Barbaree, "The Role of Pornography in the Etiology of Sexual Aggression," *Aggression and Violent Behavior* 6, no. 1 (Jan/Feb 2001): 35–53.

40. Boyle, "Introduction: Everyday Pornography," 2.

41. Clarissa Smith, "Pornographication: A Discourse for All Seasons," *International Journal of Media and Cultural Politics* 6, no. 1 (2010): 103–108. For an example of this point, the UK Home Office commissioned "The Sexualisation of Young People" report in 2010, which Clarissa Smith and Feona Attwood (2011) identify as containing similar flaws of interpretation around notions of sexualization as earlier writing (i.e., one-sided, selective, and negatively toned) and a highly negative viewpoint of sex, media, and young people.

42. MacKinnon, *Only Words*, 8.

43. Legs McNeil and Jennifer Osborne, *The Other Hollywood: The Uncensored Oral History of the Porn Film Industry* (New York: HarperCollins, 2004).

44. The term "tube sites" refers to Web sites that allow users to upload video content and watch it for free. Following the rise of YouTube, a number of tube sites focused on pornographic material emerged, including YouPorn and RedTube, where much of the material hosted was either produced by amateurs or stolen from industry pay-sites.

45. In large production studios, many of these activities take place in-house; for smaller producers, the activities are spread across several different points in the value chain. Other adult-focused organizations are scattered further afield across the United States and Canada, and further notable subsectors are present in Germany, the Netherlands, Sweden, and Japan. However, while a global consumer market for porn has emerged, the production sector itself is considerably fragmented with high degrees of variation in maturity and structure according to historical and regulatory context.

46. Robert Jensen, *Getting Off: Pornography and the End of Masculinity* (Cambridge, MA: South End Press, 2007), 90.

47. Sharif Mowlabocus, "Porn 2.0? Technology, Social Practice, and the New Online Porn Industry," in *Porn.com: Making Sense of Online Pornography*, ed. Feona Attwood (New York: Peter Lang, 2010), 69–87. "Alt" itself is now a genre in itself, as evidenced by the Vivid-Alt imprint line launched in 2006 by the Vivid Entertainment Group; and Suicide Girls has been described as "the Walmart of alt.porn." Audacia Ray, *Naked on the Internet: Hookups, Downloads and Cashing in on Internet Sexploration* (Emeryville, CA: Seal Press, 2007), 163.

48. Some elements of independent porn production have themselves become co-opted by mainstream porn. A certain amount of proamateur material involves people who want to break into the industry. Kevin Esch and Vicki Mayer, "How Unprofessional: The Profitable Partnership of Amateur Porn and Celebrity Culture," in *Pornification: Sex and Sexuality in Media Culture*, ed. Susanna Paasonen, Kaarina Nikunen, and Laura Saarenma (Oxford: Berg, 2007), 102.

49. "Interview: Tristan Taormino," *Porn Studies* 1, no. 1–2 (2014).

50. Nicola Simpson, "The Money Shot: The Business of Porn," *Critical Sense*, 2005, http://criticalsense.berkeley.edu/archive/spring2005/simpson.pdf.

51. David Slayden, "Debbie Does Dallas Again and Again: Pornography, Technology and Market Innovation," in *Porn.com: Making Sense of Online Pornography*, ed. Feona Attwood (New York: Peter Lang, 2010), 62.

52. Sanna Harma and Joakim Stolpe, "Behind the Scenes of Straight Pleasure," in *Porn.com: Making Sense of Online Pornography*, ed. Feona Attwood (New York: Peter Lang, 2010), 107–22.

53. The previous year Helmy had publically criticized the sector in a State of the Industry panel at the 2005 Phoenix Forum—a popular industry conference targeted mainly at Webmasters—for creating ever-more extreme content, a specific reference to the *United States v. Extreme Associates* obscenity trial taking place at that time.

54. "New Organization Aims to Protect Adult Industry's Image," *AVN*, May 1, 2006, http://business.avn.com/articles/video/New-Organization-Aims-to-Protect-Adult-Industry-8217-s-Image-49015.html.

55. Other aims included: Encourage producers to keep performers away from possible physical harm or from situations where they feel they have been mistreated; encourage the respect for performers on and off the set; support efforts to make performers more responsible to protect themselves from sexually transmitted diseases; and require producers to be diligent in ensuring all performers are of legal age. Pornography companies complying with these practices could also choose to use BPAV's logo on their advertising and marketing material.

56. Correspondence with Crystal Jackson, University of Nevada Las Vegas, February 13, 2013.

57. Ira Levine quoted in *Anderson Cooper 360 Degrees*, April 22, 2004, http://transcripts.cnn.com/TRANSCRIPTS/0404/22/acd.01.html.

58. Wicked Pictures, founded in 2004, was initially the only mainstream heterosexual pornography production studio that maintained a condom-only policy.

59. Terrell Tannen, "Sharon Mitchell, Head of the Adult Industry Medical Healthcare Clinic," *The Lancet* 364, no. 9436 (August 2004): 751.

60. Patient Zero was a male performer who would deliberately infect other performers and then go to the County Healthcare Centre to be anonymously tested, putting other people's names on his results. Mitchell, quoted in Tannen, "Sharon Mitchel: Head of the Adult Industry Medical Healthcare Clinic," 751.

61. This figure includes both industry members and members of the general public.

62. A parallel system, *SXCheck*, was also developed to provide similar testing services for members of the general public.

63. L. J. Williamson, "Even XXX Stars Need TLC," *Giga Granada Hills* July 24 2009, http://www.gigagranadahills.com/2009/07/even-xxx-stars-need-tlc.html.

64. Recipients of the 2003 scholarships attended local community colleges to study courses including preveterinarian studies, phlebotomy, and theatre studies. Sharon Mitchell, "LAP/LAS Scholarship Fund Spring Semester—2003," *Adult Industry Medical Health Care Foundation*, http://web.archive.org/web/20030621123038/http://www.aim-med.org/scholar.html.

65. The study found that female performers had similar rates of childhood sexual abuse and psychological health compared to nonabused women; instead the major differences emerged from aspects associated with the physical nature of their work, and actresses were more likely to have a greater number of sexual partners and were more concerned about contracting a sexually transmitted disease. The actresses also displayed higher rates of self-esteem, sexual satisfaction, and social support than nonperformers, which the researchers hypothesized may arise from both exhibitionism and personal freedoms in pornography work, and also the community support, which is bound up with being a member of a stigmatized group. Results of the research were disseminated through mainstream media and academic audiences through the subsequent article in the *Journal of Sex Research*. James Griffiths, Sharon Mitchell, Christian Hart, Lea Adams, and Lucy Gu, "Pornography Actresses: An Assessment of the Damaged Goods Hypothesis," *Journal of Sex Research* 50, no. 7 (October 2013): 1–12. Mindy Bradley, "Girlfriends, Wives and Strippers: Managing Stigma in Exotic Dancer Romantic Relationships," *Deviant Behavior* 28, no. 4 (2007): 379–406.

66. Terrell Tannen, "Sharon Mitchell, Head of the Adult Industry Medical Healthcare Clinic," 751.

67. Ira Levine, "Financial Peril Still Exists for AIM Healthcare," *Adult Industry Medical Health Care Foundation*, October 20, 2009, http://web.archive.org/web/20110615074244/http://www.aim-med.org/news/2009/10/20/1256052533/index3.html.

68. "Evasive Angles and TTB Productions Fines Range From $185 to $25K," *AVN*, September 17, 2004, http://business.avn.com/articles/video/Evasive-Angles-and-TTB-Productions-Fines-Range-From-185-to-25K-40331.html.

69. Mark Kernes, "HHS Dismisses AHF Complaint, Closes AIM Investigation," *AVN*, August 2, 2010, http://business.avn.com/articles/legal/HHS-Dismisses-AHF-Complaint-Closes-AIM-Investigation-405797.html.

70. Gram Ponante, "Labor Day in Porn Valley," *Gram Ponante: Porn Valley Observed*, September 15, 2011, http://gramponante.com/labor-day-in-porn-valley.

71. "The Free Speech Coalition: About," *FSC Blogger*, http://fscblogger.wordpress.com/about.

72. The AVA was the descendent of the earliest recorded trade organization, the Adult Film Association of America (AFAA). The AFAA was founded in 1969 by producer David Freeman with the intention of reducing the pressure being applied to the hundred-odd producers, distributors, and exhibitors of adult films who made up the nascent industry. One of AFAA's first acts was to appoint three First Amendment lawyers on retainer who helped develop an advice kit for use in obscenity trials. By the 1980s the organization had an estimated 260 members, and had changed its name in 1986 to the Adult Film and Video Association of America, reflecting the impact of this new technology, and then again in 1987 to the Adult Video Association.

73. Members span the industry, including content producers, toys and novelties companies, payment processors, and Web service providers. Sponsorship includes companies such as XBIZ and AVN.

74. "The Free Speech Coalition: About," *FSC Blogger*, http://fscblogger.wordpress.com/about.

75. "2257" is the colloquial term for the 2257 guidelines of the Child Protection and Obscenity Enforcement Act of 1988, which require producers of sexually explicit material to obtain proof of age for every model they shoot, and retain those records. Federal inspectors may inspect the records at any time of their choosing and prosecute any infraction.

76. "Code of Ethics," *FSC*, http://www.freespeechcoalition.com/code-of-ethics.html.

77. "What We Offer," *FSC APAP*, http://fscapap.com/content.html.

78. The STI-testing service runs along similar lines to AIM with results secured in a database accessible to performers and producers, and services also open to members of the public; testing is, however, outsourced to existing clinics where pornography production happens—Los Angeles, Las Vegas, and Miami—rather than kept in-house.

79. Voters were asked to vote on the proposition: "Shall an ordinance be adopted requiring producers of adult films to obtain a County public health permit, to require adult film performers to use condoms while engaged in sex acts, to provide proof of

blood borne pathogen training course, to post permit and notices to performers, and making violations of the ordinance subject to civil fines and criminal charges?" The measure passed by 57 percent supporting and 4 percent opposing in December 2012.

80. "Is Measure B necessary?" *No on Government Waste*, http://www.noon governmentwaste.com/what.html#necessary.

81. Interview with Diane Duke, January 21, 2011.

82. "Association of Sites Advocating Child Protection and ASACP Foundation," *ASACP*, http://www.asacp.org/ASACP-Foundation.html.

83. "About ASACP," *ASACP*, http://www.asacp.org/index.php?content=aboutus.

84. For example, the code requires that in the case where models are over eighteen but look younger, the statement "The models are eighteen or older" should be prominently displayed on each featured page.

85. "Code of Ethics," *ASACP*, http://www.asacp.co.uk/index.php?content=coe.

86. "RTA Verified Validation Program," *RTA Label*, http://www.rtalabel.org/? content=rtaplus.

87. Ibid.

88. .xxx domains are sponsored top-level domains (sTLD), intended to be a voluntary option for online pornography sites. The sponsoring organization is the International Foundation for Online Responsibility (IFFOR). Pornography industry critics of the scheme have raised concerns that the existence of .xxx will lead to regulation making its use mandatory for adult sites; and that the use of a single top-level domain would also make it easier for search engines and other intermediaries to block their content.

89. "Joan (asacp)," *Ambush Interview*, January 31, 2006, http://www.ambush interview.com/79/interview79.html.

90. This claim was actually by Diane Duke, following Irvine's departure (although she did not reference Irvine herself). Diane Duke, "Free Speech Says: IFFOR . . . Don't Kid Yourself," *AVN*, August 17, 2011, http://business.avn.com/articles/technology/Free-Speech-Says-IFFOR-Don-t-Kid-Yourself-444935.html.

91. Guido Palazzo and Ulf Richter, "CSR Business as Usual? The Case of the Tobacco Industry," 396.

92. "Joan (asacp)."

93. After a decade in operations, AIM was only allowed to participate in the Los Angeles AIDS walk and receive proceeds from it in 2007, with Sharon Mitchell noting that this might be because "we've been around for 10 years, so I think they realized we're not going anywhere!" "AIM Offers 'Porn 101' Online," *AVN*, September 7, 2007, http://business.avn.com/articles/video/AIM-Offers-Porn-101-Online-30843.html.

94. This localized tactic is similar to those of Nevada brothels who strive to maintain a good reputation in their local communities by "donating scholarships to high schools, buying jackets for fire departments [and] participating in local parades." In doing so, some brothel owners have become "respectable members of their community who are rewarded with trust and support from local residents." Kathryn Hausbeck and Barbara G. Brents, "Nevada's Legal Brothels," in *Sex for Sale: Prostitution, Pornography and the Sex Industry*, ed. Ronald Weitzer (New York: Routledge, 2010). The

geography of the trade organizations' work underscores the spatial elements around their activities, and the cultural context that constructs concepts of legitimacy, normalcy, and rightness. Despite the spread of the industry away from Los Angeles after the advent of the Internet, many of the FSC and AIM's activities have remained highly localized to this region. FSC's branding also draws heavily on United States' notions of patriotism. ASACP has had a wider reach, as its work focuses on the global spread of CP online rather than the physical location of porn production.

95. Guido Palazzo and Ulf Richter, "CSR Business as Usual? The Case of the Tobacco Industry," *Journal of Business Ethics* 61, no. 4 (November 2005): 387–401; Cai et al., "Doing Well While Doing Bad? CSR in Controversial Industry Sectors," 234–59.

96. These lines of argument include: Depictions of condom use would drive sales down; enforced condom use would drive producers out of state, away from the support found in Los Angeles; condoms are impractical for the type of activities that performers engage in; and the sexual activities depicted in porn should be read as performative and fantastic rather than realistic.

97. Quoted from an interview with Scott Simon, "Promoting Healthcare for the Porn Industry," National Public Radio, December 8, 2007, http://www.npr.org/templates/story/story.php?storyId=17044239.

98. Chauntelle Tibbals, "'Anything That Forces Itself into My Vagina Is by Definition Raping Me . . .' Adult Performers and Occupational Health and Safety," *Stanford Law and Policy Review* 23, no. 1 (January 2012).

When Species Meat: Confronting Bestiality Pornography*

Margret Grebowicz

In *The Pornography of Meat*, Carol Adams makes the argument that feminism in general, and the critique of pornography in particular, ought to address the condition of animals.[1] She points out that animals have historically been excluded from feminist inquiry because of the feminist rejection of denigrating comparisons between women and animals. The feminist message has been "We are not animals!" reflecting an investment in rightful belonging to humanity right down to the bumper sticker that reads, "Feminism is the radical notion that women are people too." I follow Adams in her demand to re-inscribe the animal into feminist inquiry, but critiques like hers lack a robust interrogation of the ontology of animal being in general. In other words, they fail to ask what manner of being we imagine animality to be, that then allows for the present conditions of extreme exploitation. Contemporary discourses of posthumanism, in contrast, explore "the animal" as a contingent, historical, and contested concept in dynamic and co-constitutive relation to "the human," and raise possibilities for new ontologies of animality.[2] In what follows, I argue that, in this posthumanist context, the feminist task is to construct theoretical structures in which to begin to think about not just animality in general, but animal sexualities in particular, from the vantage point of a critical rethinking of "the human."

My particular subject of inquiry is bestiality pornography, a discourse that thus far has been dealt with only in the margins—if at all—of both animal studies and feminist critiques of porn. Though the ethics of sexual relations between humans and animals warrant serious research and discussion, I am less concerned with them in this particular project, focusing instead on the interspecies imaginary that bestiality porn produces. I firstly examine the role

---

*This chapter originally appeared in *Humanimalia: A Journal of Human/Animal Interface Studies* 1, no. 2 (Winter 2010). It is reprinted with permission from *Humanimalia*.

of this imaginary in the ongoing construction of two related fields—that of femininity on one hand and of feminism on the other—and secondly attempt to organize theoretical resources for thinking about—and thus treating—animals as active co-agents in the production of meanings, rather than passive screens for our anthropomorphic projections.

GENDERING ANIMALS

Not surprisingly, Catharine MacKinnon's recent contribution to animal studies literature focuses in part on the use of animals in pornography.[3] She describes the relation of the law to animals as gendered, which in her analysis means that animals are feminized and women are figured in terms of "animal nature." Both groups are subordinated to the law of humans, the most powerful of which are biological men. This is most obvious, she writes, in the use of animals in commercial pornography, where animals and women occupy the same subordinate position. Both groups are victims of an unequal power relation, which is subsequently eroticized. The actors are men, the objects acted upon are women and animals. However, a quick survey of Internet bestiality porn shows imagery and narratives that do not align neatly with MacKinnon's schema. In fact, there is quite a variety of imagery available, making up an internally inconsistent kaleidoscope of constructs and norms, and indicating that bestiality pornography tells us little about the practice of bestiality. An analysis of the semiotics of gender particular to both cultural practices yields important information about how we view women and how we view animals.

In mythology and throughout the history of art and literature, images of women with animals (and masculine beast-men) are much more frequent than images of men with animals. But if we take commercial pornography to be a qualitatively unique, historically and materially situated phenomenon of culture, rather than, say, just another genre of literature, the proliferation of what is known as zoo porn cannot be read as just a natural extension of the story of "Leda and the Swan" or the "Rape of Europa." How do narratives of interspecies desire change when mediated by this particular technology and logic of democratization of information? The most widely available bestiality (also called "zoo") pornography depicts women having sex with male horses and dogs, two species which have evolved in close proximity to humans, and that appear as figures of masculinity throughout our culture. Indeed, horses and dogs almost always appear as the male actors in the pornography itself, situated in narratives in which animals are substitutes for men where men are missing (e.g., "horny farm girl needs horse cock"; "teen's first time with dog"). What is eroticized in this imagery is not the power difference between the male viewer and the animal, which may be trained or forced into doing (almost) anything, but something very different: the size and virility of the horse, the eagerness of the dog, and so forth. Intense anthropomorphism fuels these narratives, rather than the eroticization of the power of humans over animals on which MacKinnon focuses. There is also extensive "gay" zoo porn involving animals, with men performing the same acts as the women in the "straight" zoo porn—giving fellatio or receiving anal intercourse. In fact, the very designations "straight" and "gay" in this context signify properly only if we assume that the horses and dogs substitute quite directly and unproblematically for men. This type of imagery makes up the majority of bestiality porn on the Internet.

How do I know? I looked. In fact, the account I offer here is a result of a deliberate decision to look at and for porn sites in the way a casual consumer of Internet porn would: searching for free imagery, taking "tours" of pay sites, registering as a user of file-sharing sites, and just clicking around, getting a general impression of what is available and under what conditions. I kept a log of the search terms: animal sex, bestiality porn, zoo porn, zoo sex, animal porn—and, once I was more familiar with the terminology—farm sex, free beast toons, animal sex galleries, bestiality porn share, monster hentai, and so on. Rather than statistics about the production and consumption of this subgenre, I was interested in the intersection of this particular technological mediation with graphic narratives of interspecies desire on an experiential level. Since Foucault, philosophical theories of subjectivity have tried to trace not only how discourse is produced and circulated, but how it is productive of the subject's sense of identity, truth, and reality. *Who are the consumers of this imagery?* is a very different question than *What is it like to be a consumer of this imagery?*, and a philosophical inquiry into the production of patriarchal and naïvely humanist subjectivity conceives of the empirical in terms of the latter.

The more one clicks, the more nuanced a story emerges. There is another kind of narrative widely available, one in which the women are so insatiable that "they'll fuck anything!" Sites like *www.fuckthemall.com* and others invite viewers to watch women with "all" animals, as many different kinds as possible, penetrating themselves with snakes, eels, and other fish. The story here seems to be a bit different: The women depicted are insatiable and out of control sexually, while the masculine element is not quite as obvious, as in the bodies of the dogs and horses, often for the simple reason that we are no longer watching penises, but entire animals being inserted into orifices; animals like fish, onto whom it is more difficult to project anthropomorphic fantasies. In this kind of material, the animality of the animals is emphasized. The insatiable women will do anything to satisfy their needs, including fellating "filthy" dog penises, for instance (see *www.bestialityfacial.com*). The recurrence of the word "filthy" is important to note, because it serves to remind the viewer that this is precisely an animal penis, not a human one, marking a departure from the narratives that rely on the power of anthropomorphic projection. In one example, *www.beasttoons.com* shows a cartoon woman dressed up in a maid's outfit and a gorilla looking up her skirt. She wonders to herself, "A gorilla is so similar to a human. I wonder if he can get me pregnant?" A few Web pages later, the same site shows the same cartoon woman straddling a bucket which houses a chicken, whose head is up her vagina.

Finally, there are occasional, rare images of human penises in animal vaginas (usually those of dogs or sheep, though there are also photos of penises inside chickens). On *www.zoohan.net* there are multiple images of men having intercourse with animals, but they are tagged with the words "extreme" and "shocking." Following these photos to further links, one can also find the occasional photograph of either an entire forearm inside a cow's vagina, or even just photographs of animal genitalia alone, but with a very different appearance from today's glossy porn. They tend to be single images, rather than entire galleries or films, and the same image gets circulated among multiple sites. The fact that many are yellowed indicates that they are scanned prints, not digital photographs. They are shot in the dark with flash, usually very close up and never showing a person's face. In fact, all of the imagery of this sort that I encountered had the appearance of home-grown, amateur porn, or possibly even images made in veterinary contexts and not intended for pornographic use, but in any case, not commercial porn produced under conditions of some degree of regulation and budget. In this pornography, the animal is always on the receiving end of the sex, its vagina or anus clearly substituting for that of a woman.

Thus, in contrast to MacKinnon's claim that bestiality pornography invariably feminizes animals just as it feminizes women, it appears that there are at least three different classes of bestiality porn, in which the semiotics of gender function in different ways. To speak in broad terms, in the first class, the animals become "men." In the second, the animals become "animals" and it is the species difference that is eroticized. I would like to suggest that in this, the least anthropomorphic of the constructs, the animal is almost genderless, or at least that the erotics of the narratives and images arise not from gender difference, but from species difference. In the third, the animals are "women." Thus, we can see more than one distinct way of anthropomorphically gendering animals, and, in the case of the animalizing of animals, we encounter a de-gendering. How does this, a more nuanced reading of the gender semiotics of bestiality porn, affect feminist critiques of porn, and how does it speak in particular to a critique of this imagery as a site where the oppression of women and that of animals intersect?

MacKinnon's critique of the pornographic feminization of animals seems more like an engagement with bestiality rather than with bestiality porn. The cultural practices are quite different. The most significant difference for the purposes of my analysis is that the majority of zoo porn shows women having sex with animals, while real-life, prosecuted cases of bestiality involve men almost exclusively. The legal literature, as well as bestiality (also called "zoophilia") blogs, indicate that the people having sex with animals off-camera are in fact men. Our cartoon maid has a chicken's head in her vagina, but, as the blogs indicate, when humans have sex with chickens it is a man inserting his penis into the hen's cloaca, an encounter that is usually fatal for the hen. The kinds of rare images tagged as "extreme" are thus anything but—they show the banal truth of the sex with animals that humans actually practice. In contrast, the women having vaginal or oral sex with horse penises, at the forefront of every "zoo" or "farm" pay site, make rare appearances in the legal literature.[4] This is significant, because gender does not officially signify in the legal prosecution of bestiality cases, in the case of either the humans or the animals involved. It doesn't enter into the discussion. Moral debates about bestiality also obscure this fact, with blanket references to "humans" and "animals," as if neither were gendered, and as if gender-as-power-difference were not at work in sex acts between humans and animals.

This is certainly not the only instance in which porn does not depict the realities of sex. Lesbian porn for straight male viewers and incest porn are just two subgenres about which it is common knowledge that the actors are in fact acting, faking pleasure in the interests of a narrative, acting as "real" lesbians or members of the same family in order to produce a fantasy, in contrast to amateur straight porn, whose appeal lies in the fact (or is it?) that non-actors are experiencing real pleasure. However, one must be careful about the use of the word "real" in the context of the pornography debates. MacKinnon and others have warned at length about the tendency to figure porn as fantasy, when the sex taking place in order to produce the "fantastic" images is in fact very real. Thus, my own distinction here between bestiality porn and "real" bestiality is quite tenuous. It may be more helpful to distinguish between sex with animals for money and sex with animals for personal pleasure, focusing on distinctions between intentions, motives, pleasures, and privileges, rather than any ontological difference between more or less "real" events.

However mediated and "fake" zoo porn may or not may be, zoo sites have a particular way of linking onto Web sites about off-camera bestiality practices. They often piggyback on purported information sites about zoophilia, defined as "love" relationships with animals, usually to the exclusion of humans and including sex. Although zoophilia Web sites actively disassociate themselves from porn sites and make strong distinctions between bestiality practices and the production of bestiality porn, openly condemning the use of animals in porn as "cruelty" and "exploitation," the porn sites' invariable insistence that what they show is real ("100% real animal sex!!!") works to reinforce the connection. Bestiality is presented as something that must be kept secret, like the use of Internet porn itself. Web sites open with a sea of warnings, and the experience is that of entering ever deeper levels of something forbidden, when in fact there is nothing illegal under U.S. law about viewing most pornography, including bestiality porn and virtual child porn (decriminalized in the United States in 2002).

At the same time, however, because the cultural climate of these sites is one of repression and the failure of society to understand the viewer's alleged needs, it is also of community, file sharing, and underground trafficking of information among users who form a network. It is presented as an instance of the democratization of knowledge, where the Internet plays the part of making access to knowledge easier, faster, and less expensive than ever.[5] The Web site *www.beastwiki.com*, devoted to reviews of all of the bestiality pay sites available, looks exactly like Wikipedia.com, except that the links are red and not blue. Sites like *www.zooshare.com* are not only for file sharing, but for posting blogs, commenting on posts, and reviewing and rating the pornography. Its users often describe themselves as keeping a secret, hiding their true selves, and being deeply misunderstood. *www.beastforum.com* invites users to "share your opinions, creations, and experiences with others," and on *www.beasttoons.com*, in the very same frame in which the aforementioned French maid cartoon protagonist encounters the gorilla, she promises us an educational experience: "With your membership you'll also get full access to our extensive zoophilia database that covers everything you want to know about animal sex." Blogs often include expressions of gratitude for the forum, a place where users can finally show their true selves. While some blog posts discuss the considerable challenges of sharing one's desire for zoo porn with a sex partner, typically men writing about a new girlfriend who might be scared off, others post about something very different, namely the difficulties of a life in which animals themselves are the sex partners. Thus, the connection between bestiality porn and bestiality is further reinforced by this landscape of persecuted subculture, shared understanding, and access to important-but-forbidden information.

MEANINGFUL CONSENT IN THE CASE OF ANIMALS

In the United States, most states have laws against sex with animals, and of those, a majority deems the act a felony, not a misdemeanor. Most states classify bestiality under their animal cruelty statutes.[6] If significant money is involved, the criminality extends to property damage, as in the case in which an Illinois man confessed to having had intercourse with the mares in the stables in which he was employed over the course of twenty years.[7] MacKinnon asks the important question why laws against sex with animals exist at all. Her answer takes us out of the problematic in which both the law and so much of animal studies are explicitly located, that of suffering, and places us squarely in the problematic more proper to feminist jurisprudence surrounding rape and bodily integrity, namely that of consent.[8] Because "people cannot be sure" that animals consent to the sex, the law exists to protect the animals. More specifically, MacKinnon writes, "We cannot know if their consent is meaningful."[9] And yet, there are clearly cases when we know that the animals do not give their consent to the sex: in the Illinois mare case, for instance, the man was caught after twenty years of intercourse with the horses only because one of the mares died in the act. He had bound her in such a way as to constrict her neck, presumably in hopes of successfully immobilizing her, and the mare had fought the intercourse so hard that she had strangled herself. Or, to take a less dramatic example, in much dog porn the animal is lying down, being fellated or mounted by a woman, often with the help of at least one other person, so that the whole scene is obviously highly mediated and comes across as forced. When animals fight back or show their indifference, it seems easy to make the claim that they do not consent. MacKinnon writes, "Do animals dissent from human hegemony? I think they often do. They vote with their feet by running away. They bite back, scream in alarm, withhold affection, approach warily, and swim off."[10] So when exactly is it that "we cannot be sure" about their consent? It is when animals appear as willing participants in these acts that the question of consent becomes complicated. We know that they say no, but it is much less thinkable that they might say yes.

Indeed, in zoo porn, only those animals that are figured as intelligent enough to be agents to some degree are the ones that may be believably presented as consenting to the sex. This is most prevalent in the imagery that genders the animals as male. A dog mounts a kneeling woman from behind, or sniffs between her legs, or the horse ejaculates in her mouth—this is where the issue of consent takes on considerable ambiguity. The presentation of the animal as an agent in the sex becomes believable, and the animals are continuously described as "lucky," "hungry," and "horny." Numerous sites advertise photo galleries accompanied by narratives of dogs "raping" innocent girls or other "first timers." In all of the sites classified as "animal rape," the animal, usually a dog, is present as the perpetrator, not the victim, of a rape. This rape narrative sometimes depends on claims about the animal's intelligence, as in *www.zooshock.com*, which shows photos of a woman having intercourse with a pig. The accompanying narrative states that she was raped by the pig in a shed, a claim that is then followed by a sentence that explains that pigs are among the most intelligent animals on the planet The trajectory from intelligence to sexuality is clear: The more intelligent the animal, the more credible the narrative in which the animal is a sexual agent.

However, when we compare this pornographic valuing of the intelligence and complexity of "higher order animals" with the ways in which this densely gendered interspecies imaginary manifests itself legally, we encounter some contradictions. MacKinnon points out that "commercial pornography alone shows far more sex with animals than is ever prosecuted for the acts required to make it."[11] Indeed, though I will not offer a review of the legal literature concerning bestiality cases, it is striking that the sheer amount of bestiality porn on the Internet is disproportionately large in comparison to the number of bestiality cases that make the daily or weekly news. It is also significant that the cases that do make the news rarely describe the kind of sex that makes up the majority of the porn. Women receiving cunnilingus from dogs (and occasionally cats), women penetrated by dogs and horses, and occasionally pigs and goats, women performing fellatio on dogs, horses, goats, even camels—these acts are almost never prosecuted. Why might this be? I imagine that MacKinnon would answer that it is because the law, with its First Amendment absolutism, turns a blind eye to whatever is required to make pornography, which it is committed to protecting. This is why legislators do not go after the people engaged in the various acts required to make porn. In other words, MacKinnon's answer to the question does not depend on the contents of the imagery at all, or on its semiotics of gender, but on her reading of the Supreme Court's investment in the First Amendment. MacKinnon would argue that, just as the very real unwanted sex that must take place for porn to exist at all is virtually unprosecutable, the sex with animals remains invisible to the law. MacKinnon's equation would be simple: We don't prosecute bestiality just like we don't prosecute rape—because we hate animals just like we hate women.

Once again, an analysis of the semiotics of gender at work in the discourses yields a different answer. The legal landscape is ostensibly void of gender distinctions when dealing with bestiality, but this is not the case de facto. If MacKinnon is right that U.S. antibestiality law exists to protect animals from sex to which they do not consent, then it follows that the law is harsher on sex acts with animals in which the anthropocentric projection onto the animal is that of feminine vulnerability and passive receptivity. When the projection is of masculinity, on the other hand, as in the case of the acts required to make most animal pornography, acts that go unprosecuted, the law appears much softer. The message seems to be that if the animals are doing things that any red-blooded heterosexual man would enjoy doing—being fellated or penetrating a woman—then we are no longer dealing with cruelty. To put it bluntly, the law is more able to recognize sex with animals as cruelty when the animals are figured as female rather than male, and is thus more likely to prosecute "real" bestiality (in which men have intercourse with predominantly female animals) than the acts required to make porn (in which women have intercourse with predominantly male animals). For this reason, it could be argued, the majority of the real sex in bestiality porn goes unprosecuted.

This is consistent with MacKinnon's reading of the legal treatment of rape in general: The easier it is to establish a lack of consent, the easier the rape conviction. And as MacKinnon points out, we know when animals say no. The harder it is to prove that no consent took place, the harder the rape conviction. It is here that MacKinnon's claim that the relation of the law to animals is gendered must be turned on its head. It is gendered, but not in the sense that the animals are necessarily feminized. On the contrary, in the making of the majority of bestiality Internet porn, they are twice masculinized: once in the pornographic imagery, where they substitute for men and are (more or less believably) figured as taking pleasure in the activities, and again when the laws against sex with animals are not enforced specifically in the context of the acts required to make the pornography. The animals are made into men on two levels: once, in the pornographic narratives, and a second time, in the law's blindness to the criminal acts required to produce the narratives. The resulting equation is a bit different from MacKinnon's: When we do prosecute bestiality, it is when the animals are figured as women and not when they are figured as men. Even as the law does not distinguish among the sex of the animals (bestiality is defined as sexual activity between humans and animals, regardless of reproductive anatomy), a very predictable semiotics of gender is at work in its enforcement. Under the law, the animals' "desire" is naturalized, just as men's sexual response is naturalized. In contrast to the pornographic narrative, where desire is linked to intelligence and complexity, and so results in the anthropomorphic projection of agency, the legal one functions according to a logic in which the willing animal, as virile masculinity, is exhaustively programmed by nature and thus incapable of agency.

DENATURALIZING ANIMAL SEX

MacKinnon is perhaps best known for her analysis of meaningful consent in the case of women. She claims that in conditions of social inequality in which power differences are eroticized and women's subjugation is coextensive with their positive value as sex objects, there is no possibility of women's meaningful consent to sex.[12] This is often caricatured as her "all sex is rape" thesis. This does not mean that women cannot consent to sex. Clearly, they do so all the time. But MacKinnon asks us to consider how meaningful this consent is, how seriously we ought to take it given the cultural production of femininity as sexually available and servile. Though she has famously been criticized for denying women any possibility of sexual agency, what interests me more immediately is the paradox to which this argument leads, one which is useful for thinking through consent and thus sexual agency in the case of animals.

Note that the law does not protect entities that cannot consent, like sex dolls, vibrators, doorknobs, or watermelons, with which it is not illegal to engage in sexual activity. The only kind of creature with whom sex might be prohibited is the kind of creature that is capable of some degree of consent or dissent, an *agent* whose agency and consent cannot be established conclusively because of external mitigating factors, but who remains an agent nonetheless. In other words, only a being that is capable of consent is capable of denying its consent and thus being raped. Thus, there is something logically problematic about the very idea of the being that *always* consents (as in MacKinnon's description of the construction of the feminine in the legal imaginary, which, as she demonstrates, makes it so difficult to prosecute rape in the case of adult, sexually active women), as well as of the being that *never* consents (the child, the animal, the mentally disabled adult).

In order to escape this paradox and develop a more nuanced account of sexual agency across the board, we must pool feminist and posthumanist theoretical resources. This, I propose, points to the future of feminist animal studies: the possibility of thinking the agency (erotic, ethical, semiotic) of animals in sexual practices, in an effort to counteract the received claim that they are exhaustively programmed by "nature." Feminism has barely begun to denaturalize or queer animal sexualities. For instance, Carol Adams persuasively argues that the sexual objectification and consumption of animals and of women follow the same models. She proposes that feminism should approach the animalizing of women and the feminization of animals in patriarchal culture as a unique opportunity, namely the chance to study the oppression of animals as a particular symptom of androcentric social organization. However, Adams's work on the visual culture aspect of meat consumption is devoted to exposing the logic and structure of a pattern of oppression and exploitation, a position which depends on one important assumption: that humans are the only actors in this practice. The structure of her argument follows an identifiable Second Wave feminist formula in which power and privilege are pretty unambiguously distinguishable from subjugation. In that sense, it offers rather limited resources for a post- or neo-Foucauldian feminist analysis of power, desire, and norms, of the production of truths and practices, and the complexities of the care of the self.[13]

What happens if, in contrast, we begin from the assumption that animals are actors, too, insofar as they are the kinds of beings that cannot only deny consent, but give it? The position appears dangerous at first, as if one were on the side of the contemporary zoophilia communities I describe here, which also rely heavily on a particular rhetoric of animal consent and even "pleasure." How might we begin to distinguish between the sexual agency we anthropomorphically project onto animals (in the production of porn, for instance) and their real sexual agency, the very thing that renders them rapeable (at least in human legal terms) in the first place? Or how to think *critically* about the law, which purports to protect animals without, in the course of our critique, leaving them wide open to exploitation? And furthermore, what kind of account of agency is available in a post-Enlightenment world in which we have abandoned human exceptionalism, in which we take evolutionary biology seriously, but also in which we no longer conflate "nature" with "programming"? What is the relationship between consent, agency, and responsibility in this posthumanist landscape? And finally, does this starting point commit us to the idea that many, myself included, find difficult to swallow: that bestiality has the potential to go the way of other practices labeled "deviant" and become sexually progressive?

Donna Haraway's important book, *When Species Meet*, offers an ontology of the political subject which includes nonhuman animals, or to put it differently, demonstrates that the inclusion of nonhuman animals in the body politic will call for the radical transformation of that body. She, too, reminds us of the reasons animals were actively excluded from much early feminist inquiry, in this case Marxist feminism:[14] "They tended to be all too happy with categories of society, culture, and humanity and all too suspicious of nature, biology, and co-constitutive human relationships with other critters." Feminism never questioned the reserving of the categories of desire and sexuality for human beings.[15] But surely, it cannot be by accident that the comparisons between animals and women are made in pornographic contexts in particular. Neither is it accidental that animals are gendered in pornography—although not always in ways people assume. The patriarchal logic that depends on a presumption of woman's animal nature makes this assumption specifically in the context of sexuality, insofar as we imagine that sex is where humans are at their most animal. And we do imagine this: In his controversial piece "Heavy Petting," Peter Singer actually defends bestiality on the grounds that "there are many ways in which we cannot help behaving just as animals do—or mammals, anyway—and sex is one of the most obvious ones. We copulate, as they do. They have penises and vaginas, as we do, and the fact that the vagina of a calf can be sexually satisfying to a man shows how similar these organs are."[16] According to Singer's logic, the zoophile's desire for the animal is always already proof of our animality. Zoophilia itself becomes a symbol of the breakdown of human exceptionalism (and perhaps even proof of evolution).

But clearly, this collapsing of desire into "nature" is not where feminism will wish to end up. If the received wisdom is that woman=sex and sex=animality, and if feminism today must reinscribe the animal it has exiled from its literature, *then it must put at the forefront of this reinscription the complex naturecultural problematic of animal sexualit(ies) in particular.* Just as feminism has interrogated, historicized, and unhinged the connections between femininity and sexuality in an effort to denaturalize exploitative sexual practices, it must do so in the case of animality. The idea of denaturalizing animal sexuality is obviously problematic, at the very least because it complicates our relationship to the discourse which offers the most detailed information about nonreproductive sex among animals, namely animal behavior studies. Feminist theory will need to do much more than cite studies by empirical scientists that describe, for instance, same-sex sexual behaviors among some primates, manatees, certain whale species, and those famous big horn sheep that have made the news.[17] It will have to also examine the political and ontological commitments that underpin projects seeking to naturalize nonreproductive sex among animals.

One important task is to thematize and explore the difference between the anthropocentric projection of consent (as in the pornographic narratives, for instance), and the real agency of nonhuman animals, the agency which renders them active partners in interspecies sex and thus in the production of the posthuman sexual imaginary. What, if any, epistemological resources do we have for making this distinction? In Jacques Derrida's *The Animal That Therefore I Am*, sexuality is precisely the site of the human–animal difference and the site where both humans and animals are denaturalized. Rather than challenging the modern anthropomorphic opposition between human and animal by pointing out how very animal we are in our sexualities, as Singer does above, Derrida performs a contrasting gesture. He exposes the human as a highly mediated philosophical construct by exploring the degree to which animality poses the ultimate limit to the human. The animal is "more other than any other," and it is so precisely "on the threshold of sexual difference. More precisely, of sexual differences."[18] Animals thus become not just another Other for feminism to include in its ever-expanding list of oppressed identities, but quite possibly *the* question mark itself, the philosophical problem of sexuality par excellence. Engaging philosophically with animality means engaging with the idea of sexual differences in the plural, a bottomless heterogeneity of sexual possibilities. This undermines the modern fantasy that humans are on one side of the divide and a homogeneous group called "animals" is on the other. Derrida writes:

> Philosophers have always judged and *all* philosophers have judged that limit to be single and indivisible, considering that on the one side of that limit there is an immense group, a single and fundamentally homogeneous set that one has the right . . . to mark as opposite, namely the set of the Animal in general. . . . It applies to the whole animal kingdom with the exception of the human.[19]

Animality, understood as the site of limitless sexual differences, overturns this received order and allows a feminist engagement with animals that does not fall prey to fantasies of a Nature from which Politics is absent.

Haraway's *Companion Species Manifesto*, an account of the complexity of dog-human interdependence and co-evolution that argues for the necessity of a posthuman or animal political ontology, ends with a rather racy sex scene. Haraway makes the case that dogs are not "natural" using the example of complex, unique sexual play between two dogs, one of which is spayed:

> None of their sexual play has anything to do with remotely functioning heterosexual mating behavior—no efforts of Willem to mount, no presenting of an attractive female backside, not much genital sniffing, no whining and pacing, none of that reproductive stuff. No, here we have pure polymorphous perversity that is so dear to the hearts of all of us who came of age in the 1960s reading Norman O. Brown. The 110 pound Willem lies down with a bright look in his eye. Cayenne, weighing in at 35 pounds, looks positively crazed as she straddles her genital area on top of his head, her nose pointed towards his tail, presses down and wags her backside vigorously. I mean hard and fast. He tries for all he's worth to get his tongue on her genitals, which inevitably dislodges her from the top of his head. It looks a bit like the rodeo, with her riding a bronco and staying on as long as possible. They have slightly different goals in this game, but both are committed to the activity. Sure looks like *eros* to me. Definitely not *agape*.[20]

Haraway's political philosophy depends on the claim that humans and dogs (and many other animals) are semiotic agents.[21] They both actively create meaning in the course of their interactions, rather than just having meaning or "culture" projected onto some substratum of "nature." The central role played by nonreproductive sex play is crucial to her position, which seeks to undermine the notion that animals are programmed by nature while humans are not (and insofar as they are, they are animals). Haraway denaturalizes animal sex at the same moment that she endows the dogs with not just animal lust, but sexual agency: "They invented this game."[22] Note the importance of the claim that this is eros and not agape, perversity and not necessity—in short, a certain sense of indeterminacy, possibility, the openness that comes with the idea of choice, rather than bondage to a stable and knowable script of practices emanating from the immutable laws of nature.

Invention—in the form of nonreproductive sexual practice—appears here as an alternative to a view of nature as programming, as ordered, predictable, and thus controllable. It plays the same role in Haraway's text as the limitless plurality of sexualities does in Derrida's. In the work of these theorists the animal understood as a sexual agent becomes the figure of radical possibility and openness. If bestiality is defensible, it is not on the grounds that as animals we are all programmed by nature (and so both the bitch in heat and the man who enjoys penetrating her can't help themselves); but that posthuman sexuality means precisely the possibility of agency, resistant practices, queer bodies, and culturally unintelligible pleasures, and that within this landscape no practice may be prohibited preemptively. As philosophers know, however, agency does not erase power structures or protect the agent from exploitation. We also know that with agency comes responsibility, which means that no practice among agents is immune to ethical examination. It is precisely when we take animals to be agents that interspecies sex becomes irreducible to questions of pleasure for the parties involved, which undermines the zoophile's insistence on the pleasure of the animal partner. Thus, while a denaturalizing of animal sexualities makes it impossible to prohibit bestiality preemptively, it remains possible (and perhaps becomes even more urgent) to make postemptive prohibitions, upon ethical examination of cultural constructs, beliefs, and practices in the presence of existing power structures.

In contrast to the view that would have us believe that animality= sexuality=nature=woman, posthuman animality explodes the universalizing category of Nature as homogeneous and predictable. It is this figure of the animal with which feminist critique should engage today precisely because it unmistakably announces that we don't know what we thought we knew about any of the players in the above equation—about sex, women, and least of all about "nature." The task, then, may be more accurately described not as re-inscription of the animal in feminism, but as the inscription of a wholly new imaginary of animality, the condition for the possibility of new imaginaries of gender.

NOTES

I'd like to thank Cara O'Connor for her insightful commentary on this piece and for Anne O'Byrne for organizing the "Feminists and Other Animals" symposium at SUNY Stony Brook, February 2009.

1. See Carolyn Adams, *The Pornography of Meat* (London: Continuum, 2003) and the account of zoos as an instance of pornography in Ralph Acampora, "Zoos and Eyes: Contesting Captivity and Seeking Successor Practices," *Society & Animals* 13, no. 1 (2005): 70–88.

2. See not only Donna Haraway, but also Jacques Derrida, Bruno Latour, and Giorgio Agamben.

3. Catharine MacKinnon, "Of Mice and Men: A Fragment on Animal Rights," in *The Feminist Care Tradition and Animal Ethics*, ed. Josephine Donovan and Carol J. Adams (New York: Columbia University Press, 2007), 320–22.

4. One recent exception, the 2008 case of Diane Whalen and Donald Siegfried, in which the Oklahoma couple was charged with bestiality, was a matter of porn production: Whalen's son discovered numerous films that Siegfried had shot of the family dogs having sex with Whalen. http://www.foxnews.com/story/2008/07/22/largest-animal-shelter-in-us-will-house-2-dogs-trained-to-have-sex-with-women.

5. For more on this subject, see Margret Grebowicz, "Democracy and Pornography: On Speech, Rights, Privacies, and Pleasures in Conflict," *Hypatia: A Journal of Feminist Philosophy* 26, no. 1 (2011).

6. http://www.animallaw.info/articles/ovuszoophilia.htm.

7. http://www.zwire.com/site/news.cfm?newsid=9968062&BRD=1719&PAG=461&dept_id=25271&rfi=8.

8. My point is not that consent is a more important category, or that consent and agency are the most significant concerns to raise in the problematic of animal sexuality. My point is more modest: that *sexual* agency is an important problem to raise about animals from a *feminist* perspective.

9. MacKinnon, "Of Mice and Men," 321.

10. Ibid., 324.

11. Ibid., 321.

12. Catharine MacKinnon, "Privacy vs. Equality: Beyond Roe vs. Wade," *Feminism Unmodified* (Cambridge, MA: Harvard University Press, 1987).

13. Take the ubiquitous "Rabbit Vibrator" (made famous by the television show "Sex and the City"), which has a soft little vibrating animal attachment, working to stimulate the clitoris while the penis-shaped shaft does the work of penetration. The animals depicted are almost exclusively rabbits (hence the name) and dolphins, with occasional appearances by mice and seahorses. These products are marketed (apparently with great success) exclusively to women, arguably to sexually self-aware, adventurous, perhaps even queer or "fluid" women. The animals in play are sexy (rabbits and dolphins) or diminutive (mice and seahorses), and note the absence of any figures of masculine virility, like dogs or horses. What exactly is happening here? This

is one example of a cultural phenomenon that Adams's particular way of reading the intersection of women and animals in pop culture does not help us to analyze robustly (though, to be fair, her own analysis is concerned exclusively with the welfare of material animals, not semiotic puzzles like this one).

14. A self-described Marxist feminist, MacKinnon nevertheless offers an important resource for this conversation by opening the space for the question of meaningful consent of animals: How might an analysis of commercial bestiality pornography benefit from Haraway's writing about labor, inequality, relations of use, and freedom in the context of the work animals do in experimental labs? See Donna Haraway, *When Species Meet* (Minneapolis: University of Minnesota Press, 2007), 73–77.

15. Haraway, *When Species Meet*, 73–74.

16. Peter Singer "Heavy Petting," *Nerve*, 2001, http://www.nerve.com/opinions/singer/heavypetting.

17. http://www.time.com/time/magazine/article/0,9171,1582336,00.html.

18. Jacques Derrida, *The Animal That Therefore I Am*, trans. David Willis (New York: Fordham University Press, 2008), 36.

19. Ibid., 40–41.

20. Donna Haraway, *The Companion Species Manifesto: Dogs, People, and Significant Otherness* (Chicago: Prickly Paradigm Press, 2003), 99.

21. In future projects, I hope to work out exactly what is meant by "agency" in a Harawayan schema. This remains a difficult and ambiguous term in her work.

22. Haraway, *The Companion Species Manifesto*, 100.

12

Responding to Revenge Porn: Challenges to Online Legal Impunity

Michael Salter and Thomas Crofts

Revenge pornography is a category of online pornography that includes amateur images or videos that were self-produced or manufactured with the consent of those depicted, but then later distributed without their consent. This is typically done in revenge following the breakdown of a relationship, hence the moniker "revenge porn." There are now a range of dedicated Web sites and blogs that encourage viewers to maliciously upload material of their partners or ex-partners. Uploading and circulating revenge porn is a highly gendered activity that is primarily perpetrated by men and disproportionately impacts women, although men may also be victimized.[1] This also occurs among minors with their peers circulating images. The paradox is that minors who engage in such activity appear to be criminalized in arguably inappropriate ways by child pornography statutes while adult perpetrators have been, at least until recently, almost immune from legal sanction.[2]

Victims of revenge porn and their allies have mobilized around principles of women's autonomy and right to sexual self-expression, only to encounter a lack of specific legislative measures to protect women who are victimized through nonconsensual circulation of intimate images. If the law represents, as Durkheim argued,[3] a system of commitments reflective of prevailing moral cultures and sentiments, then the absence of formal sanctions against revenge porn perpetrators suggests at the very least an ambivalence about the victimhood status of women harmed by revenge porn. The apparent passivity of authorities in the face of victim complaints about revenge porn suggests an undercurrent of support for the worldview of which revenge porn is a product, namely that women who take and share intimate images of themselves have fallen outside the bounds of appropriate femininity and have become legitimate objects of public ridicule and disgust.

This chapter is concerned with the shifts, changes, and collisions of moral sentiment that underpin the phenomenon of revenge pornography, arguing that these reflect larger conflicts over women's formal and informal status in interpersonal and public life. Despite the legal and social advances catalyzed by the women's movement, norms prohibiting female bodily and sexual display are widespread and, in the case of revenge porn, enforced online through semicoordinated campaigns of threats and abuse designed to "expose" the woman as perverse and promiscuous. The lack of protection afforded to victims may represent a de facto endorsement of these norms. In an opposing movement, victims and their allies have instituted their own systems to provide support, build consensus, and impose informal sanctions upon revenge porn perpetrators. Recent legal reform efforts suggest that the online social solidarity among those with shared beliefs about women's rights includes a sexual ethos whose opposition to misogynist sentiment is being lent the weight of law.

THE EMERGENCE OF REVENGE PORN

In the latter half of the 20th century, technological innovations in camera, video, computing, and communication technology were made widely available to the consumer market. For the first time, individuals were able on a large scale to make and view their own media without the involvement of an intermediary. For example, the invention of the Polaroid camera meant that photos no longer needed to be processed by a chemist, and advances in video technology enabled the production of home movies without professional assistance. Consumer interest in this technology was driven to a significant degree by its applications in sexual life since it enabled confidential production of erotic or explicit material.[4] In the 1970s and 1980s, individuals, couples, and sexual subcultures began producing and sometimes sharing amateur pornographic photos and videos with others.[5]

It soon became clear that erotic material manufactured consensually could be misused in the context of an abusive relationship. One of the earliest known examples of revenge porn was a pornographic home movie of the then-married "blacksploitation" stars Jayne Kennedy and Leon Isaac Kennedy, which was circulated commercially and informally beginning in the late 1970s. The video became available only after Jayne divorced Leon and it has been suggested that Leon released the tape to punish Jayne for leaving him.[6] In the 1980s, the pornographic magazine *Hustler* began publishing images of naked women submitted by readers, sometimes accompanied by identifying information about the women including her name. Some of these images were submitted without the permission of the women, resulting in legal action (e.g., *Wood v. Hustler Magazine Inc.*, 1984). Throughout the 1980s and into the 1990s, compromising VHS tapes of other celebrities occasionally found their way into pornography stores; however, rumors about the tapes were much more widely circulated than the tapes themselves. VHS tapes can be viewed only if a physical copy of the tape, and a video player, are available, which necessarily restricts the capacity of a vengeful ex-partner to circulate tapes to others.

As the Internet was popularized in the mid-1990s (driven in no small way by consumer interest in anonymous pornography access),[7] online communities and networks formed to share and view amateur and self-produced pornography.[8] The appeal of this amateur material was that it depicted "real" people and sexual interactions as opposed to the scripted encounters of professional pornography. This appeal extended beyond consensually circulated material to images and videos shared out of malice or revenge. The Internet transcends the physical limitations of VHS and prior media technologies, enabling the almost simultaneous production and distribution of image and video to a potentially global audience. In instances where an individual seeks to maliciously distribute a sexual image or video of another, the Internet acts as what is termed a force multiplier,[9] making the material publicly and internationally available. This has been illustrated by a number of high-profile cases in which female (and some male) celebrities have found their careers destabilized after ex-partners released or sold sexual images or video without their consent. Beyond these high-profile cases are innumerable people whose images have been uploaded to the Internet without their consent, to be shared and commented upon by a largely male audience.

THE INTERSECTION OF INTERPERSONAL AND TRANSNATIONAL HARM

Revenge porn occurs at the intersection of interpersonal and transnational harm, in which the global circulation and storage of intimate images is enabled by a personal act of betrayal. Ehrenreich Brooks observed that the marginality of international crimes in legal discourse and practice, with its state-centric focus on national jurisdictions, "maps almost precisely onto equally problematic domestic law distinctions between the private and public realms of behaviour."[10] In law, transborder and transnational forms of injustice are often misframed as domestic issues,[11] while physical and sexual coercion in private relations are misunderstood as a conflict over rights rather than exercises of power and control.[12] The incommensurability of international or private harms with the hegemonic frames operating within the criminal justice system frequently leads to their exclusion from formal modes of redress. Transnational forms of gender-based victimization are particularly problematic in this regard, because women may be denied an adequate forum to adjudicate their complaint at either a national or an international level.[13]

In effect, revenge pornography occurs at the intersection of two "meta-political injustices":[14] the legal misrepresentation of gender-based forms of coercion in terms developed for contractual relations, and the lack of international mechanisms to address transborder wrongs in a globalized world. Such misframings are not accidental but instead represent prevailing assumptions about citizenship and the obligations of the state. The increasingly global flows of information and capital engendered by digital and online technology have emerged contemporaneously with, and facilitated by, a neoliberal ideology in which responsibilities previously attributed to the state are devolved to the individual. Neoliberalism enjoins citizens to adopt a "self-governing, enterprising" mode of subjectivity while the state constricts service and program delivery.[15] This excessive focus on individual responsibility and risk management obscures the gendered differentials and inequities of interpersonal relations,[16] amplifying existing cultural logics that blame women who experience gendered violence.

In the mass media, women have been exhorted to avoid the risks that supposedly inhere in the production of intimate images, alongside the message that women who take such risks are personally responsible for any harms that subsequently befall them. In a recent article for *Forbes*, law professor Eric Goldman rejects the need for a legal remedy or a policing response to revenge porn, instead advising individuals: "Don't take nude photos or videos."[17] Other commentators have asserted more forcefully that women who make such images are "dumb."[18] The position that it is women's responsibility to manage risk in sexual encounters, and that those that fail in this endeavor are dumb, carries with it a view of romantic relations as an agreement governed by deliberative negotiation between two parties (i.e., a contract). However, as Hegel noted, contract theory obscures the social and historical structures and processes that contextualize interaction by treating them as natural or given.[19] The contractual view of sexual relations as a rational-calculative exchange naturalizes male wrongdoing and gender power imbalances as the implicit backdrops to sexual negotiations that women must factor into their decision-making.

This is a poor framework in both normative and descriptive terms through which to understand sexual interaction. Not only does it hold women responsible for male perpetration, but it overlooks the spontaneous and embodied dimensions of sexual practice that do not lend themselves to calculative rationality. Furthermore, characterizing revenge porn victims as a small group of dumb women who failed at the neoliberal project of self-management is contested by social research that demonstrates the normalization of digital and online technology within sexual life. For example, a representative sample of 647 American adults aged 18 to 24 found 33 percent had sent a nude or semi-nude image of themselves to someone else[20] and surveys based on convenience samples find that up to 50 percent of adults have done the same.[21] An industry report claimed that 25 million unique users accessed online dating sites in 2011.[22] Online sex-seeking frequently involves exchanging intimate or sexual images.[23] Research suggests that a wide range of women and men around the world are making and sending nude and erotic images of themselves to others, and male wrongdoing in this arena is neither inevitable nor widespread. While revenge porn is illustrative of patterns of coercion and abuse, it would seem that the exchange of self-produced nude images is often mutual, pleasurable, and relatively harmless.[24]

Nonetheless, in the visual economy of nudity that flourishes online, it is clear that women are considerably more vulnerable than men. Female social status has historically been closely tied to chastity and modesty, and women are particularly vulnerable to humiliation when their private sexual life is made public. In revenge porn, male offenders seek to instrumentalize double standards in sexual mores to punish an ex-partner for leaving them by circulating intimate images to third parties. These double standards have also been evident in the lackluster response to victim reports. A small number of revenge porn cases have resulted in criminal prosecutions. These are likely to increase following legal reform efforts in multiple jurisdictions, as will be discussed later in the chapter. Until recently, the more typical scenario was that there were no legal consequences for the person who maliciously circulated the image, whereas the victim was largely unable to prevent or restrict the online circulation of the material.

There are a number of practical obstacles that prevent victims from minimizing the harms of revenge porn. Efforts to permanently remove such images face almost insurmountable barriers, because images may be shared via peer-to-peer services, stored on multiple computers in multiple jurisdictions, or hosted by Web sites whose servers use various means to hide their location and identity. There is no international legal standard or law enforcement mechanism to implement the removal of such material. Some victims have sought to minimize distribution of the images by making digital copyright claims, whereas others have pursued offenders through civil action, but with little confidence that the material would be permanently removed from online circulation. The absence of legal intervention or practical assistance has compounded the intended humiliation and distress of revenge porn victimization. As the following section will discuss, this distress is further amplified by the viscerally misogynist online networks that have mobilized to stalk, harass, and threaten revenge porn victims.

THE STALKING AND HARASSMENT OF REVENGE PORN VICTIMS

Revenge pornography maps onto existing power inequities in the visual economy in which men share pornography with one another to affirm masculine bonds by objectifying women, often with strongly derogatory overtones.[25] Women and gay men may also perpetrate revenge porn, but Janice Richardson suggests they are in the minority and typically motivated by financial gain, whereas heterosexual male offenders are generally seeking to punish and humiliate ex-partners.[26] In doing so, the perpetrator can draw on the support of loosely affiliated networks of anonymous men who collectively mobilize to stalk, vilify, and threaten female victims of revenge porn. While men may be subject to revenge porn, they are very unlikely to experience the coordinated campaigns of ongoing abuse and humiliation that have targeted female victims.

Such campaigns are indicative of the sexist strains of Internet culture with their origins in the early days of networked computing. Misogynist hostility and harassment are long-standing features of women's experiences online.[27] While social media has proved to be an important platform for women's online participation, female bloggers and journalists report orchestrated sexualized intimidation from men hostile to women's use of digital and online technology.[28] Such harassment and threats of sexualized violence appear designed to force the withdrawal of their targets from public life altogether. In a similar fashion, victims of revenge porn can find that images shared without their consent can serve as flashpoints for misogynist online subcultures.

The case of Holly Jacobs is illustrative. Jacobs is an American victim and founder of the advocacy group End Revenge Porn. She has described how her ex-boyfriend initially posted explicit images online by hacking into her Facebook profile for family and friends to see, before distributing more material through revenge pornography Web sites and e-mailing the material directly to her employers.[29] Revenge pornography sites were then used by groups of men to coordinate a prolonged campaign of harassment and abuse, forcing Jacobs to curtail her professional activities and adopt a new identity. She described the impact on her Web site:

> Due to this act, I have had to legally change my name, stop publishing in my field (I am a PhD student), stop networking (giving presentations, going to conferences), change my email address four times and my phone number three times, change jobs, and explain to human resources at my school that I am not a sexual predator on campus.[30]

Jacobs approached police about her ex-boyfriend's activities but was informed that they could not charge her boyfriend because he had not stolen the images from her but rather she had shared them with him. It is unlikely—if police had actually investigated her complaint—that no evidence of criminal wrongdoing would have been uncovered given that Jacobs's ex-partner published sexualized images of her on social media that launched a subsequent campaign of threats, stalking, and harassment. Other women have also reported trenchant disinterest and unresponsiveness when they report revenge porn victimization to the police.[31] Canadian teenager Amanda Todd committed suicide in 2012 following two years of extortion by a man who obtained a nude image of her and attempted to blackmail her into sexual activity, only to send the image to her classmates when she did not comply. Prior to Todd's death, her family contacted the Canadian police five times about the extortion but police did not investigate or take proactive steps to bring the harassment to an end.[32]

The lack of a police or criminal justice response has enabled a predatory online cottage industry to develop. This includes Web sites that source intimate images using coercive or illegal methods along with attempts to extort victims for money (or sexual activity, as in the case of Amanda Todd above). These images frequently catalyze a campaign of harassment and abuse conducted by misogynist online networks of men: Women can come under intense pressure to pay the blackmail money or acquiesce to other demands. In this process, the misogyny of online masculine libertinism intersects with an entrenched ambivalence to women's status as citizens and legal subjects to create a precarious position for the growing number of women whose sexual and intimate practices incorporate the use of digital and online technology.

DEVELOPMENT OF THE REVENGE PORN BUSINESS MODEL

The Web site *Is Anyone Up?* first brought the issue of revenge porn to international attention. It was founded in late 2010 and shut down in August 2012 by its American creator Hunter Moore, whose shifting rationales for establishing the site include claims that he wanted to show his friends photos of a woman he was sleeping with, and that he and his friends wanted to get back at their ex-girlfriends by distributing photos of them without their consent.[33] Moore then created a submission form that enabled others to upload nude or graphic images to the site. This form acted, in essence, as a contract in which the submitter assumed responsibility for defamatory material in accordance with Section 230 of the Communications Decency Act of 1996, which protects Internet publishers from the content posted or submitted by others.

Is Anyone Up? hosted thousands of images of men and women alongside links to their social media profiles and derogatory commentary. Moore was notoriously unresponsive to requests from victimized adults asking for the images to be removed. Perhaps his most infamous utterance is that a person who committed suicide due to exposure on his site would only boost his profile and advertising revenue.[34] One of the regular features of the site was called "Daily Hate," which contained complaints or legal threats from people who had their pictures posted on the site without consent.[35] Moore typically responded by reposting the image alongside a copy of the complaint, resulting in further distress and harassment of the complainant. In 2012, *Rolling Stone* branded Moore "The most hated man on the Internet."[36]

The site garnered international notoriety and condemnation, attracting up to 240,000 unique visitors per day at the height of its popularity.[37] Moore claimed to be earning over $13,000 a month in advertising revenue from the site.[38] In an interview, Moore confidently asserted that, because his site hosted only user-submitted content, he was protected from possible civil or criminal charges. However, a substantial proportion of women whose images were posted on his site alleged that the images had been stolen or hacked from online accounts.

Charlotte Laws, an ex-private detective, began documenting these allegations when her daughter Kayla found that personal images of her had been hacked in early 2012 and uploaded to *Is Anyone Up?*[39] After being offered little support from the Los Angeles Police Department, Laws began contacting and informally surveying women whose images were available on *Is Anyone Up?* She found that approximately 40 percent reported they were the victims of hackers.[40] After a period of monitoring Moore's online activity and social media account, she passed evidence of hacking to the FBI, who initiated a formal investigation.

Shortly afterwards, Moore shut down *Is Anyone Up?* At the time, he claimed that there were too many images of minors being submitted to the site, and that the legal requirements of age checking and contacting the police were too onerous.[41] However, it is likely that he was made aware of the FBI investigation by his lawyers. If closing the site was an attempt to forestall the police investigation, it failed. Moore's parents' house, where he lived, was raided by the FBI in early 2013.[42] In January 2014, Moore was arrested and indicted along with another man, Charles Evens, on fifteen counts of conspiracy, computer hacking, aggravated identity theft, and aiding and abetting.[43] Prosecutors contend that Moore paid Evens for photos that Evens obtained by hacking e-mail accounts.

It is notable that it took a highly motivated and skilled victims advocate in Charlotte Laws to trigger a formal investigation into Moore's alleged activities, although the hacking allegations had been regularly aired in media coverage and victims had made individual complaints to law enforcement. This provides further support for the argument that the lack of legal protections for revenge porn victims is reflective of a broader disinterest in, or even hostility to, women who are subject to harm and abuse after engaging in behavior deemed to be immodest or risky. There appears to be a continuum of what are termed subterranean values[44] (e.g., deriving a thrill from unacceptable or illegal behavior) that discourage supportive responses to revenge porn and may even enjoin others in the victimization of targeted women.

In the twelve months following the closure of *Is Anyone Up?*, Hunter Moore's Twitter following increased from 50,000 to 550,000.[45] He now has over 580,000 followers. The most ardent of these style themselves as "The Family" with Moore as "The Father." Collectively The Family can tweet hundreds of thousands or even millions of times a day.[46] His vast online support network poses a serious risk to Moore's detractors. Once Moore became aware of Law's identity, she found herself the target of a campaign of abuse and terrorization including telephone and e-mail threats of death and rape.[47] Moore enjoys the support of thousands of zealous followers who view him as a victim of the forces of "sexual repression."[48]

REVENGE PORN, BLACKMAIL, AND EXTORTION

It is clear that revenge porn is the focus of strong but conflicting sentiments that have stymied the development of a coherent policing or legal response. Efforts to protect revenge porn victims from abuse, and to hold perpetrators to account, are in direct conflict with the view that the harms of revenge porn are primarily the fault of the woman who took the picture or allowed it to be taken. This is the view articulated by revenge porn operators such as Moore, who reveled in the evident amorality of his conduct while repudiating responsibility for it. Instead, Moore assigned ultimate culpability to those who take erotic or sexual images of themselves in the first place. He articulated a sexual ethos that is a paradoxical mix of prurient conservativism and libertarian machismo, in which women who take sexual photos of themselves deserve to be publicly shamed and humiliated, and do not deserve the benefit of legal rights and protections—but those that humiliate them do. The allegations against Moore suggest that this rationale was a buffer, behind which a more complex set of calculations were at play, and in which Moore allegedly sought to meet viewer demand for more images (and thus maintain the profitability of his site) by engaging a hacker.

The convergence of conservative misogyny, libertarian sexuality, and commercial opportunism is even more readily apparent in those revenge porn sites that seek to replicate and expand the revenge porn business model brokered by Moore. *Is Anybody Down?* was a site set up by American Craig Brittain that ran from December 2011 to April 2013. Like *Is Anyone Up?*, the site hosted nude and sexual images, along with identifying information, without the consent of the person depicted. However, the victim information provided by Brittain was particularly extensive, including the woman's name, address, and, often, her phone number. Victims were catalogued according to state, country, and physical attributes, including derogatory references to sexual orientation, weight, and purported sexually transmitted infections.[49] This site was very aggressive in soliciting content, posting job advertisements for "content acquisition specialists" who were apparently tasked with befriending women on online dating sites and soliciting naked images from them, which they then provided to *Is Anybody Down?* along with the women's names and contact details.[50] Brittain himself was accused of posing as a woman online to solicit naked photos from women before posting these to *Is Anybody Down?*[51]

The site was operated in a maliciously intrusive way designed to maximize the reputational damage and harassment experienced by victims. For those women seeking to have images removed from *Is Anybody Down?*, the site recommended the services of a fictitious New York lawyer, David Blade III, who promised to remove the images for a fee of between $200 and $300. Electronic evidence indicates that that David Blade III is, in fact, Craig Brittain.[52] Brittain denied this but acknowledged that he profited from the money that women pay to "Blade" for the removal of images from his site.[53] The site garnered international media attention and the ensuing negative publicity appeared to get the better of Brittain, who in April 2013 closed the site, confessing on Twitter that he was "very, very lonely" and had been "bullied myself as a child."[54] Brittain subsequently threatened to repost the content of the site, but did not go ahead. Civil action is reportedly being considered by some of his victims.[55]

More recently, the operator of revenge porn site *Ugotposted*, Californian Kevin Bollaert, was arrested and charged with thirty-one counts of identity theft, extortion, and conspiracy. Bollaert's site hosted nude and sexual images of adults alongside identifying information, and directed victims to a separate Web site (changemyreputation.com) in which they were asked to pay between $300 and $350 to have the pictures removed. Like other revenge porn operators, Bollaert's Web site includes a submission form through which users posted content to the site. However, Bollaert's submission form went further by specifically requiring the user to submit identifying information alongside photos, including the victim's full name, location, age, and social media links. While the use of a submission form was an apparent attempt to take advantage of Section 230 of the Communications Decency Act of

1996, the specific requirement that users submit the identifying information of victims is allegedly in breach of California Penal Code sections 530.5 and 653m (b). This section makes it illegal in California to willfully obtain identifying information "for any unlawful purpose, including with the intent to annoy or harass." Bollaert has been charged in effect under laws criminalizing identity theft, while his apparent attempts to extort and blackmail people depicted on his site has yet to be the subject of a criminal charge.

CHALLENGING LEGAL IMPUNITY: IS A NEW LAW NECESSARY?

Prior to the arrests of Bollaert and Moore, criminal charges against revenge porn perpetrators and Web site operators are notable only for their absence. Unable to elicit a response from the police and the justice system, some revenge porn victims and advocates turned instead to vigilante remedies to sanction perpetrators. For example, in August 2011, a young woman whose pictures were posted on *Is Anyone Up?* found Hunter Moore's home address and stabbed him in the shoulder as he walked to the mailbox.[56] The wound was not serious but required stitches. Hunter Moore and Craig Brittain have also been targeted by the hacker collective Anonymous, which "doxxed" them by gathering and publishing their private information, and disrupting their Web sites.[57] Hacking revenge porn sites and doxxing men who post images of women online without their consent has since become relatively common, with some individuals and groups mobilizing online to uncover the names of perpetrators, document their activities, publish their details, and pass them on to law enforcement agencies.[58]

A number of women, including Holly Jacobs, have formed online support groups for victims. Jacobs's site End Revenge Porn is prominent, as is the Web site Women Against Revenge Porn, run by revenge porn victim Bekah Wells, while victims in Texas have set up Army of She. The sites vehemently resist the stigmatization of revenge porn victims by publicizing women's experiences of victimization and providing practical advice and legal referrals. The sites seek to coordinate legal action against perpetrators and Web sites, and to organize lobbying efforts for the criminalization of revenge pornography. For example, Jacobs has worked directly with California State Senator Anthony Cannella, who has sponsored a bill that recently passed the legislature to make some forms of revenge porn a misdemeanor punishable by up to six months in jail for a first offense.[59]

It is commonly thought that revenge porn is an area where the law has failed to keep up with technical and social developments and is inadequate in its current state to appropriately deal with revenge porn. Before addressing whether there really is a need for, and advantages to, new legal measures, it is first worth examining whether there are existing laws that can appropriately be applied to revenge porn. It appears that there are a number of existing legal remedies for a victim of revenge porn in civil and in criminal law; however, the effectiveness of these remedies depends on the function that the branch of law is designed to fulfill. Whereas civil law is a private matter between the individual parties with remedies designed primarily to compensate for any loss or harm caused, criminal law is a public matter generally prosecuted by the state with remedies designed primarily to punish the harm-doer rather than compensate the victim. Criminal law also has a broader, symbolic, communicative, and censuring function. Indeed, as Andrew Ashworth notes, "[i]t is the censure conveyed by criminal liability which marks out its special social significance."[60]

A person may seek remedy in civil law to compensate for the harm or loss caused by revenge porn. This may be in actions for breach of privacy, or in jurisdictions where this action does not exist (such as Australia) it may take the form of breach of confidence or possibly intentional infliction of emotional distress. *Giller v. Procopets* [2008] VSCA 236 is the first Australian case where it was accepted that a person could recover damages for emotional distress under the tort of breach of confidence as a result of the distribution of videos showing sexual intercourse. In this case, Ms. Giller lived in a de facto relationship with Mr. Procopets between 1990 and 1993. Mr. Procopets made VHS video recordings of himself engaging in sexual activity with Ms. Giller. After the relationship broke down, Procopets sought to harass Giller by showing and sending these videos to her family and friends. It was found that Giller could recover damages to compensate for the mental distress that she had suffered through the showing of these videos. Other possible civil actions include defamation, where the distributed material "injures the reputation of another by exposing him to hatred, contempt, or ridicule, or which tends to lower him in the esteem of right-thinking members of society,"[61] and breach of copyright, where a person has created, and thus has ownership of, the material.

A limitation of civil law is that the person must have enough financial and emotional resources to bring a case. More fundamentally, civil law largely lacks the symbolic, condemnatory function that is inherent in criminal law. Remedies are generally awarded only to compensate for injury and to put the person back in the position they would have been if the defendant had not committed the wrongful act. While punitive or exemplary damages, which aim to punish the defendant and to deter such behavior, are available, they are rarely awarded because they are regarded as crossing the jurisdictional boundary into criminal law without providing the protections of the criminal law system.[62]

This situation points to the obvious advantage of criminal law, which is designed to deter behavior and relies upon the state in most cases to take over the process of prosecution. There already exists a range of laws that may cover cases of revenge porn, raising the questions of whether these offenses are effectively enforced in relation to revenge porn and, if they are, whether a specific law is necessary. In many jurisdictions there are laws against publishing indecent material, for example, 578C *Crimes Act (1900)* NSW. In the 2011 case *Police v. Ravshan Usmanov* a 20-year-old man was convicted of this offense after he uploaded six pictures of his girlfriend to Facebook showing her genital area and breasts. In sentencing Mr. Usmanov to six-month imprisonment, Deputy Chief Magistrate Mottley commented:

> In relation to this matter I have regard to the purposes of sentencing, and in particular the need to prevent crime by deterring both the offender and the community generally from committing similar crimes. This is a particularly relevant consideration in a matter such as this where new age technology through Facebook gives instant access to the world. Facebook as a social networking site has limited boundaries. Incalculable damage can be done to a person's reputation by the irresponsible posting of information through that medium. With its popularity and potential for real harm, there is a genuine need to ensure the use of this medium to commit offences of this type is deterred.[63]

In recent decades most jurisdictions have also enacted laws to cover stalking. This was triggered by the murder of five women in California between 1989 and 1990. The fact that prior to their murders the women claimed that they had been repeatedly harassed by former lovers or fans (one case involved the actress Rebecca Shaeffer) and that four of the victims had restraining orders against their killers highlighted the very real harms flowing from stalking behavior and the fact that the criminal law did not provide adequate protection for victims of stalking.[64] In order to fill that gap California, closely followed by many other jurisdictions, created specific antistalking laws (California Penal Code § 646.9). These laws generally address repeatedly following or communicating with the victim and either causing the victim distress or fear for their safety or the safety of others and/or the intention to cause harassment, alarm, or distress. Such laws (e.g., California Penal Code § 646.9(g), (h)) may make specific reference to the use of electronic means of communication, covering mobile phones and similar devices.

In 2004, a law was added to the Australian Commonwealth Criminal Code to cover using a carriage service (Internet, e-mails, mobile phone, etc.) to menace, harass, or cause offense (s 474.17). There is a violation when a person publishes or distributes material in a way "that a reasonable person would regard as being, in all the circumstances, menacing, harassing or offensive." This law does not require that a person intends to menace or harass but only that they were reckless; that is, they were aware of a substantial risk that this would occur and it was not justifiable to take that risk (s 5.4). While the Commonwealth Attorney General's Department has stated that this law is adequate to address revenge porn,[65] the law has yet to be applied in a revenge porn case. However, two men in the Australian Defence Force were recently convicted of this offense after one man streamed via Skype his consensual sexual activity with a female army cadet.[66]

Despite the fact that there are already a range of legal measures that could apply to revenge porn scenarios it appears that prosecution under existing laws is still quite rare. This might be because of difficulties satisfying provisions, such as the intention to harass for a stalking offense. It may also be due to the reluctance of victims to bring forward a complaint for fear of bringing further attention to the fact that the material has been disseminated. It may also be because, as in the case of stalking, there is a lag in developing the social realization that such behaviors are indeed harmful and worthy of criminalization. In response to growing concern that the criminal law is not adequate to address revenge porn some jurisdictions have now introduced or are planning to introduce laws specifically dealing with nonconsensual distribution of material. For example, New Jersey and California are the first states in the United States to enact criminal measures with other U.S. states and the Australian state of Victoria considering the introduction of similar laws.

The California Penal Code §647(j)(4) applies where a person distributes, with the intention of causing serious emotional distress, an image that he or she took of an intimate part of another person's body in circumstances where there is an agreement or understanding that it will remain private. For this law to apply, the person must distribute the images with the intention of causing serious emotional distress and the depicted person must suffer serious emotional distress. While introducing such a law is lauded by some as a step in the right direction, there is concern that this will be of limited effectiveness because it only covers images that offenders took themselves, and thus will not apply to cases where individuals pass on images that they did not create. Furthermore, there is a need for proof that distribution is done with the intent to cause severe emotional distress, a condition that may be difficult to prove. Others are critical of whether such a law conflicts with the First Amendment right to free speech.[67]

Despite these limitations and the argument that there are existing laws that could and should be used to deal with revenge porn, there are specific advantages to new laws designed specifically for revenge porn. This advantage relates to the communicative and symbolic function of criminal law because criminal "liability is the strongest formal condemnation that society can inflict."[68] Creating such a law therefore expresses social condemnation of the practice at the core of the offense and acknowledges the harms associated with such behaviors. From a fair-labeling perspective, a new law is a positive step because it appropriately identifies and specifically names the particular wrongfulness of revenge porn. James Chalmers and Fiona Leverick explain the dual role of fair labeling, writing "It might be thought that the language of 'labelling' could refer only to the description attached to the offender's conduct, but in fact one of the considerations which is often taken to underpin fair labelling is the need to differentiate between different forms of wrongdoing."[69] Fair labeling is fundamentally important given the nature of criminal law as society's most condemnatory tool. Criminal labels operate as short-hand communication giving the public a clear indication of what the offender has done and precisely how he or she has "failed in her or his basic duties as a citizen."[70] William Wilson comments, "[p]recise, meaningful offence [sic] labels are as important as justice in the distribution of punishment. These labels help us to make moral sense of the world."[71]

On a wider and perhaps more fundamental level, criminal labels have a symbolic and educational function in society. Seeing offenders convicted according to the perceived wrongfulness of the behavior communicates society's core values and confirms in the public's mind the wrongfulness of the behavior.[72] The advantage of creating specific legal redress rather than relying on broader statutes or civil law is that a "criminal provision is better able to communicate the boundaries of socially acceptable behaviour if it packages crimes in morally significant ways."[73]

In order to be effective, a new law should focus on the intentional dissemination, or the threat of dissemination, of the intimate image without the consent of the victim (or without reasonable grounds for presuming consent) to the manner of distribution regardless of whether the person is the creator of the image or has merely come into possession of that image.[74] In recommending a new law it must also be kept in mind that there are limits to what the law can do, and there must also be a social awareness among victims, the public, the police, prosecutors, and the courts that such behavior deserves prosecution. A new specific law can, however, through its symbolic function confirm in the public consciousness the wrongfulness of distributing intimate images of another without that person's consent. A new law also functions to contest or disrupt misogynist social norms and values that deflect responsibility for the harms of revenge porn from the perpetrator and instead blame the victim.

CONCLUSION

Revenge porn raises important questions about how individuals nego-tiate responsibility, vulnerability, and trust in intimate relations. Revenge porn also raises important questions about how to respond when this trust is betrayed and amplified to international effect by new media technology. In the absence of an adequate criminal justice or law enforcement response, revenge porn has operated in a zone of legal impunity that has generated a set of countervailing forces active online. Misogynist networks of men and boys use revenge porn to harass and intimidate women online and offline, and some members of these networks seek to eroticize and commodify female dis-tress by establishing dedicated revenge porn Web sites and extorting female victims for money. In opposition, victims and their advocates are organiz-ing to provide support, formulate a political and collective response, and impose sanctions upon offenders because the justice system will not. How-ever, without the legal or practical means to disrupt the circulation of their images online, victims of revenge porn remain vulnerable to ongoing abuse and harassment orchestrated by parties hostile to women's online and public participation.

As digital and online technology is integrated into social and sexual life, it can operate as a new medium for reproducing and intensifying relational and gendered coercion. Revenge porn is one example of this. It is apparent that existing criminal laws could be applied to sanction revenge porn perpetrators, but a new legal strategy may be necessary in order to adequately label the harms of revenge porn and communicate that it is serious and deserves pros-ecution. This is the preferred response of a growing number of jurisdictions that are seeking to criminalize revenge porn. In doing so, they are challenging entrenched cultural logics that blame women for putting themselves "at risk" of victimization and endorse the public shaming of female sexuality. Judith Herman notes that it is common for sexual offenses to include a "ritualized element" designed to "defile" the victim in the eyes of others.[75] Creating laws that specifically target revenge porn may both deter perpetrators and operate symbolically to restore and affirm the dignity of victims.

NOTES

1. Janice Richardson, "If I Cannot Have Her Everybody Can: Sexual Disclosure and Privacy Law," in *Feminist Perspectives on Tort Law*, ed. Jane Richardson and Erica Rackley (Abingdon & New York: Routledge, 2012), 145.

2. Michael Salter, Thomas Crofts, and Murray Lee, "Beyond Criminalisation and Responsibilisation: Sexting, Gender and Young People," *Current Issues in Criminal Justice* 24, no. 3 (2013): 301–16.

3. Emile Durkheim, *The Division of Labor in Society* (New York: Simon and Schuster, 1997).

4. Jonathan Coopersmith, "Pornography, Technology and Progress," *ICON* 4 (1998): 94–125.

5. Mark Dery, "Naked Lunch: Talking Realcore with Sergio Messina," in *C'lickme: A Netporn Studies Reader*, ed. K. Jacobs, M. Janssen, and M. Pasquinelli (Amsterdam: Institute of Network Cultures, 2007), 18.

6. Ed Halter, "Secrets and Thighs: A History of Celebrity Sex Tapes, Real and Fake, from Joan Crawford to Paris Hilton," *Village Voice*, December 2, 2003, http://www.villagevoice.com/2003-12-02/news/secrets-and-thighs.

7. Jonathan Coopersmith, "Pornography, Videotape and the Internet," *Technology and Society Magazine, IEEE* 19, no. 1 (2000): 28.

8. Dery, "Naked Lunch: Talking Realcore with Sergio Messina," 22–23.

9. Majid Yar, "The Novelty of 'Cybercrime': An Assessment in Light of Routine Activity Theory." *European Journal of Criminology* 2, no. 4 (2005): 411.

10. Rosa Ehrenreich Brooks, "Feminism and International Law: An Opportunity for Transformation," *Yale Journal of Law and Feminism* 14 (2002): 349.

11. Nancy Fraser, *Scales of Justice: Reimagining Political Space in a Globalizing World* (Cambridge & Malden, MA: Polity, 2008), 12–29.

12. Virginia Held, *The Ethics of Care: Personal, Political and Global* (New York: Oxford, 2005).

13. Michael Salter, "Getting Hagued: The Impact of International Law on Child Abduction by Protective Mothers," *Alternative Law Journal* 39 (2014): 19.

14. Fraser, *Scales of Justice: Reimagining Political Space in a Globalizing World*, 62.

15. Yvonne Hartman, "In Bed with the Enemy: Some Ideas on the Connections between Neoliberalism and the Welfare State," *Current Sociology* 53, no. 1 (2005): 63.

16. Julia O'Connor, Ann Shola Orloff, and Seila Shaver, *States, Markets, Families: Gender, Liberalism and Social Policy in Australia, Canada, Great Britain and the United States* (Cambridge: Cambridge University Press, 1999).

17. Eric Goldman, "What Should We Do About Revenge Porn Sites Like Texxxan?," *Forbes*, January 28, 2013, http://www.forbes.com/sites/ericgoldman/2013/01/28/what-should-we-do-about-revenge-porn-sites-like-texxxan.

18. Mary Elizabeth Williams, "'Real Housewives,' Spare Us Your Sex Tapes," *Salon*, June 9, 2010, http://www.salon.com/2010/06/08/danielle_staub_sex_tape_fatigue.

19. Georg Wilhelm Fredrich Hegel, *Hegel: Elements of the Philosophy of Right* (Cambridge: Cambridge University Press, 1991).

20. AP/MTV, "A Thin Line: 2009 AP-MTVDigital Abuse Study" (2009), http://www.athinline.org/MTV-AP_Digital_Abuse_Study_Executive_Summary.pdf.

21. Bianca Klettke, David J. Hallford, and David J. Mellor, "Sexting Prevalence and Correlates: A Systematic Literature Review," *Clinical Psychology Review* 34, no. 1 (2014): 48–49.

22. Eli Finkel, Paul Eastwick, Benjamin Karney, Harry Reis, and Susan Sprecher, "Online Dating: A Critical Analysis from the Perspective of Psychological Science," *Psychological Science in the Public Interest* 13, no. 1 (2012): 5.

23. Diane Kholos Wysocki and Cheryl Childers, "'Let My Fingers Do the Talking': Sexting and Infidelity in Cyberspace," *Sexuality & Culture* 15, no. 3 (2011): 230.

24. There are important questions about the reproduction and intensification of normalized gender stereotypes that are frequently evident in consensually manufactured nude and erotic images, as well as the influence of consumer culture and bodily objectification in digital erotic self-presentation (see Jessica Ringrose, Laura Harvey, Rosalind Gill, and Sonia Livingstone, "Teen Girls, Sexual Double Standards and 'Sexting': Gendered Value in Digital Image Exchange," *Feminist Theory* 14, no. 3 (2013); Laura Harvey, Jessica Ringrose, and Rosalind Gill, "Swagger, Ratings and Masculinity: Theorising the Circulation of Social and Cultural Value in Teenage Boys' Digital Peer Networks," *Sociological Research Online* 18, no. 4 (2013); Jessica Ringrose, *Postfeminist Education? Girls and the Sexual Politics of Schooling* (Oxon & New York: Routledge, 2012). These factors may shape the contexts in which images are produced and exchanged, and the way images are interpreted and shared, in problematic ways. Nonetheless in most cases it would appear that the trust and privacy of those who share such images are generally respected by those to whom they send the images.

25. Michael Flood, "Men, Sex and Homosociality: How Bonds between Men Shape Their Sexual Relations with Women," *Men and Masculinities* 10, no. 3 (2008): 352.

26. Richardson, "If I Cannot Have Her Everybody Can: Sexual Disclosure and Privacy Law," 145.

27. Janet Morahan-Martin, "The Gender Gap in Internet Use: Why Men Use the Internet More Than Women—a Literature Review," *CyberPsychology & Behavior* 1, no. 1 (1998): 5.

28. For example, see Soraya Chemaly, "The Digital Safety Gap and the Online Harassment of Women," *Huffington Post Media*, January 28, 2013, http://www.huffingtonpost.com/soraya-chemaly/women-online-harassment_b_2567898.html; Julia Baird, "Twitter Opens a New World of Abuse Aimed at Women," *Sydney Morning Herald*, February 15, 2014, http://www.smh.com.au/comment/twitter-opens-a-new-world-of-abuse-aimed-at-women-20140214-32qyf.html; Amanda Hess, "Why Women Aren't Welcome on the Internet," *Pacific Standard*, January 6, 2014, http://www.psmag.com/navigation/health-and-behavior/women-arent-welcome-internet-72170.

29. Michael Miller, "Miami Revenge Porn Victim Holly Jacobs Demands Politicians 'Take Issue Seriously'," *Miama New Times*, May 2, 2013, http://blogs.miaminewtimes.com/riptide/2013/05/miami_revenge_porn_victim_holl.php.

30. http://www.endrevengeporn.org/my-letter-to-legislators.html.

31. Maureen O'Connor, "The Crusading Sisterhood of Revenge-Porn Victims," *New York Magazine*, August 29, 2013, http://nymag.com/thecut/2013/08/crusading-sisterhood-of-revenge-porn-victims.html; Tracey Clark-Flory, "Doxxing Victim: 'This Isn't About Porn, This Is About Humiliation," *Salon*, March 2, 2014, http://www.salon.com/2014/03/02/doxxing_victim_this_isn%E2%80%99t_about_porn_this_is_about_humiliation.

32. CBC News, "Amanda Todd Suicide: RCMP Repeatedly Told of Blackmailers Attempts," *CBC News*, November 15, 2013, http://www.cbc.ca/news/canada/amanda-todd-suicide-rcmp-repeatedly-told-of-blackmailer-s-attempts-1.2427097.

33. Alex Morris, "Hunter Moore: The Most Hated Man on the Internet," *Rolling Stone*, October 11, 2012, http://www.rollingstone.com/culture/news/the-most-hated-man-on-the-internet-20121113; Camille Dodero, "Bullyville Has Taken over Hunter Moore's Is Anyone Up," *Village Voice*, April 19, 2012, http://blogs.villagevoice.com/runninscared/2012/04/bullyville_isanyoneup.php.

34. Camille Dodero, "Hunter Moore Makes a Living Screwing You," *Village Voice*, April 4, 2012, http://www.villagevoice.com/2012-04-04/news/revenge-porn-hunter-moore-is-anyone-up.

35. Danny Gold, "The Man Who Makes Money Publishing Your Nude Pics," *The Awl*, November 10, 2011, http://www.theawl.com/2011/11/the-man-who-makes-money-publishing-your-nude-pics.

36. Morris, "Hunter Moore: The Most Hated Man on the Internet."

37. Dodero, "Hunter Moore Makes a Living Screwing You."

38. Gold, "The Man Who Makes Money Publishing Your Nude Pics."

39. Charlotte Laws, "I've Been Called the 'Erin Brockovich' of Revenge Porn, and for the First Time Ever, Here Is My Entire Uncensored Story of Death Threats, Anonymous and the FBI," *XOJane*, November 21, 2013, http://www.xojane.com/it-happened-to-me/charlotte-laws-hunter-moore-erin-brockovich-revenge-porn.

40. Ibid.

41. Dodero, "Bullyville Has Taken over Hunter Moore's Is Anyone Up."

42. Camille Dodero, "How Revenge-Porn Publisher Hunter Moore Suffered $250,000 Worth of Payback," *Gawker*, March 12, 2013, http://gawker.com/5965758/how-revenge-porn-publisher-hunter-moore-suffered-250000-worth-of-payback.

43. AP, "Notorious 'Revenge Porn King' Charged with Hacking," *Sydney Morning Herald*, January 25, 2014, http://www.smh.com.au/world/notorious-revenge-porn-king-charged-with-hacking-20140125-hv9tc.html.

44. David Matza and Gresham M. Sykes, "Juvenile Delinquency and Subterranean Values," *American Sociological Review* 26, no. 5 (1961): 713.

45. Eric Markowitz, "The 8,000 of Hunter Moore's Cult Will Do Anything for 'The Father,'" *Vocativ*, January 8, 2014, http://www.vocativ.com/culture/celebrity/8000-members-hunter-moores-cult-will-anything-father.

46. Ibid.

47. Laws, "I've Been Called the 'Erin Brockovich' of Revenge Porn, and for the First Time Ever, Here Is My Entire Uncensored Story of Death Threats, Anonymous and the FBI."

48. Brian Feldman, "How Hunter Moore Tries to Silence Critics: A Step-by-Step Guide," *Vocativ*, January 16 2014, http://www.vocativ.com/culture/uncategorized/hunter-moore-tries-silence-critics-step-step-guide.

49. Chet Hardin, "The Face of Revenge Porn: Awash in 'Honest' Porn, Colorado Springs' Craig Brittain Reigns as One of the Most Hated Men on the Internet," *Colorado Springs Independent*, January 9, 2013, http://www.csindy.com/coloradosprings/the-face-of-revenge/Content?oid=2608450.

50. Jessica Roy, "Even as He Promises to Close 'Is Anyone Down,' Craig Brittain Covertly Plans a New Revenge Porn Site," *BetaBeat*, April 5, 2013, http://betabeat.com/2013/04/craig-brittain-revenge-porn-is-anybody-down-obama-nudes.

51. Brian Maass, "Revenge Porn Website May Be 'Catfishing,' Impersonating Women to Obtain Nude Photos," CBS Denver, February 15, 2013, http://denver.cbslocal.com/2013/02/15/revenge-porn-website-operator-may-be-catfishing-impersonating-woman-to-obtain-nude-photos.

52. Timothy Lee, "'Involuntary Porn' Site Tests the Boundaries of Legal Extortion," Ars Technica, November 14, 2012, http://arstechnica.com/tech-policy/2012/11/involuntary-porn-site-tests-the-boundaries-of-legal-extortion.

53. Hardin, "The Face of Revenge Porn: Awash in 'Honest' Porn, Colorado Springs' Craig Brittain Reigns as One of the Most Hated Men on the Internet."

54. Jessica Roy, "Craig Brittain, Owner of Revenge Porn Hub Is Anybody Down, Says He's Shutting the Site," Betabeat, April 4, 2013, http://betabeat.com/2013/04/craig-brittain-owner-of-revenge-porn-site-is-anybody-down-says-hes-shutting-down-the-site.

55. Roy, "Even as He Promises to Close 'Is Anyone Down', Craig Brittain Covertly Plans a New Revenge Porn Site."

56. Gold, "The Man Who Makes Money Publishing Your Nude Pics."

57. Dave Lee, "Anonymous Target Revenge Porn Site Owner Hunter Moore," BBC, December 3 2012, http://www.bbc.co.uk/news/technology-20579728; Hardin, "The Face of Revenge Porn: Awash in 'Honest' Porn, Colorado Springs' Craig Brittain Reigns as One of the Most Hated Men on the Internet."

58. Adrian Chen, "Unmasking Reddit's Violentacrez, the Biggest Troll on the Web," Gawker, December 12, 2012, http://gawker.com/5950981/unmasking-reddits-violentacrez-the-biggest-troll-on-the-web; Melissa Jeltson, "Predditors: New Tumblr Outs People Who Post 'Creepshots' to Reddit," Huffington Post, November 11, 2012, http://www.huffingtonpost.com/2012/10/11/predditors-tumblr-creepshots-reddit_n_1955897.html.

59. O'Connor, "The Crusading Sisterhood of Revenge-Porn Victims."

60. Andrew Ashworth, Principles of Criminal Law (Oxford: Oxford University Press, 2006), 1.

61. Lord Atkin, Sim v. Stretch [1936] 2 All ER 1237, 1240.

62. See State Farm Mutual Automobile Insurance Co v Campbell, 538 U.S. 408 (2003).

63. Police v. Ravshan Usmanov [2011] NSWLC 40, 19.

64. Heather M. Stearns, "Stalking Stuffers: A Revolutionary Law to Keep Predators Behind Bars." Santa Clara Law Review 35 (1994): 1027.

65. AAP, "Revenge Porn 'Spreading Like Wildfire,'" SBS.com.au, November 22, 2013, http://www.sbs.com.au/news/article/2013/11/22/revenge-porn-spreading-wildfire.

66. AAP, "Army Sacking over Skype Sex Scandal," Sydney Morning Herald, November 9, 2013, http://www.smh.com.au/national/army-sacking-over-skype-sex-scandal-20131109-2x70k.html.

67. Mark Bennett, "Are Statutes Criminalising Revenge Porn Constitutional," Defending people: The tao of criminal-defense trial lawyering, October 14, 2013, http://blog.bennettandbennett.com/2013/10/are-statutes-criminalizing-revenge-porn-constitutional.html.

68. Ashworth, *Principles of Criminal Law*, 1.

69. James Chalmers and Fiona Leverick. "Fair Labelling in Criminal Law," *The Modern Law Review* 71, no. 2 (2008): 22.

70. Jeremy Horder, "Rethinking Non-Fatal Offences against the Person," *Oxford Journal of Legal Studies* 14, no. 3 (1994): 339.

71. William Wilson, "What's Wrong with Murder?," *Criminal Law and Philosophy* 1, no. 2 (2007): 162.

72. Barry Mitchell, "Multiple Wrongdoing and Offence Structure: A Plea for Consistency and Fair Labelling," *The Modern Law Review* 64, no. 3 (2001): 398.

73. William Wilson, "What's Wrong with Murder?," 162.

74. For a similar proposal see Victorian Law Reform Committee, "Inquiry into Sexting" (Parliamentary Paper No. 230, 2013), 152.

75. Judith Herman, "Justice from the Victim's Perspective," *Violence Against Women* 11, no. 5 (2005): 572.

Section II

Cultural Issues and Effects

13

Interpreting the Data: Assessing Competing Claims in Pornography Research

Ronald Weitzer

Much of what has been written about pornography, and commercial sex generally, is grounded in a perspective that depicts all types of sex work as exploitative, violent, and perpetuating gender inequality. This "oppression paradigm" insists that exploitation and violence are not just variables but instead are central to the very essence of pornography, prostitution, and stripping.[1] I have argued that those who adopt the oppression paradigm substitute ideology for rigorous empirical analysis and that their one-dimensional arguments are contradicted by a wealth of social science data that shows sex work to be much more variegated structurally and experientially.[2] And the oppression paradigm is not just an arcane academic notion; it has been manifested in public policy and law enforcement regarding pornography, prostitution, and commercial stripping in many societies. Former presidential candidate Mitt Romney advocated fitting all new computers with a filter that would block Internet pornography, and there have been other recent abolitionist efforts worldwide. In February 2013, a parliamentary proposal in liberal Iceland sought to ban Internet pornography from the island; the measure failed but may be reintroduced (Iceland banned strip clubs in 2010 on the grounds that they violated women's rights). In March 2013, a resolution introduced in the European Parliament would have banned "all forms of pornography" from the Internet and required Internet service providers to police their customers. Introduced by a Dutch socialist party parliamentarian, this measure also failed. Efforts such as these show that, despite the ubiquity of porn on the Internet, the war over pornography is far from over.

CRITIQUES OF PORNOGRAPHY

Many of those who write about porn make no pretense of being fair and balanced. Several of these authors are staunch antiporn academics or activists and, given their strong views, it is no surprise that they excoriate pornography, see nothing positive in it, and offer sweeping generalizations in order to condemn it. This lack of objectivity is revealed by Karen Boyle, who writes: "My antiporn politics drive what I think are the significant questions to be asked about/of pornography. These politics shape how I define pornography."[3] Following in the footsteps of Andrea Dworkin and Catharine MacKinnon, many of the writings of today's generation of antiporn academics jettison scholarship in favor of a call to action: One writer calls upon male porn consumers to reject porn and "reclaim their own humanity,"[4] and another states, "Precisely because porn has taken over the culture to such an extent it's getting to the point where a lot of people have had enough."[5] For Gail Dines, pornography is a major reason why women are subordinated in society: "As long as we have porn, [women] will never be seen as full human beings deserving of all the rights that men have."[6]

There are at least four striking features of the critical literature. The first is the claim that porn has powerful effects on men and women. According to Ann Russo, pornography "perpetuates sexual abuse and discrimination in the real world" because it legitimates "harassment and abuse as forms of sexual pleasure and entertainment"; she is unequivocal in her belief that porn functions as "a method to motivate, orchestrate, justify, and guide sexual abuse and violence against women."[7]

The second feature of the antiporn literature is that key terms are left undefined. Porn is said to be "degrading," "dehumanizing," and "body punishing," and consumers lack "empathy" with the (victimized) performers. Boyle claims that "the 'extreme' [in porn has] become increasingly mainstream."[8] Nowhere are "mainstream" and "extreme" defined.

Third, the critics are quite skeptical of empirical research; they claim to know what porn is about, thus obviating the need for data on its content, usages, or effects. Boyle writes that "it is difficult to imagine how one could be 'objective' about this."[9] Journalism scholar Robert Jensen expressly dismisses empirical research—"instead of being paralyzed by the limitations of social science"—and relies instead on his personal testimonials about porn and the distress it has caused him.[10] Regarding the issue of evidence, philosopher Lori Watson boldly proclaims that "no amount of empirical data alone will settle the question as to how best to define and understand pornography."[11] One wonders: What is Watson's alternative to empirical evidence?

Other writers, however, offer a type of evidence to support their antiporn position, and it is typically anecdotal: (1) quotations from some men and women who have viewed porn; (2) descriptions of some porn Web sites; (3) and accounts of scenes in pornographic videos. The sources are typically chosen and presented selectively, not based on a systematic and rigorous sampling or analysis of a particular body of work. Yet the critics claim that their conclusions are indeed based on typical material. Dines, for example, maintains that the materials she condemns "are all too representative of what is out there on the Internet and in mass-produced movies."[12] With so much porn available today on the Internet and elsewhere, how could anyone know that what they have observed is representative of the universe? Another issue is the veracity of some antiporn writer's anecdotal evidence. Dines quotes verbatim blocks of three to four sentences from students who spoke to her after a lecture, statements bracketed by quotation marks, without indicating how these statements were recorded. How can readers have confidence in the validity of these statements? Is Dines somehow able to remember verbatim student statements consisting of multiple sentences at a time? Are at least some of these quotations embellished or fabricated?

Fourth, critics say little about gay male porn, lesbian porn, alternative porn, women-made porn, and feminist porn—which, together, constitute a sizeable share of the market. The proliferation of these genres undermines grand generalizations about "porn."[13] But even if we focus exclusively on mainstream, heterosexual porn, most of critics' claims ring hollow, as I demonstrate below. Some of the most popular sites (xvideos.com, redtube.com, porntube.com, youporn.com) contain a very wide range of images and are hardly restricted to the images critics claim are the norm.

Missing from antiporn writings is any recognition of (1) porn's immensely variegated content, (2) how those who make porn understand and experience their work, (3) how consumers decode and engage with porn in their everyday lives, or (4) the possibility that pornography might contribute to consumers' sex education, enhance their sex lives, or catalyze greater mutuality in intimate relationships. Instead, porn critics homogenize porn (Boyle's "the 'extreme' has become increasingly mainstream"), make categorical claims about it, and depict it as a monolithic behemoth that has no redeeming value. There is no consideration of the possibility that at least some porn challenges rather than reproduces conventional gendered power relations.

ASSESSING THE CONTENT OF PORNOGRAPHY

Some antiporn writers claim to have researched its content. However, it is no surprise that this allegedly empirical work is used to legitimate their antiporn politics. As an example, Robert Jensen and Gail Dines reviewed 14 pornographic videos and 20 pornographic novels and concluded that they were demeaning toward women. Jensen and Dines provide no explanation of how they selected these items; they simultaneously concede that the materials "cannot be said to be representative" *and* then claim that "our research and experience suggests that [these videos and novels] are typical" of mainstream pornography.[14] Based on this small unrepresentative sample, Jensen and Dines leap to the following conclusion: "We found that, as the feminist critique of pornography asserts, at the core of contemporary pornography is contempt for women."[15] Notice how a small convenience sample is generalized to "contemporary pornography." Similarly, philosopher Rebecca Whisnant claims that "hostile and humiliating acts against women are commonplace" in mainstream porn, where "aggression against women is the rule rather than the exception."[16] She bases these sweeping indictments on her review of Web site postings by individuals who discuss porn, rather than a content analysis of representations in actual porn materials. She acknowledges that posters' comments may not be representative of anything, but nevertheless treats what they say as "rich" data. After quoting some of the entries, she concludes that the "contemporary pornography industry is a wasteland of lost and damaged humanity."[17]

Some critics draw conclusions that are contradicted by their own findings. While their studies can also be faulted on methodological grounds, what is particularly striking is the clash between these authors' evidence and their analysis. Two examples of this follow. Meagan Tyler examined a unique source of data on the content of porn videos: the Editor's Choice reviews of new videos, published in the industry's premier magazine, *Adult Video News*. Tyler was interested in how highly regarded films are described to those working within the industry itself, and she was particularly interested in representations of violence against women. Of the 98 reviews she analyzed, the vast majority contained *no* descriptions of violence (one-quarter [N=24] did so). And, even more telling, the most serious types of violence were, on the whole, absent from these videos. *None* of the scenes described in the reviews involved kicking, biting, attempted or completed murder, dismemberment, or torture. Only one scene depicted hitting, mutilation, or use of a weapon; two involved kidnapping; and five involved fighting or a beating. The less serious and perhaps consensual acts of bondage, slapping, sadomasochism, spanking, and verbal aggression appeared in three to nine scenes. Thus, not only were most of the videos devoid of *any* descriptions of violence but most of the violence that was described in a small minority of scenes comprised the *least serious* types, at least some of which might be categorized as nonviolent if consensual or playful. Yet, Tyler concludes from her data that "extreme and violent pornography is permeating the industry," while her own data point to the exact opposite conclusion.[18]

A similar problem colors a study by Ana Bridges.[19] In a sample of 268 scenes in 50 top-selling or -renting videos during 2004–2005, Bridges reports that 88 percent contained "physical aggression" toward women. But a closer look at the findings reveals that (similar to Tyler's results) extreme violence (torturing, punching, kicking, mutilating, threatening with or use of a weapon, murder) was either rare or nonexistent. *No instances* of murder, torture, mutilation, or threatening with a weapon were found, and almost none of the scenes (0.6 percent) depicted punching or kicking. More common were what Bridges describes as "more mild and playful" acts (pinching, biting, slapping, spanking, hair pulling). In other words, these "mild and playful" acts make up the bulk of the 88 percent total of what she labels "aggressive" behavior, and the *slapping/spanking* category itself accounted for fully 77 percent of the total aggression. Importantly, only 12 percent of the "aggressive" acts were coded nonconsensual, which raises further questions about the validity of labeling them aggressive. Another important finding, underplayed by Bridges, was that the frequency of each of the serious acts of aggression was either *identical to* or had *declined* compared to a similar study's findings a decade earlier, by sociologists Martin Barron and Michael Kimmel.[20] Judging from these two studies, depictions of the most extreme types of aggression have not increased over time, raising questions about the claim made by some writers that porn has become increasingly violent in recent years.

Bridges is troubled by the symbolic messages she discerns in these videos. She argues that if "mild and playful" acts appear consensual they might send the message that people like such treatment and, for her, this is a problem because it "may result in greater intimacy difficulties" for viewers or, worse, they "may expect that these behaviors *should* feel erotic and arousing."[21] This is an intriguing argument but clearly reflects Bridges's personal value judgments regarding "proper" sexual behavior.

Older content analyses found that most pornography in videos and magazines was nonviolent: The most sexually explicit or hard-core videos contained both the least violence and the most reciprocal, egalitarian behavior between the actors.[22] Very few photos in *Playboy* and *Penthouse* magazines depicted violence, and such depictions decreased over time (1954–1983).[23] These magazines were marketed to a fairly mainstream audience and thus sought to avoid alienating customers with content they might find objectionable.

With its ubiquity on the Internet today, it is impossible to determine how much violence, or any other behavior, exists in contemporary porn. But researchers can identify and examine the most popular materials based on records of sales, rentals, or downloads. One recent study in this vein is psychologists Catherine Salmon and Amy Diamond's content analysis of the 30 top-selling/renting heterosexual porn DVDs and the 30 top-selling/renting gay male DVDs. The study sought to determine whether there were differences between the two genres, thus testing radical feminist assertions about the uniquely degrading treatment of women in heterosexual pornography. Salmon and Diamond surmise that if heterosexual porn is about male dominance, it will feature more male than female initiation of sex, male sexual coercion of women, demeaning treatment (measured by male ejaculation on a woman's face), violent acts against women, and "little or no cunnilingus and so less overall oral sex in heterosexual as opposed to homosexual porn."[24] Using roughly comparable measures in the gay films, the researchers tested the notion that women are mistreated or subservient to men in heterosexual films.

The findings are revealing. First, the frequency of oral sex did not differ between the two genres and, in the heterosexual films, cunnilingus occurred just as often as fellatio, an average of seven times per film (suggesting mutuality of pleasure). Second, in heterosexual films female performers initiated sex just as often as their male counterparts. Third, antiporn writers claim that external ejaculation reflects male contempt for women. The study found that facial ejaculation was more frequent in the heterosexual films but that external ejaculation overall occurred more often in the gay films. Fourth, there were no significant differences in the amount of coercive sex in the two genres: it was "basically non-existent" in both. And fifth, aggression (slapping, biting, scratching) was "quite infrequent" and did not differ statistically between the straight and gay films. The researchers concluded from their comparative analysis that the two genres were similar in most respects and that none of the differences "reflect an anti-female agenda."[25]

THE PERFORMERS

Writings about those who perform in porn videos or who are depicted in photographs are usually anecdotal and often negative. As expected, what performers say about their motives for entering the world of porn or about their experiences in this profession are dismissed or disparaged if they clash with the antiporn paradigm. Boyle is a case in point:

> Whatever choices performers make about entering and staying in the industry, we need to ensure that we do not conflate those choices with desire or sexual subjectivity or let such choices (where they do exist) blind us to the physical and psychological toll of industrial sex. Because that is what commercial pornography is: it is industrial sex, and it uses (up) its constituent parts in a ruthlessly efficient way.[26]

This blatant denial of sex workers' agency is replaced with Boyle's crystal ball that tells her what is really happening in porn and that the performers' own experiences are fictional unless they admit they have suffered the "toll of industrial sex." Another reason for dismissing the voices of performers, according to Boyle, is because listening to them would "let men off the hook."[27] In other words, the views and lived experiences of the performers are basically irrelevant because what really matters is the perspective of the male consumer.

Dines imagines that there is a distinct category of "porn sex": sex that is "debased, dehumanized, formulaic, and generic." It differs from proper sex, which she defines as involving "empathy, tenderness, caring, affection" and "love, respect, or connection to another human being." Porn is almost universally "degrading," "dehumanizing," and violent, with female performers as victims and male performers as villains: "In porn the man makes hate to the woman, as each sex act is designed to deliver the maximum amount of degradation."[28] This portrayal of male performers' motivations is astonishing not only for its sweeping nature but also because not a shred of evidence is offered to support it. It is not entirely clear what "making hate" to another person means, and how does Dines know that performers intend to deliver "maximum degradation?" Actual studies of male performers contradict Dines's characterizations of them: They are motivated by the pursuit of money, fame, and opportunities for both sex and social networking.[29]

Antiporn writers make categorical claims about the female performers as well. Dines, for example, insists that (1) women in porn do not experience pleasure, (2) they "rarely" receive oral sex, (3) they are entirely devoid of agency, (4) they are forced to endure "punishing sex," and (5) they are simply vehicles for men's satisfaction.[30] "Body-punishing" sex is now the norm, Dines says, meaning that it typically involves rough sex that is perceived as harmful to women's bodies. To claim that all or most women in porn are devoid of agency, that they derive no pleasure during the sex acts, and that "body-punishing" sex is pervasive in porn are simply unsupported assertions. And it is stunning to read Dines's mistaken claim that "we never see any kissing or touching in porn."[31] Taken together, these assertions suggest either that Dines has rather limited exposure to the tremendous variety of pornography available or that she is simply distorting this material in order to support her antiporn campaign.

Recently, porn performers have been associated with another danger: *sex trafficking*. One version of this argument is that individuals are trafficked by force or deception into the porn industry, where they are compelled to engage in erotic photo-shoots or performances. This claim is made on several right-wing Web sites and in some semi-scholarly publications. An example of the latter is a piece by Robert Peters, Laura Lederer, and Shane Kelly. After presenting a handful of anecdotes, they conclude that trafficking for the purpose of producing porn is "far from trivial. . . . Women are trafficked into the production of hardcore pornography."[32] Much of their article fails to mention trafficking at all, and their conclusions about trafficking into pornography are out of all proportion to the few cases they describe. Another version of the porn-trafficking connection is more diffuse and essentialist. In an article entitled "Pornography as Trafficking," Catharine MacKinnon equates the distribution of pornography with the trafficking of persons depicted in pornography:

> In the resulting materials, these people are then conveyed and sold for a buyer's sexual use . . . Each time the pornography is commercially exchanged, the trafficking continues as the women and children in it are transported and provided for sex, sold, and bought again. Doing all these things for the purpose of exploiting the prostitution of others— which pornography intrinsically does—makes it trafficking in persons.[33]

The slippage between "materials," "pornography," "persons," and "women and children" is striking in this formulation. Conflation is even more conspicuous in MacKinnon's circular argument that "the pornography industry, in production, creates demand for prostitution, hence for trafficking, because it is itself a form of prostitution and trafficking."[34]

During the Bush administration, antiprostitution scholars and activists learned that they could get a lot of mileage out of conflating trafficking and prostitution—catalyzing a new government crackdown on prostitution—and it appears that they are now trying to fuse trafficking with pornography for the same reason.[35] Peters, Lederer, and Kelly advocate obscenity prosecutions of "the producers and distributors of adult pornography that *possibly* depicts performers who were trafficked into the production in cases where it would be difficult or nearly impossible to prove trafficking in court," but arguably easier to convict them on obscenity charges. Such a crackdown "need not await the accumulation of additional research data and other evidence of the nexus between this material and prostitution and sex trafficking."[36] In other words, even though the "nexus" has not been established, prosecutions of producers and distributors of "all hardcore pornography" should be launched because some of the performers may "possibly" have been trafficked.[37] It is important to note here that this article appeared in the journal of The Protection Project (an influential and well-funded antitrafficking organization), that Robert Peters is the president of an influential antipornography group (Morality in Media), and that Laura Lederer is a long-time antiporn activist and former official in the U.S. State Department's trafficking office—all suggesting that their views may resonate among American policy makers.

What we see here is a glaring disjunction between the claims made *about* those involved in the performance and production of pornography and data on their own *lived experiences*—which remain largely unresearched. An unknown number of people produce amateur porn or work independently of the major studios, and relatively little is known about them. We do know that approximately 1,200 to 1,500 performers are employed by 200 porn production companies in the Los Angeles area,[38] yet only a handful of researchers have interviewed porn actors, directors, or producers or conducted observations at film production sets. This means that the (usually negative) depictions of those involved in the pornography industry are rarely based on anything more than anecdotal tidbits. We do know that gender makes a world of difference, with female actors in heterosexual porn typically paid much more per film and having greater recognition and fame than their male counterparts. In-depth interviews with female performers—much like the male actors described above—reveal that their reasons for entering the business ranged from the obvious one of making money to the desire for varied sexual experiences, the freedom and independence that such work afforded them, the opportunity for socializing and networking with like-minded people, and the pursuit of fame and celebrity status in the world of entertainment.[39]

Another recent study sheds light on the backgrounds and experiences of female porn actors in the United States. Researchers sought to determine if these performers fit into the popular "damaged goods" hypothesis—i.e., that they entered the world of pornography because they were psychologically less healthy or had more adverse life experiences than the general public, hence explaining why they gravitated toward a deviant lifestyle and involvement in pornography.[40] A large sample of 177 female performers who work for porn companies were interviewed and compared to a matched sample of the female population. The findings were quite remarkable: The porn actresses were no more likely than the matched sample to report having experienced childhood sexual abuse, contrary to the conventional stereotype; the two groups reported similar alcohol use but the actresses had tried a greater variety of drugs. Importantly, the actresses had higher scores on the quality-of-life measures of sexual satisfaction, spirituality, and social support networks; the authors relate the latter to their tendency to fraternize with coworkers more than out-group individuals. One of the major findings was that the actresses had higher self-esteem scores than did women in the matched sample. The authors suggest that this may be "associated with heightened feelings of self-approval because they may be receiving reinforcement from management, coworkers, and fans." In short, the study found little support for the damaged goods notion and concluded that the porn performers "appear more similar to women not employed as porn actresses than previously thought."

CONSUMERS

Antiporn writers typically make two kinds of assertions about individuals who consume porn. First is the claim that porn has *strong, unequivocal effects on viewers*: (1) viewers are passive recipients who do not actively engage with and interpret messages and meanings and (2) ongoing exposure to porn turns male consumers into predatory beings. Jensen claims that "pornography demands that men abandon empathy" for the female performers and "a world without empathy is a world without hope."[41] Without citing any evidence, Jensen insists that male consumers simply *cannot* watch porn and empathize with the women in porn: "Men would not be able to be aroused by such material if they routinely empathized with the female performers."[42] Rejecting the notion that viewers are "sophisticated consumers who enjoy porn for the playful fantasy it is,"[43] Dines calls this a fiction created by the porn industry. Instead, males who consume porn become susceptible to a litany of harms: it "hijacks" and perverts their sexuality; "the stories seep into the very core of their sexual identity"; "the ability to keep porn women separate from the women they date is eroded"; men are "trained by the porn culture to see sex as disconnected from intimacy"; "porn trains men to become desensitized to women's pain"; and it is "fantastical thinking that men can masturbate to porn images and walk away from them untouched by the misogyny." Porn has a profoundly powerful and uniform effect on the audience, according to antiporn writers: it "leaves little room for multiple interpretations."[44]

The second claim is the *slippery slope*: Men who watch porn become "desensitized" and seek ever more extreme porn in order to satisfy themselves. Dines insists that "users need to eventually seek out more extreme acts as a way to keep them interested and stimulated . . . heightening the level of degradation is what keeps men interested in and aroused by porn." Inevitably, it seems, men "end up masturbating to images that had previously disgusted them," including bondage, violence, and child porn.[45]

Strangely, when confronted with counterevidence, some antiporn writers respond that the experiences of those who consume it do not matter, apparently because the critics already *know* what the consumption experience is truly like. Watson is adamant that we should not bother with the perceptions of "those who have the most invested in the status quo, that is, the viewers and the actors,"[46] and Boyle disparages efforts to understand consumers by pointing to the "danger of fetishing [sic] the porn enthusiast."[47]

The third claim might be called *matter over mind*—that is, porn matter contains some intrinsic power to overwhelm and negate consumers' cognitive or emotional engagement with it as well as their ability to view it as a fantasy distinguishable from real life. Instead, porn is presented as deterministically dictatorial. Antiporn writers tend to hold a rather crude and archaic view of the relationship between media representations and audience reception. Dines believes that the meaning of porn, all porn, is somehow inherent in it—hence, no need to ask consumers about their interpretations. She cites George Gerbner's "cultivation thesis" in support of her view that there is a direct causal path (stimulus→response) between the media's depictions or "messages" and audience absorption of those messages. Hence, her frequent use of terminology such as "porn tells us," porn "dictates" to us, "porn trains men," and so on. Dines seems unaware that Gerbner later aligned with those scholars who argue that media content is actively interpreted and reinterpreted by the audience.[48] Only when there is a close fit between images in the media and an audience member's pre-existing views or values do we see a potential impact on the audience—known as the "resonance thesis," where exposure to media representations interact with and reinforce pre-existing inclinations. Where this is not the case, exposure to images in the media is unlikely to affect attitudes or behavior, because audience members are agentic in interpreting and engaging with those images and do so in a wide variety of ways.[49] Dines, by contrast, insists that porn "leaves little room for multiple interpretations."[50]

Antiporn writers have long insisted that exposure to pornography contributes to hostility and violence against women because it breeds callousness and objectification. In laboratory experiments, exposure to violent acts or images, whether pornographic or not, sometimes has no effect and sometimes increases subjects' levels of anxiety or aggression when tested afterwards, whereas nonviolent pornography usually has no effect.[51] But all such lab studies are fatally flawed: they rely on small, convenience samples of volunteers instead of representative samples; many subjects have previously been exposed to porn, thus likely warping the alleged "effects" of exposure in the laboratory vacuum; and the artificiality of the setting in which these studies are conducted is at odds with the viewers' natural environment. In the lab, viewers are not allowed to engage with porn in the way they would in their private lives, and some analysts point out that not being able to masturbate in the experimental setting may itself produce feelings of frustration that researchers then interpret as aggression toward *women*—the outcome measured in most of these studies. In a nutshell, the "poor analogues provided by laboratory research may tell us little or nothing about the relation of pornography and aggression in the real world."[52] It is thus remarkable that so many experimental studies have been conducted when the results are not only dubious but also likely distortive of the experience of consuming porn in the real world.

Similar evidentiary problems bedevil macro-level quantitative studies that purport to measure porn's effects on the real-world treatment of women. These studies compare the availability of porn in a particular geographic area to official rates of violence against women—namely, (1) whether places with high availability of pornography (magazines, adult theaters, video rentals) have higher rates of sex crime than places where pornography is less available or (2) whether increased availability over time in a particular region increases rates of sexual offenses. Reviews of the literature conclude that macro-level associations between pornography and sexual aggression are mixed: Some studies find a relationship between availability and reported sex offending while other research documents a *decline* in sexual offenses with increased availability of pornography.[53] But all such studies are inherently problematic because of their inability to control for all potentially relevant influences on male behavior. There is simply no way to confidently conclude that pornography is responsible for rates of violence, particularly when it is unknown whether those who commit violence have viewed porn and, even if they have done so, whether porn or some other factor is the cause.

The larger point is that it is virtually impossible to isolate the effects of the media in the context of other influences—including individuals' demographic backgrounds and personality characteristics, socialization by family and peer groups, wider cultural influences, and so forth—and it would be impossible to include all possibly relevant influences in a statistical model for a comprehensive test of the influence of media exposure. A major literature review concluded that research has not demonstrated a link between media images—of any kind—and audience behavior: At best, media effects are "weak and affect only a small percentage of viewers."[54] What matters most is whether a person is socially predisposed to act, or "primed," in a certain way—with preexisting views reinforced by or resonating with new stimuli. Moreover, the causal direction may be the opposite of the one typically asserted (i.e., exposure to porn leads to aggression), as indicated in research that finds that men who score high on a sexual aggression scale are more likely to seek out sexually violent media and, in turn, have their pre-existing views reinforced by the latter.[55] In short, most media scholars would be shocked at the simplistic claims of the antipornography writers.

Little research has been done on porn consumers in the real world. We do know that one-quarter of Americans reported in 2012 that they had seen an X-rated movie in the past year (a figure that has been stable in the General Social Survey over the past three decades).[56] Twice as many men as women have done so (35 and 16 percent, respectively, in the 2012 survey), and young people are more likely than older age groups to have done so (44 percent of 18–25-year-olds).[57] The numbers would undoubtedly be higher if the question specified a broader array of porn than "an X-rated movie," as some consumers may not define online video clips or webcam performances as movies.

The neglect of consumers (as opposed to lab subjects) is remarkable in light of the sweeping claims about pornography's impact on them. Still, a few studies have shown that men and women decode and engage with sexually explicit materials in a wide variety of ways, which is exactly what media experts would predict.

In contrast to the charges of critics, young men in one study distanced themselves from the scenes they disliked in porn, did not try to emulate the male performers, and "asserted that sex in real life is something completely different" from porn films.[58] Compared to men, women are less likely to view porn, are attracted to a smaller range of representations, and are more critical of it. Interviews and focus group research show that more women than men feel ambivalent about porn, dislike the portrayal of women in porn, and are concerned that male consumers might compare them unfavorably to models and actors.[59] Yet other women find pornography to be entertaining, stimulating, or educational. It is not unusual for women to view porn positively, especially younger generations. In a unique survey of 688 Danish women and men aged 18 to 30, men reported significantly more positive effects of porn consumption than women but few women and men reported negative effects. Most perceived either neutral or positive effects on their sexual behavior, attitudes and knowledge regarding sex, and the overall quality of their lives. Moreover, for both men and women, the greater the amount of pornography consumed, the greater the perceived positive effects of exposure to porn.[60] If these self-reports are valid, the researchers suggest that "pornography's impact is relatively positive and that media and popular books' reports of highly negative effects on consumers are exaggerated or unfounded."[61]

A related study examined the degree to which exposure to pornography increased (1) normalization or the expansion of the boundaries of what people consider acceptable sexual behavior and (2) empowerment or engagement in a greater variety of sexual practices.[62] The study, of 245 American college students, found that the greater the frequency of viewing porn, the more expansive was the range of what were considered appealing sex acts and the greater the normalization of acts that were previously considered odd or deviant. The positive statistical association between the frequency of viewing porn and the increased appeal of a variety of sexual practices did not differ by gender or sexual orientation. Moreover, in a subsequent qualitative study conducted by the same research team—using open-ended survey questions (N=73 students)—the researchers were "especially struck by the number of women who voiced a sense of empowerment that was attributed to their pornography viewing."[63]

For some men, there is no question that exposure reinforces callous or sexist views of women, while others interpret and experience pornography in the opposite way. A major study by journalist David Loftus, based on in-depth interviews with 150 men, documented abundant variation in consumers' tastes: some viewers prefer to see idealized bodies while others like realistic ones; likewise, some want plots and the appearance of "chemistry" between the performers while others like unadulterated sex. Loftus found that most of the men understood porn as being about fun, beauty, women's pleasure, and female assertiveness and power. They did not like depictions of domination or aggression against women and were "specifically turned off by such behavior on the rare occasions they see it in pornography, and most haven't even seen any." Loftus concluded that is "important to male viewers that the women really do seem to be enjoying themselves, that they are utterly involved in the sex for their own pleasure too, and not just serving the interests of the male actors and onlookers." They also recognized porn as a fantasy world quite different from the real world in terms of people's behavior and appearance. Rather than emulating male porn performers, the men interviewed by Loftus "usually did not like the men they saw in porn" and saw them as "unsuitable models for behavior." And in stark contrast to the slippery-slope argument, these men "have not sought ever more vivid, kinky, and violent pornography, but have either stuck with what they liked from the first, investigated wilder content and returned to what they preferred, or lost interest altogether."[64] Most of these men did not gravitate toward increasingly extreme representations.

The men in the Loftus sample were largely contacted via the Internet and thus may be unrepresentative of the larger population, but the findings are consistent with another major study of consumers. Media scholars Alan McKee, Katherine Albury, and Catherine Lumby surveyed 1,023 male and female pornography consumers in Australia and conducted in-depth interviews with a subsample of 46 of them; subjects were accessed online and via a survey posted in an erotic magazine. Like Loftus, McKee et al. found variation in tastes, but a majority of respondents preferred to see realistic but attractive bodies; enthusiasm, enjoyment, and genuine "chemistry" between the performers; and about half thought that "good porn" had good production values. Other viewers prefer to see idealized bodies or straight, plotless sex. Some believe women hold the power in porn scenes while others take the opposite view.[65]

Three-quarters used porn alone, but 46 percent also did so with a partner. Over half of the respondents were currently in monogamous relationships and 58 percent described themselves as religious. The sample generally mirrored the Australian population, except that it was disproportionately male, reflecting the fact that men are more likely to view porn than are women. Two-thirds of the respondents said that they were happy with the porn they consume, 9 percent were unhappy, and one-quarter were neither happy nor unhappy. Sixty percent said that they had applied something they saw in porn to their real lives. When asked "What effect has pornography had on your attitudes towards sexuality?", 57 percent selected "a positive effect," 7 percent "a negative effect," and 35 percent "no effect at all." Of the small number who felt porn had had a negative effect on them, 2 percent said it had catalyzed unrealistic sexual expectations; 2 percent felt porn had led them to objectify people; 0.5 percent had lost interest in sex outside porn; 0.5 percent associated their porn use with a problem in a relationship; and 0.5 percent felt that they were viewing porn too often. I would point out that these are some of the problems that antiporn writers claim to be pervasive, which the McKee study finds to be rather rare. The reported positive effects, however, were much more prevalent, and included enhanced sexual pleasure, greater education about sex, becoming more attentive to a partner's pleasure, and becoming more open-minded about sex (trying different sexual positions, using sex toys).[66] In short, the existing empirical evidence on real-world consumers contradicts the antiporn paradigm's sweeping generalizations about them and shatters numerous popular stereotypes as well.

CONCLUSION

People tend to hold strong views about pornography, including those who have never seen any, and attitudes are much less liberal in the United States than in some other Western nations.[67] Yet, many who have been exposed to it, especially over time, appear from the evidence cited above to have at least some positive engagement with it. Pornography is far from monolithic, rendering vacuous any generalizations about its essential qualities (what porn is "about") or regarding its effects on consumers, on gender relations, or on the larger society (the so-called "pornification" of society). It is noteworthy that many of the most vocal critics of pornography are affiliated with universities and use their status as "scholars" or "experts" to perpetuate myths regarding all forms of sex work and to advocate for its abolition. It is clear that their antiporn goals overdetermine their claims regarding reality. Some of these individuals are unabashed in substituting their own ideology for research (e.g., Boyle, Jensen, Watkins) while others present at least some empirical material (Whisnant) but sometimes misrepresent their own findings in order to justify their critique of pornography (e.g., Bridges, Tyler). The same ideologically driven distortions are evident in some writings on prostitution and commercial stripping as well.[68] Any sound sociological analysis of pornography would clash severely with the antiporn paradigm's sweeping generalizations and many specific distortions, identified and critiqued in this essay.

NOTES

1. Ronald Weitzer, "Sociology of Sex Work," *Annual Review of Sociology* 35 (2009): 213–34; Ronald Weitzer, "The Mythology of Prostitution: Advocacy Research and Public Policy," *Sexuality Research and Social Policy* 7 (2010): 15–29.

2. Weitzer, "Sociology of Sex Work"; Weitzer, "Mythology of Prostitution."

3. Karen Boyle, "Introduction," in *Everyday Pornography*, ed. K. Boyle (New York: Routledge, 2010), 12.

4. Rebecca Whisnant, "From Jekyll to Hyde: The Grooming of Male Pornography Customers," in *Everyday Pornography*, ed. K. Boyle (New York: Routledge, 2010), 132.

5. Boyle, "Introduction," 21.

6. Gail Dines, *Pornland: How Porn Has Hijacked Our Sexuality* (Boston: Beacon, 2010), 165.

7. Ann Russo, "Feminists Confront Pornography's Subordinating Practices," in *Pornography: The Production and Consumption of Inequality*, ed. Gail Dines, Robert Jensen, and Ann Russo (New York: Routledge, 1997), 19, 29.

8. Boyle, "Introduction," 8.

9. Karen Boyle, "The Myth of Objectivity," *Violence Against Women* 18 (2012): 506–11, 507.

10. Robert Jensen, "Introduction" and "The Pain of Pornography," in *Pornography*, 5.

11. Lori Watson, "A Reply to Weitzer," *Violence Against Women* 18 (2012): 502–5, 504.

12. Dines, *Pornland*, xxi.

13. Dana Collins, "Lesbian Pornographic Production: Creating Social/Cultural Space for Subverting Representations of Sexuality," *Berkeley Journal of Sociology* 43 (1998): 31–62; Danielle DeVoss, "Women's Porn Sites," *Sexuality and Culture* 6 (2002): 75–94; Jill Bakehorn, "Women-Made Pornography," in *Sex For Sale*, ed. Ronald Weitzer (New York: Routledge, 2010); Joe Thomas, "Gay Male Pornography since Stonewall," in *Sex For Sale*, ed. R. Weitzer (New York: Routledge, 2010).

14. Jensen and Dines, "The Content of Mass-Marketed Pornography," in *Pornography*, 71.

15. Ibid., 99.

16. Whisnant, "From Jekyll to Hyde," 114, 115.

17. Ibid., 132.

18. Meagan Tyler, "Now that's Pornography: Violence and Domination in *Adult Video News*," in *Everyday Pornography*, ed. K. Boyle (New York: Routledge, 2010), 57.

19. Ana Bridges, "Methodological Considerations in Mapping Pornography Content," in *Everyday Pornography*, ed. K. Boyle (New York: Routledge, 2010).

20. Martin Barron and Michael Kimmel, "Sexual Violence in Three Pornographic Media," *Journal of Sex Research* 37 (2000): 161–68.

21. Bridges, "Methodological Considerations," 47–48.

22. Joseph Scott and Steven Cuvelier, "Violence and Sexual Violence in Pornography," *Archives of Sexual Behavior* 22 (1993): 357–71; Ted Palys, "Testing the Common Wisdom: The Social Content of Video Pornography," *Canadian Psychology* 27 (1986): 22–35.

23. Charles Winick, "A Content Analysis of Sexually Explicit Magazines Sold in an Adult Bookstore," *Journal of Sex Research* 21 (1988): 206–10; Joseph Scott and Steven Cuvelier, "Sexual Violence in *Playboy* Magazine: A Longitudinal Content Analysis," *Journal of Sex Research* 25 (1987): 534–39; Neil Malamuth and Barry Spinner, "A Longitudinal Content Analysis of Sexual Violence in the Best-Selling Erotic Magazines," *Journal of Sex Research* 16 (1980): 226–37.

24. Catherine Salmon and Amy Diamond, "Evolutionary Perspectives on the Content Analysis of Heterosexual and Homosexual Pornography," *Journal of Social, Evolutionary, and Cultural Psychology* 6 (2012): 193–202, 196.

25. Salmon and Diamond, "Evolutionary Perspectives," 193.

26. Boyle, "Epilogue: How Was it For You?," 210–11.

27. Ibid., 205.

28. Dines, *Pornland*, x–xxiv.

29. Sharon Abbott, "Motivations for Pursuing a Career in Pornography," in *Sex For Sale*, ed. Ronald Weitzer (New York: Routledge, 2010); James Griffith, "Pornography Actors: A Qualitative Analysis of Motivations and Dislikes," *North American Journal of Psychology* 14 (2012): 245–56. Abbott interviewed 19 and Griffith interviewed 105 male actors.

30. Dines, *Pornland*, x–xxiv.

31. Ibid., 64.

32. Robert Peters, Laura Lederer, and Shane Kelly, "The Slave and the Porn Star: Sexual Trafficking and Pornography," *The Protection Project Journal of Human Rights and Civil Society* 5 (2012): 1–21, 7, 14.

33. Catharine MacKinnon, "Pornography as Trafficking," *Michigan Journal of International Law* 26 (2005): 993–1012, 993, 1004.

34. MacKinnon, "Pornography as Trafficking," 999.

35. The successful conflation of trafficking and prostitution is documented in Ronald Weitzer, "The Social Construction of Sex Trafficking: Ideology and Institutionalization of a Moral Crusade," *Politics & Society* 35 (2007): 447–75, and Ronald Weitzer, "Sex Trafficking and the Sex Industry: The Need for Evidence-Based Theory and Legislation," *Journal of Criminal Law and Criminology* 101 (2011): 1337–370.

36. Peters, Lederer, and Kelly, "The Slave and the Porn Star," 18.

37. Ibid., 18.

38. James Griffith, Sharon Mitchell, Christian Hart, Lea Adams, and Lucy Gu, "Pornography Actresses: An Assessment of the Damaged Goods Hypothesis," *Journal of Sex Research* 50 (2013): 621–32.

39. Abbott, "Motivations for Pursuing a Career in Pornography."

40. Griffith et al., "Pornography Actresses."

41. Robert Jensen, "Pornography Is What the End of the World Looks Like," in *Everyday Pornography*, ed. K. Boyle (New York: Routledge, 2010), 112.

42. Ibid., 112.

43. Dines, *Pornland*, 82.

44. Ibid., xxii, 67, 92, 74, 78, 86.

45. Ibid., 68, 93, 94.

46. Watson, "A Reply," 504.

47. Boyle, "Myth of Objectivity," 509.

48. George Gerbner, "The Mainstreaming of America: Violence Profile No. 11," *Journal of Communication* 30 (1980): 10–29.

49. Peter Dahlgren, "What's the Meaning of This? Viewers' Plural Sense-Making of Television News," *Media, Culture, and Society* 10 (1988): 285–310.

50. Dines, *Pornland*, 86.

51. Robert Bauserman, "Sexual Aggression and Pornography: A Review of Correlational Research," *Basic and Applied Social Psychology* 18 (1996): 405–427; Edward Donnerstein, Daniel Linz, and Steven Penrod, *The Question of Pornography: Research Findings and Policy Implications* (New York: Free Press, 1987). Two experiments found no effect of exposure under conditions in which the researchers expected that the kind of stimuli *should* have produced misogynistic attitudes or behavior among male lab subjects: William Fisher and Guy Grenier, "Violent Pornography, Anti-woman Thoughts, and Anti-woman Acts: In Search of Reliable Effects," *Journal of Sex Research* 31 (1994): 23–38.

52. William Fisher and Azy Barak, "Pornography, Erotica, and Behavior: More Questions than Answers," *International Journal of Law and Psychiatry* 14 (1991): 65–83, 77.

53. Bauserman, "Sexual Aggression and Pornography"; Christopher Ferguson and Richard Hartley, "The Pleasure is Momentary, the Expense Damnable? The Influence of Pornography on Rape and Sexual Assault," *Aggression and Violent Behavior* 14 (2009): 323–29.

54. Richard Felson, "Mass Media Effects on Violent Behavior," *Annual Review of Sociology* 22 (1996): 102–28, 123.

55. Anthony Bogaert, Ulla Woodard, and Carolyn Hafer, "Intellectual Ability and Reactions to Pornography," *Journal of Sex Research* 36 (1999): 283–91; Neil Malamuth and James Check, "Sexual Arousal to Rape Depictions," *Journal of Abnormal Psychology* 92 (1983): 55–67.

56. The General Social Survey figures were 24 percent for 1984 and 25 percent for 2012. http://sda.berkeley.edu/cgi-bin/hsda?harcsda+gss12.

57. In 2012, the age breakdown for those who had seen such a movie in the past year was: 44 percent (18–25), 37 percent (26–40), 20 percent (41–55), and 13 percent (56–70).

58. Lotta Löfgren-Mårtenson and Sven-Axel Månsson, "Lust, Love, and Life: A Qualitative Study of Swedish Adolescents' Perceptions and Experiences with Pornography," *Journal of Sex Research* 47 (2010): 568–79, 575. (Editors' comment: The article is also reprinted in this volume.)

59. Petra Boynton, "'Is That Supposed to be Sexy?': Women Discuss Women in Top Shelf Magazines," *Journal of Community and Applied Social Psychology* 9 (1999): 91–105; Löfgren-Mårtenson and Månsson, "Lust, Love, and Life."

60. Gert Hald and Neil Malamuth, "Self-Perceived Effects of Pornography Consumption," *Archives of Sexual Behavior* 37 (2008): 614–25.

61. Hald and Malamuth, "Self-Perceived Effects," 622.

62. Martin Weinberg, Colin Williams, Sibyl Kleiner, and Yasmiyn Irzarry, "Pornography, Normalization, and Empowerment," *Archives of Sexual Behavior* 39 (2010): 1389–401.

63. Ibid., 1396.

64. David Loftus, *Watching Sex: How Men Really Respond to Pornography* (New York: Thunder's Mouth Press, 2002), xii, 249, 137–47, 61, xii.

65. Alan McKee, Katherine Albury, and Catherine Lumby, *The Porn Report* (Carlton: Melbourne University Press, 2008), 35–36.

66. Ibid., 83–87.

67. A 2008 Gallup poll reported that a majority of the population in France and Germany think that viewing pornography was "morally acceptable": 52 percent in France and 60 percent in Germany. The British public is far less tolerant, however, with only 29 percent holding this opinion. http://www.gallup.com/poll/107512/Moral-Issues-Divide-Westerners-From-Muslims-West.aspx. This compares with 31 percent of Americans who view pornography as morally acceptable, according to a 2013 Gallup poll. Age makes a difference, with 49 percent of Americans aged 18 to 34 believing that viewing pornography is morally acceptable in a 2013 Gallup poll, compared to 28 percent of those aged 35 to 54 and 19 percent of those aged 55 and older. http://www.gallup.com/poll/162881/older-americans-moral-attitudes-changing.aspx.

68. Weitzer, "The Mythology of Prostitution."

14

Why Do People Watch Porn? Results from PornResearch.Org

Clarissa Smith, Martin Barker, and Feona Attwood

FIGURING THE PORN AUDIENCE

As Henry Jenkins has argued, we know less about the audiences of pornography than "probably any other genre of popular entertainment."[1] Indeed, what little we do know often comes from representations in mainstream media where two stereotypes predominate. For example, in men's magazines like *Loaded* or in films like *American Pie*,[2] the porn consumer may be represented as "a normal bloke, having a bit of fun," but elsewhere he (and it is usually a he) is more likely to be presented as "deviant, slightly suspect and probably addicted."[3] The latter is part of a tradition of figuring those who engage with porn in negative ways as "pimply teenagers, furtive perverts in raincoats, and asocial compulsively masturbating misfits."[4] This tradition has little to say about actual audiences of porn, instead using figures of the porn user as ways of depicting the harm and danger associated with pornography. In the past, those figures have included a "falsely innocent adolescent female" and a "truly depraved adult male."[5] But the traumatized child and addicted adult male are currently the most frequently depicted figures of porn consumption. They provide the focus for much anxious press discussion of pornography, as in the well-known *Time* magazine's reporting on "cyberporn" (1995).[6] This featured illustrations of a pale, transfixed child and "a naked man, his arms and legs wrapped around a keyboard and computer monitor, seeming to dissolve into the screen." *Time* magazine's visual connection between body and screen suggested that porn is unwholesome, overwhelming, and masturbatory,[7] a trope readily taken up in stories elsewhere.[8] Consumers as victims of pornography are graphically depicted in the Josh McDowell Ministry's video *1 Click Away*,[9] where men, women, and children are shown being assailed and controlled by grasping hands and the voiceover speaks of the disintegration of the family as a result of consumption of porn leading to addiction.

The narrative of porn addiction has become a well-established way of representing porn consumption. Michael Leahy, the evangelist and author of *Porn Nation*, has claimed that porn is America's number-one addiction.[10] Writing for the *Psychologies* magazine campaign against pornography in 2010, British journalist Decca Aitkenhead describes boys sitting "in silence, staring at hardcore pornography on their phones, swapping images of astonishing sexual violence as if they were Pokémon cards."[11] The Australian parenting author, Steve Biddulph, claims that porn makes girls "compliant but disengaged," and that it is responsible for "one of the most depressed, anxious and lonely generations of young people ever to inhabit the earth."[12] This depiction of porn as a narcotic is often supplemented by claims that link it to child abuse and coercive sex work. For Australian campaigner Melinda Tankard Reist, porn and sexualized media act "as a de facto pimp for the prostitution and pornography industries,"[13] while U.S. antiporn feminist Rebecca Whisnant describes men as victims of "grooming" by pornographers—"abused" and "consumed"[14] and the "target for ruthless commercial exploitation."[15] The downward spiral of addiction experienced by young men is depicted by antiporn sociologist Gail Dines as follows:

> They neglect their school work, spend huge amounts of money they don't have, become isolated from others, and often suffer depression. They know something is wrong, feel out of control, and don't know how to stop. Some [. . .] have become so desensitized that they have started using harder porn and end up masturbating to images that had previously disgusted them. Many of these men are deeply ashamed and frightened, as they don't know where all this will end.[16]

Dines develops these themes at greater length in her book *Pornland: How Porn Has Hijacked Our Sexuality*.[17]

The representation of compulsive and disturbing porn viewing is also evident in the reporting of crimes. Support for legislation against so-called extreme pornography in the UK *Criminal Justice and Immigration Act 2009* drew heavily on the claim that viewing violent porn had fueled the murder of British schoolteacher Jane Longhurst in 2003. It further features claims that there is a general descent into cruelty in contemporary Western societies. In their book *The Porning of America* Carmine Sarracino and Kevin Scott link the torture carried out by guards at Abu Ghraib to an interest in pornography. The guards, they claim, were "intensely involved, on a daily basis, in porn" and "were fluent" in "the visual language of violent and degrading pornography."[18] Evidence that the soldiers had images of commercial porn, documented their own sexual activities, and engaged in torture is refigured as an "easy-to-imagine evening of entertainment"—"a little porn, a little abuse, a little more porn, a little torture, and then some more porn."[19] Although the authors do not at any point claim that the soldiers watched violent porn themselves, they argue that, "Given the presence of porn in their lives, it seems likely that the guards perpetrating the abuse at Abu Ghraib deliberately imitated the violent porn that now thrives on the Internet."[20] For these authors pornography's effects on those who view it can be understood by noting associations and presuming particularly destructive outcomes to behaviors. While there is no robust research basis for such claims, they circulate widely nonetheless, currently forming the basis of government action against pornography here in the United Kingdom.[21]

THE PORNRESEARCH.ORG PROJECT: MOTIVES AND METHODS[22]

Our project took a different starting point from assumptions that porn is de facto bad. Concerned with the everyday uses of pornography and how the people who engage with pornography feel it fits into their lives, our project was not based on suppositions about pornography's harmfulness.[23] We wanted to gather a collection of responses from people who use and engage with pornography—the people whose voices and stories are almost entirely absent from the debates about whether or not pornography should exist. We wanted to do this in a way that those people—who are likely to be intensely aware of the way they are talked about, categorized, and belittled—would trust us sufficiently to tell us their stories, their responses, their pleasures, and their preferences. We also needed to do this in a way that would allow us to discern patterns, distinct groupings, connections, and separations. For this, we needed to generate sufficient responses to allow us to do some secure quantitative analyses. But what mattered most to us was hearing the accounts that people would give us, in their own words, of the nature of their involvements and engagements with online pornography. We know that such accounts are not transparent truths. They are the ways that people are willing and able to tell us about themselves. That, however, is their distinctive value. Through the words that men and women, straight and homosexual, cis and trans*,[24] young and old, choose and use, we can hear their reasons and interests in sex, their sense of sexual self, what pornography means to them, and the ways in which it may matter to them. Before our questionnaire was launched, the entire research process was checked and approved by the research ethics committee of University of Sunderland.[25] Just as important to us was that we present our motives for doing the research so that people could trust that we did not have some concealed moral agenda—indeed, that our major motive for the project was to test a number of the widely circulating assumptions about the "harm" and "danger" of pornography. Because pornography is such a highly charged arena, and our research required that respondents trust us to deal fairly with their most intimate thoughts, we had to work hard to show our credentials as people who had been willing in the past to conduct research and speak out on difficult and unpopular topics. We were not surprised, therefore, when we learned that a number of people with the requisite Web skills checked our guarantee that people completing the questionnaire could not be tracked electronically. Information on our credentials circulated on Web sites and fora discussing issues around sex, sexuality, pornography, and the Internet more generally. Almost 5,500 people responded to our call for participants and, upon completing the questionnaire, 800 of them wrote to say they would be willing to carry on a conversation with us. From those conversations emerged a substantial body of further materials from almost 300 people, which we will, in due course, analyze in their own rights.

Our questionnaire used a carefully tailored combination of quantitative and qualitative questions. The quantitative questions were of three kinds: self-allocation multiple-choice questions (for example, asking people to say how important pornography was to them); personal and demographic information; and questions about possible orientations (reasons for looking at porn; the kinds of sources they used; and meanings of sex in their lives). With these quantitative questions came a series of qualitative ones. Some related directly to a multiple-choice question (for example, having asked people how important they felt pornography was to them, we simply asked them to tell us why they had answered as they had); other questions were prompted by our desire to get people to tell us about their experiences in distinctive ways (for example, we were interested in the idea of a *personal career* with pornography, so we asked people to try to tell us a "history of their engagement with pornography in ten sentences").

We also wanted respondents to tell us things that might be difficult because they were self-revelatory. So, we asked people to tell us the kinds of sexual stories that most attract them and about a pornographic moment or scenario that they found especially arousing. Finally, we added an open-ended wild-card question asking people if there was anything about them as individuals that would help us understand the answers they had given. Answers to this latter question ranged from "No" or "Nothing" to lengthy stories. These stories were important as a counter-balance to our search for patterns and tendencies. People may share many characteristics, but this is an area of very individual qualities as well—and we wanted to be able to illustrate patterns we discovered with portraits of complex individuals.

We make no claim for the representativeness of the responses we collected. This is not a sample—you can only have a sample where there is a known population from which a representative subset might be taken. We had no way of knowing what kinds and ranges of people choose to engage with Internet pornography. Indeed, one of the points of the research was to try to find out the range of people who do so. Accordingly, the questionnaire was publicized opportunistically in as wide and open a way as possible, and at the locations and via the avenues that such people would be likely to be encountering in the course of their online pornography engagements.[26] Completion rates of online questionnaires can be as low as 0.5 percent of those receiving a specific and personalized invitation,[27] and people are more likely to complete them when they feel they have some kind of personal stake in what is being asked. We cannot know how many people saw information about our research but we do know that 20,000 clicked on the questionnaire, which means our completion rate was just over 25 percent of that figure. What is so striking about our pornography research, however, is the contrast in levels of indicated Importance and Frequency of Use. Just over 50 percent reported the two highest levels of Frequency, while—very strikingly—under 25 percent reported the two highest levels of Importance. This leads us to think that we managed to attract a good range of people; and that while for many, personally, the felt Importance of porn in their lives may be quite low, they considered it significant enough to record their views on the topic, and trusted us to deal fairly with their responses.

After deriving and considering the crude overall separate totals for all headings in the questionnaire, we went through the following stages: produced cross-tabulations for every pair of quantitative questions (Gender by Relation to Age, Sexual Orientation, Frequency, Importance, etc.); produced cluster analyses of the interrelations and overlaps between the different choices within the three orientation questions (Orientations to Pornography, Kinds of Sources, and Meanings of Sex); generated word counts for all qualitative answers and for comparative groups within those answers, to discover which questions and topics had generated the most interest, and who had the most or least to say about their engagements; and random-sampled fifty responses to each of the qualitative questions, in order to gain a sense of the range of kinds of answers, and to get a preliminary sense of the accounts and explanations, and associated ways of talking about pornography, that people had given us.

SOME BASIC INDICATORS

The questionnaire was open from the end of February to the end of June 2011 and was advertised by means of social media—Facebook and Twitter (pretty much replicating traditional snowball techniques). We also sent information to various bloggers such as Violet Blue and Em & Lo (two popular bloggers who write about sex, sexuality, and sexual media). We also used whatever media opportunities came our way to publicize the research, and were able to use radio interviews in particular to get the word out about the Web site. We received 5,490 completed responses; of those, 3,743 identified as male (68.4 percent) and 1,726 as female (31.6 percent). Sexual orientation broke down as follows:

TABLE 14.1

Heterosexual	3,842	(70.1%)
Gay	186	(3.4%)
Lesbian	56	(1.0%)
Bisexual	905	(16.5%)
Queer	303	(5.5%)
Unsure	189	(3.4%)

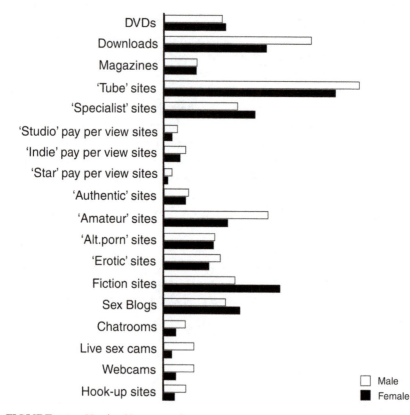

FIGURE 14.1 Kinds of Pornography Viewed.

These figures probably don't contain many surprises, aligning as they do with popular understandings of pornography as predominantly a heterosexual male pastime. Ratings for Importance are higher among men, and women give a lower Frequency for consuming pornography—again as might be expected. More interesting is the fact that cross-tabulating age with gender reveals that younger women (18 to 25) engage with pornography much more than older women, indicating a possible generational shift. When it comes to what men and women are looking at, the accompanying chart demonstrates that by far the runaway choice for men *and* women are the tube sites, supporting the popular claim, voiced by porn companies themselves, that people want free porn and plenty of choice. That said, there are some interesting variations.

Results indicate that for men, downloads are very important, as are amateur sites (at twice women's interest in these), followed by specialist sites (catering to specific sexual interests). For women, tube sites rank highest, followed by fiction sites (almost double the rate that men choose these), downloads (at half men's rate), and sex blogs. Again, these results may seem to bear out the old stereotypes that women are most interested in words rather than pictures of sex; but if we look at these in relation to our results regarding orientations toward pornography, we find some more developed patterns. Our results suggest that there are some broad, general differences between men's and women's orientations to porn. For example, men seem more inclined to

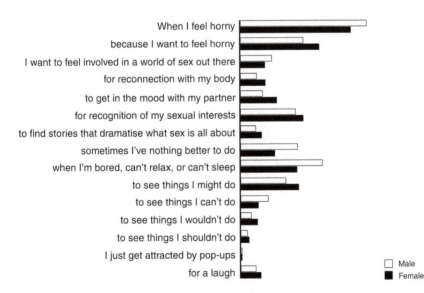

FIGURE 14.2 Reasons for Viewing Pornography.

use porn simply to *express* their arousal, but women are more likely to use pornography as a *means to arousal*. Women also seem to engage with porn as a means to reconnect with their bodies, and to use with partners. Men seem more likely to turn to pornography when feeling bored or having nothing better to do. Note, however, that very few of our respondents chose "I just get attracted by pop-ups,"—those images that interrupt intentional brows-ing to lead viewers to other sites. This seemingly insignificant result is, in fact, very important. This finding indicates that despite the attempts to frame porn as something that seeks viewers out (as so graphically illustrated in the Josh McDowell video), consumers actively pursue the sexually explicit mate-rials they choose to engage with. Moreover, far from being indiscriminate and simply opportunist, porn consumers have rich histories and tastes, which connect in complex ways with our respondents' understandings of sex and sexuality in their everyday lives.

In what follows, we explore the patterns of motivations for engaging with pornography that emerge from our research.

ENGAGING WITH PORN

Why do people engage with online pornography? The answer to that may seem too obvious to be worth asking. Yet we think it worth asking, because although sexual arousal and pleasure are aspects of people's interests in por-nography, it is not the whole story; nor is the question as simple and obvious as it might seem. But also, from previous research that we have done, we know that the reasons driving a person to seek out pornography will play a role in shaping their preferences and choices, and hence their responses.[28] To begin to understand, then, how audience responses to pornography work, we need to take a closer look at the complexities within people's stated interests.

Using our standardized procedure, we sampled our overall body of responses, focusing on answers to our first qualitative question, which asked respondents to explain in their own words their choice from the options for the Importance of pornography. In the fifty sampled responses we can see evidence for a number of different reasons people view pornography, each of which leads, broadly, to a different orientation to porn, and, from that, connects with how much and with what commitment they engage; what sources they choose; what materials (visuals, scenarios, narratives) they find interesting and arousing; and what they feel pornography adds to their lives. Of course, these orientations do not necessarily come separately, and as we look at individuals in detail we will see how these different elements may interweave. Nonetheless there is a value in first separating out these orientations to consider their separate logics.

We illustrate these briefly, using examples both from our sample of fifty, and from others in the larger sample found using keywords suggested by the fifty. First, it is significant to note that for some people the most important reason to watch pornography is that there is no real reason—they just do it. This shows in answers such as the following. "It's not a habit but something to enjoy occasionally." "Well, I don't need to view pornography for gratification—my own imagination is far better. It's great for when you are just horny and lazy, however!" "It's less that porn is important and more that it is nice to have. Were I to lose it tomorrow the funeral would be short, but it would be missed." People responding like this are marking the boundaries of their engagement. It is like Cadbury's Cream Eggs, or any other treat—no more than that. "It's not important because nothing I do relies on porn—I can function in every aspect without it." "For the same reason romantic comedy movies are not important in my life: Both are low-quality entertainment that I have no great interest in watching." "It's not important, just diversionary," said another respondent. In these responses, as we found throughout the database, there is underlying acknowledgment of the ways in which pornography and its consumption are much talked about, and that the figure of the "porn-user" is an object of considerable public concern, to be worried about, a personage who has to be managed—to protect them from themselves, and to protect others from their supposedly malign influence(s)—so that these boundary-marking answers identify the respondent as different from the stereotypical "porn-user."

But beyond these answers—almost always from low Importance respondents—there is a considerable range of reasons, as indicated by the following examples:

1. Boredom/Idleness

   "Entertainment for when I'm bored."

   "I use it regularly, sometimes to distraction. I use it out of boredom, I'm in a 'living apart, together' type of relationship—but mainly 'apart' and find porn a palliative."

   "I only occasionally look at porn, usually when I'm really bored. I hardly ever think about it."

It seems as if this is a particular kind of boredom, in which one's body asserts itself and demands some attention in and of itself. One person puts it nicely in drawing an analogy with food. According to them: "An analogy would be something like hamburgers—I enjoy hamburgers a lot, when I decide to eat them, but that's pretty much the extent of their involvement in my life." The issue then is what might be meant by "boredom" and "idleness" where this leads to looking for porn experiences.

2. Release

> "Sometimes just as a stress reliever / unable to concentrate on work."

> "I view porn multiple times a day. I feel that viewing porn reduces my stress levels, makes me feel better when depressed, and makes me feel better about myself. It also seems to allow me to re-set and re-focus quickly on important high-concentration tasks such as software development. I just feel happier and like my day is just a little bit brighter."

> "I really enjoy watching it. I use it as a coping method to cut stress."

These responses indicate the use of masturbation as a wind-down, and accessing pornography as a way to intensify this process. This idea is further exemplified by the statement: "As a college student and a virgin currently not in a relationship, I find porn as a good way to escape many of the stresses of college life." The implication here is that the body carries the load of other kinds of stress, and attending to it in itself relieves some of this.

3. Simple Intensification of Bodily Pleasures

> "While I find I can create my own fantasies outside of pornography, it does take the effort out of forming an erection, and the visual stimulation causes me to have more powerful orgasms."

> "I'm a very visual person and it increases my orgasm time by a lot (even compared to partner sex). Sometimes I just want to masturbate for the afterglow, so a quick orgasm is desirable."

> "Pornography can provide erotic stimulus or can intensify erotic feelings."

Pornography's role in the intensification of bodily pleasures might again seem obvious but, again, we don't think it is. In the answers here, we see understanding of sexual arousal as a thing in its own right, worthy of its own modes of attainment. Feeling aroused is more than a response; it is a mode of being that can be enhanced, even at its most mundane: "I masturbate regularly, and watching pornographic videos helps make it more exciting." "Life is full and complex. Most things take a small place, even eating and going to the loo. These are important, as you would likely find too, but nonetheless small aspects."

4. As a Leisure Choice in Its Own Right

"It's a leisure activity, not really 'important,' per se."

"I write porn for fun and to share, so it's an important leisure activity; I don't consume it as much as I produce it though."

"My most important leisure-time activity is coming up with new ideas for hentai. Also, I use it every day except Sundays."

"Like many leisure activities it is fun, but not all-consuming." This quote, like the previous ones, agrees with separating sex off as something with its own imperatives. But for people who enjoy sex in this fashion, it is something one can get better at, and pornography can be an important facilitator. "Fantasy is at a premium—if you have a partner with whom you can role-play some passionate and exciting scene, you'll have really hot sex. So porn, in a sense, challenges us to introduce narrative into sex, not just sensation or power dynamics." Like a sport, or like a hobby, sex can be pursued. One can choose how far one goes, but it is recognized that it could become an expertise, almost a profession where pornography can take a significant role. And it is striking that a number of those indicating this reason talk about themselves producing as well as consuming pornography.[29] This is an aspect of our responses that we will pursue in future investigations of the database; for now, we simply note its presence.

5. Inadequate Sexual Opportunities, for Various Reasons, Including Age

"Porn is necessary to supplement a lacking sexual life."

"Because my 'real life' sex-life is—after 20 years of marriage—some-what lacking, particularly in comparison to my fantasies."

"I am 70 years old with a missing human sensitivity in my life . . . erotic material (I do not particularly like the term porn) is important to fulfill a human need."

This is a very frequently given reason among respondents to explain why they choose to use porn. The condition here is usually of someone who used to have an active sex life, but for whatever reason, often due to age or a long-term relationship, has experienced a decline or absence of sex. Pornography provides a surrogate means of recovering some version of sexual experience.

For some, it is almost like an antiageing cream. According to one respondent, "I am beyond the age of being able to play in the dating/mating game. But I think it possible that the neuronal and hormonal activities that accompany desire and arousal might contribute to a healthy life." For another, "Sex was an important part of my life but age, IBS [irritable bowel syndrome], and weight gain-driven low self-esteem means that has fallen away. Porn fills that gap."

6. Within an Ongoing Relationship

"Either I or my partner and I use certain homemade porn for arousal purposes."

"My partner and I are in a long-distance relationship. We send links of porn to each other as a way of keeping things fresh and hot."

"I like trying new things with my sex partners and I learn many new things from porn."

"Both my wife and I regularly enjoy pornography." It is, of course, impossible, with an answer like this, to say to what extent a person is fairly reporting his or her partner's interests and willingness. But there are a good number of responses—from both men and women—suggesting that selective porn viewing can play a role in accentuating sexual life for some couples, both heterosexual and homosexual. Responses such as these, and the ones above, indicate that pornography can serve as a means of enabling relationships, that it contributes to the idea of sex as a particular form of sharing between individuals that can be enhanced and expanded through an external resource. While there are certainly many respondents who use pornography on their own, the thousands who talk of it as a shared activity go considerable ways to counteract the dominant discourse of pornography consumption as a "sad" or "lonely" activity.

7. Exploring One's Sexual Self/Identity

"[Porn] was really important in my sexual development; it assisted in shaping my identity and has almost always been present, but I go up and down in my use."

"I enjoy porn quite a bit, both by myself and with my partner, but other things in my life—i.e., school, social issues—are more important. I selected 'Quite Important,' however, because porn has helped me come into my identity over time, and I think porn issues can be some of the important social issues I think about."

"It helps me to express the sexual part of my identity. Since menopause I've found that my sexual responsiveness has decreased, although my desire has not. Using porn helps me."

What is interesting here is the sense of personal philosophizing that frequently accompanies answers of this kind. This is not just about sexual arousal and pleasure, it is simultaneously thinking about the meanings and significance of being aroused or feeling pleasure—the felt importance of experiencing one's own body as "sexy" in itself, for oneself and for others. The significance of pornography can, of course, decline once one has acquired a level of experience, as here: "For a time, it was quite important. It helped to clarify what excited me. Now, after many hours of 'research,' I know, so it's only of mild interest now. Still, erotic stories do hold my interest these days too." A version of this response—where people look at porn to find out if it constitutes something they want to become; for instance, young men who think they might be gay, and who experiment with gay porn to see if it arouses them—is something we might have expected to see more frequently, but it does not predominate in the opening round of fifty responses we focus on here. There are indications of it in the wider database, particularly among those respondents who identified as queer, as we discuss elsewhere.[30] For now, we note that this idea of acquiring understanding is part of people's ways of talking about fantasies—pornography enables kinds of experiments with the self, as here: "It explores my sexual fantasies." The wording of this short (complete) answer is interesting. Porn is an "it," something external which is allowed to work on this person, if we take this wording seriously.

8. As Part of a Wider Recognition of the Force of Sex

"I'm an artist/researcher. I'm fascinated with how people perform for the webcam and amateur content. I wonder why people make videos of themselves having sex to post on the Internet. I study porn but I also like to watch it. I'm aware of a whole range of fetishes that have found communities on the Internet and I'm fascinated by how people interact through it."

"Sex positivity and sexual expression are very important to me. Porn has been an important part of discovering and also defining my sexuality as a queer. Seeing other queers fuck is empowering. I write smut, am a published author and find pornographic writings and literature to be very stimulating. I also use visual porn, pictures and movies, currently on a daily basis while masturbating. So, overall, porn is very important to me! ;)"

"I do use pornography, but I also study and analyze pornography for scholarly pursuits and am in the field of porn studies, so pornography is important for my academic, intellectual, and professional life."

The idea of "studying" and learning from porn is one that frequently surfaces in our responses and clearly has several meanings both as a means of studying oneself (testing out likes and dislikes; understanding one's sexual orientation) and as a form of engaging with pornography as cultural medium in order to understand its appeal to other people, and the importance of pornography to sexual life. "I have studied it a lot. I also like watching it to feel sexually stimulated." "Sex is always around us and porn is a pretty immediate means of access." Like the previous reason, this category involves a body of wider thoughts about the meanings and purposes of sexual desire in humans—and perhaps here a sense of the simple variousness of desires, choices, acts. For some of our respondents, then, porn is not simply about feeling "aroused" but is also an important means of understanding the rich varieties of sexual attraction, interests, and practices as they exist for others. There is also, in some cases, a sense that if unattended to, lack of sex will have deleterious consequences for a person. Other aspects of his/her life will suffer in consequence.

9. As an Aesthetic/Erotic Experience

"I love beauty. I love to see beautiful women. Nature at its best, in the eyes of a man."

"The porn I view is almost entirely viewed as art by me. I rarely masturbate, but I like sexy images."

"Excitement, appreciation of human body and sexuality as an art form, fulfilment of fantasies, exploration of sexuality, comparison of desired characteristics in a mate."

This quite common response works against treating porn as something special. It is a form of taking pleasure, as with food, poetry, music, or nature. This type of response emphasizes the ordinariness of sex and the feelings that accompany it. "Porn is not only titillating, it can also be very relaxing. To me, looking at a beautiful nude model is like looking at a classic painting or a beautiful sunset. Nothing is more beautiful than the various sizes and shapes of nude human females." "Porn, for me, is a high-grade entertainment on a level with music, fine food, etc. Part of why life is sweet." Again, we see here that pornography is more than just simply a spur to physiological response, but it offers aesthetic and emotional resources that can enrich the everyday.

10. Voyeurism

"I'm a very visual person, and I also enjoy the aspect of voyeuristic visualization that porn offers . . . It helps the fantasy."

"I feel that porn is a necessary outlet for any sexual urges I get when none of my partners are available, and also as an occasional outlet for exclusively voyeuristic urges."

"I enjoy watching other people enjoying themselves sexually. I also get off on the auditory part of porn, especially when I'm jerking off."

"Looking at nude women and people having sex makes me feel good. Currently I'm single, so it's nice to have an engaging sexual outlet. Also I'm curious about how other people express their sexuality. How kind of them to share with me!"

Interestingly, this is a set of responses that does seem to have an opposite, with a number of people saying that they find this aspect of pornography difficult. The negative possibilities of being considered a "voyeur" means that looking at other people's bodies can be experienced as embarrassing (therefore watching professionals can ease their awkwardness). Or, they may prefer stories because of the distance this allows. But there are a good number of people for whom, simply, the sight—and sound—of bodies sexually engaged is an attraction in itself.

11. The Attraction of the Kinky, the Naughty, and the Dirty

"I am a single parent of young children—I'm not dating. So I masturbate to porn for my sexual release. Also, I enjoy certain kinks that I have not been able to enjoy with a partner in many years. Porn gives me access to that."

"As a lover of pegging, watching videos of the act helps set the mood for my partner and [me]. The videos also helped show her it was neither abnormal nor all that kinky so much as easy, clean and fun. Very well done porn also helps us keep up with items that aren't exactly in the local stores like sex swings."

"I don't particularly feel the need to search out porn, but will happily consume it, if it's there. Which may be somewhat more than average since I use various BDSM/kink-related social networking sites."

There is little doubt that among the motives for looking at porn is an attraction to seeing what other people do in their most private moments, sometimes balanced on a cusp between delight and disgust. It is also surely linked to the bad reputation of pornography—to seek it out and watch it is to explore a forbidden domain, and see what goes on there.

Combinations of responses, even shown in quite short answers, tell us a lot about a life story. Consider the following answer: "It stimulates my relationship with my partner and my creativity in everyday life. It makes me feel young and energetic." In this we can see the interaction of two modes: the contribution to an ongoing relationship and the sense that attention to sex provokes benefits in other parts of this person's life. But there is also a hint of awareness of another mode that has to be fended off: the possibility of waning desire that might go with ageing, though, for now, porn produces feelings of youthfulness.

Or, consider a somewhat longer answer:

> While a substantial amount of porn is mainstream and staged, there's nonetheless something voyeuristic and hot about it. The naked bodies, the sounds, just turn me on and provide my imagination with a starting point. I watch porn just about every night, and it's pleasing to fantasize right before sleep. I suppose the other reason that I find it appealing is that it's still 'naughty.' I lead such a tame life that this dirty pleasure is an outlet for me.

For this respondent, there is a very palpable sense in which pornography allows safe access to ways of being naughty, of experiencing dirty pleasures without risk. Like the sensations on a roller-coaster, pornography offers ways of experiencing thrills with limits.

CONCLUSION

In such a short chapter as this it is impossible to explore the minutiae of each of these reasons and their significances. Even so, the sheer range and complexity of reasons that respondents provide in explaining why they use and enjoy porn should give us pause. This brief foray through the range of reasons is, we believe, an important counter to the simplistic judgements about pornography and the people who consume it that we outlined in our introduction. Too often, debates about pornography revolve around whether or not porn is good or bad for us. With these differentiated reasons in view, perhaps we might begin to ask other questions: How might these different interests in porn then feed through into different patterns of choice, different preferred kinds, and different uses of pornography? Is it possible to draw out repeating threads linking wishes and hopes, sources and choices, and outcomes—even to the point of being able to link these, however tentatively, with kinds of people (by age, gender identification, sexual orientation, etc.)?

This is the task we have set ourselves in pursuing the analysis of our amassed data and responses. Inevitably this will take us some time to complete, as we have 5,500 individual responses and more than 1.5 million words to analyze. Our intentions are not to simply produce graphs and speedily accessed conclusions from the data. Rather, we are carefully sifting our way through the responses in order to do justice to the richness of the responses we have received. Whatever the confidence with which, in the end, we are able to explore different patterns of consumption, the picture that is emerging from this research is seriously at odds with the conventional figures of the aberrant, troubled, and addicted porn user that are dominating discussions about pornography at the present time.

NOTES

1. Henry Jenkins, "Foreword: So You Want to Teach Pornography?" in *More Dirty Looks: Gender, Pornography and Power*, ed. Pamela Church Gibson (London: BFI Publishing, 2004), 2.

2. Dir. Paul Weitz, 1999.

3. Alan McKee, Kath Albury, and Catherine Lumby, *The Porn Report* (Melbourne, Australia: Melbourne University Publishing, 2008), 25.

4. Laura Kipnis, *Bound and Gagged: Pornography and the Politics of Fantasy in America* (Durham, NC: Duke University Press, 1996), 161.

5. Walter Kendrick, *The Secret Museum: Pornography in Modern Culture* (Berkeley, CA: University of California Press, 1996), 261–62.

6. Philip Elmer-Dewitt, "Online Erotica: On a Screen Near You," *Time*, July 3, 1995, http://content.time.com/time/magazine/article/0,9171,983116,00.html.

7. Zabet Patterson, "Going On-line: Consuming Pornography in the Digital Era," in *Porn Studies*, ed. Linda Williams (Durham, NC: Duke University Press, 2001), 104–5.

8. Such as Liz Martin, "How Internet Porn Turned My Beautiful Boy Into a Hollow Self-Hating Shell," *Daily Mail*, April 20, 2012, http://www.dailymail.co.uk/news/article-2132342/How-internet-porn-turned-beautiful-boy-hollow-self-hating-shell.html or Leslie Bennetts, "The Growing Demand for Prostitution," *Newsweek*, July 18, 2011, http://www.newsweek.com/growing-demand-prostitution-68493.

9. Josh McDowell Ministries, *Just 1 Click Away*, http://just1clickaway.org/resources.html.

10. Michael Leahy, *Porn Nation: Conquering America's #1 Addiction* (Chicago: Northfield Publishing, 2008).

11. Decca Aitkenhead, "Are Teenagers Hooked on Porn?" *Psychologies*, June 2010, http://www.psychologies.co.uk/family/are-teenagers-hooked-on-porn.

12. Steve Biddulph, *Raising Boys: Why Boys are Different—and How to Help Them Become Happy and Well-Balanced Men* (London: Harper Thorsons, 2009), 164.

13. Melinda Tankard Reist, *Getting Real: Challenging the Sexualisation of Girls* (Melbourne, Australia: Spinifex Press 2009), 20.

14. Rebecca Whisnant, "From Jekyll to Hyde: The Grooming of Male Pornography Consumers," in *Everyday Pornography*, ed. Karen Boyle (London: Routledge, 2010), 115.

15. Ibid., 132.

16. Gail Dines, "How the Hardcore Porn Industry Is Ruining Young Men's Lives," *Sydney Morning Herald*, May 18, 2012, http://www.smh.com.au/opinion/society-and-culture/how-the-hardcore-porn-industry-is-ruining-young-mens-lives-20110517–1erac.html#ixzz23kFcaGSP.

17. Gail Dines, *Pornland: How Porn has Hijacked Our Sexuality* (Boston: Beacon Press, 2010).

18. Carmine Sarracino and Kevin Scott, *The Porning of America: The Rise of Porn Culture, What It Means, and Where We Go from Here* (Boston: Beacon Press 2008), 139–44.

19. Ibid., 149.

20. Ibid., 153.

21. The British government has enacted provisions against the possession of "extreme pornography" in its Criminal Justice and Immigration Act 2008 and is currently pushing through similar legislation that will outlaw possession of "rape porn" in its Criminal Justice and Courts Bill. This legislation is driven by an amorphous "increasing public concern," and with little acknowledgement of a vast body of work on a variety of media, including pornography, and their audiences, which would significantly complicate the picture of effects. In order to justify the legislation, the government commissioned a Rapid Evidence Assessment (Catherine Itzin, Ann R. Taket, and Liz Kelly, *The Evidence of Harm to Adults Relating to Exposure to Extreme Pornographic Material: A Rapid Evidence Assessment (REA)* (London: Ministry of Justice, 2007)), which joins a range of other government-sponsored research exercises beginning from the assumption of pornography's harms. See Reg Bailey, *Letting Children Be Children: Report of an Independent Review of the Commercialisation and Sexualisation of Childhood*. Vol. 8078. The Stationery Office, 2011; Miranda Horvath, Llian Alys, Kristina Massey, Afroditi Pina, Mia Scally, and Joanna R. Adler, "Basically . . . Porn Is Everywhere: A Rapid Evidence Assessment on the Effects That Access and Exposure to Pornography Has on Children and Young People" (press release, 2013); Linda Papadopoulos, *Sexualisation of Young People Review* (London: Home Office Publication, 2010). Each of these reviews was designed to build consensus and failed to assess the evidence for any discernable links between pornography and the normalization of violence against women. Instead, those links are assumed to be already proven. For more detail about the legislation on possession and its problematic evidence base, see Feona Attwood and Clarissa Smith, "Extreme Concern: Regulating 'Dangerous Pictures' in the United Kingdom," *Journal of Law and Society* 37, no. 1 (2010): 171–188.

22. The research was designed and conducted by the three authors. We received £1000 funding from the University of Sunderland to cover the costs of the Web design and hosting. We are still working our way through the responses we received

and are being assisted by colleagues Dr. Lynne Hall, Reader in Computing at the University of Sunderland, and Dr. Sarah Tazzyman, Teaching Fellow in Psychology at the University of Leicester.

23. See http://www.pornresearch.org.

24. Trans* is an umbrella term popularized by Sam Killerman that signifies "all of the identities within the gender identity spectrum." See Sam Killerman, "What Does the Asterisk in 'Trans*' Stand For?" *It's Pronounced Metrosexual*, May 2012, http://itspronouncedmetrosexual.com/2012/05/what-does-the-asterisk-in-trans-stand-for.

25. Most university research involving human participants is vetted by individual institutions' Ethics Committees and Institutional Review Boards to ensure that the research adheres to proper standards of research design, methodology, and reporting. Discussions of research ethics are often dominated by natural scientists and medical researchers whose perceptions of issues such as "harm" are inevitably (and for them rightly) governed by simple measurable criteria. But for researchers within the Humanities and Social Sciences the concept of harm comes laden with problematic cultural assumptions, which it has been important for researchers to question. Ethical considerations have sometimes meant that important research cannot be conducted. For example, much of the so-called evidence about young people's consumption of pornography is based on anecdote and conjecture because very few universities are willing to sanction research with subjects under the age of eighteen.

26. The research was publicized via various social media sites, including Facebook. From there individuals posted our information on their own blogs and in discussion fora such as melonfarmers.org and others focused on sexual topics and communities. It was also featured on Web sites with specifically pornographic content such as porn-rapidshare.org. The research was also discussed by traditional media, including the gay and lesbian radio station Joy 94.9 in Australia, various student radio stations, and in more mainstream publications like the UK broadsheet the *Guardian*.

27. The Head of Web Research at SPA comments that "we typically get any-where between 0.5% and 10% but this really depends on how engaged the data-base is with the company concerned, the incentive offered and how short/engaging the survey is. We typically ask our clients for sample based on a 25:1 completion ratio so 4% as an average." See http://econsultancy.com/uk/forums/best-practice/industry-stats-uk-on-line-survey-response-rates.

28. Martin Barker et al., *Audiences and Receptions of Sexual Violence in Contemporary Cinema* (London: BBFC, 2007); Martin Barker et al., *The Crash Controversy: Censorship Campaigns and Film Reception* (London: Wallflower, 2001); Clarissa Smith, *One for the Girls! The Pleasures and Practices of Reading Women's Porn* (Bristol, UK: Intellect, 2007).

29. Across our respondents we have found interests in producing written, photographed, and filmed pornographies. Sometimes these were to share with a long-term, and particularly long-distance, partner; for others, writing erotic stories had become an important pastime and means of sharing with other likeminded authors at Web sites such as literotica.com and in femslash communities. For yet others, sharing photographs with partners was a key way of fostering excitement and anticipation.

A significant minority of our respondents talked of uploading their own videos to amateur sites, while a very small number said they actually produced pornography professionally.

30. Clarissa Smith, Feona Attwood, and Martin Barker, "Queering Porn Audiences," in *Queer Sex Work*, ed. Mary Laing, Katy Pilcher and Nicola Smith (London: Routledge, 2015).

15

Pornography and Effects Studies: What Does the Research Actually Say?

Andy Ruddock

In "The One with Free Porn" episode of the hit U.S. sitcom *Friends*, roommates Joey Tribiani and Chandler Bing discover, to their delight, that they suddenly have free access to adult cable channels. The ecstatic pair spends so long watching the free fare that it eventually affects their view of reality. When they do venture outside their apartment, they expect every mundane encounter to drip with erotic possibilities; to their pornified imaginations, every woman they meet wants to have sex with them there and then. Hilarity ensues as their fantasies fail to materialize.

This may be the only sitcom gag to be based on a theory of media effects. Cultivation theory argues that because media keep telling audiences the same story about how the world works, eventually those audiences come to think there is an element of truth to what they see onscreen, and this affects their view of social reality.[1] This basic idea has been used in studies on pornography. Christina Rogala and Tanja Tyden's survey of 1,000 women outpatients at a Stockholm family planning clinic,[2] for instance, argued the spread of STIs among the group had been accelerated by the impression that unprotected anal sex is as common in real life as it is in pornography.

Of course, the joke of the *Friends* episode was that it is ridiculous to imagine that anyone would be gullible enough to believe the world is one big porn set. Similarly, whatever methods and theories they use, audience researchers who study the impact of media violence, pornography, and the like don't think that viewers are easily manipulated by what they see onscreen. Alan McKee's Australian research, for example, depicts porn consumers as a discerning bunch who know that they are watching a fantasy and use it judiciously to support healthy, respectful, mutually enriching relationships.[3]

That said, it is worth hanging on to the idea that being exposed to the same stories time and time again can affect how viewers understand themselves, their world, and the people around them: This way of conceiving media influence unifies what are otherwise different and even antagonistic views on the nature and impact of pornography. When it comes to the topic of media influence, scholars are roughly divided into two camps. Some researchers use experiments and surveys to show how pornography encourages people to be aggressive, misogynistic, and insensitive. Others prefer to use more open-ended qualitative methods, like interviews, to let audiences explain their relationship with pornography in their own terms. Unsurprisingly, the latter tend to be more sanguine about what pornography means and what it does.

But these divisions are not immutable. Surveying recent studies, it is possible to see common ground. Even if the results of various studies continue to provoke disagreement about the impact of pornography, there is similarity in the question that is being asked in the first place. In particular, there is a consensus that the "porn effects" question is fundamentally about what it means to live in a world where a sense of self and well-being depends on access to commercially produced media narratives. On this matter, cultivation theory provides a language to explain what this consensus means for understanding research into the social impact of pornography.

To demonstrate the value of a cultivation perspective on the porn effects question, this chapter:

- Describes criticisms that have been made of effects research, focusing particularly on qualitative researchers who argue that pornography is good for many of its users.
- Demonstrates how many of these criticisms are recognized *within* the community of effects scholars, noting points where this community acknowledges the complexity of the relationship between porn and its users.
- Explains how a cultivation theory clarifies the significance of an observation made in both qualitative and quantitative studies: that when you ask audiences to talk about the pornography they use, what you get are stories about what the world is like, how those users fit therein, and what it means to live in a world where, to paraphrase George Gerbner, most of the stories that most of us consume most of the time come from media businesses.[4]

WHAT'S "WRONG" WITH EFFECTS RESEARCH ON PORNOGRAPHY?

Research that uses quantitative measures to correlate exposure to pornographic material with social attitudes and behaviors has conventionally focused on the conditions that make pornography bad for people.[5] Confirming pessimism as the norm in this line of work, a meta-analysis of the results from experimental studies of porn effects concluded that research had reliably established the connection between the consumption of pornography and sexual aggression. This was especially true if the pornography was considered to be violent, and if the viewer was a man already considered at risk of offending in this regard.[6]

Recent effects studies on pornography show how this negativity has continued. It's relatively easy to find studies arguing that pornography damages its users. Moreover, the case has also been made that the ongoing infiltration of everyday life by digital media is only making things worse. Ven-Hwei Lo, Ran Wei, and Hsiaomei Wu's survey of Taiwanese adolescents is a case in point.[7] Based on data gathered from 1,688 respondents, Lo, Wei, and Wu ominously cautioned that the Internet has amplified the corrupting power of pornography. The researchers asked their subjects to report on their exposure to online pornography, to estimate how damaging this content was on themselves and other people, and to indicate their support for restricting access to it. Their results found that "the more adolescents consume pornographic materials online, the less they see the harm of Internet pornography on themselves and others."[8] They interpreted this as indicating "a state of denial among heavy users," taking this as an indicator of a powerful "desensitization" effect.[9] In all, they concluded "the harmful effects of Internet pornography are unequivocal and greater than documented in previous research."[10] Data from recent effects studies shows that the more pornography one consumes, the more one is likely to accept rape myths, to develop misogynistic attitudes,[11] to overestimate the real-world presence of common porn-world practices,[12] and to develop highly permissive attitudes toward sex.[13] Moreover, the Internet has only made things worse, for young people in particular, because it makes pornography easier to access and "edit"; the ease of access is complemented by the pleasure of being able to decide what you consume to suit your unique proclivities.[14]

In this context, Lo, Wei, and Wu's study seemingly represents the dogged determination of effects studies to show that pornography simply is bad for the world. As such, it is subject to the reservations that qualitative scholars have about the validity of effects research in general. One important criticism is that effects studies are grounded in the unstable *a priori* assumption that media culture is a fundamentally dangerous place. In contrast, audience researcher David Gauntlett[15] has argued it makes just as much sense to view media culture as a field of abundant opportunity where people know exactly how to help themselves—and others—by using the media resources that commercial culture makes ready to hand. Alan McKee's Australian research has applied the same logic to pornography, arguing that evidence from "the lucky country" suggests pornography is a boon to lifestyles that are, in every sense, healthy.[16]

Alan McKee's work is significant because it applies the general critique of effects research to understanding pornography's audience in particular. McKee used a survey of 1,023 people, and follow-up interviews with 49 respondents, to make the case that the dominant academic focus on the harmful effects of pornography was an artifact of effects methods. The case against porn, from the position of effects researchers, depended, in McKee's view, on dubious methods of sampling and data gathering. The connection made between exposure to pornography and increases in misogyny and aggression depended on a number of contingencies: being able to expose large numbers of people to pornography that they had not selected under uncomfortable conditions (surrounded by strangers) that prohibited normal reactions (i.e., masturbation). McKee reasoned that this was enough to make anyone angry. Added to the fact that these treatments tended to be administered time and time again to particular sorts of samples (such as students and prisoners—both captive audiences), and the reason for doubting the validity of effects research was clear. All that effects research had really discovered was that exposure to pornography *in experiments* makes people angry.[17]

In contrast, McKee's survey from a general population found that people who watched a lot of pornography were not more misogynist than those who did not. The interviews, which focused on the porn that people *chose* to watch in their own homes, developed many insights, including that pornography is a multifaceted genre that is hard to define. Nevertheless, the incredibly violent pornography that is frequently featured in experiments was, on the whole, alien to porn fans: McKee's interviewees simply did not watch the kind of pornography that effects researchers tend to use in their studies. Finally, porn fans are highly moral. People who like porn are highly supportive of censoring any sort of pornography that involves any form of abuse or violence, whether that be sex with minors or coercion of sex acts that the performers do not enjoy, and are extremely careful about ensuring that no one is inadvertently exposed to the content they consume.

McKee's study advocated for a new agenda for pornography research, where the possibility that pornography was a positive force in society was accepted as a legitimate hypothesis. Some years later, he developed this position further and argued that the lesson of his research on audience responses to pornography was that the genre should be approached as a form of entertainment rather than as a danger to society. According to McKee, close attention to the conventions of pornography and the pleasures that people get from it shows that the porn question is about the social function of commercial entertainment. Defining pornography as entertainment establishes an entirely different research agenda, resting on a set of different questions about why pornography matters. McKee argues that pornography encapsulates precisely the vulgarity that has always made popular culture popular.[18] Pornography is characterized by seriality, adaption, a preference for happy endings, a focus on fun, and, more importantly, a concern with what audiences want. As such, pornography demonstrates the general benefits of allowing a healthy, inclusive public culture to run through commercial systems. Having made the case to the Australian federal government that because pornography is indeed good for some people—as the foundation for healthy relationships, for example—McKee investigated the possibility of getting state-funded pornography off the ground. Having been rebuffed, yet remaining convinced of the social value of pornography—because audiences say it is so—McKee concluded, "Pornography is not suitable for subsidized culture. It must exist in the purely commercial realm, paid for by audiences and driven by audience demand."[19] Pornography, in other words, could no longer be seen as something radically different in studies of media culture; it *is* media culture, and the debates about what it is and why people like it are integral to debates about the benefits of commercial media culture itself.

At face value the concept of porn as an irreverent entertainment genre that works only because it establishes an interactive relationship with its audience confounds the general thrust of effects research. A closer look, however, shows four things. First, many of the criticisms that McKee directs at effects studies have also been made by effects researchers. Second, effects researchers agree that the pornography question is fundamentally about what it means to live with commercial public culture. Third, understanding pornography as an entertainment genre does not necessarily lead to the conclusion that porn, as a vivid exemplar of the benefits of commercial culture, is good for society. And, finally, there are ways to ask questions about why porn is bad for society that are not premised on the view of audiences as dopes.

WHAT DO EFFECTS RESEARCHERS REALLY CLAIM ABOUT THEIR METHODS AND THE INFLUENCE OF PORN?

In truth, effects researchers do not think that pornography is necessarily bad for society; it's just that their data gives grounds to think that it probably is, in various ways, for a significant number of people, given the right (or wrong) circumstances. For example, Gert Hald and Neil Malamuth's survey of 688 Danes ages 18 to 30 reaches a surprising conclusion; pornography might be good for you.[20] Most of the young people in the survey thought that using porn was a perfectly healthy thing to do, and could in fact play a positive role in building healthy sex lives that respected the needs and sensibilities of others. This finding is significant, given that the study's second author had earlier written that, based on the evidence, pornography is unequivocally bad for society.[21]

However, the 2008 Danish study is not a *mea culpa*. In its conclusion, the authors maintain that their new findings do not discredit the case for nega-tive effects; just because pornography appears to be good for young Danes, this does not mean that other studies in other places showing it is bad for other sorts of people living in different circumstances are wrong. In fact, reviews of a near century of effects studies conclude that one of the most important findings is that effects can only be addressed by attending to the differences between social groups. George Comstock, a leading figure in the field of media effects since the 1960s, argued that we can't decide whether phenomena such as porn or violence are good or bad, because the data shows that effects are best studied within social groups rather than across total popu-lations. Most of the evidence on violence, for instance, shows that harmful effects are aggregated within socially disadvantaged groups.[22] So saying porn is good for Danes, or Australians, isn't saying it isn't bad for others. Whatever the qualms about effects researchers, their methods, and their conclusions, it is not accurate to say that they are blind to the intricacies of media culture.

Actually, there two points where effects researchers agree with McKee. The first is that experiments and surveys suffer from an inherent validity problem when it comes to making inferences about what media do in the real world. Mike Allen and Tara Emmers observed that experimental studies find significant effects far more often than do surveys, which often found none.[23] Barry Gunter's lucid review of the effects case makes a number of significant points on the connections between methods and results.[24] Gunter believed that experiments and surveys are valuable resources for media researchers, as long as the inherent limitations of these methods are recognized. Fundamen-tally, the claims that can be made based on experiments are limited because:

> It remains to be convincingly demonstrated that the motives of experi-mental participants invited to use analogues of aggression in laboratory settings are psychologically equivalent to the motives of, for example, children fighting at school, husbands beating their wives, drunks in alcohol-fueled fights late at night, perpetrators of muggings or armed robberies, or motorists involved [in] road rage incidents.[25]

As far as surveys go, those associations between exposure to violence and porn and the proclivity toward antisocial attitudes or behaviors have two vul-nerabilities. The first vulnerability is a reliance on self-reporting; the second one is the absence of any evidence showing that a correlation between these variables implies causation.

On pornography in particular, Gunter observed that experiments found causative associations between exposure to violent pornography and the acceptance of rape myths among young men, and surveys found sex offenders to be heavy consumers of such fare. Nevertheless he cautioned a number of qualifications. This evidence did not establish that pornography was a trigger in their crimes (as opposed to a symptom of their predispositions). In fact, the correlation between criminality and the consumption of "bad" media content also suggested an alternative hypothesis; that for some people with antisocial tendencies "media violence may act as a distraction, and kept them out of trouble."[26]

None of this was to say that the evidence from effects research was easily dismissed, or that anxieties about media and risk were unfounded. Significantly, Gunter observed that perhaps the key problem was that effects research placed too much of an onus on behaviors. He suggested that if we are interested in what happens to most of the people most of the time, it makes more sense to focus on the nonbehavioral impact that an allegedly dangerous medium like pornography has on ordinary people who do not act out in obvious ways. What are some of the ways that long-term exposure to such content affects general perceptions of life? In other words, when it comes to porn, think less Ted Bundy and more Chandler and Joey.

The lesson, from Gunter, is that the significance of pornography is best understood by looking at the nonbehavioral responses of ordinary people, through studies that are sensitive to the notion that there are many questions that one can ask about why porn matters, and many ways of interpreting the data that is generated when we try to figure out this question. One way to follow Gunter's advice that we should focus on the ordinary is to frame pornography as a genre that reflects general tendencies in media culture. It is therefore relevant that recent effects research suggests that pornography is simply one genre among many that teach the world about sex. According to Richard Harris and Christopher Bartlett, the porn question was about what happens when commercially made pornography becomes a significant fount of knowledge about sexuality, in a world where media in general are a go-to source for how love, sex, and romance really work.[27] In other words, pornography reflects the effects of monopolized storytelling in a world where it is normal and even rational to be guided by all kinds of media on how to approach social situations.

Harris and Bartlett made two points that eventually identify common interests in research on pornography. First, the question at hand is about the role of media in sexual socialization. As such, researchers must be alert to the possibility that other genres may be far more troubling than pornography. Second, the authors sided with Gunter in maintaining that the most significant media effects take shape as nonbehavioral outcomes among ordinary populations. In particular, one of the most important effects of pornography might be the impression that we live in a world where *other people* consume huge amounts of pornography, to deleterious effect. This last position is known as the "third-person effect."

The third-person effect is the notion individuals have that onscreen sex and violence has a tremendous impact on *other* people.[28] In a study about the third-person effect, Bryant Paul, Michael Salwen, and Michel Dupagne found that around 50 percent of those surveyed believed that media had a greater effect on people other than themselves.[29] This had been tested in the field of media violence, where researchers asked if people believed that such violence was likely to make other people violent and/or aggressive.[30]

Lo, Wei, and Wu's study was notable as both an effort to apply the third-person effect to pornography, and an examination of the role that Internet pornography in particular, by dint of its sheer ubiquity, could play in reducing third-person perceptions. Conventionally, third-person effect studies have tried to identify a political response to media content. This is usually defined as a correlation between the perception that other people are affected by violence and pornography, and a readiness to support censorship legislation. Lo, Wei, and Wu asked respondents about the amount of Internet pornography they consumed, the extent to which they felt this pornography harmed them, the extent to which the same content was thought to harm others, their support for restriction on Internet pornography, and attitudes toward sex. The results found that, in general, respondents indeed thought pornography was more harmful to others than themselves, and moreover thought Internet pornography was especially threatening. However, the data also found that the more pornography people in the sample consumed, the less likely they were to hold these beliefs. In other words, the more people used it, the less worried they were about the harm pornography might do.

The question here is not about what the data says; rather, it is about what the data means. Lo, Wei, and Wu took it as an index of insensitivity, but also a measure of normalization; the tendency to accept pornography as a perfectly legitimate part of the media world. The issue with this study, then, was not so much with how the data was gathered, as how it was analyzed. Both McKee's and Lo, Wei, and Wu's studies agreed that pornography matters as a commercially available resource that people use to articulate ideas about what the world is like, and how they see themselves fit into that world. Audiences in both studies were untroubled by the pornography they used, and the more they used, the less damaging they thought it to be. The question of what this evidence means, in the context of an effects paradigm that is highly critical of its own assumptions and methods, remains open.

Qualitative and quantitative approaches to the social significance of pornography therefore share the following features. First, they are sensitive to validity issues that dog all forms of empirical research.[31] Second, they agree that the best way of understanding why media matter is to look at ordinary people. Spectacular instances where media content appears to have triggered excessive violence, including sexual violence, tells us little about what most of the media do most of the time. Third, once we focus on ordinary people, one of the compelling questions driving media research is, how do people use messages about sexuality, generated by commercial entertainment industries, to make sense of their place in the world, and indeed their relationship to commercial media culture? On the basis of these similarities, the concluding part of this chapter makes the case for thinking about pornography in terms of cultivation analysis.

CULTIVATION ANALYSIS

Recall that McKee defines pornography as a form of commercial entertainment characterized by the same features that structure other popular forms, such as television and film. There is a strong cultivation element to this position. At its core, the concept of cultivation takes the position that commercial media operations trade in formulaic stories. However, in cultivation analysis, the main effect of these tales is thought to be that they normalize the values of consumer society, and the more one is exposed to these stories, the more one accepts their values as common sense.

Most famously, this argument has been made in relation to violence. In the 1970s, cultivation analysis compiled a series of violence profiles. These profiles were a series of content analyses enumerating the number of violent acts featured on U.S. primetime television. The violence profiles found that the number of violent acts on television far outnumbered those in the real world. This violence mattered because it dramatized racialized patriarchy: White middle-class men were far more likely than any other characters to profit from this violence. Assessing the effects of these representations, survey research led cultivation researchers to believe that the main effects of television violence were political. Television violence made people believe that the world was a scary, mean place.[32]

For cultivation analysts, then, media violence was a vehicle for making a general and crucial intervention into the media effects debate. George Gerbner, who is widely recognized as the founder of cultivation analysis, believed the most important media effects were the political ones that spread among audiences who, for the most part, didn't do anything in response to the things that they saw. Gerbner believed that the least interesting, and least important question one could ask about television violence was whether or not it made a small number of people carry out the real thing. It was far more important to identify how exposure to this violence cultivated beliefs about social reality that translated into political attitudes. Fundamentally, the main impact of television was to sell the idea that the only thing we can do about a violent world full of untrustworthy people is buy things that make us feel better.[33]

Because cultivation theory was intended as a general model of effects in the realm of cultural politics, with a particular interest in gender, it wasn't long before these ideas were tested on pornography. Elizabeth Preston thought that cultivation offered a solution to the impasse between feminists and effects researchers.[34] Feminists who wanted to make the case that pornography contributed to general climates of sexual subordination were not helped in their work by effects research that tended to focus on the production of short-term aggression. Cultivation offered a solution to this problem. The idea that pornography is a symbolic dramatization of gender inequality that has long-term effects on how ordinary women and men think about and relate to one another was exactly the argument that the "mean world thesis" made about media violence: Content analysis found that women were far more likely to be portrayed as victims, meaning that television violence was at base a story about white male power. As such, for feminists "the shift to the cultivation model allows for the broad role pornography may play in the maintenance of social structures," where "the primary impact of pornography is the preservation and reinforcing of existing social structures built on sex-based inequalities."[35] The porn problem, for Preston, was simply a microcosm of the corporate media problem. Most stories that most audiences see say, "It's a man's world." The question to be answered, however, was this: Is it true that the more people see sexist bias in media, the more they believe it to be a reality that determines their place in the world?

Preston tested the question of whether pornography cultivated patriarchal attitudes in a sample of 218 and 274 male and female undergraduates. She administered a survey asking how much pornography respondents used. She then compared the amount of exposure to pornography with attitudes toward sex roles, sex traits, sex stereotypes, and attitudes to rape myths. For the men in the study, the more they used porn, the more likely they were to believe that men have a higher sex drive than women, that men are less able to control that sex drive than women, that women find it more difficult to be honest about their sexual desires, and that women sometimes say no to sex when they mean yes.

Although this was a negative conclusion, it was not one that depended on sequestering porn as a radically distinct media category. In many ways, it prefigured McKee in making the case that porn matters precisely because it works like any other piece of popular culture. Moreover, although Preston's data indicated that porn was bad for men who watched a lot of it, insofar as it cultivated beliefs that weren't true and wouldn't make for happy relationships, this wasn't the case for women in the study. Although, overall, the women used pornography less often than men, among the sexually active women in the sample, greater exposure to pornography correlated with "a more 'liberal' or 'open' attitude toward sexuality and gender stereotypes."[36] The lesson, then, was that although exposure to pornography did seem to underscore harmful patriarchal attitudes for men, it did not do so for women who brought a different set of experiences and attitudes to the same content. Preston noted, "The data suggest that the impact of pornography is neither monolithic nor uniform. Further research should continue to emphasize and explore gender differences."[37]

Preston's work was an early example of research that showed how a cultivation perspective can move the effects question beyond a narrow concern with behaviors toward a more political view, where pornography is seen as part of a broader, mediatized conversation about gender and respect. It also underlines a consistent theme in effects research: that the notion of media power does not imply that everyone responds to the same content in the same way.

THE APPLICATIONS—AND MISAPPLICATIONS—OF CULTIVATION ANALYSIS IN NEW STUDIES OF PORNOGRAPHY EFFECTS

The misapplications of cultivation analysis is an incredibly important point, because its intended meaning is lost in the way that a cultivation perspective is implied in other research on the damage that pornography does in society. Gail Dines's work is an example. In her book *Pornland*, Dines describes media influence in the following terms:

> By telling stories, images help to shape how we think about ourselves as gendered beings. . . what is of interest is not necessarily the overt message of one particular image but the cumulative effect of the subtextual theme found in the system of images, which together create a particular way of looking at the world.[38]

Cultivation analysts would agree with this view. They would also agree that one cannot simply defend or dismiss pornography as fantasy, akin to the erotic daydreams that run though most people's heads from time to time. Dines portrays pornography as an industrially produced story that attempts to standardize and monetize fantasy in a way that actually inhibits the imagination. From a cultivation perspective, the development of distinct pornographic genres, each with its own conventions, would make this a question worth exploring. Carrying on, cultivation analysts would applaud Dines's efforts to move the pornography debate beyond the question of whether it leads to rape. They would agree when she characterizes this as an "ultimately misleading question"[39]

Dines strays from a cultivation perspective, however, in presenting the statement that "taken together, pornographic images create a world that is at best inhospitable to women, and at worst dangerous to their physical and emotional well-being"[40] as an "argument" rather than a research question. Dines regards pornography as the media world's Twitter account. Systematic, long-term content analysis of prime-time TV revealed consistent patterns where women were portrayed as being less powerful than men. In pornography, according to Dines, this message is an explicit part of the appeal to men. Pornography deliberately demeans women for men's pleasure, and the men who use it like what they see. What they don't like is their inability to live up to porn-stud lives, because they physically can't and the women they meet don't want to do the things that they see onscreen. Unlike the Joey and Chandler characters, this doesn't puzzle actual men in an amusing way; it makes them angry.

The question of whether or not this happens in a socially significant number of cases, for some men, under some situations, is certainly worth asking. And Dines's description of the way that some men seem to react to some pornography underlines this. However, there are several reasons why this is not the only direction that a cultivation perspective suggests.

The first point to make is that Dines researches a very different media environment, using different methods, from those deployed in the violence profile studies. Those profiles set out to study *if* media violence was prevalent, *if* it had a negative impact on the people who saw it, and *how* this violence could be connected to the structure of media industries. This process, which took more than a decade of empirical work, made claims about what television did through a method that could reliably claim to know what most television was like, in terms of its denotative features. Its sampling strategies could reliably assume that survey respondents watched the shows that were analyzed by the content analyses. Fundamentally, cultivation analysis regarded media violence as a cultural indicator of the production processes that typified prime-time American television, and could safely assume that this content mattered because in the broadcast era, everyone was exposed to it.

It is impossible to approach the world of contemporary pornography with the same confidence. Ana Bridges, Robert Wosnitzer, Erica Scharrer, Chyng

Sun, and Rachael Liberman's analysis of aggression and harm depicted in best-selling pornographic videos illustrates the difficulties at hand.[41] Although their painstaking research does provide evidence of the prevalence of practices that are potentially injurious to women, such as slapping, gagging, and ass-to-mouth (ATM) ejaculation, the ramifications of these findings are provided with several caveats. Some are inspired by the lessons of early cultivation.

One of the criticisms directed at cultivation analysis noted the difficulty in coding screen violence because definitions inevitably involve a series of interpretative judgments. Moreover, these same judgments come into play when audiences decoded what they saw, meaning that a phenomenon like media violence can never be measured with the same precision as, say, the number of words in a series of news stories.

This criticism does not invalidate content analysis as a powerful method of describing the denotative features of the media environment. Gerbner accepted the significance of interpretation in his first model of cultivation,[42] and Bridges et al. point out that measures of aggression in pornography vary significantly according to definitions of what counts as aggression. While they maintain that their research establishes an important baseline that justifies the study of pornography as a medium that propagates gender inequality, their conclusion comes with several qualifications. Principally, any study of what pornography does must be accompanied by research on what it means to its audience. In illustration, they accept that while their model codes ejaculation in a woman's face as demeaning, it is important to ask if audiences see it as such.

It took more than a decade of empirical and survey research for Gerbner and his colleagues to develop the connection between screen violence, audience opinion, and gender inequality. According to Bridges et al., research on pornography is a long way from that point—although there are good reasons for pursuing the question. The other complicating factor in all of this is the mode of reception. The rise of online tube sites offering free clips and attracting billions of hits raises very real questions about the validity of analyzing porn content on a title-by-title basis—the approach used in this baseline study.

None of this is to say that how pornography might harm its users through the cultivation of unhealthy attitudes toward other people is not worth pursuing, or that content analysis is a futile exercise. The observation that meaning depends on interpretation does not imply that the meaning of sexually explicit materials is up to the audience. It is incredibly important to know about patterns of common scenarios, people, and acts, and the patterns of common responses (if they exist) in relation to such content. However, when applying cultivation to the assessment of the risks entailed in contemporary porn culture, it is important to note that Preston's work suggested looking for different patterns of response from audiences who had a different relationship to what they saw.

This observation has become even more important with the diversification of viewing habits. The classic cultivation studies of television violence famously maintained that there was no reason to distinguish between how the phenomenon worked between shows and genres, because in the broadcast age, most audiences watched by the clock, not by the show. With today's technology such as cable systems and DVR, it makes sense to look at the cultivating power of particular genres, shows, and media events because it is possible to immerse oneself in a particular sort of content.

In light of this, contemporary cultivation analysis would look for general effects of pornography consumption, but would also look at the *differences* between genres, and the people who consumed them. Additionally, Gerbner was committed to affecting change within commercial media cultures. He maintained close connections with industry insiders and hoped that his research would help correct unbalanced working practices. For example, he felt that his evidence about how most women tended to be portrayed on TV would provide impetus to those seeking a wider range of roles for female actors.[43]

The idea can be applied to pornography, given, for example, the rise of feminist, ethically produced porn. Just as some pornography producers and consumers enjoy humiliating women, others value the genre's capacity to promote gender equality in ethical ways. The cultivation questions here are: Does content analysis support these claims? If so, do the people who watch feminist porn tend to espouse more egalitarian views? And if not, does content analysis of the sort presented by Bridges et al. constitute a resource that can affect change within the industry and its fans? It is easy to be confused over what cultivation analysis might reveal about pornography, because the model has not responded to Preston's challenge for more work on the genre. This may be because the paradigm has largely focused on television. However, recent work on the third-person effect as a form of cultivation does indicate what contemporary practice can contribute to understanding the relationship between pornography and its users. This in particular relates to research on what motivates people to make third-person judgments—the centerpiece of Lo et al.'s project—and how the main effect of exposure to commercial media culture appears to be acceptance of that culture's right to tell us how things are. When it comes to pornography, this is represented by the observation that different studies have found that one of the main effects of consuming porn is that it is associated with acceptance of the genre. The question is, what does this acceptance mean, vis-à-vis the politics of porn research?

CULTIVATION ANALYSIS AND THE THIRD-PERSON EFFECT

Donald Diefenbach and Mark West argue that the third-person effect is a form of cultivation.[44] In other words, exposure to media convinces audiences that they are surrounded by others who are heavily influenced by what they see onscreen. The authors earlier carried out a classic third-person/cultivation study on the effects of television depictions of mental illness. Content analysis of primetime network portrayals of mental illness showed that these representations were consistently inaccurate and negative. In surveys, heavier TV viewers were more likely to think that other viewers would be more affected by these negative portrayals than they were, yet at the same time were also more likely to pronounce discriminatory views on people with mental illness. For instance, these viewers were more likely to oppose programs aimed at helping the mentally ill live in the general community. Diefenbach and West's survey showed that heavy television viewers were right about the effects of television dramas about mental illness on other people, but not on themselves. Hence, the researchers concluded that television cultivates beliefs about reality, anxieties about the power of the media, and the tendency to displace those anxieties onto others.

However, another study carried out by the same researchers produced different results. Asking a sample of 550 people how much television they watched, and how much of an influence they thought television had on perceptions about the important things in life, Diefenbach and West found that although the sample as a whole believed TV had more of an effect on others, this was not true for heavy viewers. That is, when the sample was divided into three groups—light, medium, and heavy viewers—Diefenbach and West found that the third-person effect worked in reverse: Light viewers thought television affected others more than themselves, but heavy viewers did not.

Considering what this might mean for the concept of cultivation in general, Diefenbach and West speculated that these results might indicate that Gerbner's initial hypotheses about the fundamental nature of media effects had been correct: People who watched a lot of television were most likely to consent to the power of corporate storytelling. Light and heavy viewers alike agree that media have powerful effects on what we believe to be true about our world, but the more TV people watch, the less troubled they are about this state of affairs.

Diefenbach and West's work is relevant here as a tool to situate the effects of pornography within the general influence of media culture. In essence, it is the point at which otherwise antagonistic views about what porn does to its users coalesce. McKee argues that porn should not be singled out from other aspects of corporate media, and that it's important to note that people who use it are not troubled by it. Lo et al. agree that the more people use porn, the less anxious they are about the influence of porn on either themselves or others, although they see this as evidence of desensitization. Yet, in either case, we are not simply discussing orientations toward pornography, but to the costs and benefits of commercialized public cultures in general. To research pornography, then, is to research how we feel about living in a world where we, and those around us, are heavily reliant on corporate storytelling, when we exercise our social imaginations.

Seen this way, research into the effects of pornography is a question of trust. Specifically, how much trust do we invest in commercial media, and is that trust well placed? This chapter argues that controversies over the positive and negative influence of pornography are not really about methods. Qualitative and quantitative researchers agree on the difficulties of studying media effects, just as they concur on the variability of its influence, good or bad. The common flaw in McKee's and Lo et al.'s work is that neither expends much energy into searching for alternative explanations for the patterns of response they observe. McKee quickly interprets comfort with pornography as a sign of maturity, whereas Lo et al. see it as a sign of desensitization. Neither is especially interested in exploring the interplay between general tendencies and different responses to the same content among different populations, driven by the possibility that porn, or anything else for that matter, might be good for some audiences and bad for others, depending on different matrices of factors. The problem here has nothing to do with method; it is about curiosity and a commitment to developing the conceptualization of pornography as a communication problem. In particular, this involves looking for diverging effects and the differences between audience subgroups, as they are arranged around different consumption practices and industrial organization. For example, effects researchers concede that insufficient attention has been paid to the positive outcomes of media consumption. In cultivation analysis, this observation is recognized in changing research practices, looking at how niche media and changing audience practices cultivate different reality judgments and political attitudes. Pornography was one of the first topics that indicated this shift in the model, and now is an opportune moment to reflect on what cultivation theory contributes to understanding porn's significance.

Cultivation analysis is useful in this regard as a paradigm that is interested in how any general tendencies in media cultures can be conceived and analyzed through attending to similarities and differences in responses to the same media content. Although cultivation analysis is grounded in the assumption that the main effect of media exposure is to reconcile audiences to the logic of commercial media, it has found many different types of effects within this umbrella assumption. When it comes to topics such as violence, where early research found that a heavy diet of television violence made viewers afraid of the world, more recent international studies have found that in some parts of the world, it actually makes people feel safer (because stories about violence often feature offenders being brought to justice).[45] On pornography, over twenty years ago Preston was one of the first effects researchers who began to write about the potentially positive side of consuming porn, when she noted very different responses among women and men in her studies.

But let's return to the idea that the main media effect is to promote commercial storytelling, governed by markets rather than creativity or public service, as a common-sense way of running public culture. Why might this insight be of use to researchers like McKee, who are keen to position pornography as a form of entertainment that promotes healthy relationships between people?

All of the positions described in this chapter agree that people use media narratives to paint pictures of reality. Increasingly, these pictures are also affected by how people feel about the industries that produce them. The more pornography people consume, the more they appear comfortable with it. This may be good or bad, but it may also be an index of a more general media effect, where people become increasingly comfortable with the stories that commercial culture tells us.

This is significant because, according to the people in McKee's research, pornography is an uncomfortable genre for the people who like it. Amidst the difficulties of defining what porn is, the most intriguing aspect of his research is the finding that people think good porn has to feature people having fun. The idea that performances are coerced destroys the pleasure. What this means is that good porn isn't just defined by what is onscreen, but by the stories its consumers tell themselves about how those images got there.[46]

Recently, general media audiences have been exposed to a number of stories linking the porn industry with the abuse of some of its most famed stars. For example, seasons of *Celebrity Rehab* have featured Mary Carey, Penny Flame, and Amy Fisher, all of whom claim to have been pushed into the porn industry, and claim to have been hurt by it. The confounding possibility here, of course, is that these shows, too, are performances: Carey's return to adult movies in *Celebrity Pornhab with Dr. Screw* creates confusion about which version to believe. Nevertheless, a series of questions follow. What is the reality of porn production? What are the differences between genres? Is there evidence that greater exposure to one or all of these genres tend to produce particular views of reality, in terms not only of people, but also the porn industry?

But what's at stake here is a more important question that can be directed at media culture in general. When people use media, how do they engage with issues of ethics and value? How do people use porn, and media, to reflect on how people should be treated in the world? How do people use media to think about other people, and their relationships and obligations to those people? These are the questions that are at the root of the effects tradition, and seeing that tradition through the concept of cultivation helps to clarify how that tradition connects with the concept of culture.

These questions promise to overcome, or at least address, some of the differences between researchers who view pornography as either a malicious or a benevolent force. In particular, cultivation methodology offers a compromise between the view that what matters most are general responses to general patterns of representation, versus the conviction that the interpretation of particular texts for specific reasons tells us most about what pornography does as a social entity. Studies might, for instance, do content analyses of ethically produced feminist porn, compare it with the fare of other production companies who are accused of producing degrading content, and then examine, through surveys, whether people who consume heavy quantities of the former hold systematically different views on gender equality than do others who do not view feminist and ethically produced porn. This is but one among a series of possibilities, but it leads to a few take-home lessons. An effects position does not imply that pornography is bad. Employing cultivation research could offer an empirical baseline, in terms of content patterns and user dispositions, to inform the debate on the risks and benefits of living in societies where commercial pornography furnishes powerful stories about sexuality.

NOTES

1. George Gerbner, "Cultivation Analysis: An Overview," *Mass Communication and Society* 1, no. 3–4 (1998): 175–95; Michael Morgan, James Shanahan, and Nancy Signorielli, eds. *Living with Television Now: Advances in Cultivation Theory and Research* (New York: Peter Lang, 2012); Andy Ruddock, "Cultivation Analysis" in *Handbook of Media Audiences*, ed. Virginia Nightingale (Oxford: Wiley-Blackwell, 2011), 340–59.

2. Christina Rogala and Tanja Tydén, "Does Pornography Influence Young Women's Sexual Behavior?" *Women's Health Issues* 13, no. 1 (2003): 39–43.

3. Alan McKee, "Censorship of Sexually Explicit Materials in Australia: What Do Consumers of Pornography Have to Say About It?" *Media International Australia* 120 (2006): 35–50; Alan McKee, "Pornography as Entertainment," *Continuum: Journal of Media & Cultural Studies* 26, no. 4 (2012): 541–52.

4. Sut Jhally, *Mean World Syndrome: The Media Violence & the Cultivation of Fear* (Northampton, MA: Media Education Foundation, 2010).

5. Gert Hald and Neil Malamuth, "Self-Perceived Effects of Pornography Consumption," *Archives of Sexual Behavior* 37 (2008): 614–25.

6. Neil Malamuth, Tamara Addison, and Mary Koss, "Pornography and Sexual Aggression: Are There Reliable Effects and Can We Understand Them?" *Annual Review of Sex Research* 11 (2000): 26–91.

7. Ven-Hwei Lo, Ran Wei, and Hsiaomei Wu, "Examining the First, Second and Third-Person Effects of Internet Pornography on Taiwanese Adolescents: Implications for the Restriction of Pornography," *Asian Journal of Communication* 20, no. 1 (2010): 90–103.

8. Ibid., 101.

9. Ibid., 101.

10. Ibid., 101.

11. Jack Glascock, "Degrading Content and Character Sex: Accounting for Men and Women's Differential Reactions to Pornography," *Communication Reports* 18, no. 1 (2005): 43–53.

12. Rogala and Tydén, "Does Pornography Influence Young Women's Sexual Behavior?"

13. Ven-Hwei Lo, Ran Wei, and Ran Wei, "Exposure to Internet Pornography and Taiwanese Adolescents' Sexual Attitudes and Behavior," *Journal of Broadcasting and Electronic Media* 49, no. 2 (2005): 221–37.

14. Lo, Wei, and Wu, "Examining the First, Second and Third-Person Effects of Internet Pornography on Taiwanese Adolescents."

15. David Gauntlett, *Media Studies 2.0, and Other Battles Around the Future of Audience Research* (Ebook 2011), http://www.theory.org.uk/david/kindle.htm.

16. McKee, "Censorship of Sexually Explicit Materials in Australia": 35–50.

17. McKee, "Censorship of Sexually Explicit Materials in Australia."

18. McKee, "Pornography as Entertainment": 541–52.

19. Ibid., 549.

20. Hald, Gert, and Malamuth, "Self-Perceived Effects of Pornography Consumption."

21. Neil Malamuth, Tamara Addison, and Mary Koss. "Pornography and Sexual Aggression: Are There Reliable Effects and Can We Understand Them?"

22. George Comstock, "A Sociological Perspective on Television Violence and Aggression," *American Behavioral Scientist* 51 (2008): 1184–211.

23. Mike Allen and Tara Emmers. "Exposure to Pornography and Acceptance of Rape Myths," *Journal of Communication* 45, no. 1 (1995).

24. Barry Gunter, "Media Violence: Is There a Case for Causality?" *American Behavioral Scientist* 51, no. 8 (2008): 1061–122.

25. Ibid., 1111.

26. Ibid., 1104.

27. Richard Harris and Christopher Bartlett. "Effects of Sex in the Media." In *Media Effects: Advances in Theory and Research*, ed. Jennings Bryant and Mary Beth Oliver (New York: Routledge, 2009), 304–24.

28. W. Phillips Davison, "The Third Person Effect in Communication," *Public Opinion Quarterly* 47 (1983): 1–15.

29. Bryant Paul, Michael Salwen, and Michel Dupagne, "The Third Person Effect: A Meta-Analysis of the Perceptual Hypothesis," *Mass Communication and Society* 3 (2000): 57–85.

30. Albert Gunther and Douglas Storey, "The Influence of Presumed Influence," *Journal of Communication* 53 (2003): 199–215.

31. Barry Gunter points out that researchers who study violence and pornography using experimental methods are constrained by ethical requirements to use proxies for real-world aggression in their studies. For example, Jack Glascock's study on the effects of "degrading" pornography measures sexual arousal with a survey. College men were found to be more likely to report feeling aroused after being exposed to pornography where women appear to be degraded than were women. Such measures are necessary because of ethical concerns about research assessing links between degradation and arousal. Inevitably, this raises questions about whether what one finds, through these techniques, is real arousal, which suggests a compelling connection between pornography and aggression, or something else—the tendency, for example, to want to please the researcher (by giving them the results they want, knowing that this sort of work often looks for negative effects), or to play certain gender roles. So, it isn't clear whether what this study finds is aggressive sexuality, or a response to perceptions of what media research is like, or what women and men are supposed to think, according to cultural norms.

32. George Gerbner, Larry Gross, Michael Morgan, and Nancy Signorelli, "The Mainstreaming of America: Violence Profile #11," *Journal of Communication* 30 (1980): 10–29; George Gerbner, Larry Gross, Michael Morgan, and Nancy Signorelli, "Charting the Mainstream: Television's Contributions to Political Orientations," *Journal of Communication* 32 (1982): 100–27.

33. George Gerbner, "On Content Analysis and Critical Research in Mass Communication," *AV Communication Review* 6, no. 2 (1958): 85–108.

34. Elizabeth Preston, "Pornography and the Construction of Gender" in *Cultivation Analysis: New Directions in Theory and Research*, ed. Michael Morgan and Nancy Signorelli (Newbury Park, CA: Sage, 1990), 107–22.

35. Ibid., 109.

36. Ibid., 121.

37. Ibid., 121.

38. Gail Dines, *Pornland: How Porn Has Hijacked Our Sexuality* (Boston: Beacon Press, 2010), 81–2.

39. Ibid., 82

40. Ibid., 85.

41. Ana J. Bridges, Robert Wosnitzer, Erica Scharrer, Chyng Sun, and Rachael Liberman, "Aggression and Sexual Behavior in Best-Selling Pornography Videos: A Content Analysis Update," *Violence Against Women* 16 (2010): 1065–85.

42. Andy Ruddock, "Critical Crunching: Communication, Power and Cultivation Analysis," *CommOddities* 2, no. 1 (1995): 22–27.

43. Michael Morgan, *George Gerbner: A Critical Introduction to Media and Communication Theory* (New York: Peter Lang, 2012).

44. Donald Diefenbach and Mark West, "Cultivation and the Third Person Effect" in *Living with Television Now: Advances in Cultivation Theory and Research*, ed. Michael Morgan, James Shanahan, and Nancy Signorelli (New York: Peter Lang, 2012), 347–65.

45. Markus Appel, "Fictional Narratives Cultivate Just-World Beliefs," *Journal of Communication* 58, no. 1 (2008): 62–83.

46. Andy Ruddock, *Investigating Audiences* (London: Sage, 2007).

16

"She's Totally Faking It!": The Politics of Authentic Female Pleasure in Pornography

Emily E. Crutcher

When I became interested in studying pornography as a young sociologist, I looked to see what scholarship my discipline had produced on the subject. I had read Andrea Dworkin and Catharine MacKinnon as a budding feminist, but I was eager to discover the new innovative work that feminist sociologists were producing. After I began surveying the scholarship that had been published over the last few decades, I became dismayed by the unimaginative and unreliable methods used to discover how people react to watching porn. I read the quantitative psychology research on the "effects" of pornography consumption on the male individual and society that dominated research on pornography in the 1980s[1] and found that this tradition—and its limitations—continues today in quantitative social psychology work.[2]

When I delved into the current body of sociological literature on porn, I found foregone conclusions fueled by political vitriol masquerading as research. Sociologist Ronald Weitzer provides a comprehensive critique of current research in this model, examining the methodologies and claims of two texts: a collection of critical essays titled *Everyday Pornography* edited by Karen Boyle, and *Pornland: How Porn Has Hijacked Our Sexuality* by prolific antiporn sociologist Gail Dines. Weitzer points out several flaws with the evidence presented in these texts:

> Solid original data are scarce, and anecdotes are abundant. Little secondary data are discussed as well. There is an underlying assumption that viewing porn affects both attitude and behavior, but no convincing supporting evidence is offered . . . many claims are made *about* porn performers and consumers, but these claims are superimposed on them by the writers. Consumers are rarely quoted, but when they are it is almost always negatively, and the voices of porn performers are entirely missing in the book.[3]

Antiporn feminist scholarship has also erased female consumers of porn categorically, and ignored occasional female viewers despite evidence that women do watch porn.[4] If this argument assumes that watching pornography trains men to devalue sex and women, what does it do to female viewers? Does watching porn corrupt female sexuality in some specific way, making women hate sex or men or themselves? How do women actually react in the moment when they watch pornography? I decided to do my own research to investigate.

I held two focus groups, showing participants two different types of porn scenes (one mainstream gonzo and the other from a film by a self-identified feminist pornographer) and recording the conversations that occurred during and after. I will not argue that the particular scenes I chose to show my participants are "representative" of a genre or pornography in general in some meaningful way. Nor am I making conclusions about these particular participants, or using them as representatives of their race, class, and gender to make broad generalizations. What I find most noteworthy and useful to examine as a porn scholar is their process of evaluation. In other words, what epistemic tools or knowledge of the world do these viewers bring to bear to assess what they are seeing? What kinds of past experiences (personal or anecdotal) do they find relevant to judge what they are viewing?

Unprompted by leading questions, my participants' discussions centered on measures of authenticity: the connection between pleasurable sex acts (supposedly) causing moaning, the time it takes for a female to experience what appears to be genuine moan-worthy pleasure, the verbal participation of female performers saying what they want, and the aspects of performativity that porn actors may display. These signifiers of authenticity are meaningful ways for women to process different types of pornography and show that despite the prevalence of research that denies viewers any kind of agency or reflexivity, viewers are quite capable of bringing their own beliefs and experiences to bear when evaluating different types of pornography.

FEMINIST PORNOGRAPHY AND GENUINE FEMALE PLEASURE

Although I am most concerned with participants' evaluation of pornography, it is helpful to contextualize their assessments by examining what pornographers themselves believe they are accomplishing with their work. While decades of literature have focused on "mainstream" heterosexual porn made by large production companies, an abundance of new pornography remains unaddressed. Although "feminist porn" may sound like a contradiction to some, many directors working today produce media in ways that align with feminist ideology. This means different things to different directors, but the common element that most feminist porn directors seem to agree on is the importance of showing genuine female pleasure. Indeed, to be eligible for a Feminist Porn Award, films must meet certain criteria including "the depiction of genuine female pleasure."[5]

Madison Young is one director (and performer) who echoes this commitment to showing authentic female pleasure in her work. When asked about mainstream porn (which she calls "fast food pornography") she says, "[Mainstream porn] has no emphasis on female orgasm; it's not even really focused on male orgasm or male pleasure."[6] Young locates her work as feminist by reference to her focus on the genuine pleasure of performers, especially female performers.

Feminist porn director Tristan Taormino locates her feminist intervention at the point of production itself, that is, at the site of ethical practices for making sexual media. At the same time, she has mentioned that she cannot truly influence the ways her work will be interpreted by viewers. In an interview with Danny Wylde in February 2011, she says,

> I don't know that it's possible to create a feminist image. What does that look like? Because you're going to create an image and then twenty million people—well, in my case, not twenty million people, but you know, say twenty people watch it. Everyone's going to see it differently. Everyone's going to take something different from it. Everyone's going to interpret it differently. So I don't know that there's a way to say, "This is feminist porn because that's a feminist sex image." For me, feminist porn is about how you create the product. That's really my emphasis.[7]

Despite her admission that she cannot control the way viewers interpret the images she produces, I was curious to see if Taormino's interpretation of her work as a feminist endeavor would be evident to participants without any background information about the labor conditions of the performers or the director's intent. Is a feminist approach to the production of pornography recognizable to viewers? Does authentic female pleasure matter to audiences? These are empirical questions worthy of academic attention. As it turned out, the element that my participants were most interested in was how "real" the pleasure was, especially that of the female performers.

The task of representing authentic female pleasure through pornography is fraught with complications. In her discussion of documenting female pleasure through pornography, Celine Parreñas Shimizu notes, "Pornography problematizes the difficulty of representing proof of women's pleasure, as exemplified in the search for clitoral visibility in films such as *Deep Throat*."[8] Shimizu goes on to discuss the faces of Asian female performers as the visible signifier of their pleasure. When discussing Annabel Chong as an unreliable subject, Shimizu says, "the expressive contortions of her face and body demonstrate the unreliability of representation in terms of making distinct the appearance of pain or pleasure."[9] Chong's facial expressions during *The World's Biggest Gangbang* could easily be interpreted as grimaces of pain, but are ambiguous enough to be readable as expressions of intense pleasure. However, Shimizu does not discuss audible expressions of pleasure as potential evidence of authenticity.

It is important to note the fuzzy boundary between the performance of sex and pleasure for the sake of making pornography, and sexual behavior that "real" people engage in off camera. Not only do social theorists and critics of pornography seem unable to make a clear distinction, but it may be that viewers are unable (or perhaps disinclined) to make any distinction at all. In her influential text *Hardcore: Power, Pleasure and the "Frenzy of the Visible,"* Linda Williams makes an argument about the "out-of-control confession of pleasure"[10] that pornography seeks to document: the point at which a performer loses control of the performance, and cannot help but express her true experience of pleasure. While she elaborates on the hypervisibility of male pleasure throughout the book, she only touches on the audible element of pornography very briefly in her discussion of stag films, explaining the way in which the addition of sound to pornography made theatrical facial expressions and gestures less necessary. However, she does not give examples of the ways in which sound and vocalizations may enhance the authenticity of a scene. In "Aural Sex: The Female Orgasm in Popular Sound," Corbett and Kapsalis explain, "Where male sexual pleasure is accompanied by what Williams calls the 'frenzy of the visible,' female sexual pleasure is better thought of in terms of a 'frenzy of the audible.' Sound becomes the proof of female pleasure in the absence of its clear visual demonstration."[11] If the authenticity of vocalizations signifying pleasure is at stake, how can viewers tell whether moans are "fake" (that is, performed) or "real" (that is, representations of the true bodily sensation of pleasure)?

METHODOLOGY

Antiporn feminists warn about the harmful effects of watching porn on male and female sexuality. Feminist pornographers claim that they are documenting genuine female pleasure and contributing something positive to sexual culture. How can we interrogate these disparate claims through empirical research? How do viewers actually assess the authenticity of female pleasure and orgasm in porn? Would participants recognize the effort in feminist porn to document female pleasure, and if so, how would they identify this authenticity?

This project contributes to sociological literature about women's consumption of pornography, using focus group methodology to provide empirical accounts of how women interact with different types of hardcore pornography. I explore the connection between aspects of production, particularly feminist pornographers' attempt to depict genuine female pleasure, with the experience of consumption, highlighting participants' concerns about the authenticity of female performers' vocalizations. I consider the types of knowledge women deploy to evaluate the authenticity of sexual performances, contributing to our relatively limited understanding of what matters to women as they view video pornography. This research is relevant not only for scholars of pornography consumption, but also for sociologists interested more generally in the social contexts of media consumption, gendered distributions and deployment of knowledge, and formulation of beliefs about sexuality.

Because I am interested in how people talk about and assess different types of pornography, I selected focus group methodology to explore these questions. I call my method "unfocused" groups, because I did not use a list of questions or topics to guide discussion as focus group facilitators usually do. Conducting unscripted focus groups creates an atmosphere where natural, unscripted interaction would occur between participants,[12] allowing them to shape the flow of interaction and the topics discussed. Participants were asked to watch and discuss two clips of porn that I selected. I made video and audio recordings of these discussions, including the comments made during viewings, to ensure the accuracy of participants' quotations.

My study includes a total of nine participants, including myself. Two were male and seven female, and all were between the ages of twenty-four and thirty-five. Five self-identified as white, two Latina, one African-American, one Middle Eastern. One was married at the time, and four others were in committed relationships. Six identified as heterosexual, and three as bisexual or sexually fluid. All were college educated and currently attending graduate school. None to my knowledge identified as particularly religious, though some reported occasionally attending church. I originally planned to have both groups be mixed-gender, but one of my female participants stipulated that she wished to participate in an all-female group, so my first group was mixed gender and my second group was all-female to accommodate this choice.

All of my participants identify as cisgender, and I would not want to conjecture about the experiences of trans people without their participation. In addition, because of my access to more participants who identify as straight, I chose to focus on straight porn and the experience of female pleasure in a

heterosexual context for now. While this study does not capture queer wom-
en's experiences, I hope that future research will explicitly focus on gender
and sexual subjectivities that I am not able to address here.

Further, the sample size that I draw upon for this work is limited: I held
only two focus groups including a total of nine participants. As previously
mentioned, this work is not intended to make generalizations about particular identities or communities, but to show the possibilities of a new kind of
methodological approach. Rather than show pornography to individual participants in a laboratory setting,[13] or present a streamlined lecture to a massive audience[14] and measure the presumed effects of such exposure, I showed
small groups of people two scenes of pornography in a naturalistic setting,
which produced an incredibly rich data set, one that I cannot fully analyze
here. Despite these limitations, this study points to the possibilities for future
research on porn consumption. Holding these small group discussions facilitated space for participants to share their immediate reactions to the media
and to engage in dialogue with each other on the topic, which was a valuable experience for me as a researcher and for the participants (something
I will discuss later in more detail). It also revealed the various interpretive
frameworks participants drew upon when viewing and assessing pornography,
which is my primary focus in this research.

Because this project was prompted by my own interest in feminist porn as
a medium for female sexual expression, I began by selecting a scene from that
genre. I picked a boy/girl scene from Taormino's *Chemistry 3* (released in 2007
by Vivid) between Derrick Pierce and Roxy DeVille. (I refer to this as "Scene
B.") This scene showcases Taormino's production style, which includes conducting interviews with each of the performers before and after the scene
about their desires, their feelings about their co-stars, and their sexual preferences. These interviews provide important context about the sex scene itself,
as well as representing the performers as three-dimensional people with their
own sexual subjectivities.

I found the other scene by browsing local porn stores for the most stereotypical mainstream scene I could find, and chose a boy/girl scene from *Big
Fucking Titties 6* released by Acid Rain in 2009, starring female performer
Krystal Summers. (I refer to this as "Scene A.") There was a short prescene
interview in which the director asked Krystal her name, where she was from,
and how long she had been performing in porn. The director then asked her
to stand up, turn around, and take her clothing off. Her own sexual preferences and desires were not discussed. This scene showed no relational
context, very little foreplay, and the performers barely talked to each other.
Krystal embodied the stereotypical porn aesthetic for female performers in
heterosexual porn: large surgically augmented breasts, bleached blonde hair,

artificially tanned white skin, long acrylic nails, and lots of makeup. Her non-descript white male costar was not introduced or named during the scene or on the DVD's information.

ASSESSING AUTHENTICITY

I did not select my research participants on the basis of their prior experiences and attitudes about porn. Some of my participants indicated that they watched porn regularly, while some said they had seen porn only once or twice before. Because there was no feasible way for me to track an individual's actual life experience with porn, I proceeded with the assumption that each person would bring a particular set of experiences and attitudes into the viewing experience. Instead of conveniently assuming my participants are blank slates, ready to have their opinions and tastes molded by the porn I would show them, I acknowledge that these are people laden with beliefs, experiences, values, biases, and preferences that will affect their interpretation of the media shown in complicated ways that I may not be able to anticipate or fully uncover through this research.

Therefore, instead of pulling quotes that supposedly reflect participants' attitudes out of context to support my argument, I focus on the kind of evidence they use to express their opinions and make their own claims about what they are seeing. While viewing these two clips, our conversations were riddled with assessments: One person would make a positive or negative comment about some particular aspect of the clip, and others would respond with agreement, disagreement, or requests for clarification. When formulating an assessment, people can draw from various domains of past knowledge about the topic, or personal experience. In this interaction where all participants are collectively engaged in the activity of watching the same porn together, they draw upon different kinds of signifiers (visual and aural cues) in order to assess the authenticity of the vocalizations they are hearing. I focus on four examples: a negative assessment of Scene A and a positive assessment of Scene B based upon anatomical knowledge of what kinds of sex acts produce female pleasure, and a negative assessment of Scene A and a positive assessment of Scene B based upon knowledge of the normative timeline of arousal.

Sex Acts as Pleasurable or Nonpleasurable

One belief the participants demonstrate is the cause-and-effect connection between the bodily sensation of pleasure and the vocal expression of that pleasure. Using this logic, pleasure sounds are genuine or authentic only if they are a reflection of physical sexual stimulation. After watching Scene A for about three minutes, Kaitlin (one of my female participants) makes a negative assessment of the female performer's sounds based on her knowledge of anatomy and sexual response. In the video, the male performer had just started rubbing his penis between Krystal Summers's breasts, and she moans loudly. As soon as this starts happening in the video, Kaitlin remarks upon this activity: "Like right there?" and asserts, "Unless you're particularly sensitive, there are no nerve endings on the inside of your cleavage to make you moan that way." Here, Kaitlin draws upon her understanding of sexual anatomy as the basis upon which to assess (and in this case disparage) the female performer's vocalizations. This statement is made without equivocation and claims knowledge about the location of nerve endings necessary for physical arousal. Kaitlin links this anatomical knowledge with a complaint about the moaning of the female performer as inauthentic by stating that that kind of stimulation could not cause someone to "moan that way." Matthew, one of my male participants, smiles and gives a joking explanation for the moaning of the female performer: "It's like uh, silicone nerve endings," which identifies the female performer's breasts as surgically augmented and provides the nonserious explanation that she might have had nerve endings implanted in her cleavage in addition to silicone. Carissa, a female participant, repeats Matthew's explanation and laughs. Kaitlin contributes to this joke by making explicit the nonserious claim that breast augmentation could result in "extra sensation added." I bring the sequence back to a literal treatment of this claim, asserting "Yeah that's not how it works" ("it" referring to the idea of breast augmentation surgery adding silicone nerve endings that would add sensation to the area), and appending this statement with the evaluation, "unfortunately." This attention to the sex acts performed in this scene draws upon my participants' personal beliefs about which sex acts can cause genuine bodily pleasure for females. In making a joke about the augmented anatomy of the female performer, participants show their disbelief in the authenticity of her loud moans as a reflection of her bodily experience. Kaitlin believes that nerve endings must be stimulated to "make" a woman "moan that way," and that any other reason for moaning (for example, arousing her male partner or performing pleasure for the audience) is inauthentic and therefore laughable.

In contrast, when watching the scene from *Chemistry*, my participants interpreted Roxy DeVille's vocalizations as more authentic. While watching this scene with my second focus group, the male performer, Derrick, had been performing cunnilingus on Roxy for about 30 seconds when Corinna commented on the infrequency of this particular sex act in porn: "Now you don't see him—the guy—eating her out very often." Shayla agrees, saying, "That's true—I feel like that is trying to show that they can pleasure both." Corinna then demonstrates her belief that the authenticity of Roxy's moaning aligns with this pleasurable activity, saying, "Listen to her, she is liking that!"

Women receiving oral sex can be difficult to film because the vulva of the receptive partner is at least partially obscured by the head of the person performing cunnilingus, reducing the visibility of the hardcore action central to pornographic imagery.[15] However, my female participants did not comment on the lack of visibility of the female performer's genitalia, but rather their interpretation of her moans as reflecting a genuine experience of pleasure. These participants identify cunnilingus as a sexual activity that they believe has the potential for creating real physical sexual arousal and pleasure, and that Roxy's moans are thus a believable signifier to them that she is "liking" the activity.

While the men who participated in these discussions did not make as many detailed comments about specific sex acts and the pleasure they may or may not invoke, they were attentive to the credibility of the performance. For example, about six minutes into watching the first scene, Matthew commented, "Wow she's *really* annoying." Several participants nodded in acknowledgment of this assessment. Matthew elaborated, "The best porn is when you think it's real. When you think people are actually enjoying themselves. Like this? I don't think *anyone* is enjoying themselves there." What is interesting about the phrasing of this comment is his desire for a believable performance of pleasure—not necessarily other visual or audible cues that the performers are experiencing genuine physical pleasure. While the sample size of this study limits the conclusions I could reasonably draw about the ways that desire for authenticity may be gendered, this subtle difference between the frameworks used by female and male participants highlights how critical nuanced and contextualized analysis is to the research of pornography viewership.

Abridged/Normative Timeline of Arousal

Participants were attentive not only to the sexual acts performed in each scene, but to the pace and timing of the activities being performed. In the first ten minutes of Scene A, the female performer poses for the camera and then performs fellatio on the male, with little to no stimulation of her body. After this, the male performer starts having vaginal sex with the female performer, Krystal Summers. Three or four seconds into the intercourse, Krystal begins making loud, high-pitched moans and verbalizations ("yeah! yeah! yeah!"). As soon as this occurs, Corinna notes, "That's a little soon." This comment about whether something happens early or later than expected must be judged by reference to some normative time frame. That is, for Corinna to judge the female performer's moans of pleasure as happening "too soon" reflects an abridged trajectory of the expected arousal and pleasure experience. Corinna believes that the sounds being made at that point do not match up with the expected time frame it would take to experience that level of pleasure, and thus she doubts the authenticity of those sounds. In this way, Corinna is showing that she does not identify with the experience of the female performer as an authentic expression of genuine pleasure.

While watching the second scene, Corinna draws upon the same basis for assessment to comment upon the more normative timeline of arousal demonstrated by Roxy DeVille. In the scene, Roxy and Derrick are enthusiastically having vaginal sex, and Roxy is making quiet sporadic moans. Corinna comments, "I think that's actually a more natural timeline," using the term "more" to contrast this scene with the first one. In comparison, Roxy makes quieter sounds that take longer to build in volume and intensity, and Corinna finds that to be a more "natural timeline" when having vaginal sex.

Shayla notices the agency that Roxy has in this scene to communicate with the male performer about what she wants to do and how: "She's actually saying what *she* wants, that isn't always the case." Corinna agrees, again asserting the naturalness of Roxy's vocalizations: "I feel like that's more natural sounds." The verbal interaction between participants may be a signifier of a more "natural" sexual encounter to these female viewers, contrasted with a scripted or externally directed sex scene where the performers do not speak up about what they want. At this point Linda agrees, saying, "Yeah I was thinking it is less . . . less of a show." By making this statement, Linda contrasts this scene with the last one, marking the relative performativity of the first scene. If performers are obviously putting on "a show" for the camera and the audience, viewers may conclude that this performance is just an act, just mimicry of pleasure.

LEARNING FROM PORNOGRAPHY

These focus group data start to uncover how viewers read, engage with, criticize, and possibly identify with sexual performances in pornography. Current sociological research that explores audience reactions to pornography does not capture any of this complexity. Rather, we often get second-hand reported statements like this one: "Young women have said to me, 'Porn is really positive because it shows me how to have an orgasm.' And when we talk some more it usually becomes clear that what they mean is that it shows them how to *look* and *sound* when they have an orgasm, not that it increases their sexual knowledge in any direct way."[16]

This quote above, from *Everyday Pornography*, comes from a discussion between antiporn activists Gail Dines, Linda Thompson, Rebecca Whisnant, and Karen Boyle. Here, Linda Thompson interprets this audience member's statement as evidence that the inauthentic sexual performances shown in porn are influencing female viewers to fake pleasure in their personal sexual encounters as well. This is used as evidence of the pernicious effect that watching pornography has on young women. However, if young women are looking to commercial pornography—media that is primarily produced to arouse and entertain rather than educate—to understand their own experiences of pleasure, the problem is not necessarily with the porn. In the absence of a system of comprehensive, evidence-based sex education in the United States designed to discuss arousal and pleasure with young women and men, and give them skills for exploring their sexuality, it is not unreasonable that they would turn to pornography for clues. What is unreasonable is to expect commercial pornography to do something it was never designed to do—compensate for a legacy of inadequate sex education. However, rather than accurately identifying and interrogating the inadequate system of sex education in this country, the inauthenticity of mainstream pornography has become the red herring that some feminist sociologists still cling to while completely ignoring the interventions of feminist pornography in the industry. Directors, producers, and performers have been creating innovative sexual media that prioritizes female sexual agency, showcases diverse sexual identities and gender expressions, combats pervasive and destructive racism and sizeism within the industry, and creates visibility for marginalized sexual subjectivities. If pornography ought to "increase sexual knowledge in a direct way" to be considered a worthwhile endeavor, as Thompson suggests, then ignoring or dismissing feminist pornography is quite a contradictory stance for antiporn activists to take.

That being said, my research participants were fairly sexually literate graduate students who had well-formed beliefs about what counts as "real" pleasure based on their personal sexual experiences and on their education in college sexuality classes, so they were armed with the language to interrogate the images they were seeing. Despite the difficulty of assessing the "truth" of female pleasure documented in various types of porn, my participants were able to draw on their knowledge and experience about normative patterns of arousal to assess and contrast the vocalizations of female performers in these two scenes. By focusing on the reasoning that people use to process the porn they are watching, we can get a more complete picture of how people actually process what they are seeing on the screen in that moment.

SOCIAL OPPORTUNITIES TO ASSESS PORNOGRAPHY

All of my participants ended up critiquing the inauthenticity of the performances in the first scene, and made several positive assessments of the second scene. Although my participants may not have been able to make claims about the authenticity of any given vocalization made by a female performer with absolute certainty, what matters here is their interpretation of Taormino's work as realistic, and their ability to identify with the sexual experiences of the female performers. After watching the scene from *Chemistry*, two of my female participants had the following exchange after I told them that they would get no direct benefit (such as payment) from participating in my research:

SHAYLA: You said no benefits? Well honey . . .

AMBER: We may have *found* a benefit! I mean that was just—I had never seen anything like that.

Each female participant in my focus group asked for a copy of the scene from *Chemistry 3* and expressed interest in viewing pornography that is similar in the future. The depiction of genuine female pleasure in pornography does not seem to be a discovery my participants expected to make, and they were pleasantly surprised by their positive reactions to it. In addition, each of my female participants expressed gratitude to me for creating a space for them to view and discuss pornography together, and commented on the lack of opportunities for women to have such open discussions about porn and sex. While I did not hold the focus group discussions with the specific intention of influencing my participants' beliefs about pornography in any direct or specific way (as I believe many antiporn activists do), it is crucial to recognize that simply facilitating conversations about a topic that can be sensitive and stigmatized can and will have an impact on research participants.

Media scholar Feona Attwood points out that much more empirical qualitative research on consumption is needed, with particular attention to social context: "It is the contexts of consumption which emerge here as the real areas of interest for the ways in which they construct individual and group negotiations, appropriations, and uses of sexually explicit material."[17] Attwood also suggests that some of the qualitative research methods that have been used to explore young people's relationship with pornography (such as focus groups) should be applied to adults' consumption of pornography.[18] Historically, the consumption of pornography has been a public affair limited to all-male spaces such as the viewing of stag films in men's clubs in the beginning of the 20th century.[19] The presumably legitimate spaces for women to view porn with other women are limited to educational settings, such as a classroom or conference. This is usually a mixed gender setting, though often there are more women than men in these classes. In addition, the primary purpose of watching pornography in these classes is to provide media for analysis, not necessarily to process and discuss personal reactions and preferences. Less socially legitimate spaces for women to view porn together includes porn award shows such as AVN or the annual Feminist Porn Awards. However, while viewers may express preferences and critiques of film, generally participants at these events self-select attendance for the purpose of celebrating pornography. All-male spaces still exist in men's clubs known as fraternities, or even in less formally organized male social spaces, but equivalent all-female social spaces for casually viewing pornography seem to be more limited. I have some anecdotal evidence about women watching porn together in dorms at women's colleges such as Bryn Mawr, Mount Holyoke, and Smith, as well as the occasional bachelorette party, but this kind of social space for women to watch and assess the sights and sounds of porn are relatively uncommon in our culture.

There are a growing number of college professors who teach courses on pornography that are comprehensive, rigorous, and treat pornography scholarship as they would any other academic subject. For example, at the University of California, Santa Barbara, Constance Penley teaches courses in the department of Film and Media Studies, in which she treats pornography as just another genre of film to be analyzed. At the same university, Mireille Miller-Young teaches courses in the Feminist Studies department with a focus on pornography as a type of sexual labor, with an emphasis on the experiences of women of color in the industry.

However, these courses currently seem to be the exception. In higher education, most spaces for women to gather to watch porn together are antiporn talks or rallies. These events are created and marketed with the express purpose of spreading awareness to the public about the perceived evils of pornography. Despite Taormino's speculation about her limited ability to create an image that will be interpreted as feminist, contemporary antiporn activists such as Gail Dines do claim that images themselves can be *anti*feminist. In her lectures, Dines uses terms including "morbid," "difficult to see," "increasingly violent, increasingly degrading" before showing still images of mostly naked women to audiences. When she does show slides, she refers to the models as "hideous" and fills her presentations with emotionally laden language about the danger and harms of pornography, stripping all context from those images.[20] Antiporn activists routinely quote workshop participants' horrified reactions to those images, but take their statements at face value without reflexively considering the social context of the workshops or the interactional context of those statements. As Ronald Weitzer points out in his review of Dines's book *Pornland*, "A particularly troubling aspect of the book is her quotations from men and women who have spoken to her during and after her lectures. Blocks of sentences are quoted verbatim, bracketed by quotation marks, without indicating how these statements were recorded."[21] Dines offers her recollections of audience members' statements as empirical evidence of the harm that watching porn does to people. This type of data simply does not meet the standard of meaningful sociological evidence, especially when collected in a forum specifically designed to convince audience members that pornography is harmful.

Dines furthermore utilizes a practice of manipulating or misquoting those who engage critically or curiously with her work. For instance, Dines routinely misattributes first-person quotes by women of color regarding the lack of perceived racism they experience as porn performers. Dines attributes these statements to interviewer Shira Tarrant rather than to the performers in question, giving the misguided impression that Tarrant ignores racism in media, and thus Dines is able to provoke righteous (though erroneously based) outrage among attendees.[22]

In addition, these workshops include no discussion of feminist pornography or how porn that has been produced with feminist considerations in mind, such as the depiction of authentic female pleasure, may be processed and assessed differently by viewers. Dines argues that because feminist porn does not yet make up a majority of spending in the adult industry, it is more reliable to generalize about what the biggest money-making producers of pornography are creating. However, continuing to center discourse around the mainstream, male-dominated industry at the expense of recognizing feminist efforts within the industry to subvert these norms only supports the inertia of capitalism she purports to combat. Feminist sociologists should acknowledge feminist pornographers' efforts to challenge some of the gender inequalities in the industry instead of rendering this innovative feminist work invisible.

I do not wish to suggest that viewing genuine female pleasure depicted in feminist pornography will have immediate consequences for the pleasure experienced by female viewers, or to model my argument after the effects literature that presumes a causal link between media content and viewers' attitudes. But because my participants articulated their experiences of pleasure from viewing this kind of pornography and commented on the positive impact this may have on their sex lives, I suggest that in certain social contexts of viewing, feminist pornography succeeds in its project to depict genuine female pleasure that resonates with some viewers, and may have a positive impact on female sexuality. Thus, rather than a blanket endorsement of all pornography or even all feminist pornography, I present these findings as evidence that we can—and must—do better as social scientists and feminist scholars to acknowledge both the limitations and the possibilities created by feminist pornography. Indeed, research on pornography deserves rigorous and transparently contextualized methodologies that can better capture the interpretive frameworks that viewers bring to their understanding of sexual pleasure, agency, and authenticity in pornography.

NOTES

1. See Dolf Zillmann and Jennings Bryant, "Pornography's Impact on Sexual Satisfaction," *Journal of Applied Social Psychology* 18 (1988): 438–53, and Neil Malamuth et al., "Pornography and Sexual Aggression: Are There Reliable Effects and Can We Understand Them?" *Annual Review of Sex Research* 11 (2000): 26–91.

2. See Jennee Evans-DeCicco and Gloria Cowan, "Attitudes Toward Pornography and the Characteristics Attributed to Pornography Actors," *Sex Roles* 44 (2001): 5/6, 351–61, and Chyng Sun et al., "A Comparison of Male and Female Directors in Popular Pornography: What Happens When Women are at the Helm?," *Psychology of Women Quarterly* 2 (2008): 312–25.

3. Ronald Weitzer, "Pornography's Effects: The Need for Solid Evidence, review of *Everyday Pornography*, edited by Karen Boyle (New York: Routledge, 2010), and *Pornland: How Porn Has Hijacked Our Sexuality* by Gail Dines (Boston: Beacon 2010). *Violence Against Women* 17, no. 5 (2011): 666–75.

4. Richard McCleary and Richard Tewksbury, "Female Patrons of Porn," *Deviant Behavior* 31, no. 2 (2010): 208–23.

5. "Good For Her" http://www.goodforher.com/fpa_2010.

6. Mail/Female.tv. *Interview: Madison Young*, http://www.mailfemale.tv/interviewmadisonyoung.html.

7. Tristan Taormino interview with Danny Wylde. *Trve West Coast Fiction*, February 10, 2011, http://trvewestcoastfiction.blogspot.com/2011/02/interview-with-tristan-taormino.html.

8. Celine Parreñas Shimizu, *The Hypersexuality of Race: Performing Asian/American Women on Screen and Scene* (Durham: Duke University Press, 2007): 19.

9. Ibid., 19.

10. Linda Williams, *Hardcore: Power, Pleasure, and the "Frenzy of the Visible"* (Berkeley: University of California Press, 1989): 50.

11. John Corbett and Terri Kapsalis, "Aural Sex: The Female Orgasm in Popular Sound," *The Drama Review* 40, no. 3 (1996): 103.

12. See Frances Montell, "Focus Group Interviews: A New Feminist Method," *NWSA Journal* 11, no. 1 (1999): 44–70.

13. See Richard Felson, "Mass Media Effects on Violent Behavior," *Annual Review of Sociology* 22 (1996): 103–28.

14. See Gail Dines, Linda Thompson, Rebecca Whisnant, and Karen Boyle, "Arresting Images: Anti-Pornography Slide Shows, Activism and the Academy" in *Everyday Pornography*, ed. Karen Boyle (New York: Routledge, 2010).

15. As discussed previously, see Williams.

16. Dines et al., 27.

17. Feona Attwood, "Reading Porn: The Paradigm Shift in Pornography Research," *Sexualities* 5, no. 1 (2002): 82.

18. Ibid., 82.

19. See Williams.

20. "Gail Dines website," http://gaildines.com/lectures-presentations.

21. Weitzer, 671.

22. This has occurred during Gail Dines's public presentation at the Stop Porn Culture Conference and Training, University of San Diego, June 16–17, 2012; see also Gail Dines, "From the Personal Is Political to the Personal is Personal: Neo-Liberalism and the Defanging of Feminism," https://www.youtube.com/watch?v=kDc Tt0emXhE&list=TLyS3r8VmLPwk.

17

Lust, Love, and Life: A Qualitative Study of Swedish Adolescents' Perceptions and Experiences with Pornography*

Lotta Löfgren-Mårtenson and Sven-Axel Månsson

Pornography has been a heated topic in Swedish society for several decades, especially concerning its relationship to gender roles and sexuality.[1] The societal context includes principles about gender equality and compulsory sex education since 1955, which emphasizes unrestricted rights to sexuality for both men and women. As a consequence, views about pornography are generally negative, though opinions do differ.[2] Nevertheless, Sweden became the second country in the world, after Denmark, to legalize pornography in 1971.[3] The content and dissemination of pornography has, however, changed considerably since that time.[4] One way to describe this transformation is that boundaries have been stretched. Pictures and images that society defined as pornography some decades ago now appear in mainstream media.[5] At the same time, it is clear that the visibility and accessibility of hardcore pornography in public space in the Nordic countries has increased dramatically over the last decade, not least due to the Internet.[6] Television programs, advertisements, and the music industry exploit and play with pornographic codes and scenarios. The pornography industry also launches and promotes its products via youth channels and Web sites. In other words, relationships have been forged between pornography and youth culture, which is somewhat of a new development. Even if it is a general aspect of popular culture, the so-called "mainstreaming" of pornography[7] has special significance for young people.[8]

EXPERIENCES OF PORNOGRAPHY

Research shows that the experiences of pornography among young Nordic people are extensive. The results from an Internet-based study carried out

---

*This chapter originally appeared in *Journal of Sex Research* 47, no. 6 (2010). Reprinted with permission from Routledge.

among Danish, Norwegian, and Fenno-Swedish youth in 2005 demonstrated that 92% of the respondents had seen pornography at least once.[9] These results are consistent with other recent findings in the Nordic countries.[10] Gender differences have been documented in several studies, suggesting that women are more critical of pornography than are men.[11] A recent study including more than 4,000 Swedish high school students showed that, compared with male students, a much larger proportion of the young women described pornography in negative terms such as "disgusting" and "sexually off-putting."[12] Other findings suggest that young men view pornography more frequently compared to young women.[13] At the same time, research has shown that there is a certain amount of ambivalence toward pornography among young women. For example, Svedin and Priebe indicated that, while the majority of the young women in their sample felt negatively about pornography, approximately one-third thought that it was interesting and sexually exciting. This pattern of ambivalence was also very clear in Berg's[14] qualitative interview study of Swedish 15-year-old young women. The female participants said that they could get turned on by pornography but, at the same time, they were very clear that this was not something that could be talked about openly if one wanted to be respected.

PUBLIC CONCERN

Svedin and Priebe[15] identified a group of high-frequency consumers of pornography among the young men in their sample (10%), who used pornography more or less daily. In addition, these men had more experiences of buying or selling sexual services compared to other men their own age. According to the researchers, these experiences were mediated by factors such as home background, personality characteristics, alcohol consumption, and current emotional and mental health. In addition, several studies have shown that young people are increasingly reporting experiences of sexual intercourse on the first date and a greater acceptance of more occasional sexual contacts.[16] This could be seen as a continuous disconnection of what Giddens,[17] among others, called the romantic love complex, where sexuality is legitimized by love. These and other research findings, such as reports that teenagers who watched pornography were more likely to engage in anal sex than those not exposed to pornography,[18] have caused widespread concern and public debate in the Nordic countries about the implications and consequences of pornography.

OBJECTIVES AND RESEARCH QUESTIONS

Young people's own voices are, however, seldom being heard in this debate. Our study attempted to remedy this by asking normative middle-class teenagers about their experiences, views, and relationships to pornography. We were interested in deeper knowledge and in-depth descriptions of young women's and men's experiences of pornography and how they talked about the subject. In which situations do they use pornography and what functions does it serve? What do young women and men think about the physical images and ideals displayed in pornography? What effects does pornography have on their views of sexuality and gender relations? What similarities and differences are there between young women's and men's discussions about these issues?

THEORETICAL FRAMEWORK

Guiding our analysis was an interactionist and social-constructionist perspective on sexualities, sexual expressions, and behaviors.[19] A basic assumption of this perspective is that it is through interaction with others that we learn how to think and act sexually in different situations. We employed Gagnon and Simon's[20] sexual script theory, which suggests that through sexual socialization we learn our scripts the same way actors learn their parts in a play. We learn why some things make us feel sexy and others do not. Put simply, the script is a manual for the when, where, how, with whom, and why of sexuality. However, the sexual scripts are never static, and they also differ from culture to culture. They can vary according to the situation, who is involved, and in relation to the previous experiences that an individual brings into a sexual situation. An interesting question is what role pornography plays in the development and content of these scripts for young men and young women.

The scripts occur on different levels: cultural scenarios, interpersonal scripts, and intrapsychic scripts.[21] The increased exposure to pornography in society is an example of a cultural scenario that necessitates an increased reflexivity and strategic positioning both on an interpersonal and an intrapsychic level. But, at the same time, it seems unclear to which norms and values a person is expected to conform. On the one hand, the overall societal attitude in Sweden to pornography is negative; it is regarded as something dirty and distasteful, especially if you are a female user.[22] On the other hand, pornography is part of daily life nowadays.[23] Thus, it is something that one has to take a position on, to have an opinion about, even among those who choose not to use, or who consciously try to avoid, pornography. However, an individual's actual decision to use or not use pornography is rarely independent of the influence of others. On the contrary, in addition to more or less explicitly articulated cultural scenarios regarding pornography use, attitudes to it include relational aspects on different levels.[24] Each individual belongs to, or moves within and between, different social worlds that consist of family life, friends, work, school, and leisure.[25]

METHOD

We chose a qualitative and phenomenological approach to elucidate our research questions that deal with the task of exploring meanings and consequences of pornography among young people. Bancroft[26] pointed out the importance of understanding the cultural meaning and significance connected to sexuality, which we believe to be of special value when it comes to pornography as a research area. The ambition of qualitative studies is to explain and illuminate the character of a phenomenon and its meaning,[27] which is relevant to explore young people's experiences and opinions of pornography. We used both focus groups and qualitative interviews to obtain in-depth information from participants. We wanted to gain access both to the more detailed individual experiences and to the same-sex groups' values and experiences related to pornography. By using both of these research methods we were able to compare, triangulate, and validate the data that we collected.[28] Nevertheless, the aim was not to make generalizations about youth in general, but to gain comprehensive knowledge about this sample of young men and women. An advantage of using both methods is that because of the focus group discussions, we were motivated to ask more detailed questions in the individual interviews; the interview data also generated questions we incorporated into the focus groups.[29]

FOCUS GROUPS

A focus group is commonly defined as "a research technique that collects data through group interaction on a topic determined by the researcher."[30] The rationale behind using focus groups in our case was to gain access to young people's discussions about pornography and to explore the norms and values in relation to pornography among the group members. According to Morgan,[31] focus groups are suitable when the aim is to gain insight into how people think and talk. In this study, we were particularly interested in possible differences and similarities between the young men's and women's conversations about pornography.[32] For this reason, we aimed for gender homogeneous groups. Finally, focus groups are also an appropriate approach when there is a need for a friendly and respectful research method and when the topic is sensitive.[33]

INDIVIDUAL INTERVIEWS

The aim of the individual interviews was to explore, understand, and identify different properties and meanings of pornography for the young men and women.[34] In the interviews, we wanted to get more detailed and unique information about how the individual female and male participants talked about their experiences. Also, we wanted to listen to how the young men and women expressed and described their experiences and opinions without being interrupted or influenced by other people in the room.[35]

SITE AND RESEARCH PARTICIPANTS

We decided to recruit both male and female participants, ranging from 14 to 20 years of age, to understand how gender and age matter in young people's talk about pornography. Because some of the participants were under 15 years of age, we also needed parental consent, according to the ethical guidelines and rules developed by the Swedish Research Council in cooperation with the Centre for Research Ethics and Bioethics at Uppsala University.[36] The study was conducted in accordance with four ethical principles related to information, consent, confidentiality, and usefulness.

The participants were recruited from four different schools in Southern Sweden. We sent a letter with study information to the parents of the minors (< 15 years old). All approved their children's participation. The remaining students were asked by their teachers and by invitations from the researchers during school visits to participate in the study. Two of the schools were situated in a mid-sized town, one in a suburb outside a major city, and one in a small village. The social composition of all four schools was characterized as lower middle class or middle class. Schools that were considered problematic, with high rates of truancy and other types of social limitations, were not included. This was in line with our ambition to capture the meaning of pornography among normative middle class young people. There was representation of students with an immigrant background, although the majority of the participants were ethnic Swedes.

There were 73 participants who volunteered and completed the study. We conducted seven focus groups, each comprising 6 to 10 participants (24 young women and 27 young men). There were four groups involving 14- to 16-year-olds, and three groups of 17- to 20-year-olds. With one exception, all of the groups were single-sex (one of the male 17–20-year-old groups included one woman). In addition, we conducted 22 individual interviews with 10 young men and 12 young women, evenly distributed along the age continuum between 14 and 20 years.

THE INTERVIEW PROCESS AND ANALYSIS

An interview guide was employed as a checklist for the topics and issues to be covered. We used the same guide in both the focus groups and in the individual interviews (see the Appendix). Themes were constructed according to the research questions: the participant's own experiences of using pornography, how and in which situations pornography was used, and the potential effects that pornography might have had on themselves and on others. We also included an introductory theme concerning conceptions and experiences of similarities and differences between sexuality, erotica, and pornography. This theme was primarily used as a gateway to the individual interviews and the focus group discussions, and therefore these results are not presented in this article. All interviews and group sessions were conducted on the premises of the respective schools. Both the focus groups and the individual interviews took approximately one hour. The sessions were recorded on audiotape and thereafter transcribed verbatim. In anticipation of the processing and analysis of the interviews, a synopsis was developed for each informant and each group session. Thereafter, an initial structuring of the themes in the material was conducted, which was followed by more extensive and in-depth description and analysis made by both of the researchers. The patterns that gradually emerged in the various portions of the material were then positioned in relation to other elements and to the dataset as a whole. In the process of analysis we consistently worked in a reflective manner, where we thought it was an advantage to be researchers of both sexes. Several methods have been applied: categorizing the text along different themes, condensing the individuals' statements into meaning-concentrations, and interpreting the text against the background of previous research and theoretical concepts.

A fundamental ambition of the analysis was to identify patterns and common themes, while at the same time allocate space for ambiguity and complexity. However, there was one notable difference between analyzing the individual interviews compared with the focus groups. In the latter, the group as a unit was the focus of the analysis.[37] Thus, the analysis primarily followed an inductive model, fluctuating between theoretical concepts and the emergent categorization of the data, and implied a move from the purely descriptive, to gradually analyze and develop categories at a higher level of abstraction. Validity in qualitative research is about credibility and describing the approach and the purpose of the study.[38] In this case, we have aimed for an open account of these, even though we are aware of the risk of obtaining results that agree with preconceived conceptions.

THE RESEARCHERS' INFLUENCE ON RESULTS

As a researcher in the field of sexuality, it is important to review personal starting points and conceptions. Reflections concerning how sexuality is shaped differently according to age, gender, and social class become important. The aim of the researchers, one male and one female, both of whom were middle-aged, was an open and nonjudgmental attitude to attain a constructive and permissive atmosphere in the interviews and the group sessions. Nevertheless, we were aware that our age and gender status could potentially make the participants too embarrassed to discuss a topic seen as charged and sensitive. In addition, some of the participants may have felt more at ease with an interviewer of the same, or the opposite, sex. Thus, we listened with respect and carefully avoided any leading questions. We also maintained a more reserved stance in the focus groups than in the individual interviews to capture how the participants talked about the subject. In the focus groups and in the individual interviews, we used follow-up questions from our interview guide to clarify some of their comments, and to elicit more information.

PRESENTATION OF RESULTS

The results are presented as themes, connected to the patterns that emerged during the process of analysis. Each theme starts with an overview of the results that were consistent across the focus groups and the individual interviews. Thereafter, the findings are presented separately for the focus groups and the individual interviews, even though they shared many characteristics. The focus group data contained, to a greater extent, opinions that mirrored or contradicted cultural norms negotiated among the participants. In the individual interviews, more detailed or unique personal experiences are described in the participants' own words, without influences from the group.

RESULTS

"Girls Are Getting the Wrong Picture of Us Guys": Gendered Aspects of Pornography

All of the young participants reported that they had come into contact with pornography, voluntarily or involuntarily, primarily on the Internet. They had either gone looking for it themselves or had encountered pornographic textual messages or pictures without actively seeking these out. However, compared with young women, men were much more likely to actively seek out pornography, irrespective of age. The young women in our study who did consume pornography also stated that they did so infrequently.

Focus groups: The young men spoke openly in the groups about their experiences of pornography. Their statements were without shame, embarrassment, or hesitancy, and the atmosphere was playful and humorous. The general opinion was that everyone, especially young men, was in contact with pornography from a very young age. However, they sometimes disagreed about the age at which young men usually first experienced pornography:

R: How old were you when you first got in contact with porn?

M2:   I don't remember. Seven years or something [laughing]!

      (Everyone starts laughing)

M2:   No, but 13–14 maybe . . .

M3:   I was 10–11.

M8:   It depends if you had it [porn] at home or not.

M1:   Or when you discovered your "dick"!

R: When did you do that then?

M4:   He has not done it yet [laughing]!

                              (*Male focus group, aged 17–20 years*)

The male participants agreed that young men today do consume pornography. However, opinions differed regarding the extent of pornography use. The atmosphere was more charged and uncertain in the younger male groups, including questions such as, "Do all young men really consume porn everyday? And for several hours?" This was a topic of some interest. Some of the male group participants were anxious to provide a balanced picture of their consumption:

M4:   Girls are getting the wrong picture of us guys. They think that we are looking at porn all the time.

M3:   Well, some of us might look . . .

M4:   Yes; some think it is macho . . . Those who don't commit themselves to school work . . .

                              (*Male focus group, aged 14–16 years*)

The discussion in the female focus groups was more hesitant and negative toward pornography consumption. However, if a participant expressed a contrary opinion, the general view might shift and new, different statements surfaced in the groups. Some argued that women do not like pornography because "it is not allowed in society" for women to do so. Others claimed that it is because pornography is produced in a way that does not attract women (e.g., porn is made by men, for men). Many ambivalent feelings and opinions were expressed:

F1: I think that a lot of girls do get turned on by porn . . .

F3: But I have never felt that! Actually, I have never seen a porn movie. I saw the movie *Language of Love*, but I didn't like it.

(Female focus group, aged 14–16 years)

In addition, some of the female participants maintained that pornography consumption among young women depended on the context. For example, when in the company of somebody they liked and felt secure with, most often a boyfriend or a girlfriend, some of them would consider viewing pornography. Among our participants, only a minority of those between 17 and 20 years of age said that they had watched pornography together with a partner. No participants in the 14- to 16-year-old groups reported this experience. Nevertheless, this was discussed in the female focus groups. Some pointed out that they thought that love and sexuality belong together and that this was a reason they did not like pornography. Pornography was perceived as sexuality without emotions and too "rough":

F2: It [porn] should be nicer, kind of.

F1: With lit candles.

F3: Yes, less hard, quite simply!

F2: Yes, they almost hit the girls in the porn movies.

(Female focus group, aged 17–20 years)

Individual interviews: There was considerable hesitancy and ambivalence in the individual reflections of the young women, as well as in the groups. Again, if the situation was right, which means if they were together with a partner or someone they like, some of the young women said that they might consider viewing pornography. This pattern may also explain why some of the positive views expressed about pornography were more conditional.

One young woman reflected: "I don't know, but actually I think I would do it. I haven't done it, but maybe" (Female interview, aged 18 years).

On the other hand, feelings of doubt and insecurity were expressed among the young women. Looking at pornography together with a partner, when one was lacking in sexual experience, might lead to unfulfilled expectations. Some of the participants were also afraid that their potential partner would be disappointed: "You might be a virgin, and then having sex together after watching porn. It might be better in the porn movie then . . . " (Female interview, aged 15 years).

The young men who did consume pornography stated that they regarded these experiences as something completely different from sexuality experienced in more conventional situations and relationships. They discussed the subject more thoughtfully in the individual interviews than in the focus groups. In addition, several of the young men stated that they were tired of pornography and also of portrayals of the stereotypical female body. This was confirmed by experiences reported by the young women: "There are guys that are sick and tired of silicone breasts and do get tired of all this plastic (in porn movies)" (Female interview, aged 18 years).

"You Might Learn a New Way of Having Sex": Reasons for Pornography Consumption

In our study, we identified three main functions of pornography in young people's lives. These were pornography as (a) a form of social intercourse, (b) a source of information, and (c) a stimulus for sexual arousal. Pornography as a form of social intercourse was primarily focused on the interaction between the viewers.

Pornography as a Form of Social Intercourse

Focus groups: Looking at pornography together with friends, either on the computer or in movies on television, was a common experience, according to the focus group discussions. Sometimes these situations occurred during meetings for computer games, a so-called local area network:

M1: Half of the guys were playing games . . . half were looking at porn.

M7: I have never seen as much porn as then!

(Male focus group, aged 17–20 years)

These situations were, for the most part, not discussed as involving sexual arousal. Instead, the young men described these shared experiences as a way of testing one's own and others' reactions to the actors' and actresses' behaviors, appearances, and bodies. The jokes, laughs, and sighs became a normative guideline for the young and perhaps sexually inexperienced viewer. This phenomenon was recognized and discussed in the female focus groups as well:

F1: They probably sit on the sofa, making fun of the women in the porn movie.

F2: Yes, (say the other girl) even if the guy hits the woman they say, "well, she likes it!"

(Female focus group, aged 17–20 years)

Pornography as a Source of Information

Focus groups: The content of the pornography was usually described in both the male and female focus groups as rather violent and rough. Nevertheless, some of its substance also functioned as a source of information for the young people. The discussions illustrated that pornography as a source of information was critically reviewed by the young people. Sometimes it was perceived as a reliable source; more often, it was judged as exaggerated, distorted, or downright false: "Sure, you can get some tip-offs by pornography . . . But, they do it completely brutally! Ok, you can do it fast, kind of . . . But in the porn-movie they do it ten times faster! (Female focus group, aged 17–20 years).

Individual interviews: Information on sexuality is acquired in different ways, depending on access to sources and consideration of what is reliable and useful, which, in turn, depends on one's previous experience. Some of the participants explained that behaviors could be depicted in pornographic movies that they did not know about beforehand—for example, different sexual positions and techniques about how to satisfy a partner sexually: "We didn't learn much in school about sex education, so one has to look in porn magayyyyyzines. But the only good thing is that you might learn a new way of having sex, kind of . . . " (Male interview, aged 18 years).

Pornography as a Stimulus for Sexual Arousal

Focus groups: The third function of pornography was as a stimulus for sexual arousal, either alone or in the company of someone else. This was primarily described as a private activity but, all the same, a subject that was permissible to talk about in the focus groups. Overall, the young men described becoming sexually aroused by pornography more often than the young women did, and they also said that they used it for this reason. Sexuality was often described by the men as a frustrating need that had to be satisfied. In addition, the general opinion was that young men are more interested in sex (and, therefore, in pornography) than are women:

M1: Well, you know . . . we as guys are horny all the time . . .

R: Is it really that way, or is it something that guys are just saying?

M1: Not all the time . . .

M6: No, but it is not an awkward thing to say if you're a guy . . . compared to if you were a girl.

M2: It is a funny thing to say!

(Male focus group, aged 14–16 years)

Individual interviews: The male participants were more taciturn and reserved in the individual interviews. They still talked about pornography consumption without expressions of shame or guilt, however, and often described it as an easy way of getting sexually satisfied: "Sometimes I just want to get rid of the energy in my body . . . And then it [porn] is a fast way of doing that! Afterwards I can do other things . . . go to school, exercise and so on" (Male interview, aged 15 years).

As mentioned earlier, the women in our study were generally more ambivalent regarding pornography than the men. It is important to point out that some of the young men also told us that they were not sexually excited by pornographic pictures or films but, concurrently, said that this was expected of them as men. Thus, just as the women felt that they were expected to react to pornography in a negative way, some of the men articulated the opposite: "It is humiliating . . . that is the way I see it. And when you see a porn movie with six guys and one women . . . How fun can that be?" (Male interview, aged 18 years).

"I Save a Little Tuft to Show That I Am a Woman": Ideal Bodies and Perfect Performances

Our participants described what we called a "pornographic script" for physical appearances and sexual performances. Participants of both sexes agreed that women and men in porn were portrayed unequally in sexualized images in the media, particularly in pornography.

Focus groups: The task of women in pornographic movies was described by both the female and male participants as "to satisfy the men's sexual need." The image of the woman was that she is less valued than the man. This opinion was criticized by both the young women and the men, across the different age groups:

M1: It is kind of weird . . .

M2: Girls are inferior.

M3: It doesn't have to be like that, but it is often that way . . . Well, the guy says to the girl, "Do that and that!" Most of the times the girl does everything for the guy!

(Male focus group, aged 17–20 years)

In particular, the young women reacted negatively to what they perceived as a lack of sexual pleasure portrayed by the women acting in pornographic films. They were also critical of the physical ideals displayed in pornography. Some of our participants, again mostly the young women, encouraged active involvement against pornography. They encouraged each other in the groups to stand up against men's persistent demands about how to look and act sexually. However, the young men stated that they do not always perceive the female physical ideals portrayed in pornography as attractive, even if these are supposed to be sexually arousing for the average male:

M1: I mean some of the women in porn videos are totally shabby . . . with wave permanents and bodies destroyed by too much plastic surgery! They are neither attractive nor good looking girls!

(Male focus group, aged 14–16 years)

A topic of heated discussion in the male focus groups was that in pornographic movies, it seemed as if men were always sexually willing and able to perform sexually for hours. How was this possible? How can one stay aroused and erect for so long? The explanations put forward varied:

M1: Usually the male porn actors are gay.

R: So?

M1: That is why they can go on for hours. They don't feel horny with women.

(Male focus group, aged 17–20 years)

We were confronted with two parallel, intersecting discourses in the interviews: one that critically described the physical ideals in pornography and one that highlighted the impact that these ideals have on young people. One example cited by the participants was the importance of having not only shaved axillae and legs, but also shaved genitals.

Individual interviews: In the individual interviews, we obtained more detailed information on feelings and experiences of shaving one's body, particularly before a potential sexual encounter. It is important to mention that it was not only young women who shaved their genitals. Young men also shaved their entire bodies, even though masculinity was ultimately measured by performance. However, it was the young women who expressed concerns regarding this topic: "If I meet a guy for a one-night-stand . . . then I am afraid that he will say "no" because I have hair between my legs! But, I save a little tuft to show that I actually am a woman and not a ten-year-old girl!" (Female interview, aged 18 years).

Overall, it was the young women that admitted being influenced by the physical ideals displayed in pornography. They expressed some insecurity about their own bodies and about whether they would be considered adequate in the eyes of their sexual partners. They worried that they would be compared against the physical standards of the women in pornography and that they would be found lacking. A young woman recalled a situation when she was watching a pornographic movie together with male friends:

Q: How did you feel then?

F: Well, like very unattractive . . . you can say that you aren't influenced by this, but no one can resist. You do want to have these ideal bodies.

Q: Why does one think like that?

F: Well, even though I don't think it is good looking to have huge silicone breasts, but . . . everyone in the movies have those and they all have shaved bodies . . . so, well . . . they have what is regarded as gorgeous bodies.

(Female interview, aged 15 years)

The young men stated that they were not affected by these physical ideals. The young women, however, thought that the men were not willing to admit this and maintained that "nobody can resist the influence of these ideals." Apart from being compared in appearance, the women were also concerned that young men would expect them to act in a similar way to the women in pornographic movies. Engaging in anal sex was cited as one example of this, clearly influenced by porn, the female participants argued. A young woman related an episode when her boyfriend wanted to try anal sex: "Well, I told him that neither I nor my girl friends want to do that [anal sex]. But because I knew that the boyfriend to one of my girl friends also wanted to try it, I told my boyfriend to do it with him!" (Female interview, aged 19 years).

However, most of the male participants in our study did not agree with the views of the female participants. They fervently denied, both in the focus groups and in the individual interviews, that they wanted to do everything that is shown in pornographic movies. Furthermore, they asserted that sex in real life is something completely different and they can keep the two things apart from each other. Once more, we see how pornography differs from the participants' experiences of sexuality in more conventional relationships.

"Self-Esteem Is Important": Navigation in the Pornographic Landscape

We use the metaphor of navigation to describe the participants' accounts of having to sail upwind between contradictory norms and values regarding sexuality in the pornographic landscape. Even though most of the participants declared that pornography does affect everyone to some degree, especially when it comes to physical appearance and sexual performance, they argued that the majority managed to avoid becoming psychologically harmed. In other words, they navigated successfully and the older they became, the easier this was to do.

Focus groups: With increasing age, the curiosity about pornography diminished, and its role was downplayed in the young participants' lives; they reported that life experiences, rather than specific sexual experiences, contributed to experiences with pornography becoming more nuanced and defused. Most of our participants, regardless of gender, said that young people's interest in pornography decreased with age:

M2: I do pornography myself instead of looking at it nowadays [laughing]!

M4:   Yes, that is pretty common when you get older.

Q: So you don't look that much if you have a partner of your own?

M4:   That is the way it is.

(Male focus group, aged 17–20 years)

Our participants also pointed out the importance of including pornography in sex education in schools to reach those who do not have anyone else to discuss the subject with, as well as those who believe the subject is important and interesting to discuss.

Individual interviews: Our participants reported that their self-confidence and self-esteem increased as they grew older. In addition, they found it easier to assert their own sexual preferences and sexual desire: "It is important to be able to say that I don't want to do that! And if you don't respect my wishes, so . . . well, drop off! But, also it's important to sometimes stretch your borders and try . . . because then you know more about what you like and dislike" (Female interview, aged 19 years).

Our participants also described anxiety that pornography consumption could lead to abuse for some people, even though none of them declared that they were at risk from this. They told us about a small group of young people, young men in particular, who were at risk. According to descriptions from our participants, these individuals suffered from social isolation and loneliness, which, in turn, may lead to vulnerable situations: "If you have poor self-esteem . . . and don't dare to date girls in real life . . . Then, if you are drinking beer and looking at porn instead . . . and get the idea that you just can go out and fuck a girl. Then you will end up with a thick ear!" (Male interview, aged 18 years).

The majority of our participants stated that they could handle exposure to pornography satisfactorily because they have friends and close relationships with family members. In addition, they had positive life-experiences that made it possible to develop good self-esteem: "It is important to have someone to talk with . . . and to have a family as a support and someone in the same situation. And of the same age . . . And not being alone. Friends are very important!" (Male interview, aged 20 years).

DISCUSSION

Overall, the young participants seemed to enjoy talking about this subject, both in the individual interviews and in the focus groups. Initially, we believed that the interviews would provide an opportunity to talk more openly and freely about the subject. However, the topic seemed easy for participants to discuss both in the focus groups and in the interviews. Indeed, we noted a tendency for participants to speak more unreservedly in the focus groups and also for individuals to sometimes change perspective on a subject in response to comments from others in the group. This has also been reported by other researchers using focus groups.[39] The openness in both the focus groups and in the individual interviews could also be a consequence of the research situation. The participants were expected to discuss pornography in front of the researchers. Furthermore, they seemed to appreciate the opportunity to talk about a subject that they valued as important and absorbing. Similar observations have been made in previous sexuality studies.[40] The interview situation can become an occasion to systematize and organize experiences and to create a context and overview about one's own sexual conduct.

NORMALIZATION AND AMBIVALENCE

The results from this study illustrate that the cultural script concerning pornography seems to have changed from having been regarded as shameful and morally reprehensible to something socially accepted. Primarily due to the Internet, pornography has become an integral part of the everyday life of young people, which is supported by other research.[41] Consistent with several studies,[42] actively seeking out pornography was significantly more common among the young men than among the women, irrespective of age. One reason for this could be the cultural context,[43] where it is more socially accepted in Western society for men to consume pornography than it is for women.[44] Historically, consuming pornography is a male act and seldom done by women; this may reflect Gagnon and Simon's "homosocial reinforcement of masculinity."[45] Heterosexual masculinity is then a central part of the ethnography of pornography and also illustrates the connection to the social world of roles, values, and social structure in society.

On the whole, the young women in our study expressed a restrictive, hesitant, or critical stance in relation to pornography. However, they also expressed ambivalent feelings similar to the female participants in Berg's[46] qualitative study, who described physiological reactions associated with sexual arousal concurrent with negative feelings toward pornography. This could be a consequence of the current cultural script, which makes it more difficult for women to acknowledge a positive attitude toward pornography.[47] However, some of the young men in our sample were also ambivalent, which may, in part, be a response to the societal context, which has generally negative attitudes to pornography.[48] On the other hand, the young participants' ambivalence could also be understood as a substantial critique of the content of pornography that usually is produced by men, with men as potential consumers.[49]

Our study indicated that the so-called love ideology,[50] where love legitimates sexuality, still seems to have a rather firm grip on our participants, especially on the young women. Pornography was perceived by the female participants as sexuality without emotions, whereas the male participants seemed far more open to pure sex or to sex just for the sake of it. This pattern may also explain why some of the women's positive views on pornography were more conditional. If the situation was right, which meant if they were together with someone they liked, they might consider viewing pornography. In the spirit of Gagnon and Simon,[51] the sexual potential in pornography is defined as appropriate for women if consumed in a socially accepted environment or with a socially accepted co-consumer. Another way of understanding our participants' different reactions and descriptions of their experiences of pornography is to see how they defined situations as "sexual." According to Gagnon and Simon, the basic question in the integration of sexual elements in the social script is about "who does what to whom in what kind of relationship, and to what consequence."[52] Among our participants, it seemed that their individual scripts differed in varying degrees, regardless of age and gender, depending on how much they related to the cultural level, where violent or unequal sex is not socially accepted in Swedish society.

THE PORNOGRAPHIC SCRIPT

This study highlighted the functions of the pornographic script as a frame of reference for young people in relation to physical ideals and sexual performances. The participants agreed that women and men in pornography are portrayed in an unequal manner. They were also critical of the physical ideals displayed in pornography, foremost for women who are supposed to be thin with large, surgically enhanced breasts. According to their reports, these ideals do influence young people. One example of the impact of physical ideals was the importance of shaving one's genitals. Even though men were seen as also measured by these ideals, they were primarily influenced by performance ideals of the actors' performances in pornographic movies. Consistent with previous studies,[53] anal sex was cited as one example of this. Even though our participants agreed about pornography's influence on young people, other studies have suggested that young people usually think that this is something that concerns others and not themselves.[54] More detailed knowledge about how and to what degree these ideals influence young people in the long term would be interesting research questions to pursue.

NAVIGATION IN THE PORNOGRAPHIC LANDSCAPE

Our findings indicate that young men and women nowadays have to cope with different parallel norms regarding sexuality. Forsberg[55] discussed the task of acting in congruence with what is seen as appropriate behavior as influenced by different factors (e.g., gender, age, family culture, and religion). Several of our participants emphasized the connection between sexuality and love and argued that sexuality in real life was more exciting than pornography; some of the male participants also stated that they were tired of pornography. Possible consequences of early extensive consumption of pornography in relation to interpersonal and intrapsychic scripts are important to investigate. Further research including young adults who have grown up in the pornographic landscape might contribute to our understanding in this area.

Our findings suggest that most of our participants had acquired the necessary skills of how to navigate in the pornographic landscape in a sensible and reflective manner. The way they reasoned about the exposure and impact of pornography indicated that most of them had the ability to distinguish between pornographic fantasies and narratives, on the one hand, and real sexual interaction and relationships, on the other. To validate these results might require another research method, such as field observations or interviews with other people (e.g., parents and teachers).

The participants described a small group of individuals that they judged as being at risk for abuse of pornography, even though none considered themselves in this group. To admit problems in a focus group or in an individual interview might be difficult, and those who are at risk might not volunteer to participate in a study such as this. This "at-risk" group, however, warrants attention and further research. Notwithstanding this, daily consumption of pornography is not automatically problematic or risky. Research indicates that the potential problems of high-frequency porn consumption depend on the situation and the circumstances in which it is consumed.[56]

LIMITATIONS

This qualitative study has several limitations. First and foremost, it is not possible to generalize from the results because the sample was not random and, in addition, recruitment was restricted to schools in lower middle-class or middle-class areas. The young men and women volunteered for the study and we do not know the views of those who did not want to talk about the subject. However, through using a combination of focus groups and interviews, we obtained a rather varied and multifaceted sample that provided us with the opportunity to explore and analyze the different navigational strategies in relation to pornography used by the participants. Nevertheless, it would be of interest to conduct further research with more diverse samples. Another limitation is that we did not collect demographic data from the participants. If we had done so, we might have highlighted other factors of importance such as social class or ethnocultural background. Also, an initial choice of a different theory might have highlighted other aspects of the interviews concerning sexuality, gender, and pornography. As Gagnon[57] pointed out: "theory remains a map that is not to be believed, or held on too fiercely, or forced on anyone else. It is a way of constructing or inventing a world rather than discovering it."

Finally, it is not possible to know how the young people would have talked about pornography without the researchers present. We have tried to link the young participants' voices about pornography to the social context in which they live and act. However, it is hard to say if the map of the pornographic landscape that we have constructed is the same as the one the young people used and responded to. Clearly, the picture of the young participants' experiences of pornography is both complex and far from unambiguous and needs further research.

APPENDIX

Interview Guide

Theme: Similarities and differences between sexuality, erotica, and pornography

- Is it possible to distinguish between sexuality, erotica, and pornography? If so, how would you define the differences?
- Have you ever come in contact with pornography and/or erotica? Where and how, in that case (e.g., on the Internet, on the television, in magazines, at movies)? If not, how come?
- Do you talk with friends, family, or others about pornography, erotica, and/or sexuality? Why or why not, and how do you talk, in that case? Is there a gender and/or age difference?
- Other comments

Theme: Experiences of using pornography, how and in which situations

- Do you think it is common or unusual for young people to consume pornography? Is there a gender and/or age difference? Why and how, in that case?

- How would you describe young people's feelings toward pornography in general and toward consuming pornography more specifically (e.g., excitement, curiosity, shame, embarrassment, or acceptance)?
- What do your own experiences with pornography look like? How would you describe your own attitude towards pornography?
- Do you consume pornography? Why or why not? What function(s) does it fill (if answered yes)?
- In what situations do you consume pornography (e.g., not at all, alone, together with friends, together with a partner) (if answered yes)?
- Other comments

Theme: The effects and influences of pornography

- Are there differences in the ways that young men and young women are described and pictured in pornography, and how in that case (bodily ideals, performances etc.)? Does this affect you and/or your friends, partners, etc.? Why or why not?
- Do you think that pornography and/or erotica have influences on your own sexuality? How, for instance (e.g., positive, not at all, negative)? Why not, otherwise? Are there gender and/or age differences?
- Is it necessary to have strategies to handle the effects of pornography? Can you describe these, in that case?
- Other comments

NOTES

1. M. Forsberg, "New Challenges in Sex Education," in *Generation P? Youth, Gender, and Pornography*, ed. S. V. Knudsen, L. Löfgren-Mårtenson, & S.-A. Månsson (Copenhagen, Denmark: Danish School of Education Press, 2007), 328–34.

2. Forsberg (2007); N. Hammarén and T. Johansson, *Könsordning eller könsoordning landskap [Gender Order or Disorder. The Sexual Landscape of Youth]*. Report No. 2. (Kungalv, Sweden: Centrum for Kulthurstudier/Forum for Studier av Framtidsstudier, 2002).

3. S.-A. Månsson, L. Löfgren-Mårtenson, & S. V. Knudsen, "Introduction," in *Generation P? Youth, Gender, and Pornography*, ed. S. V. Knudsen, L. Löfgren-Mårtenson, & S.-A. Månsson (Copenhagen, Denmark: Danish School of Education Press, 2007), 8–18.

4. Månsson et al. (2007); S.-A. Månsson and P. Söderlind, *Sexindustrin pa nä tet. Aktö rer, innehå ll, relationer och ekonimiska floden [The Sex Industry on the Internet. Actors, Contents, Relations and Economical Torrents]* (Växjö, Sweden: Egalite, 2004).

5. B. McNair, *Mediated Sex* (London: Arnold, 1996); B. McNair, *Striptease Culture. Sex, Media and the Democratization of Desire* (London: Routledge, 2002);

A. D. Sørensen, "'Porno-chic'—Sex and Mainstreaming of Pornography in Mass Culture," in *Generation P? Youth, Gender, and Pornography*, ed. S. V. Knudsen, L. Löfgren-Mårtenson, & S.-A. Månsson (Copenhagen, Denmark: Danish School of Education Press, 2007), 87–102.

6. A. Hirdman, "'Please vote nicely . . .' Visualizing Gender Online," in *Generation P? Youth, Gender, and Pornography*, ed. S. V. Knudsen, L. Löfgren-Mårtenson, & S.-A. Månsson (Copenhagen, Denmark: Danish School of Education Press, 2007), 151–70; G. H. Kolbein, "Exposed — Icelandic Teenagers' Exposure to Pornography," in *Generation P? Youth, Gender, and Pornography*, ed. S. V. Knudsen, L. Löfgren-Mårtenson, & S.-A. Månsson (Copenhagen, Denmark: Danish School of Education Press, 2007), 103–17; S.-A. Månsson, K. Daneback, R. Tikkanen, & L. Löfgren-Mårtenson, *Karlek och sex pa Internet [Love and Sexuality on the Internet]. Nätsexprojektet [Net Sex Project]* (Göteborg, Sweden: Göteborg University and Malmö University, 2003).

7. McNair (2002).

8. Sørensen (2007).

9. A. D. Sørensen and V. S. Kjorholt, "How Do Nordic Adolescents Relate to Pornography? A Quantitative Study," in *Generation P? Youth, Gender, and Pornography*, ed. S. V. Knudsen, L. Löfgren-Mårtenson, & S.-A. Månsson (Copenhagen, Denmark: Danish School of Education Press, 2007), 87–102.

10. For example, E. Häggström-Nordin, U. Hansson, and T. Tydén, "Association Between Pornography Among Adolescents in Sweden," *International Journal of STD and AIDS* 16 (2005): 102–107; Hammarén & Johansson (2005); C. G. Svedin and G. Priebe, *Ungdomars sexualitet—Attityder och erfaneheter. Avsinitt: Sexuall exploatering. Att salja sex mot ersattning/pengar [Young People's Sexuality—Attitudes and Experiences. Section: Sexual Explotation. Selling Sex for Compensation/Money]* (Lund, Sweden: Avdelningen for Barnoch Ungdomspskiatri, OPUS-Institutionem, 2004).

11. G. M. Hald, "Gender Differences—Behavioral, Situational and Interpersonal Patterns in Pornography Consumption," in *Generation P? Youth, Gender, and Pornography*, ed. S. V. Knudsen, L. Löfgren-Mårtenson, & S.-A. Månsson (Copenhagen, Denmark: Danish School of Education Press, 2007), 118–32.

12. Svedin & Priebe (2004).

13. Hald (2007).

14. L. Berg, "Det dubbeltydiga talet. Unga kvinnor samtalar om pornografi [A Contradictory Talk. Young Women's Discussion of Pornography]" *KvinnoVetenskaplig Tidskrift* 21, no. 3 (2000): 41–54.

15. Svedin & Priebe (2004).

16. M. Forsberg, *Brunetter och blondiner. Om ungdom och sexualitet i det mangkultuerella Sverige [Brunettes and Blondes. On Youth and Sexuality in the Multicultural Sweden]* (Gotenberg, Sweden: Gotenborgs Universitet, Institutionem for Socialt Arbete, 2005); N. Hammarén, "Horor, players och de Andra. Killar och sexualitet I det nya Sverige [Whores, Players and the Others]," in *Sexualitetens omvandlingar*, ed. P. Lalander and T. Johansson (Göteborg, Sweden: Daidalos, 2003), 95–124; C. Herlitz. *Allmanheten och HIV/AIDS: Kunskaper, attiyder och beteenden 1987–2004 [Members of the Public and HIV/AIDS: AIDS: Knowledge, Attitudes and Behavior 1987–2003]* no. 2004.7 (Stockholm, Sweden: Statens Folkhälsoinstitut, 2004).

17. A. Giddens, *Intimitetens omvandling. Sexualitetet, karlek och erotik I det moderna samhallet [The Transformation of Intimacy: Love, Sexuality and Eroticism in Modern Societies]* (Nora, Sweden: Nya Doxa, 1995).

18. Häggström-Nordin et al. (2005); Hammarén (2003); C. Rogala and T. Tydén, "Does Pornography Influence Young Women's Sexual Behavior?" *Women's Health Issues* 13 (2003): 39–43.

19. J. Weeks. *Sexuality* (London: Routledge, 1986).

20. J. H. Gagnon and W. Simon, *Sexual Conduct. The Social Sources of Human Sexuality*, 2nd edition (Chicago: Aldine, 2005).

21. J. H. Gagnon, "The Explicit and Implicit Use of the Scripting Perspective in Sex Research," *Annual Review of Sex Research* 1 (1990): 1–43; J. H. Gagnon and E. Laumann, "A Sociological Perspective on Sexual Action," in *Conceiving Sexuality. Approaches to Sex Research in a Postmodern World*, ed. R. Parker and J. Gagnon (New York: Routledge, 1995): 183–214; W. Simon and J. H. Gagnon, "Sexual Scripts," in *Culture, Society, and Sexuality: A Reader*, ed. R. Parker and P. Aggleton (London: University College London Press, 1999), 29–38.

22. N. Hammarén and T. Johansson, "Pornotopia—Theoretical Considerations and Young Pornographers," in *Generation P? Youth, Gender, and Pornography*, ed. S. V. Knudsen, L. Löfgren-Mårtenson, & S.-A. Månsson (Copenhagen, Denmark: Danish School of Education Press, 2007), 33–46.

23. Månsson & Söderlind (2004); Sørensen (2007).

24. L. Löfgren-Mårtenson and S.-A. Månsson, *"Sex overallt, typ!?" Om unga och pornografi ["Sex Everywhere, Kind Of ?!" On Youth and Pornography]* (Mö lnlycke, Sweden: Gothia Forlag, 2006); Rogala & Tydén (2003).

25. Gagnon & Simon (2005).

26. J. Bancroft, "Introduction and Overview," in *Researching Sexual Behavior: Methodological Issues*, ed. J. Bancroft (Bloomington, IN: Indiana University Press, 1997), ix–xvi.

27. B. Starrin and B. Renck, "Den kvalitativa intervjun [The Qualitative Interview]," in *Kvalitativa studier i teori och praktik*, ed. P.-G. Svensson and B. Starrin (Lund, Sweden: Studentlitteratur, 1996): 53–78; K. Widerberg, *Kvalitativ forskning i praktiken [Qualitative Research in Practice]* (Lund, Sweden: Studentliterratur, 2002).

28. D. L. Morgan, *The Focus Group Guidebook* (Thousand Oaks, CA: Sage, 1998); V. Wibeck, *Fokusgrupper. Om fokuserade gruppintervjuer som undersokningsmetod [Focus Groups. Focus Groups as a Research Method]* (Lund, Sweden: Studentlitteratur, 2000).

29. Cf. Wibeck (2000).

30. D. L. Morgan, "Focus Groups," *Annual Review of Sociology* 22 (1996): 130.

31. Morgan (1998).

32. Wibeck (2000).

33. Morgan (1998).

34. Starrin & Renck (1996).

35. Cf. Wibeck (2000).

36. S. Eriksson, "CODEX—Rules and Guidelines for Research," *The Swedish Research Council in cooperation with the Centre for Research Ethics & Bioethics at Uppsala University, Sweden*, December 12, 2008, http://www.codex.vr.se

37. Wibeck (2000).

38. S. Kvale, *Den kvalitativa forskningsinterjun* [*The Qualitative Research Interview*] (Lund, Sweden: Studentliterratur, 1997).

39. E.g., Wibeck (2000).

40. B. Lewin, "Studiens genomforande [The Implements of the Study]" in *Om sexuallivet i Sverige 1996*, ed. B. Lewin (Stockholm, Sweden: Folkhälsoinstitut, 1998, 29–60); L. Löfgren-Mårtenson, *Får jag lov? Om sexualitet och kärlek i den nya generationen unga med utvecklingsstörning* [*"May I?" About sexuality and love in the new generation of young people with intellectual disabilities*] (Lund, Sweden: Studenlitteratur, 2005).

41. E.g., Häggström-Nordin et al. (2005); Hammarén & Johansson (2002); Sørensen (2007).

42. Häggström-Nordin et al. (2005); Hald (2007); Svedin & Priebe (2004).

43. Gagnon & Simon (2005).

44. Hammarén & Johansson (2002).

45. Ibid., 201.

46. Berg (2000).

47. Cf. Berg (2000); Hammarén & Johansson (2007).

48. Cf. Hammarén & Johansson (2007).

49. Månsson & Söderlind (2004).

50. Giddens (1995).

51. Gagnon & Simon (2005).

52. Ibid., 206.

53. Häggström-Nordin et al. (2005); Hammarén (2003); Rogala & Tydén (2003).

54. Häggström-Nordin et al. (2005); Rogala & Tydén (2003).

55. Forsberg (2005).

56. Svedin & Priebe (2004).

57. Gagnon (1990).

18

Race and the Politics of Agency in Porn: A Conversation with Black BBW Performer Betty Blac

Mireille Miller-Young

Porn performer Betty Blac straddles both the mainstream adult industry and the feminist-queer independent side of U.S. porn production.[1] As an African American Big Beautiful Woman (BBW) performer who also identifies as queer, Blac has pursued opportunities to work in both the heterosexual, BBW market—which typically fetishizes the bodies of voluptuous women—as well as in the market for porn made by and for queers. Nominated for the first Adult Video News Award for BBW Performer of the Year in 2013, Blac's performances for queer productions like Courtney Trouble's *Lesbian Curves* series and Shine Louise Houston's *Crashpad* series have garnered the University of Sydney educated actress increasing attention. Blac, an avid writer and video-blogger with a large fan following, also works in the digital side of the adult entertainment business as a webcam performer for *Kink.com*—one of the few black women or BBWs to do so. Extremely thoughtful about the politics of race, body size, and women's agency in the adult industry, Blac offers important insight into why a critical lens for racial, sexual, and feminist issues matters to those studying the role of pornography in society and the nature of the business itself. For Blac, being an African American woman in porn means negotiating sex work organized along hierarchies of race, where black women are often at the bottom. While BBW exists as a specialty genre of porn, often the companies producing films for black and interracial BBW markets are exploitative. In the conversation that follows, Blac discusses the ways that she contends with this tricky terrain and how she seeks out greater economic value, autonomy, respect, and pleasure, often in queer pornography where issues of identity and embodiment tend to be more fluid. Finally, Blac describes her vision of a kind of porn she would like to produce, one based on the sexiness of diversity and imagination rather than the routine and often uncreative logic of what sells.

Mireille Miller-Young: What are some of the ways in which race plays out in the adult industry?

Betty Blac: There's one director who shall remain nameless. He offered my white friend three scenes but he only offered me one blowjob scene [because] he didn't really feel like black Big Beautiful Women (BBW) were as marketable. He was only willing to work with me because I was light skinned. I sent him an e-mail and said basically, "You're a racist."

MMY: His logic seems counterintuitive because so much of BBW features black women or women of color. BBW seems to be one space where more women of color are able to get entry because we can have bigger bodies, or at least more of us can kind of fit into that genre. Do you think white BBWs are more marketable than women of color BBWs?

BB: No, I don't think that white BBWs are more marketable. As I told the director, "You guys are the generators of the porn. You are creating the marketing." I feel like there are more companies that bother to market white women more [than women of color] but that doesn't mean that [white women] are [more] marketable.

I have [white] friends who have worked for the same companies as me. I may have shot more for those companies but their photo shoots will be the ones that are in the ads, the ones that are in *Adult Video News*. They're the girls who get the covers. That's not necessarily the case with a lot of women of color in the industry.

If you go to the "plumper" Web sites and take a look at the women who are in the ads and on the splash page, it's not that there aren't women of color. But companies tend to promote white women more. Especially with Web sites like *Score.com*, where they have the "Girl Next Door" look that they're going for. Models are fighting to even be included and they're just so happy to get shoots that they don't even care that they're not going [to appear] on the main pages.

MMY: It's the same story in mainstream, non-BBW-oriented porn. For the more prestigious shoots and feature opportunities, black women and women of color tend to be shut out.

BB: That's definitely true. I mean BBW is already a subculture and then being a woman of color and a BBW—that's a subculture of a subculture. It also depends on who you're willing to work for. I personally don't want to work for really ghetto companies. I don't want to work for companies where I'm going be referred to as a "nasty ho" or any of that stuff. I want to work for the main respectable companies or for the local indie companies.

It is interesting that the only video cover I ever made was for one of the kind-of ghetto companies. That was probably the least amount of money I have made for a shoot. I didn't realize until after the fact that they are a company who will regularly find women who are down on their luck, and especially young, pregnant black women who are beautiful, and offer them $1,000 to do four shoots.

MMY: So those women are only getting paid $250 per shoot?

BB: Yeah, there's a lot of that. There's a lot of pregnancy porn. There's a lot of exploitation in the industry. It depends on what company you work for. A lot of these companies (and the company I was working for) [shoot] multiple kinds of porn. The shoot I was in was all-black BBW. That company mostly produces porn with black women in a variety of settings.

MMY: What were the things that offended you about the working conditions? How were you treated?

BB: I was new to the industry and I didn't really know how much you're supposed to make and things like that. A friend set up the shoot and she was honest about saying it was going to be a little bit less money. If I had the wisdom that I have now, I probably wouldn't have done it. I did it because I wanted to appear on a video cover. That was the deal. But what ended up happening was that the cover [photo] made me look really light and I don't think it was a flattering picture of me. It's not something that's made my career any better. I don't feel ashamed about it or anything, but when I look back, I really didn't need to do it. I only made six hundred bucks for two scenes. [The scenes] were super awkward and, you know, they're two scenes that no one probably even sees.

MMY: And you got paid $600 for two scenes?

BB: A lot of what I've made has been ridiculous, which is why I'm at this point now where I've made this decision recently that I'm not going to do any more condom-less work. This means that I'll be mostly shooting stuff for myself or for local or Indie companies. It means that I won't be working for a lot of the major companies. I feel so proud about that [decision] because most of the shoots that I was on were not [paying me] that much money at all. It was partly to do with me being black and BBW, and partly to do with porn. Porn just does not pay that much money anymore, especially with shooting in Los Angeles. I would have to pay to travel to get to L.A., I would have to pay for a place to stay, I would have to pay for all of the things that I needed to maintain myself—waxing, nails, whatever. I have to pay $200 for testing. And by the time that I've done all that I better have at least three or four shoots lined up even to cover my expenses, let alone be able to come home with anything.

MMY: I'm interested in the resources that it takes to be in the game, especially for black women. In addition to the waxing and the nails we have hair, which costs a lot to do. How much money would you say that it takes you to actually do all the self-care necessary to even work?

BB: It takes a lot. [In terms of how much it costs] I guess it depends. When I've shot for Los Angeles companies, they don't pay for you to get out there, but when I've shot in Miami, the companies fly you out, they provide room and board, and they have someone who does make-up.

MMY: Black women earn half to three quarters of what white women make. The difference in earnings involves a lot of overt and covert racism. Performers tell me about the micro-aggressions they experience, how they feel treated poorly in general and made to seem undesirable compared to white women. Do you think that racialized exploitation impacts you? How does that make you feel?

BB: It is really isolating. When I had that disagreement with that director [who I mentioned earlier], an amazing friend of mine also had a shoot with him the next day and she called him to the carpet about his racism. She was offered $1,700 for the same work that I was offered $1,500. At first, when I tried to point out to her the racism in the industry she kind of didn't say much. When the director said that he was only willing to work with me because I was large, she started to see that the industry was racist, but she still stayed friends with him.

So that kind of thing is what hurts me and makes me infuriated. I feel isolated because there are so many people who don't know how industry racism works, and I sense them judging me when I speak out about it. They say I'm complaining or that things are all in my head or that I'm just not trying hard enough.

I've had really great experiences [working in porn], but the amount of racism and the amount of frustration that I have around this, has gotten to the point where I'm not having fun anymore.

At times I find myself comparing myself to other women in porn. I was really bringing my self-esteem down before I realized that it was the racism. These other women have so many scenes and all the banners and I would think, "Is this person better than me?" I don't like to be in that headspace. I don't like to compare myself to other women or bring the other women down to make myself feel better.

MMY: That's understandable. The industry has created a system of racial hierarchy where your only option is to compare yourself to other women. Women are pitted against each other in this effort to get in a better position.

The black women I have interviewed are frustrated and feel that white women use their skin privilege all the time, especially those that charge more money for performing a scene with black men. Black porn performer Marie Luv went to her director and demanded an interracial rate like the white women and they just kind of laughed her out of the room.

BB: It's interesting that interracials are, for the most part, seen as black man, white woman. None of the other mixed-race porn is really seen as interracial. Someone pointed out to me the other day that there are these sites called "reverse interracial" with black women and a white man. So, okay, a white man and an Asian woman, or a Latina woman and an East Indian man are not interracial? I was totally appalled.

MMY: I'm curious about how the racial issue overlaps with the BBW issue, in that you kind of are put in this double category. Do you feel confined in that category?

BB: I feel confined. Maybe if I had more resources and I put myself out there in a different way, I might be able to cross over and be featured in films other than specifically BBW or specifically black. But I just don't have the time and the resources now. I don't like to be labeled in my regular life, so being in this industry—which relies on labels—is frustrating because that's not how I have sex in my [real] life and I know that that's not how a lot of my fans have sex.

But a lot of my fans will come to my work or things that they've seen me in because they specifically have a thing for BBW porn or they specifically have a thing for black women. If I produced porn, I would use that opportunity to include all these beautiful big black women. I like a wide range of women and I like a wide range of men, and I would want to see that in anything that I produce. I get exhausted with the fact that a lot of porn is the same thing—the same looks, the same formula, the same way of expressing sexuality.

MMY: Absolutely. How did you like working with Courtney Trouble and Shine Louise Houston in *Lesbian Curves* or the *Crashpad* series? And how do you compare working in indie and feminist/queer porn compared with the mainstream industry?

BB: It's completely different. I like working with Courtney and Shine because they treat their performers better. We have complete control over whatever we want to do. I'm not saying that other companies necessary treated me badly . . . When I work with indie companies and I want to use barriers or condoms, or I want to be comfortable or to shape the scene [I can do so]. I can have a say in how I am portrayed.

I also felt really proud of the last thing that I shot for Courtney Trouble, not only because it is with somebody that I know and love [but also because] Courtney set the frame for how they wanted [the scene] to be done, what they wanted to get from us out of the scene. We communicated all along. I felt like I had agency and like I was really sexy in the scene. I also feel that I really stepped up as a performer. I was able to come out of my shell a little bit. Because sometimes, the mainstream stuff that I do, I just look like a deer in the headlights. [*Laughs*] [The] penis comes and it's just like everything. It's just not the same [sense of] empowerment. I love the co-stars that I work with [in mainstream productions]—that's not what I'm saying—it's just a different structure.

MMY: It seems like it would be in the interest of producers to be ethical and treat their talent well so that they get the best performances. But there is this industrial aspect in the mainstream industry that really does not treat most workers with care, except for the people that they see as most valuable. And everybody else seems to feel pretty disposable. Do you agree?

BB: Yes, definitely. BBWs don't even have agents. It's like we aren't seen as valuable at all. Being black and a BBW, I feel doubly disposable. You are pretty much dime a dozen because you're brown. I wish that indie companies had the money that mainstream companies have because then I would have more jobs.

MMY: Do indie companies pay the same or do they pay less than mainstream companies?

BB: They pay comparable rates. If you are doing a queer scene you're not going to be getting paid the same as if you're doing a straight scene. You'll probably get paid $200 or $300 [at the lower end of the mainstream market] and considering that [both indie companies I worked with] pay $300 a scene, that's pretty comparable.

MMY: How do you feel in your performances? Do you enjoy the boy-girl scenes as much as the girl-girl scenes?

BB: It really depends on the co-star. Some of my co-stars were super fun. I am queer and I enjoy relationships with both men and women, but I think that my attraction to men is a bit stronger. Technically speaking, sometimes the straight scenes are a bit easier because I'm lazy and it's less work. If I'm doing mainstream, they're not typically looking for me to top. They're not looking for me to take control of the scene and so I really just have to get into different angles and make noises. With the queer performances, more stuff has to happen.

MMY: I read your writing on your blog about your experiences performing. It looks like it's supposed to be easy. But it's not, is it?

BB: It's definitely not easy! But I feel like I am becoming more confident as a performer and learning a little bit more about how not to make horrible faces at the camera.

It really is a shame to me how horrible the industry pays and how difficult it is for me to put myself out there as a viable performer. But my way of dealing with that is to create my own projects, because I don't really want to have my money filtered through a lot of other people. I don't really want to be seen through other people's lenses anymore. I want to have more control and agency and creativity. I don't want to have a generic porn-girl Web site; I want to have something out there that's creative and different and that has the same values that I have. I'm a highly political person; I'm very passionate, and I don't want to downplay that to be in mainstream porn.

MMY: When I started doing porn research there were no black women directing. It's fascinating to watch how with changes in technology there is a cadre of black women who matured in the industry and who were able to move behind the scenes. People like Vanessa Blue and Diana Devoe who became important directors, and Shine Louise Houston and Nenna Joiner coming into the picture. The first black woman to become a director was Angel Kelly who was the first black woman with a contract in the 1980s. What kind of porn would you like to make?

BB: Well, I work at an adult store and we have this whole spiel that we tell people when they're trying to buy porn. Specifically when it's guys trying to buy porn for their girlfriends and they have no idea what women like, it's always like, "Women like story lines," or "Women like feature films." Or [we show them] very weird versions of porn produced by women. It's [supposedly] more gentle, more romance novel-y, or erotica. And I don't like any of the shit! [*Laughs*] I don't identify [with it] at all.

So, I think that part of what I want to produce is hardcore. It might have a storyline—there are some cute campy things that I would like to do—but I think that [my porn] would dispel the idea that women like [story lines or romance-y erotica] in porn.

The other thing I'd include would definitely be diversity. I'm so tired of white women being *the thing*. I would have white women, but they wouldn't be the focus. There wouldn't be ten scenes with white women and then an Asian person thrown in for diversity. There wouldn't be one type of look that would be acceptable. I definitely want hot people but hot people from a variety of different subcultures and ethnicities.

I want to play with the format. When some people masturbate or fantasize, they think about short images, like focusing on specific acts or on specific body parts. So, I want to play with that. I want to have images overlaying in scenes in a way where there's a lot of condensed erotic imagery. So that it's not just one scene that plays out from start to finish. When I look at trailers for porn I see all the hot stuff all at once and I get totally into it. I don't know why there can't be porn that's the length of a trailer where they just have the juicy bits all put together.

MMY: I love that idea because most people spend somewhere between six and ten minutes watching porn for masturbation, so films don't need to be that long. Let me ask you about kink and BDSM. It's one of your interests and I think that it's getting more attention these days but there's still, at least from an academic perspective, not a lot of research done on people of color and kink. I think that it's really interesting and complex because, given black women's history and the history of slavery, a lot of people from the outside see ropes and it's automatically associated with the history of violence used against us. We add a layer to our experience of fantasy that maybe other people don't have. I just wonder how you would describe your fascination with, or desire for, kinky sex.

BB: The shoots that I've done haven't really involved anything kinky. In the scene that I did with Kitty [Stryker], there was a little bit of butt slapping and spitting, but that's as kinky as it got. Most of my fans are not looking for that from me. I do have a photo shoot that has me in ropes and I actually had some conflict with my friends (and with myself) about what it means to be por-trayed [tied up] in rope. It's a challenge for me because I really enjoy being in bondage. I like the sensation and I like that sort of play. But I feel this pressure from people of color to see more images of black dommes or black women in power, and they are rallying behind those images more than behind [images of] black submissives. This makes it so it's not okay to be submissive.

I'm not necessarily submissive or dominant, but I definitely feel like if I did a dominant shoot everybody would be excited about that. Maybe it would be different if I was shown being submissive to another black person [rather than to a white person], but other than that it's interesting; it's a challenge to figure out. I cam for *Kink.com* and everything is managed through them, [but] they don't have big girls on any of their main sites.

MMY: Tell me about camming. What is the exchange framework?

BB: Basically, with the exchange framework, users have the option of tipping in the public room or taking me private. I think it is $5.99 a minute. I get

40 percent of any money made. I know some of the major companies stream [the cam sessions] and get 20 or 30 percent. There are smaller, more feminist companies, like Skin Video, where you make 80 percent, but they don't have the traffic that *Kink.com* or *Streamit.com* have.

There [has been] a lot of controversy, especially with feminists in the porn community, [over representation issues] at *Kink.com*. Ultimately it was important for me to be aligned with a major company [like *Kink.com*] and I wanted to increase their portrayal of [BBWs] because I was the only BBW model on their cam site initially. Now they have more, and that was important to me. I know that there is a huge BBW contingent in the kink community and especially in the local [San Francisco] kink community so it's interesting that our local kinky site doesn't really have that many BBWs on there.

MMY: Yes, *Kink.com* is known for being overwhelmingly white. Are you seeing a shift in that?

BB: I'm seeing a few more people of color. There's a lot more diversity among the cam models. I think that's because we are making our own money and [the company is] not having to invest as much. They're okay with making the cam models more diverse. But the shoots can still be pretty homogenous. I've only been in one of their shoots and that was as an extra.

MMY: What are the kinds of things that the webcam viewers or consumers write you when you're in chat?

BB: For the most part I spend a lot of time in public chat and I would say that a lot of fans just want to talk with me. One person regularly comes and picks me just because he likes to find out what's going on in my life. We talk about everything under the sun. Because I know a lot about sexual health and sex toys, I'll tell people about pegging or toys they can use with their partners. The majority of the audience is male and the guys don't normally feel safe or comfortable talking about [sex] and so they're behind their computer and they can hear this weird, quirky girl talk about pegging or whatever. That part I enjoy.

I also like that at the end of the day people are paying me to pleasure myself. A majority of what I do in private is just play with my Hitachi [Magic Wand] and that's it. Sometimes people will give me instructions, like, I'll have to spank myself, or whatever, but I'm in control. I can hit myself as hard as I want to. My skin gets red pretty easily so I'm really not using that much force.

MMY: It's interesting that you're doing sex education on webcam as well. In my research on black women performers on a token-based webcam site, it seemed to me that when compared to white women, black women were being asked to do so much more for the tokens, whereas a lot of the white women sex workers who were doing really well and were listed at the top of the list remained clothed. The white women were just chatting and typing, but the black women were going full throttle just to get a token, and it seemed that they were asked to do a lot more for less.

BB: I think that it really depends. Porn stars will [be treated differently] than non-porn performers doing cam work because we already have a fan base that's like, "Oh, right. I can cam and talk to you." When I first started camming my experience was a little different than it is at Kink. I'm definitely still not as desirable as some of the white women on the site, so I'm not going to paint it like it's always fun. There are times when I'll come home with two hundred bucks after three hours and there are times when I come home with twenty bucks or no bucks! I guess I don't know what I'm being asked to do compared to white women. Typically I'm not asked to do a lot of crazy things. I don't do shit that I don't want to do and I make that clear to people. I set boundaries around what I'm willing to do. Like in the public room, when I do things for tips, I'll say, "I'll do this and then you can tip this amount." That way, if they're into that act they'll tip and if they're not they won't. I won't be in a private and wanting to make money but being asked to do some shit that I don't want to do.

MMY: That gives you a sense of control?

BB: Yeah, I feel in control. A lot of what I've been doing lately is public shows where I'll just say, "If we get up to a hundred bucks then I will play with my Hitachi in public," and that way they all get to see and interact [with me] even if they can't afford a private. And I get to decide how much I want to do or what I want to do and that agreement is made ahead of time. Before I was doing it differently. I was really pushing for privates—and I still do privates—but I'm finding that if I raise money in public I get to do what I want and I'm guaranteed a certain amount of money. I just like that better. It also depends on what site you work for. Every site has a different structure. They have different rules.

Ultimately, guys will come to the room and if they are attracted to me they're going pick me for a private if they have the money. Most people just want to see me masturbate and that's it, or see me spank myself. It's very, very basic. There's a subset of people that want me to dominate them, but I don't that often and I'm not as good at it [as others]. Some people will pay me just to sit there in a ball gag or some people are just lonely and they'll pay me to chat.

MMY: Do you feel like you can express yourself in this genre of sex work? Is there a creative aspect to it?

BB: There's definitely a creative aspect to it. I have control over everything—how I style myself, how I do my hair, how I dress myself, what I say, what I decide to talk about. I can sit with people and talk to them about *Star Trek* if I want to and there are guys who will totally jack-off to that.

When I first started [camming] there was this one period where it would get really slow in the room and I would just blow up a bunch of condoms and make balloon sculptures and then people would start tipping for that. I feel like when I just do something weird they're going to tip for that because they're like, "I've never seen anything like that on cam before." I definitely feel like it's fun.

MMY: Your master's degree in Creative Writing is from the University of Sydney and your undergraduate degree is from Mills College. Do you think your educational background gives you an advantage in the kind of work that you're doing?

BB: It gives me a disadvantage sometimes because it distances me from other people who think that I think that I'm better than them. Or it disappoints other people because they're like, "Why are you in porn if you're smart?" I don't think my education gives me any advantage in my work but it helps me articulate my oppression sometimes.

MMY: In your YouTube videos, you talk about Trayvon Martin, institutionalized racism, and mental health. You have profound things to say about your life and about the way that you see the world. And to me, although you might feel like your education does not give you an advantage, I think that it's given you the capacity to think through your life and experience and to put your voice out there in a way that does make a difference.

BB: It does make a difference a little bit. It gives people a little bit of an idea of what it means to be in this industry. I think it definitely gives people a different face for porn performers. I think that because I'm educated, I bring something to the table when I deal with fans and when I tell them about what it's like to be in this industry. I hope that [my education] will really serve as an advantage when I start producing my own stuff.

MMY: I want to ask you about your YouTube videos about mental health. It's really wonderful to hear mental health talked about because this is totally taboo and silenced in communities of color. The subject has also been totally silenced in terms of how it impacts us as sexual beings, as women of color who are sexual. How do you feel your mental health struggles shape your sexual identity or the practices that you are engaging in? How does it shape how you have to take care of yourself as a worker in the industry?

BB: I didn't see [my sexuality and mental health] as interlinked really until I realized that I probably was more promiscuous as a woman of color and as a fat woman because [sex] is a form of validation. I felt insecure or disempowered in the world or I felt depressed or sad and [sex] was just immediate gratification. I'm sure that it has to do with how my sexuality was shaped, but not all of it. I don't feel like when I do a shoot or anything like that it really affects my mental health. It's more the politics around porn, the industry, the money, and that kind of stuff that affects my mental health. That's where I don't feel supported or I feel anxiety and depression around those things. I think also there just isn't an understanding of mental health in general in the world, let alone what comes with being [porn] performers. People will just assume that mental issues are a factor in [my entering porn], "Well you're doing something that's taboo and [part of the] subculture, of course you're crazy."

MMY: Right. The misperception is that you have to have something wrong with you to be there in the first place. Actually the thing that makes something wrong mentally or emotionally for you is the politics of the industry in devaluing your labor. The bigger problem is the structural inequality that then creates this situation. I love that argument to counter antiporn feminists who assume that (a) you must have been abused, and therefore you must be living out this problematic traumatic childhood, and/or (b) that the abuse occurs in the way you are objectified by the representation, by the image itself, which then traumatizes other women.

BB: If I was valued the same as my white counterparts, and seen as beautiful and sexy, and if I was making the same amount of money, then not only would I not struggle with financial issues, but [I wouldn't struggle with] insecurity issues as well. Some people say that money doesn't buy happiness, but I definitely feel that's said by people who have money. That is not something that is said by poor people.

Of course you can't literally buy happiness, but you can definitely buy mental health medication and the resources that you need. With money, you can buy a lot of things that can get you pretty damn close to happiness.

NOTE

1. On the latter and the relationship between the two sides of the porn industry see Tristan Taormino et al., eds., *The Feminist Porn Book: The Politics of Producing Pleasure* (New York: The Feminist Press, 2013).

19

Positively Fat and Queer: An Interview with Indie Porn Insider Courtney Trouble

Lynn Comella

Porn performer and director Courtney Trouble has been blazing trails in the world of feminist and queer pornography for more than a decade. Trouble's films are often described as gender-bending and genre-bending, fat positive, and transracial; they deliberately explode the very identity categories that typically define how pornography is made and marketed. Their[1] growing repertoire of films, which includes *Fuckstyles, Trans Grrrls: Revolution Porn Style Now!* and *Lesbian Curves*, among others, eroticize what is often fetishized and feature groups of people—not to mention queer desires—that are often underrepresented, if not entirely absent from mainstream porn.

Trouble got her first camera when she was eight years old and spent much of high school and college in the darkroom. When she was nineteen she applied to be a model for the alt porn Web site SuicideGirls, and was rejected because she was too fat. It was a turning point for Trouble. Were they going to try to fit into a standard of beauty and desirability that didn't reflect who they were or were they going to create a new mold? Trouble decided it would be the latter. They wanted to make an alternative to alt porn, in which performers didn't have to pretend they were straight or starve their way to thinness. Trouble embraced their curves, their queerness, and their sexual desires, and set about making pornography that encompassed the very things that most mainstream porn either rejects or marginalizes. In this interview, Lynn Comella explores Courtney Trouble's views on how feminist and queer pornography interrupts normative stereotypes about beauty, sexuality, and desire.

Lynn Comella: Feminist pornography recently had a breakout year. In 2013, there was the publication of the *Feminist Porn Book* and the first international Feminist Porn Conference was held in Toronto. Feminist porn was also a topic for conversation in the mainstream media, from *Cosmopolitan* to the *Huffington Post*. What does feminist porn mean to you and how do you think it's changing the adult industry?

Courtney Trouble: My definition of feminist porn has gotten a lot richer recently. Before, I could really only describe it from my own point of view. Meaning, I am a feminist and I make a certain kind of pornography. For the most part I make queer porn. I work with lesbian, gay, bisexual and transgender (LGBT) people and alternative, sex-positive people. But I don't think all feminist porn is like mine. I see feminist porn as a movement more than a genre. It is about having conversations about the right to access pornography, our right to make it, to enjoy it, and our right to work in the industry as sex workers. What really matters is that the feminist porn movement is moving toward deeper conversations about women's relationship to pornography, [including] how we watch it and why.

If you think about it, porn has always been for guys—but that isn't because women didn't want to watch it; it was because we weren't offered it. For example, when I was a kid, the boys in my middle school had all seen pornography because their dads had ushered it in. Society has said that porn is for boys and that girls are not supposed to like porn. We were socialized around that idea. Feminist porn is breaking those rules. It's not [only] about the kind of porn that's being made, but [also] about who gets to watch it.

Feminist porn [involves] a group of people making pornography that looks different than everybody else's. [Still,] a lot of the feminist porn movement is based on heterosexual ideas and made by heterosexual filmmakers. So I am working overtime to make as much queer content as I possibly can. Aside from a few smaller filmmakers and, of course, people like Shine Louise Houston and Jiz Lee, there are really only a few of us right now who are making queer porn and representing this sector of feminist porn.

LC: Why do you think queer porn is still somewhat underrepresented within a broader feminist movement that's all about changing the types of sexual representations that are available?

CT: I think you have to look at the larger spectrum of privilege when it comes to the opportunities that heterosexuals are offered compared to the opportunities that queer people are either offered or feel safe taking. A lot of queer pornographers, or aspiring queer pornographers, just don't have money to start a company, make their first film, or build a Web site. These things take a lot of money. Traditionally, queer people are not the richest people in the room. I think that's a huge part of it. I started from nothing when I was nineteen. I was privileged enough to be able to get a couple of day jobs here and there at [sex toy retailers] Babeland and Good Vibrations, but I really had to save my pennies to make my projects happen. I am not saying that all straight people have a bunch of money, but I do see a lot of projects popping up that are heterosexual-focused and that get great funding. A lot of heterosexual-focused female directors get jobs with larger companies.

LC: Do you think more mainstream companies will start making and marketing feminist porn?

CT: They are hiring us. I am in the process of becoming a crossover director. I signed a contract this week with Smash Pictures to be the director of their lesbian line. I am getting a beautiful budget. I am going to be putting something out once a month. What I am excited about is that instead of these larger companies just being inspired by feminist porn and trying to create their own versions of it, we are succeeding in getting people who are already making feminist porn to be hired by these companies. Instead of just taking my ideas and executing them in their own way, they have actually hired me to implement my own ideas with a lot of financial backing and production help. They could've just taken it from me. I think people have tried that and discovered that it's not how our porn looks that makes it different, but how it's made.

LC: That's an interesting point. Can you say more about this idea that it's not just that feminist porn looks different, but how it's made?

CT: When speaking about feminist porn it's clear that it all doesn't look the same way or elicit the same reactions. Some feminist pornographers make luscious, cinematic short films with great lighting and meaningful or emotionally driven content. Others point their handycam at two people having sex and put it up unedited on the Internet for money. So what's the difference? What really sets feminist porn directors apart from mainstream porn companies?

[A] feminist porn set is one [where the people on it are] aware of sexism and intersectional oppression, and how it affects sex work, porn, modeling, marketing—basically everything. A feminist porn set generally allows for performer and crew agency. Ideally, nobody would get asked to do something they weren't comfortable with; [they would] feel like they left set and had a good day at work and that they were compensated at a level that fits the work they did [and] how long they did it. This is what people talk about when they speak of the ethical porn movement. I think it overlaps with feminist porn because providing a sexism-free workplace for porn makers is part of being ethical, not just being feminist.

A feminist porn set would allow for a potentially diverse audience. For instance, in a traditional straight boy/girl scene, a feminist porn set would make sure to get wide shots, and close and medium shots of the man—keeping in mind that a woman who likes men might be watching the video and want to see him, and not just a dick coming into the screen from stage left. They may also make room after the male orgasm [to showcase] more female pleasure, which is something I do in my own work often, to gently remind people with penises that sex isn't over by default after they've come.

For a queer porn scene, feminist pornographers would pay close attention to people's gender identities, sexual orientations, pronouns, and interests. [They would] also attempt to carry the performer's preferred identities throughout the marketing and selling of the finished work. For an example, we can look at Jiz Lee's career. Many companies that Jiz has worked for have not respected their gender identity or pronoun preference through to the final product. Jiz gets called a "woman" and "lesbian" in many, many mainstream [productions]. A decidedly feminist porn set, however, would or should create information for their customers to let them know that Jiz is genderqueer.

LC: A lot of queer porn, including the porn you make, deliberately interrupts normative assumptions about gender, sexuality, race, and bodies. Can you talk about this?

CT: I started making porn because I wanted to see my fantasies and my body represented in porn. It was really just for myself. Because I'm a creative person, photography and video was a natural way to go. It was a way for me to document my sex life and my desires. I wanted to have fun and I wanted to desire myself. I wanted to create a project that wasn't built on any norms whatsoever. I was saying, "This is a small collection for us."

That slowly grew and now my work does get compared to various norms and standards all the time: Why aren't there transwomen in lesbian porn? Why aren't there women of size in lesbian porn? Why aren't there transmen in straight porn? There are now all of these questions, but I never set out to challenge norms from the get go. I wanted to make porn that queer people could enjoy.

For a lot of queer people and people of size and people of color or transpeople, it doesn't matter what kind of medium we are participating in, be it television, music, porn, anything, it is incredibly difficult to see yourself reflected back in any way other than a joke or tragedy or an inspirational coming out story. The narratives for us are really limited. To be able to create media that doesn't reflect any of these stereotypical images, whether it's porn or not, is incredibly valuable to marginalized people. Even if it is just porn, even if it's just sex, we can see ourselves reflected in it, and we are not being made fun of or marginalized or portrayed as a tragedy. We are being respected and desired. We are being given agency. We are given a voice to tell a story that is ours. And maybe we see something that we connect to. If you look at a lot of queer cinema, outside of pornography, like *Hedwig and the Angry Inch* or the L Word [on television], that stuff doesn't represent queer people either. In a lot of ways I think pornography has an option to create sort of a side story.

LC: It's interesting to hear you talk about storytelling. I think people who haven't watched a lot of pornography don't necessarily see porn as a form of storytelling. They might see it as fantasy or escape or something they watch to get turned on. So when you think about the stories that you most want to tell through the medium of pornography, what are some of those stories?

CT: I should preface this by saying that I am probably the worst narrative filmmaker I have ever met! I am really, really horrible with a script. And honestly, most of my porn starts with kissing and then leads right into sex. It doesn't have a script. It is very much documentary-style filmmaking. The stories are sort of told through the sex. So when I say, "People telling their stories," it might be a lack of a storyline, because what they might be doing is just being honest and truthful in their performances. So the story you are getting is the true story of someone's desires. It's not a script I've written or a cheesy lead in—although I do some of those now. I'm currently doing a movie called Wet Dreams, which is all fantasy. None of it requires much work on my end. It's giving somebody an opportunity to be themselves and a medium through which they can express their desires and their sexuality and their gender identity on screen, which tells the story without a script. For me personally, as a performer, I really want to tell my story, with or without words.

I am a survivor of sexual abuse; I am gender queer; I am incredibly tied to feminine presentation. I am strong. I am fat. I am complicated and queer and obsessed with girls. I am perverted. There are also words I use to describe myself that [people wouldn't guess] like "Daddy" or "boy." So that's the story I want to tell as a performer. I try to let that out of the hat whenever I get in front of the camera. A lot of porn directors will stop you at a certain point. They say, "Be yourself, but don't . . . well . . . you're being too quirky." [I've experienced this] even with indie feminist performances, when I've been directed to dress conventionally feminine and told to leave the strap on at home, or wear feminine underwear, not boy's underwear. It's only in my own productions that I have been able to perform my own story. There's a lot of my own personal shit that I work through when I am performing. I can only imagine that every person who comes to my set goes through the same thing. How can I present myself through my clothes or my body or the way I fuck or who my costar is? How can I put my true queer story out there?

I shot some established lovers for Trans Grrrls: Revolution Porn Style Now. We didn't have any set up; [the performers] just started the scene. Halfway through the scene, Tobi said to her date, "I want you to muff me."[2] This was something I had never seen before in my entire life, so there's no way I could have directed it. Over the course of forty-five minutes, she proceeded to tell Quinn how to dig into her body to fuck these nerves under her skin that were so deeply embedded inside of her that she had to be very specific about her internal map. She was talking the whole way through it. She was literally giving a speech while getting fucked and then coming.

LC: In terms of questions and feedback, what kind of fan mail do you get? Is there anything that stands out to you in terms of hearing from someone who saw something in one of your films and felt the need to share with you the impact it had on them?

CT: Absolutely. I recently had a couple e-mail me after buying my movie *Girl Pile*. *Girl Pile* involves four femme women having an orgy of their own design. This couple, a guy and a girl, bought the DVD and watched it together. They sent me an e-mail and said they loved it. It was the first time they'd ever watched a DVD together. Then they sent another e-mail saying that the male partner had discovered that he likes wearing women's underwear while they are watching *Girl Pile* and pretending that [he is] one of the girls in the pile. This is a conversation that arose while they were watching *Girl Pile* together as a heterosexual couple, and now they are lovingly and appreciatively exploring erotic cross dressing. Because of this video, this couple got to go down this path together. I get a lot of e-mails, but this one really stopped me in my tracks.

It goes back to the argument about whether porn is educational or just entertainment. I think people get a lot of inspiration from the erotic media they watch. *Girl Pile* was not intended to be an educational movie in any way. But somebody learned something from it. Porn can inspire people to pursue their desires. I never know what my movies are going to inspire for the people who watch them.

The majority of my fans, though, are queer femmes. [Their e-mails go] beyond saying, "Hey, I like your porn," and include things like, "I like your porn, but what lipstick are you wearing?" Or, "You are the first femme-presenting genderqueer that I've ever heard of in my entire life. I've never felt like a woman, but I've always been femme. Thank you." Since I've come out publicly as a genderqueer femme, I've gotten more of this fan mail, which makes me wonder why I waited so long to come out.

LC: These are really interesting examples, and are a reminder, I think, that the experience of watching porn isn't one-dimensional. There are lots of different entry points and paths that someone might take to connect with or experience one of your films—and it might not even involve sex. On another note: You're doing a lot of college speaking these days. What do you hear from students when you visit campuses and screen your porn?

CT: I've been on a lot of speaking tours recently. I just got back from presenting and screening hardcore pornography at the University of Calgary, which was an awesome experience. We watched my movies uncensored, and I did a presentation on finding genderqueer identity through porn performance. It's my story about how performing in porn has given me options to explore my gender, and getting to a place where I feel really comfortable identifying with a nonbinary gender identity. Most of the questions I get from college students really center on nonbinary gender identity. A lot of college students are interested in what it means to be nonbinary, and this might be what attracts them to queer porn in the first place. A lot of them relate to not identifying as 100 percent male or female; they exist somewhere along a gender spectrum or identify with having a fluid gender. I have to thank [gender queer porn performer] Jiz Lee for coming out and being very vocal about this. They were really the only person [in porn] who was speaking about being a non-binary gender queer person, and they did a lot of the initial work for me. The emergence of gender queer identity really seems to resonate with students, and queer porn seems to be playing a role in these conversations.

LC: Do you think that's because there's an ambiguity in queer porn, and the bodies we see aren't necessarily anchored to any predetermined set of cultural meanings?

CT: Exactly. The bodies aren't anchored to any particular gender identity or story. In my presentation about gender identity through porn performance [that I've been giving at colleges], I show clips and quote some gender queer porn stars that I've worked with in the past. One of these is Papi Coxxx. They say that before doing queer porn when anyone saw their body they would describe Papi as a woman. It was only when Papi started doing queer porn that they could say, "I am not a woman," and really have that resonate. Porn allowed them to break away from that structure. If you see only breasts and a vulva or see no breasts and a cock, you are often projecting yourself onto those bodies. If no one is telling you who they are or how they identify, you as a viewer have the freedom to play with that. It's not a documentary where someone is saying, "I am this." With [queer] porn, no one is telling you [the limits of] what is or is not possible.

LC: It's almost like you're describing an idealized version of queer identity, in which there is no stable or predetermined gender or sexual identity. It's like taking the idea of queerness to its most logical conclusion.

CT: Basically, yes. Amateur porn or nonscripted porn or documentary porn features people who are generally doing what they love to do. The cameraperson is just kind of there. There's a lot of freedom to get into an animalistic zone as a performer. When you are not being assigned a particular gender or role to play . . . when that happens to me as a performer I feel like an animal. It's bringing humanity closer to what we are, which is animals. It's taking us back down to that level where we don't have to critique or problematize anything. It's just people having sex and you can make whatever you want out of it as a viewer. The performers aren't telling you who they are and who you are, and the director isn't doing that either. I think queer porn allows for sex to feel like more of a universal act and not separate us into different kinds of humans. I mean, if you want to talk about representing diversity this really gets at how we separate all different types of bodies into categories. The porn industry does that all the time. I understand why they do it, but I don't think human sexuality is as cut and dry as the porn industry makes it out to be. A person is not only one thing sexually. I don't think human sexuality is as specific as porn has tried to make it.

The diversity I present in queer porn just has to be. And it's actually really appreciated by audiences, because it includes a lot of different things at the same time, which makes it hard to categorize. [The representation in my queer porn is] not just trans; it's not just lesbian; it's not just fetish; it is not just romance. It's actually all of these things at once. I allow these things to exist alongside of each other, because I think that viewers are just as complex as we are, so why not play to their curiosities as much as we possibly can.

LC: The idea that human sexuality is not as cut and dry as the porn industry presents it as gets tricky with marketing. To market something you have to categorize it, and you have to use language to construct categories that are recognizable and therefore marketable. This happens all the time with porn— "Teen," "MILF," "Amateur," "Ebony," "Blonde" —and, as you point out, these categories aren't necessarily a good barometer of how complex people's sexual desires are. So how do you, as director, negotiate this? You're exploding these boxes in an industry where these boxes very much exist. What does that mean in terms of reaching audiences? Do you do a complicated dance or do you shrug your shoulders and say, "I'm just gonna put it out there"?

CT: I have been experimenting with the adult industry for the past decade. The best way that I have been able to get new customers, new fans, and new audience members has never been within the porn market. It's been going out and meeting my customers. Queer Porn TV does dance parties. We hand out stickers and market our site. I immerse myself in the community that might ultimately be an appreciative customer base for queer porn. This has been so much more lucrative to me than advertising in porn magazines, because there's no category for what I do. I am being hired to make a lesbian film [by

Smash Pictures] and that's awesome. That's only the second lesbian film I've ever done, but people see me as a lesbian director so I've used this market in different ways. I do community outreach, which has been the best way for me to grow my business. My political work and academic work has also been important. I've also experimented with different ways that I can enter the adult industry and compete. *Lesbian Curves*, for instance, was the first movie I ever made that had a theme. It was my thirteenth movie, and it was the first one that had a genre-specific theme: a BBW lesbian movie. It was the first time I ever made a film that actually fit into a category. Before that it was indie, alt, woman director, but those categories had nothing to do with what the movie was about. *Lesbian Curves* was the first movie I made that was really tailored to adult industry marketing. It was the same thing with *Trans Grrrls*. I thought, "Okay, I am going to experiment with entering the category of the adult industry that it will probably sell in, but I am going to make it my way and see where it goes." *Lesbian Curves* got nominated for an XBIZ award and so did *Trans Grrrls*—and the punch line? Not in the BBW category or the trans category, but in the "Best Feminist Film" category. That's a great punch line: I do genre movies to compete in the adult industry, and [the industry] ends up creating a new award category for films like mine, which ironically was the category that I came from to begin with.

LC: This really circles back to where we started, which was a conversation about some of the ways in which feminist and queer porn is seeping into the mainstream adult industry. That XBIZ would even think about generating an award category for "Best Feminist Film" says something quite powerful, I think, about the growing influence of feminist porn. But there's an irony here: You make these genre-specific films to fit into these predetermined marketing categories, only for someone to turn around and create an entirely new category.

CT: *Fuckstyles* won the "Most Deliciously Diverse Cast" at the Feminist Porn Awards in 2012. That movie had everything in it: gay boys, trans boys, plus size people, skinny white girls. It had absolutely everything. It is the first Trouble movie to go out of print. The most diverse film I've ever made is the one that went out of print. There was no category for it. There are warnings about that film all over the place. On the lesbian DVD sites, it says, "Warning: This movie has cock in it." In a straight store is says, "FYI, this has transsexual content in it." It's a really hard movie to put in a category and yet it's been my most popular film. I think people want variety. I think people are really sick of being told what they should and should not want from porn. Viewers, customers, porn stealers—whoever they may be—they don't give a fuck what category it's in, they just want to see good sex. We all have our own secret keywords. I really like "POV Blowjobs," because I like to pretend that I have a penis. But aside from that, if there's enough light and people are humping, it does the trick. It often doesn't matter who those people are, and I think that's becoming more and more of a universal realization about pornography: Watching people have sex is hot. It doesn't matter if you are straight or gay, trans or disabled, or white or whatever you are. If porn shows respect and has good lighting, I think it's all enjoyable.

NOTES

1. Trouble's preferred pronouns are "they" and "their."
2. Muffing refers to penetrating the inguinal canals. The inguinal canals are a pair of internal tubes extending through the lower abdominal wall.

20

Bare-ing Witness: Bareback Porn and the Ethics of Watching

Gregory Storms

In the years of HIV/AIDS, condom use in pornographic video has become a matter of ethical and financial concern for porn producers, viewers, and various social and public health organizations. Although the topic reemerged for straight porn production in Los Angeles in early 2012,[1] the general standard for straight porn has been condomless on-screen sex combined with recurring HIV (and other STI) testing. Most mainstream gay porn companies, on the other hand, have had a mandatory condom use policy for filming since the 1990s. The emergence of HIV/AIDS, however, did not completely eradicate the production of condomless gay porn.[2] Rather, lesser-known producers of gay porn marketed what would come to be known as "bareback porn."

This chapter examines the return of bareback porn during the late 1990s as a social and political commentary regarding the dominant representations of the gay male body and sex between men. In a period of gay men's history symbolically marked by disease and death, one in which unprotected sex was viewed as dangerous and irresponsible both for an individual's health and the well-being of the gay male community as a whole, the rise of bareback porn represented a protest against the denigration of the HIV+ body and uninhibited sex between men. Further, it reflects a nostalgic return to the Golden Age of Gay Sex, a brief period encompassing the 1970s to the early 1980s, in which many gay men (primarily those living in or visiting urban centers) were able to celebrate their sexuality with greater openness than before. This period of time, which coincided with the growth of the gay cinematic porn industry, created a genre that today is typically referred to as "classic gay porn" or "precondom porn."

In recent years, the topic of bareback porn has become an increasingly controversial issue. Some argue that its mere existence and availability normalizes condomless sex between men and contributes to the ongoing persistence of HIV transmission. Others argue that bareback porn acts as one mechanism to maintain freedom of artistic expression and to give representational value to *all* men who have sex with men, including those living with HIV. However, in communities and subcultures attempting to ban access to bareback porn, such as the International Mr. Leather competition and convention of 2009, as I discuss below, precondom porn has tended to remain an accessible genre. Given the arguments for prohibiting sales of bareback porn in various venues, why is precondom porn so often left out of the conversation? This chapter examines the historical similarities and differences between precondom and bareback porn and considers what lessons might be learned in the process.

THE SEXUAL POLITICS OF BAREBACKING

Barebacking, or unprotected anal sex between men, has its origins in a particular gay male subculture that began to coalesce around 1997. For many gay men who lived through nearly fifteen years of cultural messages that sex between men meant certain death, the persistent public health initiatives to remind gay men of the importance of condom use was also a constant reminder to many that gay male sex was akin to jumping out of a plane: If you did it without your parachute, you were as good as dead. "Condom fatigue," combined with medical innovations that improved treatment of the AIDS virus, "cleared a space for the growth of bareback sex, both as a subcultural practice and as a commercially viable pornographic genre."[3]

Thus, bareback sex and bareback porn is charged with the social and political energies of the 1990s, a reaction to the growing anger among some gay men concerning the practical and ideological responses to the AIDS epidemic. This cultural impact is reflected in the filming techniques employed by bareback porn producers. For example, the standard practice among bareback porn producers is to ensure maximum visible proof—to the extent physically possible using cameras positioned outside the body—that anal insemination has occurred during bareback sex.[4] This usually involves scenes in which the "money shot," so vital in porn as scholar Linda Williams has famously argued, is visibly seen outside the body, often directly on the bottom's anus, while the top then reinserts his penis to ensure the viewer can see there is semen exchange.[5]

There are other ways that films provide this evidence, including felching scenes, in which a man ejaculates inside another person's rectum and then proceeds to lick or suck out that semen. Yet another common way of depicting insemination is to have the penetrated/inseminated man excrete the semen on camera as proof of the deed. In reality, however, these scenes are often produced using techniques that do not include actual semen. Different mixtures of fluids to simulate semen have been used in enema-like ways to intensify the intended effects of proving insemination—whether or not it actually occurred.[6] Whether actual semen is present or not seems to be less important than providing visible evidence of its presence. Much of the erotic charge of these scenes, therefore, is not simply the presence of semen, but the understanding that what appears before one's eyes is considered by some to be taboo. In light of the continual threat of HIV infection, cinematic depictions of insemination provide a gateway to vicariously experience uninhibited sex between men, an act that allows fluids to mix and bodies to truly become one.

Semen has taken on an important symbolic and social character for queer men, even—perhaps especially—in the years of HIV/AIDS. Ellie Reynolds explains, for instance, that the meanings of HIV-positive semen for "bugchasers" (HIV-negative men who actively seek to be infected) and "giftgivers" (HIV-positive gay or bisexual men actively seeking to infect HIV-negative men, usually by consent) seemingly concern "effecting social ties (kindred) through the exchange of a primary metaphor for western personhood: DNA contained within semen."[7] But whether HIV is actually present or not, it continually haunts sex between men. Even among men who claim to be free of HIV, there can remain uncertainty as to whether one's partner truly is HIV-negative, especially because an estimated 18 percent of the 1.1 million people living with HIV in the United States are unaware of their status.[8]

Although semen has significant metaphoric meaning for this particular subset of gay men, in most cases it is not merely the semen itself that has such power, but the *act* of exchange—real or imagined. In forging new forms of kinship based on HIV transmission, the modes of transmission matter equally if not more than the actual medium itself. The draw for bugchasers and giftgivers exists in the social ties that are formed in the process of being infected, including the context of such transmission and, ultimately, in the physical effects of infection.

In the cinematic realm, bareback porn is widely available on multiple platforms. The difference between contemporary bareback porn and precondom classic gay porn is important. Tim Dean explains that "despite what is said by its critics in the gay community, bareback porn also may constitute one valid way of thinking about a virus. Unlike 'pre-condom' gay porn produced during the '70s and '80s, bareback porn is far from oblivious to HIV. Bareback porn, in other words, is no more simply a case of 'denial' than bareback sex is simply a case of irresponsibility."[9]

Comparing gay bareback porn to straight hardcore, Dean argues that the two genres share "an intense curiosity about the body's interior."[10] Dean focuses, however, on the special meanings internal insemination have for many queer men (and barebackers in particular) given the unique connections that HIV has for queer men. Describing pornography as barebackers' only visual form of self-representation, pornographers are charged with the difficult task of representing internal insemination through a variety of sexual and cinematic practices. These range from what Dean terms a "compromise shot," in which the ejaculating partner pulls out immediately before orgasm and then reinserts his penis to continue ejaculating internally, to the use of subtitles as signposts about the events occurring on screen.

Dean separates classic gay precondom porn from bareback porn for important reasons. As a distinct genre that often challenges the viewer to confront sentiments of disgust and overcome taboos about (potential) transmissions of HIV, bareback porn provides a special opportunity for examining the politics of sexual representation. But actors in the precondom era were not immune to contracting HIV, both on and off camera; and yet still, in many arenas bareback porn is treated as particularly vile and socially irresponsible, while precondom porn is excused as naïve in its lack of attention to the epidemic. By treating these two genres differently, men living with HIV today become further marginalized through the inhibition of openly expressing their sexuality on camera for public consumption. In particular, while precondom era actors tend to be excused for their lack of knowledge regarding HIV, actors in bareback porn who acknowledge and accept risk are often regarded as irresponsible and dangerous, a threat to the fight against the disease, rather than men who deserve equal access to representational regimes and sexual freedom.

CENSORSHIP CONTROVERSIES, BAREBACK PORN, AND GAY LEATHER EVENTS

My interest in distinguishing between precondom gay porn and bareback porn extends beyond the mere expansion of pornographic taxonomies; the differences between the two genres have led to not only differences in representational style and spectatorship, but social legitimation of distinct sexual practices and the bodies engaged in them. Take, for example, the actions of the Executive Committee for the International Mr. Leather (IML) competition in 2009, which serves as a useful case study about how the politics of representation impact real world social and sexual relations. As a result of controversy both within and outside the gay leather and related fetish communities over the status and appropriateness of bareback porn, most of which initially centered around the topic of public health but quickly extended to debates about censorship, the IML Executive Committee decided to issue a public statement to all potential vendors of the annual event, one of the largest in the gay male leather community.

This statement, officially signed by leather legend and IML president Chuck Renslow, briefly discusses the history of HIV/AIDS for queer men noting, specifically, that younger queer men differ in their experiences with HIV/AIDS: "Not having experienced the deaths—the loss of loved ones—which preceded these [antiretroviral] medications, we have an entire generation who may not fully appreciate or comprehend the severity of the situation." The statement continues:

> Too many of our community believe HIV/AIDS is curable or manageable. Too few understand that HIV/AIDS infections dominate life. We believe that it is our duty to inform and educate. Several years ago when 'Meth' was the scourge of our community, IML drew a line in the sand and raised awareness and used all our influence to try and stop this addictive madness. As is the case with HIV/AIDS, we believe it is our further obligation to do everything in our power to prevent future infections.
>
> To that end, after considerable discussion, the Executive Committee of International Mr. Leather has decided that it will no longer allow participation in the IML Leather Market by any entity which promotes barebacking or distributes/sells any merchandise tending to promote or advocate barebacking. This restriction will also apply to distribution of gifts, post cards or any other information via our facilities. This policy takes effect immediately.[11]

Following the decision to ban promoters of barebacking from IML festivities and commerce, public reactions exploded in all corners of the blogosphere both supporting and criticizing the announcement. Take, for example, the opinion of Will Clark, a blogger, pornographic and nonpornographic actor, emcee, and producer. Immediately following the decision, Clark wrote a blog post on his Web site in support of the decision. He opened his statement with the following: "Today the International Mr. Leather (IML) group out of Chicago made history by stopping the sale of bareback porn at their event. This is truly phenomenal." After providing some background information about Renslow and the impact of HIV/AIDS in the gay community, Clark continued: "But although six years later [after Renslow's 2003 speech condemning unsafe sex practices at IML], it's good news that IML is taking a healthier/ active approach to this situation. You can call it censorship and that's your prerogative but whatever. I don't care. If you want to blow your brains out, I don't have to be the one to hand you the gun."[12]

Clark was certainly not the only vocal supporter of the IML decision. Take Eric Leven's post on his Canadian blog KnuckleCrack, which I quote from at length below:

> This has always been about **more** than just sex.
> further [sic] I throw myself into this topic the more I understand this is a never ending uphill battle. ~~Unsafe sex~~ Bareback never went away, anyway. It's just that at one time striving to have safe sex and the idea of protecting oneself and their partners, mattered.

I know men have the ability, and right, to watch ~~unsafe~~ bareback sex videos without ever practicing it in their real lives and I know that sex is between two people having it. But this is more than that. This is more than just sex.

This is taking a stand. Slowing down, knowing your risks, communicating, wearing a condom—all of that is taking a stand! This is yet another person putting their foot down, swimming upstream in his *own* fetish-based event and declaring he will no longer participate or facilitate in the growing complacency toward unsafe sex in the gay community and HIV/AIDS. This is yet another person who actually cares how their actions impact a younger generation.[13]

Even on Web sites such as Leatherati.com, a well-known site dedicated to leather and BDSM enthusiasts, there was support for the decision to ban bareback porn vendors. Steve Lenius, for example, wrote that "[t]his announcement set off a firestorm of discussion. Is it censorship? (No.) Will it drive barebacking underground, thereby making it more attractive because it's forbidden? (I hope not.)" Lenius defended Chuck Renslow, referring to him as a community leader: "[T]his is exactly what community leaders ought to be doing, and I applaud Renslow and IML for having the courage and the willingness to take such a public stand, even when it could seriously and negatively affect the IML organization's finances. This is what leadership looks like, folks."[14]

Not all opinions sided with IML and/or Renslow or agreed there was a need to ban bareback porn. Contradictory opinions were expressed on Leatherati, for example. While Lenius and others expressed support for the IML decision, commentators like Editor in Chief of Leatherati, Loren Berthelsen, had varying opinions on the matter. Berthelsen took a moderate, though decisive, stance on the subject: "So did Chuck and the IML Executive Committee make the right decision? We wish we could say yes, however we think it was absolutely the wrong decision motivated by all the right reasons." Berthelsen provides other potential actions the IML Executive Committee could have taken such as creating a "hot, sexy education effort around barebacking issues. And NOT one that only advocates glove love and ignores reality," because, as he says of people in the BDSM world, "when we see someone doing something badly we usually try and teach them the right way to do it, not pretend they're not doing it."[15]

Renowned leather writer Race Bannon also weighed in on the discussion via Leatherati. While he believed the actions behind the prohibition were well intentioned, he disagreed with the actions taken. He argued "there is a place for meaningful HIV prevention at IML (and other similar venues), but it can only be taken in an atmosphere of accepting reality and nonjudgmental engagement with those who might take in such messages." He also questioned denigration of barebacking as a sexual practice. Serosorting, or the practice of engaging in sexual behavior with someone who is (or is thought to be) of the same HIV status, is one practice he discusses. Though based on anecdotal evidence, Bannon writes, "Based on my interactions with countless gay leathermen, I believe, with rare exception, this practice [barebacking] is taking place between HIV+ men. Yes, I know there are negative men who have chosen to accept the risk of barebacking with other negative men. And yes, there are the occasional negative 'bug chasers' who actively try to seroconvert. But I contend the vast majority of barebacking takes place between positive men."[16]

Like a number of other commentators, Bannon questions what other avenues the Executive Committee of IML could have taken to avoid outright prohibition of vendors deemed to be promoting barebacking. "What if IML had taken all this energy and done something different?" he asks, listing a number of potential options including having safer-sex educators staff booths with porn companies, providing extensive literature on barebacking to everyone who registers for the event, or providing private spaces for safer sex educators to speak with individuals confidentially. Bannon concludes that "instead they chose what I consider the 'easy way out.' Just say no. No discussion. No community engagement."[17] The alternative modes of addressing the topic of barebacking at IML that Bannon offers are fairly representative of many suggestions I found during the course of my research. Other arguments depended heavily on the characterization of the IML decision as a form of censorship.

And yet, as Bannon also notes, the censorship is not total. "I also wonder if IML's policy extends to older vintage porn," Bannon asks. "It was all raw fucking. Is any vendor selling older porn also to be excluded? What about vintage imagery from leather eras past? Since they were captured or drawn in the time of universal barebacking, do they 'promote' barebacking?" Here, Bannon uses the more current and widespread definition of "barebacking" as simply condomless sex. As I have noted, however, the history of the practice and its linkages to pornographic productions are more complex. The IML policy did not seem to extend to "older vintage porn." Whereas the decision to ban bareback porn (and other "promotions" of the practice) prevented a number of vendors from selling their wares, my 2010 fieldwork at the IML Leather Market revealed that those selling precondom porn, including Bijou Video, were permitted to have a continued presence at the event. Thus, the date of original production and its symbolic relationship to HIV/AIDS appears to be of critical importance.

IML is only one example of the industrial differentiation of bareback and precondom gay porn. Titan Media, a well-known gay porn studio, issued a statement denouncing bareback porn, seemingly unconnected to the IML decision. In it they state that any model who previously appeared in bareback films would no longer be eligible to work at Titan. The company also chimed in regarding the status of precondom films, offering their support:

> These films were produced at a time when sex without condoms was not a life threatening behavior. In the same manner that mainstream films of the 1950's and 1960's feature cigarette smoking, but yet are still widely distributed and enjoyed, we will continue to support the availability of 'Pre-condom' adult features . . . Today's 'bareback' films depict and eroticize high risk behavior as the centerpiece of their sensuality—risking HIV is the fetish and foundation of these presentations. We find this to be reprehensible and an attempt to profit at the risk of the health and safety of performers and the community at large.[18]

Working under the premise that bareback porn is a genre distinct from precondom porn, Titan Media sees the latter as a safer genre in terms of its position to HIV/AIDS. Titan's statement becomes problematic, however, under closer scrutiny. The studio's statement that "sex without condoms in these 'pre-condom' features was not a health hazard" is somewhat misleading. Ignorance about the sexual modes of HIV transmission certainly did become a health hazard, both within and outside the pornographic industry; a great number of adult film actors contracted the virus on set. And even though the mainstream gay porn industry was quick to adopt mandatory condom use policies for its actors, there was a considerable lag between known modes of sexual transmission and the instatement of these policies. It was not until the early 1990s that most mainstream gay porn studios began enforcing mandatory condom use among actors, because, as Escoffier writes, early on in the epidemic "porn producers seemed loath to accept the limits imposed on gay men's sexuality by HIV/AIDS."[19]

There are important thematic and stylistic differences between precondom and bareback porn, including the eroticization of risk, as Titan Media proclaims; but it should come as no surprise that actors engaging in condomless anal sex in precondom films made in the 1970s and 1980s were at risk of contracting HIV, regardless of whether it was a known risk at the time. From the perspective of the viewer several decades later there remains the haunting specter of HIV/AIDS in classic films like *One in a Billion* and *A Few Good Men.*[20] Though the typical viewer will not likely know which actors were infected on screen (or even off), or what scenes present a visual record of a moment of transmission, the possibility of transmission is indeed there. As with bareback porn, the reason precondom porn maintains its erotic charge is at least partly due to the risk involved. Though also marketed as vintage and classic gay porn, the fact that the genre is so often referred to as "precondom" heightens the importance of HIV/AIDS in critical discussions of these films.

So why is it that this genre is treated differently in terms of its relation to HIV controversies? Although the reasons are multiple and complex, one factor is the conflicting roles precondom porn generates as a historical archive of sexual fantasies and practices, nostalgia for a more innocent past, and queer men's confrontation with issues regarding HIV/AIDS today.

IGNORANCE IS BLISS: NOSTALGIA, HISTORY, AND PORN

In my research I have encountered two dominant perspectives on the "essence" of porn. The first conceptualizes porn as a purely fantastic venture. In other words, porn is meant to give fantasy some kind of tangible representational form. Pornography is an artistic project intended to incite erotic responses in the spectator. The second perspective, as epitomized by directors such as Paul Morris, understands porn in documentary terms. Morris, for example, is a widely controversial figure in the porn industry because he films some of the most extreme sexual practices that exist in gay male porn.[21] Discussed at length in Dean's account of bareback porn, Dean likens Morris to a visual anthropologist, whose films serve as an archival record of the actual and preferred sexual practices among distinct populations of gay men.

Precondom porn from the 1970s and 1980s functions today in a similar way. These films, viewed and understood several decades after their production, act as a sexual documentary of the times. This by itself is nothing unusual; all films, to one degree or another, are documents of their times, and of the artistic, fantastic, or realistic trends of their days. What makes precondom porn special can be found in the name of the genre: The entire cinematic subspecies acts as a temporal index. These films document a time when gay men were able to live sexual lives without the fear of sex equating death. Actors enjoyed a certain level of security and privilege not afforded to actors today; a privilege of ignorance. For a number of years, the modes of HIV transmission were not well understood; and even when semen was revealed to be one source of transmission, many studios held off on mandating condom use among actors. These early years reflect a period of time in which those in the industry were aware of the risk, but continued to shoot condomless sex.

Precondom porn compels the viewer to remember a past that blends elements of reality and fiction. These films are structured narratives. They make use of stock characters, plots, and environments. They build upon fantasies and fetishes, but they also depict actual sexual acts. The films that remain with us today thus provide celluloid and digital archives of real sex acts carrying with them a valence of death. Precondom porn indexes a time when sex between men did not automatically mean engaging in practices that involved a conscious risk of contracting HIV. At the same time, I suggest that these films cannot be understood without noting how HIV/AIDS haunts the frame. In other words, precondom porn gains its status as a different kind of genre by invoking the specter of HIV/AIDS, while these films simultaneously create nostalgia for a past.

Despite any attempts to engage in what gay novelist Zea Miller calls "amnesic nostalgia," precondom porn is all about history. For culturally marginalized populations such as gay men, a sense of collective history is often tenuous. Except in unique contexts, we are not taught gay history at home or in school. Even at the university, it is not uncommon for gay historians to struggle in offering courses in queer history and culture. In many universities, explicitly antiqueer activism has arisen—together with antisex activism generally—to prevent such courses from being offered. Many queer people today learn their history and culture in nonstandardized ways, including through pornography. As Jeffrey Escoffier claims, "gay pornography contributes to the education of desire—it provides knowledge of the body and of sexual narratives, and examples of gay sexuality and of sexuality within a masculine framework. Since most gay men have become adults without having been socialized in the social and sexual codes of their communities, pornography can contribute to that as well."[22]

Pornography is by no means a complete resource for history—or a comprehensive means of sex education. But, at the very least, pornography provides a window into commercialized sexual fantasies in particular eras and among specific communities. The fantasies dispersed through the market clearly depend on who had the opportunity, capital, and desire to make porn and how those people chose to represent gay male sexuality. For early gay porn producers, such as Wakefield Poole or Chuck Renslow, artistic vision and legal restrictions structured what was possible to create and disseminate for public consumption.[23]

But what can be said about the ethics viewing porn made in an era before HIV was known to exist? When engaging in a spectatorial fantasy that simultaneously backgrounds yet occludes HIV as an eroticizing force, how do we reconcile the need to accept the presence of HIV as a fact of life (and death), yet ignore its potential presence in the film? Again, for most viewers of precondom porn the HIV status of the actors is neither known nor necessarily a concern. And yet there remains the fact that performers such as John Holmes, who died from complications from HIV/AIDS, were acting in porn while infected.[24] While the onscreen narratives are works of fiction, the potential consequences of HIV infection are real. In a way, then, the story continues for the actors off-camera. Given that pornography incorporates elements of fantasy and reality, the relationship between spectator and screen becomes all the more complicated.

In viewing precondom porn, the typical viewer is likely to ignore the potential yet invisible presence of the virus. This invisibility, both literal and metaphorical, allows for a guiltless form of viewing. Whether the film in question was recorded before or after 1981 is somewhat irrelevant. The gay porn industry did not begin to have a strong commercial face until the 1970s at the earliest, and because HIV and other sexually transmitted infections were being unknowingly transmitted at this time en masse,[25] there still exists a chance that it was circulating on porn sets. In viewing precondom pornography outside of its orgasmic aims and instead as a form of sexual archive, we may begin to pay homage to a period of gay history that many would rather we leave in the past.

For queer men, the primary mode of HIV transmission has long been sexual; and yet despite actions taken to prevent new transmissions, assist those living with the virus, and remember those who have lost their lives to AIDS, as a culture we have set the actual modes of transmission apart as an untouchable topic of visual representation. Depicting the movement of HIV from one body to another has largely been prohibited. Aside from early bareback porn, where the explicit depiction of men with signs of having HIV are shown inseminating other men with all its sociopolitical dimensions, the notion of potential transmission on camera is utterly denied—hence the ability of precondom porn to maintain its protected status in light of more restrictive regulations.

Rather than censoring our interpretations or the actual films themselves, I propose a direct engagement with precondom pornographic images on their own terms. It is not a stretch to note that the point of porn is to facilitate orgasm. But that is not its only possible use. By viewing precondom films in historical perspective, we can take in more than just what is offered on the surface. Precondom pornography is an archive of the sexual inclinations, fictions, and realities of their time; its continued presence in our lives bears even more importance in the context of HIV/AIDS.

When we allow ourselves to recognize the potential presence of HIV when watching such films, we also allow ourselves to inhabit a place of cultural pain. We must recognize not only the erotic joys present on screen but also the haze of potential death. Bareback porn produced decades later originally had this goal in mind. By prohibiting the circulation of recorded acts of condomless sex between men who might be living with HIV, a direct statement was being made about the ways in which our society views HIV-positive people—as being unworthy of living sexually autonomous and fulfilling lives and engaging in the same forms of sexual expression on camera as men supposedly living without HIV.

The social and political consequences of actions like those taken by IML, various porn studios, and myriad cultural commentators contribute to a culture in which the HIV virus is looked at with contempt—and so, too, are the bodies of those infected. By distancing precondom and bareback gay porn from one another under the guise of public health concerns, we obscure the longer history of HIV. The virus, present or not, ought not dictate who is permitted to be represented in pornographic film. Embracing both genres on sexual and social levels, gives respect to those living with HIV in the past and today, even when our ultimate goal is to end its grip on our lives in the future.

NOTES

1. On June 17, 2012, the City Council of Los Angeles passed a proposed ordinance to require condom use during vaginal and anal sex on all porn sets within the city's domain. In order to receive a permit to record commercial pornographic film in Los Angeles, producers must now require actors to wear condoms, provide water-based or silicone-based personal lubricant, and may be subject to additional fees to pay for on-set inspectors who ensure compliance with the ordinance. The ordinance gained national attention and called into question the practicality and usefulness of such city-level laws. Workplace safety regulations applied to adult film actors is the primary motive mentioned in favor of the law. Those opposing the law note a discomfort with what can be described as a biopolitical intervention and increased state regulation of sexuality. Others, however, have also raised concern about the actual practical implementation of the law. Whether this will drive porn companies to leave Los Angeles remains to be seen.

2. This pattern has been noted by Tim Dean, *Unlimited Intimacy: Reflections on the Subculture of Barebacking* (Chicago: University of Chicago Press, 2009); Jeff Escoffier, *Bigger than Life: The History of Gay Porn Cinema from Beefcake to Hardcore* (Philadelphia: Running Press, 2009); Casey McKittrick, "Brothers' Milk: The Erotic and the Lethal in Bareback Pornography" in *Porn: Philosophy for Everyone: How to Think with Kink*, ed. Dave Monroe (Malden, MA: Wiley-Blackwell, 2010), 66–78.

3. Casey McKittrick (2010), 69.

4. This practice is noted by both McKittrick and Dean, the latter in his controversial, yet important book, *Unlimited Intimacy: Reflections on the Subculture of Barebacking* (2009). See Endnote 1 above.

5. Linda Williams, *Hard Core: Power, Pleasure, and the "Frenzy of the Visible"* (Berkeley, CA: University of California Press, 1989).

6. A variety of mixtures are known to have been employed such as combining water, flour, cornstarch, milk, and methylcellulose (a chemical used, for example, to make the slime in the *Ghostbusters* films). Computer-generated semen has even been used in many pornographic images to create or enhance its presence before the eye.

Personal lubricants have also been marketed to gay men that look and feel like actual semen. These products appear to be enjoying some level of success, both in the bedroom and on the film set.

7. Elsie Reynolds, "'Pass the Cream, Hold the Butter': Meanings of HIV Positive Semen for Bugchasers and Giftgivers," *Anthropology and Medicine* 14, no. 4 (2007): 259–66.

8. Centers for Disease Control and Prevention, "Basic Statistics – HIV Basics," Centers for Disease Control and Prevention, http://www.cdc.gov/hiv/basics/statistics. html.

9. Dean (2009), 105.

10. Ibid.,110.

11. Chuck Renslow, "Vendor Policy Change for 2010," International Mr. Leather, http://www.imrl.com /downloads/vendorforms.php.

12. Will Clark, "IML Makes History," *Will Clark World*, http://willclarkworld. typepad.com /will_clark_world/2009/07/iml-makes-history.html.

Care has been taken to re-create all blog citations verbatim. All nonstandard grammatical practices appear in the original.

13. Eric Leven, "Bareback the Fuck Up!" *Knucklecrack*, http://knucklecrack. blogspot.ca /2009/07/bareback-fuck-up.html.

14. Steve Lenius, "IML Says Bye Bye to Barebacking," *Lavender Magazine*, 2013, http://www.lavendermagazine.com/our-lives/iml-says-bye-bye-barebacking/?doing_ wp_cron=1348514659.0811560153961181640625.

15. Loren Berthelsen, "The Three Little Bares," *Leatherati*, http://www.leatherati. com/ leatherati_issues/2010/05/the-three-little-bares.html.

16. Race Bannon, "The Raw Controversy," *Leatherati*, http://www.leatherati.com /leatherati_issues/2010/05/the-raw-controversy.html.

17. Ibid.

18. Bruce Cam, Keith Webb, Harold Creg, and Brian Mills, "Titan Media Public Policy Statement—'Bareback' or High Risk Behavior," *Titan Media*, http://www.titan-media.com/promo-images/public/NEWS/pages/barebacking.pdf.

19. Jeffrey Escoffier (2010), 187.

20. *One in a Billion*, directed by Al Parker (1984; Chicago: Bijou Classics, 2013); *A Few Good Men*, dir. Steve Scott (1983; Surge Studio).

21. Morris's studio, Treasure Island Media (TIM), was founded in 1997 and released its first commercial feature-length film, *Raunch Lunch*, the following year. As of 2012, TIM has released over one hundred films, including *Dawson's 50 Load Weekend*, *The 1,000 Load Fuck*, and *Breeding Season*, as well as several series like *Drunk on Cum*, *Plantin' Seed*, and *Ass Stretchers*. Among the more extreme acts depicted is a scene in which a Tupperware container, filled with the semen of numerous men who are shown ejaculating into it, is poured into a funnel positioned in the anus of a young man. The semen is then released and enters the mouth of another man (for a more detailed description and analysis of this scene, see Dean 2009, 138–40). In online social networking profiles, TIM provides a chronology of film releases together with other important events. Among these are notations of TIM being banned from

the 2009 Folsom Street Fair and Dore Alley—both leather and fetish street fairs held annually in San Francisco (see also Witchka 2009). In 2011, the company was fined by the California Occupational Safety and Health Administration. The acknowledgment of these incidents indicates at least desire on TIM's part to call attention to the ways in which barebacking and transgressive porn are subjected to social and legal regimes regulating what may be deemed legitimate forms of sexuality.

22. Jeffrey Escoffier, "Gay-for-Pay: Straight Men and the Making of Gay Pornography," *Qualitative Sociology* 26, no. 4 (2003): 536.

23. Wakefield Poole is among the most important figures in the history of gay male video porn production. His 1971 surrealist pornographic film *Boys in the Sand* gained popularity in mainstream film, making it one of the first pornographic films to cross such a threshold. Chuck Renslow was also a leading figure in the history of gay pornography. Primarily dedicated to still photography, Renslow founded a number of businesses catering to sexually explicit imagery of men, including the physique photography from Kris Studios and *Mars Magazine*, the latter largely considered to be the first gay leather magazine.

24. Actors with HIV during the precondom era were engaging in condomless sex on camera typically without knowledge of their HIV status.

25. William J. Woods and Diane Binson, "Public Health Policy and Gay Bathhouses," *Journal of Homosexuality* 44, no. 3–4 (2003): 2.

21

Ambient XXX: Pornography in Public Spaces

Ryan Bowles Eagle

In this chapter, I examine the diverse manifestations and uses of pornography in public spaces. There is a strong tendency to deem certain media technologies and forms as being inherently private or domestic. Among these are the television apparatus and pornography, and yet both also have important public histories that media scholars have begun to recognize. An important example of this is Anna McCarthy's *Ambient Television: Visual Culture and Public Space*, in which she calls for extending the study of the television apparatus beyond the domestic space.[1] McCarthy's reconceptualization of the ambient television screen as both ubiquitous and socially transformative has significant implications for porn studies. As with other modes and genres of media, pornography is exhibited and viewed in public spaces on a number of devices that, collectively, I refer to as *ambient porn screens*. While public pornography is neither a new nor uncommon phenomenon, as it becomes more recognized, it is met with impassioned discourses of shock and panic that play upon anxieties about the protection of children and the common good. These discourses emphasize the social dangers of pornography, and are largely characterized by calls for regulation that are rooted in false and inflexible notions of public and private. What I demonstrate in this chapter is that ambient porn screens are neither as new nor dangerous as they have been framed in popular discourse. Instead, the outcry over porn in public spaces arises from the lack of an ethical code covering the use of mobile devices in public; these concerns extend beyond porn viewing to a larger practice of conducting personal affairs on mobile devices in loud, highly visible ways. And most important for my arguments here, such efforts to control and render invisible displays of sexuality primarily arise when those displays are perceived as a threat to normative heterosexuality, and even when they serve a communal function among adult participants.

I argue that porn studies should be expanded to better encompass the diverse ways of looking at pornography, challenging its dominant conceptualization as a private viewing experience. Though media consumers may certainly experience pornography as intimate, that intimacy can also be tied with or shared with other people, connecting individuals rather than isolating them from one another. While popular press coverage tends to focus on anecdotes that best garner support for panic-driven regulation efforts, there are other concerns to be addressed. In order to best ensure equal access to public resources for technology and information, and protect adult communal spaces, it is important to examine the classist assumptions and normalizing discourses that pervade calls against porn in public. In order to support my claims, I analyze three very different contexts for ambient porn screens: (1) the mobile "anywhere" created by digital devices including smartphones, tablets, and laptops; (2) the public library; and (3) a gay leather-fetish bar in Los Angeles. Before examining these three sites individually, I map out some of the important scholarly work that prompts recognition that, despite recent panic about its role in public life, pornography has never really just been private.

PRIVATE VERSUS PUBLIC

The majority of the moral outcry around public porn centers on the claims (both implicit and explicit) that: (1) private and public can be clearly defined in simple opposition to one another and (2) pornography has a history of belonging in the private/domestic realm. To address the first point, it is important to recognize that notions of public and private are far from neutral. Rather, the decision of who and what to relegate to the private realm is intertwined with social power. Assumptions about who should be allowed visibility on a public stage and a voice in public discourses align with intersectional privileges possessed or challenges faced by certain genders, ages, ethnicities, and social classes.

Scholars such as Lynn Spigel have worked to reveal the gendered nature of "public" and "private," taking valuable steps toward undoing the constructed separations between the two realms of media studies. In her introduction to *Welcome to the Dreamhouse*, Spigel notes that ideological distinctions between public and private spaces coincide with ideological distinctions between "high" and "low" arts; hence, television has historically been devalued as a low art. McCarthy shows the ways that television was misconstrued as belonging solely to the domestic sphere. In deeming porn private, it is also deemed low art (or not art at all). While the categories public and private may seem stable in any one cultural moment, they are actually quite flexible, each with its own unique histories in which visibility has been differentially allowed for particular identities.[2] With regard to the claim that porn has always been private and thus should remain so, film scholar Linda Williams has made significant contributions to the historiography of public porn.

In *Hard Core: Power, Pleasure, and the Frenzy of the Visible,* Williams's examination focuses on several historical moments for the ambient porn screen, from the earliest "stag film" exhibitions that arrived with the beginnings of motion picture film, to the adult arcades where Super 8 mm porn films were projected on the wall, to the "Golden Age" of pornographic narrative films being screened in cinema theaters, the pinnacle of which was the 1972 release of *Deep Throat.*[3] Williams's work reveals that alongside the history of mainstream/Hollywood cinema, public pornography has followed its own—and not entirely separate—historical path. Some public screenings of pornography, such as stag films, were explicitly tied to shared social rituals. Williams cites Al Di Lauro and Gerald Rabkin, who describe stag film screenings as characterized by "collective banter and bravado," and frame the primary pleasure of the gatherings as the formation of a "gender-based bond with other male spectators."[4] Williams's chapter on the stag film refers to the illicit public screenings as both Genital *Show* and Genital *Event.*[5] By choosing to use the word "event," she highlights the social interaction involved in the viewing of the "silent, one-reel, illegally made and exhibited" stag film.[6] Unlike mainstream films whose narrative was often intended to satisfy spectators, the stag film, Williams asserts, does not aim to achieve sexual satisfaction. Instead, Williams argues, "its role seems rather to arouse and then precisely *not* to satisfy a spectator," but to leave the spectator in a state where satisfaction must be sought elsewhere, often by "channeling sexual arousal into communal wisecracking or verbal ejaculation of the 'homosocial' variety."[7] Di Lauro and Rabkin argue that these bonding rituals also served an instructive, and self-affirming purpose: "By sharing the mysteries of sexual data through collective rituals of masculine emergence, American and European males . . . received through the stags a non-credit course in sexual education."[8]

Public porn exhibition also has its history in the adult arcade, where patrons would watch films in a loop from side-by-side booths, encouraged to feed coins for continued viewing time. In the arcade the viewing experience was more cut off from the surroundings of the public space than in the stag screenings, and thus more individualized. Still, the arcade was far from private, often resulting in what Scott MacDonald refers to as a sort of "shared embarrassment" between viewers.[9] In the 1970s, pornography's "Golden Era," feature-length pornographic films were screened openly in theaters where, shielded only by the darkness and illuminated by the flickering of the projection, viewers again sat and watched side by side. For Williams, these historical sites demonstrate the differential development of porn viewing practices, which have always been private and public, not one or the other. Citing the emergence of "more private and furtive way(s) of experiencing hard core," Williams also attends to the "relatively open mode of viewing for the new feature-length pornos as well."[10]

Williams's scholarship, in conversation with other historians of pornographic media, demonstrates that public pornography is not a recent phenomenon. And yet, it seems likely that the intensity of the protest and panic that public pornography inspires must in some way be attributed to a cultural change. I propose that while the sale, exhibition, and consumption of pornography in public is not new, what is new is the level of accessibility of a wide array of pornography at home, via the Internet. With a massive library of pornographic content now easily in reach for those with high-speed Internet access, the cultural expectation has shifted: now, it is largely assumed that because porn can be private, it should be private. But this logic is exclusionary, assuming the only people who should be watching porn are those who have both the means and the desire to watch it privately, a designation that obscures class-based issues of access to technology as well as community rights to shared media rituals. The following examinations of porn in the bar, porn in the library, and porn that travels "anywhere" via mobile technology illustrate the ways in which the declaration that porn can (and should) be private obscures the very complexities of where and why ambient porn screens exist.

ANYWHERE XXX: AMBIENT PORN SCREENS GO MOBILE

Since the advent of the first 3G smartphones, the adult industry has been working to make its content available to users of mobile technologies, touting these devices as "the ultimate sex machine for personal portable pleasure."[11] Industry heads saw big moneymaking potential if they could seamlessly merge pornographic content with what were fast becoming our most personal devices—devices that in many ways enabled people to feel and act in public space as if they were alone.

In the early 2000s, *Adult Video News* (AVN), imagined porn's "portable future," urging "forward-thinking Webmasters to contemplate this coming shift in the wind, if not actually [to set] sail to catch it."[12] Such articles served as both friendly tip and an implicit threat; those who did not take interest in porn's mobile possibilities would find themselves left in the dust. One article cites Stephanie Schwab, CEO of Erotigo.com, who says, "If you think back to '93, the people who aren't interested in this [smartphone technology] now are like the people who said no to web back then. They were all wrong." The article later stresses, "Be forewarned. Find a great partner and pay attention."[13] Smartphone manufacturers have been successful in promoting the smartphone as the first communications device capable of becoming one with its user, a conception that aligns well with assumptions of porn viewing as private and intimate. AVN called the smartphone "the truly personal device the computer really isn't,"[14] and in 2005 AVN predicted that "as the one device that a consumer carries with him or her 24 hours a day, a mobile phone has been positioned as able to offer the most far-reaching yet most intimate experience the adult industry has ever witnessed."[15] For producers of pornographic content, this utopian discourse of privatized mobility represented a gold mine.

The hope that the adult industry placed in mobile media technologies mirrors the utopian discourses that tend to follow the emergence of new media technologies in general. For instance, media scholar Lynn Spigel addresses the utopian discourses surrounding the release of an earlier mobile technology, the portable television. Spigel notes a shift from the home television as a "window on the world" to the portable television as "a vehicular form, a mode of transport in and of itself," a technology that was able to free the user from the boundaries of place.[16] Spigel's earlier visions for portable television are now compounded by the emergence of laptop computers, tablets, and smartphones. Spigel demonstrates how much mobile media technologies have reconfigured understandings of public and private space, resulting in what she calls the "privatization of public space," and providing users with a version of "portable public privacy."[17]

But these visions of liberation were contradicted by dystopian fears of isolation and disconnectedness that also accompany mobile media technologies. The same elements of the mobile phone user's experience that Spigel characterized as freedom are framed by media scholars Gary Gumpert and Susan Drucker as displacement and *a-location*.[18] They note that media technologies have enabled individuals to shift their attention inward, even in public, dramatically changing social interaction.[19] Gumpert and Drucker envision that with such transformation new challenges will arise for those concerned with maintenance of communities and the "regulation and design of places facing transformation by mobile media."[20] Gerard Goggin argues that mobile devices can incite a moral panic similar to those associated with pornography; while the panic is not new, the smartphone presents "new pathways for the circulation of anxieties."[21]

These anxieties surrounding the mobile ambient porn screen gained prominence in recent years when the introduction of both 3G technology and onboard Wi-Fi allowed airline passengers to access and view their personal viewing choices. Since air travel became available to the general public, it has been associated with both physical and social mobility.[22] But in a post-9/11 climate, air travel has transitioned from symbolizing ideologies of freedom and movement to surveillance and control, leaving travelers nostalgic for an imagined time when air travel was about freedom. In "Stripping for the State: Whole Body Imaging Technologies and the Surveillance of Othered Bodies," Shoshana Magnet and Tara Rodgers debunk this nostalgia, arguing that it was Americans' "romance with flying" that began in the 1920s that masked and thus enabled practices by which government and industry restricted access to flight and implemented highly regulated, carefully choreographed practices to manage travelers.[23] By this logic, today's intense governmental control over air travel is not new, but rather part of a much longer lineage of the surveillance and discipline of bodies, which have been largely disguised through discourses of freedom and mobility. In other words, to retain the freedom to travel via plane, passengers give up control over many things they would never dream of under normal circumstances. This interplay between imagined freedom and lived experience of surveillance sets the complex context for the mobile ambient porn screen.

American Airlines was among the first to make Wi-Fi available on its transcontinental flights. Though the airline announced that it only planned to provide Internet access for a trial period at first, even that initial attempt caused quite a stir, inciting much debate, almost all of which surrounded the topic of pornography.[24] Around that time, I was boarding a Delta flight to a conference at the University of Notre Dame (during which I was to present my work on the ambient porn screen), and found that the airline's newly available onboard wireless was fittingly named "Go-Go." The airline employee who enthusiastically shared with me the features of the new service declined to be interviewed; when I pointed out Go-Go's coincidental double entendre, she was not amused. While some airlines, such as Jet Blue, did employ filters on their flights from an early stage, American Airlines decided to leave the pornography issue for the flight attendants to deal with. Immediately after its planes went online, representatives from the union asked why the role of porn regulator should fall on the flight attendant: "Why should [flight attendants] be put in the position to police, [to] deal with the people offended and in a position to view objectionable people in their workplace?"[25] Amid speculation came fears over the exposure of children to pornography, and the question of how to protect them. One letter to American Airlines from an antiporn organization took issue "with the fact that children and passengers might be exposed to pornography in the already cramped quarters of the plane."[26]

In the initial months of its first Wi-Fi trial, American Airlines was sued by a passenger for allowing porn to enter the in-flight space. The passenger sued for $200,000 alleging that, "while resting they awoke to find a substance in their hair from another passenger who was allegedly masturbating."[27] This story of airplane wireless gone horribly wrong would be capable of causing disgust in most individuals. Such "gross-out" anecdotes surrounding the ambient porn screen are precisely the sort to rally citizens around regulation of the mobile porn screen. As of October 2008, American Airlines decided to ban Internet pornography during flights, and was working with an outside software company to implement filtering technology.[28] American Airlines' debacle over wireless Internet access and porn is just one of many recent debates that negotiate the utopian visions of limitless access to the Web through mobile devices with the dystopian fears that tend to accompany pornography's rupture of public space.[29]

Adult industry professionals described early adopters of smartphone porn as being few, but devoted.[30] Even porn industry trade magazines seemed ignorant of pornography's public history, with articles expressing doubts as to the comfort level required to view porn in public space. These moments of anxiety were generally glossed over with reassurances about massive profit potential and a fast-growing adult industry sector, and yet their mere presence reveals notable anxieties. One contributor worries, "With the Internet having become the ultimate place to match anonymity with sizzling pictures and video, it might be hard to believe anyone would want to take their porn habits mobile."[31] Here, the logic again emerges that because pornography viewing can be private, everyone must prefer that privacy. An article that AVN pulled from Forbes.com likewise acknowledges, "Not everyone is convinced that portability is that much of a plus when it comes to porn. Even if you can watch Jenna Jameson on an airplane or in a doctor's waiting room, that doesn't mean you'll feel comfortable doing so." In addition to ignoring the history of public and communal porn viewing practices, this article also noticeably relies upon assumptions of an intended purpose for pornography, concluding that, "Practically speaking . . . [the mobile device is] never going to supplant any kind of large-screen home format."[32]

Even the adult industry's speculations about early-adopters of smartphone technology demonstrate the underlying assumption that if it is possible to watch porn in private, privacy is preferable. By generalizing and thus over-simplifying the possible motivations people have for watching porn, the industry fails to account for viewers who take pleasure in viewing pornography in public and with others. The motivations for and meanings of the ambient porn screen are diverse. Yes, there are people who would watch porn in small public spaces simply because they can, and because they genuinely do not care about the comfort or preferences of the people around them. But there are also people who yell into their devices in a library or doctor's waiting room, and who continue their cell phone conversations once they have reached the front of the line at a coffee shop. There are inconsiderate ambient porn viewers, but not all ambient porn screens can be attributed to such a lack of consideration. In the following section, I argue that if we set aside moral judgment, pornography becomes one kind of media content among many that are differentially accessible based on social class and income. In keeping with this, public librarians, who are known to be advocates for free and equal access to information, have been at the forefront of a discussion surrounding the use of library computers as ambient porn screens.

ACCESS, AFFORDABILITY, ANONYMITY: THE CASE OF THE PUBLIC LIBRARY

My second site for examination of ambient porn screens is the public library. While an online identity and participation in online spaces are now in many ways requirements for active citizenry, there are very few places where all people, regardless of financial means, can access the Internet. The public library is one of those remaining places. The public library is a community space, but it is certainly not without its share of rules. Users are provided with resources at no cost, and in turn they are expected to abide by community codes (such as the silencing of cell phones, refraining from eating, etc.). Public libraries operate on the principles of freedom of information and equal access, yet they are also committed to serving as a welcoming space for everyone, including children, and the maintenance of "community standards," however difficult to define.[33] And so, when a member chooses to view pornography on the library's shared computers, several of the institution's core values are put at odds with one another.

These tensions became apparent as I began to speak with librarians around Los Angeles, California. "Oh, there's a *lot* of porn watching going on," one library clerk at the Will and Ariel Durant Library, located in Hollywood, told me. I followed her gaze to the rows of computers next to us; they were surprisingly busy, I thought, for early Monday afternoon. The librarian shared that when she first began working in the library, she had walked past the computers and saw a man looking at pornography. Concerned, she quickly told her supervisor but was informed that there was nothing for her to do. As long as this man was not breaking the rules of the Los Angeles Public Library system's "code of conduct" (e.g., looking at anything illegal), the staff would respect his privacy.[34] In her discussion of porn in the public library, librarian Sue Banks notes, "Libraries embraced the internet with great zeal in the 1990's," and still provide no-cost Internet access to those who cannot afford computers or an Internet connection of their own.[35] No-cost Internet has likewise meant no-cost streaming of pornography for some patrons. *Adult Video News* has closely followed public debates surrounding the ambient porn screen's presence in the library. These debates have tended to reflect larger cultural divides over censorship versus free access to information and whether to protect community standards or individual rights. Public institutions, in particular when funded by taxpayer dollars, raise difficult questions about whose desires they should prioritize. Is the library's ambient porn screen a symbol of how "morally bankrupt" people have become, or is its presence a reminder that the library is the most "democratic" space left? Banks describes the library as "the last bastion of freedom of thought in an aggressively conservative society bent on moral homogeneity."[36] In 1999, the American Civil Liberties Union (ACLU) demonstrated its own commitment to protect institutional freedom in the debate over library porn. A concerned parent (identified only as "Kathleen R.") filed a law suit against the Livermore Public Library in Virginia; Kathleen R. argued that the library's "open net access" had created a "public nuisance," and later added that libraries "'have a constitutional obligation' to protect minors from pornography by blocking *all patrons'* Net access."[37] The Virginia federal appeals court did not agree, however, finding that a library's blocking software violated free speech, in particular because imperfections in the software resulted in the blocking of not only porn Web sites but also nonporn sites as well, including the *San Francisco Chronicle* and the American Association of University Women. AVN celebrated this win for the porn industry, quoting staff attorney for the ACLU, Ann Beeson, who said at the time that the Livermore Library Board recognized "that requiring the use of blocking software in libraries creates, rather than solves, constitutional problems."

Libraries have faced significant pressures to install porn filters on its computers, often in the form of monetary reward or punishment. For example, in 2003, the Supreme Court approved Congress's Children's Internet Protection Act (CIPA). CIPA mandates that public libraries install "anti-porn filtering software" on their computers or "lose federal funds for technology," playing upon fears for the safety of our children.[38] While CIPA does not explicitly require libraries to filter pornographic content, it puts libraries, which are already facing financial hardships, in a tough spot. CIPA uses the power of the federal dollar to strong-arm them into filtering, a practice that librarians would otherwise resist for a number of reasons. Refusing to filter would come at a high cost: in 2003, when the Act was put into law, "Federal grants to libraries for electronic access [were] in the neighborhood of $150 million annually."[39] According to Chief Justice William H. Rehnquist, "Public libraries' use of Internet filtering software does not violate their patron's First Amendment rights . . . [the CIPA] does not induce libraries to violate the Constitution, and is a valid exercise of Congress's spending power"; and so the legislation has been able to stand, with the FCC further updating and implementing the rules in 2011.[40]

Still, whether or not CIPA is constitutional, the question remains what exactly the filters can and should do. What is their role in limiting and regulating potentially pornographic content displayed on the library's ambient screens? In theory, the purpose of such filters would be to prevent pornography from making its way into the public space of the library. However, when the lower court in Philadelphia initially reviewed CIPA, it ruled against requiring what were referred to as "defective filters that block protected speech and don't filter all objectionable material." There are important technological limitations to consider. For instance, the filters are not actually capable of detecting material based on the graphic nature of images; also, they function primarily to weed out sites that are explicitly tagged as pornographic, lacking the capability to detect user-generated pornographic content placed on blogs or message boards. One librarian shared with me in an e-mail that filtering is "a much contested issue because filters don't work well and generally end up acting as a censorship technology (e.g., a patron needs to search for information on 'breast cancer' and has it blocked by the filter)." In what he described to me as a "well known case" among librarians, a patron "couldn't find information about Dick Cheney because the filter blocked the occurrence of 'Dick.'"[41] CIPA has forced librarians to choose between (1) limiting their patrons' access to information with a technology they know to be inherently flawed, or (2) losing valuable federal funding. It's a lose-lose decision. Banks poses this: "At the heart of the argument is the heart of democracy—what are citizens willing to sacrifice or compromise to live the life they choose? If Americans want Internet access in the public library, they're going to have to put up with a little porn. Even the best filters don't filter everything."[42]

Still, it is important to note that a refusal to install filters does not mean that a library relinquishes control over the content on its ambient screens. Indeed, libraries that choose not to abide by the CIPA and thus lose that federal funding often still employ nonfiltering strategies that serve to regulate porn viewing in the library. I separate these strategies into two main categories: (1) *user-driven*: those that prioritize the privacy of the user and the user's right to information and, ultimately, right to look at what he or she chooses and (2) *community-driven*: those that prioritize the protection of "community standards" within the library through diverse surveillance techniques intended to control patrons' viewing. While these two categories are certainly not entirely discrete, user-driven strategies tend to include installation of privacy screens and strategically hidden or masked computer monitors in an attempt to reduce the ambient nature of onscreen porn. I witnessed both of these strategies at work in my visits to the Central Library located in downtown Los Angeles. Privacy screens are useful insofar as they can shield the content of a user's computer screen from nearby onlookers—so long as the person looking on is not standing directly behind the user. Coupled with the library's privacy screens, I noticed that in several Internet computer areas, the screens were strategically turned on a diagonal away from the walkway, so much so that the user must work his or her body into what appears to be quite an awkward and uncomfortable position in order to view the content of the screen. This arrangement of the screens (and the resulting hidden-ness of their content) is markedly different from non-Internet (i.e., reference) computer screens in the library, which are often fully visible not only in each room, but also from the central escalators that provide a view of each floor through its glass windows. I asked a librarian on the History floor if she thought the computer arrangement was able to guarantee privacy to Internet users. She said that every effort was made to ensure that it was, expressing that patron privacy was a high priority for the library. As to why the monitors were all arranged at such a sharp diagonal angle on the desks, she replied that, to her knowledge, this was not the result of actions by the library staff but rather, that the patrons tended to place them that way.

While my visits to several Los Angeles Public Libraries confirmed librarians' commitment to protecting patron privacy and access, nonfiltering strategies used by other libraries reflect a different set of priorities—those that are perceived to best uphold the standards of the community within the space of the library. These strategies include having a librarian patrol the space on a regular basis, employing a shoulder-tap policy should he or she encounter a patron viewing porn.[43] The librarian's actions after the shoulder tap vary, ranging from logging the patron out of his or her Internet session from the librarian desk, to explaining to the patron why he or she was logged off and what is appropriate to view in the library (this applies primarily to young viewers), to writing up an incident report, to revoking the patron's library privileges and banning him or her from the library (this last tactic is generally reserved for repeat offenders).[44] However, librarians have argued that these workplace tasks lay outside their job description. For example, in the year 2000, the American Library Association's Director For Intellectual Freedom, Judith Krug, said that "to place criminal liability on those whose role it is not to serve as the Internet police, but to provide information, is inappropriate . . . a librarian's job is bringing people together with information and resources they can use."[45] In 2003, Minneapolis library officials had to pay "$435,000 to 'a dozen librarians,' to settle a lawsuit charging the presence of Net porn on library computers equaled a 'hostile' environment," an event that speaks to the risks involved for libraries that force librarians to act as porn police.[46]

Another strategy used by libraries is the careful arrangement of computers and screens to give the appearance of the constant possibility that their content could be seen by a librarian or fellow patron. During my research, I was provided with various opinions on whether or not this strategy works. One public librarian, who works for a small library in Massachusetts, describes how she perceives changes in computer arrangement and screen placement as having an apparent effect on the amount of porn watching:

> For a while there was a surge of looking at porn on the Internet, and the library went a long way to staunching the epidemic by facing all of the computer monitors in a direction where they *could be viewed* by a librarian or patron passing by. I think this is one of the most interesting things about public libraries and porn—something about a *collective conscience* being present keeps people from accessing those sites as much. It's not like the librarians patrol the computer lab . . . but having the monitors face out instead of away from the public makes a huge difference. Also, for a while the library had the kind of monitors set into a desk to provide privacy—the result was a lot of porn watching, and then the switch to monitors and an arrangement that faced out was made.

Though it is unclear whether it was intentional, this librarian's mention of the "collective conscience" harkens Jeremy Bentham's Panopticon, with its particular model of surveillance famously taken up by Foucault in *Discipline and Punish*; though the librarian cannot be everywhere in the library at all times, the very possibility of surveillance via the hypervisibility of the computer's screen is "permanent in its effects,"[47] which are meant to include regulation of oneself. Still, not every librarian I spoke with thought that such visibility of screens made much of a difference in user activity. The same library clerk who emphasized that there was "a *lot*" of porn watching going on in the LAPL was referring to computers that are very much out in the open, in plain view of fellow patrons and the main circulation desk. There is even the possibility that another patron might be sitting right behind the user, looking at the screen while waiting for his or her turn.[48]

In the library, the ambient porn screen raises significant questions about government intervention, censorship, and individual and community rights. Yet there is another space where these questions become even more complex, and more personal, a space where the ambient porn screen takes on different meanings than I have discussed so far: the gay bar.

"IT JUST FITS": PORN AS MEANINGFUL AMBIENCE ON THE GAY BAR'S TV SCREEN

One of the most intriguing sites for a discussion of the ambient porn screen is the adult leisure space of the bar. For me, the ambient porn screen calls to mind one particular bar in Los Angeles, a leather-themed fetish bar that caters to gay men. In order to gain access to the owners and bartenders for interviews, I promised not to name the establishment; in this section, I will refer to the bar as Leather. Here, the ambient porn screen speaks to a long struggle for both belonging and visibility in public space.

At Leather, the ambient porn screen, along with the explicit sexual content it displays, is a central component of the ambience. Sexuality is always already central to the meanings of a bar space. However, Leather's ambient porn screen represents a purposeful attempt to foreground sex as part of the feel and décor of the space. My interest here is not strip clubs or topless bars (i.e., locales where public nudity and sexualized display of workers for the benefit of paying customers is the norm), but rather bars like Leather where the ambient porn screen is tasked with bringing explicit sexual content into the communal space. Here, the ambient porn screen does not merely seek to connect the patrons to its "dirty" content, but uses the content as an extension of the existing aesthetics, ambience, and culture of the space.

In order to understand the particularity of Leather's ambient porn screens, it is important to consider the social function that bars have historically served for marginalized communities, in particular the gay community. Within the gay bar space, the ambient porn screen becomes associated with ideologies long attached to taverns and bars in general. McCarthy notes that historically, bar spaces have been imagined to be more democratic or nonhierarchical than other public spaces.[49] Feminist scholars have also considered the ways that bars have been able to serve as subcultural spaces; because they were "on the margins of—but not outside—the economy, such spaces partially circumvented normative race and gender hierarchies."[50] Because of their potential as non-normative spaces, bars have also been a significant cultural space where gay men could display their sexuality in public. Queer theorists, including Michael Warner, have argued that gay politics needs to take into account the importance of public sexual culture, including pornography.[51] The use of ambient porn in the gay bar is one way to keep sex visible and public.

In a nation where the legal tradition has claimed to protect sexual freedom by keeping it private and where public displays of homosexual affection are deemed "private acts" to be relegated to the home, public space becomes a vital site for sexual minorities to stake their claim for understanding and visibility.[52] In this context, a primary function of the gay bar's ambient porn screen is to contribute to the creation of a unique public space of comfort, safety, and community for its patrons—issues that historically have been central to gay politics and organizing. In the gay bar space, ambient porn, along with all public displays of sexuality, is imbricated with gay identity politics.

Gay bars like Leather that make use of, or, more daringly, foreground, the ambient porn screen open themselves up to persecution under the guise of content regulation. For instance, in California, pornography in bars used to be regulated by the California Alcohol and Beverage Commission (ABC)— the body with the authority to give, or take away, an establishment's liquor license.[53] Essentially, this body has the power to put a bar out of business by stripping it of its right to serve alcohol. The California Code that regulates visual displays was repealed in January 2001, and now it is left up to each community to police based upon its own set of standards, as the obscenity test vaguely implies.[54] Business owners' fear of regulation has not disappeared— quite the opposite, in fact.[55]

These fears surfaced in my own research process. When I first contacted the owners of Leather about their ambient porn screens, they were very responsive, even offering to meet with me in person to discuss my project. However, just a few days after that initial e-mail correspondence, I was informed that we would need to have a phone conversation first in order to "clarify a few things" before meeting. As the weeks went by, and the set times for our calls came and went, I began to wonder if I had scared them off somehow. While I was well aware that pornography is a topic that can make some people nervous, these were businessmen who had chosen to make porn a part of their bar's aesthetic, and so I waited to hear back, more than a little confused. When I finally did get a call, I tried my best to make it clear that in no way did I plan to defame their establishment, but that I was only interested in writing about the screens and the way the content of the media they displayed seemed to function in the space. As it turns out, I had not been totally off base in my worries; the owners wanted to make clear that I could not use their names or the name of their establishment in my paper. In addition, they asked that I not take any photographs. The owners said that the reason for their concerns is that while the local vice squad is well aware that the bar shows pornography, they still fear that antiporn forces within the community will come after them and try to shut them down. Even within adult spaces that stake an explicit claim in sexuality, displaying and viewing non-normative sexuality can never take place without engaging with issues of power.

A reasonable question might then seem to be, "Why do these establishments take the risk? If the vice squad or a Christian community leader can target a bar and the content it plays at any time, threatening to shut the place down, why make the choice to show porn in the first place?" I think there is some insight to be found in the way that the owner and bartender of Leather describe how they conceptualize porn as functioning within the space of their establishment, and how they perceive their patrons' responses and relationship to the pornographic content.

In their respective interviews, both the owner and bartender of Leather expressed an understanding of the way that the ambient porn screen can take on different functions and meanings, even within the same space. For instance, I asked the bartender if Leather's onscreen porn functions as wallpaper (e.g., something in the background, part of its décor) or if it is more of a conversation piece, or perhaps even a distraction from awkward conversation. He laughed and said that, depending on the night, it is all of these things. In addition, the bar owner told me that on their "biggest night" each month, the ambient porn takes center stage in the space. In addition to the usual television screens located at a high angle above the barstools, they hang a massive white backdrop on a wall behind the bar, and project some of "the most hardcore fetish scenes" at larger-than-life size. The owner described a memory of one of these "big nights," during which he watched two women sitting at the bar experiencing what he described as "shock and awe" as they took in the blown-up onscreen image of one man lying on the ground nude while three other men urinated on him. Both owner and bartender agreed that on these nights, there would be no way to consider the porn as merely wallpaper; it is difficult, if not impossible for patrons to ignore.

When discussion in the interviews turned to what sort of content the bar's regulars like to see on the screens, it became clear that the pornographic content is an extension of the aesthetic, ambience, and even culture of the bar itself. The content is mostly vintage porn that, according to the bartender, features "muscular, hairy guys" rather than "skinny, shaved boys," stressing that "for our bar" there is a focus on "hairier, tattooed, muscular men." The distinction he makes is important, because it reflects the bartender's understanding that the content onscreen must be in keeping with the experience and identity the bar cultivates for those who have come to rely on it as a space of belonging. According to the bartender, "People have a definite idea of what's supposed to be up there—and if it's not there, they let you know." I asked him if people are just joking when they speak up about what is on the screens, or if they actually get upset. He said, that "some people genuinely mind," but added: "That just shows their level of comfort [in the bar]." Because some of the patrons have been coming to the bar for so long, he explained, "they can get indignant." For these patrons, then, the bar is no longer just a place to gather for a beer, but it becomes a shared community space in which individuals stake both a personal claim and a sense of ownership; thus, the bartender offered, "they can get possessive [of the screens]." For the owner of the bar, the onscreen porn and the bar's overall leather theme go hand in hand; the pornography they screen "just kinda fits."

There are times, however, when the bar owners do make the conscious decision not to show porn on their ambient screens. For instance, I once visited Leather on a late Monday afternoon, just after opening. The space certainly had a darker mood than the bright California December day outside, with its walls painted black and biker accoutrements decorating the shelves above the bar. Yet, the feel inside the bar space was comfortable, not intimidating; the bartender that day—a woman with a friendly laugh—wore a big fur hunter's cap that jostled as she mixed drinks and poured happy-hour pitchers from the tap. A handful of regulars, some wearing leather jackets, some not, sat on bar stools. The television screens just above them were not playing gay porn, but instead, the 4 o'clock news with closed captioning running along the bottom of the screen. As the bartender opened up tins of holiday cookies and put out small bowls of popcorn and chips, I actually felt my own expectations being turned on their head. One of the owners explained to me that while their patrons enjoy the ambient porn, and it is a big part of the nighttime ambience, the bar does engage in self-regulation, choosing not to show porn during the day, or during local street festivals when passers-by might wander in for a drink.

Being that there are nights when Leather will show something other than all-male porn, I was especially curious about the bar's girls'/lesbian night. Now obsolete, the "girls' night" was a weekly event for several years, drawing a crowd of between 200 and 300 women, diverse in age, gender expression, and ethnicity. It was during a particular girls' night a few years before conceiving this chapter that I walked into Leather for the first time. Somewhere between the friendly introductions at the pool table and a walk to the bar, I noticed that the television screens overhead were showing hardcore, fetish, all-male porn. Upon realizing that the bar owners did not change the usual content on the ambient porn screens for the girls' night, I started to pay attention to the reactions of the women in the bar, as their eyes would drift from casual conversation upward, to the screens. Women would suddenly become transfixed by the sex acts displayed. Eventually, the period of fascination would end, and, perhaps with a casual laugh, their eyes would meet again: "What was I saying?"

As I studied the ambient screens, I wondered why the decision was made to show the same type of pornographic content during the lesbian night. How did the owners imagine it to function, and how did this particular group of patrons react to and interact with the content? It seemed the women enjoyed, or at the very least were not bothered by, the presence of the ambient porn. Both the bar owner and bartender said that the choice to keep the all-male porn was made in response to the women patrons themselves. The men running the bar have, they said, always been willing to change the type of content—offering to simply take the porn off, or put on girl/girl porn; however they told me that on the occasions when they would do this, the majority of the crowd would ask for them to "Put the boys back on!" As to why the women prefer the all-male content, the bartender offered that perhaps the sex is just better in all-male porn. While this hypothesis is suspect on its surface, it might also speak to the lack of girl-on-girl porn that reads as "authentic" rather than a straight male fantasy of lesbian sex. It could also reflect the extent to which gay male fetish porn strives for non-normative sexual displays, which in turn does "just fit" with a space that actively asserts its difference from other spaces. It also seems plausible to me that perhaps encountering gay male porn in the setting of the bar allows the women an opportunity to study the ambient porn, to talk about and engage with sex openly in a public space while, at the same time, not being implicated in or sexualized by the sex acts themselves—indeed, there are limited cultural spaces available for women to do just this.

Leather's ambient porn screens may seem strange to an individual who understands sex as something to be relegated entirely to the private realm. But for those personally invested in the gay bar space, the porn fits what the bar is and does, in terms of building community and fostering a public sexual culture. The owner described the forty-year history of the bar and said, "I have customers who would come here when it was illegal for a man to touch another man in public," when members of vice would just wait around inside the bar for someone to touch someone else, and then would raid the place. For him, the prohibition of public-ness for gay men is something that Leather and its patrons consciously work against and subvert. It is a space where gay male sexuality is brought to the fore, and actively made public. The ambient porn screen plays a central role in confirming the validity and acceptability of such public sexual expression.

At the same time, however, a disconnect remains between the ease with which the bartender spoke with me about the place of public pornography in the bar and the desire of the bar owner not to have the name of the bar publicly disclosed. This disconnect reveals an undercurrent of antiporn intimidation and the resulting fear of regulation. Despite the central role that the ambient porn screen can play in a space, it is still kept in the background of a space's public identity. Since the ABC lifted the ban, the responsibility of regulation has shifted to law enforcement within the community. While no longer in fear of losing their liquor license, bar owners that show porn are left with a precarious sense that that their business could be shut down, if, at any point, antiporn activists in the community came together to make it happen. And yet, despite its potential risks for the establishments that house it, the ambient porn screen has the potential to bring a community together around its pornographic content and the sexual desires and identities it visualizes.

By examining three very different sites for ambient porn—the "anywhere" of personal mobile devices, the public library, and a Los Angeles gay bar—I hope to have shown that these screens are much more complex than a newspaper headline about airplane Wi-Fi gone wrong would imply. Incidents of forgotten etiquette mask the cultural significance of the ambient porn screen. While the loudest voices in the debates over porn-in-public emphasize its social dangers, in particular for children, there are other issues at stake. In the case of the library, the ambient porn screen raises questions about the rights of all citizens, despite class status or financial means, to access legal media content, as well as the right of librarians to exercise their expertise and good judgment in how best to regulate the library space without the risk of losing their already limited funding. In the gay bar, public pornography, as a component of public sexuality, is intimately intertwined with a history of advocating for gay visibility and contributes to the sense of belonging that space can provide for the community it serves. While I do not question the general need to protect children and consider the possibility of a common good, I reject the value of using them as unstoppable rhetorical devices. If we allow the conversation about public pornography to be halted out of fear, we contribute to a larger—and dangerous—cultural habit of privileging individual comfort before equality of access, expression, and community.

NOTES

1. Anna McCarthy, *Ambient Television: Visual Culture and Public Space* (Durham, NC: Duke University Press, 2001).

2. Joseph Couture, *Peek: Inside the Private World of Public Sex* (New York: Haworth Press, 2008), vii.

3. Linda Williams, *Hard Core: Power, Pleasure, and the "Frenzy of the Visible"* (Berkeley, CA: University of California Press, 2009).

4. Ibid., 73.

5. Ibid., 58.

6. Ibid., 73.

7. Ibid., 74.

8. Ibid., 58.

9. Ibid., 75.

10. Ibid., 76.

11. Brandon Zack, "A Moveable Feast: Skeptical About Adult Cell-phone Content? It's All in How You Sell It," *Adult Video News*, October 1, 2005.

12. Mark Logan, "Would You Like Fries With That?: An Overview of Porn's Portable Future," *Adult Video News*, August 1, 2001.

13. Ibid.

14. "Cell Porn Could Outstrip Net Porn, If . . ." *Adult Video News*, April 12, 2005.

15. L. R. Clinton Fayling, "Carpe Diem: The Time is Now For Adult Content Providers to Work with Carriers to Seize Cell Porn Profits," *Adult Video News*, October 1, 2005.

16. Lynn Spigel, "Portable TV: Studies in Domestic Space Travels," in *Technological Visions: The Hopes and Fears that Shape New Technologies*, ed. Marita Sturken, Douglas Thomas, and Sandra Ball-Rokeach (Philadelphia: Temple University Press), 121–122.

17. Ibid., 110.

18. Gary Gumpert and Susan Drucker, "The Parable of the Mobile Rock: Displacing Mobile Communication in the 21st Century or 'Everybody, Everywhere, at Any Time,'" in *Displacing Place: Mobile Communication in the 21st Century*, ed. Sharon Kleinman (New York: Peter Lang Publishing, 2008), 11–12.

19. Ibid., 19.

20. Ibid., 19.

21. Gerard Goggin, *Cell Phone Culture: Media Technology in Everyday Life* (New York: Routledge, 2006), 115.

22. Shoshana Magnet and Tara Rodgers, "Stripping for the State: Whole Body Imaging Technologies and the Surveillance of Othered Bodies," *Feminist Media Studies* (April 2011): 1–18.

23. Ibid., 4.

24. Todd Lewis, "American Airlines Flight Attendants Ask for Help in Policing Porn," *Adult Video News*, September 11, 2008.

25. Ibid.

26. Justin Bourne, "Organization Claims the Public Wants In-Flight Porn Filters," *Adult Video News*, September 18, 2008.

27. Ibid.

28. *Los Angeles Times*, October 8, 2008.

29. In researching this topic, I have found the debate about wireless technology and pornography on mobile devices has entered discussions on wireless in airport waiting areas, including the Denver Airport and the Melbourne Airport (where a man was arrested for viewing child pornography online), as well as the hopes and fears surrounding the FCC's National Broadband Plan, which, it has been discussed, would need to be "porn-free." The plan does not make clear how access to pornography over the national broadband would be prevented.

30. Charles Farrar, "The Few, the Devoted: Adult Mobile Service Customers," *Adult Video News*, July 6, 2005.

31. Zack, "A Moveable Feast."

32. "Forbes.com Discusses iPod Plans for Vivid, Others," *Adult Video News*, November 7, 2005.

33. Confidential e-mail correspondence with anonymous librarian.

34. At the time my observation was conducted, the Los Angeles Library Rules of Conduct with regard to computer usage could be read in full at http://www.lapl.org/about/computer_policy.html. Today, that site content has been replaced with an Internet Use Policy. "Los Angeles Public Library Internet Use Policy," http://

www.lapl.org/about-lapl/internet-use-policy. The updated policy makes no explicit mention of pornography but does note that the Library cannot control Internet content and that users should not remove privacy screens from library computers.

35. Sue Banks, "Your Privacy's Showing: Pornography at Your Local Library," in *Pop-Porn: Pornography in American Culture*, ed. Ann C. Hall and Mardia J. Bishop (Westport, CT: Praeger, 2007), 164.

36. Ibid., 164.

37. "ACLU Joins Library Net Censorship Suit: Files Brief Against Parent Trying to Impose Library Blocking," *Adult Video News*, October 20, 1999.

38. Charles Farrar, "Libraries Have Till Next July to Install Porn Filters," *Adult Video News*, July 25, 2005.

39. Clyde DeWitt, "The Supreme Court and Porn on the Library Computers," *Adult Video News*, October 1, 2003. See also Charles Farrar, "Congress Can Make Libraries Filter Out Porn," *Adult Video News*, June 23, 2003, and Sue Banks, "Your Privacy's Showing."

40. Farrar, "Congress Can Make Libraries Filter Out Porn." The full text of the "Children's Internet Protection Act" can be accessed at the FCC's page, http://www .fcc.gov/guides/childrens-internet-protection-act.

41. E-mail correspondence with anonymous librarian.

42. Banks, "Your Privacy's Showing," 164.

43. Justin Bourne, "Library-Porn Issue Addressed at Board Meeting," *Adult Video News*, April 27, 2008.

44. E-mail correspondence with anonymous librarians, November 4, 2008, and December 5, 2008.

45. "S.C. Law Would Prosecute Librarians for Porn," *Adult Video News*, February 1, 2000.

46. Charles Farrar, "Library Settles Net Porn Complaint for Six Figures," *Adult Video News*, August 19, 2003.

47. Foucault, *Discipline and Punish: The Birth of the Prison* (reprint), ed. Alan Sheridan (London: Vintage, 1995).

48. Whether or not a library works to protect the individual adult's right to view pornography in the library, it is important to note that every library that I visited and every librarian I spoke with communicated the commitment on the part of the staff to do all they can to prevent children from being exposed to pornographic content. Thus, children and teen areas are placed away from the adult computers (sometimes even with their own room or wing) and in view of the librarian. Adults are not allowed to use these computers (although, interestingly, there is no rule in the LAPL that children cannot use adult computers). Conscious efforts made by libraries to simultaneously keep children away from adult areas *and* place children's computers in view of an adult seem to both underscore the library's priority of protecting children and at the same time acknowledge the likelihood that children will attempt to view pornographic materials if left unattended.

49. McCarthy, *Ambient Television*, 33 and 35.

50. Anne Enke, *Finding the Movement: Sexuality, Contested Space, and Feminist Activism* (Durham, NC: Duke University Press, 2008), 28.

51. Rich Cante and Angelo Restivo, "The Cultural-Aesthetic Specificities of All-Male Moving Image Pornography," in *Porn Studies*, ed. Linda Williams (Durham, NC; London: Duke University Press, 2004), 145.

52. Cante and Restivo, "The Cultural-Aesthetic Specificities of All-Male Moving Image Pornography," 144, and Williams, *Hard Core*, 288.

53. E-mail correspondence with Joseph Cruz, Assistant Director, California Alcohol and Beverage Commission. See also "Official California Legislative Information," www.leginfo.ca.gov.

54. E-mail correspondence with Joseph Cruz.

55. When I spoke with both the owner and head bartender, they revealed that there was a crackdown on pornography in gay bars happening right at that moment in Palm Springs, California. The bartender had recently visited an establishment that usually plays pornography, and found the screens instead playing alternative "sexy" content. Unable to show porn any longer due to recent raids by the local authorities (that had been, according to rumor, fueled by a mayor and a jaded ex-bar owner), the ambient screens instead showed a sort of "glam shot" male model slideshow. This sort of nonporn "sexy" montage content is similar to what was shown in the L.A. gay bar before the ABC ban was repealed, and is used to fill the porn lack; after all, it's still, the bartender tells me, "provocative wallpaper."

22

Pornography and Pedagogy: Teaching Media Literacy

Shira Tarrant

In the spring of 2012, a tenured professor at Appalachian State University was placed on leave after screening a well-known documentary critical of pornography and its impact on society and relationships. After showing *The Price of Pleasure*[1] in an Introduction to Sociology course, professor Jammie Price was accused of engaging in inappropriate speech and conduct in the classroom when four students complained.[2]

Spurred by events at Appalachian State University and subsequent controversies, media debates about the merit and legitimacy of including pornography in academic curricula appeared in the *New York Times*, *The Atlantic*, *Jezebel*, and *HuffPost Live*. News coverage of the professor's suspension raised a number of questions: Is it appropriate for faculty to teach the subject of pornography? If so, under what conditions? In university classrooms, these are important issues in regard to free speech, academic freedom, and the tension between the open exchange of ideas and protectionist perspectives that emphasize shielding students from potential discomfort. Beyond the classroom, teaching skills in porn literacy promotes more sophisticated and nuanced understanding about sexual politics, health, pleasure, and safety. As actor and feminist activist Jane Fonda writes, if pornography is the main source of sex education for teens (and adults; and for many it is), there is a risk of "learning from porn how to be in a sexual relationship, what is sexy, how to look and act."[3] This chapter surveys how and why pornography is a crucial component in developing critical media literacy skills beginning from the position that porn literacy promotes stronger abilities to navigate sexual and gender politics in the 21st century. Pornography is an important media genre for both questioning normative expectations and exploring forms of resistance that challenge racism, classism, ageism, and related intersectional subjugations.

CONTEMPORARY ISSUES

As a university professor I regularly teach courses on the philosophy of sex and love, the politics of sex in popular culture, and contemporary issues of gender and society. These classes blend media literacy skills with critical analyses of race, gender, sexual orientation, class, disability, size, and beauty.

Students arrive in class having been immersed in a normative consumer culture that pushes narrow stories and stereotypes about sex and gender. Many of my students have not been taught basic information about sexuality when they were in middle school or high school; often what they know about reproduction, sexual health, and sexual pleasure is in spite of—not because of—their earlier education. Classroom conversation reveals that, at best, students received "the condom talk" in high school, and not much else. They arrive at college, therefore, as young adults who are missing crucial information about sex, gender, safety, and pleasure.

Quantitative data supports these anecdotal observations: There were ten times more pornographic films produced in 2005 than 1988 (13,000 versus 1,300)[4] while, at the same time, a survey of teenagers conducted by *Psychologies* magazine found that 75 percent of parents never talked with their children about pornography.[5] The Kaiser Family Foundation finds that as these teens become adults, few take seriously the idea that marketing is a force from which they must wrest creativity, individuality, and autonomy. This creates generations that are "generally unprepared to think critically about both sexuality and the role of media in their lives."[6] As political scientist Caroline Heldman and sociologist Lisa Wade write about media culture more broadly, "The negative effects of sexual objectification and self-objectification, once merely theoretical, have now been documented empirically, linked to problems with mental health, physical health, confidence, cognitive, sexual, and motor function, access to leadership, and political efficacy."[7] At the same time, and against this backdrop of heavy media saturation and limited media literacy programming, sex education in the United States is uneven, at best. Nevada exemplifies the inconsistency in sex education that is provided for students: One Cimarron Memorial High School teacher "went beyond the district's curriculum, bringing in her own videos and other materials. She also debunked myths, like the idea that you can't get pregnant if you have sex in the shower because hot water kills sperm." Her student Maria realized her teacher was not the norm: "Her method wasn't to say, 'Don't have sex.' Rather, it was, 'If you have sex, you need to know this stuff. You need to know what is true and what is not true.'" In contrast, other classes focus on showering, hygiene, and nutrition rather than providing medically accurate information about sexuality or reproduction. None of this surprises Amanda Morgan, and neither are the schools entirely to blame. A sexual-health educator who teaches human sexuality at the University of Nevada, Las Vegas, Morgan reports that adult students "come into my class and they don't know the proper name for their genitals. They call it a 'cookie,' a 'flower' or just 'down there.' And that's because their parents taught them it was a cookie or a flower."[8]

Yet these inconsistencies and shortcomings are neither unusual nor limited to Nevada. According to the Guttmacher Institute, as of March 2014, twenty-two states and the District of Columbia mandate that public schools teach sex education; only thirteen states require that sex-education content (when mandated) must be "medically, factually or technically accurate." Thirty-five states, however, allow parents to remove their children from sex-education instruction, only two states prohibit sex education programs from promoting religion, thirty-seven states require that abstinence information be provided, and nineteen states "require that instruction on the importance of engaging in sexual activity only within marriage be provided."[9] None of these policies stipulate that sex education must include an emphasis on pornography (or other sex-related media technologies). In its policy statement on sexuality and the media, the American Academy of Pediatrics explains that abstinence-only education is a waste of time, especially "when the media have become such an important source of information" about sexual activity.[10]

When I ask my college students for anecdotal reports about the sex education they received when they were teenagers in high school, most proudly proclaim that they experienced progressive education, that abstinence-only is a relic of the past, and that their teachers were open and engaged about the issues. When pressed further, these same students share that by "sex education" they mean there was a condom-and-banana demonstration or "the priest acknowledged there might be sex outside marriage, but he really hoped that didn't happen." In other words, the baseline expectation for comprehensive sex education has been pushed quite low. When I ask my students if their high-school sex education included frank conversations about pornography and media literacy, the consistent response has involved uncomfortable shuffling and resounding silence.

It is not a stretch to suggest that in dorm rooms and apartments—and from the back of some WiFi-ed classrooms—college students are Internet-cruising with the left-handed mouse. The pop-culture industrial complex thrives on churning out imagery attempting to bring sex-infused fantasy and pleasure, as well as shock-value, into our living rooms and smart phones. Pornography itself is a ubiquitous and easily accessed part of our media landscape. Yet for all the punditry and moral panic about young-adult sexuality,[11] there is little opportunity for teens and young people to discuss how to critically watch and think about pornography.

The use of Internet porn hardly represents the first time people have used pictures to learn about sex. *Playboy* launched its first issue in 1953 and *Penthouse* has been around since 1969. *The Joy of Sex* became a best-selling book when it first hit the shelves in 1972, in no small measure for its how-to illustrations. But access to high-speed, live-action visuals ups the ante. With laptops overtaking sales of desktop computers and the proliferation of smart phones and ongoing technological developments such as Google Glass, sexually explicit media is available to many of my students anywhere, anytime.

Anecdotally, it is said that "sex" is the number-one search term used around the globe, and one reporter goes so far as to state that "porn," "free porn," and "porno" are blowing other Google search terms out of the water. *Ghostery.com* reports that 25 percent of all Web searches are for pornography and 891 million unique users were tracked on the top adult Web sites during the summer of 2013.[12] Data reveals that these four terms were collectively searched nearly twenty-three million times each month in 2011,[13] while other data indicates that every second, people spend $3,000 on Internet porn. It should be noted that this latter figure is contested and reliable figures on porn use and revenue are difficult to assess; however, it stands to reason that the click-through rate is reasonably high.[14]

But along with its popularity, there is also cause for deep concern about the effects of mainstream pornography on our culture. Whether we individually like porn or not—and based on the figures, many people like it—we would be smart to figure out strategies for dealing constructively with pornography's ubiquity by teaching media literacy skills and providing education about the impact of this media genre instead of trying to silence it, shut it down, or uncritically supporting it.

Given that pornography is ubiquitous, that the state of sex education is dismal, and moral panic runs high,[15] there is a potentially dangerous combination at play. In light of the data, it is easily argued that improving media literacy skills provides important foundations for navigating the sex-tech nexus. Including pornography as a specific component of media literacy is crucial to promoting sexual health, pleasure, and safety in a media-saturated culture.

MEDIA LITERACY FOUNDATIONS

When the semester begins, the students in my pop culture class often start out thinking they will learn the secrets to subliminal advertising, or that I will present PowerPoint lectures on how to find hidden pictures of naked women in liquor-ad ice cubes.

To the contrary, I begin by explaining that decoding pop culture does not mean finding the hidden pictures. Rather, it means learning how to understand the messages and meanings of the images that are clearly in front of us. The goal is to pull back the curtain on normative assumptions and naturalized imagery in order to think more deeply about what media teaches about who we are and how we relate to others. Critical analysis of media images, including pornography, requires understanding concepts of sexual fantasy, consent, air-brushing, and the illusion that a camera angle can present.

My pop-culture class provides foundations in theory, politics, data, and competing ideologies. The class specifically includes a focus on television shows, advertising, music lyrics and video, mainstream movies, social media, and pornography. My usually talkative students tend to clam up when we get to the latter topic. It's awkward. I get it. But this is all the more reason for educators to find productive pedagogical strategies for engaging in difficult dialogues about what is easily framed as a quite popular—and profitable— aspect of contemporary pop culture. Pornography is now included in courses across the country at campuses such as Spelman College, Indiana University, Texas A&M, Rutgers, and the University of Pennsylvania (to name a few). Classes go by titles such as Sexual Economies, Sexuality and Race, Hip Hop Feminism, and The Politics of Pornography in a range of departments including fields such as Political Science, Gender and Women's Studies, and Communications. The content of these classes includes diverse emphases including labor issues, industry structures, public policy, public health, sexuality, sexual politics, and the law. Yet for all its growing academic popularity, pornography arguably remains among the most used products but least taught topics on a college campus. Bobby Noble writes that "pornography has been a consistent staple of university curricula since, at the very least, the mid-twentieth century," but as a field of studies on its own, pornography is a fairly recent arrival on campus. More open for debate are the "kinds of pedagogical and epistemological ends" pornography has served as an element of academic focus.[16]

Film scholar Constance Penley, who has taught courses on pornography at the University of California, Santa Barbara, for more than two decades, explains that porn is "a genre of film and media that has been central to the development of technology, culture, and society over the last one hundred years." In 1993, Penley suggested to her colleagues that, although UCSB was lauded as one of the foremost media and film programs, they had neglected to teach "the most enduring and prolific of genres." Faculty agreed that to remain among the strongest academic leaders in film and media, they needed to include pornography in the curriculum.[17] Where scholars in other fields are expected to have extensive expertise and breadth and depth of knowledge, pornography may be discounted as a legitimate area of expertise, as relevant as it may be to film studies, psychology, politics, or any number of academic fields.[18] As Penley explains:

> I teach [pornography] as a course on film and popular culture. For the most part, students who take the class are advanced film and media majors, so I want them to be able to ask of pornographic film and media all the questions they normally ask of all other forms of film. How have the style, strategies and content changed over the decades? What have been the audiences and venues? What have been the modes of production, consumption and distribution? How has the legal climate in any given era shaped all of that? Exactly the kinds of things they'd ask of Hollywood filmmaking or any kind of filmmaking. What I want my students to do is something that not many people can do. As a society, we debate, legislate, regulate pornography in almost a total vacuum of knowledge about what it really consists of historically, textually, institutionally. I tell my students that they can have their opinions, but only after they know what pornography is.[19]

Although Penley initially intended to teach a university pornography course in the context of film history, her first run of this course inadvertently became a class on sex education. This, Penley explains, was due, in no small part, to the dismal sex education provided to students before they arrive at college: "In one of my first [pornography] classes," Penley recounts, "I remember sitting next to one of my students, and it was the first scene of anal sex we had seen in the class. She whispered to herself, 'I didn't know you could do that.'"[20]

Although teaching porn literacy may be delegitimized[21] or perceived as risky,[22] done well, the subject can be an important conduit for discussing consumer culture, progressive politics, democracy, contention, and free speech. Because pornography is often a de facto source of information about sexuality, this provides all the more reason to consider the importance of teaching porn literacy and developing ethical best practices. This does not necessarily mean defending pornography but rather "to show its diversity, complexity, and historicity . . . and to educate students about pornography as a popular field of representation and a political economy informed by gender, race, class, and culture."[23] The growing tradition of porn education includes documentary films, slide shows, and video compilations of road shows dating back several decades. These encompass a range of political and ideological perspectives. Among these are "Not a Love Story" (1982), Susie Bright's "How to Read a Dirty Movie" and "All Girl Action, The History of Lesbian Eroticism in Hollywood" (1987), Focus on the Family's "Learn to Discern" (1992), Gail

Dines's "Who Wants to be a Pornstar?" (2007),[24] and a recent resurgence in books, blogs, and articles on the topic.

In the 2014 inaugural edition of *Porn Studies*, journalism and media expert Kath Albury comments that pornography is increasingly the subject of educational texts; debates about porn education or porn literacy tend to presume that young people under eighteen "should be provided with porn literacy education that promotes critical disengagement from pornographic texts. In contrast, sexuality education targeting adults has drawn on pornographic imagery to promote sexual learning—particularly in relation to safer-sex practices."[25]

From this context emerge two main areas of concern in regard to teaching porn literacy: The first is intended to promote critical engagement with pop culture and media, with a focus on pornography in particular. The second prong of teaching porn literacy is intended to foster healthy engagement with sexual safety and an understanding about sexual pleasure. Although the two goals clearly overlap, it is not at all clear that these ought to be demarcated among those older and younger than eighteen. Issues such as possible relations between pornography and self-perception, self-objectification, risky sexual behavior, or consent and sexual decision-making all presumably impact sexually active individuals and those who intend to be. Secondary schools and university classrooms are well advised to incorporate a broadbased attention to pornography's impact on our lives and our culture.

To this end, in early 2014, the U.K. released a study about sex education that included advice for educators. Updated for a new era in which sex and technology routinely collide, these government-supported recommendations urge educators to address various contemporary issues.

The release of *Sex and Relationships Education for the 21st Century* (SRE) marks the first time in fourteen years that sex education guidelines have changed in the U.K. The SRE is accompanied by supplemental advice and support provided by three organizations that are leading experts in sex and relationship education. Parliament member Nick Clegg is quoted as saying, "It is vital that we safeguard the health and wellbeing of our young people to help them get on in life. That's why we need all schools teaching sex and relationships education that is absolutely up to date, particularly when teenagers' lives are so dominated by advances in technology."[26]

The SRE notes that children, teens, and young people "are naturally curious about growing up, how their bodies work and how humans reproduce. Their questions need to be answered honestly, using language and explanations appropriate for their age and maturity, thus avoiding unnecessary mystery, confusion, embarrassment, and shame."[27] The SRE program will include information about the intersections between sex and technology, specifically in regard to sexting and pornography.[28]

The British guide stipulates that high-quality sex education is required in all schools, "including those with a religious character," and must include "medically and factually correct information, treating sex as a normal and pleasurable fact of life."[29] Acknowledging the impact of technology in the 21st century, the SRE advises teachers to discuss pornography by emphasizing that porn is "not the best way to learn about sex because it does not reflect real life."[30] Further, the SRE outlines greater inclusion of children and young people who are lesbian, gay, bisexual, and transgender, advocating for sex education to tackle prejudice, including homophobia. In particular the SRE states that teachers should never assume all intimate relationships are among heterosexual partners.

While sex education in the U.K. is mandatory for secondary education, in comparison, U.S. sex-education policies fall well behind the curve. If U.S. state laws regarding sex education reflect both medical and cultural naïveté, then arguing for porn-literacy curricula might very well seem to be a stretch. There is reason to hope, however, that the U.K. guidelines might serve as a constructive model for teaching teens and young adults to be savvy, educated media consumers. By teaching that pornography is "not the best way to learn about sex because it does not reflect real life," as the SRE recommends, the framework is consistent with feminist pedagogy and critical media tools that emphasize active engagement to better understand media constructions of gender, race, class, and sexuality. The study states that discussions about pornography are important opportunities to talk about the media's impact on distorting concepts of bodies, beauty, and perfection.[31]

TEACHING MEDIA LITERACY

Pornography both shapes and reflects assumptions about masculinity, female sexuality, gendered power, expectations of beauty, and how women are treated—particularly women of color. Porn has the potential to affect the sexual pleasure and safety of all. Mobile technology and abstinence-only education guarantee that more young people get their sex education from pornography. It is time to talk with them about what they're watching. [32]

Like all forms of pop culture entertainment, mainstream porn often reenacts bias about gender, race, and power. In this sense, porn is no different than most Disney films, primetime television, popular streaming Netflix shows, or the sports section of the local paper. But because porn is explicitly focused on sex instead of infused with sex-power innuendo, porn can blur the line of consent by making nonconsensual domination sexy.

In a liberal democracy, we trust adults to make their own best decisions about their sexual choices. Whether this involves spanking, teasing, topping, or switching—or even nuzzling, fondling, spooning, or kissing—it is not clear that porn is an evil culprit. Certainly there's nothing wrong with human proclivity for both cuddle and kink. But what matters most crucially is accurate information and consent.

Better information about the politics of media creates in young people—and all of us—stronger abilities to distinguish between fantasy and reality, yes and no, coercion and consent—lines that can be fuzzy in porn and in real life. The more we understand how to "decode" porn media, the better situated we are to know the difference. The more willing we are to teach age-appropriate media literacy to children and young adults, the better able they are to navigate the sexually mediated world we live in.

When I speak at universities across the country, students enthusiastically contribute their questions and concerns. They *want* to talk about the impact of porn on our most intimate lives, our most casual hook-ups, and our most long-term desires. A PowerPoint I present, culled from decades of porn stills, shows changing expectations of breast shape and nipple location as cosmetic surgery becomes more common; it charts the path of increasingly vanishing pubic hair (and its on-trend return); it presents sexual images that, without explicit consent, could be considered rape or sexual assault. While a full Brazilian is neither necessarily good nor bad, teaching how porn fashion can become bedroom style goes a long way toward expanding—and explaining—beauty expectations for ourselves and for our partners. In describing his experience traveling in Japan, one student recounted his experience with women crying or whimpering during sex, an auditory practice more common among Japanese porn clips compared to the stylistic moaning of women in U.S.-based pornography. This led to a robust class discussion about how we learn what sex ought to look like, sound like, and feel like—and the relation between these expectations and pornography. This class session is powerful evidence that open conversation about the personal politics of porn happens best when the room is free from judgment or shame. Based on what young adults share about their pleasures and their fears, we know there is a serious need for media literacy and porn education and for providing new language to articulate our preferences and our sexual boundaries.

The answer is not to eradicate porn or to silence education about it. While, on the one hand, Appalachian State University sanctioned Jammie Price for screening an antiporn documentary, groups such as Stop Porn Culture would like to obliterate pornography altogether by using both education and policy measures.[33] Pedagogical strategies such as those promoted by the Stop Porn Culture slide show depict the dangers of porn and what the group calls "body punishing sex."[34] This approach to media literacy presents a homogenous viewpoint about what pornography is and what kinds of effects it has. Even if motivated by concerns about safety, sexism, and well-being, strictly antiporn approaches to the subject risk silencing discussion and debate rather than fostering productive dialogue that promotes nuanced analysis of critical sociopolitical issues. Given our consumerist culture that promotes mainstream product and media content—that which so often replicates the problems of sexism, racism, ageism, and narrow tropes of beauty, class, and status—pedagogically sound approaches to media literacy help students understand that porn (like much else in a consumer-saturated society) is not solely limited to mainstream genres, but also includes feminist, queer, ethical, and indie content.

As Mike Pearl, writing for *Vice* magazine, comments, "Porn is a part of culture, and whether one likes it or not, it has and will continue to be a part of our culture throughout our lifetimes. It behooves us as a society to critically engage it without a predetermined agenda."[35] Rather than fostering silence and further taboo, it is crucial to provide critical media literacy, increased access to sexual information, and greater conversation about gender, race, consent, and power. This promotes sexual pleasure and productive solutions to sexual harm. This goal is strengthened by continued development of pedagogically successful strategies.

Porn literacy requires that we have brave conversations that are in sync with our cultural realities. These include topics that maximize open discussion and accurate information. For example:

- If porn is not "real sex" then what is so-called real-life sex? The online video *Porn Sex vs. Real Sex: The Differences Explained With Food* does a terrific job using humor and fact to dispel assumptions and correct the record about basic questions that many young people have such as penis size, arousal rates, and the percentage of nonporn sex involving lesbian relations, anal intercourse, or what they refer to as light bondage.[36]
- If objectification is a problem of sexism, racism, and heteronormative assumptions, then what is self-objectification and why does it matter? Research conducted by Caroline Heldman and Lisa Wade finds that female sexual objectification undermines men's perceptions of women's competence. Female *self*-objectification, they argue, is linked to problems with cognitive development, sexual satisfaction, and grade point averages. This aspect of Heldman and Wade's research is more nuanced than other studies setting out to prove that pornography causes violence against women. Their framework is promising in regard to media literacy education: Heldman and Wade, both of whom oppose pornography, suggest ways of understanding possible media harms. This strategy can lead to media literacy solutions and feminist education about gender and objectification, without demanding censorship.[37]

- If we reject sexism, racism, trans* hatred, and homophobia—and we also object to censorship and silencing—what models can we draw from to encourage critical media literacy? This requires pedagogical strategies and education materials that teach how to think as critically and as seriously about pornography as any other form of media and cultural information. The documentary *Mickey Mouse Monopoly* helps to reveal embedded tropes of violence, abuse, and racist and sexist stereotypes in everyday children's movies. This enables consumers to become active in our choices without demanding that we "Stop Disney Culture" or eradicate Disneyland. Communications professor and executive director of the Media Education Foundation Sut Jhally comments "that all of us present ourselves to be watched and gazed at." We all "watch attractive strangers with sexual desire. To treat another as an object of our desires is part of what it means to be human." The challenge is when women are presented as nothing more than objectified sexual desire, men are presented as only agents of sexual objectification, and trans* individuals are fetishized.[38] The answer, Jhally explains, is more conversation about sexuality, not less.
- If pornography is an unreliable source for accurate information about sex and sexual politics, what is a better option? *Our Bodies, Ourselves* is a leader in providing frank, positive, and accurate information about body image, sexuality, reproductive health, and related issues.[39] Scarleteen.com, which bills itself as "sex ed for the real world" provides inclusive, comprehensive, and accessible sexuality information geared toward teens and young adults.[40]

Fortunately, the list of resources for information and suggestions for pedagogical strategies is growing. As digital technology increasingly shapes our analog relationships and pop culture infuses our everyday lives, we must put media literacy at the top of our cultural to-do list. Doing so provides the critical skills that enable children and adults (young, or otherwise) to identify sexism, misogyny, and racism in all forms of pop culture, including pornography. As a generation of Internet porn-watchers comes of age, it is to society's benefit that they are taught a kind of "porn literacy" that encourages an understanding of what constitutes mutually consensual sex in real life. The ubiquity of porn requires a willingness to start talking out loud about the sex-tech nexus. Talking won't solve all our problems overnight. But shifting our cultural conversation matters—particularly when these are difficult dialogues.

Censorship violates our most fundamental principles of free speech. Instead, what is necessary is greater conversation to confront crucial issues of equality, safety, health, and consent while promoting agency, autonomy, and free will.

NOTES

1. Miguel Picker and Chyng Sun, dir., "The Price of Pleasure: Pornography, Sexuality, and Relationships" (Northampton, MA: Media Education Foundation, 2008).

2. For a summary of this case and the academic freedom issues at stake, see "FIRE letter to Appalachian State University Board of Trustees Chair Michael A. Steinback, March 19, 2013," *FIRE*, March 19, 2013, http://www.thefire.org/fire-letter-to-appalachian-state-university-board-of-trustees-chair-michael-a-steinback-march-19-2013.

3. Jane Fonda, *Being a Teen: Everything Teen Girls and Boys Should Know About Relationships, Sex, Love, Health, Identity and More* (New York: Random House, 2014), 29.

4. Caroline Heldman and Lisa Wade, "A Call for a Twenty-First Century 'Sex Wars'" (paper presented at the annual meeting of the Western Political Science Association, Los Angeles, March 28, 2013), 6.

5. https://psychologies.co.uk/put-porn-in-its-place. See also Jerome Taylor and Jane Ryan, "We Need to Talk About Porn," *The Independent*, April 28, 2012, http://www.independent.co.uk/news/uk/home-news/we-need-to-talk-about-porn-7685283.html#.

6. Art Silverblatt, Jane Ferry, and Barbara Finan, *Approaches to Media Literacy: A Handbook* (New York: M. E. Sharpe, 2009). Quoted in Heldman and Wade, 8.

7. Caroline Heldman and Lisa Wade, "A Call for a Twenty-First Century 'Sex Wars'" (paper presented at the annual meeting of the Western Political Science Association, Los Angeles, March 28, 2013), 1.

8. Lynn Comella, "Sex, Lies, and Public Education," *Vegas Seven*, May 31, 2013, http://vegasseven.com/2013/05/31/sex-lies-public-education.

9. Guttmacher Institute, "State Policies in Brief: Sex and HIV Education," March 1, 2014.

10. Victor C. Strasburger, MD, The Council on Communications and Media, "Policy Statement—Sexuality, Contraception, and the Media," *Pediatrics: Official Journal of the American Academy of Pediatrics* 126, no. 3 (September 2010): 576–82.

11. Aline Zoldbrod, "Why a Sex Therapist Worries About Teens Viewing Internet Porn," *Commonhealth*, November 15, 2013. http://commonhealth.wbur.org/2013/11/sex-therapist-internet-porn.

12. https://purplebox.ghostery.com/post/1016023854. See also http://www.covenanteyes.com/pornstats.

13. Alan Dunn, "Top Google Searches—What Do People Search For?" *Business Insider*, December 21, 2011, http://www.businessinsider.com/top-google-searches-what-do-people-search-for-2011-12.

14. Aarti Shahani, "Hurting for Cash, Online Porn Tries New Tricks," National Public Radio, February 17, 2014, http://www.npr.org/blogs/alltechconsidered/2014/02/17/276897125/hurting-for-cash-online-porn-tries-new-tricks; Dan Ackman, "How Big Is Porn?" *Forbes*, May 25, 2011, http://www.forbes.com/2001/05/25/0524porn.html.

15. Despite widespread fears about allegedly deranged versions of human sexuality depicted by online porn, research on the effects of pornography on children and young adults remains inconclusive. See Amanda Hess, "How Does Internet Porn Affect Teens? New Study Says: We Have No Idea!" *Slate.com*, May 31, 2013, http://www.slate.com/blogs/xx_factor/2013/05/31/internet_porn_study_the_affect_of_pornography_on_kids_and_teens_remains.html.

16. Bobby Noble, "Porn's Pedagogies: Teaching Porn Studies in the Academic-Corporate Complex," *Porn Studies* 1, no. 1–2: 97.

17. Lynn Comella, "Film Professor Constance Penley on Sex, Education . . . and Sex Education," *Las Vegas Weekly*, November 7, 2012, http://www.lasvegasweekly.com/news/2012/nov/07/film-professor-constance-penley-sex-education-and-. See also Constance Penley, "A Feminist Teaching Pornography? That's Like Scopes Teaching Evolution!" in *The Feminist Porn Book: The Politics of Producing Pleasure*, ed. Tristan Taormino, Celine Parrennñas Shimuzu, Constance Penley, and Mireille Miller-Young (New York: The Feminism Press, 2013), 179–99; "Truth Claims About Porn: When Dogma and Data Collide" in *The Pornography of Pornography: Contemporary Perspectives*, ed. Lindsay Coleman and Jacob M. Held (Lanham, MD: Rowman & Littlefield, 2014).

18. Lindsay Coleman and Jacob M. Held, "Introduction: Why Pornography?" in *The Philosophy of Pornography: Contemporary Perspectives*, ed. Lindsay Coleman and Jacob M. Held (Lanham, MD: Rowman & Littlefield, 2014).

19. Lynn Comella, http://www.lasvegasweekly.com/news/2012/nov/07/film-professor-constance-penley-sex-education-and-.

20. Ibid.

21. Lindsay Coleman and Jacob M. Held, "Introduction: Why Pornography?" in *The Philosophy of Pornography: Contemporary Perspectives*, ed. Lindsay Coleman and Jacob M. Held (Lanham, MD: Rowman & Littlefield, 2014).

22. Mireille Miller-Young, "The Pedagogy of Pornography: Teaching Hardcore Media in a Feminist Studies Classroom," *Signs* 2, no. 2 (Fall 2010). http://www.signs.rutgers.edu/miller-young_essay_1_2-2.htm.

23. Ibid.

24. Eithne Johnson, "Appearing Live on Your Campus! Porn-Education Roadshows," *Jump Cut: A Review of Contemporary Media*, no. 41 (1997): 27–35.

25. Kath Albury, "Porn and Sex Education, Porn as Sex Education," *Porn Studies* 1, no. 1–2 (2014): 178.

26. This trio of expert organizations comprises Brook, the PSHE Association, and the Sex Education Forum. See "SRE Supplemental Advice," http://www.brook.org.uk/index.php/information/sre-supplementary-advice.

27. Brook, PSHE Association and Sex Education Forum, "Sex and Relationships Education (SRE) for the 21st Century: Supplementary Advice to the Sex and Relationship Education Guidance DfEE," (2014) www.sexeducationforum.org.uk/media/17706/sreadvice.pdf: 8.

28. "New U.K. Sex Ed Guidelines to Become More Progressive than U.S. Programs," *Nerve.com*, March 4, 2014, http://www.nerve.com/love-sex/new-uk-sex-ed-guidelines-to-become-far-more-progressive-than-us-programs.

29. Liana Aghajanian, "Revised U.K. Sex Ed Guidelines Now Address Pornography, Sexting," *Takepart*, March 2, 2014, http://www.takepart.com/article/2014/03/02/revised-uk-sex-ed-guidelines-include-pornography-sexting.

30. Quoted in ibid.

31. Brook, PSHE Association and Sex Education Forum, "Sex and Relationships Education (SRE) for the 21st Century: Supplementary Advice to the Sex and Relationship Education Guidance DfEE," (2014) www.sexeducationforum.org.uk/media/17706/sreadvice.pdf: 10.

32. A previous version of the following discussion appeared on AlterNet.org. See Shira Tarrant, "Pornography 101: Why College Kids Need Porn Literacy Training," *AlterNet*, September 15, 2010, http://bit.ly/cjZpYr.

33. Stop Porn Culture (SPC) is a feminist antipornography group based at Wheelock College in Massachusetts. SPC is arguably the most visible feminist antipornography organization currently working in the United States, with impact in Australia, the UK, and elsewhere around the globe. Launched by professors Gail Dines and Robert Jensen, filmmaker Chyng Sun, and additional affiliated scholars, members of SPC regularly appear in international media promoting their opposition to pornography. As part of an organized effort to shut down pornography, members of SPC actively publish in such left-leaning and general-interest media as the *Guardian*, *Time* magazine, *Al Jazeera*, and the *New York Post*. See Shira Tarrant, "Truth Claims about Porn: When Dogma and Data Collide," in *The Philosophy of Pornography: Contemporary Perspectives*, ed. Lindsay Coleman and Jacob M. Held (Lanham, MD: Rowman & Littlefield, 2014).

34. For further discussion about Stop Porn Culture, see Feona Attwood and Clarissa Smith, "Emotional Truths and Thrilling Slideshows: The Resurgence of Anti-Porn Feminism," in *The Feminist Porn Book: The Politics of Producing Pleasure*," ed. Tristan Taormino, et al. (New York: The Feminist Press, 2013); and Christopher Boulton, "Antiporn Agendas: Feminism, Internet Filtering, and Religious Strategies" in this volume.

35. Mike Pearl, "'Porn Studies' Is a Serious Academic Journal for Serious Academics," *Vice*, March 26, 2014, http://www.vice.com/read/porn-studies-is-a-serious-academic-journal-for-serious-academics.

36. Kbcreativelab, *Porn Sex vs. Real Sex: The Differences Explained with Food*, https://www.youtube.com/watch?v=q64hTNEj6KQ.

37. Caroline Heldman and Lisa Wade, "A Call for a Twenty-First Century 'Sex Wars'" (paper presented at the annual meeting of the Western Political Science Association, California, March 28, 2013).

38. Shira Tarrant, ed., *Men Speak Out: Views on Gender, Sex, and Power* (New York: Routledge, 2013), 70; Sut Jhally, dir., *Dreamworlds 3: Desire, Sex and Power in Music Video* (Northampton, MA: Media Education Foundation, 2007).

39. The Boston Women's Health Book Collective, *Our Bodies, Ourselves* (New York: Touchstone, 2011). See also http://www.ourbodiesourselves.org.

40. http://www.scarleteen.com.

23

The Science and Politics of Sex Addiction Research

Nicole Prause and Timothy Fong

This chapter explores the science and controversy around sex addiction. While some medical and counseling professionals emphasize an addiction model for grappling with compulsive use of pornography, Nicole Prause and Timothy Fong explain that the research does not support an addiction framework. Although sex addiction was rejected as a psychiatric diagnostic category in the most recent edition of the *Diagnostic and Statistical Manual of Mental Disorders* (*DSM-5*) based on lack of credible scientific evidence, rejecting the addiction model has political ramifications, including, in this instance, attacks on the authors by what they call "proaddiction, antipornography stakeholders."

Readers will note that the term "pornography" is replaced in this chapter with the phrase "visual sexual stimuli" (VSS). This is based on the view that "pornography" is biased to suggest that sexual images are inherently negative. For example, the classification of visual representations as "pornography" has been used to restrict information about homosexuality in some countries, or even to prosecute gay businesses. Therefore, rather than using the term "pornography," the authors follow others by using visual sexual stimuli to refer to visual representations likely to provoke a sexual response.

–eds.

Laws regarding the viewing of visual sexual stimuli[1] (VSS) suggest a strong sociocultural context in which the pathologizing of VSS viewing occurs. Viewing such images is not legal until age eighteen in many countries, including the United States. The legal age to view sexual images is fifteen in Denmark. Viewing sexual images is never permitted at any age in the People's Republic of China. As a result, most research on the effects of VSS has occurred in Europe and the United States, usually with individuals over the age of eighteen, who were aware they would be viewing or asked about VSS. Within the United States, there is a history of government-sponsored research to identify harmful effects of VSS, government efforts to withdraw funding from studies of VSS, and government regulatory agencies reshaping sexuality research.[2] Thus, when individuals report that their VSS use is getting them into trouble and want help regulating their use, social context must be considered in delineating pathology.

At the level of the individual, cultural influence is probably most clear from the relationship of religious identification and VSS use problems. Stronger religious beliefs and moral disapproval of VSS predicted a person's belief that they were "addicted" to VSS, above and beyond the actual level of VSS use. Those with stronger religious values also are more likely to seek treatment to reduce their VSS viewing.[3] These individuals are not necessarily citing religion as the reason they struggle with their VSS use; rather, their religious background appears to have influenced their perceptions of what is normal or acceptable. For example, researchers relayed reports of a Catholic man who identified as sexually addicted due to his bimonthly masturbation, behaviors which actually are well within the statistically normal range.[4] With these contextual factors, defining pathology, if it exists, becomes increasingly complex.

Stepping back, sexual arousal occupies a unique space in psychological theory important to understanding the possible effects of VSS. Some have proposed that sex is an emotion.[5] While sex shares many features with other emotions, sex differs in the key respect that it is not consistently pleasant or unpleasant. This inconsistency might be due to people experiencing both pleasant and unpleasant emotions during sexual arousal, or that sexual arousal is, itself, sometimes experienced as pleasant or unpleasant.[6] Others have described sexual arousal as a drive that can be deprived, like sleep or hunger.[7] This view has been largely rejected on both theoretical[8] and empirical[9] grounds, as sex cannot be deprived like other drives. A final popular perspective is that sexual arousal can be characterized as a drive and deprived, but that the deprivation state interacts with the incentive, rewarding aspects of sexual cues.[10] In sum, sexual arousal is not clearly a drive or an emotion. Thus, it is often difficult to know how to best conceptualize sexual arousal in experimental protocols as compared to other emotions or drives.

SEXUAL AROUSAL IN THE BRAIN

Physical responses can be useful as one method to objectify and characterize responses to sexual stimuli. Four types of sexual stimuli that have been studied in the laboratory include cognitive (fantasy or story), visual (photographs or films), mechanical (vibratory, manual, or electrical), and partnered (manual-genital or intercourse) stimuli. Unfortunately, no study has yet contrasted these stimuli in the brain directly, even in animal studies. Thus, it is not yet possible to characterize similarities or differences of these different sexual cue types directly. Given the focus of this chapter on VSS, we limit this discussion of the sexually aroused human brain to VSS.

Brain responses to VSS share some features with other very activating, negative emotions. For example, very activating negative images showing dismemberment enhance brain potentials, as do VSS, relative to emotionally neutral images.[11] Evidence also exists that VSS share unique features with other pleasant stimuli that are different from unpleasant stimuli, such as uniquely increasing activity in brain areas associated with reward.[12] VSS also share some features with reward drives, such as commonalities in the brain areas activated by food and VSS.[13] It is also worth noting that brain responses to VSS appear very similar in men and women to the same VSS.[14] Brain response pattern to VSS suggest that VSS are processed most commonly as pleasant, hedonic, motivating cues.

Differences in brain responses to VSS appear primarily driven by differences in the level of sexual desire the individual experiences day-to-day. Evidence increasingly suggests that women with low sexual desire do not respond, or respond more weakly, to the rewarding properties of sexual cues than women with high or statistically normal sexual desire. Women with lower desire exhibit not only lesser activation of brain areas associated with reward, but also greater activation of areas associated with executive control.[15] These functional differences are supported by structural differences that may contribute to supporting the functional difficulties.[16] Cancer survivors who are distressed about their low sexual desire demonstrate less activation of anterior cingulate and dorsolateral prefrontal cortex to sex cues than do survivors not distressed about their sexual desire.[17] These patient differences are supported by basic science demonstrating that, in those without sexual desire problems, greater neural responsiveness to sex cues is associated with having more sex partners and sexual desire levels.[18]

Brain responses to VSS also vary by sexual orientation. Broadly, brain areas associated with processing rewards tend to be more active when viewing pictures of genitalia of the preferred sex in both heterosexual and homosexual men and women.[19] Other brain studies have tended to support some specificity, although the effects are not always so clear in men[20] or women[21] when controlling for responses to other pleasant, arousing visual stimuli. Some have demonstrated that these brain responses are so specific that they allow high-accuracy classification of sexual orientation as well as preferences for target age.[22] Animal models have demonstrated that sexual preferences can be strongly influenced by early conditioning, although it is not clear whether this extends to gender preferences in humans.[23] Sexual arousal is unique from other cognitive states, because high-specificity genital response measures are available to index sexual arousal.[24] Brain measures remain useful to complement these investigations, as they allow us to contrast responses to VSS with other "border" construct stimuli (nonsexual pleasure, rewards, etc.).

SEARCHING FOR A MODEL OF PROBLEMATIC VSS USE

Many have attempted to propose criteria for a disorder that reflects high VSS involvement. The proposed criteria arise from two different areas of research: Internet Use Problems or Sex Problems. In the popular model from the Internet perspective, "Internet Addiction" defined dependence largely on an untested, eight-item questionnaire directly derived from criteria for pathological gambling.[25] Criteria included items like preoccupation with thoughts about Internet use and staying online longer than originally intended. Other models have been suggested,[26] and remain largely similar to one another in their proposed criteria.[27] In this view, VSS represent "a specific form of sexual computer-assisted behavioral addiction."[28] From the Sex Problem perspective, VSS problems are "associated with increased or excessive expression of biologically mediated human behaviors or pathological conditions."[29] In this light, VSS problems would be specifying the type of high-frequency sexual problem. The sex framework seems popular with patients in the United States with the overwhelming majority of those presenting for treatment for high-frequency sexual behaviors reporting problems with their VSS viewing.[30] Some attempts have been made to bridge these literatures with Internet and sex, suggesting that both share features by labeling a new "internet sex addiction."[31]

There are some clear differences in the proposed criteria from popular models in each of these domains. Internet Addiction criteria generally include some reference to a withdrawal state, while withdrawal is not explicitly described in Martin Kafka's model.[32] Kafka, on the other hand, offers "personal distress" as one way to meet criteria related to having "impairment" due to the behaviors. Personal distress is not generally a part of the Internet Use problem models. Given the social taboos surrounding VSS viewing, the use of a personal distress criterion is potentially very important in describing the type of sample studied. For example, one study found that distress was strongly related to measures of Internet VSS "addiction," but later found this perception of addiction was driven by religious beliefs.[33] It may be that changing this distress criterion would result in very different samples.

Aside from the issue of whether VSS problem use arises from characteristics of the Internet or characteristics of sex, it also is unclear what model best characterizes VSS problems. Terms used that could describe models include "addiction,"[34] "disorder,"[35] "compulsions,"[36] and many others.[37] Unfortunately, the terms are used to refer to proposed clusters of symptoms, but are not described as testable models. Given that neither the framework nor the model for VSS use problems were clear, it was difficult to design a neuroscience test of a model of VSS problem use.

Some resistance seems to exist to testing models of VSS problem use, although there are established empirical methods for delineating amongst these models.[38] Some researchers such as Patrick Carnes explicitly argue against testing by suggesting that terms are interchangeable. Carnes, for instance, writes "To call the addiction a compulsion may have been politically expedient."[39] As experimentalists, we disagree.

Psychologists in clinical practice often profess an orientation. They may describe their orientation as "behavioral" or "psychoanalytic." These labels generally describe a school of thought about psychological problems. A schism exists in psychology between those who believe treatments must be supported by research supporting a treatment model and others who believe their orientation/model works better than any research formula.[40] Richard McFall critiqued practitioners for failing to use empirically supported treatments.[41] Practitioners continue to be resistant to using research-supported treatments for many nonempirical reasons.[42] A similar process appears to be occurring with high-frequency sexual behaviors. Many have adopted a sexual addiction model and base their treatment approach on it; surprisingly, few data support an addiction model.

What makes a good model? Good models make specific predictions. In fact, the predictions must be so specific that a scientific test could prove them false, often referred to as a "risky prediction" required for good science. By Popperian science, falsifying any risky prediction of a model means that the entire model is incorrect.[43] This may seem straightforward in fields like chemistry, where balanced chemical equations provide highly replicable yields. Medicine, psychology, social sciences, and many other disciplines, however, rely on constructs.

Constructs refer to concepts that cannot be directly observed, but whose existence is supported by observable, empirical relationships. Addiction is such a construct. One cannot study the effects of a "cup of addiction" or say a person is infected with "three addictions." Rather, debate should surround what model best characterizes the converging observables. Instead, sex addiction literature argues about symptom lists for disorders, rarely fully considering the implied model. For example, Kathryn Jones and Katherine Hertlein write extensively about "symptom distinction," discussing the importance of hours of viewing, without providing any comprehensive model to support why these symptoms would ever be expected to cluster or be pathological.[44] A better example of a broad conceptualization is reward deficiency model, which provides a framework for making clear, falsifiable predictions.[45]

The biggest challenge for a model of pathological VSS viewing is how to distinguish it from the construct of reward. While viewing VSS, the areas of the brain that become more active strongly resemble other nonsexual rewards. Viewing a preferred brand of chocolate as compared to a less-preferred chocolate results in brain differences[46] similar to those VSS with higher or lower sexual desire (see review above). Consider that Florida students respond with larger brain potentials to images of their adored Gator team over images of other sports[47] and extreme sports enthusiasts respond with larger potentials to images of extreme sports.[48] A similar comparison could be made in the sexual domain where those who have more sexual partners respond with larger brain potentials to VSS.[49] Using a different EEG measure, those who have no problems with their eating exhibit greater frontal alpha asymmetry to images of delicious, hedonic foods,[50] just as those with higher sexual arousal exhibit greater alpha asymmetry to sexual films.[51] In summary, any enjoyed, rewarding activity like sex will evoke stronger brain responses, and these will be accentuated in fans of that particular reward, thus accentuated responses to VSS alone are not evidence of pathology.[52] Consequently, stronger activation to VSS in those reporting liking VSS more is both expected and nonpathological.

An addiction model applied to VSS viewing (i.e., "pornography addiction") makes several predictions that can be tested. For example, addiction models usually include a tolerance component. Tolerance would be demonstrated if those who are said to be addicted to VSS exhibited lesser sexual arousal to VSS than those who do not report a problem. To date, evidence indicates that those who believe they have a problem with their VSS use actually exhibit higher sexual arousal in response to the same VSS viewed by others.[53] Our study tested another prediction of the addiction model.

The responsiveness of the brain is enhanced to pictures ("cues") representing the addiction of the affected person. At first glance, this appears to contradict the tolerance prediction above. However, this early response to a cue is thought to reflect reorientating according to the motivational relevance of a cue, whereas tolerance refers to the later, developed response to the cue. Thus, a number of studies have demonstrated increased neural orienting to cues of cocaine,[54] cigarettes,[55] and gaming[56] in problem users. Problem VSS users also should exhibit enhanced brain responses to VSS.

We collected a large sample of men and women with and without problems regulating their viewing of VSS. Our original plan to recruit patients was thwarted when the Institutional Review Board prohibited us from recruiting these patients on the grounds that showing them VSS could cause them to relapse. These data were collected at Idaho State University.

Three publications were planned from different data within these studies. One would use a within-participant control to examine whether a relationship existed between continuous indicators of hypersexuality and neural responses. The authors included Cameron Staley, who designed the study and collected these data for his doctoral dissertation; Vaughn Steele, a postdoctoral scholar with strong programming and EEG skills; Timothy Fong, an addiction psychiatrist; and Nicole Prause, a sexual physiologist and fellow programmer with EEG skills. A second paper was planned by Prause, which would use a between-subject control. Finally, a third paper would examine the brain response to the sexual films over time to test for the presence of a tolerance response.

As this would be the first neural responsivity study of sexual addiction, there were many tough design and analytic decisions that had to be made with minimal empirical guidance. For example, there was a need to control for sexual desire levels, which had recently been more strongly associated with sexual responses to VSS than hypersexuality levels.[57] There also was no consensus on the best questionnaires for measuring these problems, so three had been included. Previous research did suggest that clear predictions could be made regarding the P300 magnitude in VSS problem users. Specifically, the P300 is known to be the largest to sexual images in nonproblem users as compared to other pleasant images, and the P300 is known to increase in magnitude in those reporting problems with their use (see above).[58] Thus, a clear, falsifiable prediction could be made: Those reporting problems with VSS viewing should exhibit P300 responses to VSS even greater than controls, and this difference should be proportionate to the severity of the problem experienced. Prause had been invited to submit a manuscript to the journal *Socioaffective Neuroscience and Psychology* for peer review. Given that the within-subject design was closer to completion, Steele took the lead to complete this paper first to test the latter prediction: Was the severity of VSS problems related to the P300 response to VSS?

The results in the paper were presented in two steps. First, results from the evoked response potentials, specifically the "P300" had to be shown to mirror previous P300 research to demonstrate that the data were collected properly. We demonstrated this clearly in our data first (see Figure 23.1). Second, we attempted to relate the size of the P300 with the measures of sexual desire (desire for sex with a partner, desire for solo sexual activity) or hypersexuality (three

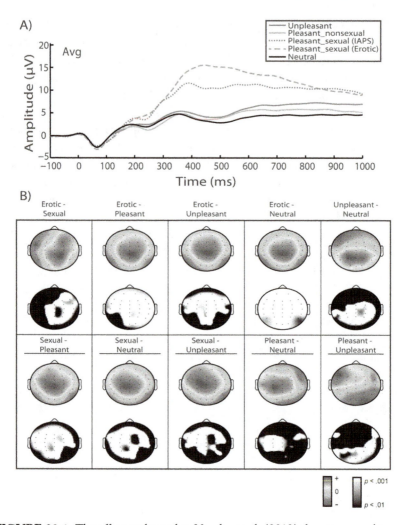

FIGURE 23.1 The effect replicated in Vaughn et al. (2013) showing sexual images provoking the highest brain response in the range of 300+ milliseconds. Topographical plots show the source of the component.

different scales) using regression techniques. The only questionnaire related to the P300 size was the measure of desire for sex with a partner (see Figure 23.2).

This was the first functional neuroscience study of those who claimed to experience problems with their VSS use, so we had inquiries from a few colleagues and media prior to its appearance in print. One blogger posted a story with the results on *Psychology Today* unexpectedly, which we requested be corrected to make clear the paper was awaiting final notification. At this point, we became aware of proaddiction group tactics for the first time. Proaddiction,

P300 Amplitude and Sexual Desire

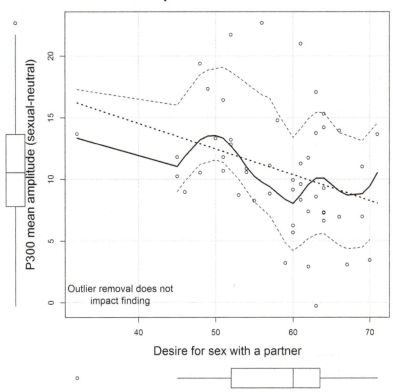

FIGURE 23.2 An ERP difference score, plotted at CPz, between Pleasant-sexual and Neutral stimuli plotted against the measure of sexual desire (dyadic).

antipornography groups across the country rapidly attacked the study despite having no access (nor having requested any access) to it, creating false details of the study design to allow critique. Having seen this preview of the response, we decided to request a press release through UCLA with the publication of the study to reduce the chances that the study would be misrepresented. It was our first press release, and we hoped it would decrease the ability of motivated groups to intentionally misrepresent the findings. On the day the study was published, the phone calls and e-mails started and did not stop for about two months. Recall that this was for a null result: none of the questionnaire assessments of hypersexuality were related to the P300 response.

The vitriol from the religious groups, treatment clinics, and bloggers was remarkable. The accusations were extreme, including that we had falsified our results, forced homosexuals to view heterosexual VSS, secretly excluded questionnaires, and recruited from churches. Morality in the Media, LLC, and the Society for the Advancement of Sexual Health sent e-mails to their members with talking points concerning how to best refute our study to the media and patients. Some individuals repeatedly e-mailed the authors after we had requested the contact to stop, resulting in a harassment complaint filed with local police. The chancellor of UCLA was written five times with accusations that data had been falsified and requesting disciplinary action be taken against one author. They threatened retribution in the forms of legal avenues and "exposing" UCLA if disciplinary action was not taken. The same female author had personal photographs stolen by the blogger and posted on Web blogs with sexist diatribes against her person. Individuals mapped routes to the laboratory address and there were multiple (blocked) attempts to gain access to the laboratory server space, sparking repeated security alerts at the laboratory. Because the accusations were false, UCLA was able to support its scientists. The research was never stopped by these attempts. Noticeably absent from these attacks are published critiques from any scientist.

The larger between-participant design paper currently is under review. The new paper will generally show a reversal of the prediction of addiction models of VSS viewing. Given the strong reaction to the initial paper showing merely a null result, the proaddiction cabal may fail to note that this new paper actually supports a pathology model. Specifically, the pattern reported could be interpreted as evidence of hyporesponsivity in those who report problems with VSS viewing, and such lower arousal has been associated with higher impulsivity.[59] Those interested in helping individuals reporting these problems may be able to identify/develop more effective treatments if the addiction model is inappropriate.

In summary, the first publication of an electroencephalographic result failed to support an addiction model of visual sexual stimulus viewing. Sex research has historically faced unusual political challenges, but this finding was additionally attacked by many proaddiction, antipornography stakeholders. Few financial resources are accessible to conduct sexuality research in general, and financial resources that are made available are under constant political threat for rescission.[60] The addition of personal threat and attacks make it especially unlikely that strong scientists who might publish challenges to addiction models of VSS would choose to work in this area.

NOTES

1. For discussion about the use of the terms "visual sexual stimuli" or "pornography" see J. D. Brown and K. L. L'Engle, "X-Rated: Sexual Attitudes and Behaviors

Associated with U.S. Early Adolescents' Exposure to Sexually Explicit Media," *Communications Research* 36 (2009): 129–51.

2. Edwin Meese, *Attorney General's Commission on Pornography: Final Report*, Department of Justice (Washington, DC, 1986); S. Epstein, "The New Attack on Sexuality Research: Morality and Knowledge Production," *Sexuality Research and Social Policy* 3 (2006): 1–12; J. M. Irvine, "Can't Ask, Can't Tell: How Institutional Review Boards Keep Sex in the Closet," *Contexts* 11 (2012): 28–33.

3. This is documented by J. Grubbs, J. Exline, K. Pargament, J. Hook, and R. Carlisle, "Transgression as Addiction: Religiosity and Moral Disapproval as Predictors of Perceived Addiction to Pornography," *Archives of Sexual Behavior* (2014): 1–12; Michael W. Ross, Sven-Axel Månsson, and Kristian Daneback, "Prevalence, Severity, and Correlates of Problematic Sexual Internet Use in Swedish Men and Women," *Archives of Sexual Behavior* 41 (2012): 459–66; J. Winters, K. Christoff, and B. B. Gorzalka, "Dysregulated Sexuality and High Sexual Desire: Distinct Constructs?" *Archives of Sexual Behavior* 39 (2010): 1029–43.

4. M. Reece, D. Herbenick, V. Schick, S. A. Sanders, B. Dodge, and J. D. Fortenberry, "Sexual Behaviors, Relationships, and Perceived Health Among Adult Men in the United States: Results From a National Probability Sample," *The Journal of Sexual Medicine* 7 (2010): 291–304.

5. W. Everaerd, "Commentary on Sex Research: Sex as an Emotion," *Journal of Psychology & Human Sexuality* 1 (1998): 3–15.

6. Z. Peterson and E. Janssen, "Ambivalent Affect and Sexual Response: The Impact of Co-Occurring Positive and Negative Emotions on Subjective and Physiological Sexual Responses to Erotic Stimuli," *Archives of Sexual Behavior* 36 (2007): 793–807; N. Prause, C. Staley, and T. Fong, "No Evidence of Emotion Dysregulation in 'Hypersexuals' Reporting Their Emotions to a Sexual Film," *Sexual Addiction & Compulsivity* 20 (2013): 106–26.

7. F. J. Allport, *Social Psychology* (Cambridge, MA: Houghton-Mifflin, 1924).

8. F. A. Beach, "Characteristics of Masculine 'Sex Drive," in *Nebraska Symposium on Motivation*, ed. M. R. Jones (Lincoln, NE: University of Nebraska Press, 1956), 32; R. Whalen, "Sexual Motivation," *Psychological Review* 73 (1966): 151–63.

9. A. H. Leiman and S. Epstein, "Thematic Sexual Responses as Related to Sexual Drive and Guilt," *Journal of Abnormal and Social Psychology* 63 (1961): 169–75; N. Prause and G. H. Proudfit, "A First Study of Human Sexual 'Deprivation' Suggests Improved Regulation," *Emotion*. Manuscript under review.

10. B. Singer and F. M. Toates, "Sexual Motivation," *Journal of Sex Research* 23 (1987): 481–501.

11. J. T. Cacioppo, S. L. Crites, Jr., and W. L. Gardner, "Attitudes to the Right: Evaluative Processing Is Associated With Lateralized Late Positive Event-Related Brain Potentials," *Source Personality & Social Psychology Bulletin* 22 (1996): 1205–19; A. Weinberg and G. Hajcak, "Beyond Good and Evil: The Time-Course of Neural Activity Elicited by Specific Picture Content," *Emotion* 10 (2010): 767–82.

12. Dean Sabatinelli, Margaret M. Bradley, Peter J. Lang, Vincent D. Costa, and Francesco Versace, "Pleasure Rather Than Salience Activates Human Nucleus

Accumbens and Medial Prefrontal Cortex," *Journal of Neurophysiology*, 98 (2007): 1374–79.

13. Kathryn Demos, Todd F. Heatherton, and William M. Kelley, "Individual Differences in Nucleus Accumbens Activity to Food and Sexual Images Predict Weight Gain and Sexual Behavior," *The Journal of Neuroscience* 32, no. 16 (2012): 5549–52.

14. Sabatinelli et al., 2007; S. Wehrum, T. Klucken, S. Kagerer, B. Walter, A. Hermann, D. Vaitl, and R. Stark, "Gender Commonalities and Differences in the Neural Processing of Visual Sexual Stimuli," *Journal of Sexual Medicine* 10 (2013): 1328–42.

15. B. A. Arnow, L. Millheiser, A. Garrett, M. L. Polan, G. H. Glover, K. R. Hill, A. Lightbody, C. Watson, L. Banner, T. Smart, T. Buchanan, and J. E. Desmond, "Women With Hypoactive Sexual Desire Disorder Compared to Normal Females: A Functional Magnetic Resonance Imaging Study," *Neuroscience* 158, no. 2 (2009): 484–502; F. Bianchi-Demicheli, Y. Cojan, L. Waber, N. Recordon, P. Vuilleumier, and S. Ortigue, "Neural Bases of Hypoactive Sexual Desire Disorder in Women: An Event-Related FMRI Study," *Journal of Sexual Medicine* 8, no. 9 (2011): 2546–59; T. L. Woodard, N. T. Nowak, R. Balon, M. Tancer, and M. P. Diamond, "Brain Activation Patterns in Women With Acquired Hypoactive Sexual Desire Disorder and Women With Normal Sexual Function: A Cross-Sectional Pilot Study," *Fertility and Sterility* 100, no. 4 (2013): 1068–76.

16. Jos Bloemers, H. Steven Scholte, Kim van Rooij, Irwin Goldstein, Jeroen Gerritsen, Berend Olivier, and Adriaan Tuiten, "Reduced Gray Matter Volume and Increased White Matter Fractional Anisotropy in Women With Hypoactive Sexual Desire Disorder," *The Journal of Sexual Medicine* 1, no. 3 (2013): 753–67.

17. F. Versace, J. M. Engelmann, E. F. Jackson, A. Slapin, K. M. Cortese, T. B. Bevers, and L. R. Schover, "Brain Responses to Erotic and Other Emotional Stimuli in Breast Cancer Survivors With and Without Distress About Low Sexual Desire: A Preliminary fMRI Study," *Brain Imaging Behavior* 7, no. 4 (2013): 533–42.

18. N. Prause, V. R. Steele, C. Staley, and D. Sabatinelli, "Late Positive Potential to Explicit Sexual Images Associated With the Number of Sexual Intercourse Partners," *Social Cognitive and Affective Neuroscience* (2014b): manuscript in press; Demos, Heatherton, and Kelley, 2012.

19. J. Ponseti, H. A. Bosinski, S. Wolff, M. Peller, O. Jansen, H. M. Mehdorn, C. Büchel, and H. R. Siebner, "A Functional Endophenotype for Sexual Orientation in Humans," *Neuroimage* 33 (2006): 825–33.

20. A. Safron, B. Barch, J. M. Bailey, D. R. Gitelman, T. B. Parrish, and P. J. Reber, "Neural Correlates of Sexual Arousal in Homosexual and Heterosexual Men," *Behavioral Neuroscience* 121 (2007): 237–48.

21. M. Costa, C. Braun, and N. Birbaumer, "Gender Differences in Response to Pictures of Nudes: A Magnetoencephalographic Study," *Biological Psychology* 63 (2003): 129–47.

22. J. Ponseti, O. Granert, O. Jansen, S. Wolff, H. Mehdorn, H. Bosinski, and H. Siebner, "Assessment of Sexual Orientation Using the Hemodynamic Brain Response to Visual Sexual Stimuli," *Journal of Sexual Medicine* 6 (2009): 1628–34; B. Schiffer,

T. Krueger, T. Paul, A. de Greiff, M. Forsting, N. Leygraf, M. Schedlowski, and E. Gizewski, "Brain Response to Visual Sexual Stimuli in Homosexual Pedophiles," *Journal of Psychiatry & Neuroscience* 33 (2008): 23–33.

23. James G. Pfaus, Tod E. Kippin, Genaro A. Coria-Avila, Hélene Gelez, Veronica M. Afonso, Nafissa Ismail, and Mayte Parada, "Who, What, Where, When (and Maybe Even Why)? How the Experience of Sexual Reward Connects Sexual Desire, Preference, and Performance," *Archives of Sexual Behavior* 41 (2012): 31–62. For arguments against this position, see D. F. Swaab, "Sexual Differentiation of the Brain and Behavior," *Best Practice & Research Clinical Endocrinology & Metabolism* 21 (2007): 431–44.

24. R. Savin-Williams, G. Rieger, and A. M. Rosenthal, "Physiological Evidence for a Mostly Heterosexual Orientation Among Men," *Archives of Sexual Behavior* 42 (2013): 697–99.

25. K. S. Young, "Internet Addiction: The Emergence of a New Clinical Disorder," *CyberPsychology & Behavior* 1 (1998): 237–44.

26. M. Griffiths, "A 'Components' Model of Addiction Within a Biopsychosocial Framework," *Journal of Substance Use* 10 (2005): 191–97; R. Tao, X. Huang, J. Wang, H. Zhang, Y. Zhang, and M. Li, "Proposed Diagnostic Criteria for Internet Addiction," *Addiction* 105 (2010): 556–64.

27. A. J. vRooij and N. Prause, "A Critical Review of 'Internet Addiction' Criteria with Suggestions for the Future," *American Psychiatry*. Manuscript under review.

28. A. Weinstein and M. Lejoyeux, "Internet Addiction or Excessive Internet Use," *The American Journal of Drug and Alcohol Abuse* 36 (2010): 280.

29. M. P. Kafka, "Hypersexual Disorder: A Proposed Diagnosis for DSM-V," *Archives of Sexual Behavior* 39 (2010): 378.

30. This included 81.1 percent of the patient sample according to R. C. Reid et al., "Report of Findings in a DSM-5 Field Trial for Hypersexual Disorder," *The Journal of Sexual Medicine* 9 (2012): 2868–77.

31. M. D. Griffiths, "Internet Sex Addiction: A Review of Empirical Research," *Addiction Research & Theory* 20 (2012): 111–24.

32. Kafka (2010).

33. J. B. Grubbs, F. Volk, J. J. Exline, and K. I. Pargament, "Internet Pornography Use: Perceived Addiction, Psychological Distress, and the Validation of a Brief Measure," *Journal of Sex & Marital Therapy* 1 (2014): 1–24.

34. Patrick Carnes, *Don't Call It Love: Recovery From Sexual Addiction* (New York: Bantam, 1991).

35. Kafka (2010).

36. E. Coleman, "Sexual Compulsivity: Definition, Etiology, and Treatment Considerations," *Journal of Chemical Dependency and Treatment* 1 (1987): 189–204.

37. J. Bancroft and Z. Vukadinovic, "Sexual Addiction, Sexual Compulsivity, Sexual Impulsivity, or What? Toward a Theoretical Model," *Journal of Sex Research* 41 (2004): 225–34; S. N. Gold and C. L. Heffner, "Sexual Addiction: Many Conceptions, Minimal Data," *Clinical Psychology Review* 18 (1998): 367–81. For review see

T. E. Mudry et al., "Conceptualizing Excessive Behaviour Syndromes: A Systematic Review," *Current Psychiatry Reviews* 7 (2011): 138–51; and D. J. Stein, "Classifying Hypersexual Disorders: Compulsive, Impulsive, and Addictive Models," *Psychiatric Clinics of North America* 31 (2008): 587–91.

38. For examples, see D. Ley, N. Prause, and P. Finn, "The Emperor Has No Clothes: A Review of the 'Pornography Addiction' Model," *Current Sexual Health Reports* (2014): 1–12.

39. Patrick Carnes, "Addiction or Compulsion: Politics or Illness?" *Sexual Addiction & Compulsivity* 14 (1996): 130.

40. B. Kleinmuntz, "Why We Still Use Our Heads Instead of Formulas: Toward an Integrative Approach," *Psychological Bulletin* 107 (1990): 296–310; P. E. Meehl, "When Shall We Use Our Heads Instead of the Formula?" *Journal of Counseling Psychology* 4 (1957): 268–73.

41. R. M. McFall, "Manifesto for a Science of Clinical Psychology," *The Clinical Psychologist* 44 (1991): 75–88; R. M. McFall, "Elaborate Reflections on a Simple Manifesto," *Applied & Preventive Psychology* 9 (2000): 5–21.

42. S. O. Lilienfeld, L. A. Ritschel, S. J. Lynn, R. L. Cautin, and R. D. Latzman, "Why Many Clinical Psychologists Are Resistant to Evidence-Based Practice: Root Causes and Constructive Remedies," *Clinical Psychology Review* 33 (2013): 883–900.

43. Karl Popper, *On the Sources of Knowledge and of Ignorance, Conjectures and Refutations: The Growth of Scientific Knowledge* (London: Routledge & Kegan Paul, 1963).

44. Kathryn Jones and Katherine Hertlein, "Four Key Dimensions for Distinguishing Internet Infidelity From Internet and Sex Addiction: Concepts and Clinical Application," *American Journal of Family Therapy* 40 (2012): 115–25.

45. K. Blum, E. R. Braverman, J. M. Holder, J. F. Lubar, V. J. Monastra, D. Miller, J. O. Lubar, T. J. H. Chen, and D. E. Comings, " Reward Deficiency Syndrome: A Biogenetic Model for the Diagnosis and Treatment of Impulsive, Addictive, and Compulsive Behaviors, *Journal of Psychoactive Drugs* 32, Supplement (2000): 1–68.

46. M. Schaefer, M. Knuth, and F. Rumpel, "Striatal Response to Favorite Brands as a Function of Neuroticism and Extraversion, *Brain Research* 1425 (2011): 83–89.

47. C. H. Hillman, B. N. Cuthbert, J. Cauraugh, H. T. Schupp, M. M. Bradley, and P. J. Lang, "Psychophysiological Responses of Sport Fans," *Motivation & Emotion* 24 (2000): 13–28.

48. A. M. Fjell, M. Aker, K. H. Bang, J. Bardal, H. Frogner, O. S. Gangås, A. Otnes, N. M. Sønderland, A. K. Wisløff, and K. B. Walhovd, "Habituation of P3a and P3b Brain Potentials in Men Engaged in Extreme Sports," *Biological Psychology* 75 (2007): 87–94.

49. Prause et al., 2014b.

50. P. A. Gable and E. Harmon-Jones, "Relative Left Frontal Activation to Appetitive Stimuli: Considering the Role of Individual Differences," *Psychophysiology* 45 (2008): 275–78.

51. N. Prause, C. Staley, and V. Roberts, "Frontal Alpha Asymmetry and Sexually Motivated States," *Psychophysiology* 51 (2014a): 226–35.

52. J. D. Salamone and M. Correa, "Dopamine and Food Addiction: Lexicon Badly Needed," *Biological Psychiatry* 73 (2013): e15–e24.

53. M. Brand, C. Laier, M. Pawlikowski, U. Schächtle, T. Schöler, and C. Altstötter-Gleich, "Watching Pornographic Pictures on the Internet: Role of Sexual Arousal Ratings and Psychological–Psychiatric Symptoms for Using Internet Sex Sites Excessively," *Cyberpsychology, Behavior, and Social Networking* 14 (2011): 371–77.

54. J. P. Dunning, M. A. Parvaz, G. Hajcak, T. Maloney, N. Alia-Klein, P. A. Woicik, F. Telang, G. J. Wang, N. D. Volkow, and R. Z. Goldstein, "Motivated Attention to Cocaine and Emotional Cues in Abstinent and Current Cocaine Users—An ERP Study," *European Journal of Neuroscience* 33 (2011): 1716–23; M. C. van de Laar, R. Licht, I. H. A. Franken, and V. M. Hendriks, "Event-related Potentials Indicate Motivational Relevance of Cocaine Cues in Abstinent Cocaine Addicts," *Psychopharmacology* 177 (2004): 121–29.

55. M. Littel and I. H. A. Franken, "The Effects of Prolonged Abstinence on the Processing of Smoking Cues: An ERP Study among Smokers, Ex-smokers and Never-smokers." *Journal of Psychopharmacology* 21 (2007): 873–82.

56. R. Thalemann, K., Wölfling, S. M. Grüsser, "Specific Cue Reactivity on Computer Game-related Cues in Excessive Gamers," *Behavioral Neuroscience* 121 (2007): 614–18.

57. Winters, J., Christoff, K., Gorzalka, B. B., "Conscious Regulation of Sexual Arousal in Men," *Journal of Sex Research* 46 (2009): 330–43.

58. A. P. Anokhin, S. Golosheykin, E. Sirevaag, S. Kristjansson, J. W. Rohrbaugh, A. C. Heath, "Rapid Discrimination of Visual Scene Content in the Human Brain," *Brain Research* 1093 (2006): 167–77; J. J. van Lankveld and F. T. Smulders, "The Effect of Visual Sexual Content on the Event-related Potential," *Biological Psychology* 79 (2008): 200–8.; Y. Vardi, E. Sprecher, I. Gruenwald, D. Yarnitsky, I. Gartman, and Y. Granovsky, "The P300 Event-Related Potential Technique for Libido Assessment in Women with Hypoactive Sexual Desire Disorder." *Journal of Sexual Medicine* 6 (2009): 1688–695.

59. Stenberg, G., "Personality and the EEG: Arousal and Emotional Arousability," *Personality and Individual Differences* 13 (1992): 1097–1113.

60. S. Epstein, "The New Attack on Sexuality Research: Morality and Knowledge Production," *Sexuality Research and Social Policy* 3 (2006): 1–12.

About the Editors and Contributors

EDITORS

LYNN COMELLA, PhD, is an Associate Professor of Gender and Sexuality Studies at the University of Nevada, Las Vegas, where she teaches courses on gender, sexuality, media, and popular culture. Her research examines the adult entertainment industry, with a focus on the history of the women's market for sex toys and pornography. Her research has been featured in the *International Journal of Communication*, *The Feminist Porn Book*, *Sex for Sale: Prostitution, Pornography, and the Sex Industry*, *New Sociologies of Sex Work*, and *Feminist Media Studies*, among other venues. She serves on the editorial board for the journal *Porn Studies*, and writes a regular column on sexuality and culture for *Vegas Seven*.

SHIRA TARRANT, PhD, is an Associate Professor in the Department of Women's, Gender, and Sexuality Studies at California State University, Long Beach. Her books include *Men Speak Out: Views on Gender, Sex, and Power* (Routledge), *Men and Feminism* (Seal Press), *Fashion Talks: Undressing the Power of Style* (SUNY Press), and *When Sex Became Gender* (Routledge). Read more at http://shiratarrant.com.

CONTRIBUTORS

FEONA ATTWOOD is Professor of Cultural Studies, Communication and Media at Middlesex University, UK. Her research focuses on onscenity, sexualization, sexual cultures, new technologies, identity and the body, and controversial media. Feona is the editor of *Mainstreaming Sex: The Sexualization of Western Culture* (I.B. Tauris) and *Porn.com: Making Sense of Online*

Pornography (Peter Lang), and the co-editor of *Controversial Images: Media Representations on the Edge* (Palgrave Macmillan). She co-edits the journal *Sexualities* and is the founding co-editor of the journal *Porn Studies*.

MARTIN BARKER is Emeritus Professor at Aberystwyth University, UK. He retired from teaching in 2014, after forty-five years. His research has spanned a wide range of subjects, across contemporary racism, media controversies and moral campaigns, comic books, and films. His work has in particular focused on advancing our questions and methods for studying audiences within a cultural studies frame. In 1996, he collaborated on a project to study UK audience responses to David Cronenberg's film, *Crash*, which had been the object of a year-long censorship campaign. In 2006 he was invited by the British Board of Film Classification to design and lead a project on audience responses to screened sexual violence. In 2003 he was one of the organizers of the international *Lord of the Rings* audience project. He is now among the leaders of a forty-six-country follow-up study of responses to the films of *The Hobbit*. In 2011, he worked with Clarissa Smith and Feona Attwood on the design of their study of porn audiences.

CHRISTOPHER BOULTON is an Assistant Professor in the Department of Communication at the University of Tampa where he teaches critical media studies and nonfiction video production. Before entering the academy, Boulton worked at Mister Rogers' Neighborhood, Travel Channel, CourtTV (now TruTV), and Discovery Channel. His most recent film, a collaboration with the Media Education Foundation entitled *Not Just a Game: Power, Politics, and American Sports*, screened in Austin, Frankfurt, Havana, London, New York, and Toronto. Boulton's research focuses on the intersection of communication, inequality, and activism and his writing has been published in the *International Journal of Communication*, *Advertising & Society Review*, and *The Routledge Companion to Advertising and Promotional Culture*. His previous work on pornography, "Porn and Me(n): Sexual Morality, Objectification, and Religion at the Wheelock Anti-Pornography Conference," appears in *The Communication Review*.

RYAN BOWLES EAGLE is Assistant Professor of Media Studies in the Communications Department at California State University, Dominguez Hills. She earned her PhD in Film and Media Studies at the University of California, Santa Barbara. She specializes in documentary, film festivals, global media activism, and feminist theories. Her current book project is a media ethnography that examines a global network of human rights film festivals called the Human Rights Film Network. She offers sincere thanks to Constance Penley and Lisa Parks, whose respective graduate seminars on pornography and new media theories were the inspiration for the chapter in this book.

CAROLYN BRONSTEIN is Associate Professor of Communication at DePaul University. She is the author of *Battling Pornography: The American Feminist Anti-Pornography Movement, 1976–1986* (Cambridge University Press), for which she received the 2012 Emily Toth Award for the Best Single Work in Women's Studies, given by the Popular Culture Association/ American Culture Association. Her scholarship on gender representation, social responsibility, and feminism has been published in a wide range of media, history, and communication journals, such as *Journal of Mass Media Ethics, Journal of Popular Romance Studies, Camera Obscura,* and *Journalism and Mass Communication Quarterly.* She is currently at work on a collection of essays, which examine the impact of pornography on American culture and politics in the 1970s.

Associate Professor THOMAS CROFTS is Director of the Sydney Institute of Criminology. He is a graduate of University College London (LL.B.), the Bayerische Julius-Maximilians-University Würzburg, Germany (LL.M.), and the European University Viadrina in Frankfurt/O., Germany (Dr. iur.). His research in criminal law, criminology, and criminal justice centers on criminalization and criminal responsibility, exploring why and how behaviors are defined by, and governed through, criminal law. Within this broad field his interests are the criminal responsibility of, and for, children, comparative criminal law, criminal law reform, and the relevance and role of labeling. He has published in English and German in these fields in national and international journals. In 2011 he was awarded the Australia and New Zealand Society of Criminology's inaugural Adam Sutton Crime Prevention Award. Currently, he is conducting a collaborative project, funded by the Australian Institute of Criminology, studying young people's perceptions of sexting.

EMILY E. CRUTCHER is a doctoral student at the University of California, Santa Barbara, in the Department of Sociology, where she completed her master's thesis, "The Pleasure Gap: A Sociological Analysis of Evaluating Female Pleasure in Pornography." Emily currently does interpersonal violence prevention at UC Santa Barbara as Prevention Education Coordinator, and is interested in connections between violence prevention and sex-positive education. Her other interests include sex work and sexual labor, gender representations in media, sexual literacy, qualitative research methods, kink and consent culture, and trying a cupcake from every major city in California.

TIMOTHY FONG, MD, is an Associate Clinical Professor of Psychiatry at the Semel Institute for Neuroscience and Human Behavior at UCLA. Dr. Fong completed his undergraduate and medical education at Northwestern University in Chicago. He then came to UCLA and finished his residency in adult general psychiatry in 2002 and was the first accredited addiction psychiatry fellow at the UCLA Neuropsychiatric Institute (2002–2004). Currently, Dr. Fong is the co-director of the UCLA Gambling Studies Program. He is the director of the UCLA Addiction Psychiatry Fellowship, a program designed to provide a leading-edge clinical and research training experience. Dr. Fong's research interests include understanding hypersexual disorders, pathological gambling, and behavioral addictions from a biopsychosocial perspective.

MARGRET GREBOWICZ, PhD, has published extensively on many topics in contemporary philosophy. Her current projects focus on two areas, cybersex and environmental aesthetics, and she is working overtime to trace the connections between them. Her recent books include *Why Internet Porn Matters* (Stanford University Press), *Beyond the Cyborg: Adventures with Donna Haraway* (Columbia University Press), and *The National Park to Come* (forthcoming). She is Associate Professor of Philosophy at Goucher College, where she teaches courses on feminism, postmodernism, animal studies, and environmental philosophy. She is also an avid translator of poetry from her native Polish, and her work appears regularly in journals such as *Agni*, *Literary Imagination*, *Quarterly West*, *Field*, and *Third Coast*, among others. She lives in Brooklyn, NY.

KIMBERLY A. HARCHUCK, Esq., LLM, is a Senior Associate Attorney with Walters Law Group in Metro-Orlando, Florida. She focuses her First Amendment practice on Internet law issues, such as Web site operations, cyber law policy, and free speech advocacy. Ms. Harchuck regularly counsels clients involved in the adult entertainment industry. She is a member of the First Amendment Lawyers Association, acts as Legal Counsel for Woodhull Sexual Freedom Alliance, and volunteers as an advisor to Planned Parenthood of Greater Orlando. Ms. Harchuck has authored several publications and lectured on various topics addressing contemporary freedom of speech and censorship issues, and is a regular co-blogger for the adult industry's XBIZ.com. She can be reached at Kim@FirstAmendment.com.

KEVIN HEFFERNAN, PhD, teaches media history and culture in the Division of Film and Media Arts at Southern Methodist University. He currently is at work on a book, *Channels of Pleasure: American Moving Image Pornography*

After 1994, and another book titled *From Beavis and Butt-head to Tea Party Nation: Dumb White Guy Culture and Politics in America*.

JESSICA JOHNSON, PhD, is a Lecturer at the University of Washington teaching in the Departments of Anthropology; Gender, Women, and Sexuality Studies; and Comparative Religion. Her article, "The Citizen-Soldier: Masculinity, War, and Sacrifice at an Emerging Church in Seattle, Washington," won the Political and Legal Anthropology Association Student Paper Award in 2009, and was published in *PoLAR: Political and Legal Anthropology Review*, November 2010 (Vol. 33, No. 2). She is writing a book based on her research at Mars Hill Church in Seattle entitled *Biblical Porn: The Affective Labor of Popularizing Evangelical Culture*.

LOTTA LÖFGREN-MÅRTENSON is Professor of Health and Society, specializing in the field of sexology, and the Director of the Centre of Sexology and Sexuality Studies at Malmö University, Sweden. Her research areas consist of youth and sexuality, sex education and sexual health, disability and sexuality, and sexology as a profession. She has written several articles and books on these topics, including *Får jag lov?* (May I? On love and sexuality in the New generation of young people with intellectual disabilities), *Kärlek. Nu* (Love.com. On Internet and young people with intellectual disabilities), *"Hur gör man?"* (How do I do? Sex education in special schools), *Sexualitet* (Sexuality), and co-editor of *Sexologi* (Sexology), *Generation P? Youth, Gender and Pornography*, and *"Sex överallt, typ?!"* ("Sex everywhere?!" On youth and pornography).

SVEN-AXEL MÅNSSON is Professor Emeritus of Social Work at Malmö University in Sweden. He has written several books and articles on gender and sexuality, with special emphasis on issues of commercial sexuality, trafficking, pornography, sexual violence, and Internet sexuality. His books include *Cultural Conflict and the Swedish Sexual Myth* (Praeger), *Vägen ut!— Om kvinnors uppbrott ur prostitutionen* (The Way Out!—On women exiting prostitution), and the co-authored *Sexindustrin på nätet* (The Sex Industry on the Internet), *'Sex överallt, typ?!'—Om unga och pornografi* ('Sex everywhere?!' On youth and pornography), and co-edited *Sexuality and the Internet: A Collection of Papers 2003–2013* (co-edited with Kristian Daneback). Sven-Axel Månsson is also senior advisor at the Centre of Sexology and Sexuality Studies at Malmö University.

MIREILLE MILLER-YOUNG, PhD, is Associate Professor of Feminist Studies at the University of California, Santa Barbara. She received her doctorate from New York University in History of the U.S. and African Diaspora and her bachelor's degree from Emory University's Department of History. She is co-editor of *The Feminist Porn Book: The Politics of Producing Pleasure* (The Feminist Press). Her book, *A Taste for Brown Sugar: Black Women in Pornography* (Duke University Press), examines African-American women's representations, performances, and labors in pornographic media from the 19th century to the present.

JENNIFER C. NASH is Assistant Professor of American Studies and Women's Studies at George Washington University. She is the author of *The Black Body in Ecstasy: Reading Race, Reading Pornography* (Duke University Press), and articles that have appeared in journals including *Social Text, Feminist Review, Scholar and Feminist, Meridians: Feminism, Race, Transnationalism,* and *Feminist Studies.*

NICOLE PRAUSE, PhD, is a scientist at the University of California, Los Angeles, with a continuing Scientist appointment at the Mind Research Network in Albuquerque, New Mexico. She was trained as a clinical scientist with a training emphasis in statistics and neuroscience from Indiana University, Bloomington, with joint supervision from The Kinsey Institute for Research in Sex, Gender, and Reproduction. Her research focuses on HIV risk behaviors, substance use and sexual functioning, approach motivation, and reward processing using a variety of psychophysiological methods. She co-authored the "Sexual Response chapter" in the *Handbook of Psychophysiology* (Cambridge University Press) and is also interested in psychometric developments that can forward the field. The overarching goal of this work is to characterize how sexual arousal impacts decision-making that can lead to health risk behaviors.

CAROL QUEEN, PhD, has been working at Good Vibrations since 1990, where she currently serves as staff sexologist. She is also the curator of Good Vibrations' Antique Vibrator Museum. She writes regularly for *Good Vibes Magazine*, has authored or edited over a dozen books, including *PoMoSexuals* (Cleis Press), and *Real Live Nude Girl: Chronicles of Sex-Positive Culture* (Cleis Press), and is a frequent lecturer at colleges, conferences, and community organizations. She is also co-founder of the Center for Sex & Culture in San Francisco. See more at www.carolqueen.com, www.sexandculture.org, and www.goodvibesblog.com.

SHAR REDNOUR worked with *On Our Backs* magazine and Fatale Media as an editor, writer, and in video production. In 1998, Shar Rednour co-founded

S.I.R. Video Productions with her wife, Jackie Strano. They created the revolutionary *Bend Over Boyfriend* video series, *Healing Sex: A Mind Body Approach to Healing Sexual Trauma*, and the award-winning *Hard Love & How to Fuck in High Heels*. Of all her video work, *Sugar High Glitter City* is Shar's personal favorite. Shar's publications include the controversial essay "Losing It," which originally appeared in *On Our Backs* and was reprinted in *The Last Sex: Feminism and Outlaw Bodies* (Palgrave Macmillan) and *Virgin Territory 1 and 2* (Masquerade Books). Shar's book *Starf*cker* (Alyson Books) was nominated for an ABA award and her fabulous femme "bible," *The Femme's Guide to the Universe* (Alyson Books), was nominated for a Lambda award. She is interview host and co-producer of the biographical audio series *The Deeper Truth with Shar Rednour*. Shar has been featured in HBO's *Real Sex, Pornucopia, Hot and Bothered: Feminist Pornography*, and in the historical documentary *San Francisco: Sex and The City*, among others. Shar is very proud to be an original member of Sister Spit. Jackie Strano and Shar Rednour have been together for twenty years and have three children.

ANDY RUDDOCK is Senior Lecturer in Communications and Media Studies at Monash University, Australia. He has also taught in the United States, the UK, China, South Korea, and New Zealand. He is author of the books *Youth and Media, Investigating Audiences*, and *Understanding Audiences*, all with Sage Publications, and is currently working on a fourth title, *Exploring Media Research* (Sage). Ruddock's studies of media audiences, youth, mass communications theory, research methods, social media, reality television, violence, school shootings, celebrity, alcohol, politics, sport fans, media education, and the politics of comedy have been published in several anthologies and scholarly journals. He is best known for his work on cultivation analysis.

Dr. MICHAEL SALTER is a Lecturer in Criminology at the School of Social Sciences and Psychology and a member of the Centre for Health Research at the University of Western Sydney. He teaches on gender, crime and violence, and on critical theories of media and consumer culture. His research is focused on the intersections of gender, violence and culture, and how crime is constructed and made meaningful by victims, perpetrators, and others. Current research projects include a study of young people's sexual use of digital and online technology, and best practice in the primary prevention of violence against women. He specializes in the study of multiperpetrator forms of gendered violence and his book *Organised Sexual Abuse* was published in 2013 by Routledge.

CLARISSA SMITH is Professor of Sexual Cultures at the University of Sunderland, UK. Her research focuses on sexual cultures, practices, and representations. In particular, she is interested in pornography and other sexually explicit media, their institutional practices, representational strategies, uses, and meanings. Her publications include *One for the Girls! The Pleasures and Practices of Pornography for Women* (Intellect) and *Studying Sexualities: Theories, Representations, Practices* (Palgrave Macmillan, with Niall Richardson and Angela Werndly). She is the founding co-editor of the journal *Porn Studies*.

GREGORY STORMS is a doctoral candidate in the Department of Anthropology at The University of Michigan. Based on two-and-a-half years of ethnographic research in Chicago, his current work looks at queer male fetish subcultural transformation and intergenerational social relations. Focusing on a developing fetish subculture of primarily gay and bisexual men known as "puppies"—individuals who take on dog-like characteristics for both erotic and nonerotic social purposes—Greg's research looks at the history of transformation from fetish ("puppy play") to an institutionally robust subculture and the interplay with other fetish subcultures and older generations of fetishists. When not writing his dissertation, Greg spends time working on a short documentary film based on his research interests. Greg also enjoys mixing drinks in one of Chicago's gay leather bars, The Cell Block, or relaxing at home with his cat Jaeger and some good science fiction.

JACKIE STRANO is the Executive Vice President of Good Vibrations, the feminist sex-positive retailer founded in 1977, and the Executive Producer of Good Vibrations' digital content channel. Strano is an award-winning adult filmmaker and feminist pornographer. She has created best-selling, critically acclaimed, and culturally influential titles with her partner Shar Rednour including *Hard Love & How to Fuck in High Heels* and the pop culture phenomenon, *Bend Over Boyfriend*. Strano is featured on HBO and Channel 4 UK documentaries including *Hot and Bothered: Feminist Pornography* (USA), *San Francisco: Sex and the City* (USA), *The Truth About Lesbian Sex* (UK), *Pornocopia: Down in the Valley* (USA), and several publications including *Playboy*, *Cosmopolitan*, Salon.com, and *The Village Voice*. Strano has lectured at universities and international film festivals. In addition to being a 20-plus-year sex industry veteran, Strano is also a singer/songwriter/musician (http://jackiestrano.com) with original music featured in mainstream and alternative movies and has published essays in various anthologies. Strano has toured and performed on stages from CBGB's to the Fillmore. Jacki Strano and Shar Rednour live in the San Francisco Bay Area and are the proud parents of three sons.

WHITNEY STRUB is an Associate Professor of History at Rutgers University, Newark, where he also teaches American Studies and Women's & Gender Studies. His books include *Perversion for Profit: The Politics of Pornography and the Rise of the New Right* (Columbia University Press) and *Obscenity Rules: Roth v. United States and the Long Struggle over Sexual Expression* (University Press of Kansas), as well as articles in *American Quarterly*, *Journal of the History of Sexuality*, *Journal of Women's History*, and *Journal of Social History*. He blogs at http://strublog.wordpress.com.

GEORGINA VOSS is an interdisciplinary researcher, based at the Royal College of Art. Her work explores intersections around technology practices, politics, and ethics; industrial sociology; and gender and sexuality. She was awarded her PhD in Technology and Innovation Management by SPRU, University of Sussex, where she is currently a Visiting Fellow. Prior to joining the RCA, Georgina held research positions at the Faculty of Arts, University of Brighton, and was Research Manager at Tinker London where she ran the "Homesense" project, which was featured in the "Talk to Me" exhibition at MoMA, New York City. Her work has been published in *Wired* and the *Guardian*; and in journals including *Science and Engineering Ethics*, *Journal of Urban Technology*, *Journal of Homosexuality*, and *Sexualities*. Her work also appears as chapters in books including *The Oxford Handbook of the Creative Industries* and as innovation policy reports for bodies including NESTA, the EU, and BIS.

RONALD WEITZER is Professor of Sociology at George Washington University in Washington, DC. He has published extensively in the sex work area, especially on prostitution and trafficking. He edited *Sex for Sale*, now in its second edition (Routledge), and is the author of *Legalizing Prostitution: From Illicit Vice to Lawful Business* (NYU Press). His current research examines laws and policies related to prostitution in various European nations.

Index

CPSIA information can be obtained
at www.ICGtesting.com
Printed in the USA
LVHW020311300120
645188LV00011B/338